THE EARLY CHRISTIAN EPOCH

Edgar Cayce

THE EARLY CHRISTIAN EPOCH

The Edgar Cayce Readings

VOLUME 6

Compiled by

The Readings Research Department

ASSOCIATION FOR RESEARCH AND ENLIGHTENMENT, INC.

VIRGINIA BEACH, VIRGINIA

Copyright © 1976 by Edgar Cayce Foundation

All rights reserved

(ISBN) 87604-089-X

The Edgar Cayce readings are quoted verbatim from the originals except for minor changes in spelling and capitalization.

PRINTED IN THE UNITED STATES OF AMERICA

CONTENTS

Foreword	vii
Preface	xi
HISTORICAL BACKGROUND	3
PREPARATION FOR HIS COMING	9
The Essenes	9
John the Baptist, Elizabeth and Zachariah	38
THE CHOOSING OF MARY	49
THE BIRTH	67
Background	67
The Inn	75
The Shepherds	86
Consecration in the Temple	89
The Wise Men	93
The Flight to Egypt	99
HEROD'S COURT	109
THE YEARS PRECEDING HIS MINISTRY	122
HIS INCARNATIONS	128
HIS SISTER AND BROTHERS	142
EVENTS IN THE MINISTRY OF THE MASTER	168
Random Followers	168
The Seventy	178
The First Recorded Miracle	185
The Samaritan Woman at the Well	191
Peter's Mother-in-Law Is Healed	196
A Leper Is Healed	204
A Widow's Son at Nain Is Healed	205
The Parable of the Tares	207
The Tempest Is Stilled	207
Gadarene Demoniac Is Cast Out	208
Jairus' Daughter Is Healed	210

    The Woman Who Touched His Garment 215
    The Feeding of the Multitudes 216
    The Teachings at Bethsaida 226
    Daughter of Syrophoenician Is Healed. 244
    An Example for the Disciples 247
    The Adulteress 251
    Lazarus Is Raised 260
    The Rich Young Ruler 281
    Blind Bartimaeus Is Healed 283
    Zaccheus Entertains the Master 286
    The Triumphal Entry 287

THE LAST HOURS 295
    The Betrayal 295
    The Last Supper 297
    The Trial 300
    The Crucifixion 303
    The Preparation of His Body 315
    The Resurrection 319

THE PENTECOST 328

THE FOLLOWERS AND THE CHURCHES 338

THE ROMANS 517

Footnotes 575

Index 581

Foreword

Edgar Cayce was a student of the Bible; he read the Bible cover-to-cover once for each of the 67 years of his life. It may be said that he was Bible-centered to an extent that few other people have been. Although he is widely known for his extraordinary psychic sensitivity and accuracy, his greatest attribute was probably the consistency of his purpose to be of service to others. His simple habit of daily Bible study was no doubt a great factor in centering his life on this purpose. It should be recognized that the validity and spiritual depth of his readings were "fruits" of his daily prayer and Bible study, and not the other way around.

Even as a child, Edgar Cayce's desire was to be of help to others. One morning, while studying the Scriptures, young Edgar experienced a vivid vision of an angel who assured him of his life's work, a life of service to mankind. Subsequently, there were other visions. His most treasured life experiences through the years would be those several visits of the Master, so real, in his garden or study. And so, besides being Bible-centered, Mr. Cayce was most assuredly Christ-centered, so much so that Dr. Richard Woods, a Dominican friar and an expert on mysticism, has called him "one of few true American mystics, in the mold of Jonathan Edwards." Dr. Richard Drummond, a Midwestern Presbyterian theologian, has likewise called Edgar Cayce a true prophet, comparable in his life experiences to Jeremiah of the Old Testament.

While still a very young man, Edgar Cayce had a memorable and propitious meeting with Dwight L. Moody, the leading evangelist of the nineteenth century. This encounter with a great religious leader of his time may symbolize the special way in which the unconscious mind of Edgar Cayce seems to have been in continuing dialogue with the leading Biblical scholars and theologians of the first half of this century. Consciously, he had probably never heard of these men, but his readings seem to reflect a response to the questions they were raising.

In 1926, as the Cayces settled into their new home in Virginia Beach, Albert Schweitzer was publishing his scholarly work, *Quest of the Historical Jesus*. Dr. Schweitzer was addressing himself to one of the major issues occupying the theological world of the first half of the twentieth century. "Could the Jesus of History," he asked, "be known apart from the Christ of faith?" In unknowing dialogue with Schweitzer's question, Edgar Cayce was answering with a resounding "yes." Through many of the readings in this volume, scores of people were counseled that they could know Him from within themselves and their memories, as a real person, a brother, as well as knowing Him through the historical events of two thousand years ago. It was stated in such a way as to affirm that anyone believing could know Him. For this reason, these readings can inspire the same affirmative knowledge in a reader today.

Paul Tillich was addressing the problem of making the Christ principle actual in society's present situation and was writing eloquent articles to this point; during the same period, Edgar Cayce was giving readings for the formation of the first *Search for God* group. These readings said in part, "In whatever state we find society . . . may we meet it . . . and lift it." This indeed was a practical application of Tillich's concern. But the strongest link of these two minds was reflected in a mutual assertion that a very special opportunity existed for a lasting world peace following World War I. "A time of Kairos existed," said Tillich, a time of special transcendence of the Divine Christian principle. "The Christ sat with that person [Woodrow Wilson] at the negotiating table" for the League of Nations, said a Cayce reading. That special opportunity for peace was lost, and Paul Tillich was forced out of Hitler's Germany in 1933.

Time was crucial, people were being oppressed and, in the midst of growing tensions, Martin Buber spoke tenderly but insistently for strong interpersonal relationships based firmly on the relationship of God with man, the *I and Thou*. It was now 1937 and many who came to Edgar Cayce were told that the Christ light was seeking increased expression in the earth and that it depended on them as individuals to spread this light to the "classes and then the masses."

In the early 1940s, Rudolph Bultmann proposed a method of

"de-mythologizing Scriptures," or treating the Bible as we would an archaeological site. By sifting through the various layers of progressive translations, additions, or changes within Scripture, perhaps scholars could discover the primary voice of Jesus as separate from things of secondary or tertiary importance. But the readings were saying to the droves of people now applying for them that the individuals themselves were the archaeological site, telling each person that his memories, dreams, and reflections must be de-mythologized so that the true self might be discovered in the Christ.

As you read this volume, remember that this is the product of a man who consciously was a simple, Christ-centered mystic, while at the same time he was subconsciously carrying on a cogent discussion with the world's greatest Biblical minds. Keep in mind that this is an encyclopedia of readings given over many years, and not a narrative. Remember as well that "who one was" or "what one has done" is not nearly as important as what one does today about what he or she believes in these special days of opportunity.

In the final chapter of the Gospel of John, Mr. Cayce's favorite, John the Apostle says that if all things that Jesus did in the presence of His apostles were written down, the world itself could not contain the books that could be written. Perhaps this book lies in the direction of one of those many books "that could be written." In any event, this volume, *The Early Christian Epoch,* is humbly offered to the same end, "that ye might believe that Jesus is the Christ, the Son of God; and that believing ye might have life through His name." (John 20:31)

> The Reverend Ralph W. Spears, Pastor
> Christ the King Lutheran Church
> Kendall Park, N. J.

Preface

This material has been selected from those Edgar Cayce life readings which give incarnations in Palestine paralleling the New Testament period. The extracts are arranged in chronological order according to Biblical events in all cases which did not interfere with the continuity of the individual's reading. Footnotes have been added to those passages which show correlation with Biblical events. Selection of the information and compilation of the text was made by Mae Gimbert St. Clair and Erma G. Cook. Bible references were prepared by Mark Vieweg.

Each extract is identified by a case number which denotes the individual or group for whom the reading was given or, in certain instances, a general category. The number following the hyphen indicates the sequential number of the series. Notation of "M" or "F" indicates the sex, and the number following shows the person's age at the time of the reading. The date on which the reading was given follows. The final point of identification is the person's name in the Palestine incarnation.

Certain seemingly conflicting details in the information have been included in the text to permit each reader to reach his own conclusions.

It is hoped that this collection will provide a deeper appreciation of the Scriptures and broaden the reader's understanding of the New Testament period.

THE EARLY CHRISTIAN EPOCH

Historical Background

5749-7   6/27/37

Much might be given as to how or why and when there were the purposes that brought about the materialization of Jesus in the flesh.

In giving then the history: There were those in the faith of the fathers to whom the promises were given that these would be fulfilled as from the beginning of man's record.[1]

Hence there was the continued preparation and dedication of those who might be the channels through which this chosen vessel might enter—through choice—into materiality.

Thus in Carmel—where there were the priests of this faith—there were the maidens chosen that were dedicated to this purpose, this office, this service.

Among them was Mary, the beloved, the chosen one; and she, as had been foretold, was chosen as the channel. Thus she was separated and kept in the closer associations with and in the care or charge of this office.

That was the beginning, that was the foundation of what ye term the Church.

Then, when the days were fulfilled that the prophecy might come that had been given by Isaiah, Malachi, Joel [2] and those of old, she—Mary, espoused to Joseph—a chosen vessel [3] for the office among those of the priests, the sect or group who had separated and dedicated themselves in body, in mind, in spirit for this coming—became with child.

Then, as the record is given, that is the common knowledge of most, there was born in Bethlehem of Judea that entity, that soul, Jesus.[4]

There was the period of purification according to the law, and then the days in the temple and the blessing by Anna and by the high priest.[5]

And these made for those days of the beginning of the entity called Jesus—who becomes the Christ, the Master of Masters—in the days when there was the return to Nazareth and then the edict that sent them into Egypt that the prophecy was fulfilled, "My son shall be called from Egypt."

There five years were spent, as ye term time—by the mother, Joseph, and the child.[6]

Then there was the return to Judea and to Capernaum, where dwelt many of those who were later the closer companions of the Master.[7]

Here, after the period again of presentation at the temple, when there were those questionings among the groups of the leaders,[8] the entity then was sent first—again—into Egypt for only a short period, and then into India, and then into what is now Persia.

Hence in all the ways of the teachers the entity was trained.[9]

From Persia he was called to Judea at the death of Joseph, and then into Egypt for the completion of the preparation as a teacher.

He was with John, the messenger, during the portion of the training there in Egypt.

Then to Capernaum, Cana, and those periods of the first preparation in the land of the nativity.

The rest ye have according to Mark, John, Matthew and Luke; these in their order record most of the material experiences of the Master.

Many of details may be given in the varied fields of the preparation, but these were the experiences.

5749-8   6/27/37

[Relative to] the understanding and knowledge of the physical experience of the Master's in the earth.

In those days when there had been more and more of the leaders of the peoples in Carmel—the original place where the school of prophets was established during Elijah's time,[10] Samuel—these were called then Essenes; and those that were students of what ye would call astrology, numerology, phrenology, and those phases of that study of the return of individuals—or incarnation.

These were then the reasons that there had been a proclaiming that certain periods were a cycle; and these had been the studies then of Arestole, Enos, Mathias, Judas, and those that were in the care or supervision of the school—as you would term.

These having been persecuted by those of the leaders, this first caused that as ye have an interpretation of as the Sadducees, or "There is no resurrection," or there is no incarnation, which is what it meant in those periods.[11]

In the lead of these, with those changes that had been as the promptings from the positions of the stars—that stand as it were in the dividing of the ways between the universal, that is the common vision of the solar system of the sun, and those from without the spheres—or as the common name, the North Star, as its variation made for those cycles that would be incoordinant with those changes that had been determined by some —this began the preparation—for the three hundred years, as has been given, in this period.

Those in charge at the time were Mathias, Enos, Judas.

In these signs then was the new cycle, that as was then—as we have in the astrological—the beginning of the Piscean Age, or that position of the Polar Star or North Star as related to the southern clouds. These made for the signs, these made for the symbols; as would be the sign as used, the manner of the sign's approach and the like.

Then were the beginnings, and these were those that were made a part of the studies during that period.

Then there were again those soundings—that is, the approach of that which had been handed down and had been the experiences from the sages of old—that an angel was to speak. As this occurred when there was the choosing of the mate that had—as in only the thought of those so close—been immaculately conceived, these brought to the focal point the preparation of the mother.[12]

Then when there were those periods when there was the dumbness to the priest [13] and he, Zacharias, was slain for his repeating of same in the hearing of those of his own school, these made for those fears that made the necessary preparations for the wedding, the preparations for the birth, the preparations for those activities for the preservation (physically) of the child; or the flight into Egypt.

5749-15   6/22/41

[Relative to] events surrounding the birth of Jesus, the son of Mary, in Bethlehem of Judea.

The purposes are well known, for which the journey was made in the period. The activities of Joseph are well known. The variation or difference in their ages is not so oft dwelt upon. Neither is there much indicated in sacred or profane history as to the preparation of the mother for that channel through which immaculate conception might take place. And this, the immaculate conception, is a stumbling stone to many worldly-wise.[14]

The arrival was in the evening—not as counted from the Roman time, nor that declared to Moses by God when the second passover was to be kept, nor that same time which was in common usage even in that land, but what would *now* represent January sixth.

The weather was cool, and there were crowds on the way. For, it was only a sabbath day's journey from Jerusalem. There were great crowds of people on the way from the hills of Judea.

The people were active in the occupations of the varied natures in that unusual land. Some were carpenters—as those of the house of Joseph, who had been delayed, even on the journey, by the condition of the Mother. Some in the group were helpers to Joseph—carpenters' helpers. Then there were shepherds, husbandmen, and the varied groups that had their small surroundings as necessitated by the conditions of the fields about Nazareth.

In the evening then, or at twilight, Joseph approached the inn—that was filled with those who had also journeyed there on their way to be polled for the tax as imposed by the Romans upon the people of the land. For, those had been sent out who were to judge the abilities of the varied groups to be taxed. And each individual was required by the Roman law to be polled in the city of his birth.[15]

Both Joseph and Mary were members of the sect called the Essenes; and thus they were questioned by those not only in the political but in the religious authority in the cities.

Then there was the answer by the innkeeper, "No room in the inn," especially for such an occasion. Laughter and jeers followed, at the sight of the elderly man with the beautiful girl, his wife, heavy with child.

Disappointments were written upon not only the face of Joseph but the innkeeper's daughter, as well as those of certain groups about the inn. For, many saw the possibilities of an unusual story that might be gained if the birth were to take place in the inn. Also there was consternation outside, among those who had heard that Joseph and Mary had arrived and were not given a room. They began to seek some place, some shelter.

For, remember, many of those—too—were of that questioned group; who had heard of that girl, that lovely wife of Joseph who had been chosen by the angels on the stair; who had heard of what had taken place in the hills where Elizabeth had gone, when there was the visit from the cousin—and as to those things which had also come to pass in her experience. Such stories were whispered from one to another.

Thus many joined in the search for some place. Necessity demanded that some place be sought—quickly. Then it was found, under the hill, in the stable—above which the shepherds were gathering their flocks into the fold.[16]

There the Savior, the Child was born; who, through the will and the life manifested, became the Savior of the world—that channel through which those of old had been told that the promise would be fulfilled that was made to *Eve;* the arising again of another like unto Moses; and as given to David, the promise was not to depart from that channel. But lower and lower man's concept of needs had fallen.[17]

Then—when hope seemed gone—the herald angels sang. The star appeared, that made the wonderment to the shepherds, that caused the awe and consternation to all of those about the inn; some making fun, some smitten with conviction that those unkind things said must needs be readjusted in their relationships to things coming to pass.

All were in awe as the brightness of His star appeared and shone, as the music of the spheres brought that joyful choir, *"Peace on earth! Good will to men of good faith."*[18]

All felt the vibrations and saw a great light—not only the shepherds above that stable but those in the inn as well.

To be sure, those conditions were later to be dispelled by the doubters, who told the people that they had been overcome with wine or whatnot.

Just as the midnight hour came, there was the birth of the Master.

The daughter of the innkeeper was soon upon the scene, as was the mother of the daughter, and the shepherds that answered the cry—and had gone to see what was come to pass.

Those were the manners, and the ones present soon afterwards. For, through the period of purification the mother remained there, not deeming it best to leave, though all forms of assistance were offered; not leaving until there was the circumcision and the presenting in the temple to the magi, to Anna and to Simeon.[19]

Such were the surroundings at the period of the birth of Jesus.

Preparation for His Coming

The Essenes

489-1   F.53   1/17/34   Veronicani

. . . the entity was during those periods when there was much turmoil in the land of Judea, when there was the announcing of the prophet, of the new teacher, and all Judea had gone out to John.[1]

The entity then was among those that had been of the students of the Essenes, and in direct connection with many that had been prophesying, had been searching the records of or for the coming of the new light to those that had been hemmed in by tradition and by the acts of peoples in a political and religious purpose in the land.

Hence rather did the entity act in the capacity of one that counseled with those of its acquaintanceship, of its surroundings; for there was the inactivity until there had been within self found that which would answer to the calls that were being proclaimed by the various individuals moved by the teachings of a strange man who had renounced his position, who had renounced his activities in the material world to proclaim the acceptable year of the Lord is at hand. This to the entity brought many peoples in the counsel given, and when the lowly Nazarene came to know the entity, then in the name Veronicani, the entity became of those that, though weak in body, brought much counsel to many that saved many in their approach to this new understanding.

489-3   F.53   5/24/34   Veronicani

In that experience we find the entity was a soul seeking through those associations and activities that brought the entity into the environ of the Grecian-Syrophoenician surroundings; and in the activity in Palestine grew into womanhood there as one—that would be termed in the present—in the household of the counselor of those that traded with the peoples in that land.

With the advent of the Roman rule, the activities of such people became much more important; for there was the necessity of keeping a balance with both the Jew, the Greek and the Roman.

When the ministry of the forerunner began, that of itself brought into the association of the entity many of those that were in that particular sect of peoples to whom the entity then was joined—the Essenes.

The meeting of the mother of John and Veronicani brought about one of those friendships that made for a great deal of change in that experience, both for the entity Veronicani, ([489] in the present) and the peoples both of the Essenes and the Syrophoenicians and Grecians of that particular land.

When there were the meetings of those in the various lands where the Master taught, this caused an interest that made for much that is as the religious and commercial history of those peoples. And it is seen how that the activities of the associations brought to bear during the experience changed even the thought of the teachers in that land.

When the Master's ministry began, after the beheading of John by Herod,[2] the entity being in the position that there were relations both in the commercial and social activities of the people made for a closer relationship that gradually grew between the sisters of Lazarus and Elizabeth and the mother of the Master.

And when there were the teachings and activities in and about Bethany and in Jerusalem, there were those groups—of which the entity was a part—that gave their time in the main to making for the better associations and relations with those that particularly had been among the numbers that were healed during the ministry in that particular land. And where it is at present held as being the well or house of David in Bethany and Bethlehem, is where there was what would be termed today a place of refuge. For, as may be noted, it was one of the cities of refuge when the land was first proclaimed as the abiding place of Israel.[3]

It then became a refuge or hospital for those that might become the teachers, the ministers, for the activities of the

Essenes or teachers of which the Master was a member during the sojourn in Palestine.

With the coming of the trial [4] and the crucifixion of the Master,[5] when there were the periods of turmoil among those that had been the followers and teachers, and when the Roman pontiff under Cleodius disbanded or broke up the place of refuge during those periods when the trial was being brought about or being planned by the peoples, the entity then suffered the persecutions; not only because of the associations but for the heritage of the land or peoples from which the entity had been a native and a sojourner and had gained much for the native friends and associates.

When the trial arose, and when there was the preparation for the burial of the body, the entity Veronicani bathed the face of the Master.[6] And thence arose much of that which has come as an ability in the healing and in the ministry of the soul force to those with or for whom the entity may pray or seek to aid in an hour of turmoil.

What more could be asked for, from the material, than to have bathed the face even of a dead Lord! Yet with the resurrection morning, how much greater was it to be among those to whom it was given, "Go tell my disicples that I go before them into Galilee. There shall I meet them as promised." [7] To be among those with the mother, with the cousins, with Mary Magdala, and those that had come to anoint again the body, and find the dead Lord a risen Christ! This was the experience of the entity during that particular sojourn.[8]

Hence oft do we find the entity and those of that particular group met in the chambers of the father of James and John, in Zebedee's rooms or hall where they met.

The entity was that one who opened the door for the doubter, Thomas, when on the third meeting with the disciples and the people in the upper chamber there was that conversation which ensued between that individual disciple and those gathered there.[9]

During the periods when there were more and more of the persecutions that arose, the entity more and more gave of self and of those activities as related to the periods and times. And gave her son also, Stephen, that came as among the first of the martyrs for a cause.[10] And this, while making for that period in the experience of reaching to the higher soul development, wrecked the body—and it went out into the inter-between soon after the persecutions of one Saul of Tarsus began.[11]

Then, what meaneth that experience in the life that may be manifested in the present?

How oft comes the opportunity for the word here, there, that there may be the open door for some soul seeking to know that peace, that joy, that comes into the experiences of those who become *aware* that it is a living, a risen, a personal, a worthwhile *Christ* that is worshiped in the hearts and souls of men!

Thus was the experience of this entity, this soul, during that sojourn in Palestine.

2441-2   F.36   3/11/41   Durkon

. . . entity was in the Promised Land, during those periods when there were those cryings aloud because of the persecutions being wrought by those who overran the land.

There it may be said that the entity so fostered those activities of that group later known as the Essenes, as to have been the influence that made the whole ideal and idea possible.

That, too, was a noble and an enlightening service to the world; that has made and does make for a strength of purpose so oft manifest.

From that experience there may be the same influence; for the entity gained from the teachings of many outside the pale of the tenets of the Mosaic law—those things that were good in the purifying of the body, not only through the mastering of activities in thought but through the diet, through communion with the universal forces as manifested or expressed in nature itself.[12]

The name then was Durkon.

1391-1   F.62   6/22/37   Eloise

. . . the entity was in that land of the *nativity,* when the Master walked in the earth, when there were those who gathered to listen, to interpret, to seek not only physical but mental and spiritual relief and understanding.

The entity then was among those of the holy women and

those in close acquaintanceship with many who were the teachers or the apostles or the disciples, many of those women — as Mary, Martha, Elizabeth; all of these were as friends, yea companions of the entity during the experience.

For the entity then was in that capacity as one of the holy women who ministered in the temple service and in the preparation of those who dedicated their lives for individual activity during the sojourn.

The entity was then what would be termed in the present, in some organizations, as a sister superior, or an officer as it were in those of the Essenes and their preparations.

Hence we find the entity then giving, giving, ministering, encouraging, making for the greater activities; and making for those encouraging experiences oft in the lives of the disciples; coming in contact with the Master oft in the ways between Bethany, Galilee, Jerusalem. For, as indicated, the entity kept the school on the way above Emmaus to the way that "goeth down towards Jericho" and towards the northernmost coast from Jerusalem.

The name then was Eloise, and the entity blessed many of those who came to seek to know the teachings, the ways, the mysteries, the understandings; for the entity had been trained in the schools of those that were of the prophets and prophetesses, and the entity was indeed a prophetess in those experiences — thus gained throughout.

Hence the stories of the experiences and activities of the holy women mean oft more to the entity, through the intuitive forces, through the impelling force of *good* in relationships to others.

So we will find that in this experience the greater gain, the greater promise, the greater satisfaction, the greater hope comes to the entity in its ministering to others; not in the way of an overflow of sympathy, not in the way of laudation of any particular activity, but the encouragings here, the aiding there, in encouraging words, encouraging deeds, that they press on.

For all, as has been given, are as one before the throne of grace and mercy and peace and justice. For God is not the respecter of persons or of places or positions.

For to fulfill that purpose for which an entity, a being, has manifested in matter is the greater service that can possibly be rendered.

Is the oak the lord over the vine? Is the jimson beset before the tomato? Are the grassy roots ashamed of their flower beside the rose?

All those forces in nature are fulfilling rather those purposes to which their Maker, their Creator, has called them into being.

Man—as the entity taught, as the entity gave—is in that position where he may gain the greater lesson from nature, and the creatures in the natural world; they each fulfilling their purpose, singing their song, filling the air with their perfume, that they—too—may honor and praise their Creator; though in their humble way in comparison to some, they each in their *own* humble way are fulfilling that for which they were called into being, reflecting—as each soul, as each man and each woman should do in their particular sphere— *their* concept of their Maker!

This is the purpose—as the entity taught; this is the purpose the entity may find in giving its comfort, in giving the cheery word, in giving the lessons to those in all walks of life.

Fulfill thy purpose in thy relationship to thy Maker, not to any individual, not to any group, not to any organization, not to any activity outside of self than to thy Creator!

For it is the reflection of Him.

5264-1   F.40   6/14/44

The entity was among the Essenes who made for, built up for, the experiences which were to bring a greater interpretation, and these were those activities when there were the gatherings of those for ideals and the entity ministered to the needs of those at that period.

1450-1   M.19   10/6/37   Philo

. . . during those periods when the Master walked in the earth, the entity was among the Essenes that made for the predictions—yes, the preparations—for the activities that would bring about His entering into the activities in that period.

There we find the entity acted then in the capacity of keeping the records and the temple service where the maids as well as the men were kept, or directed or taught according to the tenets of the law as pertaining to *material* things and the law or tenets pertaining to the *spiritual* things.

We find the entity's activities there brought into the experiences of many that which has influenced and will ever influence the affairs of man, as man, in the earth—a great revolutionary period. . .

Then the name was Philo . . .

5337-1   F.40   7/8/44   Leonax

. . . the entity was in the Holy Land during the period when there were those expectancies for the coming of the Master, when there had been those changes for the varied groups because of the land being overrun by the Romans.

The entity was among those who made peace with both the Romans and those of the Jewish land and also the Syrophoenician group.

The entity then was among those of what today would be called the customs, of those making it possible for the Roman and the Jew, the Roman and the Syrian, the Roman and the Samaritan to get together, as it were; and thus a "go-between". . .

In the experience the entity gained throughout, though in the opposite sex; in the name then Leonax.

1869-1   F.46   5/1/39   Zenda Lumi

. . . the entity was in the Promised Land, as now called; during those periods when the Master walked in the earth.

The entity then was among those peoples who looked for, through those who were endowed with the inner vision, a helper, a master, a leader, a teacher; being a student of what ye would term astrology.

Thus we find that all phases of such natures that tend towards the mysteries of the universe outside of man's own material vision become conditions and experiences to be sought. These should ever be, as we have indicated, assurances rather than those things upon which to build thy determinations or thy activities even.

In that experience the entity knew much of those things that dealt with the activities between the various religious factors —as those termed the Sadducees, the Essenes, the Pharisees, those who worshiped beauty and those who knew of and—yea —presented those things of the mythological nature that gave to the material world concepts of the ethereal and terrestrial spheres of activity.

All of those were portions of the entity's experience, as Zenda Lumi.

There we find the entity gaining and losing; gaining during those periods in which there was the entertaining of those tenets set by the followers of the Nazarene; losing when those were turned to self-indulgences.

2067-11   F.56   2/22/43

Q-3. For literary purposes, please describe a secret Essene meeting before Christ, at which Judy, or her parents, or Thesea, or some Bible characters were present.

A-3. This might be described very well as by any authentic meeting of certain groups founded by Solomon. But the description should not be from here, for it would be quite at variance to much of the data prepared. Draw upon the own imagination.

The Essenes were a group of individuals sincere in their purpose, and yet not orthodox as to the rabbis of that particular period. Thus such a meeting would be described by the meditations, certain ritualistic formulas, as may be outlined very well from some of those activities as may be gathered from the activities of the priest in the early period when there was the establishing of the tabernacle.

Remember, recall, the first two didn't do so well, even under the direction of the high priest; for they offered strange fire.[13]

Let not, then, that as would be offered here, become as strange fire, but as in keeping with the precept of Jesus, "I and the Father are one"; not individually, but in the personal application of the tenets, commandments, being one in purpose, one in application.

Thus such a meeting would be the interpreting of each promise that has been made; as to when, as to how there would come the Promised One.

Analyze in the mind, then, that from the third of Genesis through to the last even of Malachi. Set them aside. Use them as the basis of discussions, as the various groups may be set in order; each rotating as a teacher, as an instructor for that particular meeting; remembering all were secret meetings.[14]

2072-15   F.34   6/20/44

Q-4. Were we [2072 and 1861] Essenes in the Palestine period?

A-4. The names [Ruth and Alec] themselves imply it, yes. But remember the Essenes had the divisions, just as you will find that most churches have their groups and divisions, these were in opposite groups of the Essenes. One held to—that it can happen—the other that God makes it happen. Which comes first, the hen or the egg? As was implied in that same question.

254-109   5/20/41

Q-2. What is the correct meaning of the term "Essene"?

A-2. Expectancy.

Q-3. Was the main purpose of the Essenes to raise up people who would be fit channels for the birth of the Messiah who later would be sent out into the world to represent their Brotherhood?

A-3. The individual preparation was the first purpose. The being sent out into the world was secondary. Only a very few held to the idea of the realization in organization, other than that which would come with the Messiah's pronouncements.[15]

Q-4. Were the Essenes called at various times and places Nazarites, School of the Prophets, Hasidees, Therapeutae, Nazarenes, and were they a branch of the Great White Brotherhood, starting in Egypt and taking as members Gentiles and Jews alike?

A-4. In general, yes. Specifically, not altogether. They were known at times as some of these; or the Nazarites were a branch or a *thought* of same, see? Just as in the present one would say that any denomination by name is a branch of the Christian-Protestant faith, see? So were those of the various groups, though their purpose was of the first foundations of the prophets as established, or as understood from the school of prophets, by Elijah; and propagated and studied through the things begun by Samuel. The movement was *not* an Egyptian one, though *adopted* by those in another period—or an earlier period—and made a part of the whole movement.

They took Jews and Gentiles alike as members—yes.[16]

Q-5. Please describe the associate membership of the women in the Essene brotherhood, telling what privileges and restrictions they had, how they joined the order, and what their life and work was.

A-5. This was the beginning of the period where women were considered as equals with the men in their activities, in their abilities to formulate, to live, to be, channels.

They joined by dedication—usually by their parents.

It was a free-will thing all the way through, but they were restricted only in the matter of certain foods and certain associations in various periods—which referred to the sex, as well as to the food or drink.

1472-1   F. 57   11/6/37   Judy

. . . the entity was in the Palestine land, during those days when the Master walked in the earth; and when there were the peoples about those activities of not only the birth but His sojourns before and after the return from Egypt—those whom Judy blessed, that labored in the preserving of the records of *His* activities as the Child; the activities of the Wise Men, the Essenes and the groups to which Judy had been the prophetess, the healer, the writer, the recorder—for all of these groups.

And though questioned or scoffed by the Roman rulers and the tax gatherers, and especially those that made for the levying or the providing for those activities for the taxation, the entity gained throughout.

Though the heart and body was often weary from the toils of the day, and the very imprudence—yea, the very selfishness of others for the aggrandizing of their bodies rather than their souls or minds seeking development, the entity grew in grace, in knowledge, in understanding.

1472-3   F.57   11/18/37   Judy

Here we may give even portions of the records as scribed by the entity called Judy, as the teacher, as the healer, as the prophetess through that experience.

Some four and twenty years before the advent of that entity, that soul-entrance into material plane called Jesus, we find Phinehas [?] and Elkatma [?] making those activities among those of the depleted group of the prophets in Mt. Carmel; that begun [17] by Samuel, Elisha, Elijah, Saul, and those during those early experiences.

Because of the divisions that had arisen among the peoples into sects, as the Pharisee, the Sadducee and their divisions, there had arisen the Essenes that had cherished not merely the conditions that had come as word of mouth but had kept the records of the periods when individuals had been visited with the supernatural or out of the ordinary experiences; whether in dreams, visions, voices, or whatnot that had been and were felt by these students of the customs, of the law, of the activities throughout the experiences of this peculiar people—the promises and the many ways these had been interpreted by those to whom the preservation of same had been committed.

Hence we find Phinehas and the companion, both having received the experience similar to that received by Hannah and Elkanah, had drawn aside from many of the other groups.[18]

And then as in answer to that promise, the child—Judy—was born.

That the entity was a daughter, rather than being a male, brought some disturbance, some confusion in the minds of many.

Yet the life, the experiences of the parents had been such that still—fulfilling their promise—they brought the life of their child, Judy, and dedicated it to the study and the application of self to the study of those things that had been handed down as a part of the *experiences* of those who had received visitations from the unseen, the unknown—or that worshiped as the Divine Spirit moving into the activities of man.

Hence we find the entity Judy was brought up in that environment; not of disputations, not of argumentations, but rather as that of rote and writ—as was considered necessary for the development, the influences, the activities of the life, to induce or to bring about those experiences.

That much had been to that period as tradition rather than as record, appeared—from the activity of the entity, Judy—to have made a great impression.

So there was the setting about to seek means and manners for the preservation, and for the making of records of that which had been handed down as word of mouth, as tradition. Such channels and ways were sought out. And eventually the manner was chosen in which records were being kept in Egypt rather than in Persia, from which much of the tradition arose —of course—because of the very indwelling of the peoples in that land.

Hence not only the manners of the recording but also the traditions of Egypt, the traditions from India, the conditions and traditions from many of the Persian lands and from many of the borders about same, became a part of the studies and the seeking of the entity Judy early in the attempts to make, keep and preserve such records.

The manners of communication being adverse, owing to the political situations that gradually arose due to the Roman influence in the land, made more and more a recluse of the entity in its early periods; until there were those visitations by what ye call the Wise Men of the East—one from Persia, one from India, one from the Egyptian land.[19]

These reasoned with the brethren, but more was sought from the studies of the entity Judy at that experience.

Then there was the report by the Wise Men to the king.[20] Has it been thought of, or have you heard it reasoned as to why the Wise Men went to Herod, who was only second or third in authority rather than to the Romans who were *all* authority in the land?

Because of Judy; knowing that this would arouse in the heart and mind of this debased ruler—that only sought for the aggrandizement of self—such reactions as to bring to him, this despot, turmoils with those then in authority.

Why? There was not the proclamation by the Wise Men, neither by Judy nor the Essenes, that this new king was to replace Rome! It was to replace the Jewish authority in the land![21]

Thus we find, as it would be termed in the present, attention was called or pointed to the activity of the Essenes such that a little later—during those periods of the sojourn of the Child in Egypt because of same—Herod issued the edict for the destruction.[22]

This brought to those that were close to the entity those periods that were best described by the entity itself, in the cry of Rachel for her children that were being born into a period of opportunity—yet the destructive forces, by the very edict of this tyrant, made them as naught.[23]

Hence during those periods of the ministry of John, and then of Jesus, more and more questioning was brought upon the recorder—or Judy—by the Roman authorities, or the Roman spies, or those who were the directors of those who collected and who registered taxes of those peoples for the Roman collection.

Consequently, we find the entity came in contact with the Medes, the Persians, the Indian influence of authority—because of the commercial association as well as the influence that had been upon the world by those activities of Saneid and those that were known during the periods of Brahma and Buddha.

These brought to the experience of the entity the weighing of the counsels from the traditions of the Egyptians and of her own kind—and then that new understanding.

Hence we find the entity in those periods soon after the crucifixion not only giving comfort but a better interpretation to the Twelve, to the holy women; an understanding as to how woman was redeemed from a place of obscurity to her place in the activities of the affairs of the race, of the world, of the empire—yea, of the home itself.

Those all became a part of the entity's experiences during that portion.

Hence we find many have been, many are, the contacts the entity has made and must make in this present experience.

For, as then, the evolution of man's experiences is for the individual purpose of becoming more and more acquainted with those activities in the relationships with the fellow man, as an exemplification, as a manifestation of divine love—as was shown by the Son of man, Jesus; that *each* and every soul *must become, must be,* the *Savior* of some soul! to even *comprehend* the purpose of the entrance of the Son *into* the earth—that man might have the closer walk with, yea the open door to, the very heart of the living God!

The entity's activities during the persecutions aroused much in the minds of those that made war again and again upon the followers of the Nazarene, of Jesus, of the apostles here and there.

And the entity, as would be termed, was hounded, yea was persecuted the more and more; yet remaining until what ye would call the sixty-seventh year *after* the crucifixion; or until time itself began to be counted from same.

For the records as were borne by the entity, it will be found, were *begun* by the activities of the entity during what ye would term a period sixty years *after* the crucifixion.

And then they were reckoned first by the peoples of Carmel, and then by the brethren in Antioch, then a portion of Jerusalem, then to Smyrna, Philadelphia, and those places where these were becoming more active.

The entity—though receiving rebuffs, yea even stripes in the body—died a natural death in that experience; at the age then of ninety-one . . .

Q-1. How close was my association with Jesus in my Palestine sojourn?

A-1. A portion of the experience the entity was the teacher!

How close? So close that the very heart and purposes were proclaimed of those things that were traditions! For the entity sent Him to Persia, to Egypt, yea to India, that there might be completed the more perfect knowledge of the material ways in the activities of Him that became the Way, the Truth!

Q-2. How can I extend the scope of my writing opportunity to use this ability in more important channels and wider service than at present?

A-2. As may be gathered from that as given, by putting into first thine own experience, thine own activity, those teachings of Him; not as tenets but as *living* experiences! So manifesting same in the lives and minds of those whom the self may meet day by day, learning that lesson as He so well manifested, that it was not in the separation as John,[24] not in the running away as Elijah,[25] not as in sitting in high places as Isaiah,[26] not as in that form of Jeremiah—mourning,[27] not in that lording as Moses [28]—but *all things unto all men!* reaching them in their own plan of experience; and not with long-facedness!

For as He—He wined, He dined with the rich,[29] He consorted with the poor,[30] He entered the temple on state occasions [31]; yea He slept in the field with the shepherds, yea He walked by the seashore with the throngs,[32] He preached to those in the mount [33]—*all things;* and yet ever ready to present the tenets, the truths, even in those forms of tales, yea parables, yea activities that took hold upon the *lives of men and women* in *every* walk of human experience!

So ye will find that the lessons ye gave then may be used today! Why? Because truth is *truth, ever*—in *whatever stage,* in whatever realm of evolution, in *whatever* realm ye find same; it is as He gave—the little leaven.

Think not, even as He, to do some great deed that would make the welkin ring throughout the earth. Rather *know* it is the little line, the little precept, the little lesson given into the lives and experiences that brings the awareness into the hearts and souls of men and women; that consciousness of the *nearness* in the still small voice within.

For as proclaimed of old, it is not in the thunder or lightning, it is not in the storm, it is not in the loudness—but the still small voice within!

So as ye write, so as ye talk, so as ye love—let it be in meekness of spirit, in *purposefulness* of service, in an activity and an eye single to the *glory* of the Father through those that are His children.

For "Who is my mother, my brother, my sister? They that do the will of the Father, the same is my mother, my brother, my sister."

What is the will? Love the Lord with all thy heart, thy mind, thy body; thy neighbor as thyself!

Sow the seeds of kindness, helpfulness, long-suffering, gentleness, patience, brotherly love; and leave the *increase* to the Father, who *alone* can give same either in the spirit, the mind *or* the body!

Being patient even as He.

This is the manner in which ye may reach, O the whole earth, even as ye did—Judy—in thy counsel as given thee by thy father then in the flesh, as ye learned, as ye gathered from the counsel of the lessons from the patriarchs of old, by the lessons of tradition that ye first—even as he—set to be in order; yea have heard as of old, an eye for an eye, a tooth for a tooth; ye have heard he that does the good, do the good to him; but "I say, he that would smite thee on the right cheek, *turn thou* the other also! He that would sue thee and take away thy cloak, give him thy coat also."

Did ye not set these as the very words given by Him who is the Lord of Lords and the King of Kings?

For to him who hath overcome—and He standeth at the door and knocks—and *ye,* as all His servants, His children, His sisters, His brethren—may be co-laborers with Him in the harvest that is ripe.

1472-6   F.58   6/19/38   Judy

Q-17. If, as you have said, I was a prophetess, healer, teacher and writer in my Palestine sojourn, why does so-called sacred history give no record of me or my work?

A-17. Ye were of the Essenes; not of the Jews nor even the Samaritans!

2067-11   F.56   2/22/43

Q-4. Tell of the work, the prophecies, the hopes of Phinehas and Elkatma, Judy's parents, at Carmel, as Essenes.

A-4. These were those activities that may be illustrated very well in the ministry of the parents of the strong man—that a parallel may be drawn; as to how first there was the appearance to the mother, and then the father, as to what should be the ministry, the activity of the entity that was to lead that group, and aid in the early teaching of the prophecies of the life of the child Jesus, as well as of John. For, John was more the Essene than Jesus. For Jesus held rather to the spirit of the law, and John to the letter of same.

Q-5. Was Judy immaculately conceived, as perhaps was Samuel?

A-5. Neither were immaculately conceived.

Q-7. Why was Judy not a boy as expected?

A-7. That is from the powers on high, and gave the first demonstration of woman's place in the affairs and associations of man. For, as were the teachings of Jesus, that released woman from that bondage to which she had been held since the ideas of man conceived from the fall of Eve, or of her first acceptance of the opinions—these were the first, and those activities that brought about, in the teachings materially, that as Jesus proclaimed.

Q-9. *Describe any outstanding points or unusual abilities Judy had.*

A-9. Only as one brought into those activities—as it may be well described as the feminine of Samson.

Q-10. *Where did Judy receive her education, in what subjects, and who were her teachers?*

A-10. The Holy Spirit, and the mother and father; not from other sources, though there were those activities from all of the teachings of the East, through those early periods before there were those acceptances of Judy as the leader of the Essenes at Carmel at that period.

Q-11. *During the lifetime of Jesus where did Judy live and with whom?*

A-11. In Carmel; with the companion and the mother.

Q-12. *Please describe Judy's personal appearance, her dress, her personality, her faith.*

A-12. Draw upon the imagination for these. As would be the dress of Samson, making it feminine.

Q-13. *Tell of Judy's marriage, the name of her husband, his work—names of children and their accomplishments.*

A-13. His work had to do with the records that were translated for the various groups. The activities of Judy through these experiences were much as might be termed those of Hannah, during those periods when there were those seekings for that from the Lord that might give a recompense for those doubts brought out by others.[34]

2795-1   M.28   8/9/42

Q-6. [*When, where, and what has been my association in past incarnations with the following people; what are the present urges from same; and how may we be of mutual help to each other here and now?*] . . . [*1472*]?

A-6. Ye were the son of Judy in the Palestine experience . . . . . . the son of that entity Judy [1472] that led the Essenes' activity. Yet with the persecutions the entity became as one paralyzed from fear—bodily fear. These brought disappointments . . .

2067-11   F.56   2/22/43

Q-15. *What were the "fears" that wrecked Judy's son who is now [2795] and why was Judy, the healer, unable to heal him?*

A-15. It was not disease, other than that within self. Why were Samuel's sons sinners?[35] These may only be answered within the individual, or from the seeking of the individual himself.

1472-6   F.58   6/19/38   Judy

In the Palestine sojourn, then the [present] daughter was the sister—and averse to the entity's making those activities in associations with the sect or group with which the entity was then affiliated or associated.

2067-11   F.56   2/22/43

Q-16. *Tell about the angels appearing to Judy, when, where, and what they said.*

A-16. Which period? These were many and oft.

Q-17. *Please describe Judy's home life as well as her Essene activities.*

A-17. That as might be the description of an individual who had set self aside as a channel for such activities. These are very hard to be understood from the material mind, or from the material understanding or concept, especially in this period of consciousness. For, then man walked close with God. When there were those preparations—it is possible in the present, but not *acceptable*. Consequently, to describe the home life as to say they sat in the sun, ate three square meals a day and wore little or nothing, or that they dressed in the best—it must be that as from the spirit. May best be described as given by Luke, in his description of those things that disturbed Mary. "She kept these things and pondered them in her heart." She kept those experiences, those teachings—she pondered them in her heart.[36] This did not prevent her from being, then, a material person, nor one with the faculties and desires for material associations—as indicated in the lack of celibacy.[37] Is this indicated in any condition in the book, or man's relationship to God? Nowhere is this indicated!

Q-18. Tell about Judy teaching Jesus, where and what subjects she taught Him, and what subjects she planned to have Him study abroad.

A-18. The prophecies! Where? In her home. When? During those periods from His twelfth to His fifteenth-sixteenth year, when He went to Persia and then to India. In Persia, when His father died. In India when John first went to Egypt—where Jesus joined him and both became the initiates in the pyramid or temple there.

Q-19. What subjects did Judy plan to have Him study abroad?

A-19. What you would today call astrology.

Q-20. At what major events in Jesus' life was Judy present— such as casting out of demons, healing, feeding five thousand, etc.?

A-20. At His teaching—for a period of some five years.

Q-21. Was she present at any of the healings or the feeding of the multitudes?

A-21. Those where she chose to, but she was very old then. She lived to be sufficiently old to know, of course, of the feeding of the first five thousand.[38] She was present, but rather as one that brought the crowds together, than as contributing to the activities at the time. For, there the divisions arose, to be sure.

Q-22. Was Judy present at the crucifixion or the resurrection?

A-22. No. In spirit—that is, in mind—present. For, remember, Judy's experience at that time was such that she might be present in many places without the physical body being there!

Q-23. Tell of instances when Judy and Thesea, the Essene, worked or planned together.

A-23. Only at the regular periods, or meetings of the Essenes, as we find.

2880-1   F.56   1/12/43   Zermada

. . . the entity was in the land of promise, in those periods when there was the looking forward to the coming of the Holy One, in association with those who had been and who were the leaders of those groups known as the Essenes.

Thus the entity was closely associated with Judy in that

particular period of experience, though the entity was more in the keeping and the application of spiritual tenets of the Syrophoenician, or the Persian and the Syrophoenician peoples. And the entity then was a prophetess, a seeress, in its study of astrology—as is called today—or the effect of planets, the sun, the moon, the stars, upon the habits of men. And these took the form of activity as the counselor, the guide, the instructress to those through that period of activity.

And the entity set much of its findings to poetry, yea to music also. Thus the high evolving of the psychic forces, though to the entity it has ever been accredited to the occult. But these in their higher estate attain to one, even as the worship of First Cause or the first principles are one.

In the experience the entity gained much, suffered much, experienced much; but gave much to the peoples of the various periods and various groups with whom it was associated.

The name then was Zermada.

2880-2   F.56   3/22/43   Zermada

As indicated, the entity now called [2880]—then Zermada—was rather of the Syrophoenician, or the Persian and the Syrophoenician peoples—as they were known in that experience.

In its unfoldment during the period the entity, as would be called now, took on the study of astrology, or astrological activities; growing in the early period in the experiences as a dreamer, as a meditator, as a seeress or prophetess; making those associations with the peoples of the Far East.

Coming early in its experience to the conclusions, from its own experiences, that the looked-for changes were coming in the Holy or Promised Land, the entity—before the birth of the Christ-child—made many journeys, and finally there were the closer associations with the leader of the Essenes and the entity dwelt in Carmel.

Through those associations there came more communications and interpretations of those records or signs that eventually brought the journeys of some of the Wise Men, of which we have records.[39] These were the highlights of the entity's experiences through that particular period of activity.

As to the associations, many of those of other lands came to the entity, with the counseling together. The associations with Judy as the leader of the Essene peoples only intensified or made the preparations as to choosing the groups that were to be the channels through which there was the possibility, the probability that the awakening should come to the peoples of that period; as well as to the world.

There were many of those who were a part of the associations in those activities; some where there were disputations, some where there were agreements. And as indicated for the entity, in the application or use of the findings, studies or interpretations of the various combinations of astrological influences—the Persian manners of interpretation should be used. These would come to be more in keeping with those that were the unfoldments and developments of the entity through that particular period . . .

After the birth of the forerunner,[40] and the problems that such brought to the priests that had conformed to or become a part of the experience, the entity was not altogether a dweller in Carmel—or the Promised Land, for fear of those in political power as to the activities. This caused the entity to go back and forth a great deal. Much of these were secret meetings, or what would be called not open visitations. Yet the entity throughout its experience continued to be one to whom many in places came seeking information, for direction and counsel.

The entity lived to be nearly ninety years of age in that particular period, passing into the other consciousness in a period of journey coming toward the Carmel retreat.

Q-6. Please give a fuller account of my association in Palestine with the entity now known as [1472]—then also called [1472] —and interpret the frequent vision in which I see us together on a high tower or battlement looking out over what seems to be a desert land, giving the significance of the fact that, in the vision, [1472] wears a headdress with her robe, while I wear a similar robe without a headdress.

A-6. There's little more than that as given. They counseled together oft, but they each considered self as an authority in or among their particular group. Do not get the idea that there was whole consideration of either, but that each had her own inner groups to which the counsel meant much, when to others at that period it meant little. Yet there was kept ever that bond of sympathy, that bond of purposefulness between the two; for each realized in the experience the less of self—or as was aptly given by the forerunner, "He must increase and I decrease." Neither finds that in self in the present, but that must be the principle. In the interpretation of the Christ Consciousness, it must increase while self is lost in the giving to others. Neither holds to this, but you will find it in the end.

As to the vision—this is an interpreting of experiences when individuals met in Carmel. The battlement was where the two entities met in their discussions of their findings, and for their choice as to which each is to give to her own particular group. The vision of the headdress merely represents the customs and the differences of the peoples or tribes or groups to which the two belonged.

1602-1   F.40   5/30/38   Eunice

. . . the entity was in the land now known as the Promised Land, during those days when there were the great expectations among certain groups of the peoples of the land, and among the peoples of which the entity then was a part—in the Galilean and the Judean land where the entity lived.

And when there were the activities with the wife of Zachariah, the mother of John, the entity was a companion, a friend.

And when there were those visitings, those associations with the mother of the Master, the entity Eunice became acquainted with those activities.

And the entity's son, Eunice's son, then, was among those who were taken by the edict of Herod.[41]

These brought great disturbances into the experience of the entity, and troubled periods as there were questionings as to whether or not there *was* the consideration given by those who were said to have brought protection to Mary and to her Son, the Master—and the willingness to give away to easier paths became too prominent in the experience.

Yet in the latter portion of the sojourn the entity's experiences came in good stead. For the associations of the entity with those who acted in the capacity of the data gatherers for the Romans, for the taxing, became as that which enlightened some of those who became the friends of those who accepted the Master's teachings, when there were questionings by those in authority.

1602-4   F.41   9/26/39
. . . in the Galilean land—in which the entity found itself, as it became aware of the tenets and the changes that had come about—there was less of what would be termed the orthodox Jewry or the adherence to the tenets as had been established with the return of the peoples to the Palestine land from the Persian.

Yet, the entity was of those peoples who had united with the remnant left in that land of Zebulon during the period of captivity; thus being a mixture (as understood according to the history of the theological nature or phase) of the Jewry and the Samaritan.[42]

However, with those adherents of the land becoming more and more imbued with the ideals and tenets of the Essenes, the entity's family then had embraced that phase.

The Essenes were a religious order within Jewry *and* the adherents and near adherents of same, see?

This then was to the entity in its early years a problem; because there were the continued reports of happenings that were handed down as a part of the family records (for these were by word of mouth rather than from books), happenings in the Promised Land, as well as to the preserving of a people of promise—though they were in captivity—and as to how there had come the interference of providence on the one hand, in returning one portion of the family to the land of promise, and on the other as to how that portion had been preserved—though they had maintained their adherence through the changes which had been wrought.[43]

Then, with the looking for the Savior,[44] through the tenets of that new order, it became something which to the entity induced the feeling, or the attempt to make such a combination that, to be sure, through the self must be the lineage that were to see and know and hear of this fulfilling of the promise in the day and age and period of the entity's experience.

Thus, with all such expectancy there was the betrothal; and

then the birth of the son, that to the entity must be one especially endowed with those privileges that were to mean and to bring such an awakening to the people—through the very associations of the entity with Elizabeth, the mother of John, and the friendships with Mary and Joseph in a portion of *their* experience that was a part of not only the conversation but the wonderments and the study of the entity through those early periods of experience in that particular land.

And then there came the edict that robbed *all* the mothers of that particular portion of the land, through that which had been a part of the activities of one in the position to direct the activities and counseling of the Wise Men and their conversation and convocation with the king who made the edict; and then the happening.[45]

This brought into the experience of the entity a spirit of hurt, of hate for those who had—according to the entity—betrayed that knowledge as pertaining to those who were in those positions, whose sons were in those periods in which there was the expectancy and the desire for their fulfilling a long-looked-for promise.

Into the experience in the present, then, this has brought the little jealousies, the little disputations that are to be eliminated if there would be the full knowledge of and at-onement with the Creative Forces.

During those periods, as conditions developed, when John and Jesus were receiving their trainings in other lands, the entity kept close in touch with the household of Elizabeth.

And through that period when she, too, was affected by the very edicts of the king, and when there was the change that brought about the death of the king,[46] and through those periods when the Romans robbed Elizabeth of her mate—through the death even at the altar [47]—there began to be changes in the outlook of the entity; and the attempt to understand *why* those who were supposed to be endued with powers and activities divine should have such things happen to them, brought still greater resentment and wonderment.

Then again in the periods when Mary and Elizabeth were so desirous of those activities within their homeland as the changes came about, and the journey from the upper part of Galilee to Capernaum, the entity there entered rather into not wholly the intrigues but rather what might be called in the present more of a social activity—owing to the abilities of the entity's mate to make friendships with those who were in power.

With the rebuking of Jesus in the house of worship,[48] and the imprisonment of John,[49] the entity—with the expectancy again of motherhood—sought greater counsel with Mary, Martha, and those who were closer to the activities—not only of those who had renounced their relationships with the priests but those who were in the position of keeping alive the order of the Essenes.

Then in the latter days of Jesus' sojourn in the material plane, the entity saw her child blessed by Him, among those who were set as the ideal manner in which all individuals were to accept their relationships with others, in that pronouncement, "Unless ye become as little children, ye shall in no wise enter in." [50]

These brought periods of searching of self, and the adherence closer to those tenets which had been a part of the experiences of the entity.

Yet, with the knowledge that such an one as Magdala had become a close companion of those of the household, there again was brought to the entity that questioning as to "How can such things be?"

Such questionings, though, were blotted out in those periods when the entity, with Mary, Josie, and the other Mary, learned of those things which had brought the conditions to pass in Jerusalem.

And as the entity journeyed there, and became aware of the turmoils which surrounded those periods of activities, there was a greater leaning upon those who were of that land.

For, remember—of the twelve, seven of them came from the entity's *own* land, and own acquaintances.[51]

As the days passed, the entity was among those who were turning then more and more to the tenets pertaining to the activities in Jerusalem; and the Pentecost came.[52]

Then the entity was among those who heard her own kinsmen speak in tongues, seeing the great tumult and the activities wrought.[53]

Thus there was builded that determination within the experience and heart of the entity to bring the greater knowledge, the greater awareness of the spirit of truth—as was indeed manifested by Him that shed through the tenets of His disciples and apostles the new light to men; that hate and those things that make afraid may be put away, and that positions or power or wealth or fame may be set at naught compared to the peace that came and *is* the understanding of those who have seen and known and become aware of His presence abiding—even as the entity heard promised, "Lo, I am with you always, even unto the end of the world." [54]

Through the latter portion of its experience, then, we find that the entity ministered to the needs of the saints, as they were called, or those who dedicated their lives and their activities wholly to the ministering to the fields about the whole of that land.

The entity thus gained in the giving—giving of self; in just being kind to those who were heavily burdened by the cares of life, whether in illness or in the vicissitudes of relationships, or in wants of the body, or in needs in the activities of others that brought desperate circumstance in the experience.

These then should be analyzed, and the petty jealousies and hates made less and less a part of the attitudes of mind and body and activities in the present.

Meeting all of those forces in the experiences, we find that the entity—Eunice—was among the elderly mothers of the church in the latter portion of the experience, in the southernmost portion of Palestine.

Thus we find that the associations with those who were in authority of the Romans, and those who were brought to a better understanding by the associations of the wife of Cornelius, who brought the greater activity and blessings to many of the entity's household and associates and friends—these brought into the experience of the entity the joys in which it passed into the greater realms of activity in that experience.

Ready for questions.

Q-1. Who are the individuals with whom the entity was most closely associated in this Palestine period with whom a closer relationship should be developed in the present? That is: Would it be best to develop the relationships now with those who were close to John in the Palestine period; with those who were spreading the teachings of the Master then; or with those who were in high places at that period? Explain and direct the present activities towards such associations.

A-1. All of these must be met by circumstances. These may be found, as individuals, by paralleling the lives and experiences of those who were in that particular period. Not that these are to be chosen as individuals, but they are the activities that are a part of the experience. To be sure, there is what may be called an excess of that urge arising from such activities, but as to whether it shall be applied in the direct associations of individuals or as a cause or purpose, and in contact with those things and influences that bring a united effort, is to be the choice of the entity itself.

For, this: Because of the associations with those in authority then, as counselors, we find that in the presence of such individuals in the present there is felt the urge, "Well, I can't get that, nor those activities." But these are principles, and not things to be applied as to individuals.

If there are things to be worked *out,* with individuals, because of the knowledge of same—then as to whether or not this is attempted depends upon the choice in self, as to whether such knowledge is to be a stumbling block or a stepping-stone for greater development.

Test not self beyond that it is able to bear. Rather develop for the *principle,* than for the activity of individuals.

In analyzing the present experience and environ, it will be seen that the associations are with some to whom the entity ministered much, and brought through such activity greater blessings to many. Then, where such are needed, apply self.

Where there is the urge because of the personalities of individuals that renew the urge for activities known within self to be such as to cause or make one to err—as He gave, "Being forewarned, be forearmed, and allow not thine house (thine self) to be broken up."

Q-2. *I have had visions and impressions of a Roman experience during the period immediately following that of the Palestine. Is this so, or is it the same?*

A-2. As we find, it is rather the visioning of the experiences the entity had with those who were in authority. Remember, as was first given, in the early portion of the experience the entity heard both sides that were handed down — as the experience of those in the Chaldean land as well as those in the land of promise. In the latter portion the entity heard from those in authority (as Cornelius and those of his household) [55] about the activities in Rome, and how such were carried on. Hence it is rather as a vision by the entity, than an experience of being in the position. For, as we find, if analyzed, the vision is rather the awareness of such a position, yet not being just in Rome itself.

Q-4. *In my relation to my Aunt . . . will you explain karmic relation and what I should do for her in this present life?*

A-4. Just as in that experience in which ye found thyself blocked and mocked because of that experience as Eunice, because of the loss of thy son, by thy present aunt, ye find periods when there could not be hard enough or bad enough sayings, or even things done. And yet as He taught, these are not the manners nor the ways to meet same, but rather in applying what ye would have her do if the conditions were reversed. If conditions were reversed, what would you have her do? Then, *that do.*

2505-1   M.53   5/21/41   Jarael

. . . the entity was in the Promised Land, during those periods when there were the activities among special groups that had been preparing themselves, materially as well as mentally, as channels through which there might be the fulfilling of that which had been the promise to those of old.

Thus the entity was with that group of peoples known as the Essenes, and acquainted with those in the positions of the priests as well as those in authority among the various groups.

Hence the entity was acquainted with Zacharias, with Judy [1472], with those of the household of faith, with Anna, as well as others who sought and who interpreted for the peoples of the day that happening.

Thus the *innate* psychic force that is a part of the entity's interest, as well as from the astrological aspect in Uranus.

Thus the entity was a part of that activity as brought into that experience those influences from which arose the awareness that brought not only the Wise Men of the East [56] but those of other groups who were looking for the awakening which might again bring hope into the lives and hearts of men; that light which shines in the darkness ever, since God became manifested in the earth . . .

Throughout that experience there were material hardships at times, yet great mental and spiritual understanding was attained by the entity . . .

These were the experiences of the entity throughout that sojourn, as Jarael—among those that led in that group that aided John, as well as the Master, Jesus, in their early periods of education and interpretation of the various tenets that were the experience of that group during that particular period.

And it was owing to much of the efforts of the entity that *that* group became one with that known as the Christian way—or Christianity.

1949-1   M.45   7/6/39   Betrili

. . . the entity was among those of the natives of the Palestine land, it was neither a Jew *nor* a Roman, but rather of the Grecian and Parthenian way of thinking. And the studies of the various sects or groups during the experience made for the background of the activities of the entity in association with many of those who came into authority—as the groups of the Essenes, as well as the Pharisee influence upon various groups, as well as the more select set of the Sadducees holding to the various influence or forces.

Hence we find the entity was in the capacity of an active force in importing and exporting during those periods when there were the needs for the general activity with those in authority.

Hence ships, as well as the degrees of activity in religious and political thought were a part of the entity's experience then.

The entity was a student also, because of the associations with those who had been of those peoples of other lands. For the entity was brought in contact with those who were in power or authority in the various lands which the entity visited—

about the Mediterranean; and greater and greater became the searching into those impelling forces in the lives of those with whom the entity came in contact. And the activities in the Alexandrian library were of special interest.

Then the name was Betrili. In the experience the entity gained and lost, and the entity gained. As the abilities were applied in his search for the greater hope in the lives of the masses, there was advancement. As they were applied in his search and in his labors for the secular and the advancing of self alone—losing.

1851-1   M.65   3/27/39   Zacheus

. . . among those who crowded about the Master, especially upon the mountainside.

We find the entity, as one Zacheus, not the little man, but was of the Judean country where those activities were just beginning, during that early portion of the ministry, to become a thought or tenet of those peoples.

There we find the entity holding both to the form as well as to the principle that was being proclaimed. For the entity was of that group of Essenes of which John and others had been a portion. Hence to many of the peoples, especially of the Pharisee group, the entity was termed a rebel, a radical. Yet the entity gained through those activities much that brought—while disturbing forces and hardships in the material activities—the love of nature, the love of the beautiful, the listening to the voices as for the interpreting of the message from the teacher that proclaimed, "Blessed are the peacemakers—for they shall inherit the earth."

John the Baptist, Elizabeth and Zachariah

2156-1   F.4½   3/30/40   Elizabeth

. . . the entity was in that period from which the greater hope may be expressed; as Elizabeth, the mother of him of whom the Master said, "Among them that are born of women there hath not risen a greater than John the Baptist." [1]

So, as the entity was a chosen vessel, a chosen channel for

that one who *proclaimed* the day of the Lord to be at hand,[2] the entity now—manifested in that body known as or called [2156]—may indeed be kept as a channel, by those about the entity, that it, too, may arouse and bring the consciousness in the minds of many that the day of the Lord is indeed at hand.

For, whosoever will may come and take of the cup, even as He. For as He hath promised to stand in the places of those who are discouraged, disconsolate, who have lost a vision, lost hope —so may this entity be that channel through which *many* may take hope, many may be aroused to the awareness that the Lord is nigh, that He standeth at the door of thy consciousness, that ye may be awakened!

Then, let there not be a worshipfulness as of the body of the entity, but rather as of its abilities to *arouse* in the hearts and minds of others the *knowledge* that the day of the Lord is at hand!

[See page 355 for incarnation as St. Cecilia.]

2156-2   F.4½   4/16/40   Elizabeth

... the entity was a channel for the forerunner of the Master, Christ; and, as there is sanctioned, as there is realized in the minds, the hearts of those who would and do distribute the words of the prophetess, *His* ways, God's ways, Christ's ways, are not past finding out, but are ready for those who will harken —and then live in their own lives that as the messenger gave —"The day of the Lord is at hand!" to all that will harken, that will heed His call!

Then—let all who would sponsor, who would aid this entity in *any* manner, put away from themselves all hate, all malice, all that would cause any to err, and bring *themselves*—in *their* conversation—in keeping with the messages that will come.

Thus may that entity as proclaimed to Elizabeth speak to those who are honored with the care of this prophetess . . .

Q-1. *In past incarnations, what has been the present mother's association and connection with the entity?*

A-1. Close in attendance and care, oft; else the conditions in the present would be too great a burden for any! . . .

[The present mother] was as the closest friend to the entity,

Elizabeth; caring for her through that period when the prophet came.

Also there have been many other close associations; for, remember, many sojourns have there been for a little while; but these as indicated are the ones that need to be impressed, and pondered in the hearts and minds and purposes of those who foster, who care for the entity—those who would see God's way among those where strifes, turmoils, disappointments and fears arise in the present.

Take warning, then—and as the mother has gathered in the present, let its prayer oft be, *"Thy will, O God! Have Thy way with me!"*

Q-2. *What has been the association of [1837] with the entity?* [*1837 was not given a Palestine incarnation.*]

A-2. In the experience especially as Elizabeth we find the associations with most of those who would sponsor, who would crown the entity with their voice.

But hold not malice against any who deny, lest ye bring condemnation to thyself!

We find that the entity was a friend to the entity, especially during those periods when there was the sacrifice of the father Zachariah; and it is he that ye see shadowing the entity oft.[3]

2175-1   F.28   4/23/40   Sofa, nurse to John

. . . the entity was in the Promised Land, during those periods when there was the looking for, and the expectancy of the peoples for the fulfilling of the promises which had been a part of the Scripture, as well as a part of the things that were hearsay.

The entity was closely associated with the mother of the forerunner of the Master—and the entity made itself, by choice, the nurse of John.

Thus the message of John—"Prepare ye the way, the day of the Lord is at hand!"—is a part of the entity's seal of life, as we have indicated in the Arabic inscription on the ribbon.[4]

Then the entity was in the name of Sofa, and gained; though at times very discouraged at the happenings and the misunderstandings of those peoples because of the inabilities to know of the teachings of the Master as well as of John.

And when there were those days of persecution and imprisonment, the entity suffered—in body, in mind.

2175-6   F.32   10/17/42   Sofa

In giving the outline and the activities of the entity through the experience in Palestine, something of the history of the period must be interpreted, for this to be a helpful experience for the entity.

There were, in the period, those political turmoils with many of those peoples of the holy family, or the house of the Lord.

Zachariah was a just man, then living in the hills of Galilee; yet the priest who offered sacrifice for the month Nisan. And when there were those visions or experiences,[5] and his wife Elizabeth conceived, these brought into the experience of those groups—of which this entity, Sofa, was a part—the Essenes—a great deal of questioning—as to what manner of individual would be required or needed as the helper, or director, or nurse, in the circumstances that would naturally arise if these visions were to be fulfilled.

When there had been the experience, then, of the happening of the visit of Mary to Elizabeth,[6] there was the choosing of the dedicated women for this office.

This was a reminder to many of what and how the maiden had been chosen on the stair.[7]

The entity then, Sofa, was one of the women dedicated to service in the temple; not as one that would be called a caretaker, yet these were the offices of the entity—to "touch up" or paint, or to keep certain portions of the temple in order for the activities of the priest.

Thus the entity appealed to Zachariah to use his period of preparation as the one to offer the sacrifice,[8] as the time when there would be the choosing of the attendant or nurse to the babe.

Hence the entity was chosen by what would be termed, or is termed in the Cabala, the moving of the symbols upon the vesture of the priest.

This, then, prevented *any* of those confusions as might have arisen with the entity.

When there was the birth, then, of John (for, remember, he

was not called the Baptist until after his death), in the periods of training, the entity also acted as the instructor; as in the position of one who looks after or cares for those through such periods.

And (this aside), too often there is not sufficient thought taken as to the care of a developing body through those first eighteen months to two years.

Here, though, this entity was chosen by those directing forces as from the temple service itself, or by divine guidance.

Thus did the entity fulfill, until the boy, John, was weaned at six years of age.

Then the entity was associated with Jesus with the last year of the experience in the household of Mary and Joseph. While the offices here had been fulfilled by that one as we have indicated, the entity was especially given this office to indicate to the developing child the nature, the character of the cousin.

After that period, and the period of education, and the periods when the labor began—from the periods of twelve years to that of seventeen—when the entity John went to Egypt for the dedication and the preparation there—the entity was known among those who were as holy women, who acted in the capacity of the mourners at the various functions of the order, as would be called, of the Essenes.

Later the entity was among those, not *the* first but *among* the first, to be baptised by John in Jordan.[9]

The entity also ministered to the needs of John when he was cast in prison,[10] and was among the chief mourners when he was beheaded.[11]

The entity also was among those who, during his period in prison, sought Jesus for counsel.[12] And with the answers given, the entity was confused—until there were those reclaiming activities upon the day of Pentecost.[13]

Then the entity was old in years, and among those first disturbed by the first edicts that brought death to James [14]; the entity dying in that period from exposure by the abuse of soldiers in that first raid.

As to the period, no losses in spiritual or mental progress might be indicated; rather those periods of confusion that may be the experience of any that are dedicated to an idea, and who in sincerity give of their best through a material sojourn.

As to the entity's parents—these were of the Levites, and those acquainted with many of the activities in the temple.

And from same, ceremony means much to the entity. Whatever the preparation, for whatever function, to the entity there must be some ceremony.

Ready for questions.

Q-1. To what extent, and over what period of time, did I have a close association with Jesus?

A-1. As indicated, during a year the entity gave most of the time to indicating to the child Jesus the life, the preparation, and the character of John. Then *only* meeting same in those periods when, as indicated, coming to Him for counsel.

Q-2. In choosing to be the nurse of John the Baptist—

A-2. [Interrupting] Chosen; not choosing but *asking* that there *be* a choosing, and chosen by the office, or upon the ephod.

Q-3. Did I take the vows of celibacy?

A-3. They didn't take the vows of celibacy! Not to have children during those periods was considered to be ones not thought of by God!

Q-4. Concerning the fulfillment of those promises which had been a part of the Scripture, please outline the promises for purposes of study. (That is, where in the Bible?)

A-4. *All* of those recorded by the writers respecting the visit of the disciples of John to Jesus.[15] Then especially 14th, 15th, 16th and 17th of John. *There* are the promises that are a part of the promises to the entity, and to all.

Q-5. As indicated, in '42 the influence of my children will enter in, especially when there will be the awakenings as to their relationships, or as I unfold the story of both of those who took the vows of celibacy. What were the associations with each of my children that bring about this influence in the present? First, [2308]—then Sister Duene?

A-5. A younger sister of the entity; and this means very much younger, as you would count by years today. And as the entity experiences, [2308] oft appears more in the role of the sister than as the daughter.

Q-6. [1566]?

A-6. In the experience [1566] was among the acquaintances of the entity, rather than being closely associated—as was the older.

Q-7. Were there associations in that period, and of what nature or activity, which brought—or would bring about—the deep friendship between me and the following: [2390]?

A-7. When there were those visits of the entity now called [2390] to Jerusalem, the acquaintance began. And from the entity they learned of the life of John, the purposes, the fulfilling of prophecies, the fulfilling of those things that brought about the associations or friendships in the present.

The entity then, of course, was older, much older, than the entity now called [2390].

Q-8. [1523]?

A-8. Known of, through the associations with the acquaintance made; and when there were the reports later of the activities in the church, it was close to the period of departure of this entity.

Q-9. [578]?

A-9. Knew of, but not close together.

Q-10. [413]?

A-10. The entity now known as [413] was among the holy women, then; thus among those groups who were oft together in the offices as the mourners in those periods.

Q-11. Was I associated with Lucius, now [294]? If so, how?

A-11. Acquaintance, and advisor to Lucius.

1581-1   M.11   4/26/38   Xaneres

The entity then was among those of the priesthood, and closely associated or affiliated with the activities of Zacharias.

And the entity was the one who announced, by the blowing of the ram's horn, the various services or activities in the temple when there were the morning and evening periods for the sacrifice; when there were the announcings of those various periods when the offerings might be accepted by the priesthood activity—or those who acted in the capacity of the sacrificial priests at the altars.[16]

Hence the entity knew much of those experiences of John

and the activities as connected with same, as also of those activities in the temple when the child Jesus was presented before the priests—as was necessary under the Jewish law.[17]

Again we find ritual and those things pertaining to the mental or spiritual conditions and experiences becoming a portion of the entity's whole activities during that sojourn.

The name then was Xaneres—yes, a Grecian; for the entity was of those activities that were of the pure household of the children of Judah but who had been taking on other names in their activities for the preservations of those activities of the Parthenians as well as the Samaritans and those particularly who had accepted the Jewish tenets through the study of those things of that particular sect of same, called the Essenes.

Hence we find, though the entity held himself in good repute with the rest of the leaders through those periods of service, there were the acquaintances with all of those mysterious influences that were given as a portion of the reasons for the coming of the Wise Men and their teachings, as well as the educational values and activities in the experiences of John and of Jesus to become teachers or leaders in and during that experience.

2167-1   M.23   4/13/40   Jochaim

. . . the entity was in the land of promise, during those early periods of the Master's walk in the earth. There we find that the entity was among those of noble birth in the land, being among the sons of the priests of the land.

Hence the entity was close in those things pertaining to music, art, and those that would arouse within the hearts and souls of individuals the hopes for finding expression within and without themselves; as the songs of the shepherds, the songs of those who watched upon the mount for the visions as had been proclaimed.

Thus the entity was close to the activities of Zachariah, who was the announcer of those things to come into the experience of the peoples. The entity found itself following closely in these, and—like Zachariah—lost its life in the defense of those principles for which it stood; in that God never fails to speak to the children of men through man.[18]

In the experience the entity gained, the entity lost; and the entity brought to others the power and the ability to hope. The name then was Jochaim.

1643-1   M.21   7/20/38   Simean
 . . . the entity's appearance was during the activities of the now called Palestine period, just in the early portions of the preparation for and the early activity of the Master's walkings in the earth.

The entity was better associated or acquainted with the hills peoples there, or those who were in the processes of having political as well as factional meetings during those experiences.

The entity was known as one Simean [?], well acquainted with the activities of Zachariah, his persecution, his final death as he took hold upon the altar [19]—as well as the activities of the holy family in their flight into Egypt.[20]

There the entity was acquainted then with many of those conditions and activites that surrounded the earlier portion of those who were and are to be such a factor in the affairs of the human race.

The entity's interest then was more than that of a passive nature, yet according to the circumstances and surroundings and environs the entity was hindered from carrying on . . .

While the desires of the spirit were attuned, the flesh or the body was weak; and persecutions overcame much of the beauty that ye were able to give—and yet did not give—during that experience.

1000-14   F.47   7/4/36   Adahr, sister of John the Baptist
The entity then was among those in the Palestine land associated more particularly with the entity known as or called John the Baptist, or Elias that was for to come, for the announcing of the necessity for the preparations of individuals in their spiritual lives, making through their material associations ways and means and manners for the knowledge of the relationships of man to the Creative Forces in the earth.

The entity in those periods was among those who proclaimed those activities, proclaimed those teachings with those in John's own household, John's own undertaking.

For the entity then was a sister of that teacher, and a daughter of Elizabeth and Zacharias—in the name Adahr.[21]

In the experience the entity gained much; the entity had much confusion, owing to the teachings of the priests and the rejecting of same by the brother and the acceptance of the teachings of the Essenes; making for doubt and confusion in the experiences of the entity.

And only in those answers that came to the inner self was there brought an understanding; for through the entity's *own* expression and seeking there came that answer, "Go tell John the things ye have seen and heard; the lame walk, the blind see, the sick are healed, the poor have the gospel preached unto them." [22] *Then* there came in the entity's experience the full meaning of the priesthood in Israel, and how that the lowly Nazarene was that fulfilling of that priesthood in His offering of Himself as the lamb that was not to roll back but to take away the sins of the people. Not as an escape but as an atonement in which each soul does find, would find, the lamb standing *ever* as that offering in its relationships as an individual to its fellow man.

There the entity gained the most; and these influences, these forces that ever bear witness in the experience of the entity, make in the present experience for the greater help, the greater glory in the activities.

And when it is considered how that the entity then made for those oppressions owing to the manner of dress of the brother,[23] that in the next experience bore evidence of the attempts of the entity to adjust itself—by dealing with that of which it berated its brother for his dress, it may be seen how that the law carries through.

In the present experience then, those influences bear a part.

Hence in the dealings with those things that have to do with dress, that have to do with skins, or have to do with furs, there should ever be carried in the background of each association, each activity, that those who use such influences or things may become even as self—*aware of* that influence of the lamb in the experience of man's sojourn in the earth.

5330-1   F.43   7/17/44   Smantehn

. . . the entity was in the days when the Master walked in the land. Yes, when there were those teachings by the forerunner of the Master, John, the entity was then among those who were the entertainers, or danseuse at the court of Herod, or the entity was one of those with the one who asked for John's head, Salome.[24]

In the experience the entity gained, even under the periods when there were such good changes in the activities. The entity was then in the name Smantehn.

5749-8   6/27/37

Q-16. Were the parents of John the messenger members of the band which prepared for Jesus?

A-16. As has just been indicated, Zacharias at first was a member of what you would term the orthodox priesthood. Mary and Elizabeth were members of the Essenes, you see; and for this very reason Zacharias kept Elizabeth in the mountains and in the hills. Yet when there was the announcing of the birth and Zacharias proclaimed his belief, the murder, the death took place.[25]

262-120   8/28/38

Q-4. What did Jesus mean when He said that the least in kingdom of heaven *was greater than John the Baptist?*[26]

A-4. John was still the doubter.

1158-6   F.46   1/25/37

Did not John come as the voice of one crying in the wilderness and in the spirit of Elijah? Yet he *was* Elijah.[27]

The Choosing of Mary

254-109   5/20/41

Q-7. Please describe the process of selection and training of those set aside as holy women such as Mary, Edithia, and others as a possible mother for the Christ. How were they chosen, were they mated, and what was their life and work while they waited in the temple?

A-7. They were first dedicated and then there was the choice of the individual through the growths, as to whether they would be merely channels for general services. For, these were chosen for special services at various times; as were the twelve chosen at the time, which may be used as an illustration. Remember, these came down from the periods when the school had begun, you see.

When there were the activities in which there were to be the cleansings through which bodies were to become channels for the new race, or the new preparation, these then were restricted—of course—as to certain associations, developments in associations, activities and the like. We are speaking here of the twelve women, you see—and all of the women from the very beginning who were dedicated as channels for the new race, see?

Hence the group we refer to here as the Essenes, which was the outgrowth of the periods of preparations from the teachings by Melchizedek, as propagated by Elijah and Elisha and Samuel. These were set aside for preserving themselves in direct line of choice for the offering of themselves as channels through which there might come the new or the divine origin, see? [1]

Their life and work during such periods of preparation were given to alms, good deeds, missionary activities—as would be termed today.

5749-8   6/27/37

Q-4. How were the maidens selected and by whom?

A-4. By all of those who chose to give those that were perfect

-49-

in body and in mind for the service; and as Ann—or Anna—gave the same, and in the presentation could not be refused because of the perfectness of body, though many questioned and produced a division because she proclaimed it had been conceived without knowing a man.

Thus came the division, yet the others were chosen—each as a representative of the twelve in the various phases that had been or that had made up Israel—or man.[2]

Q-6. Describe the training and preparation of the group of maidens.

A-6. Trained as to physical exercise first, trained as to mental exercises as related to chastity, purity, love, patience, endurance. All of these by what would be termed by many in the present as persecutions, but as tests for physical and mental strength; and this under the supervision of those that cared for the nourishments by the protection in the food values. These were the manners and the way they were trained, directed, protected.

Q-7. Were they put on special diet?

A-7. No wine, no fermented drink ever given. Special foods, yes. These were kept balanced according to that which had been first set by Aran [?] and Rata.[3]

5749-7   6/27/37

Q-7. How long was the preparation in progress before Mary was chosen?

A-7. Three years.

5749-8   6/27/37

Q-5. How old was Mary at the time she was chosen?

A-5. Four; and, as ye would call, between twelve and thirteen when designated as the one chosen by the angel on the stair.[4]

5749-7   6/27/37

Q-8. In what manner was she chosen?

A-8. As they walked up the steps!

Q-9. Was there any appearance of the angel Gabriel in the home?

A-9. In the temple when she was chosen, in the home of

Elizabeth when she was made aware of the presence by being again in the presence of the messenger or forerunner.[5]

Again to Joseph at the time of their union.[6] Again (by Michael) at the time when the edict was given.[7]

5749-8   6/27/37

Q-13. Give a detailed description for literary purposes, of the choosing of Mary on the temple steps.

A-13. The temple steps—or those that led to the altar, these were called the temple steps. These were those upon which the sun shone as it arose of a morning when there were the first periods of the chosen maidens going to the altar for prayer; as well as for the burning of the incense.

On this day, as they mounted the steps all were bathed in the morning sun; which not only made a beautiful picture but clothed all as in purple and gold.

As Mary reached the top step, then, then there were the thunder and lightning, and the angel led the way, taking the child by the hand before the altar. This was the manner of choice, *this* was the showing of the way; for she led the others on *this* particular day.

Q-14. Was this the orthodox Jewish temple or the Essene temple?

A-14. The Essenes, to be sure.

Because of the adherence to those visions as proclaimed by Zacharias in the orthodox temple, he (Zacharias) was slain even with his hands upon the horns of the altar.[8]

Hence those as were being here protected were in Carmel, while Zacharias was in the temple of Jerusalem.

3652-1   F.22   1/12/44   Macha

. . . the entity was in the Holy Land, when there were those periods of choices being made among the Essenes of those for the channel through which there might come the Expected One.

The entity was among those mothers, whose daughter was in that group on the stair, even when Mary was chosen.

Then the entity was very active in those groups. And with

the coming of the expressions from Elizabeth and Mary, the entity was a companion to each of them in the giving out to other groups. And the entity was among those who were much disturbed by the edict when many of the "daughters of Rachel" wept because of the edict in that district.[9]

The name then was Macha. The entity gained. And from there comes the great balance in mind, in body, in purpose of the entity.

Do not starve either of these phases of thy unfoldment, for all that is in mind and body first appears in spirit. Keep each, then, in its proper relation one to another, if the entity would contribute the more to the activities in the earth.

2173-1   F.50   4/19/40   Sofa

. . . the entity was in the land of promise; being among those peoples who had accepted the teachings as to the manners in which there was the looking for a messiah, a prophet, which had been proclaimed of old.

The entity was among those of the household of faith in that direction; not only embracing the Jewish activities but the Essenes' interpretations of same.

Hence the entity was acquainted not only with those of the house of David through whom there came the forerunner, the prophet, but the Messiah, Jesus Himself.

Thus the entity was acquainted with many of those whose children were destroyed, though none of the entity's were offered, for in the experience the entity was never wed but led the life of the celibate.

And the entity counseled with the mothers of many of those who hoped for the selection of their offspring as the channel for that prophecy; also caring for many of those.

Hence the entity was among those of the period who are termed in the present as the holy women; counseling with the mothers and the young during that period.

The name then was Sofa. The entity gained, the entity lost; for with the activities which apparently allowed the edict of the king that brought destruction, was it not even the prophetess itself—*this* entity—who wrote that song of Rachel's weeping for her children?

In that the entity brought into the minds of many disturbing forces; not intentionally, not purposely, but because of overzealousness.

2608-1   F.56   10/18/41   Japhter

... the entity was in the Promised Land, during those periods when there were the preparations for changes as predicted by many of those who studied the cycles of time for the changes and the incoming of that promise to the world.

The entity then was among the Essenes, yet also among those close in the temple that was temporal. This made for a division in the entity's material experience. For, being convinced in mind, the body was surrounded by the material ethics and traditions of its own household, so that it brought turmoils. Yet the entity—not secretly, yet not openly—espoused the cause when there was the gathering of the twelve that were offered as channels through which the Holy Spirit might make manifest. . .

But that thou hast, use as thou didst in thy experience in that sojourn—as Japhter.

2408-1   F.38   11/25/40   Anna

... the entity was in the Promised Land, in the days preceding and just following the entrance of the Prince of Peace into the material manifestation in the earth.

The entity was among those of a group, an organization as it would be called in the present, who sought—through the mysteries of the sages—to interpret time and place according to the stars and the numerological effects upon the period in which the entity found material expression.

Thus, while not as one who set itself above others, the entity was much sought after, and interpreted much for those in material authority of that group. Hence, as there were those applications of individuals who were prone to interpret and apply that knowledge for material benefits, disturbance arose with the entity and some of those in authority among the Essenes. . .

Then the entity was in the name Anna; not the one in the temple, but that one who made the choices eventually of the twelve maidens who were to be chosen as the channels that might know that truth so thoroughly as to be moved by the Holy Spirit.

2520-1   F.38   6/23/41   Shalmar

. . . the entity was in the Promised Land during those periods when preparations were being made by those groups to which the entity belonged, for the coming of the Son of man, the Prince of Peace, the heralds for the new day.

The entity was closely associated with the priests who were active in the Carmelian area, where there had been the early teachings established years ago by Elijah, Elisha, Samuel; that taught the mysteries of man and his relationships to those forces as might manifest from within and without.

The entity then was among the sages who chose the young that were to be set apart as channels through which that blessing might come to the world.

Thus the entity was acquainted with the teachings of those groups in Persia, India, Egypt and even of the Hebrews and the activities in Olympus and the isles of the sea.

These brought at times periods when the entity needed long periods of meditation, and the setting aside of activities necessary to induce the submerging of the physical to the spiritual in its relationships to materialization. . .

In that experience the entity was known as Shalmar.

2603-1   F.67   10/15/41   Anna

. . . the entity was in the Holy Land, during the early periods and activities when there were those preparations for the incoming of He that is the way, the truth and the light.

The entity was among those who were later known as the holy women, being associated with the Essenes as well as those of the temple activity; being a part of the influences that made for choices especially of those who were to be channels in the activities that were to bring about that proclaimed and looked for consideration from and of the Creative Forces.

Then the entity was in the name Anna; not in the temple, but an associate of those in authority in the temple, and saw the Holy One blessed there.

1981-1   F.18   8/22/39 "third upon the stair"

. . . the entity was in that now known as or called the Promised Land, during those periods when there were the preparations of the channels through which the Essenes looked for choice to be made of one, from those who had been consecrated for the service of being the channel, through which He, the Prince of Peace, might come.

Hence we find the entity was in the temple or house of lodgement where the maidens were brought for that consecrated service, and the entity was the third upon the stair when the choice was made of Mary.

Hence the entity was closely associated throughout that experience not only with the close followers of the Master, but the entity was also the wife of James—the brother of John, the beloved; the wife of the first of the martyrs for the Christ, the wife of him who brought many of the Romans to the greater interpretation[10]; and hence closely associated with especially the wife of Cornelius,[11] as well as the entity who acted with the disciples on the walk to Emmaus[12]; giving then that entitlement there as being among the holy women who sought for the preparations of the body, as well as those who came with the disciples and the mother at that first Easter morn.[13]

Is it then any wonderment to the entity that Easter has been at times most significant? And at others as a period to be observed, and yet felt within as not being observed wholly in a proper manner?

These were, then, the experiences when the entity again instructed many of all classes, of all stations in life, in the needs of individual service that brought to the varied groups the greater understanding.

Is it any wonder, then, that oft in pronouncements by individuals as to the life, as to the activities during those periods, the entity questions, "By what authority is this or that said?"

Keep that faith as ye expressed, as ye manifested. For did ye not oft receive blessings, as it were, firsthand from the Master Himself?

Let that which has been thy watchword be ever close with thee, "It is I, be not afraid." For if His hands are guiding (as ye have known and have felt), if His words are thy understanding, there needs never be fear for aught in thy experience; for He, with His promises, standeth nigh!

1479-1   F.54   11/17/37   "among the twelve maidens"
. . . the entity was in the land now called the Promised Land, during those periods when preparations were being made for those entrances, those activities in which there came that Holy One, the man called Jesus.

The entity was then among those that were first chosen, among the twelve maidens that ascended and descended the stairs upon which Mary was chosen.

To be sure, the entity was of the Essenes—of the household of one Joseph; not of that Joseph that was chosen later, of course, but a kinsman—in the correct line from David.

Hence the entity throughout its experience came close in contact with those that kept the records, yea with those activities when the persecutions arose.

And when the entity's own son was among those that were destroyed by Herod, the great cry of the heart that went up in rebellious forces to a consciousness that would allow such, made for an experience that has oft been met in this experience in many ways in disappointments.

That lesson of humbleness, that lesson of self-sacrifice seems to have been drained to its very dregs oft in the present. But know the *light* as ye gained from those teachings and those persecutions and those sacrifices made among those holy women, and thy association with those in search for same.

For ye were among those that *first*—in thy latter years—recognized the freedom brought to thy sex by the very *manner* of the entrance of the Son of man, the Son of Mary, to the material world!

Hence there are those abilities for activities in the present to uphold the *purposes* for or in the relationships of man and woman; not condoning things that become questions, but rather showing that love that arises in the hearts and activities, in those influences that should be *necessary* in such unions as to bring into preparation those channels in mind and body through which souls may manifest in the material world. Not just the aggrandizement of a material or earthly or body passion, but that they each must give of their own bodies, their own blood, for such; that may bring to their consciousness the necessity for a training for such — even as thy training in that experience, even as thy fellows in those choices made because of their fitness, thy fitness in body, because of the fitness of thy father and thy mother, their fathers and mothers, during those experiences.

And these cry aloud then in thy experiences in the present, through what may be called eugenics — or the preparations for the entrances of souls that make the earth *better* in the material ways, yea the spiritual ways.

For God is not mocked, and whatsoever ye sow, that must ye also reap.

Preach, practice; give of thy strength in making these forces known in the hearts and minds of men *everywhere!*

2425-1   F.21   1/3/41   Sophie

. . . the entity was in that land now called by some the Promised Land, during those days when there was the looking forward to the channels through which there was expected to be the coming of the Messiah.

The entity was among those of that group chosen as ones to present themselves as a channel worthy of acceptance to be such.

Hence in its youth, as well as through those periods of girlhood, motherhood, the entity knew many of those who were so active — as was the entity — in those periods for a *definite* religious experience, as would be called today.

The entity then was of that sect or group known as the Essenes, and of those who were of the house of David, but of the kinship little to Joseph or Mary — and yet of those same groups.

The entity was among those who saw that vision on the stairs, when the first choice of the maidens was made. The entity knew then of the voice of the unseen forces as were aroused within the groups, that made for the speaking with the unusual tongues; not unknown yet unusual tongues, or the ability to make known their wishes to many in many tongues.

Throughout that experience the entity gained, though — as many that were of definite groups that set metes and bounds for their activities in relation to groups or masses, or even individuals — there were periods when the entity doubted.

But with the advancing of the activities which brought about the fulfilling to the entity of the various experiences, that answered to all phases of not only the material but the spiritual and mental phenomena, the entity was a believer, and among those who in the last day stood at the cross.[14]

The name then was Sophie.

649-1   F.17   9/4/34   Andra

... the entity was in that land known as the Holy Land, during the period when there had been those peoples who had looked and longed for, been expectant of, the coming of the promise to a people that sought relief from material bondage as well as from the spiritual activities of those that gormandized themselves and their own interests in the sale of privilege in the activities of those things that were of the letter of the law without the spirit thereof.

The entity then was in the household, and of the sisters that were in the temple with that one chosen as the channel through which the Spirit would manifest in the Holy One; hence a daughter of Elois [?], or the priestess that blessed the Holy One in the temple with Simeon [?].[15]

Then the entity, in the latter portion of the experience in that land, joined in that band who made for what would be termed in the present a prayer band, or ladies' aid or circle, that made the preparations for those that had separated themselves to become the followers of those peoples. And the entity then was with Simon Peter's mother, wife, the children of Zebedee, and their families—as well as Thomas and Luke; for Luke and Thomas were brothers.

In that experience the entity, in the name Andra, gained throughout; and the entity aided in preparing much of that which came later in the form of visualizing the paintings on the walls, the drawings that might be carried hither—and that became as banners that might be shown; also the wrappings for the last of the anointing of the body of the Holy One—rather the wrappings than the spices, for Magdalene and Mary and Jose [Josie], and the mother of the Lord prepared these. The napkins that were about His head, and with those seals that were later made as raised figures, did the entity prepare.[16]

THE CHOOSING OF MARY

649-2   F.18   8/8/35   Andra

Q-11. Please explain my relation with Mary, the mother of Jesus.

A-11. The activities then were as one of those who *grew* up with those affiliated in that order which bound together that particular group of individuals that were all associated at the time. To elucidate:

In the preparation for the coming of the Son of man, there were those during those periods who joined in their efforts to consecrate their lives, their bodies, for a service; for a channel through which activities might be had for the perfecting, as it were, of the material channel through which such an expression of the Creative Forces might come into the earth. See?

There were, then, twelve maidens in the temple, or of the *order* of the temple, who were dedicated for such preparation.

The entity, then, was one of the twelve so associated with Mary in the preparations.

Q-17. Please give the reason for my dream about the children on the double staircase.

A-17. This might be interpreted by some in one way, others in another!

In this particular experience, if this is experienced again it will go farther. For it was as the children (as self) on the staircase that led to the ordination or coronation room, in the dedicating of those twelve, at the time that Mary was *indicated*— by the walking up the steps, with the other children on the other—as the one being chosen or led by the Spirit.

This is rather, then, an *experience;* not a dream! Pray that it may be thine experience again. Let the deeper self, the real self, enter into the deep meditation that the I Am consciousness may make more and more aware of how the purposefulness of the experience may be applicable in the activities of the entity in the present. This is most to be desired.

379-3   F.54   9/17/35

Q-12. Whose choice was it that my daughter, [649], was in the temple in the Galilean experience?

A-12. Her own!

649-2   F.18   8/8/35

Q-12. Was Elois, as mentioned in my life reading, and Anna mentioned in the Bible, one and the same?

A-12. No. Anna was the older, or what would be termed the supervisor, or what would be termed by *some* as the lady superior of the group at the time.

587-3   F.44   11/21/34   Edithia

. . . the entity was in the Holy Land itself, during those periods when the Master walked among men, when there were the gatherings of those that questioned—even during those periods of the enunciation, when there was the wonderment as to whether the mother had escaped into Egypt or not, whether the mother had fled in time for the saving from the edict of Herod.

The entity was among those of that household in which Mary, the mother, had come when the Babe was born.

Throughout those sojourns in the experience the entity held that vision, that experience; not only those words of the shepherds, not only those voices heard, not only those words of the Wise Men, but that experience in itself from being in the *presence* of that which was about that inn.[17]

In the latter portion of the entity's sojourn there, the entity became closely associated with those who gathered there—or here and there, when those had wrecked their own selves upon the Body through the activities of the Romans' influence.

The entity gathered with those people that held to those tenets of the period, and *gained* throughout that sojourn, in the name then Edithia.

In the present from the experience, oft have there been the visions of the lights, the sounds, at certain seasons, at certain characters of the evening when the lights are low, and when those very voices—as it were—of the spheres are ringing in those periods that were experienced by the entity; and the heart grows heavy or glad—when there come those periods of turning within, and the wonderments of those experiences through which the entity passed in all of its activities; bringing to the inner self that peace, that joy, that harmony that was experienced when the understanding and the awakening came during that sojourn.

From that experience in the present we find the abilities within self to bring to others the sensitive understanding of the awakening for good that good may come, that all the virtues that have within themselves their own rewards bring to the inner man, to the inner soul, that peace, that harmony, that joy. Hence the beauties of the experience come in those periods when day is done, when there are the shades of the evening and the periods of quiet. Hence as the entity turns within self these may be raised to a better understanding . . .

. . . Then, give oft of self in the deeper service as thou taught and heard in Nazareth . . .

Q-3. *Why am I helpful and attractive to people professing atheism?*

A-3. As that inner self experienced in every thought during that sojourn in that particular land, how oft told the entity the story of the voice as heard, of the star, of the light, of the shepherds, of the Wise Men; and these be those tenets, those lessons *all* seek to hear. The entity gave same. Why would not there be that calling—calling—seeking ever by those who profess atheism, or who doubt. *Give!* As thou hast blessed Him, He hath blessed thee.

587-6   F.45   10/18/35   Edithia

In giving the interpretation of that as we find as a record in the experience of this soul-entity, it is well for the moment that there be given some conception of the conditions that surrounded that particular portion of the earth's spheres and activity of the period; also as a background, as it were, for this entity, this soul's experience as Edithia, in that particular phase of its development.

We find, then, the entity was of the household of those that had been a portion of the lineage where there had been set aside the men of the household for a definite service in the activities of the peoples of the day. Not merely in the thought of that termed in the present as the people of Israel, but rather that as understood by those peoples of the day—the greater meaning of the word Israel—those called of God for a service before the fellow man.

Then, that group, those of the particular sect to which the household of Edithia belonged, had—through study, through experience, through longing and desires—been among those that had been prepared. And there had come those periods when there were to be the changes in the order of things. Man as man had been looked upon as the only correct line of understanding or application, and woman (or women) as an individual was only to obey the master of the house. There had been, then, the understanding of that which had been promised from the beginning of man's interpretation of his relationships to a Creative Force or God, a *correct* interpretation of "and the seed of the woman shall bruise his head." [18]

There was then the choosing of those from the varied activities of that brotherhood, for those that might be chosen of the Lord for the channel through which there might come that beloved Son, who would make the paths straight, who would bring then *man out* of darkness into light; with the understanding that there must be—and would be, through the very expression of that Being in the earth—the understanding that the law was written in the hearts of men, rather than upon tables of stone; that the temple, that the holy of holies was to be within. Also that which had been given as the pattern to those that had made for the calling as of the voice of one in the wilderness for the people that were scattered as a flock without a shepherd. And behold the day, the hour, the time had come when that shepherd must lead forth His flock, His brethren again into the light of the countenance of an all-merciful Father.

This entity then, Edithia, was among the daughters that were chosen as those that were to dedicate, consecrate their bodies, their minds, their service to become a channel. And with others was chosen in the earlier period of its earthly activity.

Hence in that environ, in that atmosphere of expectancy, in that atmosphere of promise was the directing of the entity's thought, the entity's activity made during those experiences.

And when there was chosen that one to whom there had come that as a gift from on high, the entity *knew* then Mary, Martha, those of the household of Cleopas, those of the household of Anna, of Joseph, and those of the brotherhood of that order called the Essenes in that particular land.

There were those periods through which the entity as one

chosen or called among those for the dedicating of their activities, experienced not only those periods when the law demanded that the children, the sons were to be destroyed, but that even those who were consecrated might be abused the more by those activities of Roman power, or the authority that had been given among that brotherhood as that *from* which man was to be cleansed.[19]

In that environ, then, with those conditions that arose about the entity, did the early years, the early experiences come to this entity.

During those years of preparation of the Master in the various fields of activity, again there were the years of longing, the periods of oppression, the periods of fear and doubt, the periods of the attempt to be disbanded by those more and more in authority.

Hence when there was proclaimed of the son of Elizabeth that he had through the prayers, the activities of those consecrated souls, become one capable in the flesh of renouncing the priesthood and to become as an outcast that there might be made known what had been promised by those of old, that he should be as the voice of the one crying in the wilderness, "Prepare ye the way, for the day of the Lord *is* at hand," the entity was among those that aided in those preparations.[20] And it was a follower of same, owing to those periods of the preparation and the depressing periods when there had been the persecutions of those that scattered those chosen for those offices.

Then, in applying these to the urges that appear in the present experience, is there little wonder that the doubts and fears from those in authority should not make those recurrent activities in the very soul of the entity; that unless there arises some one who would defy custom, one that would defy authority, one that would defy in a manner even that which has become as the natural experience of those to keep harmonious experiences? For the day will arrive, even as it arose with the entity then, when he that separates himself becomes rather the one that declares to all.

And the entity has found self oft contemplating the face of the Master, on that day when John declared, "Behold the lamb of God that taketh away the reproach of His people!"[21]

This brings to the entity that awakening in the present; and more and more the entity should hold to those experiences that arise from those that walked and talked with Him as a man, *as* those that would become ones with that activity that *changed*—as it were—the course of the stars in their movement about the earth, and that becomes in the hearts and souls of men that hope which *quickens* as the water of life, that heals as does the touch of His hand upon the brow, that awakens as does the kind word spoken to those that are in doubt and in fear. For this is His teaching, "As ye do it unto the least of my brethren ye do it unto me."

The entity from those experiences in the periods of waiting, as many, doubted; yet in the presence of Him—as He increased, and as many of the disciples of John became doubtful when Herod putting forth his hand slew him that there might be the appeasing of a selfish desire because he had spoken against that which answered to the aggrandizing of a fleshly lust—there came the days when Edithia was with those great crowds that cried, "Hosanna! Ye come in the name of the Lord!" [22]

And though they turned into troublesome days, when He—too—was taken from His loved ones, Edithia remained with the holy women that in the period acted for the family as the mourners for Mary, who had been the companion of Edithia in the dedication of self, of self's abilities, of self's body, for those services.

Those experiences become in the present, then, as lights, as halos about the deeds done in the body to show forth His love to *His* brethren till it be fulfilled and He comes again[23] . . .

Q-5. What were my experiences with the shepherds who came seeking the Master, and describe my understanding of their experience at that time.

A-5. As indicated by the records, and as seen here, the shepherds came from the very fact that all nature, all the heavenly hosts, proclaimed that glorious period for man. And as the entity came with the Wise Men to do honor, to give of their substance, the entity—realizing within self that self, in body, in mind, had been dedicated to that service to man, that self might be a channel of blessing—found an awakening in the praise of that given by those shepherds who had *experienced* that cry of the heavenly hosts, "Behold a son is given, and his name is wonderful, counselor!" This awoke within the entity that as may be found in the present, how all nature—the face in the water, the dew upon the grass, the tint and the beauty of the rose, the song of the stars, the mourn of the wind, all proclaim—*now*—the mighty words of a merciful, a loving God.[24]

1904-2   F.52   8/16/39   Anna

. . . the entity was in the land now known as the Promised Land or Palestine land, during those periods when the preparations were being made by the many who had heard—as it were—the call from nature, and the harkening of the spirit for the preparations of the children of men that their bodies might furnish a channel through which the spirit of the Creative Forces might make manifest.

And there we find the entity was among the mothers who gave of themselves in body, and in the preparation of those things that had been handed down as of old, as to how—through the concentration of thought, and through the preparations by bodily exercise, as well as diet and physical activity—there might be the closer communion; or the consecrating of themselves that on the morrow there might be the greater preparations for the receiving of the message from the living forces or God.

Hence we find the entity, as one Anna, making overtures to the peoples—with the companion Jebocel (who has been, who is in a manner, associated with the entity in a portion of its experience)—as channels—being the cousin of the entity who became the channel through which the Prince of Peace came.

In the experience the entity made for the longings, and yet there were those innate feelings as of being denied something throughout. And there is the innate feeling in the experience of the entity through this sojourn that if there could but be the other side of a something deep within seen, there could be aroused a greater light.

Know that the spirit of truth lies within—not that it may descend from without or even from heaven. It's self! For, lo, it lieth within—and must—by the love, the application, the desire, the harmony—be aroused to that attunement, "I will abide with thee always!" Know that this means thy own self! For He hath not left thee comfortless, but the spirit of truth abides ever with thee.

1222-1   F.34   7/17/36   Anna

. . . Remember thou art in the same signs, omens, as the mother of Him; that gave to the earth the physical man, Jesus —Aquarius in its *perception,* perfection.

Hence when those experiences arose in that life, ye find it said, "She pondered these in her heart."[25] . . .

. . . the entity was in that known as the Holy Land, or the Promised Land, during those experiences when there were those expectancies and those activities when there was the activity that brought the Prince of Peace, the Christ, Jesus, into the earth.

The entity then was among those, or that *one* that would be termed as the waiting maid with Elizabeth *and* with Mary when they each were heavy with child; and at their meeting when there was the awareness of that as was to come to pass, the entity then was the one that blessed them both and made those prophecies as to what would be the *material* experience of each in the earth.

Then in the name Anna, the entity waited in the preparations for the maidens that consecrated their lives for this expectancy in those periods.

Hence the entity was then known as a seeress, a prophetess; and is one in the present that may find oft innate experiences coming through voices, through sounds as of music, through the rushing of mighty winds. But *know,* O my child, their *source,* when such things come to pass!

The Birth

Background

5749-8   6/27/37

Q-20. Do we celebrate Christmas at approximately the right time?

A-20. Not a great variation, for there having been the many changes in the accounting of time, or accounting for the periods from the various times when time is counted—not far wrong —twenty-fourth, twenty-fifth of December, as ye have your time now.

587-6   F.45   10/18/35

Q-1. When and where in Palestine was Jesus born?

A-1. In Bethlehem of Judea, in that grotto not marked in the present but called a stable; rather in the den where shelter was had did the *entity,* to be sure, look upon the child Jesus.[1]

Q-2. When was He born?

A-2. On the 19th day of what would now be termed March.

Q-3. And the year?

A-3. Dependent upon from what calendar or from what period ye would judge. From the Julian calendar, the year 4. From the Hebrew or the Mosaic calendar, the year 1899.

2067-7   F.53   6/25/41

Q-5. In one reading we are told Jesus' birthday was on March 19 according as we would reckon time now. In another reading we were told that we keep Christmas about the right time, the 24th or 25th of December as we have our time now. Please explain seeming contradiction.

A-5. Both are correct according to the time from which same were reckoned. How many times have there been the reckonings? Take these in consideration, with the period of events being followed in the information indicated. Just as there was the reckoning from the various groups for their individual activity, so was the information given as to the records from that source with which those seeking were concerned.

262-116   12/19/37

As ye approach the Season that to every student of Christian thought means so much, know that the birth of the Christ-child in Jesus has meant and does mean more and more in the thought and the activity of the world as a whole. And you each here may judge within yourselves as to whether the world is growing better or not according to that conviction, that feeling within thine own self that what the Christ-mass or Christmas spirit means is being manifested in thy daily life and thy associations with thy fellow men.

For unless this fact is a personal experience, then to you—as an individual—it is not being accomplished.

5749-8   6/27/37

Q-21. Who were the parents of Joseph?

A-21. That as recorded by Matthew, as is given, you see; one side recorded by Matthew, the other by Luke—these on various sides but of the house of David, as was also Mary of the house of David.[2]

254-109   5/20/41

Q-6. How did Mary and Joseph first come in contact with the Essenes and what was their preparation for the coming of Jesus?

A-6. As indicated, by being dedicated by their parents.

5749-8   6/27/37

Q-22. Were Mary and Joseph known to each other socially before the choosing for them to be man and wife?

A-22. As would be chosen in a lodge, not as ye would term of visitations; neither as only chosen by the sect or the families. In those periods most of the Jewish families, the arrangements were made by the parents of the contracting parties, you see; while in this—these were not as contracting parties from their families. For Ann and her daughter were questioned as to belonging to any, you see! Then it was not a choice altogether as that they were appointed by the leaders of the sect or of the group or of the lodge or of the church; for this is the church that is called the Catholic now—and is the closest.

These were kept then in that way of choice between them, and choice as pointed out by the divine forces . . .

Q-10. How old was Joseph at the time of the marriage?
A-10. Thirty-six.
Q-11. How old was Mary at the time of the marriage?
A-11. Sixteen.
Q-17. Where was the wedding performed? of Mary and Joseph?
A-17. In the temple there at Carmel.

254-109   5/20/41

Q-9. Please describe the Essene wedding, in temple, of Mary and Joseph, giving the form of ceremony and customs at that time.
A-9. This followed very closely the forms outlined in Ruth. It was not in any way a supplanting but a cherishing of the sincerity of purpose in the activities of individuals.[3]

When there was to be the association, or the wedding of Joseph and Mary—Mary having been chosen as the channel by the activities indicated upon the stair, by the hovering of the angel, the annunciation to Anna and to Judy and to the rest of those in charge of the preparations at that time—then there was to be sought out the nearer of kin, though *not* kin in the blood relationships. Thus the lot fell upon Joseph, though he was a much older man compared to the age ordinarily attributed to Mary in the period. Thus there followed the regular ritual in the temple. For, remember, the Jews were not refrained from following their rituals. Those of the other groups, as the Egyptians or the Parthians, were not refrained from following the customs to which they had been trained; which were not carried on in the Jewish temple but rather in the general meeting place of the Essenes as a body-organization.

5749-8   6/27/37

Q-8. In what manner was Joseph informed of his part in the birth of Jesus?
A-8. First by Mathias or Judah. Then as this did not coincide

with his own feelings, first in a dream and then the direct voice.

And whenever the voice, this always is accompanied with odors as well as lights; and oft the description of the lights is the vision, see?

Q-9. *Why was he disturbed when Mary became with child while yet a virgin?*

A-9. Owing to his natural surroundings and because of his advanced age to that of the virgin when she was given; or as would be termed in the present, because of what people say. Yet when assured, you see, that this was the divine, not only by his brethren but by the voice and by those experiences, he knew. For you see there was from the time of the first promise, while she was still yet in training from the choice, there was a period of some three to four years; yet when he went to claim her as the bride, at the period of—or between sixteen and seventeen, she was found with child.[4]

Q-18. *Where did the couple live during the pregnancy?*

A-18. Mary spent the most of the time in the hills of Judea, portion of the time with Joseph in Nazareth. From there they went to Bethlehem to be taxed, or to register—as ye would term.

Q-19. *Who assisted as midwife?*

A-19. This has been touched upon through these sources; and as the daughter of the innkeeper and those about assisted and aided, these have seen the glory, much, in their experiences.

1648-1   F.57   7/28/38   Margii

... the entity was in the land now called Palestine, during the periods when the Master walked in the earth.

The entity then was very close to those activities of both Elizabeth and Mary, during those periods when there were the preparations and confusions in the minds and activities of those who were to be the channels through which activities were to come to mean that in the experience of the world, and the hearts of men and women as individuals, that would arouse them to their relationships to the Creative Forces, as well as to the manner in which same may be expressed—only as we deal with our fellow men!

Then it may be said that the entity was the midwife for both

Mary *and* Elizabeth. While there were not those immediate activities, there was the counsel with them as to that purpose for which each had been chosen as the channel for the manifestations. Such was the counsel of the entity during that particular experience.

Is it any wonder, then, as to what the home, or the young, in the lives of those who are just beginning the building of homes, or the building of activities, has meant and does mean to the entity in the present?

Yet denied so much of these that oft it becomes the longing for the entity to be in that position in which the minds of the young might be directed by self, in the choice of their directing of activities for such!

Hence the very great activity of the entity in the present in directing the minds and the hearts and the purposes and the ways of those who counsel with all such in their individual channels or places of service in the world.

Not then that the peoples of the present are responsible, but rather that which they create in the minds and the hearts and the activities of those who are to become the mothers and the fathers of the future generations! In *those* rests the responsibility as to what the thoughts and actions of such are to be!

Such were a portion of the entity's experience then, as Margii —who was *of* the priestly—yea, the kingly peoples; yet the purposely mothers of the peoples of that experience.

In the present from those activities we find, as indicated, while disappointments have arisen and do arise, the entity should hold to that as it practiced, as it preached in counsel with those mothers—as to the thought—yea, of spiritual truth; as it counseled with those then, so may it in the present counsel with those who direct the flocks of Israel—or those that direct the flocks of those who are seekers after truth.

Thus the entity may again fill that longing, fill that purpose for which each soul enters a material experience, that it may be a channel through which its portions of the material earth may be bettered because of its having lived in same!

Then so live and so act that each individual, each day, each place in which ye find thyself, day by day, may be better for thy having passed that way!

Sow the seed of the Spirit. Be not overanxious about same. For the Father alone can and does bring such to fruition in His own way and manner.

And only the try, only the purpose, only the desire is necessary in thy individual activity . . .

Let, first, self counsel with self as to keeping in all good conscience before thy Ideal; and that being He who became the material manifestation through the material motherhood with whom ye counseled—for not once but twice, yea three times have ye seen Him coming to the earth in the various spheres of activity; He that is the way, the manner, the how man approaches his relationships to God!

1158-5   F.46   12/2/36   Ruth, sister of Jesus

Q-1. Was Jesus the natural son of Joseph?

A-1. As just given, as ye questioned in Athens as regarding these; a conception through the Holy Spirit. For the pouring out of the body of thy *natural* mother, the natural daughter of Joseph the Carpenter—these brought to the consciousnesses of the entity the fact that there were, there are, there can be such to those who *open* themselves into the will of the Father-God, that *their* wills are one with His.

And in such even in the earth there comes the natural to be unnatural, and the unnatural natural. For Nature proclaims God, as the unnatural in nature magnifies God.

Q-2. If not, how can the rest of humanity be expected to reach His perfection when they start with a less divine origin?

A-2. O that the children of men would gain that which is the purpose for procreation in the earth! and start within their own selves in those periods of activities that bring about the channel for or the means of the entering in of the holy ones that ideal! For He *is* the way, and He asks that all follow in that way.

And as two souls come in a union of purpose—not a gratifying of earth, not a gratifying of the earthly impulses and desires but that they, too, may be used as channels through which souls may enter—there may be brought into the earth those that may quicken. For all must be lifted up even as He.

But through the natural, the unnatural means as He entered, all become then in that purpose, in that oneness as the natural way, the natural source.

THE BIRTH

Q-3. Does this mean that the world will evolve into bringing souls into the world in the manner that Mary did?
A-3. Souls will evolve into the manner to be able to bring into the world souls, even as Mary did.[5]
And these may come as the souls of men and women become more and more aware that these channels, these temples of the body are *indeed* the temple of the living God and may be used for those communications with God, the Father of the souls of men!

5749-7   6/27/37
Q-1. Explain the immaculate conception.
A-1. As flesh is the activity of the mental being (or the spiritual self and mental being) pushing itself into matter, and as spirit—as He gave—is neither male nor female, they are then both—or one.
And when man had reached that period of the full separation from Creative Forces in the spirit, then flesh as man knows it today became in material plane a reality.
Then, the immaculate conception is the physical and mental so attuned to spirit as to be quickened by same.
Hence the spirit, the soul of the Master then was brought into being through the accord of the mother in materiality that ye know in the earth as conception.
Q-5. Does the immaculate conception, as explained, concern the coming of Mary to Anne, or Jesus to Mary?
A-5. Of Jesus to Mary.
Q-6. Was Mary immaculately conceived?
A-6. Mary was immaculately conceived.

2067-11   F.56   2/22/43
Q-6. In Jewish history was anybody but Mary and Jesus immaculately conceived?
A-6. Mary was not immaculately conceived [according to Jewish history]. Jesus was. There have been others, but not in Jewish history.

5749-3   6/17/33
Q-1. Please explain the virgin birth of Jesus, the Christ.
A-1. In that there had been the manifestation in the earth of that which completed the cycle for the necessary manifesta-

tion in the earth of the holy influence necessary for the sustaining of a backsliding world, there was then that choosing of the influence through which there became manifest (in and through those channels that comply with the laws of spiritual forces) that which brought into being the conception, that made for the living influence of the spirit through the body that became the child Jesus; and through the manifesting of the spirit of the oneness of the Father became a manifestation of the Christ spirit in material surroundings.

5749-8   6/27/37

Q-2. Was Ann prepared for her part in the drama as mother of Mary?

A-2. Only as in the general, not as specific as Mary after Mary being pointed out.

See, there was no belief in the fact that Ann proclaimed that the child was without father. It's like many proclaiming today that the Master was immaculately conceived; they say "Impossible!" They say that it isn't in compliance with the natural law. It *is* a natural law, as has been indicated by the projection of mind into matter and thus making of itself a separation to become encased in same—as man did.

Then, that there has been an encasement was a beginning. Then there must be an end when this must be or may be broken; and this began at that particular period. Not the only—this particular period with Ann and then the Master *as* the son; but the *only* begotten of the Father in the flesh *as* a son of an immaculately conceived daughter!

Q-3. Neither Mary nor Jesus, then, had a human father?

A-3. Neither Mary nor Jesus had a human father. They were one *soul* so far as the earth is concerned; because [otherwise] she would not be incarnated in flesh, you see.

2067-7   F.53   6/25/41

Q-23. Please explain more about Mary being the twin soul of Jesus and her refusal to reincarnate, and her deity?

A-23. We do not find such as even being true.

5749-8   6/27/37

Q-1. Is the teaching of the Roman Catholic Church that Mary was without original sin from the moment of her conception in the womb of Ann, correct?

A-1. It would be correct in *any* case. Correct more in this. For, as for the material teachings of that just referred to, you see: In the beginning Mary was the twin soul of the Master in the entrance into the earth!

281-54   5/28/41

Q-3. The mother of Jesus in being a channel for material desires was making practical her spiritual activities.
A-3. Correct.

The Inn

1196-2   M.58   6/23/36   Apsafar, Abel-Tean

. . . the entity then was that man, the keeper of the inn, to which Joseph made application for a place for the birth of the Master of men.

Much of that as has been recorded as we find is not so well, nor in keeping with that the entity did then—as Apsafar; who was of the Essenes, though of a Jewish descent, though a combination of the Jewish and the Grecian.

For the entity then made a study of those peoples, knew of those things that had been foretold by the teachers of the Essenes, and made all preparations as near in keeping with what had been foretold as possible.

While among the entity's stables was indeed the place of rest, it was because of the very rabble, the very act of those that were in authority—both as to the Roman as well as the various groups that were in their discussions making for the very things that would hinder or prevent those experiences that had been foretold. The entity did this rather for protection, than because—as has been said—there was "no room in the inn." [1] But this was meant to be implied or conveyed, that they were "turned away." Yet in the entity's activities it was really for the protection. For the entity, too, had seen a vision; the entity, too, had heard, had known of the voices that were in the air. The entity, too, had seen the star in the east. The entity, too, had known of those experiences that must befall those that were making all the preparations possible under those existent conditions for Him that should come as a teacher, as a shepherd, as a savior.

Hence the experiences of the entity were as of those that are ever present in the entity's inner self. And when there is sorrow, when there are cares for others—these become rather as an appealing experience in the entity's activities.

For these are innate and are builded from those experiences in that land about Bethany, in which the great development, the great experiences came. And much might be given as to the history. For the entity was in that position where it stood rather not as one that made for a spy, either upon the Jewish or the Roman or those of its own peoples, but rather as a counselor to those that sought to overcome those oppressions that were of a political as well as of a religious nature, owing to those conditions existing between the Pharisees, the Sadducees, the Essenes, the Romans, and those teachings that were gradually being presented from the Grecians—or the entity's peoples, for the correlation of the philosophies that were of the Grecians and those activities with the Teacher, the Nazarene.

Hence the entity—though in years—came to know the experiences, and there did the entity know its present companion or wife. For their relationships then were rather as father and daughter in the experience; for *she* stood watch.

In the experience then, there comes in from those activities the very nature of the religious influence, yet the adherence to any particular sect or any particular denomination—as ye term—or any particular group, seems to have a drawback to the entity, because of those very experiences of contentions that arose during that sojourn . . .

First know thine own ideal, as thou didst find in thine studies as the innkeeper upon the gateway to the city of learning.

As thou didst keep in touch with those from Carmel's gates, so in thy dealings with thy fellow man in every walk of life thou mayest become as the gateway to understanding for many . . .

Yet carry with these the basic forces as make for that as ye heard in thy declining years in the Bethany land, for thou wert present when he was raised from the dead, the friend Lazarus,[2] as well as a friend to those that suffered through the experiences and the oppressions of those in authority . . .

Q-1. What was my name as innkeeper in the time of the Master?

A-1. Abel-Tean.

Q-2. What was the name of my daughter, who is now my present wife?

A-2. Anna.

Q-3. Did I do any special work in that life besides as innkeeper?

A-3. As has been indicated, the entity was as a go-between between those in authority in the religious influences in the Roman and the Jewish faith; or a *keeping* of a watch, as a counselor to those that sought the way.

2550-1   F.38   4/28/41   Sodaphe

. . . the entity was in the Promised Land, during those early periods of activity in which there were the expectancies for the coming of the Master.

The entity then was closely associated with the innkeeper and those activities there; being the wife of the innkeeper, thus the mother of the daughter who spoke to and who directed the Wise Men, and who saw and held the young Child first.

In the experience the entity was pulled between confusing influences. Though the customs of the day called for the entity's position to be rather hidden, the entity in its purpose and in its very activity was quite outspoken. Hence with the visions, the experiences that came about during that particular period, the entity was awed—and was then kept in that constant air of expectancy because of those periods through which there were the days of purification for the mother of the Son of God.

Throughout that sojourn the entity, as Sodaphe, brought betterments in the experience of the mother of the Lord.

1152-1   F.60   4/20/36   Jenife [see 1152-3 giving her name as Sarapha or Sara]

. . . the entity was in the earth during that period when great changes, great opportunities were coming to man by the fulfilling of time and of the prayers of many.

At the period there were turmoils and strifes in many directions, and the peoples of the land were pulled between the truths or lessons being presented by the Romans as well as by the new interpretations by the peoples of the land.

But when the Prince of Peace came into the earth for the completing of His *own* development in the earth, *He* overcame the flesh *and* temptation. So He became the first of those that overcame death in the body, enabling Him to so illuminate, to so revivify that body as to take it up again, even when those fluids of the body had been drained away by the nail holes in His hand and by the spear piercing His side.

Yet this body, this entity, *too,* may do these things; through those promises that were so new yet so old, as given by Him. "Not of myself do I these things," saith He, "but God, the Father that worketh in me; for I *come* from Him, I go to Him."

He came, the Master, in flesh and blood, even as thou didst come in flesh and blood. Yet as He then proclaimed to thee, there is a cleansing of the body, of the flesh, of the blood, in such measures that it may become illumined with power from on high; that is *within* thine own body to *will!* "Thy will, O God; not mine, but Thine, be done in me, through me." [3]

This was the message as He gave when He, too, overcame; surrendering all power unto Power itself, surrendering all will unto the will of the Father; making of self then a channel through which others taking hope through the knowledge that He hath perfected Himself, may bring to thee that grace, that mercy, that is eternity with Him and in Him.

Then in the name Jenife (as would be interpreted in the present), the entity was a daughter of the innkeeper, that stood by—and was the second of those that took the Babe into their arms.

What should such mean in thy experience?

Is it any wonder that thou hast looked long into the face of those that were newly born and wondered, wondered what *their* purpose, *their* hardships, their joys, their sorrows would be in the earth?

In the experience the entity beheld not only the experiences of the shepherds but the words of the sages of the East who came bringing those gifts to Him that had been proclaimed from old should come again!

THE BIRTH

And He will come again and again in the hearts, in the minds, in the experiences of those that *love* His coming.

But those when they think on Him and know what His Presence would mean and become fearful, He passeth by — even as the experiences of the entity through that sojourn found many that harkened not to the simple words of Him who gave, "Know thyself, know that thy Father abideth in thee. And if ye love Him, ye may know His ways, His experiences."

1152-3   F.61   11/27/36   Sarapha or Sara [see 1152-1 giving her name as Jenife]

In that sojourn we find the entity then was, in time, just a year younger than the little mother who came to the inn where the entity then was an aid to the parents.

And the entity knowing of same through the meetings that were half forbidden by those in the Jewish law and questioned by those in authority for the penal law, there was caused not only the wonderments but — as seen from the nature of the natural development — a seeking to know. Also the entity *felt* the emotions of some great thing in the experience of the world about to come to pass.

The entity then, in the name Sarapha (or Sara), requested that she might aid in the preparation of those quarters to which that mother-to-be, that father, might come — that were revered by all.

For it was well known to the innkeeper that which had been set by those high superiors or leaders, as to the care that must be given to those as they wended their way to fulfill the needs of an overlord demanding that all register for their contribution to an alien land.

Yet as the entity waited, expectant, there was the general rabble; and there were the discussions of those that journeyed to Jerusalem for the meetings, as well as to the centers for their taxing-registration — as ye would term in the present.

The entity was comely in person and was sought by one that would today be called a registrar, as companion; yet rejected him — though the entity has met him in this present experience; and the association has meant much, and much disturbance too.

Then the entity aided, so that all was in readiness, when in the evening—just before the sun in all its glory of the Palestine hills gave forth almost into the voice of nature, proclaiming the heralding of a new hope, a new birth to the earth, and the glorifying of man's hope in God—the spectre of His star in the evening sky brought awe and wonder to all that beheld.[4]

And the entity, being anxious, gazed with wondering awe at that *unusual* experience to all, and wept with *joy* of those unfoldments within self, of the emotions that made for the expectancy of glory surpassing what had been told of all the glories of her peoples in the days of old.

There the entity felt what may be very close akin to the experiences in self in the present—that a new light, a new vision, a new experience was *being born* in every atom of its being.

Then when it was known to the entity that the den, the cave, the stable had been occupied—Oh, the rush, Oh, the desire to be off to see what that experience might be, held the very being of the entity!

And as soon as its duties were cleared about the home, as the space was very near, the entity started. But as the entity walked into the open upon that Eve, the brightness of His star came nearer and nearer. And the entity heard, even as the shepherds, "*Peace* on earth, *good will* to men." [5]

There came again that awe, that feeling of a new creation, of a new experience, as the entity among those—only with the closer attendant of the mother—hastened; while all the rabble, all the jeers of a world were stopped!

As it hastened to the quarters where the mother lay, in all that awe of a new experience, and the light as from His star filled the place, the entity then first beheld the *Babe*. That was the crowning experience, until the plea that she—too—might hold that glorious child in her arms also!

Then as this became a reality, there were those feelings, those experiences—O that the world might know the beauty, the joy, the glory of the experiences of His Life in their own hearts and minds and beings!

There the entity also saw the shepherds gather, there the entity also saw on the morrow the Wise Men—with their ladened beasts or camels, with all their praise for those who had kept the faith, in making and preserving, in keeping and helping those that were in need, that were alone—yet *God* with them!

There were those experiences of the presence as well as that expressed in those strange tongues to the entity, though the entity knew and thought and felt and experienced the reverence and awe as shown by all.

As the entity sought to find, to keep in touch with the mother, the Child, and then when the edict went forth, indeed was the entity's heart rent with fear. For that experience became then as something to be cherished, yet the fear of the law and the hatred that would naturally arise in the hearts of those that were persecuted.

For oft was the entity's father questioned as to which way, as to what amounts, as to what *were* the activities of those men who had defied the authorities of Rome as well as of Herod the king at that experience.

Those made for days and weeks and months when the entity wondered and wondered and wondered.

And the necessity for menial labors by the great demands made upon those with whom the entity sojourned, and those activities roundabout, brought mental and material distresses. Yet oft the entity in the stillness of the evening reviewed the happenings, and there was the seeking more and more as to what had become of His star, His light.

And as there was followed the receding of His star, and the flight into Egypt through the devious ways and manners in which there came the news through word of mouth, yet in awe and quiet kept, it made for that in the experience of the entity—when it sits alone in the twilight, and there is almost again felt the music of the spheres, the singing of the morning stars, as the earth is quieted—there enters oft again that peace, that is only troubled by the cares of a workaday world.

In the days and months and years that followed, eventually the entity became closer to those in Bethany and those upon Mount Olive. For *there* the entity took up its abode, upon the edge of Olivet [?], on the road that led to the great city.

And there word was sought again of what had become of that

glorious, that marvelous experience which to the entity became more and more a burning experience in the heart.

Yet when persecutions came, and the influence more and more of the Romans, and more and more of the sects and activities of the Sadducees that persecuted especially those groups to which the entity had belonged, and in which it had found so much help, so much wonderment—then doubt and fears arose.

For apparently, from the words that were heard, the Child had become only as another of those that were of the peoples, yet was it for *all* the peoples!

For as other children came, and as other experiences were brought about, not until in those days when again as a child He went with His parents and those of the great company to again register did the entity realize and know the truth of what had been experienced.[6]

For at the time or period when the passover feast was demanded to be kept by all of the children of Israel, then the entity sought again that Child, that young man, that glorious child that questioned the doctors. And the entity kept close, that she—too—might hear. For it had put away then all thoughts of association or union with *men;* though beset and though disturbed, and though those forces of the periods were brought about. For the entity became what may be said to be as the first body to dedicate its mind, its body, its *being* to a purpose, to a Child!

Throughout those experiences, then, the entity wondered; and sought for word as to His progress, in following that which had become almost as a story; yet the entity held to those visions, those experiences in the evening before, during those periods when they beheld the light, when they beheld the Child in the mother's arms—and that glorious moment when it had been placed in her own, and the entity had pressed its own lips to the brow of that Babe!

When there began then the ministry of Jesus the man, the entity held fast—and stayed close to every word that might be gathered from those who heard the more oft.

But when the visits brought Him near, and yet the cares kept

THE BIRTH 83

the entity closer to the abode near the highways through which throngs now oft passed, the entity pondered, pondered—grew fearful for the things that were being said.

And then the rejection by His own peoples, when He first began His ministry, brought tears of scalding shame to the entity for those very ones that seemed to doubt when they should know.

When there came at last those days when there was the triumphal entry from Bethany into Jerusalem, to the temple, the entity was among that mighty throng that cried, "Hosanna to the Highest—the King cometh." [7]

And there the entity met those disappointments again, when that mighty force, that glorious creature, that mighty man among men was not proclaimed king. And He seemed to exert so little of that necessary material application of a glorious power and might over those things in man's experience of sickness, of doubt, of fear!

For many of those were known to the entity who had been healed. And the entity was especially joined closer then to that one Bartaemus [Bartimaeus?], who had rested oft by the way, close to where the entity abode.

When the days of the crucifixion were passed, and the entity stood then with the holy women and those that aided in sustaining those of the household that were beginning to feel that possibly the mother, Mary, had misjudged. Yet the entity *knew* from her own experience, had not forgotten that choir before the celestial throne that sang, "Glory, *glory* in the highest—peace—*peace* on earth, to all men of good will."

Those experiences the entity held, and they are innate in the present; though the entity was first among those to suffer martyrdom by the roughness of the Romans that attempted to disperse the crowds. For through the injuries that came, broken of body, the entity suffered in the flesh; but then it was even as now—the entity looks ever to Him who *is* life, light and immortality to those who put their trust wholly in Him!

In the application then, we would give counsel to those and to the entity who have tasted, who have felt, who have known within themselves that He is the Way, He is the Truth, the

Light, and no other name is given under heaven whereby man may be made whole, or whereby man may know his true relationships to God.

Hold *fast* to that, O daughter of the innkeeper, O the beholder of His glory; O the joyous, gracious feelings that fill thy soul and being with the richness of the earth poured out at His feet, with those that experienced the lowly shepherds that came to see that glorious sight, and they—too—were not hindered from beholding the face of their Savior. And ye, too, O daughter, may know His face—but turn *within!* For *there* ye may meet Him, as so oft ye did in those days, those weeks, those months, those years ye recounted in thine inner self those glorious experiences, those glorious happenings of that day when the Babe, the child Jesus lay in thy arms.

For He is very nigh unto all that call on His holy name. He has promised and His promises are sure, to *you*—to *YOU*—to Y-O-U; and *in* you may you know! Not listening to those fears, but listening to those things even as ye heard during those days when those wonderments were so close a portion of thine experience. Embrace him *now,* even as ye did upon that glorious day when the earth saw and heard and felt her King, her Maker, had taken on the earth and become a part of same.

So may ye, too, take on God—in Him, and become a part of *His* dealings with man!

Ready for questions.

Q-1. What did I do as the innkeeper's daughter?
A-1. As indicated throughout, the care in the home—and yet those many activities as indicated. And with the persecutions, and at last the death of the father, the entity then prepared or kept an inn herself, upon the Mount of Olives nigh unto Bethany, on the road from Jerusalem to Gizeh.

Q-2. What in my previous appearances merited my being born as the innkeeper's daughter?
A-2. As has been indicated in those appearances before, there was brought about that seeking, that desire to be *so close,* and to be willing to dedicate self. O that man would but gain that willingness in self to be a channel to be used, even as He gave,

THE BIRTH

"Not my will but Thine, O God, be done in and through me." That has been the cry and is the experience of all, even as that entity then, that may come to know His face!

Q-3. What experience did I have with the three Wise Men?
A-3. As has been indicated.

Q-4. How did I contact them?
A-4. As has been given. The entity was there at the time when they came as from the King, and saw—as given—not only the glories and the gold and the precious things of the earth poured at His feet, but saw also the adoration as from the lowly shepherds that were bewildered by those in power or in authority, and yet—as the entity—saw indeed that there was no respecter of persons in the face or heart of that Babe! And indeed He is today no respecter of persons! For Jesus, the Christ, as God, is the same yesterday, today and forever!

Q-5. How long did the holy family remain in Bethlehem?
A-5. Until the time of purification was passed. Twenty-nine days, as ye would count suns today.

Q-6. How long was I closely associated with them?
A-6. Throughout the period, and in those ways and manners as has been indicated.

Q-7. Was I associated at that time with the entity who was my husband in this life?
A-7. As has been given, he was the registrar—rejected by the entity.

Q-8. How was I associated with Ruth, the sister of Jesus?
A-8. As has been indicated, there were some periods or changes in between—there were some doubts and some fears, some not understandings as to why the other members of the family could not see in the child, in the man, that which had been experienced by the entity.

Only when the days of the crucifixion, the resurrection were passed, and there was the greater knowledge that indeed—as many of the Romans gave—"*Indeed* this was the Son of God," did the entity become very closely associated with Ruth—and that only for very short periods.

For, as indicated, she was among those of a different class or group, and of those peoples that had joined with those that to the entity were to be hated for their part in her own father's death and the persecutions and questions that had been brought in the experience.

Q-9. Why is it, having had such an experience, that I have not become purified and more as I should like to be?

A-9. If—*if* ye will but empty thyself, ye may be *filled* with that glory even as then! Count not judgments as the judgments of man. For man looketh on the outward appearance, but God seeth—even as ye have experienced in those moments of thy closeness—the heart, and that purpose, that *will*, that desire there!

The Shepherds

2562-1   M.35   5/9/41   Thaddeus

... the entity was among the shepherds who heard the voice, who saw the light, and who experienced the choir of the angelic hosts that pronounced His advent.[1]

In its activity then the entity was closely associated with one of the writers of the Gospel; in fact, the one who addressed most of his writings to Theophilus.

The entity gained through the experience, in power, in might, in the ability as a speaker, as an interpreter of the teachings of the Roman as well as the various groups and sects of people.

These made the tendencies for doubting, and yet the holding fast to those principles that bespeak of what the individual entity accepts as the ideal.

The name then was Thaddeus.

1815-1   M.15   2/8/39   Eucuo

... the entity was among the shepherds who heard the cry of "Glory to God in the Highest—peace on earth and good will to men."

These were as those forces that made for abilities in the harp, the reeded instruments; and the greater songs that were played in those periods were part of that intuition, that motivative force which arose from the activities of the entity under that experience.

Hence he beheld Him as a babe! . . .
The name then was Eucuo.

519-1   M.39   2/20/34   Slocombi

. . . the entity was in the land now called or known as the Promised Land, during those periods when there were the destructive forces owing to the visits, the star that came from the East, and those reports, when the children were put to death that there might be the destroying of those things that had been foretold or told by the Wise Men of the East.

The entity then, in the name Slocombi, was among the kinsmen of the father and mother of the forerunner of the Master —or of John, called the Baptist.

In that experience the entity was among the shepherds that were in the hill country, and among those that heard the song of the angels, "Peace on earth, good will to men."

While the entity suffered, as to those destructive forces brought into the experience at the time, in the latter portion of the experience the entity came very close in touch with the activity of the Nazarene, the Prince of Peace, the Savior of men, as He walked in the earth; and among those that gathered at the feast when it was made by those that had been called the disciples or the representatives of the peoples in that particular experience.

1859-1   M.26   4/7/39   Joel

. . . the entity was in the earth during the days when the Master walked in the land, and especially in those activities when there was the enunciation, the announcing at those periods in the Bethlehem hills.

. . . the entity, though a musician, a dreamer, was a herdsman—and among those who heard the singing, as well as the lights—and was among those who viewed what came to pass in the stable in Bethlehem.

In the experience then the entity was known as Joel—elderly in that period when this came about, yet so impressed with the ability for song, poetry, the telling of those experiences, that it becomes as it were a part of the activity.

2125-1   F.62   10/19/31   Josie

. . . in that land during those periods when there were the gathering together of the peoples that were taxed in those days, and the entity then among those who came to the same town in which the shepherds gave to the peoples thereabout the message of the angels in that land. The entity then among those who came and saw the mother and the Babe in the manger, and carried to the peoples in the hills *that* thought, *that* experience, that was not forgotten by the entity. Later in the experience we find the entity among those who led many to the understanding of those *lessons* as were being given by the Master, by the Teacher, leading those; even that one who became the power, or tower of strength, in the defense when persecutions arose, leading the blind Bartimaeus to the road when the Master passed by.[2] In the name Josie. Much may be read in those teachings of the entity during that experience. The entity gained throughout the experience by the service that was given to others in bringing the understanding of the teachings to those of the period.

509-1   F.65   2/5/34   Myra

. . . the entity in that land when the Master came as the babe, and the entity was then in the household of Salome — as a sister of Mary, the mother of the Lord.

The entity was a babe that viewed the body and played as a child with the Holy Child, and yet taken — as if by the angels themselves — that the body then might know the realms of aid to those that would counsel in the flesh and in the spirit with *our* Lord.

Hence in the name then Myra, yet that experience, that viewing in the flesh of that glory made manifest by God among men, that there might be the intercession for man through his waywardness has given to the entity in the present experience an ideal of tolerance that is seldom found in the hearts and the souls of those in an earthly sojourn.

So in the soul is ever the glory of that the entity enjoyed *in* the earth and among those that ministered, of the angels of mercy and light, *to* that body during its earthly sojourn.

[See page 475 for incarnation at time of Saul of Tarsus.]

Consecration in the Temple

1521-1   F.1 wk.   1/22/38   Anna

... it was a prophetess as Anna ... it was the *mother* of the *prophet* as Hannah! [1] ...

... the entity was in the land and period when there were those expectancies for the coming of the Lord, the Master, the promise of those influences in the experience of men.

The entity then was the prophetess Anna, that waited in the temple and held and blessed Him in the days when there was according to the law the presenting of, the purifying of the mother by the material and the spiritual law of the people in that experience.

The entity gained throughout that experience, though suffering in body, suffering in many of those things that arise from those activities in a materialistic world of a spiritual-*minded* individual given to a purpose and a cause that is in the spiritual and mental sense to be the source of redemption for the great numbers rather than the few.

2629-1   F.55   11/29/41   Anna

... the entity was in the Promised Land, when the Master walked in the earth, when there were the enunciations that there was to be the coming of the Savior.

The entity then was among those peoples who chose the activities about the temple service. For, the entity was she that blessed Him in that day when He was presented in the temple for consecration to the Lord—Anna.

In the experience the entity longed for, and saw in its latter period, that fulfilling; yet knowing what were to be the material trials, the material sufferings—yea, even to the death on the cross.

Know, then, as ye counsel with thy fellow man—know ever, and depart not from that faith—it is Jesus the Christ and Him crucified! and as to how each soul, each entity, each physical being *must* crucify in their minds, their hearts, their bodies, that as would separate them from the love of Him who hath shown the way, the truth and the light.

For, He so loved the world as to give His Son. Ye have loved, ye do so love thy fellow man as to give thy mind, thy body, in counsel, in instruction, in those activities that enable the individual souls to think better of themselves and the reason thereof. For, they must learn to live with themselves, even as did He, and to know—though the prince of this world may come, may tempt, may even declare the joy of self-elation—he has no part in them.

For, thou didst show the way to many; many of those who through that consecration of self, gained in such a manner as to declare unto others that as was to become, in their experience, the hope of man.

And know today there is no other than that found in the admonition given by Jesus of Nazareth, Jesus the Christ—"If ye believe in God, believe also in me." Hence He is that to which the mind of the individual entity responds. He is the way, the mind is the way. And as the mind dwells upon the fruit of the spirit—faith, hope, gentleness, kindness, patience—it may blossom into that which brings the hope of man, the confidence in his brethren, the faith in his God.

2166-1   F.80   4/11/40   Ananan

. . . the entity was active in those periods when the Master walked in the earth; among those of that land where strife had arisen, and where the peoples of the land had hoped for a redeeming power in the affairs of the peoples of promise.

As the entity was among the holy women in the temple, it brought comfort and consolation, and proclaimed ever to the peoples of that period, "Harken to the voice of Him who has called, 'If ye will be my people, I will be thy God!' Turn ye to that way in which ye may bring *again* the sunshine of God's purpose among this people!" This was the message the entity gave.

And as the entity had prayed, as the entity had lived that it might indeed see the day when that promise was fulfilled— thus when the mother, Mary, presented the Babe in the temple, the entity blessed same, and saw that face! . . .

So the entity gained through that experience, not only by its waiting upon the activities in the temple in the Holy City, but as it ministered to the peoples in many of the lands thereabout, through that particular sojourn.

The name then was Ananan.

1938-2   F.78   6/29/39   Sathamantha

... the entity was in the land now known as the Promised Land, during those periods when there was much expectancy, much preparation on the part of those who were looking forward to the redeeming of the peoples from not only the bondage of the Roman rule but the misconception and misapplication of the laws of individuals or peoples who professed to be in the way of the chosen people.

The entity was among those who were the musicians in the temple where Anna and Simeon saw the consecration of the one Lord, the one Master.

Then the entity was a harpist, or what would be called a harp today . . .

The name then was Sathamantha. In the experience the entity gained throughout.

1283-1   F.61   10/31/36   Zadok

... the entity lived in the earth during those periods when there were the activities just previous to the advent of the Holy One into the earth's experience, among those peoples of that group then called the Essenes.

The entity was active among those in aiding to gather the data from the various teachers of the varied lands for the interpretation of that for that particular group.

Then the entity was very close to one Anna, in the temple service. For it was of the same household, of the same activity, yet varying somewhat in the manner of their presentations. Yet when the ministry began in the latter days of the entity's experience in and about that portion of Bethany and a part of Jerusalem, there became much of that the entity had given, the entity gave, that became as a part of that to those who looked for the activities of the minister, the teacher, the Holy One.

For the entity then was a prophetess as well as among those, as it might be said, who were the recorders or who kept the records of those peoples.

Hence the associations with John, as well as with the various individuals that led with those groups, became as a part of the entity's experience.

1032-1   F.62   10/25/35

The entity then was among those who were nigh unto the priests that ministered in the temple, that made for the associations of man's relationships to the individuals who sought for the quieting of the longings within, for the expressions of a divine love shown among men.

And in those days when there was the presenting in the temple, when Anna blessed the Son, the entity aided in that service in such measures that to the entity in the present experience the birth of a son, the birth of any one to those about the entity, has meant and does mean a purposefulness of opportunity that seldom finds expression in the material world as to the understanding of motherhood among the children of men.

Hence the entity in its activities during those periods when there were the persecutions by those in authority, that the fear might be allayed, made for experiences that find expressions in the manner in which the entity in the present *honors* motherhood in all its relationships. And *oft* has the entity seen and found and aided in bringing such expression in many strata of experience to those that might never have had the opportunity, without the expressions the entity has given in its aid by word, by act, and by the very activities in which the entity has engaged.

However, through those very expressions, as experience, there have come those periods—not of anger but of hurt, and a longing for that healing force which was experienced by the entity during that sojourn in Jerusalem, Judea, and in those portions of Galilee to which the entity's activities carried the entity; as the associate or Zadok, the priest that worked opposite—as it would be termed today—to Zachariah, who waited on the temple service.[2] . . .

And ye will find—even as He called to thee when there were those varied activities in Cana, in the City, in those periods even when thou didst behold Him upon the cross of shame (that to thee has become, does become through those very activities, *not* as a cross)—the *beauty* of a life well lived. For what have been crosses to others, to thine self may be as stepping-stones for not only the appreciation but the comprehending of the glory of the Lord.

The Wise Men

5749-7   6/27/37

Q-2. Explain the relationship of the Wise Men and Jesus' birth.

A-2. As indicated by the travels of the Master during the periods of preparation, the whole earth, the whole world looked for, sought the closer understanding. Hence through the efforts of the students of the various phases of experiences of man in the earth, as may be literally interpreted from the first chapters of Genesis, ye find that those that subdued—not that were ruled by, but subdued the understandings of that in the earth —were considered, or were in the position of the wise, or the sages, or the ones that were holy; in body and mind, in accord with purposes.[1]

Hence we find the Wise Men as those that were seekers for the truth, for this happening; and in and through the application of those forces—as ye would term today psychic—we find them coming to the place "where the child was." Or they were drawn as those that were giving the thanks for this gift, this expression of a soul seeking to show wayward man back to God.

So they represent in the metaphysical sense the three phases of man's experience in materiality; gold, the material; frankincense, the ether or ethereal; myrrh, the healing force as brought with same; or body, mind, soul.

These were the positions then of the Wise Men in their relationship, or to put into the parlance of the day—they were the encouragement needed for the mother and those that had nourished, that had cherished this event in the experience of mankind.

They came during the days of purification, but to be sure

only after she was purified were they presented to the Child.

Q-3. What relation did they have with the later travels of Jesus?

A-3. As has just been indicated, they represented then the three phases of man's experience as well as the three phases of the teacher from Egypt, from Persia, from India.[2]

2067-7   F.53   6/25/41

Q-24. In one reading we are told the Wise Men came from India, Egypt, and Gobi; in another reading we are told the Wise Man who brought the incense came from Persia. Which is correct, and besides the Wise Men Achlar and Ashtueil, what were the names of the other two Wise Men?

A-24. Both are correct. There was more than one visit of the Wise Men. One is a record of three Wise Men. There was the fourth, as well as the fifth, and then the second group. They came from Persia, India, Egypt, and also from Chaldea, Gobi, and what is *now* the Indo or Tao land.

587-6   F.45   10/18/35

Q-4. What was my association with the Wise Men that came seeking the child, and what influence does that have on me now?

A-4. As indicated. The entity was among those first chosen to be presented before the Lord as *possible* choices or channels through which those great blessings were to come. So, when the birth came, the *natural* associations were such that the entity was drawn to and about those activities of the parents. And when the Wise Men of the East, or from India, Egypt, the Gobi, came to Jerusalem where there had been the gathering of those that had been of that consecrated group, the *entity* went *with* the Wise Men. For it *awakened within* the entity then that there had been the fulfillment, the completion of that which had been impressed upon the entity in the years of its preparation.

1908-1   M.49   6/15/39   Achlar

In those periods that preceded the advent of the Prince of Peace in the earth, we find the entity was among those of the land that would now be called the Persian—as a wise man, a counselor, a sage, that counseled with those peoples; using the

THE BIRTH 95

mathematical activities of the ages old as well as the teachings of the Persians from the days of Zend and Og and Uhjltd, bringing for those peoples a better interpretation of the astrological as well as the natural laws.

Hence we find the entity was associated oft with those who looked for the day, the hour when that *great purpose,* that event, was to be in the earth a literal experience.

Then we find the entity was among those of the fabled as well as real experience, seeking with the Wise Men that came from the East during those periods.

In the present experience of the entity, then, we find that those oft told tales are accepted deep within because of the conviction and purpose such have produced and do produce in the hearts and the minds of individuals.

We find this entity was the one who brought the incense to the child Jesus[3] — in the name then Achlar. In the experience the entity gained, the entity manifested its love for its fellow man through those periods of activity in the search for the helpful influences, mentally, spiritually, materially; though the entity then lost sight oft of materiality . . .

Q-1. Please give me a detailed explanation of any past associations in previous lives with [1472] [Judy] . . .

A-1. Draw upon the parallel of the purposes of each through those experiences in the Palestine land, and ye will have that as may be a detail of how there are and were those periods of the oneness of thought, of purpose, through the varied channels of activities that enabled one to become as a helper to the other.

In the present, then, we find each lending that strength in what may be sought in the closer study and the closer application of those tenets taught by Him whom ye both sought, who lives and gives and promises to all that seek to know His ways.

256-1   M.32   8/14/29   Ashtueil

. . . the entity was among those who were of the Wise Men coming into Jerusalem and to Bethlehem when the Master came into the earth. The entity then in the name Ashtueil, coming in from the mountains of what is now known as Arabia and India. The entity gained through this period in pointing out that through the various forces as were added in the experiences of man with that creation of forces necessary to keep the balance in the universal forces, the earth must bring forth that that would make man's balance of force with the creative energy as one, and the Son of man appeared. The entity brought the frankincense and gave same to the Master at that period.[4]

256-5   M.37   8/31/34

Q-2. What incarnations will be the source of the most compelling urges during the next few years?

A-2. The Persian, where the studies were of the influence of stellar space or the sojourns of souls in the environs about the earth that made—and make—for the mental urges in the souls of men.

1293-1   F.39   11/17/36   Astaid

. . . the entity was in the land now called the Persian, during those days and experiences when many were studying, looking for those indications that had been proclaimed by not only the seers of old but by the new visions. For *His* star had appeared!

And the entity then was among those that *today* would be called soothsayers. Yet rather from the experiences in the earth the entity was a prophetess then of no mean estate; aiding —though misunderstood—those peoples then and now called the Essenes.

And the entity gave an understanding as those activities were for those that sought in the city of Bethlehem for the meaning of those experiences during those days.

In the name then Astaid, the entity gained throughout that experience; for those applications of self were in those aids to those that were seeking the knowledge of the experiences, of the new life in the promises then . . .

Q-1. What was the relationship in the past with my present husband, [1297]?

A-1. How oft has the entity lifted that entity up! How oft has the entity reckoned with those influences that the present companion used to make for disturbances with the Essenes! For *then* he, the present companion, was a Jew that made for disdaining of those meetings, those understandings.

As again in Chaldea, the entity then aided in the activity.

THE BIRTH

1297-1   M.42   11/25/36

. . . the entity was in the land now known as the Persian or Chaldean, during those periods when there were the seekings for an understanding and a comprehension of what was to take place in the experience of the *world* by the entrance of an unusual, unheard of as it were (only by tradition) influence from another source upon human experience, human relationships, human activities; or when the Wise Men of India, Persia, Egypt—yea, of the Mongoloids—were seeking to know the promptings of those activities.

The entity then was among those of the Jewish race, yet had withdrawn as it were from those teachings of tradition—or the mere service in the temple—and had joined rather with those who had become of the understanding as handed down by the old Persian teacher, Zoroaster.

2148-7   M.2   11/19/42   Eliajah

. . . the entity was in that period just previous to the advent of the Master in the earth.

The entity was a student of, and a worker with, especially the Essene groups that were making those preparations for the coming of these particular events in the experience of man.

Thus those intuitive forces. For, the entity was a worker in the chemical and the metal attributes, and thus called an alchemist.

The entity reached an old age in that period, knowing or seeing in the temple those periods when Anna and the priest blessed the Son. These brought to the entity a satisfaction, in seeing those things the entity had worked for.[5] Thus those communications that went from this entity to the Wise Men. Thus we come to those interpretations of the periods when the Wise Men visited the activities of the Christ, or Jesus who became the Christ.

The name then was Eliajah. In the experience the entity gained throughout. And the interest will be found, in the unfolding years, in those things that are of the mysterious nature, the entity's interest in telling stories, fairy tales, those experiences where the unusual happened.

And the intuitive forces that will be manifested in the present experience of this entity arise from those innate forces there.

2397-1   F.42   11/13/40   Rebkah

. . . the entity was in the Promised Land, during those early periods of the looking for the incoming of the Prince of Peace, the Master of masters.

There the entity was among those who directed the Wise Men to the inn, to the place where *His* manifestation of light, of hope, of joy, was proclaimed by the sages of old.

Thus the entity in its present experience, through its material and physical activities, may give light to not only those of high estate but those of the common peoples also.

For, as ye learned so well in that experience, He—thy Lord, thy God—is not a respecter of persons, but of hopes, of desires, of purposes in the *individual* lives.

Thus, learn the *individuality* of thy purpose as being at one with His; that all men may know the glory of the Lord, that it may fill their lives also!

The name then was Rebkah. In the experience the entity was a seeker after knowledge, a seeker for the way of truth. Thus the entity was used as the channel; not spoken of, and yet in patience it may become the way through which *so many*—as self does at times in the present—may find hope, cheer, joy; in merely being a means whereby others may take hold again.

1220-1   M.23   7/14/36   Puloaus

. . . the entity was in the land now known as the Holy Land, during those periods when there were the preparations of those activities when the Prince of Peace, the Son of man, the Son of God, came into the earth.

The entity then was among those that were of the Roman peoples, yet had been stationed in the Palestine or the Jewish land that there might be the reckoning for the customs sought.

And the entity then was in the position of overseeing the establishings of those that would be as the collectors of same, and the first to make for that overture of there being chosen individuals from the various faiths so that not only the Romans or the Jewish or the Grecians, the Helvetians, the Egyptians were part in charge of those collectings of same.

During those experiences that there were those turmoils from the uprisings of the Jews that rebelled, the entity not only as a soldier but as one that made for the *commanding* of those that made for the putting down of such raids.

And when there came the answer for the service rendered, the entity was in that position of "all a clean record." And when the enunciation was made, when the Wise Men came to seek out that answer, the *entity*—as Puloaus—was given the *Roman* charge that these Wise Men be conducted to that place they sought.[6]

Then the entity became even as they, a worshiper, a follower of those influences wrought in the minds and the souls and the hearts of men during those experiences.

There the entity came to honor and dishonor, to hold that those in authority, those in power that trampled upon the hearts of men and women for their faith and their belief made almost a rebellious one in the entity's experience.

Asking for a recall that there be not those greater temptations, yet again in those latter portions of the activities the entity came into the land of Judea and in and about Jerusalem and Bethany.

Hence the story, the legend, the influences of that story of the Wise Men, the influence of that story of the edicts of the Jew, the attempts of the Romans to stay this destruction, became to the entity as something that riles and brings within self a sentiment, a tenderness, a truism, a fact that establishes much in the heart of this entity.

The Flight to Egypt

5749-16   9/10/41

In interpreting the life of the Master, Jesus—as has been indicated, His birth, His advent into the material world brought satisfaction, and yet consternation to the many.

This was indicated a few months afterward, when—with the return of the mother and Joseph to Nazareth—there was the edict that all children up to two years of age were to be destroyed. Indeed did Rachel weep for her sons.[1]

Through the experience, though, as has been indicated, there were those precautions. There was that journey into Egypt, which is recorded in the varied manners in Matthew and in Luke. To many there might be questionings as to whether Mary was informed of the necessity for the flight, or merely Joseph — as Matthew records. However, as we find, they were of one mind, and the flight into Egypt — as is recorded — was the fulfilling of the prophecy. For, it had been said, "and my son shall be called from Egypt." [2]

The period of stay in Egypt was something over two-and-one-half years — until another ruler was in authority or power. Then there was the return.

Through that period there were many of the stories that have come down as legends, even of those people in some portions of Egypt and of Arabia, as to the happenings along the way, as to how there were the unusual happenings — indicating not only the divinity of the Child but that purpose later recorded, "And she kept all of these and pondered them in her heart." [3]

1992-1   F.38   9/5/39   Mateal

. . . the entity was among those peoples *to whom* the entity — *as* the mother of the Master — came for help when it was necessary for the fleeing from the hands of the decree of Herod.

We find the entity there *physically* acting in the capacity of fulfilling, in the material expression, God's plans.

Think on that! And live that also today.

For it was from this entity's own activity and urge that the beasts were obtained upon which the infant and the mother fled into Egypt.

Hence the interest the entity bore to the activities of those who were bereft by the edict, in which the entity's *own* child had become a part of that destruction; and the influences which brought later into the experience of the entity the comprehending of and the application of the teachings of Him during those experiences.

The name then was Mateal. In the experience the entity gained in soul development. For who may be the channel, or have the full knowledge of being used as a messenger of the all-powerful, and not comprehend some development of the soul?

THE BIRTH

1010-12   F.67   4/13/38   Sophie or Josie

... the entity's sojourn was during the period when the Master was born in the earth, in Bethlehem of Judea, of the city of Nazareth; and when there had been those proclamations made by Herod for the destruction of the young; when Joseph had been warned to flee into Egypt, that the prophecy might be fulfilled, "Lo, my son has been called from Egypt," or "Lo, the Messiah has been called from Egypt," as given by Jeremiah as well as Isaiah.[4]

The entity then chose to join with the holy family, and acted in the capacity of the handmaid to the mother, the child, and waited on Joseph during those sojourns; dwelling by the brooks or the portions where there were wells, in the upper portion of the Egyptian land to which they fled.

During those periods of the journey the entity ministered; and it was no mean distance for a very young child, and a very young mother—during such delicate conditions.

And the very ministering of the entity throughout that sojourn, first to the mother and to the child, and later to the aging Joseph, has caused those abilities which the entity finds in the present experience to minister to the needs of those ill in body, in mind. And such applications are those that may be made by the hand, and nursing and care, and the consideration of the body as subsisting upon *natural* or nature's activities in the material world.

In that experience the entity was known as Sophie, or Josie, and very close to the activities of the innkeeper who made the preparations—owing to the close associations of the family to which the entity then joined, from the activities of the Essenes and the holy ones, for the protection of the individual activity.

Through the experience the entity gained. And with the return to Capernaum, and when the other children of the mother came, the entity still ministered.

And with the activities of the growing child Jesus, His teachings and His ministerings became all a portion of the entity's experience; yet so disturbed by the close activity of others *and* the manner in which the members of the family deserted the teachings owing to the needs of prominence from the economic standpoint during that experience.

In the application of self in the present respecting same, study those portions that have been written, again and again; and there will gradually come into the consciousness an awareness of the entity in the present that in Him is indeed the light that lightens the world, and that only in just living His way may we indeed by like Him. Only may the awareness come in being that character of individual, with that purpose, that attitude which He manifested ever. Though He came to His own and His own received Him not, never— *never*—did He rail at them! Never did He manifest any other than just gentleness, kindness, brotherly love, patience, with those who were the most unkind.

The entity's activities then were even in the preservation or the keeping of the family intact, with the death of Joseph. For this the entity saw; closed the eyes and laid him to rest.

Hence, as the entity reads of those activities there will come more and more an awakening. Read especially the first chapter of John, the first and second and third John. For the second epistle of John (as a letter) was directed to this entity, Josie, by John the beloved!

Read then the fourteenth, fifteenth, sixteenth and seventeenth of John. And reading it, not as rote, ye will find that even He is speaking, even as to thee!

1010-17   F.71   6/21/42   Josie

. . . there were those special groups of individuals who had made some preparations for the expected activities that were to come about during that particular period; especially those of the Essenes who had chosen the twelve maidens to indicate their fitness. This choice was to be made by those selections indicated by the spirit, and Josie was the daughter of Shem and Mephibosheth that was among those.

This entity, Josie, was close to Mary when the selection was indicated by the shadow or the angel on the stair, at that period of consecration in the temple. This was not the temple in Jerusalem, but the temple where those who were consecrated worshiped, or a school—as it might be termed—for those who might be channels.

This was a part of that group of Essenes who, headed by Judy, made those interpretations of those activities from the Egyptian experience—as the Temple Beautiful, and the service in the Temple of Sacrifice. Hence it was in this consecrated place where this selection took place.

Then, when there was the fulfilling of those periods when Mary was espoused to Joseph and was to give birth to the Savior, the Messiah, the Prince of Peace, the Way, the Truth, the Light [5]—soon after this birth there was the issuing of the orders first by Judy that there should be someone selected to be with the parents during their period of sojourn in Egypt. This was owing to the conditions which arose from the visit of the Wise Men and their not returning to Herod to report, when the decrees were issued that there should be the destruction of the children of that age from six months to two years, especially in that region from Bethany to Nazareth.

Thus this entity, Josie, was selected or chosen by those of the Brotherhood—sometimes called White Brotherhood in the present—as the handmaid or companion of Mary, Jesus and Joseph, in their flight into Egypt.

This began on an evening, and the journey—through portions of Palestine, from Nazareth to the borders of Egypt—was made only during the night.

Do not understand that there was only Joseph, Mary, Josie and the child. For there were other groups that preceded and followed; that there might be the physical protection to that as had been considered by these groups of peoples as the fulfilling of the Promised One.

In the journeys to Egypt, little of great significance might be indicated, but the care and attention to the Child and the mother was greatly in the hands of this entity, Josie, through that journey.

The period of sojourn in Egypt was in and about, or close to, what was then Alexandria.

Josie and Mary were not idle during that period of sojourn, but those records—that had been part of those activities preserved in portions of the libraries there—were a part of the work that had been designated for this entity. And the interest in same was reported to the Brotherhood in the Judean country.

The sojourn there was a period of some four years—four years, six months, three days.

When there were those beginnings of the journey back to the Promised Land, there were naturally—from some of the records that had been read by the entity Josie, as well as the parents—the desires to know whether there were those unusual powers indicated in this Child now—that was in every manner a normal, developed body, ready for those activities of children of that particular period.

But do not interpret same in the light of childhood in thine own land in the present—more in the light of the Oriental. For, remember, Egypt as well as parts of Galilee were the customs and activities of those to whom the care of this physical entity was entrusted through that early sojourn in the earth.

The return was made to Capernaum—not Nazareth [6]—not only for political reasons owing to the death of Herod but the division that had been made with the kingdom after the death of Herod; and that there might be the ministry or teaching that was to be a part of the Brotherhood—supervised in that period by Judy, as among the leaders of the Essenes in that particular period.

Hence much of the early education, the early activities, were those prompted or directed by that leader in that particular experience, but were administered by—or in the closer associations by—Josie. Though from the idea of the Brotherhood the activities of the entity were no longer necessitated, the entity Josie preferred to remain—and did remain until those periods when there was the sending or the administering of the teachings to the young Master, first in Persia and later in India, and then in Egypt again—where there were the completions.

But the entity, Josie, following the return, was active in all the educational activities as well as in the care of the body and the attending to those things pertaining to the household duties with every developing child. And Josie was among those who went with Mary and Joseph when they went to the city, or to Jerusalem, at the time of the age of twelve. It was thought by Joseph and Mary that it was in the care of Josie that He had stayed, when He was missed, in those periods when there was the returning to find Him in the temple.[7]

Josie was with Mary throughout those activities. And is it any wonder that when there were those preparations of the body for burial that Josie was the one who brought the spices, the ointments that were to consecrate the preparations of this body for whom it had cared through those early periods of its experience in the earth? [8]

Through that period Josie never married, and was known among the holy women throughout the period; coming and persuading the mother, Mary, when there was the arrest, to come to Jerusalem.

The entity passed on through those periods of riots following the beheading of James, the brother of John.[9]

Ready for questions.

Q-1. What association with the entity who is now [294] did I have in the Palestine experience?

A-1. The teacher of the Master knew only of Lucius through those activities in Laodicea—for he came at the time of Pentecost, see?

Q-2. What was the nature of the records studied by Josie in Egypt?

A-2. Those same records from which the men of the East said and gave, "By those records we have seen His star." These pertained, then, to what you would call today astrological forecasts, as well as those records which had been compiled and gathered by all of those of that period pertaining to the coming of the Messiah. These had been part of the records from those in Carmel, in the early experiences, as of those given by Elijah —who was the forerunner, who was the cousin, who was the Baptist. All of these had been a part of the records—pertaining not only to the nature of work of the parents but as to their places of sojourn, and the very characteristics that would indicate these individuals; the nature and the character that would be a part of the experiences to those coming in contact with the young Child; as to how the garments worn by the Child would heal children. For the body being perfect radiated that which was health, life itself. Just as today, individuals may radiate, by their spiritual selves, health, life, that vibration which is destruction to dis-ease in any form in bodies. These were the characters and natures of things studied by Josie.

For, is it not quoted oft, "All of these things she kept and pondered them in her heart"? With what? With the records that Josie as well as herself had seen. These records were destroyed, of course, in a much later period.[10]

Q-3. Can any more details be given as to the training of the child?

A-3. Only those that covered the period from six years to about sixteen, which were in keeping with the tenets of the Brotherhood; as well as that training in the law—which was the Jewish or Mosaic law in that period. This was read, this was interpreted in accordance with those activities defined and outlined for the parents and the companions of the developing body. Remember and keep in mind, He was normal, He developed normally. Those about Him saw those characteristics that may be anyone's who wholly puts the trust in God! And to every parent might it not be said, daily, dedicate thy life that thy offspring may be called of God into service—to the glory of God and to the honor of thy name!

1458-1   F.49   10/15/37   Hunduen

. . . the entity was in the earth when the Master walked in the land, and when there were the needs that the holy family flee from the wrath of man.

In those portions nigh unto what later became a part of the educational experiences of the Master, in Egypt, did the entity then reside. And the entity came to know the holy mother, yes the child Jesus; so that those cares during that sojourn in the portion of the land became a part of the entity's experience— in that which is held innate in the experience of the entity; that is, the emotions as to the care for those that are called for an individual activity . . .

In the experience the entity then gained and lost and gained.

Only with the turning of the spiritual laws into self-indulgence was there brought the misapplication in the experience, as Hunduen; as to make for the losing of the hold in that experience.

Yet when there came the greater knowledge of the purposes

for which there were those activities of those peoples who had taken to themselves the training, the entity became an aid to those in Delphi [Delhi?] for the interpretations of the mysticisms of the East as combined with those of the Egyptians in that period.

578-2   F.21   6/9/34   Jacobinus

. . . the entity was in the Palestine land, or the Promised Land, during those periods when many in the land about Nazareth and Bethany and Capernaum suffered from the edict of the ruler that only ruled with a reflected power—or Herod, the Great.

The entity then was among those mothers whose young were taken from them at the edict, for the destruction of the children that the son of Mary might be destroyed also.

Then in the name Jacobinus, the entity came to know Elizabeth, the mother of John the forerunner, as a real friend; and later knew the activities of many of those that followed in the teachings of Him of Capernaum and Galilee.

In the experience the entity gained, for though suffering in body in the real activities of the soul the entity gained throughout; and when there were the needs for the ministering to the ones that labored in the field of the teacher, the entity supplied much to those peoples in that experience throughout the sojourn . . .

In that experience also did the entity find much pertaining to the activities of the open field, or the garden, or those things that partook of the fields that supplied the needs of the body . . .

Q-6. Why do I have fear especially in darkness?

A-6. This is from those periods when there was the destruction by the soldiery; for the young was hidden in darkness and they took the body unaware.

Q-7. Are the eyes I see when meditating an optical illusion or something with meaning?

A-7. Rather of meaning; for that soul thou lost in Nazareth may again come to thee in this experience—if ye would make thyself as a channel for such an event in this sojourn.

Q-9. Why do I have such a great love for children?

A-9. For He gave, "It is as Rachel weeping for her children and is not comforted until she knows that which was lost there is in here arms materially again." So may this bring to the self the awakening as nothing or any experience may, for in him will be the blessings to many.

Herod's[1] Court

953-13   M.53   3/20/25   Zxenaw

In the one [incarnation] before this we find in the judge in the courts in Herod's rule, and the counselor to that judiciary at that time. The entity in this shows the weaknesses of the flesh, in that the ruler was given to the exercise of the earthly desires and the entity then sought to assist in gratifying these, from the position of the individual to which he sought to give service . . .

[953-6, 12/4/23]: . . . In this was the [entity] counselor in Herod's Court, and the member of the San Hedron [Sanhedrin], and in this the name was Zxenaw.

3424-1   F.47   12/20/43   Adynthe

. . . the entity was in the earth during those periods when Herod the Great was king, in those periods just preceding and at the birth of John and of Jesus.

The entity then was among the courtiers of that group or court; not of the Jewish peoples, though attaining to the abilities to act in the capacities of those of that particular group; being a Cyrenian by birth.

In that experience the entity was among the favorites of the court; not of the king but of the court, and in those periods of entertainment the entity was the danseuse . . .

The name then was Adynthe.

1207-1   F.13   6/22/36   Cleopeo

. . . the entity lived in the earth during the days when the Master walked therein, especially in that period just previous to His teachings that became as the examples to all—through not only the material benefits for the secular life but those that made for the answering to that longing that arises ever within the human breast for the continuation of a consciousness that will live on and on.

The entity then was among the entertainers at the court of

Herod. And if the entity will read oft the record of the dance of those that asked for the head of John the Baptist, there will come—with meditations—a feeling of emotions that may not be aroused by any other sort of experience.[2]

Yet when those of that court came under the influence of the teachings of the Master, when there were the healings of Pontius Pilate's son by the Master, the entity then joined with those that are rather later spoken of as the *holy* women—that followed afar, yea and made for many preparations for those that were to come under the persecutions of those in the latter days.

The entity then, in the name Cleopeo, gained throughout; for those experiences in pomp and power, in the lowly walks among the needy, the persecuted, brought for the entity an inner feeling that should be kept even as the light burning within the heart ever, that may make for that as its ideal in all of its experiences in the present, even as it in the former appearances and experience held to the Law of One which was exemplified as the same through those teachings given by Him who was to the entity the friend and the Savior.

764-1   F.38   12/18/34   Dumuru

. . . the entity was in the earth during that sojourn when the Master walked in the land, in the periods when there were the persecutions of those that were the followers of Him who walked in Galilee.

The entity then was in the associations with those of Herod's household, that one who questioned so oft as to the one who made the persecutions of the forerunner of that Teacher.[3]

Through those experiences the entity suffered in the mental associations. For had not there been in the experience of the entity, in the formative years, the message of the Wise Men that had come seeking?[4] And they came to that very court in which the entity then heard those things that aroused within self that longing to know more of the mysteries, that made for the arousing and the awakening in the hearts and minds of men and women everywhere that longing for the raising of those forces or powers that would loose them from the bondage—not only of material things but of that wonderment, of doubt, that so oft beset the minds of those who have been called for a

HEROD'S COURT   111

purpose, for an ideal. Though the surroundings of the body were such that its position did not allow the defying of custom, nor yet the judgments of people, the entity wondered and wondered—seeking with those ever that might gather together those things that passed from the lips of those that had been close with that man that preached first, "Seek the Lord while He may be found! Make thy paths straight! Turn ye while ye may, for the acceptable year of the Lord is at hand!" [5] And to the entity these words *ring* as something that takes hold upon the inner self. Yea, with those periods of persecution of those that had become the teachers and the ministers to those that were in material bondage—and were still in doubt as to those teachings of that man, the entity then—in the name Dumuru—was among those people that listened and harkened; and, being rather in a position of power, became the friend of her that suffered as the wife of Pilate—and of those that suffered in the household of Herodias, also those that were enjoined with Magdalene in the periods beyond Berea and among those that aided when Lazarus spoke as from the dead.[6]

3577-1   F.56   12/29/43   Rhadahr

. . . the entity was among the dancing girls at the court of Herod—and was the only one who could even outdance Salome.[7]

The entity taught, yes the entity encouraged even those activities at that period.

During the period in the larger market place (not recorded) when the Master dined with a leader, the entity was among those with Mary of Magda who bathed the Master's feet with tears. And the entity will never be away from same, for those whom He blessed may still be blessed if they will hold to His promises.

Then, keep that faith which prompted thee to change. For it has held thee in good stead in this experience. But let it be purposeful for Him, and not for [3577]. Let it be as appreciation, love, honor, glory to the blessings that have been and may be in thy present experience. These appeal as in those days to the entity, the tendencies to be all things to all individuals. Yet there have been those restrainings within self, as it were a harking back to that hour when His blessings caused thee to renew a life of purpose, a life of cause, a life of hope, a life of beauty—through those periods of activity in the earth as Rhadahr.

1626-1   F.29   6/29/38   Viola, or Vi

There we find the entity was among those peoples of the land, and associated with those activities about the court of Herod; though not *of* the thought nor the purpose of same. The entity was among the dancers before Herod; acquainted with Salome, and with all of those activities.

Those periods were as drudgeries oft to the entity. For coming of those peoples that were in authority, yet within self seeing the miserableness from that of self-indulgence, the appetites gratified for bodily forces alone produced revulsions in the experience of the entity.

Hence, as has been the warning, do not call in associations or have as thy associates those who oft indulge in gratifying of appetites; or we will find such revulsions arising as to make the experiences and the beauties of life become hardships and stumbling stones.

The entity was acquainted then not only with the ministry of John but with the work of Judy and the activities of the holy mother, and the teachings of the Master . . .

There the entity learned tolerance. Well to hold to that ye gained. The entity gained and lost during the experience, but he that hath gained somewhat even of tolerance—without losing hold on purpose and principle, and ideal—hath gained much.

Then the entity, as would be the interpretation in the present, was named Viola, but called rather Vi.

1629-1   M.45   2/25/28   Quienllo

. . . in that period just before the Prince of Peace came. The entity then among those who were in power in the land in which this took place. Then among the rulers in Herod's court and among those who carried out the search for the decree as was given for the beheading or the death of the male children in the land, when the cry went up to the powers on high for the weeping in Israel.[8] The entity then in the name Quienllo. The entity lost and gained and lost through this experience, for in the service as rendered gain came. In the exercising of personal gain, through the oppressions brought, the entity lost. Through the ability to have presented that which was truth, and rejecting same for those of power, the entity lost . . .

308-3   F.12   7/15/36   Ruth
. . . the entity was in the Palestine land, during those periods when there were those turmoils and those preparations that had been made by individuals and by groups when there had been those expectations of the coming of the Prince of Peace.

The entity was among those of the mothers of Nazareth that suffered under the edict of Herod, and made for during those portions of the experience a rebellion as against those of religious freedom or of religious rote.

Hence we find in the latter portion of the entity's experience that only when there came the influence under the teachings of Bartholomew and of Titus that the entity gained the real import of those purposes, those activities, and why and how that the entity even as a mother was a martyr to a cause. And in the latter portion of that experience the entity became rather as a *personal* aid to those of the Church as was established in Jerusalem, suffering with those of the persecuted yet making for strength in those that became weak through the persecutions that came during those periods.

In the name then Ruth.

775-1   F.19   12/29/34   Salonica
. . . the entity was in that known as the Roman land, during those periods when there were the activities in what is now the Palestine or Holy Land, when the Master walked in the earth.

The entity then was among those of the same sex as in the present, but with the soldiery of the Romans that were encamped and engarrisoned in that particular portion of Palestine where there were the activities of Herod during the periods of destruction of the children that there might be the carrying away of those that were supposed to be of that line from which there would be the calling of the ruler. For only the children of the household of David in Judah were destroyed.

That experience, then, caused the entity—in the name Salonica—to study that particular or peculiar people, or the Jewish race. For the entity then adopted not, but became very closely associated with some of those that aided in the preservation of those that were questioned as to which household they belonged, Ephraim or Judah, Benjamin or Issachar—and this caused those interests to become accentuated.

Coming later in contact with those people that became the followers of that teacher, the Master, the entity joined with those and forsook rather the teachings of the Romans that were being adhered to by the various sects of people from the Athenian land. And when there was the return to the Roman land, the entity aided those people; especially Paul, Titus, Timothy, in the latter portion of the entity's sojourn.

2486-1   F.22   4/3/26

... in the plain of the country when the Master came in the world ... the entity in that of the rule of the Herodians in that day, only remaining in the earth's plane a few days, for among those destroyed in the edict for destruction of the young.

2400-1   F.51   11/14/40   Elenor

The entity was among those who grew up among those peoples when there were questionings and fears as concerning the edicts even of the children that were to be a part of that experience of peace.

Oft is it indicated by man that the era was a period when peace reigned in the earth—yea, *true,* politically; but in the minds, in the hearts of many individuals there was strife and turmoil and wonderment as to what *must* be that aid that could bring the comfort to those when their children, by the edict of a ruler, might be put to death!

This was the environ in which the entity first knew the longings of the mothers, the fathers of that experience; and yet there gradually grew, but all too seldom, that awakening within the entity—through the telling of the mysteries of the experiences of Zachariah, of Joseph and Mary, of the return from Egypt, of the things that had been a part of man's experience.

Later the entity became the companion of those close to the Master in His walks in the earth; and there grew the realization within the entity, or the knowledge of how, of what manner His teaching was to be—not ritualistic, not pertaining to that which had only been as part of ritual; but just being kind, just meeting the needs of the individual day by day, as to bring hope and cheer and joy, even under hardships. For, He will bear thee up, if ye hold to that faith in Him.

Thus—as Elenor—the entity brought hope and help and cheer—as those days of persecution began—to the holy women, to Mary the mother, to *all* of those about the entity—even to those who were rather of the aged who had prophesied, who had kept clear and clean the activities of those who were set aside as the channels through which the activity might come.

Thus the entity knew the old and the new concepts of "The day of the Lord is at hand."

2067-7   F.53   6/25/41

Q-4. Why do historians like Josephus ignore the massacre of the infants, and the history of Christ, when they record minute details of all other historical events?

A-4. What was the purpose of Josephus' writing? For the Jews or for the Christians? This answers itself!

2067-1   F.52   12/22/39   Thesea

. . . the entity was in the land of the Master of masters' sojourn in the earth.

During those periods the entity was a queen of no mean estate, and took hold upon the words of the Master—though never personally coming in contact with Him. For the entity then was the companion or wife of Herod, who sought His destruction. Yet the entity's experience there, as Thesea, sought a closer comprehending of the Wise Men.

Thus the entity will, or may in this experience find, even by the conversation with one of these—that is in the city of its own birth—the interpretations of those experiences and periods that brought about the determinations to cry out, as it did, that brought material or physical extinction—and bore in its activity the very same influences and forces that were upon the minds of many by Calvary.

For as the entity reasoned with the Essenes, as well as conversed with the Wise Men who came with the new messages to the world, the entity proclaimed—yea, that pronouncement that He Himself then being announced had given—"Others may do as they may, but as for me and my house, we will serve the living God." [9]

Do not interpret this to mean those who may be in thine own physical household. Thy house is indeed thy body—*that* is the temple of the living God. *That* is the whole house made to conform to the will, the way. "He that loves me keeps my commandments," in body, in mind, in soul.

Through the experience the entity gained, the entity lost; yet those very happenings of that land were written by the entity —as to how there were the longings in the hearts of those peoples, especially from the days of the return to the Holy Land, through the provisions of those forces that were as in answer to a law, "If ye call, I will hear, saith the Lord of hosts."

Hence the entity wrote concerning those peoples through those periods from the prophets to the period when the announcing had been to those groups who sought for His coming. And these were a part of the records (as destroyed by her own children) in the Alexandrian library, as well as in the "city in the hills and the plains."

In those things again, then, the entity may find an outlet, by the conversation with and the recording of the experiences of self in the various activities as impelled peoples of different lands, different environs. And yet, as has been before indicated, know that the message is *one;* for the Lord thy God is one, and that Jesus *is* the one who was promised from that day, "—and her seed shall bruise his head."

2067-7   F.53   6/25/41

Q-6. A reading states that the historic events from the time of the prophets until Christ were written by Thesea, Herod's wife. Why did her children destroy these writings in the Alexandrian Library, and are there any of these writings left on earth at the present time?

A-6. Her children did not destroy them. They were destroyed by the Mohammedans and the divisions in the church, who were of the Jews and not the Romans nor the mixture of the Roman and Jewish influence. There are not those records save as may be attained from some present in the Vatican.

2067-6   F.53   4/7/41

Q-17. . . . can you tell me what Thesea's other name was, by which she was known to history (which one of Herod's nine wives was she?), and can you tell how she was killed?

A-17. She was the third wife of Herod, killed by exposure and starvation. The name was just Thesea, or the entity was known by that name.

2067-2   F.52   9/3/40

Q-25. Was my mother Jewish and my father a Roman?

A-25. Mother was Jewish, the father Roman—of the soldiery; thus the entity was brought or kept in the Palestine experience, and with the close relationships to Caiaphas the elder and Alexandria.

2067-7   F.53   6/25/41

Q-28. Is Herod the Great now on earth, and will he be located through the readings?

A-28. We haven't Herod the Great. [Herod's records were not requested in the suggestion.]

254-109   5/20/41

Q-8. Please tell of the contacts of Thesea [2067], Herod's third wife, with the Essenes, her meeting with one of the Essene wise men, and what were the names of the two wives preceding her?

A-8. There was the knowledge of same through the giving of information by one of those in the household who had been so set aside for active service. Through the manner and conduct of life of that individual, and the associations and activities, the entity gained knowledge of that group's activities.

2067-1   F.52   12/22/39

Q-1. I have been told that I got my idea of a brotherhood colony, which I expect to start, when I was a man in the temple at Smyrna. Is there any relation of this incarnation to the life I am to live now?

A-1. We never find the entity as a man! The hatred of men, and of men's understanding, comes from Thesea, and not from a man. We do not find the man in this entity's material understanding.

Q-5. Can you tell me what relation my former husband was to me . . . ?

A-5. . . . In the Palestine or Promised Land, a guard or a protector in the household of the companion at that time.

Q-8. My son, M . . . ?

A-8. Here we find close associations through the Palestine experience, for he was among the children who came under the care of the entity—by the edict of Herod.

Q-11. Can you tell me my own mother's former relationship to me and the part she plays in my present life?

A-11. She was among the children thy husband beheaded; for she was a relationship of the Master.

2067-2   F.52   9/3/40   Thesea

In giving the interpretations of the experience as Thesea, it is well that some of the background, which brought about the entity's activities through that experience, be at least indicated.

That portion of the Palestine land in which the entity was born, and over which the companion was ruler or dictator, had more recently (in comparison to the entity's experience) come under the direction or dictation of the Roman empire.

The entity was not entirely Jewish, not entirely Roman; but chosen because of the beauty, as well as the political influence that the family of the entity had with those in power as the priests.

For, the entity's brother-in-law was a priest; and he, Caiaphas,[10] made overtures to Herod in his proclaiming the closer relationships to the Roman rule.

This, with the education or training of the entity through the early experience, fitted the entity in its social as well as political affiliations for the companionship with one in such a position. Yet these were never very close, as would be considered from the experiences of companions during that period.

The entity was well acquainted with many of that group of the Essenes during that time; for the entity was a seeker not only for the unusual but for the mystical powers proclaimed by many of that group through those periods of activity.

Then there came those periods of persecutions, for these were the attempts of the companion to court favor with the dictators or procurators who were in charge during those periods of the entity's experience or activity.

This, as indicated by the Scripture, brought some disturbing conditions with those of the Roman rule, because of the changes that were very probable, or that later came about, as to the emperors and their policies for handling those conditions and situations through the land.

Thus the entity became one acquainted with activities of a political and religious nature, and as to the *general* relationships of the populace to those changing situations.

When there were the orders for the destruction of the individuals, that their blood might be a portion of the sacrifice that was attempted, these brought abhorrence, and the turning away from the close associations with the activities of the companion at the period.

This brought great disturbances as to whys and wherefores of activities by or through the divine interference, or divine progress among men at the time; and these are a portion of the entity's own disturbing forces in the present—which have never, as to the entity, been completely answered.

For, there has not been the full concept as to the meaning of the blood as shed for the eternal sacrifice, or the law being of none effect in the law itself; that as individuals, in body, in mind, in spirit *become* the law, it is then as void in *their* experience—for they *are* the law! And the law is love, the law is God, the law *is* circumstance—as experienced in the activities there.

Through those periods the entity gained and lost; gained when self was put in the place of preserving or saving the individuals from special servitude, and aiding in making it practical for the various groups to become more and more in accord with the tenets of some of the priests' activity; condemning the priests in their only making their office as a means for the gaining of material and social prestige.

Thus it was not an easy life through the sojourn; for the entity was wedded when only fourteen—as would be termed today, and lived until the experiences of that announcement of the Christian or Christ experience.

As to the application of that experience in the entity's present activity—there needs to be—as we have indicated—the analyzing of the needs for that entrance of a God in materiality, and as to why at that period it was possible—through the aptitude and union of purpose in individual preparation; and how same *is* applicable in the experience of individuals today.

Throughout the experience, as indicated, the entity *gained* the more; though turmoils in the mental (as the builder) are still a portion of the entity's *own* personality . . .

Q-14. Just what are the dates of my life as Thesea, the Roman Queen of Palestine, and who were my children?

A-14. Beginning of 28 B.C. and extending to 6 A.D.

As to the children—there were only two, and neither of these became the ruler—but were associated with the ruler in a portion of the divided district.

Q-15. Can I find my name Thesea written in any history?

A-15. Best to find it written in the tablets in the burial places about Jerusalem. There it will be found, as with The Great.

Q-16. What books are best to read on the period?

A-16. Josephus, of course, is among the best; but those that have been a part of the experience of individuals are very good —as Asch.

Q-18. Please describe Thesea's character and appearance.

A-18. The character may be drawn from the portion of the entity's activities as indicated. As to appearance—five feet six inches in height, *black* of hair, and almost blue of eyes; prominent cheeks, but a great deal of color in the general or whole figure and make-up; in weight, 129 pounds.

Q-19. Was Herod the Great cruel to me, how was I fated to marry him, and what was his general character?

A-19. It has been indicated as to how the entity was fated to marry him because of the political relationships with those in power. He was cruel in the aversions that were a part of the experience, because of the *non*-activity or non-conformity to any general rule, and the rumors caused with the Romans—which were a portion of the entity's whole experience in education as well as in training and in the general activities.

On the whole, the association was more of a mental than a physical nature; though the death was brought about by the decrees that were issued before the sarcoma germs brought death to Herod himself.[11]

Q-21. Can you give details of Herod's and Thesea's deaths?

A-21. Herod, as indicated, died of sarcoma. Thesea died by the destruction wrought because of the aversion for her living *beyond* the period of Herod, and the order issued by him before his death.

Q-22. Can you give some of the details of my saving my present son M . . . and other children from the cruel Herod?

A-22. This was because of the edicts for the destruction of those seeking to become as channels through which there was to be the perfect generation of individuals through which the Messiah was to come. The entity saved those children through the preparing of means and ways for their being transposed or brought to other portions of the provinces.

The Years Preceding His Ministry

5749-2   6/28/32

Mrs. Cayce: You will please give at this time an outline of the life and activities of Jesus the Christ from the time of His birth until the beginning of His ministry in Palestine at approximately thirty years of age; giving birth place, training, travels, etc.

Mr. Cayce: As seen from the records that were kept then regarding the promises and their fulfillments in many lands, "Thou Bethlehem of Judah—the birth place of the Great Initiate, the Holy One, the Son of man, the Accepted One of the Father." [1]

During those periods in accordance with those laws and rulings, in the household of the father.

Then in the care and ministry from the period of the visit to Jerusalem, in first India, then Persia, then Egypt; for "My son shall be called from Egypt." [2]

Then a portion of the sojourn with the forerunner that was first proclaimed in the region about Jordan; and then the return to Capernaum, the city of the beginning of the ministry.

Then in Canaan and Galilee.

In the studies that were a portion of the preparation, these included first those that were the foundations of that given as law. Hence from law in the Great Initiate must come love, mercy, peace, that there may be the fulfilling wholly of that purpose to which, of which, He was called.

2067-7   F.53   6/25/41

Q-16. Why does not the Bible tell of Jesus' education, or are there manuscripts now on earth that will give these missing details to be found soon?

A-16. There are some that have been forged manuscripts. All of those that existed were destroyed—that is, the originals—with the activities in Alexandria.

5749-16   9/10/41

After the journey to Jerusalem [from Egypt], there were the periods of education in Syria, India, the completing again of the activities in Egypt; and the passing of the tests there by those who were of the Essene group, as they entered into the service — as did the Master and John before Him.

2067-7   F.53   6/25/41

Q-7. Was Jesus as a child also able to perform miracles, as the Catholic Church claims, and was he clairaudient, clairvoyant, and did He remember His past incarnations?

A-7. Read the first chapter of John and you will see. As to the activities of the child — the apparel brought more and more the influence which today would be called a lucky charm, or a lucky chance; not as a consciousness. This began (the consciousness) with the ministry from that period when He sought the activities from the entrance into the temple and disputing or conversing with the rabbi at the age of twelve.[3] Thus the seeking for the study through the associations with the teachers at that period.

Q-9. Please give facts about Jesus' education in Palestine, the schools He attended, how long, what He studied, and under what name He was registered.

A-9. The periods of study in Palestine were only at the time of His sojourn in the temple, or in Jerusalem during those periods when He was quoted by Luke as being among the rabbi or teachers. His studies in Persia, India and Egypt covered much greater periods. He was always registered under the name Jeshua.

Q-13. Please describe Jesus' education in Egypt in Essene schools of Alexandria and Heliopolis, naming some of His outstanding teachers and subjects studied.

A-13. Not in Alexandria — rather in Heliopolis, for the periods of attaining to the priesthood, or the taking of the examinations there — as did John. One was in one class, one in the other.

5749-2   6/28/32

Q-4. [Under whom did Jesus study] In Egypt?
A-4. Zar [?].

2067-7   F.53   6/25/41

Q-30. Please describe Jesus' initiations in Egypt, telling if the Gospel reference to "three days and nights in the grave or tomb," possibly in the shape of a cross, indicate a special initiation.[4]

A-30. This is a portion of the initiation—it is a part of the passage through that to which each soul is to attain in its development, as has the world through each period of their incarnation in the earth. As is supposed, the record of the earth through the passage through the tomb, or the pyramid, is that through which each entity, each soul, as an initiate must pass for the attaining to the releasing of same—as indicated by the empty tomb, which has *never* been filled, see? Only Jesus was able to break same, as it became that which indicated His fulfillment.[5]

And there, as the initiate, He went out—for the passing through the initiation, by fulfilling—as indicated in the baptism in the Jordan; not standing in it and being poured or sprinkled either! as He passed from that activity into the wilderness to meet that which had been His undoing in the beginning [6]. . .

Q-14. Please describe Jesus' contact with schools in Persia, and did He at Persepolis establish a method of entering the silence as well as demonstrating healing power?

A-14. Rather that was a portion of the activity in the "city in the hills and the plains." [Persian incarnation as Zend]

Q-15. Name some of His outstanding teachers and subjects studied.

A-15. Not as teachers, but as being *examined* by these; passing the tests there. These, as they have been since their establishing, were tests through which ones attained to that place of being accepted or rejected by the influences of the mystics as well as of the various groups or schools in other lands. For, as indicated oft through this channel, the unifying of the teachings of many lands was brought together in Egypt; for that was the center from which there was to be the radial activity of influence in the earth—as indicated by the first establishing of those tests, or the recording of time as it has been, was and is to be—until the new cycle is begun.

5749-2   6/28/32

Q-1. From what period and how long did He remain in India?

A-1. From thirteen to sixteen. One year in travel and in Persia; the greater portion being in the Egyptian. In this, the greater part will be seen in the records that are set in the pyramids there; for *here* were the initiates taught.

Q-2. Under whom did He study in India?

A-2. Kshjiar [?]. [Kahanji?]

Q-3. Under whom in Persia?

A-3. Junner [?].

Q-5. Outline the teachings which were received in India.

A-5. Those cleansings of the body as related to preparation for strength in the physical, as well as in the mental man. In the travels and in Persia, the unison of forces as related to those teachings of that given in those of Zu and Ra. In Egypt, that which had been the basis of all the teachings in those of the temple, and the after actions of the crucifying of self in relationships to ideals that made for the abilities of carrying on that called to be done.

In considering the life physical of any of the teachers, these should not be looked upon by students as unnatural conditions. Rather as, that the righteous Father *calling* to those that had builded in their experience that enabling them to *become* what each individual must in their own little sphere, gradually enlarging same to become inclusive until they—the individuals—are one in purpose, one in aim, one in ideal, with Him.

2067-7   F.53   6/25/41

Q-10. Please describe Jesus' education in India, schools attended—did He attend the Essene school in Jagannath taught by Lamaas, and did He study in Benares also under the Hindu teacher Udraka?

A-10. He was there at least three years. Arcahia was the teacher.

Q-11. Did He attend the schools in Jagannath—

A-11. *All* were a portion of the teachings as combined from the Essene schools, but these were not the true Essene doctrine as practiced by the Jewish and semi-Jewish associations in Carmel.

Q-12. Did He study in Benares also under the Hindu teacher Udraka?

A-12. Rather that as indicated—Arcahia.

Q-22. Did Jesus study under Apollo and other Greek philosophers, and was it through educational contacts that the Greeks later came to Him to beg Him to come to their country when the Jews cast Him out?

A-22. We do not find such. Jesus, as Jesus, never appealed to the worldly-wise.

Q-29. Were Mary and Elizabeth taught in a sacred grove in Egypt for a time by teachers, Elihu and Salome, that they might better instruct their sons, Jesus and John?

A-29. We do not find this to be true. Their education was rather with those headed by the Essenes through which Zachariah was called as the one to and through whom would come those influences as became the forerunner of the Christ. These were rather in the Palestine land. They were in the Holy Land, and at Mount Moriah.

2037-1   F.32   11/6/39   Jose

The entity then was a helpmate to Mary, the mother of the Lord—and there were the ministerings during those periods of the childhood, from the return from Egypt to those activities when there was the separating for the studies in other lands.

And we find that the general ministering, and the maternal love, as well as the awakening to those great influences which arose through those periods of association and activity, builded that into the experience of the entity which was never—and may never be—eradicated!

Keep those trusts, those ideals.

Though there were periods during that sojourn in which there were fear and doubt, these were rather for others than for self . . .

The name then was Jose—in associations with those who became the followers, yea, as the teachers of His tenets. The entity was closely associated with many of these; becoming the wife even of one of the apostles . . .

Q-5. To which of the apostles was the entity wed?

A-5. Thomas.

5749-2   6/28/32

Q-6. In which pyramid are the records of the Christ?

A-6. That yet to be uncovered.

Q-7. What relation was there in the training with the three Wise Men?

A-7. Representing the three phases of the development, for these were those that looked toward that development; as is symbolized by the character of that given as the blessings were made upon the infant in the manger.

Q-8. Are there any written records which have not been found of the teachings?

A-8. More, rather, of those of the close associates, and those records that are yet to be found of the preparation of the man, of the Christ, in those of the tomb, or those yet to be uncovered in the pyramid.

Q-9. When will this chance be given for these to be uncovered?

A-9. When there has been sufficient of the reckoning through which the world is passing in the present. '36—'38—'40.

His Incarnations

5749-3   6/17/33

Q-3. Discuss the various phases of spiritual development before and after reincarnation in the earth.

A-3. This may be illustrated best in that which has been sought through example in the earth.

When there was in the beginning a man's advent into the plane known as earth, and it became a living soul, amenable to the laws that govern the plane itself as presented, the Son of man entered the earth as the first man. Hence the Son of man, the Son of God, the Son of the First Cause, making manifest in a material body.

This was not the first spiritual influence, spiritual body, spiritual manifestation in the earth, but the first man—flesh and blood; the first carnal house, the first amenable body to the laws of the plane in its position in the universe.[1]

For, the earth is only an atom in the universe of worlds!

And man's development began through the laws of the generations in the earth; thus the development, retardment, or the alterations in those positions in a material plane.

And with error entered that as called *death*,[2] which is only a transition—or through God's other door—into that realm where the entity has builded, in its manifestations as related to the knowledge and activity respecting the law of the universal influence.

Hence the development is through the planes of experience that an entity may become one *with* the First Cause; even as the angels that wait before the throne bring the access of the influence in the experience through the desires and activities of an entity, or being, in whatever state, place or plane of development the entity is passing.

For, in the comprehension of no time, no space, no beginning, no end, there may be the glimpse of what simple transition or birth into the material is; as passing through the other door into another consciousness.

Death in the material plane is passing through the outer door into a consciousness in the material activities that partakes of what the entity, or soul, has done with its spiritual truth in its manifestations in the other sphere.

Hence, as there came the development of that first entity of flesh and blood through the earth plane, he became *indeed* the Son—through the things which He experienced in the varied planes, as the development came to the oneness with the position in that which man terms the Triune.

2072-4 F.31 6/23/41

. . . First, He was created—brought into being from all that there was in the earth, as an encasement for the soul of an entity, a part of the Creator; knowing separation in death.[3] Then He was made manifest in birth through the union of channels growing out of that thought of the Creator made manifest, but so expressed, so manifested as Enoch as to merit the escaping of death [4]—which had been the result as the law of disobedience. He was made manifest in Melchizedek by desire alone, not knowing body, not knowing mind—save its own; brought into being in materialization as of itself; passing from materialization in the same manner.[5] Then there was perfected that period again in *body* when the other soul or portion of self was made manifest by the consecration of the mother; meeting then self by that same quickening power as had been made manifest in the beginning—or at first.[6]

Hence the cycle. Hence the circle. Hence the emblem of same becomes as the channel through which such takes its form, its expression, its symbol.

2072-8 F.32 6/23/42

. . . "For this purpose came I into the world." So He came on other occasions, but failed to keep the whole law . . .

442-3 M.57 1/26/34

. . . For, since the foundations of the world He has paved the ways, here and there entering into the experience of man's existence that He may know every temptation that might beset man in all of his ways. Then in that as the Christ He came into the earth, fulfilling then that which makes Him that channel, that we making ourselves a channel through Him may—with the boldness of the Son—approach the throne of mercy and grace and pardon, and know that all that has been done is washed away in that *He* has suffered that *we* have meted to our brother in the change that is wrought in our lives, through the manner we act toward him.⁷

262-82   5/26/35

Q-2. Please explain what is meant by Jesus being tempted in all points like we, yet without sin. Does this refer to more than one incarnation? ⁸

A-2. That as the Son entered into the earth throughout the ages, as man counts time, there was the growth; the growth that made for that purposefulness that the world, the earth and the fullness thereof might be a *living* example of the *glory* of the Son. And as Man counteth shortcomings *many* there were, yet tempted in all—even in that experience when "yet without sin" He presented His body before the throne of grace and mercy (as is the promise of every man) and offered it up— without question; offered up the blood of that body, in same becoming pure. So does every soul that offers its body, its mind for a cleansing, become pure in that thing. He, through all, grew to where, "This is my beloved son; hear ye him," for He hath the words of life.⁹

364-7   4/5/32

Q-5. What was meant by "As in the first Adam sin entered, so in the last Adam all shall be made alive"? ¹⁰

A-5. Adam's entry into the world in the beginning, then, must become the savior *of* the world, as it was committed to his care, "Be thou fruitful, multiply, and *subdue* the earth!" Hence Amilius, Adam, the first Adam, the last Adam, becomes—then —that that is *given* the *power over* the earth, and—as in each soul the first to be conquered is self—then *all things,* conditions and elements, are subject unto that self! That a universal law, as may be seen in that as may be demonstrated either in gases that destroy one another by becoming elements of the same, or that in the mineral or the animal kingdom as may be found that destroy, or *become* one *with* the other. Hence, as Adam given

—the *Son* of God—so he *must* become that that would be able to take the world, the earth, back to that source from which it came, and *all power* is given in his keeping in the earth, that he has overcome; self, death, hell and the grave even, become subservient unto Him *through* the conquering of self in that made flesh; for, as in the beginning was the word, the word was with God, the word *was* God, the same was *in* the beginning. The word came and dwelt among men, the offspring of self in a material world, and the word *overcame* the world—and hence the world *becomes,* then as the servant of that that overcame the world!

Q-6. Please give the important reincarnations of Adam in the world's history.

A-6. In the beginning as Amilius, as Adam, as Melchizedek, as Zend [?], as Ur [?], as Asaph [?], as Jesus [Jeshua]—Joseph —Jesus.[11]

5749-14 5/14/41

Q-19. Please list the names of the incarnations of the Christ, and of Jesus, indicating where the development of the man Jesus began.

A-19. First, in the beginning, of course; and then as Enoch, Melchizedek, in the perfection. Then in the earth of Joseph, Joshua, Jeshua, Jesus.

2072-4   F.31   6/23/41

In Adam that expression was given by the Father in its individual activity, as well as in its relationships to the conditions about the entity . . .

Again it was manifested in Enoch, who oft sought to walk and talk with that divine influence; with the abilities latent and manifested in self to find self in the varied realms of awareness, yet using the office of relationships as a channel through which blessings might come, as well as recommendations and warnings might be indicated to others . . .

Again there may be drawn to self a parallel from the realm of spiritual enlightenment of that entity known as Melchizedek, a prince of peace, one seeking ever to be able to bless those in their judgments who have sought to become channels for a helpful influence without any seeking for material gain, or mental or material glory; but magnifying the virtues, minimizing the faults in the experiences of all with whom the entity comes in contact day by day . . .

We would turn again to that realm of awareness in material experiences from which the entity may gather those lessons, those instructions which arose from the activity of the entity called Joshua; that though in the earth's place or period of advancement, there may be the collective activity of that as would do good even unto those who persecute thee . . .

Then again the expression was in that entity as he entered through those channels indicated as necessary for the functioning of the material, mental and spiritual mind, for the advent of that influence manifested in what ye call the Christ Consciousness, the Christ awareness (Jeshua).

For, *this*—the Christ Consciousness—is the basis.

364-8   4/15/32

. . . Be thou, then, a channel that may oft walk with Him that gave not of else than, "Let not your hearts be troubled; neither let it be afraid. Let not thine right hand know what thy left hand doeth." Rather giving self to seeking, day by day, to *know* the will of the Father as was manifest in Him, and may be manifest in thee, for He will not leave thee desolate, but will come to thee—but not unless invited; for, as in the periods, as we find, when He walked with men as the Master among men, or when as Joseph in the kingdoms that were raised as the saving of his peoples that *sold* him into bondage, or as in the priest of Salem in the days when the call came that a peculiar peoples would proclaim His name, He has walked and talked with men. Or, as in those days as Asapha [?], or Affa [?], in those periods when those of that same Egyptian land were giving those counsels to the many nations, when there would be those saving of the physical from that of their own making in the physical; or in the garden when those temptations came, or as the first begotten of the Father that came as Amilius in the Atlantean land and allowed himself to be led in ways of selfishness. Hence, as we see, all the various stages of developments that have come to man through the ages have been those periods when He walked and talked with man.

In this, then, when—as we find—that those periods began in a like period from that of Joseph to Joseph, or Jesus, then again we see the cycle when perfected in body, overcoming the world in the body of man, will He appear in those *varied* experiences; for He tarries not, and the time draws near.[12]

364-9   4/28/32

Q-1. In what country, and in connection with what religion or philosophy, did Jesus live as Ur?

A-1. Ur was rather a land, a place, a city—and the thought, or intent, or the call was from Ur. Ur, then, as presented or represented in the experience of Jesus, as one that impelled or guided those thoughts in that period, or experience.

Q-2. What part did Jesus play in any of His reincarnations in the development of the basic teachings of the following religions and philosophies? First, Buddhism:

A-2. This is just one.

Q-3. Mohammedanism, Confucianism, Shintoism, Brahmanism, Platonism, Judaism.

A-3. As has been indicated, the entity—as an entity—influenced either directly or indirectly all those forms of philosophy or religious thought that taught God was one.

In the first, as one that associated with—in the meditation or spirit of—that one guiding same, and those things that have been added to are much in the same manner that was added to in Judaism. Whether in Buddhism, Mohammedanism, Confucianism, Platonism, or what—these have been added to much from that as was given by Jesus in His walk in Galilee and Judea. In all of these, then, there is that same impelling spirit. What individuals have done, do do, *to* the principles or the spirit of same—in turning this aside to meet their *own* immediate needs in material planes, or places—has made for that as becomes an outstanding thing, as a moralist or the head of any independent religious force or power; for, as has been given, "Know, O Israel, the Lord thy God is *One!*" whether this is directing one of the Confucius' thought, Brahman thought,

Buddha thought, Mohammedan thought; these are as teachers or representatives, or to make more of the distinct change—as was in that as given by the apostle to the gentiles: "I hear there are divisions among you. Some say I am Paul, another I am Apollos, another I am of Caiaphas. Paul may minister, Apollos may have watered, but it's *God* that gives the increase!" [13] The spirit of the Creative Force, and as such the Son represented in the spirit in that as was made manifest in the earth. Not as *only* one, but *the* only one; for, as He gave, "He that climbs up any other way is a thief and a robber." As the spirit of the Master, the spirit of the Son, was manifest—as was given—to each in their respective sphere. As it is today. As it was of yore. God calls on man everywhere to seek His face, through that channel that may be blessed by the spirit of the Son—in whatsoever sphere this may take its form. Because there are contentions, because there is the lack of the giving and taking as to others' thought, does not change God's attitude one whit; neither does it make one above another; for, as has been given, there *is only* one—the others are as those acting in the capacity of the thought that was given to them through that same power, that "In the last days has He spoken unto us through the Son, as one born out of due season." We find the same contentions arising in that called in the present denominationalism, and each one crying, "Lo, here is Christ—Lo, this is the manner of approach—Lo, unless ye do this or that ye have no part in Him." "He that loves me will keep my commandments." [14] What are the commandments? "Thou shalt have no other *God* before me," and "Love thy neighbor as thyself." In this is builded the whole *law* and gospel of every age that has said, "There is *one* God!"

5023-2   M.45   7/18/44

... the entity will find that the promises are true which have been made in that which is foolishness to the scientific or wise, the simple story of Jesus of Nazareth. But when or if the entity takes this as its study (and set this as its thought and then read, then study the Book which tells of Him, Jesus born in Bethlehem of the Virgin Mary), know this is the same soul-entity who reasoned with those who returned from captivity in those days when Nehemiah, Ezra, Zerubbabel were factors in the attempts of the reestablishing of the worship of God, and that Jeshua, the scribe, translated the rest of the books written up to that time. Then realize that is the same entity as mentioned who as Joshua was the mouthpiece of Moses, who gave the law, and was the same soul-entity who was born in Bethlehem, the same soul-entity who in those periods of the strength and yet the weakness of Jacob in his love for Rachel was their firstborn Joseph. This is the same entity, and this entity was that one who had manifested to father Abraham as the prince, as the priest of Salem, without father and without mother, without days or years, but a living human being in flesh made manifest in the earth from the desire of Father-God to prepare an escape for man, as was warned by the same entity as Enoch, and this was also the entity Adam. And this was the spirit of light.

1825-1   F.54   2/19/39

[Egyptian incarnation] For the entity was acquainted with and oft associated with Joseph, the incarnation of Him whom the entity later served so well in Thessalonica!

362-1   M.19   6/27/33

The entity was an associate and friend of the leader in that land, or a friend of Caleb, and through Caleb the entity had an acquaintance with Joshua the prophet, the mystic, the leader, the incarnation of the Prince of Peace.[15]

833-1   F.70   2/19/35

Hence we find in the present those interests that are arising from the expressions from the eastern thought, as well as that which was established by those peoples in the Egyptian land that found the expression in the Law of One—in which He that walked in the Egyptian, the Indian, the Persian land, yet known as Him of Galilee, founded His material tenets.

294-142   M.55   4/23/32

. . . there developed that ability for the entity [Uhjltd] to call upon the unseen sources for the information necessary to aid those individuals so succored, so aided in this experience. And when joined with the companion — that later brought forth that leader [Zend?] who was to become the power that has ruled this portion of the land in some directions — then greater became the *power* of the abilities of that entity in that experience to manifest that in the various ways and manners as called psychic forces, psychic abilities. In that there was, then, the conscious *and* unconscious activities that gradually became the ability to become as one *well* endowed with the abilities to be the teacher of that one who became the world teacher and the Savior of men [Jesus] . . .

3054-4   F.50   2/16/44

. . . Apply thyself in such a way and manner as to know what ye will do with this man, Jesus of Nazareth — Jeshua of Jerusalem, Joshua in Shiloh, Joseph in the court of Pharaoh, Melchizedek as he blessed Abraham, Enoch as he warned the people, Adam as he listened to Eve.

288-29   F.27   4/16/32

Q-13. Was the entity of Adam and Eve —

A-13. We are going too far back!

Q-14. [Continuing] contained in the one body San [sic] during that period, or was it separated?

A-14. Not asked correctly! These were all together in Amilius. They were material bodies as came in Adam. They were as associated in body as came in Zan, or that that eventually became — through its incantations, incarnations, into the earth, those forces as the Savior in all periods.

452-3   M.28   8/25/32

Q-7. Explain the harmony between the "Atonement of Christ" and Reincarnation.

A-7. That as is the experience must be met in the activity of that soul, that is an *individuality,* that may be one *with* God, yet *not* God — yet one *with* Him in its individuality. Hence as the Son of man — made in the flesh — in Adam brought sin, or separation from God — in the last Adam, the Christ, brought that *at-onement with* God. So does this, then, make the atonement with those that, as He, make themselves — through Him — in the same activity, the same atonement,[16] *with* Him.

2067-7   F.53   6/25/41

Q-19. When did the knowledge come to Jesus that he was to be the Savior of the world?
A-19. When he fell in Eden.

262-55   10/1/33

Q-4. Was Jesus, the Christ, ever Job in the physical body? May this information be given?
A-4. No. Not ever in the physical body the Jesus. For, as the sons of God came together to reason, as recorded by Job, *who recorded same?* The Son of man! Melchizedek wrote Job!

993-3   F.41   10/21/31

Q-3. Have I in any experience through the earth plane been associated with Jesus Christ before He became the world teacher? If so, where?
A-3. In this same experience, that of the brother, the incarnation previous to the Master's entry into the earth's plane, for He became *then* the leader in those lands, and *much* is *still* gained in thought from those of the Persian efforts in this direction; or, as is termed in the *present* day, the Persian philosophy.

Q-4. What was His name at that time?
A-4. San [?]. [Gladys Davis' note: Zan (?) or Zend (?); sound rhymed with Wan.]

538-32   F.52   7/19/32

Q-6. [Give the associations with] Zan in that period.
A-6. Zan—that one who became the leader—trained in physical and mental much by the entity, and closely associated with the entity. Zan not in the earth's plane in the present. Came again as those that were the Sons of man, and—the Savior of the world. In the reappearance, many that were among those will be called blessed; for their place has been prepared, if they will but remain faithful. As He gave, "Who is my mother, my brother, my sister? He that doeth the will of my Father, the same is my mother, my brother, my sister."

364-8   4/15/32

Q-2. In the Persian experience as San (or Zend) did Jesus give the basic teachings of what became Zoroastrianism?

A-2. In all those periods that the basic principle was the Oneness of the Father, He has walked with men.

2982-4   F.35   6/19/44

... The manners of approach have oft been given. There is the one approach to the Father through the Son, who manifested in the earth through the activities which were later, in the son of Uhjltd, the manifestations of that which eventually became the consciousness in the Nazarene. For this was outside of that accepted in some centers as the only channel, but "Who is my mother, my brother, my sister? He who doeth the will of my Father in heaven, be he of this or that group." Not the outward measures only as did those who made, as He gave, a mockery of the principles.

1968-10   F.33   6/19/44

Q-3. What is meant in my life reading by the statement, "God brought such as thee into material experience to be the mother of God Himself?"

A-3. This indicated that through the channel of the entity as the mother in the descendant came those who were in the lineage of Jesus of Nazareth.

5070-1   F.23   5/6/44

The entity then [Old Testament incarnation] was among the sisters of Rahab who made for the entertainment of the spies who were sent into Jericho, and was among the few who were preserved because of the kindnesses shown ... For in that experience the entity was among those accepted into the tribes of Judah, and the sister became physically a lineal mother, or her lineal descendant became physically the mother of Jesus.[17]

2402-2   F.56   11/16/40

... the entity was in what is called the Gobi land, with the children of the Sun.

Then in the name Taoi, the entity was a priestess in the Temple of Gold—that is yet to be unearthed, that there may be more known of those things that are as old as the earth itself. For, the love of God as made manifest in the souls of human beings in the earth, is as old as the earth itself.

There the entity was the priestess making overtures to those of other lands — as in the Indo-China land, what is now the land of the setting sun in the Japanese and Chinese lands, that are so close at times in the inmost thoughts and being of the entity. For, *all* that ever was and ever is to be learned is "The Lord thy God is one—*one.*" O that it could and would be manifested as this entity can—by word of mouth, by demonstration of the powers and the hopes within—to bring to the consciousness of those it meets, that law "The Lord thy God is one." No matter in what clime, under what name, all must come to that as was from the beginning. For, know that He—who was lifted up on the cross in Calvary—was also that Son in the land of the setting sun; also he that first walked among men at the beginning of man's advent into flesh! For He indeed was and is the first Adam, the last Adam; that is the way, the truth, the light!

991-1   M.39   8/16/35

Q-9. Why do I have a leaning more towards Christianity than Judaism?

A-9. Hast thou not tried both? Hast thou not found that the *essence,* the truth, the real truth is One? Mercy and justice; peace and harmony. For without Moses and his leader Joshua (that was bodily Jesus) there *is* no Christ. *Christ* is not a man! *Jesus* was the man; Christ the messenger; Christ in all ages, Jesus in one, Joshua in another, Melchizedek in another; *these* be those that led Judaism! These be they that came as that child of promise, as to the children of promise; and the promise is in thee, that ye lead as He has given thee, "Feed my sheep."

315-4   M.27   6/18/34

. . . the entity may be said to have been the first to begin the establishment of the library of knowledge in Alexandria; ten thousand three hundred before the Prince of Peace entered Egypt for His first initiation there. For, read ye, "He was crucified also in Egypt."

1158-5   F.46   12/2/36

Q-4. Is it true that Jesus is the only begotten son of God, and what does this mean?

A-4. In this to give the full concept is to give the history then of all those who have entered into flesh *without* that act which man knows as copulation. For as those experiences Jesus, known as Jesus, the brother of this entity, came into the earth, the *first* that were of the sons of God to enter flesh, *there* the first and only begotten of God. Again, as names would say, Enoch walked with God, became aware of God in his movements — *still* that entity, that *soul* called Jesus — as Melchizedek, without father, without mother, came — *still* the soul of Jesus; the portion of God that manifests.

But each son, each daughter, through these very acts of the only begotten, of the son of Mary, of the first in the earth, of that without father and without mother, without days, without years — becomes then as the elder brother to all who are *born* in the earth, as the maker, as the Creator, as the first, as the last; as the beginning, as the end of man's soul's experience through the earth and throughout the spheres of consciousness in and about the earth.

Thus is He the only begotten, the first-born, the first to know flesh, the first to purify it.

And so man in his concepts, in his understandings, in his wisdom of God, purifies — here a little, there a little.

2067-1   F.52   12/22/39

... Jesus *is* the one who was promised from that day, "—and her seed shall bruise his head." [18]

1158-14   F.47   11/28/37

Hence as He gave in the last hours — and *sang* the psalm of praise, yea and as He joked — as ye would say — to those about Him, about the beauties of the garden; yet all of these filled a portion of the experience of those that made them *stronger* in purpose, in *determination* to be as He Himself had proclaimed hundreds of years before [as Joshua] "Others may do as they may, but as for me and my house, we will serve the *living* God!" [19]

364-9   4/28/32

Q-4. What name was borne by Jesus in His reincarnations in France, England, America?

A-4. Rather these have been as the spirit of the Christ, or the

Master walked among men, than incarnated in these different countries; for whether among the priest, as it were, in France — or among the lowly monk in England, or the warrior bold in America, the *spirit* that "God is *one!* Prefer thy neighbor, thy brother, before thyself!" These, as we find, took possession of — or rather labored with, until their own *personalities* were laid aside in individuals. Do thou likewise, would thou have Him walk with thee. "Not my will, O Lord, but thine, be done in me — this day, now!"

His Sister and Brothers

5749-8   6/27/37
Q-12. At what time after the birth of Jesus did Mary and Joseph take up the normal life of a married couple, and bring forth the issue called James?
A-12. Ten years. Then they came in succession; James, the daughter, Jude.[1]

Q-15. Was Mary required to wait ten years before knowing Joseph?
A-15. Only, you see, until Jesus went to be taught by others did the normal or natural associations come; not required—it was a choice of them both because of their *own* feelings.

But when He was from without the roof and under the protection of those who were the guides (that is, the priests), these associations began then as normal experiences.

5749-7   6/27/37
Q-4. Did Mary and Joseph have any other children?
A-4. James, Jude, and the daughter.

262-62   5/6/34
Q-9. Is Mary, the mother of Jesus, on the earth plane?
A-9. No.

1250-1   F.51   8/15/36   Hannas
. . . the entity was in the now known Palestine land, during those days when there were the turmoils between the Roman influence and the religious influence, the activities of those that would collect custom or tribute from those peoples of the land; and during those periods when the Master walked in the earth.

The entity then was among those that were nigh unto the peoples in the Master's own household, and yet the entity held both to the old customs and to the new. The entity held that those conditions, those experiences could *not possibly be true* of that one whom the entity had seen and known. And yet when those changes came about, when those activities came that made for persecutions, the entity began then to know—even as some of the friendships of the household of Joseph.

For the entity then was a cousin of Joseph by the flesh, of the household then of David, and in the name Hannas.

1709-3 F.20 11/11/39 Puella

... the entity was in the land now known as the Promised Land, during those periods when there were the activities following the sojourn of the Prince of Peace.

The entity was among those children of that period, and of those who were the close followers and associates of those who were of the household of the Master.

For the entity was among the daughters of the sister of Joseph, that was called the companion or husband of Mary, the mother of Jesus.

Hence the entity was acquainted with the hardships, the edicts of the Romans, as well as of the Jewish leader of the experience; knowing of the hardships as brought on by those who were the priests of the experience ...

The name then was Puella.

1158-2 F.46 5/31/36 Ruth

Before that, then, we find comes the experience that is the outstanding one—of a glory, yet of a suffering; turmoils, yet joy; beautiful experiences, yet sorrow and shame.

For the entity was in that land where the Master walked, and the daughter of Mary the mother of the Lord—Ruth.

In the experience from those joys, those sorrows that came with the changing scenes of the activities of the entity during the experience, there came much that finds in self today the harkening to the experiences in vision; this listening, this expectancy that so oft becomes as a part of the innate self, this sensitive force for helpfulness; yet at times of questions, at times the rumble as of disturbances, the fearful things that come from activities of those in authority that make the ways of men as a fearful thing rather than the expressions of the glory of the love of the Father through Him that made the way straight, that gave the understanding that there *is* a way that seemeth right but it may lead to misinterpretations. But he that leaneth upon the strong arm of the Father knoweth the Son, and knoweth the way. And His ways, though to the world are hard, to the soul become as stepping-stones for those great glories that come as it ministers; as the entity through that experience in its material activity ministered to those that were in want, that were in need of the material things.

Hence there comes in the experience in the present the helpfulness to the individual, to the masses, to those that have been as less fortunate in the material things of life. The heart goes out in adoration to those that, though in sorrow they smile, though in their turmoils and strife they remain faithful and pure in heart. These become as *helpfulnesses* to the entity in its influences in its relationships to others.

But learn ye patience with thyself!

In the experience as the entity became the more closely associated with those in authority from the civil forces, or the Roman influences through those experiences after the death upon the cross, and after the periods of those beautiful experiences with the disciples and the apostles, there came then that helpful aid in the entity's activity as it journeyed with those that would aid and bring to account much of those forces that brought to the powers of the Roman period the awareness of the Christ influence as exemplified in the *man* Jesus.

In the experience in the present, those influences will and do remain as the more beautiful, those to which it will hold the more.

Yet the forces as in the experience of Ruth, that co-laborer with the mother of the Master, are the outstanding ones.

Keep that faith of Ruth, that period when there came almost all experiences that may be said to be heir to the flesh. But as thy brother, thy Master, thy Lord, *learn ye patience!*

Q-1. *What is the significance or explanation as to why Dr. H. R. Charlton of Bronxville, N.Y., was the central figure in the mystical experience which I had in the Bronxville Hospital in May 1927?*

A-1. He was one that aided the entity in the experiences that followed the resurrection of the Master, that brought together the entity and its companion [1151] in that experience, that aided in the material as the entity aided in the spiritual welfare of all.

Q-2. Did the entity know the man from Rome—

A-2. [Interrupting] Married a Roman!

Q-3. Did I know the Roman who walked with Christ to Emmaus? [2]

A-3. Married the one. With him then the entity returned to Rome, as has been indicated, aiding in the interpreting, in helping others to understand the message that Jesus brought.

1158-4   F.46   11/19/36   Ruth

Q-1. Have I contacted the entity now known as Dr. H. R. Charlton of Bronxville, N.Y., in other incarnations besides the one in Palestine?

A-1. As a passing experience, yes. As a contact that made for close, active service, that influences the experiences in the present, we do not find so. But then he was the associate, the companion in the meeting of not only thy husband but in the understanding of thy brother in that experience.

Q-2. What was Dr. H. R. Charlton's official title or profession in the Palestine experience?

A-2. As indicated, a physician—and a teacher of Luke.

Q-3. Is there any constructive use to either of us, or to others, in Dr. H. R. Charlton and myself contacting further in this present life experience?

A-3. Much might be said respecting this. Necessary that as experience, as circumstance in the present presents opportunities, there be the presenting of tenets or truths in accord with those teachings; that by even the calling forth of the Son, even the bonds of death are rolled back. And yet not all are ready, not all are called; and neither do all that are called arise. But in the associations as we find, great help may come to others in gaining the understanding that—not by material things, but the arousing through material application oft—the spirit of truth may bear witness in a material world!

Q-4. Would it be helpful and right for me to tell Dr. H. R. Charlton about the Cayce life readings? If so, when?

A-4. As the opportunity may present itself. Approach not from that—remember thine approach as has just been indicated, as to how through Dr. Charlton ye were led to thine own brother! So may *ye* lead Dr. Charlton to thy brother, through those experiences that may be his—if he within himself seeks even as thou in thine *inner* self sought then. Part because of curiosity, part because of resentment; and yet—as the face in the water answereth as face to face—ye were drawn. So in thine expression may ye draw even he as face to face to self.

For ever is there constantly the meeting of self, in the experience of each soul. How few can so separate themselves as to watch themselves go by!

So analyze thine associations then, so analyze thine associations in the present, that ye may ask in faith of Him the wisdom, the manner, the way to present that thou hast found helpful or hopeful in thine experience to thy friend. For these are the manners and means that are in accord with all He hath given—face answers to face! and that seeds sown must be reaped in thine own experience!

Q-5. *Is the physician, who was my father in a recent incarnation* [*early America*], *known to me today?*

A-5. Known to the entity in this very experience of Charlton, yet—as has been indicated—not the greater influence of power then as during that to which there is an *eternal* tie to *life* itself! For He, then thy brother as manifested in life, in earth, in physical body, *is* life! . . .[3]

As has been indicated, that experience as Ruth, from the records we find, was a very full experience; and one from which much may be gained in the present. Not only by the material associations, but it may be seen as to how and why the teachings of the Master *must* become *the* factor in the experience ever—as well as in the present.

That there may be the proper interpretation, much of that recorded here as a background becomes necessary to be interpreted also:

With the return of Joseph and Mary to Palestine from the Egyptian sojourn, and with the return of the *active* service among the peoples, there was created quite a different environ for Joseph and Mary—the father and the mother then of the entity, Ruth.

For soon after the return, and that recorded in Writ of the journey to the city for that period of the Passover teachings, we find that James—the elder brother of the entity—was born into that experience.

In the next year, when there had been by the Wise Men of the East the beginnings of the teachings of Jesus and his sojourn in Persia, India, and when those activities brought about the change in the material or financial status of the family, Ruth then was born—in that city of Capernaum; and surrounded with the activities that befitted the peoples of that period, that day.

There was awe in the minds of the peoples as to what had taken place at the birth of the mother's, or Mary's, first son.

Hence the entity, Ruth, was rather in awe of the suggestions, the intimations that surrounded that experience; and questioned the mother concerning same.

As the entity grew into maidenhood, and after the birth of Jude, then the death of Joseph brought that brother—Jesus—home! and there were those activities that surrounded the entity concerning that unknown, that strange kinsman; that kinsman whom the peoples held in awe, yet said many unkind things about him.

With the departure of that brother to Egypt for the final initiations or teachings, with John—another kinsman who had been spoken of and held in awe, his mother having been a chosen vessel by the priests of the Essenes, and he, John, being the lineal descendent of the high priests of the Jews—we find that in the entity's latter teen-ages such ponderings brought a great many disturbing influences to the entity, Ruth.

As the circumstances from the material angles began to alter, or as the position of the family began to fall away or change as it were, they again brought to the entity the experiences that have found expression in the experience of this entity in the present; that is, the necessity of expending self's efforts mentally, materially, for the aid and understanding of those that are in less fortunate circumstance from the worldly angle—or to bring a knowledge to those in sundry places as to the cooperation that might be attained or gained by those in such circumstances with those in authority politically as well as religiously.

Hence we find the entity was divided in thought and activity between those tenets held by the elder brother, James, those held by the mother, and the actual activities of the entity as one among those of a peoples that were being questioned and doubted.

With the return of John, the cousin, and the beginning of his ministry—one that had renounced his position as a priest that might serve in the temple, to become an outcast and a teacher in the wilderness—to the entity, Ruth, there was brought consternation.[4]

And again there was a questioning with the mother as to those experiences of the mother preceding the birth of that Jesus.

Then the return of Jesus to the Palestine land, after those periods of the tests in the wilderness, after his meeting with John; and then the return to Capernaum and the teachings that he, Jesus, accorded there.

The entity then for the first time heard in the synagogue His first utterances, as to the prophecies of Isaiah, Jeremiah, and the teachings of the lesser prophets, and as to how they applied in the experiences of that day.[5]

Returning from that meeting, where a tumult was raised owing to the utterances of that new teacher, the entity encountered that entity now the husband; a collector, not in the sense of the "taker in" but the supervisor as to the abilities of various individuals in various positions to pay that tribute; a Roman.

Being not only beautiful of body but active in those conditions that were accorded to those peoples in the less fortunate circumstance, which became a part of the interests of that unusual Roman, the natural consequences of the age, the material circumstance, brought about a bond of sympathy between the two.

At that meeting, the introduction was made by one who has been very close in the cares of the entity in the present experience, as then—a minister to the bodily needs of those whom oft Ruth, as well as the then new companion, had met.

In the haste to acquaint the mother with the sayings of that teacher, or the brother, of whom so much had been asked, by whom so much had been said but so little understood by Ruth, the entity with those two companions acquainted Mary with what had taken place; warning her of the possible entanglements with those new authorities—or the Roman activities.

Hence those again made for questionings in the experience of the entity.

When the associations had advanced then from those periods of the first timidity of the entity, Ruth, with one of other foreign or alien groups, there came about an experience of some resentment towards the mother—as to the advice or counsel given. Yet there was the persistence in the activities, for to the entity, Ruth, the new-found friend to *her* bespoke of a greater knowledge of the needs of human experience than that held to either by the Essenes or by the orthodox Jewish peoples.

Hence the continuations of those activities, in association oft with that friend.

Then came those periods when the entity, with its friend, its companions, began the travels to ascertain the truth of what had been told by the mother as to the experiences in Bethlehem, those activities of friends in Bethany.

And when there came the period when the raising of Lazarus at Bethany was experienced by the entity as well as the companions, that brought a change which made for a *new life*, a new understanding, a new conception of the manifestations of the Creative Forces or God among the children of men! [6]

Then, just before the crucifixion, there was the consummation of the wedding between Ruth and that friend, now the husband—then the husband [1151].

And *Jesus* attended *that* wedding also; blessed them.

And with the recall of the companion to Rome, during those experiences in Rome, the crucifixion came about.

With the return and the recall of Pilate before the authorities in Rome, with the meeting again of Ruth with the mother and the holy women—and Lazarus, Mary and Martha, the friends of the mother—and those periods with Elizabeth, the mother of John the kinsman—there were the greater effects from the emotional as well as the active forces brought into the experience of the entity, Ruth.

Hence as it has been given the entity, hold fast to that thou hast gained in Him. For as the entity knew those that were ministers with Him, as the entity was then in the flesh associated with that kinsman and beloved one of Jesus, John — study that as He has given, in those last words of His with His disciples, the apostles, who became — as self and as the companion did — not only by word but by act the living examples of that as He taught, "As ye do it unto the least of thy brethren, ye do it unto thy Maker."

In the latter portion of the entity's sojourn, while children were born in Rome, in those activities of the entity and the companion much aid was brought to those who accepted those new teachings in the Roman experience. Much that gave help and strength to those to bear the persecutions later was established in the hearts and the minds and the experiences of those peoples during the entity's sojourn in Rome — as well as in the Grecian quarters.

And those experiences may be recaptured, as it were, by the entity; by introspection. For He has given, they that call upon Him or upon the Lord in His name may *know* what has been the experience from the foundations of the world!

Hence the love of the Father createth the pure understanding. And they that lack wisdom may ask of Him who faileth not to give that necessary for the more perfect knowledge, the more perfect activity in the experiences of self day by day.

For even as He hath given, it is not by some great influence from without. For there are three that bear witness in heaven; the Father, the Word, the Holy Ghost. There are three that bear witness with thee in thine indwelling in the earth; the spirit, truth, and the understanding in Him. These are one; these are *as* one.

When an individual entity, as this, may apply those tenets, those truths, indeed doth "My spirit bear witness with thy spirit that ye are the sons, the daughters of the living God."

And how much more in thine experience, thou daughter of Mary, thy elder brother the Christ — may ye know; for He standeth at the door!

Even as thou hast seen Him before those peoples that doubted, so may ye see Him in this experience standing before the door of those that would proclaim some other way.

But He is the word, He *is* the way, He *is life!* and thou hast a hold upon Him, in such manners that many another soul would *proclaim*—even as some do already—that intercession might be made through *you,* because of thy closeness with the heart of the Son of the living God!

Then hold fast. Turn not away because of those who would give thee this or that, to bring thee to material understanding. For as thou didst bring the heart of thy people to Him, as thou didst bring thy younger brother—though he faltered much; as thou didst give strength to thy elder brother to head the church under all those vicissitudes of distress without, turmoils within, so thou may find in thine inner consciousness that door opened that *He,* Jesus, will not pass thee by!

1158-5   F.46   12/2/36   Ruth

. . . it would be well here to give for the entity, as well as general information for those that seek to know more of how experiences in any individual sojourn may affect an entity or body in this particular experience in the earth.

Know that each sojourn or indwelling may be compared to that as ye have in your mental experience as a lesson, as a schooling for the purposes for which each soul-entity enters an earth experience; and why an entity under such environments came into that experience.

Each study of each lesson then adds some phase of development for the soul. And each merits then the opportunity; for it has been given as to the graciousness of the divine oneness in not willing that any soul should perish or lose sight of its identity or lose its hold upon those purposes for each soul's entrance into an experience.

Thus in the study of the activities of the entity previous to the periods of activity as ye would term the Christian era in Palestine, in Rome, in Sicily, in Athens; we find these are as human nature, the natural thing—or nature's expression.

For that which has been given man for his interpretation of the Creator is ever before him in the things about him that respond to the emotions; not mental or bodily emotions as having to do with some activity, but those deeper emotions or urges arising from those very influences that have and do become a part of the entity's experience as a growth, or an outgrowth of what each entity has done, does do, respecting its knowledge.

For what brought dissension? Knowledge misapplied!

Hence the wisdom of God; that surpasseth the understanding of man save in the meditations upon, or meetings within, his own divine self.

This is the lesson, this is the study that all that has been given is to point out. As the study of any individual experience is brought to the consciousness of an entity it becomes more applicable in the material experience of the entity at that time. Just as if there is a discussion of music or of sculpture or of the artist's brush in his depiction of any of the phases of human emotions, there may be discussed through the mental mind those studies, those meditations. But the applying of the principles of that being discussed becomes a portion of the entity and influences same in its relationships to its fellow man.

For as has been so aptly given oft, it is not what we know that counts but what we do about that we know, in our dealings with our fellow man. For as ye do it unto the least ye do it unto thy Maker.

For when honor or preference or thought is given a friend, an acquaintance, a neighbor, for *self*-glorification, it becomes not spiritual but temporal. But if such preference, such love, such honor is given that there is glorified the emotions of the knowledge "As I do it, I am doing it to my Maker and not for self," then the honor comes upon the individual soul and the growth, the new buds of hope, of life, are a part of such an entity.

So in the experiences of this entity in giving that which is so near, so dear to the heart of God, in that the entity was given the privilege, the opportunity—not alone of itself but for those purposeful opportunities—to use, to give, to spread the gospel of good tidings, as the entity did in its associations with those in authority politically and economically, so does the experience in the present—in the knowledge of its activities—become a part of the entity's being.

Much has been given as to the doubts and fears that arose in the mental experience of the entity during the experience or sojourn in that as a national association with those that were considered heathens, yet who by their practical application brought hope and the possibility, the opportunity for those that were afraid bodily yet imbued with the spirit of truth by that reflection of the Son, of the Holy One, the Holy Child who came as *fearless*. Yet as is the experience of human nature in the present, to be doubted, to be fearful for the livelihood of the day, for the suffering that may be brought to loved ones, for the separations that might be brought about by those that considered it not—these have and do become then in a much modified form to be sure, yet just as piercing, just as questioning. For as the individual entity or soul becomes the more sensitive to the attunement of itself with divinity, the more the hurt there be.

Then for the moment, as the entity saw during those periods when there was a relating to same of that walk to Emmaus, when there was the conviction brought that this indeed was the son of a living God, so in the experiences in the present so oft those periods of conviction come in that those lives, those souls touched by the entity in its associations, in its activities, are indeed even as they in those experiences were *convicted* not of themselves but by that as of a closer walk with *life* itself!

So these become so much a part of the entity, yet owing to its relationships, its positions in those periods of activity when by the very companionship necessitated the journeying to other lands where less of the experiences had come into the hearts and minds of individuals, so the entity in its present experience finds, when having been touched by the holy light of the way and the word and the Christ Consciousness, and it comes in contact with the various groups (though these may be presented by just around the corner, or just another meeting), and sees the groping and feels that longing in the hearts of those acquaintances or those that are merely seen as other groups seeking much of that as was the experience during that life or that sojourn as Ruth—these become, and will more and more, as indicated, upon the finger-tips of the experience of the entity, as would be termed in the modern parlance.

Yet hold thou fast, O child of grace and promise, to those tenets—not as tenets but as living truths, that it *is* through the grace and the gift of thy Brother, thy Father-God, thy consciousness within self is being awakened and aroused, that life in its expressions and manifestations becomes as sweet savour, the incense of the Lord in the lives of individuals!

And hold thou fast to those truths as ye gained in the greater knowledge from that conviction of the walk to Emmaus.

And as ye saw in those intents and purposes when thy elder brother James [7] became as the head of what is termed the church; not as that *ye* understand in thy present surroundings as an elder, a teacher, a minister. For how has it just been given? He, thy brother James, was exalted to the position of the leader because the *honor* was to Jesus, the Christ, to Him to whom all honor and all glory are due; to whom all patience, all suffering, all humbleness became so much a portion of His demonstration in life—and for which He only asked that we as His be a part of, that He may be strengthened in the earth. For to those of the earth hath He given the message, "Lo, I am with thee always—*always!*" To *you*, to *all* who have named and do name His Name is given that charge, "Feed my sheep, care for my lambs." And even as in thy activities when in the face of those in authority and with the changing scenes in Rome with the death of that one who had given and made it possible for the closer associations of His representatives with those in political and religious authority in thine own land, then with those changes came the checking up on those that had become imbued with the spirit of these new teachings. Yet thy light was not hid under a bushel, but the quietness, the gentleness, the patience that was shown by thine activities even in the courts of Bacchus and those revelries that were brought to bear that there might be a satisfying and a gratifying of the material appetites of men and women during those periods that to thee were debaucheries. As ye looked on these and saw not the vileness but the flow of those influences of wine and strong drink that excited the passions of men, rather did ye see the blood of thy Brother *spilled* in a wanton manner that the earth might know that He lived not in vain! For those that honor, those that love Him even as He loved the world, would give, do give their own heart's blood that the world may know that He *lives* and is at the right hand of the Father; that ye—yea, thy brethren, thy friends, thy enemies—may have an advocate before that

Throne of mercy, pleading the cause of the wayward, hearing the cry of those that are persecuted, and saying "Be patient — be patient, my child; for in patience know ye thine own soul and become aware that I am able to sustain thee, even though ye walk through the valleys and in the shadows of death." For death hath no sting, it hath no power over those that know the resurrection, even as thou hath seen and as thou hast known, as thou hast heard, how the resurrection brought to the consciousness of man that power that God hath given to man, that may reconstruct, resuscitate, even every atom of a physically sick body, that may resurrect even every atom of a sin-sick soul, may resurrect the soul that it lives on and on in the glory of a resurrected, a regenerated Christ in the souls and hearts of men!

As ye saw these even in Rome through those periods of lasciviousness, as ye saw in Athens in the unwarranted flow of blood for those of thine own peoples because they held to that, whether it is right that "I should listen to the voice of God or harken to the voices of men."

Then farther and farther away do ye grow from the voices of men and closer and closer do ye come to the voice of the Christ in the lives of those that are weary with the toils of the physical, that are sick with the doubts of the spiritual through the mental activities of the worldly-wise. And as ye give that gentle smile of assurance and of understanding, even as He looked upon thy mother and thy friends and gave, "Behold the woman," and to thy cousin and to thy friend gave, "To you she is given. Be to her a son in my stead." And as ye are to those about thee in thy daily life the mother, even as in thy associations the soft word that turneth away the wrath of those that are worldly-wise or that are in fear because of the doubts of their bodily needs, ye bring to thyself more and more those consciousnesses of thine experiences in that atmosphere of thine experience as Ruth.

For as it brought, even as the name implies, *hope* and new life, *ye* may bring—and ye *do* bring in this thine experience just that in the experiences and into the lives of many. And as the little leaven leaveneth the whole lump, so do thy gentlenesses, thy kindnesses, thy long-sufferings, thy patience, bring into this world that for which He gave His life, His hope—into thy hands and to thy friends' hands, and into those that have named His Name, the *power* to bring to the consciousnesses of others that awakening to the glories of a risen Lord.

But ye seek thy specifics . . .

Much again might be given in this vein of those varied experiences. As in Sicily ye came upon those activities that were from a peoples that were so bound by that of tradition that only those who were of the household of promise through the lineal descendants that had not been crossed by the blood of those that had been heathens might be saved; that even pointed to thee that *thou*—as a blood sister of His—had mingled thy blood with the Romans.

And yet as in thine reasoning that God is God of the just, and hath no patience with mere rote, hath no patience with that which is only of such and such line—but *everywhere* calleth, "Whosoever will, let him take of the cup of my son and learn of me. For thou, too, art my son if ye will but drink and be renewed in body, in mind, in soul to the purposefulnesses of that Son's entering—that *all* men, *everywhere*, might know the love the Father hath for the children of men, and that the Father is not the respecter of persons but rather as He hath given to the women of the Saracens, the crumbs indeed of the Master's table are not cast out but are become even as He, the head of the corner, the keystone to the building of that life that is aware of its relationship to the Godhead, that is aware of how ye treat thy brother and the god in him—ye know and experience the God-love in thyself."

And as ye hold this or that as mere rote or as being endowed, ye set a barrier. For He made Himself of no estate, though He came into a world created by His very breath. The *world* knew Him not, but *ye* have known Him—ye *know* Him; for thou hast seen, thou hast tasted, thou hast heard, thou hast felt, thou hast proclaimed, do proclaim, the love of God through the Christ, even Jesus the man, thy Brother!

And as ye questioned and were questioned again in Athens, where there was given the proclaiming to all the forces and powers of nature that then ruled over this or that portion of man's experience—whether as the god of the storm or of the rain or of the sunshine or of the harvest or of the winter or of the elements about the earth, ye saw, ye heard, ye were questioned even *how* the Holy Spirit upon thy mother's body was quickened to that influence to which there came conception, that is unknown and only a myth in the gods of the ancients or of the unseen forces. And why not these be worshiped then as well as this unseen force that acted as ye claim, then?

From the very foundations of thy faith then ye were questioned, but ye stood steadfast; for as ye had heard and as ye proclaimed—and as is in the experience of man even today—that which to man with *all* his knowledge is impossible, to God is but as the breath or the wind in its passing, yet in its passing may quicken to each atom. For as each cell in each atom of the body *knows* its purpose, if it is imbued with the spirit of *life*, yet knoweth naught if it is condemned by the desires of flesh only to its mere rote of activity—yet quickened by the Spirit bringeth, even as in thine experience, that of the unnatural to the natural. Hence as the body grew, as the body was held by the mother in its whole purpose of "Thy handmaid, O God; use me—Let my cup be filled with Thy purpose, Thy desire, because of Thy love for man, that I may be the channel, a channel, through which the world may know; though I be doubted, though I be spurned by those that are worldly-wise and say all manners of things."

So thou in thine experience in the present, as ye may be questioned as to thy gentleness to this or that experience of individual activities, become aware of those experiences through which ye passed, even there—as not only the sister in the flesh of Jesus but as the helpmeet to a heathen; yea, a Roman! Yet the foolishness of the world and of the earth is the wisdom of God! Just as the foolishness of man may be turned into the wisdom of the ages, the wisdom of God. For the wisdom is indeed to be willing to be led by the spirit of *God* rather than to be guided by thine own concept *of* paralleling or classifying or reasoning.

For the worldly-wise oft destroy themselves, as ye saw among the leaders of thine own peoples, as ye saw among those in authority among thine own associates. And these ye see oft. But even as He, thy Brother; though He wept bodily over Jerusalem, though He sighed with the very blood of His body in Gethsemane, He smiled upon the cross—as He smiles upon thee and gives, "*I* am with thee; be not afraid, it is I—even I who *am* the life, who Am the way, who Am the word!"

And in Him, (and "In me," as He gave) ye can put thy trust. "Were it not so, I would have told you. I prepare a place for those that are faithful, are patient, that they—too—may be with me as from the foundations of the earth. Ye have been, even as I, in and out—in the shadow, in the light; yet the purpose, the desire of the soul itself is to be at an at-onement with Him."

1158-9   F.47   3/28/37   Ruth

In giving further interpretations of those records as we find in the experience of the entity, and their application in the present, it is very well, very befitting that such should come at a season or time when there were the experiences of the entity as the sister of the risen Lord; that there may be in the experience of the entity those practical experiences and practical applications . . .

How much more then should this mean to self? For even as He in the consciousness of the separations bade John to take her, thy mother, His mother, as his own, how much more would be that consciousness in self that the life, the self, the experience is dedicated to His at-onement with the Father in thee; that the glory as He had before the world was is His.

How much more may it shine in thee, that would make such an application of self? Not unto self-glory, not unto self-indulgence. These are only that thy name may be well-spoken of, or that thou might be different, or that in self there might be that even as He hath given to thy friend in the mother of John and James when He said, "That these may be upon the right or the left is not mine to give, but is prepared for those who are able, who are willing to drink of the cup even as I" . . .

In that particular period then, of which ye seek to know more —as to the occasions, in a physical manner, when there were the contacts with the *individual* as a personality—that ye experienced physically:

As has been given, while the physical body or entity Jesus was studying in Egypt, in Persia, in India, ye came into the experience—or were born in the earth.

When there was the death of Joseph, He returned to thee— yea, then a lassie—as a stranger; yet there was a binding influence from those very tendernesses, those very influences as brought to bear that draw upon thine inner self.

Yet thine orthodox teachings (as ye would term today) held thee aloof. The first appearances then were at the burial of Joseph.

At those periods when there was the first preaching in Capernaum, ye again heard His words. Then with the attempts of all of those in authority, even those of thine own faith, to dispute, to do bodily harm, again there arose that cry—as ye oft asked of Mary—"How *can* such things be? How *can* he without father come into the world?"

It was against nature, against thine own reasoning. Yet as has been given, as has been shown, Creative Forces bring into being that as of the Father through the *purposes,* through the intents, through the desires! Then as He hath made, He hath builded and without Him there was nothing made, does it become strange to thee that He entered into His own to become a part of same?

Yet this ye could not comprehend, and yet ye say ye may see a manifestation of the presence or power of God in moving, in activating, in the hearts and minds of peoples and of individuals, animate and inanimate things. Yet He came to His own and His own received Him not!

Then again with thine own training ye were separated far, as has been indicated; and only was there the comprehending in the last days when there was the triumphal entry, when there was the evening of the night in the garden, and ye came to thy mother in her physical bereavement, and ye understood, ye comprehended—*when* there was related to thee the walk to Emmaus!

Those were the periods. In life ye saw Him, in experience and manifestations as when He healed Peter's wife's mother, just before the rising of the rulers of the temple against Him. Then in death. Thus ye could not, ye did not comprehend.

How if He is life, could He die? Why did He die? These were the burdens. *Why* should He die?

Yet as He gave, "For this purpose came I into the world." Just as He gave, "If ye would have life, give life."

If ye would know Jesus, God, be *that, be that,* to thy fellow man!

For it has ever been and is, even in materiality, a reciprocal world. "If ye will be my people, I will be thy God." If ye would know *good,* do good. If ye would have life, give life. If ye would know Jesus, the Christ, then be like Him; who died for a cause, without shame, without fault yet dying; and through that able to make what this season represents—*resurrection!*

Resurrection means what? It is reciprocal of that which has been expressed. How hath it been put again by him whom ye knew but disliked (for ye loved Peter the better)? "There is no life without death, there is no *renewal* without the dying of the old." Dying is not blotting out, it is transition—and ye may know transition by that as comes into the experience by those very activities, that "With what measure ye mete it shall be measured to thee again." That was His life, that is thy life, that is each one's life. Then how near, how dear has grown in the hearts, in the minds of all, those who put away self that they may know Him the better?

He put away self, letting it be nailed to the cross; that the *new,* the renewing, the fulfilling, the *being* the law, becomes the law!

For it is the law to *be* the law, and the *law* is love! Even as He showed in all of His manifestations, in the material experiences in the earth; that ye doubted, honestly—that is in the eyes, in the heart, in the soul even of the Creator counted—even as of old—desire, honest desire (not because faults did not arise in material world but they were meted to Abraham, even as He said)—as *faith!*

Faith is manifested by that evidence of things not seen, but the hope in the promises of that which is creative in thine inner self, thine own soul, as it seeks expression, hopes for in the life, yea in the blood of the Lamb which is the life that lights the whole world!

Ready for questions.

Q-1. Was I an eye witness of any of the miracles of Jesus? If so, please designate?

A-1. As has been indicated; the resurrection, the healing from fever.[8] Hast thou not felt, hast thou not seen, hast thou not experienced those things from what even the world today calls fevers as the periods when He was the closer to thee? Is it strange? Is it not a reciprocal world? What ye sow, ye reap. What ye *are,* ye are by purpose of the will given thee that makes for seeking a way, yea seeking the city without foundations whose builder and maker is God, and whose manifestations of self are given. For as ye have seen, as the Father, the Son, the Holy Spirit are one, so ye being one in purpose, in desire, in hope, in faith, *by* thy deeds, by thy hopes, by thy long-sufferings, by thy patience, by thy enduring, by thy beliefs, show what indeed *are* thy hopes, thy fears, thy desires, thy purposes, thy aims.

Q-2. Can you give me more details of my personal contacts with Jesus?

A-2. As has just been given.

The closest personal contacts came only at deaths. Remember, these are conditions—remember all that has just been given, and the aloofness of self (not a fault. This is not given as a fault, but there was the aloofness of self, owing to the variations in age, in the times, in the periods). But the personal contacts were at death, at deaths. The death of the father, when in thine own physical purposes there was the reasoning, "If He healed, why did He let Father die? If He is such as so many proclaim, *why* hath He been so long away? *Why* does He continue to go here, there? Why do those that are in authority appear against Him?"

These are questions then, they are questions ever. Is it not a reciprocal world?

Q-3. Did I see Jesus after the resurrection?

A-3. Saw Jesus upon the Mount, as did many.

Q-5. Are the children who were born to the entity in this Palestine period known to the entity today, and in what connection?

A-5. They may be known, as grandchildren.

Q-6. Is Peter known to me today?

A-6. Not known. There are many of the apostles, as has been indicated, or disciples, that may be known. There's Bartholomew that may be known. There is Andrew, there is Jude (thy brother) that may be known. There is even Judas—don't know him, shouldn't know him; not as a fault in his, but better not. John may enter, and will be known—and as one that may be proclaimed by the entity. These come only, to be sure, as conditions—but may become personal experiences. Just as this: How personal is thy God? Just as personal as ye will let Him be! How close is the Christ as was manifested in the physical body, Jesus? Just as near, just as dear as ye will let Him be!

Oft ye may ask, from thy enquiring mind, when I so desire to know Him, why then do I not see, do I not hear?

How long, O Lord, how long? Look not for a sign, as a *sign*, as He gave, but *be*—and ye *are* as one with Him!

These become not as trites, not as sayings—they must be *experienced* by self! They may not be experienced by merely being told. Ye live them! "As ye live in me and I in the Father, ask what ye will and it will be done unto thee."

Ye wait, then, knowing. He knoweth what thou hast need of before ye ask. Then ye say, Why ask?

In the love of thine own children, is it those who ask or those who do not ask that make a response? Not that ye love one more than the other; not for impunity, but a reciprocal reaction!

Those things are as God is. And they that would know Him must *believe* that He is; and most of all *act* that way!

Q-7. *Should I hope and seek for personal experiences or contacts with Jesus as a personality now?*

A-7. As has been indicated, this may be—but this ye live. Not as a desire for self-exaltation; that is, self-proof, self-evidence; but it is evidenced *in* thee when ye *are* (in thy living, in thy thinking, in thy acting) one with Him.

Then, and thus—how hath the angel given? "As ye have seen Him go, so will ye see Him come." Were those just as words? No.

Thou hast seen Him oft in the acts of others and the personality ye called by another name, yet ye may see Him. And when

He speaks, "Be not afraid, it is I." Know He is near. And in the breaking of bread ye may know Him!

1158-10   F.47   11/15/37   Ruth

As has been indicated, one stands out so beyond the others —not only because of the experiences and activities of the entity in that period, but because of the associations of the soul-entity in relationships to individuals who had so much to do with the opportunities of that sojourn—as they do in the present.

Hence we will find many of these making for that which will offer, does offer, the opportunities for not only the development in the lives and experiences of others but opportunities for that awareness so long sought within the experience of self.

For the moment, review some of those activities as already intimated in the experience of this entity, as the daughter of Joseph and Mary, in the Palestine land; when there were those turmoils and confusions as to what ye would term in the present the orthodox faith or view of the relationships of individuals; as well as those activities with a new regime, a new idea, a new approach to the very influences that have changed and will ever change the course of human thought and experience among the children of men; the lessons, the tenets, the teachings, yea the very life of Jesus, the brother, the entity.

And those activities of the companion of this entity in the experience, when—through the very associations—the entity gained those *new* awakenings of not only the spiritual and mental thought of the period but as to its dealings with individuals.

For as He taught, it becomes in the experience of the entity in the present, "As ye do it unto the least of these, my children, my brethren, ye do it unto me."

And, "As ye would that others should do to you, do ye even so to them."

These become, in the experience then, more and more as living truths; so that as the course of their application runs in the dealings with others, in the actual experiences, there is seen the arousing of those things which He and His loved ones presented as the fruits of the spirit. For they bring hope where none has been, they bring cheer where confusion has existed, they bring the longings for peace where turmoil or misunderstanding has existed; and the result becomes more and more as the entity heard, not only from the mother, from the friends, but from the companion also, "Peace—I leave with you; not as the world giveth peace," but the peace that makes the heart glad, that brings the renewing of hope, that brings the understanding of joy unabated in the lives and the hearts of all that *will* come and take of the water of life freely. For the spirit and the bride say "Come, and whosoever *will* let him take of the water of life freely."

Ready for questions.

Q-1. Why do I, in my imagination, often feel like kneeling before, or kissing the hand of Jean Alexis Teslof, now resident at 200 West 57th St., N.Y. City?

A-1. As has been indicated for that entity Teslof, he was among the first of those to make or create in mosaics the activities—or depict same in this manner—of Him as He gave, "If ye will not believe because I have told you, believe for the very works' sake." [9]

Then as the entity Teslof made into this form those concepts of that activity of the teacher, the master, the brother, there *dawned* upon the entity now called [1158] the real, *real* service.

And as all that did vision same, there is felt then the reverence for the mind and hand that could so visualize a manifestation of His work and service in such a beautiful manner.

Then is it so hard to understand, or is there any great wonder that in the presence of such there is felt that obeisance in the present? because of the awakening and the assurance that "Indeed, it must be true!"

Q-2. What have been the relationships in former lives with Jean Alexis Teslof?

A-2. Again it may be said that one experience so overshadows others as to become that channel, that awareness—which the activities of the entity called Teslof aroused in so many during that experience.

And if the entity Teslof will in the present paint that description given of the Lord's Supper, as it has been outlined through this channel, or seek to have it awakened or aroused in the consciousness to undertake same, yea the whole of Christendom will again understand that the entity Teslof was so *close* to those teachings in that experience as to bring the awareness to many such as may not be given by another.

Those were the activities, in that experience, that were so close to the entity, now [1158] and that which is felt in the present arises from same.

Q-10. Was Jean Teslof's Greek name Pinneas, or Cineman?
A-10. Cineman.

137-4   M.26   10/28/24   Jude

Just before this, we find in the days when the Master came into the Promised Land. This entity one that followed close in the ways of the teachings as set by Him. In the personage of the brother in the flesh, Jude.

137-64   M.27   3/10/26   Jude

. . . there have been times and occasions when there was the physical resistance against the accepting of the tenets as presented; yet in this latter view there is seen that which brings to the subconscious forces that awakening of the experiences of the entity, in the death of that One that presented the *way* to the giving of self to the service of man, in the Son of man, and the brother of entity; and in the flesh there comes, in the year and a half after this death, the acknowledgement of the Master as the Master of the entity, and in that day the entity then only nineteen, as is viewed by the entity. As is seen by reading that as was composed by the entity in that period, and set down now in the sacred scriptures [Jude 1-25], there is seen that the entity in that period was the deep thinker, and one that sought out many conditions as had been presented through the knowledge of ancient days . . .

Q-2. Did I live on earth at the time of Christ's crucifixion?
A-2. As the brother.

137-125   M.31   11/15/29   Jude
Q-9. Will I be able to see Jesus?
A-9. You will.

Q-10. In John, thou saidest, "After my death, the comforter will come." Who is the comforter today?

A-10. The comforter is the gift of the Holy Spirit, for it sheds abroad in dark places, and Him that keepeth my counsel is brought to the full understanding, and is brought to remembrance of that walk with Him.[10]

Q-11. Which of the disciples was the one you loved the best?

A-11. John. Upon this one Jude leaned in days when chains and bonds held thee. Freed with Him and then sent into the wilderness for thy tenderness. He (John) will aid you.[11]

137-123   M.30   7/28/29   Jude

Q-16. Is [5767] one of the prophets or disciples of the Master?

A-16. Bartholomew.

Q-17. He was Bartholomew?

A-17. Bartholomew.

Q-18. Why is my liking for him so marked?

A-18. On account of those associations that endeared all of the apostles or disciples to this entity Jude in that experience when, through hardships, many gained the better concept of those experiences through which each were passing. As is seen in the present experience, this—or these entities, thrown together under different circumstances, yet each find in the other that confidence that is not wholly understandable to either—yet, were these to read together, even this as is given by the Beloved—"The Father pitieth those that would seek after Him"—or again in "In my Father's house are many mansions; were it not so I would have told you. I go to prepare a place, that where I am ye may be also. Me ye have known, and the way ye know, for I am the way, the truth, and the light. Had ye not known me ye would not have known the Father, but seeing me, in me ye see the Father also. If I go not away the spirit will not come unto you, but I go to the Father and the spirit will *abide* with you and bring to your *remembrance* all things whatsoever I have said unto you." These—this, mine son—and thou wilt see, even in the counsel of thine own hearts, as men, *this* fulfilled in the street, in the market place, or in thine *own* home.[12]

137-12   M.26   1/12/25   Jude

Q-2. Give names, relationships and influences existing between this body, [137], and those with whom he was associated in past experiences on earth's plane, and with whom he is now associated on the same plane.

A-2. In this, we find many, many, many, with whom he has been, and is, associated with, wherein there was association in other planes in earth plane . . .

137-121   M.30   5/12/29   Jude

Question: . . . *who in the earth plane now was his [137]'s wife as Jude?*

Answer: His mother-in-law [4255]! . . .

Q-2. Then, his conclusion regarding that written by Jude to his wife is correct?[13]

A-2. Correct. This has been given the body, that in the reading of that written, as has been translated—this not all the letter as printed, and the body may in the days to come gain physical possession of much more that was written by the entity in that period; for with the breaking up of the groups, the body served in the land that is to become soon a source of knowledge to peoples seeking to know of the records as were put away during the 90th, 96th and 97th year after the Lord's ascension. The entity (Jude) wrote much in the confinement at that place now called Achaiah [Achaia (?), Acts 18:12, Province of Rome in Greece?], and with the unearthing of those tombs to which the body was then confined, there will come—on the tablets in the rolls that will be taken from these in the days to come—much more of the writings of the body.

137-126   M.31   11/30/29

Q-6. Are these [physical] conditions of [140]'s inevitable in her development . . .?

A-6. Each must meet that builded in the body. In the counsel and the aid of those able to bear comes succor and help. Hence that as was preached by Jude in the days by the hillside.

Q-7. Where can these preachings of Jude be found?

A-7. These will be found, or a continuation of these, near Ur of Chaldees.

Events in the Ministry of the Master

Random Followers

3180-2   F.19   9/1/43   Ukle

. . . the entity was in the Promised Land, in those throngs that followed closely after the Master, during those first two years especially of His popularity, through those periods in the choosing of the disciples, the periods when there were the teachings such as the Sermon on the Mount and those relating subjects given by those closely associated with the families of the entity.[1]

Thus we find the entity saving many of those that were persecuted; eventually leading to martyrdom because of what might be called indiscretion in regard to those with whom the entity discussed such material or spiritual application of truth in a material world.

The name then was Ukle.

1646-2   M.59   12/18/39

Q-1. *How may I be most useful to Jesus Christ?*

A-1. In applying principles. He spoke not in individual cases, but principles. These, too, ye may apply in thy daily life in dealing with thy fellow men.

2481-1   F.Adult   3/22/24

In the one [incarnation] before this, we find in the country of the Gadarenes,[2] when the Prince of Peace entered in that country, and was a messenger for the Master in that country, being one close in contact to the one receiving the influence of the Prince of Peace.

5354-1   F.34   7/24/44

The entity was in one of the experiences when the Master walked through the wheat fields on a Sunday morning among those who heard the disputations between some regarding the Sabbath day, regarding the labor on the Sabbath day, and saw and heard.³ These make in the consciousness of the entity a vision of the Master as might be put on canvas if the entity were to attempt to do so and be entirely different from all these which have been depicted of the face, the body, the eyes, the cut of the chin and the lack entirely of the Jewish or Aryan profile. For these were clear, clean, ruddy, hair almost like that of David, a golden brown, yellow-red, but blue eyes which were piercing; and the beard, not cut, but kept in the proportion at the contour of the face, and the head was almost perfect.

That in wheat and in nature would be something the entity might give if it would attempt to do so.

3360-1   M.67   11/12/43   Ardath

. . . the entity was in the Holy Land, during the periods when the Master walked in the earth.

The entity then was among those throngs that gathered at times for the interpreting of the new teachings, and the watching of their application in the experience of Him—who gave such hope to the world.

In those periods the entity followed close, and yet was easily dissuaded for fear of bodily force. These find expressions in the present rather in the physical conditions than in the spiritual natures. Hence these will and do become at times hard to be understood.

The name then was Ardath. The entity gained throughout, save when the fear prevented the full cooperation with those that were set in authority in many places . . .

Q-4. Did I contact Jesus, if so, in what activity and under what conditions?

A-4. Knew the man Jesus as He went about the countryside. As to the application, as just indicated, the entity blew hot and cold through the periods of development. With the resurrection, when the entity saw Him again, the entity became very active in the churches established—first in Caesarea and then in Caesarea-Philippi.

2015-3   F.15 days   10/12/39   Magan

. . . the entity was in the land of promise, during those periods when the Master walked in the earth; and in that land not as a Jewess but rather of the mixed peoples.

Thus the entity was not understood by many when there were the blessings to the entity by the Master in the household of the ruler, when the great service was indicated through the entertaining of the Master by those who were rulers in those portions of the city—not in Jerusalem but nearby.

The entity was not that one who was considered as an outcast, but with those same groups—though not of those peoples.

Hence we find the entity's appealing to those who need to be reasoned with, and in kindness and gentleness as it will manifest or express in its associations—in its wanting to give away, as well as to be given to, everything in and with which it is associated.

Do not hinder this, but do not let it become an extravagance in the experience in the early years; for then in the formative periods for greater development will come great blessings from the experience.

And let that ever be a part of the training, the teachings of the entity—that in Him is the life and the light, and that His whole command is *sincerity* and love.

The name then was Magan.

2459-1   F.3   3/7/41   Naneoi

. . . the entity was in the Roman land *and* the Palestine land. For, the entity was among the companions of those in authority in the Palestine land when there were the activities, the tenets, the beliefs being presented by the Prince of Peace.

The entity then was a companion of one of those in authority in that land; knowing the holy women, knowing the Master Himself. For, the entity was that companion that brought the periods of activity for the great dinner for the Master, His disciples and His followers, during the latter portion of the Berean [Perean?] ministry. This was the greater occasion of an individual dinner given in honor of the Master during His early ministry. While in the record nothing is given as to the entity's part, owing to the custom of that period or age, it was from the *entity's* choice, the *entity's* desire to know firsthand, to see *all* characters, all groups of individuals that were not only the followers but the listeners, as well as the character of the apostles—or disciples as they were called at that particular period.

Thus we will find that oft the entity will ask questions, when in the teachings there are the lessons given as He gave to the little ones or in any given direction. The entity will ask, at times, "What did Jesus say?" Never, never refrain from taking advantage of such opportunities to fully explain this to the entity. For, as it did then, the entity will gather much that is missed by many in making practical application of the principles and tenets of His teachings.

The name then was Naneoi. The entity gained—and much should be given the entity of that period in its own developing through this particular sojourn and period.

2427-1   F.58   1/16/41   Judith

... the entity was in what is known as the Promised Land, during those periods when the Master walked in the earth.

The entity knew, the entity entertained the Master in its own household—but as the companion of the Pharisee, in the land of Perear [?]. Because of the customs of the day, the women were kept, socially, in obeisance to the dictates of their companions —until there had been changes wrought by the undertakings of many of the peoples. Yet with the interpreting of the law, the moral and social relationships as understood by the entity through the periods of entertainment, a great awakening came to the entity then—in the name of Judith.

Throughout that experience the entity gained. For, with the convictions of the entity—that there was not only a state of consciousness as related to conditions about one, or as rote, but an activity according to that believed—the entity's activity brought—while not always material comforts—the greater ability of understanding, the greater appreciations of the activity of creative forces in the influence of the entity.

Thus, throughout the experiences of the entity in the material plane since those periods, there has been the returning to that determination to be as He of old, "Others may do as they may, but as for me and my house, we will serve the living God." [4]

Hold fast to those experiences, to those urges which arise so oft — not as in one that would set self away from activity, but as He gave, the fields are white unto the harvest, the laborers are few. Labor *thou* in the vineyard of thy Lord! . . .

Q-9. What has been the association with my husband in the past, and how can I best handle this situation and the urges now?

A-9. . . . When thy activities were in the Promised Land, ye worked together — *after* ye had found thyself . . .

513-1   F.35   2/10/34   Marian

The entity then was of the Sidonian peoples when the teachings from the Master came to those peoples when he journeyed into Thyatira and the upmost coast of the land. The entity followed with those teachings and returned to the land of the upper portion of Galilee during that sojourn, in or with those peoples where the Master and some of His disciples made their home — in what was then Shilo, near the upper end of the lake or the sea of Galilee.

The entity then, in the name Marian (be well if it had been named that this time), gained through the greater portion of the sojourn, only losing when there were the threatenings to the body and especially to those of its own household — then the weakenings; yet being strengthened later by those that came up from the city, the entity furnished aid to many that were persecuted by those in material authority.

From that experience into the present has come much in the entity's inner self, from even hearing the songs of Galilee or the rugged cross. They *do,* as it were, something to the inner self of the entity when these are sounded; as also does the combination of certain vowels that were used by His followers to warn others as to the approach of danger.

1741-1   F.42   10/15/30   Lystia

. . . the entity among those who sat by the river, as the gatherings on the feast days, and listened to the speech and the exhortation by those who gave a new message from the foreign land to the women of Thyatira and Sidon, for the entity was then a seller of lace, purple brocade and linens, and in the *city* as of Lystra did the entity dwell — a maiden throughout the experience, and the entity gained through this experience, for much as was gained in the service set—and in the applications of the new rule or ideal as was given in this experience—did the entity apply and use in that experience. In the name Lystia.

3640-1   F.27   1/1/44   Tharha
. . . the entity was in the *Holy Land* when there had been the edifying of the peoples in the outer areas of Palestine. From Thyatira the entity came, hearing of the healings and of the Master's activities through portions of the land.

With some of its own household the entity then came to Galilee that there might be a healing from a possession, and the entity ever gave thanks for the manner in which the Master indicated His interest in others, their sorrows, their joys, their uprisings, their littleness and their abilities to appreciate.

Then the entity in the present may learn first of all the meaning of appreciation of the blessings, the opportunities that are given thee in thy present environs, thy present surroundings. The one healed in thy association then is the one ye need to heal in the present, thine own companion whom ye have rejected! Find him! Save him, and in same save thyself! If you don't, you'll be sorry!

The name then was Tharha.

3407-1   F.40   12/16/43   Samanteherlequen
. . . the entity was in the Holy Land during those periods when the Master walked in the earth, when people of varied lands were interested through those activities, especially when the entity came in contact with those whom the Master healed when He went to the North country.

For the entity was not of the Jewish people, not of Samaritans, but rather of those lands nigh unto those—among those designated by the Samaritans and the Jews as heathens, but the entity was not a heathen—for the entity accepted the teachings. Though it brought turmoils when there were the persecutions the entity aided in caring for many of those as they fled from those in authority in Jerusalem as well as in other portions of Palestine.

Then in the name Samanteherlequen, the entity gained throughout—and it would be well for those tenets, those truths, those activities to be manifested in all forms in the present. Let those tenets and truths be the basis, the beginning, the end of those things it would teach, it would preach, it would practice in its own life. For those activities of man or woman in the earth may not excel that ideal, may not excel the individual's ideal.

Choose then, and keep in those ways . . .

Q-7. [*Would appreciate details of associations in past experiences with*] *My daughter,* [*3053*].

A-7. In the Holy Land ye saw the daughter healed. Ye loved the daughter—ye acquired her for yourself in the present. Keep the faith with those experiences in which ye saw the healing.

618-3   F.61   3/6/35   Abighael

. . . the entity lived during those periods when the Master walked in the earth. While the entity came not in direct contact with the individual, there were those visions, those aids that came to the household of the entity, and to those about the entity; and the entity's activities during the period made for a greater development in the experience than has been experienced in any material or earthly sojourn.

The entity then was in the household of the centurion whose daughter (the entity's daughter) was healed; in the name then Abighael. In the experience the entity made for, through the associations not only in state craft, the native activities, but the understandings that have come to the entity have enabled the entity from those sojourns to be more than ordinarily tolerant with the various activities under which individuals may be subjected in their daily life; enabling the entity to counsel with others. And this should be the life work, as a teacher; for in this the entity would have done well, as a teacher in those of spiritual tenets or lessons or crafts, and in these may the entity even yet gain much in self and in self's development in the present experience, making for those things in the activities with others that may enable many to understand the real tenets of the lesson of love as taught by Him who healed the daughter that was already in the coma of fever . . .[5]

Q-5. [*What were the past associations*] *With my grandchild Virginia?*

A-5. The daughter that was healed.

2181-1   M.31   4/26/40   Mathias

... the entity was in the land of promise, and among those who were of that group who met the Master in the way. The entity, then, was one who was healed; but did not return to give thanks, *after* having complied with the penal and moral law for such healings.[6]

The name then was Mathias; and the entity gained and lost through the experience; gained in the fact of coming in contact with that influence, force or power in which there were the demonstrations of the entity—through and within itself, by and through the spoken word—becoming aware of creative forces or energies within the own experience; lost in not making a practical application of same in its experience among its fellow men, not bearing witness to those assurances, those experiences, in its activity.

3216-1   F.64   9/15/43

... the entity was in that land where the Master walked in the earth, among those who had brought their loved ones to the Master for healing. The entity brought its son that had been afflicted, and was so hard for those who were the Master's companions to know why they themselves could not heal when He had withdrawn in the mount that there might be material evidence in the flesh to His faithful three. Thus was the power or the might withdrawn and as was indicated in the admonition, fasting and prayer also must cast such conditions out.[7]

So in thy own experience in the present, be oft in prayer. Be patient, be persistent for, He will not suffer thee to see corruptions until many of thy hopes, many of thy aspirations are fulfilled in thy consciousness. For, He is mindful of those who keep His ways, even as then He supplied that as would bring happiness and joy; not gratification but contentment and peace to the hearts and souls of those that sought to know His biddings.

2035-1   F.58   11/2/39   Sophia

... the entity was in the land of promise, during those periods when the Master walked in the earth.

There we find the entity was acquainted with much and

many of the happenings of that experience; yet not until there came the meeting of many of the holy women were those experiences as the greater awakening influences in the experience of the entity—as Sophia—in that sojourn.

For, the entity was not of the Jewish peoples, but rather of the combination of the Grecian and Saracen peoples, or those about the northernmost portion of that particular land.

There again we find the entity losing, gaining; gaining because of its abilities to relate to the many during that experience the stories and experiences of those who had been in close contact with the Teacher of teachers, the Lord of lords, the Brother of man!

For the entity, as is understood from the records that are indicated, was one that could tell such in a manner as to induce the individual to live with those experiences.

Practice these in thy daily life in the present, and in the telling of them ye will not only find Him alive in thine own heart and consciousness, but that His words become *living* water, quenching the thirst of those who are disturbed or troubled as to the meanings of His parables, His lessons that He taught.

2661-1   M.9   8/4/31   Suel

. . . in that plane when the Master walked in the land, and during that sojourn into the land of the Saracens, and through those periods when the entity *followed* the Master through the land. The entity gained in that experience, for coming under the tutelage and the direction of Him as was, as is, the life, the light in this material world, the entity then in the name Suel became one of those leaders of that sect in this land. In the present, as will be seen from the experience, those of **that as** pertains to these teachings will find a fertile soil; for those **that** do not ring true will be rejected *by* the entity, even **in** *this* experience, for having *been*—as it were—the example, **or** *presenting* self in the one to *become* the example, as a **martyr, in** the present this will find—unless there is truth in those **presented** to the entity—that which would separate **the entity** *from* the understanding in the present. In those applications, then, may the entity be that as was in that land where **those** peoples harkened *to,* and understood that that heard came from the *sources* divine.

478-4   M.45   11/7/35   Phylos

"My Spirit will, does, bear witness with thy spirit whether ye be the sons of God or not."

Again, saith the Master, "He that loveth me and keepeth my words, with the same will I come and abide; that he—or *you* —or *ye*—may know I am *indeed* thy brother."

Hence in self the *experiencing* of those words in the mental and the spiritual and the material *self* WILL BE the answer to self in no *uncertain* terms.

For the way of the Lord is not past finding out. While the experience of man with his fellow man may indicate to an individual that this or that manner may be a *means of* approach, yet from the individual viewing same his experience being different, has not made it different as to the point of contact nor as to those definite laws; for the *vision* is of the individual.

Look upon those experiences of Him who is not even questioned by those that proclaim, profess, or are active in any moral aptitude of life, when He gave, "There be some standing here that will see me come in my glory. And He taketh with Him Peter, James and John and goeth into the mount, and *there* was transfigured before them."

What is happening then, as is in thine own experience, when thou art listening to those—as were those of the nine left in the valley? Were they not great preachers, great ministers? Did they not have a close contact with the very truth and life itself? Yet it is not that He had departed, not that He was withdrawn. Yet their ability to heal as in former times, as in experiences later, did not become effective. Did it take from the activities or add to the activities of Peter, James and John— their being in the Presence? Peter denied. John held to himself. James—by his very exertion—Herod laid his hands upon him.[8]

All of these should be as ensamples, as lessons in thine own experience; that ye may be either upon the mount in thine experience with Him, or in the valley with the nine, and still of Him, should not disturb thee. For hath He not given (and His promises are sure), "Believe in me, abide in me, and I will bring to thine remembrance *all* necessary that *ye may know* the way"? His words are *true!*

Hold *fast* to that thou hast set in thine *heart* as concerning Him. For He has promised to come to thee, to all who seek, who live, who act in such a manner that His presence is *acceptable* to those who seek.

The Seventy

1529-1   M.62   2/4/38   Silvanus

. . . the entity lived during that period when the Master walked in the earth, and when there were those gatherings about the disciples and the followers, and when the Master blessed the seventy that were to go abroad and teach and minister to others and preach repentance, that the day of the Lord was at hand.[1]

Ye then were among that seventy, and again on the days or day of Pentecost ye rededicated thyself—as Silvanus.[2]

And as a teacher and a minister in the churches of lower Asia and the upper portions of the Palestine land, ye ministered to thy fellow men; and gained and *gained* through those experiences; bringing encouragement and hope and faith again and again into the hearts and minds and experiences of those that from the very stumbling forces of life from the political and social and economic forces became weak and stumbling.

And indeed to thee may it be accredited that in Caesarea were those followers first called Christ-like, or Christ-ians!

In thy associations with the Twelve, the bishops, the deacons, ye brought counsel and strength.

And so may ye in the present, even as was bidden to thy neighbor, thy brother in the Lord, "Feed my lambs—feed my sheep." This is the work of thy hands in the present; and these directed not by the eye-service of man but to the oneness of purpose of desire to bring into the hearts of men again and again *hope,* encouragement; and to *sow* again and again the seed that bear the fruits of the Spirit—patience, gentleness, kindness, brotherly love, long-suffering! For against such there is no law.

For it is the law that as ye sow, so shall ye reap. And ye are the sower; but leave what may be the results to thy Father!

For He alone may increase. For unless the souls be quickened by the precept and example, and the Father calleth, how can they know Him?

2285-1   M.16   6/24/40   Cleopas

The entity was among those closely associated with, and among those endowed of, that group of seventy who were sent as emissaries through the land to proclaim periods in which there would be activity of the Master as combined with the teachings and ministerings of many of the apostles.

Hence the entity was acquainted and associated with many of those activities . . .

The entity gained throughout that experience, in the name then of Cleopas.

622-4   M.33   6/18/38   Pilos

. . . the entity was among those who were close with many of those who became the disciples, the apostles. The entity was numbered among the seventy that were sent for ministering to the needs of the peoples of the land during the Galilean as well as the Judean ministry.

There the entity's activities, during the latter portion of its sojourn, were of the greater import. For as we find, the entity joined close with the activities of Barnabas, Paul, Silas, Mark, Luke and Lucius in the ministerings. For the entity then was endowed with a voice that made for the *creating* of song service with the ministry and teachings of the disciples, the apostles. For the entity was acquainted with those activities in the various churches.

And there should be the application of self in those directions in the present, by the singing of psalms; not as of dolefulness but of praise, and the psalms themselves — *all* of those activities in which there may be depicted either the activities through the Passion or through the praise as in the Hosannas during the journeys to Jerusalem and throughout the experiences . . .

The name then was Pilos . . .

Then, study to show thyself approved with all good conscience towards those things as ye proclaimed during thy activity in the Palestine land.

For as He blessed thee in body, in mind, so may ye receive — now, in this experience — those blessings in thy dealing with thy fellow man.

3541-1   M.53   1/10/44   Bethelda

. . . the entity was among those that were of the seventy, and yet turned back. But later in the experience, the entity became one of those who aided in activities in establishing united efforts in Bethesda.

Not known or spoken of in the records we have, he was yet ever the figure behind those who were the moving influences of causes and purposes.

And so may the entity yet be the leader, as he was in those experiences in the name Bethelda.

3347-1   M.53   11/1/43   Joel

The entity was among those that were oft in the Master's presence, yea one of those commissioned or sent out with the seventy.

The entity was then advanced in years, being among those elders sent out in the second period of activity.

Hence that feeling oft in the present for those that are sick, those that are bereaved, those that are distressed in mind or in purpose. The entity's kindness of words, gentleness of speech, the entity's very manner has brought quietude when others have failed.

The entity has oft belittled these abilities within self. Yes, of self they are naught. But in the doing, in the being of that which is ever in the way, ye walk in the way even as He walked. Just being patient, just being kind, just showing brotherly love, ye manifest His love until He comes again. And ye may be sure ye will be among those who will meet Him in the way.

The name then was Joel.

2031-1   M.31   10/28/39   Alphus

. . . the entity was in the Promised Land, during those periods when the Master walked in the earth—in those periods when there was the choosing of those who were accredited with the activities of the Master; having a knowledge of, and the entity's friendships were counted among, *all* of the Twelve.

For the entity was among the seventy who were sent—yea, set apart for that contemporary service with Him.

Inasmuch as ye have been given that opportunity, then, by Him who *is* the life, the light of men, *fail not* again in the present to hold that tenet—yea, that truth which He so thoroughly exemplified in the experiences of man; namely, to love the Lord thy God with all thy heart, thy mind, thy body, and thy neighbor as thyself—which is the whole law.

Because of those confusions that arose, ye went back; and again and again did ye continue to condemn thyself.

He condemned not; only as He expressed in those periods when He questioned all—"Indeed offenses must come, but woe unto them by whom they come."

Then, keep those trysts oft with thy Lord, thy Maker. For thy body is indeed the temple of the living God, and there—within thy holy of holies—He has promised to meet thee oft. Fail Him not!

The name then was Alphus. In the experience the entity gained, lost, gained.

Then, keep this experience in such manners that, day by day —not so much by proclamation of thyself, but by thy gentleness, by thy kindness, by thy tenderness of words, of hope, of cheer, of that ever giving of creative forces in their experiences —others may be led to know that ye walk and talk with Him!

4016-1   M.42   3/22/44   Elias

The entity was among the seventy to whom there was given a mission to perform through the land. The entity was among those who could not interpret upon the return. "Except ye eat of my body, ye have no part in me." Literal, it becomes disturbing. Mentally and in a spiritual sense, it may be interpreted.[3]

The name then was Elias and the entity was a friend of Peter and Andrew, and leaned more towards the staid Andrew than to the boisterous Peter; for he argued with Peter and reasoned with Andrew.

The associations with these entities in the present, if there were the better understanding, would in the present bring for each a better interpreting and understanding of activities as related to mental, spiritual and material things in this particular life. The interpretation to either would be well; the stress may not be put too strongly that there should be association with these entities when there are those better conditions for interpreting the law of the Lord. For the law of the Lord is perfect, it converteth the soul. It should be used, not abused, in the application. For unless one makes the application (as the entity found through that experience, as Elias), healing of the physical without the change in the mental and spiritual aspects brings little real help to the individuals in the end.

Though the entity rejected the first tenets, the entity was among those who aided in caring for the numbers who were added to the activities of the disciples on and after the day of Pentecost. All of these incidents appear very close to the entity.

5328-1   M.21   7/6/44   Joseph

The entity was among those who were of the "seventy" who were chosen—not among the "Twelve"—but acquainted with and knew of most of the activities. But with announcements or pronouncements, when there was the return, that one must eat of the body, and drink of the blood if they are to know the Lord, like many others the entity went away, but kept in touch with the activities; and with the day of Pentecost, when many were turned, the entity again became one of those associated with organized work. For then the entity understood, when there had been explained how on the night He was betrayed He took bread and broke it saying, "This is my body," and with the cup, "This is my blood."

For the Christ, as manifested in Jesus, was the first, is the foremost, is the essence of both bread and of wine. For that element which is life-giving physically of bread, or that giveth strength to wine, is the source of life itself. Thus in partaking, one does literally partake of the body and of the blood in that communion.

In these the entity was known as Joseph—not a companion of any of the disciples—but rather from the land of the Galileans and thus of the Samaritan group. In the experience the entity gained, lost, gained.

The experience was of the interest in the healing, being able, by the blessing of the Master, to heal physically and mentally; which brought, has brought, still brings that interest in the spiritual side, yet don't ever attempt to be a preacher, ye failed then, ye would fail again. The activities must be, then, not ever as that which is called too practical; not that ye are not to be practical, but the basis, the spirit of a thing, the purpose of an ideal, rather than the purpose itself or what is done.

1188-2   M.6   12/19/36   Gamaliel

But rather as the entity proclaimed in the experience before that, as Gamaliel—one of the seventy as presented during those experiences when the Master was in the earth and His activities were there in the temple, and during those periods when there were those distressing conditions as arose from the persecutions of those that had been His disciples or His apostles and His followers.

For Gamaliel then was a teacher, yea a rabbi; but had held to that principle that if it be of God, then man had better *not* interfere, and if it is only of man's imagination and not founded in the truth it will come to naught of itself.[4]

Throughout that experience the entity gained, because of those activities and those sojourns throughout. For there was not only the individual development, but those activities or developments which gave the opportunity for others to express themselves in their relationships to their fellow men—as to that held as their ideal of their Creator, and their relationships to same.

Much might be given as to the activities and the associations of the entity during that sojourn, and as to the study and the reading—which so easily becomes a part of the entity in the liking of stories, in its search for unusual things.

Let there be put into the hands of the entity those things as pertain to the activity of *this* entity as Gamaliel in its dealings with the Jewish law as might be applied in the experience of the Roman citizens, and the beauties of the Roman law as might be applied in the experiences of the Jewish followers in those periods of the entity's activity [5] . . .

Q-2. *Was the entity known to his present parents,* [1158] *and* [1151], *in other lives?*

A-2. Especially in that as indicated in those periods when the entity rose to the defense of the apostles, and the study of the entity as a leader of Israel of the Roman's application to that land.

Then the entity was personally known, and admired them for their sincerity.

3344-1   M.46   10/29/43

Well if such had then [English incarnation during first Crusade] learned the lesson given of old by Gamaliel, "If it be of God it will carry on, if it be of man it will of itself fail, and if of God we would only be fighting against God." The influences and powers then in the earth indicate purposes, purposes! O what crimes have been committed in the name of religion! [6]

933-1   M.16   7/28/31   Gamaliel

. . . the entity passing through that period where much was given, much was required of the entity, being in that position in the days when the Master walked in the land; the entity then among those of the teachers in the city [1188 also?], in the name Gamaliel. To him went many for counsel. To him was given the teaching of those that *became* as mighty in the land, and in the name of Him who came as the Lamb to the world. The entity then gave counsel as of justice to all, counseling much in that as held innate, *losing* only in that of persecutions as came to the entity from those in power, as the lawyers and the changes came about in the rulers from the Roman land. The entity lost in becoming weak, that there might not be suffering in self and those near and dear to same. Hence in the present many of those to whom the entity held close in that known as filial relations, or parental relations, has been in that experience of farther and farther away, that become as was in that period [Was 933 the father or son of 1188, whose name also was Gamaliel?], that of the *dream,* that of that experience in the loneliness of the night, in the waking, and in the going out and the coming in, these become as turmoils not wholly understood. Hence that study as the entity may give, the entity may find in self's study, in the application of those things as were given in the counsel to those about the entity [by 1188?] in that of the Sanhedrin, as in that period—that, that must come to naught that is not founded in the living God; for who could fight against the living God, and who is on the Lord's side is not alone though he may stand as one! [7]

The First Recorded Miracle

5749-16   9/10/41

As to the healings, the miracles performed by the Master—of course, the first recorded begins with that in Capernaum, or in Cana and nigh unto Capernaum, when He had so recently returned from the wilderness—or the visit to John—when the water was turned into wine.[1]

5749-15   6/22/41

A great deal of that leading to the experience [wine miracle], to be sure, is being skipped over. For, that came about soon after the return of the Master from the Jordan, and his dwelling by the sea, his conversation with Peter—after Andrew had told Peter of the happenings at the Jordan; and there was the wedding in Cana of Galilee.

The girl was a relative of those close to the mother of Jesus, who prepared the wedding feast—as was the custom in that period, and is yet among those of the Jewish faith who adhere to the traditions as well as custom of those people chosen as the channel because of their purpose with God.

The girl [Clana, 609] to be wed was a daughter of the cousin of Mary, a daughter of a younger sister of Elizabeth, whose name was also Mary. And she was the one spoken of as "the other Mary," and not as some have supposed.

The customs required that there be a feast, which was composed of the roasted lamb with the herbs, the breads that had been prepared in the special ways as were the custom and tradition of those who followed close to the faith in Moses' law, Moses' custom, Moses' ordinances.

The families of Mary were present, as well as those of the groom.

The groom, in the name Roael, was among the sons of Zebedee; being an elder brother of James and John who later became the close friends and the closer followers of Jesus.[2]

The Master, returning with those who were hangers-on, naturally sought to speak with His mother. Learning of this happening He, too, with the followers, were bid to remain at the feast.

Much wine also was part of the custom. The day was what ye would call June third. There were plenty of flowers and things of the field, yet only a part of those things needed. For, the custom called for more of the meats prepared with certain herbs, and wines.

The day had been fine; the evening was fair; the moon was full. This then brought the activities with the imbibing more and more of wine, more hilarity, and the dance—which was in the form of the circles that were a part of the customs, not only of that land then but that are in your own land now and then being revived.

With those activities, as indicated, the wine ran low. Remember, the sons of Zebedee were among those of the upper class, as would be termed; not the poorer ones. Thence the reason why Mary served or prepared for her relative the feast.

From those happenings that were a portion of her experience upon their return from Egypt—as to how the increase had come in the food when they had been turned aside as they journeyed back towards the Promised Land—Mary felt, knew, was convinced within herself that here again there might be such an experience, with her son returning as a man starting upon his mission. For, what was the pronouncement to the mother when Gabriel spoke to her? What was the happening with Elizabeth when the mother spoke to her?[3]

This might be called a first period of test. For, had He not just ten days ago sent Satan away, and received ministry from the angels?[4] This had come to be known as hearsay. Hence the natural questioning of the mother-love for the purposes; this son—strange in many ways—had chosen, by the dwelling in the wilderness for the forty days, and then the returning to the lowly people, the fishermen, about this country. It brought on the questioning by the mother.

3361-1   F.61   11/15/43   Matada

The entity was among the holy women that prepared for the Master in many periods where entertainments took place in people's homes—as in the home in Cana, where there was the beginning of the miracles indicated in some interpretations of the experiences of the man Jesus in the earth, when water saw its Master, blushed and became wine even by activity! Remember, only as it was poured out would it become wine. Had it remained still, no wine would have filled those conditions where embarrassment was being brought even to the friend of the entity in that experience. For this was one of the brethren of James and John, and the entity was acquainted with the bride at that period.

With this activity there came true faith, but at times static. For there came the dependence upon the spirit without the use of the spirit by self at times. Yet the entity in the name Matada, brought much help to those activities of the early church in the various centers; not only the church in Jerusalem but also in other places where there was the setting up of individual activities.

609-1   F.45   7/12/34   Clana

. . . the entity was in that land now known as the Promised Land, during those periods when the Master walked in the earth, and among those people in Cana when the wedding feast was made.

The entity then, as Clana, was the bride for whom the first of the miracles was performed by Mary's son who became the Christ, the Lord.

In that experience we find the entity gained throughout, for —as there were the associations with those that were of the household of the carpenter and of the fishermen in Cana and in Capernaum, and later in Galilee—the entity gained in the understanding and the relationships that grew and grew with the women that followed in the way.

The entity ministered in material activities, material welfare and things, that there might be carried on much of those teachings in that period; losing only by the dissensions with those of its own kinspeople—of John, called the Baptist, that disputed oft with those concerning who was the greater, he that abstained and thus purified the body or he—as the Master taught—that indulged in those things that to some became questioned, but keeping the body for those purposes alone whereunto He had called same to be beautiful in its relationships with that which brings the promises of the Master.[5]

For, as the Master gave, to which the body then answered, "One came not eating, not drinking," clearing self from the ways of the world; the other associating self with those activities in the material things and thus becoming, through the application of that, that which brought peace, harmony, strength and vitality to those to whom the entity and the teacher came. Thus did this entity become, through those discussions, as one versed in what has been called the Scripture of these particular peoples . . .

2946-2   F.48   5/16/43   "The Other Mary"

. . . the entity was among those of the household that entertained the Master oft; then being an aid to "Mrs. Zebedee," as would be ordinarily termed. John and James were charges or cares of the entity during that experience, and the entity was among those spoken of and referred to as "The other Mary," when no other indication is given as to the place from which the entity came, or as to the groups to which the entity belonged.[6]

These brought the entity close in contact with the holy women. Especially during those periods following the crucifixion, the entity became acquainted the better with the mother. For, as the mother became a part of that care, that charge of John, the associations became close.

Thus the imbibing of those tenets that were indicated so oft by John in the repeating, especially, of the last hours of the

Master. These, then, endear to the entity that latter portion of the record of His activity, as given in a portion of the epistle of John; not entirely as given, yet that lacking may almost to the entity at times be supplied. And there is builded in the consciousness—as the walk in the garden, as the repeating of the 91st Psalm that He sang with His disciples—such that these become almost heard at times by the entity.

As to the accomplishments, materially—little may be added; yet the aid, the inspiration the entity gave the disciples and apostles through that period may be counted as much that has been and may be the strength of the entity in the present.

2946-3   F.48   6/18/43

We find that the entity was among those of the group selected as channels considered worthy for the incoming of the promise of God with man.

Thus the entity from its early experience was dedicated to a service to the promises which had been made from the days of the mother of men, until Malachi; that the great, the dreadful day of the Lord would be at hand.

The entity, then, was [the mother of ?] that one at whose wedding the water was turned to wine, as the bride of the brother of James and John, the sons of Zebedee—Roael, as the individual entity, the elder of the children of Zebedee, a zealot for those principles of the law.

Thus, with those activities that brought about the questionings because of John the Baptist making those charges against those in political authority,[7] the husband of the entity was among those that suffered persecution and death . . .

Thus the close association of the entity in the household of Zebedee. For, especially John, the younger of those chosen, that one beloved of the Master, was as a favorite of the entity, with the sorrows that had come—even though the faith, the doubtings had been indicated in the blessings of having the Master present at the wedding.

Hence weddings—the unions of hearts and minds and bodies—take on an unusual significance to the entity. And yet oft, as the entity studies, there are doubts arising.

Know, in thine heart of hearts, as bodies and minds are

drawn together, these are not purposeless but purposeful; that the glory of God may be made manifest. They are opportunities, as ye so well exercised through those periods in thy anxiety as to those, not only of the material things. For, as has been interpreted correctly, the sons of Zebedee were among those sufficiently able financially, as would be termed in the present, to leave their work, their home (and all of the apostles, save Matthew); for these, the sons of Zebedee, were in favor with those in political authority . . .

In those periods, then, when there had been the crucifixion, the entity was drawn closer in association physically with the mother of Jesus, the Lord.

When there had been those activities by those pronouncements made upon the cross, they became then as bosom friends. Thus, as was reiterated again and again to the mother, Mary, and the other Mary, the last hour in the garden, on the way to the garden—these have a special meaning:

"Let not your heart be troubled—ye believe in God, believe also in me; for in my Father's house are many mansions—if it were not so I would have told you. I go to prepare a place for you, that where I am there ye may be also. The *way* ye know." [8]

He, then, is indeed the way, the truth, the light. And, as indicated to the entity in the latter portion (for the entity lived to be of great age, even in that experience—and many may be the years of active service of the entity in its magnifying among men—) that which is addressed to her by John in the letter to the "lady elect." [9]

This indicates that reverence which the beloved of the Master held for the entity through that experience.

504-3   F.53   2/12/34   Cleoapas

. . . the entity was in that land where there were those that were called upon to give of their body those that were of age, when there had gone out the decree from Herod that all males from the suckling to two years old should come under the power of that edict.[10]

The entity then was a neighbor to Mary, the mother of the Lord, and to Joseph. And the husband of the entity was then a carpenter also, and an aid to Joseph, in the name Cleoapas.

Hence the entity knew much of those things that have remained to the *world* a mystery, and oft in the quietness of the hours of the early morn, when as during that period, the entity suffered in the body as for the loss of the offspring, and as has been given that the cry of Rachel went out to the Father for the deeds done in the body of those that professed to be the followers of the living God.[11] Hence doubts and fears arose during the entity's sojourn in that experience, yet when there again arose those in the activities of the forerunner and later when the son of Mary had again gathered at Cana in Galilee, the entity was among those present and as an intimate friend of the mother of the Lord, and saw the first of the miracles of the Lord in Cana of Galilee! And these experiences through that sojourn, as indicated in the early morning hours, have often come; sometimes as beautiful visions, at others—when turmoil and strife arose within the experiences of the day—they have come rather as beating upon the mind that made for the influences of those that would hinder, the influences of the evil that would make of these as nightmares—and there has been in the experience often as one torn from the very breast in the destructive forces. This has made for a quieting within and at others a turmoil and strife within the self. Yet, if these will be turned and viewed from those experiences in that sojourn, there may be built that strength; for His promises ever remain, "Whom I *will* raise up—he that loveth the Lord's ways and hateth or careth not for what may be said in ridicule," for he that will not abase his own personality for the love of the Christ child is not worthy of His love.

The Samaritan Woman at the Well

451-2   F.23   11/5/31   Jodie

. . . this entity that one to whom the Master spoke at the well in the way and a sister then of those that later became messengers and understanders of that being taught.[1] The entity lost and gained, and gained, through this experience; for as the entity had wielded its influence for that which brought those of distorted emotions and ideas in the minds of individuals during that period, so with the awakening of the water of life springing anew in the hearts and souls of those that made Him as the ideal, did the entity bring into the minds, hearts and souls of those first of its own household, then of the multitudes, then of the greater masses, that of the *beauty* of *life* in Him, of the glories of the Father in Him, as may be manifested in the lives of individuals who have Him as their ideals—whether pertaining to the secular things of life or otherwise—for the crust of bread glorified by Him feeds in the physical body those things that bring glories in the hearts and minds of individuals, where the sumptuous board of those that wander far away must bring dimness of eye, solemn-ness of feeling, want and desire in the hearts of those that follow such; but keeping in that way and that understanding as gained then, as Jodie in this experience . . .

428-4   F.47   2/20/31   Josie

. . . The entity was among those of the city who came to the well to hear those truths as propounded in that day, and was a *sister* of the woman at the well. In the name Josie. In this experience the entity gained, after coming under the influence of this individual experience; for *reason*—with the faith that was implanted by this meeting—brought peace, joy, understanding, and the ability to suffer, even in silence, whether in physical, in mental, or the material things of life; being in the position, in the latter portion, of those who sought, those that sent—being sent to the lost sheep of the house of Israel. The entity gained in the giving of an understanding and an experience to those whom the entity contacted, being in the household of a ruler of one in command of those that administered the laws, secular laws of the land, yet bringing peace to her own household, quietude to those disturbed in body and mind, and being of that *family* that worshiped in the mount—the entity gave much to others . . .

2112-1   F.58   6/2/31   Selmaa

In the one before this we find in that land now called the Holy Land, and about that land where the Master walked—the entity then a sister of she whom the entity [Jesus?] met at the well in the land, and the entity came to know of that ministry, following afar; yet later becoming one of those that *spread* those glad tidings to those in Mount Seir. In the name Selmaa. In this experience the entity lost and gained. Lost in the early portion when there was the aggrandizing of selfish interests; gaining in crucifying of *ideas* for ideals, and gained much through the latter portion of that experience. In the present there is felt that awe that comes with the hearing of that particular portion of the Scripture, the Gospel, the message read, of the journey *through* that land; and the *abilities* with the needle, with the making of things that have to do with adorning of body, also come from this experience.

379-3   F.54   9/17/35   Phoebe

The entity then was among those women who in the latter portion of His sojourn journeyed from afar; being of those who came to the sojourns in the land from the teachings the Master had given to those about the well, in the land of the Samaritan peoples. The entity was not of the household of that one spoken to but rather the associate and companion of one of those who joined in the message given by the woman at the well.

Throughout the experience, then, the entity gained much in the mental and spiritual aspects of its sojourn; while to those peoples (and according to the present day of thought) the entity became one who wandered, as it were, from place to place. It became a singer, a dancer, that there might be the wherewithal that more and more of the messages, more and more of the teachings of *this* man, might be a part of the entity's experience.

Hence in the activity the entity became, in the latter portion of the experience, joined with those who met in the upper chamber.[2] And the feelings, the innate expressions that arise in the entity from the reading of those particular activities in the first chapters recorded in Acts, have to the entity a significance that is not experienced in other portions; save in those that deal with the visits of the man of Galilee, the man who walked among His fellow man that others might be shown the way for the more perfect understanding.

Then the entity was in the name Phoebe, and in the latter

portion of the entity's sojourn—when the persecution activities began in the city, the entity again journeyed into the land of its birth, or into Galilee, to become associated rather with Andrew, Bartholomew, Jude, and those who became the ministers in that land.

Then the entity acted in the capacity of one to aid in bringing the words that had been gained by such associations to those that were in despair in body, in mind, and those that were troubled in spirit.

2809-1   M.55   9/9/42   Teular

. . . the entity was in the Roman land, during those periods when there were those expansions of the Roman empire into northern Africa, into western Asia, into the Holy Land; during those periods when the Master walked in the earth.

Then the entity was among those put in authority of a garrison in the Judean hills, portions of Galilee as well as portions of the land over which the Master went.

The entity then was in the name of Teular, and was garrisoned in the old city of Samaria.

In that experience the entity became very hard, very severe; attempting to keep the letter of the law, rather than listening to or applying the spiritual aspects of same.

Not that the law is to be set aside, but brotherly love is the spirit of the law, as well as the letter—then, as in the present. For it is a universal law, and is the basis of that freedom as He gave in those ministrations through His material manifestation in the earth; that ye shall know the truth and the truth shall make you free.

1592-1   F.56   5/16/38   Maryon

. . . the entity was in what is now known as the Holy Land, during those periods when there were the turmoils arising among the peoples owing to the various teachings that came to be a part of the entity's experience.

It was during the turmoils arising from the settlings of the land by the Roman rulers, and the variations between the teachings from the Persian and the Roman and the Egyptian lands, and the native peoples.

The entity was among those who were called the Samaritans, and of that city which later turned a great deal of its activity because of the visit of the Master to the woman at the well.

The entity was among those who in the earlier portion of the experience became imbued with the desire, *by* the associates, to be among those from whom the channel was to be chosen *through* which there might come the promised seed . . .

. . . during the latter portion of the entity's experience in the land did the entity come very close to the teachings, the leaders of the Essenes; coming close to the entity known as Judy in that experience.

Until its latter days the entity did not wed; choosing rather the life of celibacy for the preparation of self to be a teacher; and yet felt in the latter portion as though a great deal had been lost that might have been gained through filial and material love in those periods.

The name then was Maryon, or—as would be interpreted in the present—Mary, Mayan, or Myra.

1552-1   F.40   3/18/38   Jeaniel

The entity came in close contact with the Master when the Master spoke to the woman at the well and many of those in the city who came out to see Him.

Though then young in years, the entity was impressed not only by the gentleness and kindness of the disciples, especially the Master, but later when there were the gatherings of the many in Jerusalem for the feasts—that more and more became a part of the Samaritans as His teachings had advanced—the entity then was among those of the crowd that were in the triumphal entry into Jerusalem [3]. . .

Throughout the experience the entity gained. For the entity was in close associations with the leaders of the churches in the many varied lands, during the latter portion of the experience . . .

The name then was Jeaniel—of the Samaritans but closely associated with Lucius, Luke, Mark, John, Mary the mother as well as Mary and Martha in that experience, as the other disciples—but closer with those of the household at Bethany.[4]

322-2   M.58   4/26/33   Pleadila

. . . the entity was then among those of the citizenry in the Samaritan land, in Gadara, when the people of that city came to hear, to understand, that taught those by the well.

The entity then was among those that acted in the capacity of what would today be called the chief of counsel to the police, or those that kept order; known then among the elders of the land, and in the name Pleadila.

In this experience the entity gained and lost; gained throughout those periods of activity in the official capacities. With the accepting of the teachings, and when there arose dissensions, the entity was falsely accused of turning divers positions, divers solutions, into self's own interests, and faults arose — or the judging that arose brought *suffering* in the mental; yet satisfaction and strength when the entity was able to *prove,* through those records made, that all *was* right.

Is it any wonder, then, the tediousy or accuracy with which the entity makes marks? or bespeaks that which is nearest and dearest to the ideals of self?

The entity then became a teacher, and one who aided in the establishing and building of a city — alone — separate from those, even of the peoples of that particular land.

In that experience the entity became an old patriarch, living to be an hundred and nine years of age.

Peter's Mother-in-Law Is Healed

5749-16   9/10/41

Then there was the healing of Simon Peter's wife's mother, of a fever. It was one of the few instances where healings were performed among His own people, among His own kindred.[1]

1541-11   F.62   7/31/41   Esdrela

. . . the entity was among those of the group called the holy women, or those that saw, that knew many of the associations with the disciples, the apostles, and the helpful, direct influence of the Master Himself.

For, the entity then was the mother of Peter's wife, once healed by the Master Himself.

Those periods brought to the entity the closer associations through the latter periods of the activity. For, being healed as it were, physically, by the Master Himself, the entity's sojourn in the earth was long and varied, and would make a book in itself.

The entity's ability to write in the present should be manifested, especially in the stories as concerning the life of the Master as might be read by children. For, these the entity would be able to do; as it brought through those experiences the channel through which the early church attracted others; as many lived and drew upon those truths as illustrated by the entity.

During that experience the entity had *two* activities; the growing of plants, especially adaptable for the healing of the body, and flowers; and also the ministering to the sick. Not as a nurse — rather as a comforter. For the entity at periods acted in the capacity as a hired mourner, as was the custom of that period.

The name then was Esdrela . . .

Q-1. Why do I feel such an abhorrence of the Catholic religion, and how may I overcome this?

A-1. This arises from those periods of the controversy which arose between the followers of Cephas and the Paulites; that made for those changes wrought in the foundation of that first or early group.[2]

Overcome same in giving expression in those manners in which the young will weigh well in their own lives the teachings of the Master, without condemning any as He, yet requiring that all be sowers in the life journey.

Q-11. What was my past association with my father . . . deceased; and why do I feel he was so much ahead of his time?

A-11. Closely associated; for he was the younger brother of Peter and Andrew.

Q-12. Also my daughter . . . whose short experience with the family brought so much love, and left our lives so empty upon leaving?

A-12. The daughter in the Palestine experience, who suffered martyrdom there.

2358-1   F.38   5/20/30
[Suggestion for physical reading given]
Mr. Cayce: We have the body here, [2358]. There be many conflicting conditions here, and well were there for *this* body and entity an understanding of its relationships to the material world, through its associations in a material life; for [2358] was Peter's mother-in-law. Hence in the physical we find conditions at present. *Not* that the fever during that period, nor the reactions of the body during the present *experience* as related to temperature as has been existent in the body at various times —but these conditions *have* had, *do* have, an *unusual*—not peculiar, but *unusual*—effect upon the physical forces of the body, and this—were medical or the application of purely medical science applied to the physical forces—would be that tendency of which the body is most heir apparent to, or is an heir *to* such conditions. Not that the healing was not wholly, and holy, in the touch of the Master, but that again the force as may make manifest through this entity's application of itself. . .

As for the mental body, *much* might be said. The body *should* associate itself with those attempting to carry out those very same principles as were given by Him who has meant, does mean, *must* mean, so much to the entity; for in the abilities to raise within self those of the vibrations sufficient to heal those that are *unstable* in their mental forces, as related to those conditions where especially combativeness lies between the physical body and the mental body. The body means much to many, and keeping itself in the channel through which the forces of the very Creative Energy itself may operate; even as it did in the physical body so may it do in the present physical experience.

The *life* reading here would be the most interesting to the body. [Life reading was not requested]

3175-1   F.42   8/25/43   Martha
The entity was acquainted with the Master, being a sister of

Peter's wife's mother. Thus the entity was acquainted with the first of the outward miracles of healing in that experience, and has looked for and may find in its own hands the abilities to heal others in His name. Not of self but in His name.

In the experience the entity ever remained through the period one of those of the holy women. The timidity, the backwardness, and yet the exaltation that may be the experience of many by merely being in the presence of the entity, arises from that sojourn.

For, as has been indicated all feel a variation, a difference, by the very presence of the entity in any company. This is not to be used other than as given; kindness, gentleness, patience, persistence and brotherly love. These are the fruits of the spirit. These ye then made manifest. These ye may again make manifest.

There, too, the entity made for much color, and it was this entity that prepared the robe of one piece for the Master.[3]

The name then was Martha.

3175-3   F.43   6/17/44   Martha

Yes, the entity's experience in the earth plane as Martha, the sister of Peter's wife's mother. Yes, we are again given the records here of that entity now known as or called: [3175]. A lovely body!

In giving the experiences of the entity in the earth plane as Martha, the sister of Peter's wife's mother, it would be well that much of the happenings or history of the times be included, that there may be the more perfect understanding of the conditions and as to how and why urges from that experience apply in the experience of the entity in the present.

As is understood by many, there had been long a looking forward to or for the advent of the promised Messiah into the earth and there had been those various groups through one channel or another who had banded together to study the material which was handed down through the varied groups in that day and period.

Here we find there had been, for the mother of Martha, an experience of coming in touch with Judy who had been the first of women appointed as the head of the Essenes group who had the experience of having voices, as well as those which would be called in the present experiences communications with the influences which had been a part of man's experience from the beginning, such that the divine within man heard the experiences of those forces outside of man and communicated in voices, in dreams, in signs and symbols which had become a portion of the experience.

When the children of Martha's mother, Sophia, were in those periods of development these had become a part of what would be called today a play-experience for the entity, Martha.

For Peter's wife's mother was many years the senior of Martha but the coming of John, and the birth of Jesus, the dispensation of Jesus and John in Egypt, all had an impression or imprint upon the mind of the entity Martha, who built in her own mind how the king and how the announcer of the king should be dressed, (as this had been a part of the experiences of the entity in other periods and thus the choice of things in this direction).

Then there came those great changes in the life experience of Martha. For one among those of the rulers of the synagogue sought the entity in marriage and through the individuals who made these arrangements the entity was espoused to Nicodemus [3021]. Through his activities, and personality, Martha learned first of what had happened to the peoples in the homes of John the Baptist and of Mary and Joseph and Jesus.

Thus, when there were later the experiences of those entering into activities, and then when the message was given out that Martha's older sister had been healed from a terrible fever by this man, Jesus, this brought about great changes in Nicodemus and Martha, as they had to do with the temple and the service of the high priest. Martha began the weaving of the robe that became as a part of the equipment the Master had. Thus the robe was made especially for the Master. In color it was not as the robe of the priest, but woven in the one piece with the hole in the top through which the head was to be placed, and then over the body, so that with the cords it was bound about the waist.

This robe Nicodemus presented then to the Master, Jesus,

after the healing of the widow of Nain's son, who was a relative of Nicodemus.[4]

In the activities, then, when Nicodemus went to the Master by night [5] and there became those discussions in the home, for Nicodemus and Martha there began the communion as man and wife rather than man and his chattel or his servant. They were more on a basis of equality, not in the same proportions which were established a bit later by some of the rulers from the Roman land but more in keeping with the happenings which had brought about the activities in the Essenes group.

Though Martha was an Essene, Nicodemus never accepted completely the tenets or the teachings of the Essenes group. These were a part of the principles and applications of Martha. The acquaintanceships, the friendships which were established between Mary, Elizabeth and the other Mary, all were parts of the experience and because of the position of Martha throughout those activities she was considered rather one of the leaders, or one to whom others made appeal to have positions or conditions set in motion so that there was given more concessions to the holy women who followed Jesus from place to place when there were those periods of His Palestine ministry.

The only differences which arose were with Martha and Mary in the household of Lazarus, Martha and Mary.[6] Because of conditions there from which Mary had returned, from the houses which were a portion of her activity in various cities, questions as to morality arose. And yet, after there were the healings, or as it was discovered how she out of whom seven devils were cast became changed,[7] or how there were even changes then and there, we find there was a greater working together with the activities of Mary, Martha, Lazarus and Mary the mother of Jesus, Elijah and many of those others, including John Mark's mother. These were parts of the experience of the entity.

The entity stood, as indicated by the accomplishments of the robe from Nicodemus, as one particularly honored even by the Master.

During the periods of activity, during the missions after the crucifixion and resurrection of the Master, the entity Martha gathered with those in the upper room looking for the promise of the coming of the outpouring of the Holy Spirit. This, too, became a part of the activities.[8]

For the entity later was among those who aided Stephen and Philip, as well as others of the various lands. For it was with these that the entity first became acquainted with Luke and Lucius who later became the heads of various organizations in other portions. These acquaintances were then rather as counsel from those to whom Luke, Lucius, Mark as the younger of the disciples (not apostles, but younger of the disciples), went for counsel.

For the entity was one acquainted with the law, the entity Martha, taught the law to the young ones, the children who sought knowledge.

The entity had its own family, two sons and one daughter. These became ministers in the church in Antioch, aiding the peoples who worked with Barnabas, and it is mentioned that one, Theopolus learned from the entity Sylvanus, and those who labored in the church in Jerusalem with John, James, Peter and the others, as a child. As a child, this one was known as Thaddeus. The daughter was wed to one of the companions of Paul, Silas [707], who was engaged in a portion of the activities with Paul.

As to the activities of the entity, then:

The abilities are indicated in weaving, in color. The color of the robe was pearl-gray, as would be called now, with selvage woven around the neck, as well as that upon the edge, as over the shoulder and to the bottom portion of same; no belts [bells? Ex. 28:34], no pomegranates, but those which are woven in such a manner that into the selvage portion of the bottom was woven the Thummim and Urim. These were as the balance in which judgments were passed by the priest. But these were woven, not placed upon the top of same. Neither were there jewels set in same.[9]

With the persecution the entity withdrew more and more because of its associations with those in authority, but its home became more and more a place of refuge and help for all of the young of the church.

The entity lived to be an elderly person, something like seventy-nine years of age in the experience, and was not among those ever beaten or placed in jail, though persecuted by only the Romans, feared by those of her own peoples . . .

Q-2. *What place did I occupy at the crucifixion?*

A-2. As one of those upon the right hand of Mary, the mother of Jesus, and the other Mary upon the left hand.[10]

Q-3. *In the meeting on the day of Pentecost?*

A-3. Among those who heard all of the various places announce their hearing Peter in their own tongue.[11]

Q-4. *In what way was I acquainted with Lucius?*

A-4. As indicated, as a teacher, as a helper, an advisor, when he was destined by being joined in the church activities in his own home areas. The entity never visited there.

3357-1   F.50   11/13/43   Salamar

. . . the entity was among the sisters of Peter's wife, yea, one who received from the Master the care of her sister when Peter's wife's mother was healed.

The entity gained that ability, which is exhibited in the present, of minding not high things but condescending to things of low estate, knowing that such may also find glory in praise of the divine within . . .

. . . All types and characters may the entity aid, as through those days when it ministered not only to the weaknesses, but to the strengths even of those that one day gathered at the feet of the Master.

And in the early periods when there were those activities in Capernaum as well as in Bethsaida, the entity—as Salamar—made the greater contribution to the helpfulness of those organized groups through that period.

910-4   F.37   9/19/40   Ruth

. . . the entity was in the land when the Master walked in the earth; when there were those activities about Galilee; and when there was the entering in and the calling of the disciples about Peter's home.

The entity was among those who were present and saw Peter's mother-in-law healed. This to the entity, then, has never been as a mystery—instantaneous healing. While never fully understood, there is the belief and the willingness to act in that direction without questioning; which is latent and manifested as a part of the entity — to be sincere, to be in the house of faith.

In the experience the entity knew many material hardships, and many of those activities to which those of the faith were called through persecution by those in the political as well as social activities . . .

The name then was Ruth; and *well* is the name for the entity in the present. The entity was a niece then of Peter, but *not* Andrew's daughter — rather the daughter of Barjon.

2448-2   F.25   5/31/41   Josie

The entity was among those of Peter's household, and one that was called when Peter's mother-in-law was healed.

In the experience the entity suffered physically, yet in its inner self there were the desires for might and power and physical ability to meet emergencies. There was that determination (though delicate in body as in the present) which brought the experience of the stalwart Bruce; who found that "it is not by might nor by power, but by my spirit, saith the Lord of hosts."

The entity had acquaintanceships with all of those who led in the many ways of activity, both pro and con in the experience. For, the entity saw much, hoped for much, and yet felt in self that it was accomplishing so little. It prayed oft for a physical body to meet physical conditions.

The name then was Josie; and of those who saw not only the beginning of the miracles but the mightiest one of all — the cross, the tomb and the resurrection; which once gathered in and becoming a part of the soul may never be lost.

A Leper Is Healed

2482-1   M.45   3/3/26   Mahaieol

. . . in those days when the Master walked in Galilee. The entity then among those healed, in that of the leper at the gate. Then in the name of Mahaieol, and the entity gained much in that period, for with the cleansing there came the desire to manifest that as was found in that period [1]. . .

Through the study of those forces in which the entity was *healed* (physical), made clean (moral) . . . the entity would gain the better understanding of self, through those lessons taught by that Teacher . . .

5749-16   9/10/41
Respecting the miracles of healing, there were many instances where individual healings were of the nature as to be instantaneous—as that when He said to him sick of the palsy, "Son, thy sins be forgiven thee." When the questionings came (as He knew they would), He answered "Which is it easier to say, 'Thy sins be forgiven thee,' or 'Arise, take up thy bed and go unto thine house'?" *Immediately* the man arose, took up his bed and *went* unto his house! Here we find that it was not by the command, but by His own personage. For, the question was not as to whether He healed but as to whether He had the power to forgive sin! The recognition was that sin had caused the physical disturbance.[2]

Then, these are part of the experiences of each and every soul in their search for, in their relationships with their fellow man.

Ye may ask, does this apply in the present? "In Him ye live, ye move, ye have thy being—If ye love me, saith the Master, ye will keep my commandments. My commandments are not grievous; my commandment is that ye love one another, even as I have loved you. If ye love me, I—and the Father—will come and *abide* with thee."

Believe ye His words?

A Widow's Son at Nain Is Healed

601-2   F.48   8/1/34   Deul
. . . during those periods when the Christ—or Jesus—walked in the earth.

The entity then was among those peoples that were aided by the ministry of this teacher, this master, during that sojourn; of those peoples to whom the entity received back alive the son—as they walked from Nain at those periods of His ministry there.[1]

Then in the name Deul, much of turmoil and strife came into the entity's experience; yet in the soul and mental forces of the entity much was gained during that sojourn. There was the embracing of those activities, yet following very closely in what—in its own activities—may be called the very orthodox in the presenting of self to the peoples for the service during that activity; yet being enjoined to those that were of a different faith brought much of turmoil in the mental and in the soul forces, though developments were gained by the entity in and during that sojourn in that land. For much of peoples' minds, much of peoples' activities, came under the vision and the experience of the entity during that particular sojourn; making for an experience wherein there has been oft in the experience of the entity—even during the present—those things pertaining to the activities seen and viewed by the entity during that period, that have brought into the experience much that has been the *saving* influence—it may be said—as to its *belief,* as to its activity in relationship to those things pertaining to what is termed religious thought. Not, then, as an orthodox individual nor a fundamentalist, but rather as one that has seen a vision, an experience, and has *not* let it pass without those things that have added to the greatness of the abilities to which the entity may give itself to others during this sojourn.

5248-1   F.36   6/16/44

. . . the entity was in what is now known as the Holy Land and among those who were the courtiers when the widow of Nain was stopped by the Master, among the holy women who were mourners for this particular occasion was the activity of the entity in that particular period, but the application of many of those things which were heard and applied was and is part of the consciousness of the entity, and in these directions only need the application of self to become that which would be a helpful experience for many.

2454-3   F.43   7/15/42   Pegler

. . . the entity was among those who came under the direction of the teachings not only of the Master Himself, but of the apostles; having that deep sympathy with—and in association with—the disciples, the apostles, and the gatherings with those activities during the experience.

Coming into the experience as a professional mourner, the entity came in contact with the teachings first through an association with the widow of Nain, when the son was delivered again to the mother.

In the name then Pegler, there came the greater development; yet turmoils were brought following the persecutions, and the entity following those into the Persian land.

The Parable of the Tares

3308-1   M.63   10/22/43   Petros

. . . the entity was in the land during those days when the Master walked in the earth, when there were the ministerings to the multitudes.

The entity was among those spoken of, that the seed fell among the tares and it sprang up, yea, though with persecution, hardships for the material things, the ideals and purposes were choked out.[1]

Thus the greater admonition that may be given to the entity —less and less of self, and more and more of the spirit of truth should be in thy ministering, in thy attempting to direct others.

The entity gained, the entity lost in letting self be persuaded that to know and keep the truth is better than protecting the physical body from suffering. For, oft men forget, "Though He were the Son, yet learned He obedience through the things which He suffered."[2] Count thyself then rather as being remembered, when ye suffer for His sake.

The name then was Petros.

The Tempest Is Stilled

5276-1   F.56   6/17/44   Mathias

. . . the entity was in the activities, in the experiences, when there were those administrations indicated in the Holy Land, when the Master walked in the earth.

And the entity was among those groups chosen as companions upon many of the missions which the Master took.

The entity was then in the name of Mathias, not Matthew, but Mathias. The entity saw that experience of the wind, of the storm, the elements, the thunder, the lightning obey the voice of the Master; and thus may the entity find an attunement in same in the present.[1] The entity was a man, or of the opposite sex, in that experience, and this causes much of the distress, as well as the ability to become most of the man in its thoughts and in its expression with others . . .

[This] one outstanding experience, if it would be undertaken by the entity, may bring that which has been longed for by the entity, of an outward expression or material manifestation of divinity manifested in activities of the entity. The why of this may be indicated in the pattern, as to why such an experience would attune the entity in body, mind and soul to the infinite. That to be used in a storm over the moor, or over a rugged mountainside, wind and rain, thunder and lightning. Be out in same. These are the elements which were under the influence of those closest to Him, who is the God of the storm, God of peace, God of the wind, God of the rain, yea the Lord of the earth of whom the disciples said, "What manner of man is this, that even the wind and the rain, the sea and the elements obey His voice?"

Ye followed, ye experienced with Him those facts, those activities, and to be in same again would awaken the closer coordination between body, mind and soul. For as the entity finds, as it analyzes itself, it is in a three-dimensional consciousness in the earth. Hence in self it finds body, mind and soul in the material or the earthly experience, or in the expression of the Godhead, it is Father, Son, Holy Ghost or Holy Spirit. This, then, is the counterpart or the shadow of that which is expressed or manifested in self. Yet in self it is one, and yet there have been and are periods when confusions arise and when some individual expression has drawn off the entity to seek its activity, even as Moses turned aside to see the bush on fire and yet not consumed.

Gadarene Demoniac Is Cast Out

1934-1   F.32   6/21/39   Mayrah

. . . the entity was among those who were of the land of the

Master's nativity in that experience, but rather of those to whom the Master came in the outer coasts of the land.

And the entity was in the land of the Gadarenes when there were the experiences with those who came from the tombs, as well as those experiences recorded as that the spirit of those— or of that one possessed—entered the swine.[1]

The entity then was of the household of the *owner* (not the keeper) of those swine.

Hence through that experience the entity came directly under the touch and acquaintance of Jesus of Nazareth. For, as was a part of the experiences of the peoples of that day or period, the entity was among those who at times looked after such of their household effects.

In the experience and under those activities the entity learned gentleness, kindness, patience—as was shown in the gentle manner in which *all* were answered who raised their voice in criticism of the activities of that particular experience.

Hence we find in the present a longing for the unusual—the experience of being aroused deep within by things that happen from the unseen sources; yet the entity attempts—even though the Uranian influence makes for the interest within self in the occult forces—to keep itself away from phenomena of a questionable nature to the mental self—and yet a longing deep within to know if there is not some touch, some attunement with a something that answers from within self—*from* that experience on that morn when the master called Mayrah.

1616-1   F.44   6/14/38   Sarai

. . . the entity was in the earth during the days when the Master walked in the earth, and in and about those portions where there were the journeyings of the Master into strange lands—or out of the Palestine or Galilean land.

The entity was among those who heard, yea that saw the activities when the influences were driven from the man in the Gadarene land.

There the entity caught hold upon the very foundations of that as He gave, "Father, God!" Those were new experiences to the entity, yea to those influences during that experience. For hate and recompense, and sacrifice to satisfy the appetites, had been the tenets of the entity.

Yet as Sarai, in the experience the entity set about the teachings and gatherings of the young as well as the stranger, to give those tenets and lessons that were gathered here and there by that visit into that land.

Jairus' Daughter Is Healed

1968-1 F.28 7/27/39 Maipah

... entity was in the Palestine land, during those periods when the Master walked in the earth; and the entity was aware of those influences of His life in that experience.

For was not the entity then the mother of Jairus' daughter [559?] who became aware of His presence to heal body, mind and soul? [1] ...

How much more, then, may thy body in the present find in thy arms that which may indeed be the channel to tell the story of His love for man, of His filling the whole life purpose of man! How well does such fit the entity to tell to those who are young and old, the stories of the patience of the man of Galilee—yea, of how stern He might be when He put the entity out of the room, as well as those of the household, because of doubt—and then there are those lessons we will gain from the experience, as to putting the whole trust in the faith of Him that *is* the way and light and truth and understanding!

The entity was a joy to many throughout that experience; suffering oft in disputations—being disturbed oft by the other individuals who caused the disturbance—and yet the entity in heart and mind was at peace because of His blessings to thee!

Hold fast to that as ye gained in seeing in body the love in the flesh presented to thy arms, by the love of the Son of the Father, God!

1968-4 F.29 9/18/40 Maipah

The indications here are rather unusual (in comparison); an experience of an entity entering the earth's plane, filling those purposes or opportunities as gained from other sojourns.

The entity was among the daughters of the children of Ishmael. And the associations, the wedding with Jairus in the early portion of the entity's experience in the earth plane, came through the journeying of Jairus with those influences established in the western portion of the country now known as Turkey; and the activities of the entity through those experiences were of a social as well as political nature.

There was quite a variation as to the position of women in a household as was the entity, Maipah, and those in a household of those in authority—as was Jairus, because of his position politically. He was not merely the captain of a guard, or of a garrison, but as one who was in authority pertaining to the supplying of the commercial, the social and the political relationships of the land; when the entity joined in the activities, in portions of that now known as the Galilean land.

The entity was some twenty years of age when the first child was born; then the second and third—and the third child was the daughter, Touhpar by name.

When the companion or husband, Jairus, became aware of the teachings and tenets of the Master, Jesus of Nazareth, and knowing the conditions surrounding the companion and the "delicate" condition (as would be called), for there was the expectancy of the fourth child to be born—the anxiety as manifested brought the commendation from the Master, as well as wonderment from his associates or companions in his office. This showed rather the unusual interest of man for his mate, and for the offspring, for the period or time. But Jairus had been influenced by those tenets which he had heard expressed, not only by John but by the followers of—and the Master Himself.

This brought into the experience of the entity, Maipah, that of humbleness, patience, desire for expression in some manner. Yet, because of the early teaching, the early training, wonderment and fear and doubt were also a part of the consciousness through that particular period.

And it was that period, and that following—as to what the entity did about it—which brings the urges within the manifested activities of the entity in the present.

For, with the coming of the Master to the home, and with the conditions and environs of self as well as the counsel or advice of others, there came doubt and fear. Yet with the command that those who would hinder by their adverse thought or expressions be put away, the entity and companion had their loved one given again to them as a *living* example of His indeed being the resurrection.

Thus the entity sought to know and aid those who were the leaders or teachers—of course, the holy women, the prophetesses, and those who had been instrumental in every form or manner in keeping the tenets alive in the experience of others.

Throughout the rest of its sojourn, then, the entity lent self in aid of every manner; in the social manner as well as in the *practical* helpfulness to all who sought to keep the faith.

The entity lived to a ripe age for those periods, and the persecutions. But being of those in authority the entity was protected or shielded in some ways; for, with others that came to know more of the blessings to be had materially and mentally from the embracing of those principles and tenets of the teacher, greater opportunities came for the entity throughout its sojourn . . .

Q-1. What were some of the tenets which were used by the entity and [264] in our Palestine experience, and how can we use them in the present in order to bring about the better associations and activities to each and with others?

A-1. The practical application of those things, ideas, ideals that are justly called the seed of the spirit; gentleness, kindness, long-suffering, patience, brotherly love, temperance in all things. These were rather unusual in that experience or period, for those of the sex—or the women—to make practical application of; yet the freedom given to the companions of those in authority (politically and socially) aided them in making such applicable.

For, who sought physical associations with those who were of the low caste, or low estate, save as applied to the mothers of faith, those of the holy women, through that experience, of which the entity was one!

559-7   F.6   5/25/34   Jairus' daughter

The entity then was that one whom the Master called again from the deep sleep—Jairus' daughter. Before and after that happening, we find that the entity was one in the experience who gave much of self to make for the closer association and relation with the mental attributes of the spirit as related to the material things, rather than to the thoughts of material things themselves.

2485-1   F.44   10/4/29

The entity then in that period when the Master passed through the land, and the entity [was of] the one[s] to whom the Master spoke and said, "Arise, maiden," [to] then the daughter of Jairus. In *this* experience the entity gained, and in the present ever the desire to know more of that love, that force, as emanated through that experience, has the entity sought much—and those influences as have to do with powers of the innate influence does the entity seek, yet fears from within. Here would the entity dwell long upon that experience, could the entity draw much from *that* experience, and ever does there appear to the entity a peculiar sensation when that is read.

1968-8   F.31   7/31/42   Maipah

Q-10. Please clarify information in my life reading regarding the experience as wife of Jairus. Was I the mother of the entity now known as [421], or the entity now known as [2485]?

A-10. The entity was one of the wives of Jairus, see, and the mother of that entity now called [421]. The entity [2485] was then also a wife of Jairus, but not the mother of the daughter that was healed; rather being desirous that *her* daughter receive a blessing; and because of seeming indifference or change, brought disturbance to *both* entities for a period.

1246-2   F.52   8/9/36   Fillipe

. . . the entity was in that land now known as the Promised Land, during those periods when the Master walked in the earth; when the entity then distressed—as the wife of Jairus, as the mother of Jairus' daughter—had that awakening within of the powers that may bring life again to that which has fallen away. And *there* was established the seal, the bridge of the cross that led from sorrow to gladness, that led not only in the material experiences but in that quickening that came with the presence of life within the presence of the entity.

And how oft has the entity in the present experienced upon

the meditations not the experiences and activities of the man called a lowly one but rather the man of might and power through Galilee. And these experiences have brought to the entity, as then—in the name Fillipe [?]—the feelings of the raising of self from within to the realms of that "Awake, my daughter, to the abilities of thyself through the might of the God-force within thee," or "Arise, and minister."

421-5   F.21   10/20/31   Jairus' daughter

... during that period when the Master walked in the land. The entity then of the household of the ruler to *whom* the entity [the Master] came, and the entity heard that Voice that *called* the entity [559] back to service in that experience, "Talitha, Talitha, Arise!" the daughter of Jairus in that experience. *Gaining* throughout, for the service as rendered to others through that life, that hope, that understanding, given by that touch ...

5347-2   M.35   7/14/44   Julius

... the entity was in the Roman land when there were those activities in which many individuals were required to look after the protectorates in various portions of the empire.

The entity was set among those who were in portions of Palestine, following the period when the Master walked in the earth.

The entity became acquainted with, heard of, understood much of that which had happened. For, in the entity's own household the Master had come—before the entity was born, though. For the entity, as Julius, was a son of Jairus, whose daughter was healed.

3307-1   F.50   10/19/43   Elada

... the entity was in the Holy Land among those people when there was the calling of Jairus' daughter.

The entity was among those that were the hired or paid mourners of that day ...

The name then was Elada. The entity was a changed person in those days because of the happenings there, and was among those active in the early church as helpful groups for training the young.

The Woman Who Touched His Garment

1353-1   F.Adult   3/26/37   Eloise (or Lois)

. . . the entity was in the land now known as the Promised Land, during those periods when the Master walked in the earth.

There the entity found and had that which made for the greater activity, in the innate forces as well as in the urges from the emotions of the entity.

For the entity then was not only healed by the Master but made for those activities that brought the greater understandings in those of the entity's particular circle of associations with those of other lands.

For the entity while in the experience was sojourning in the land, it was not of the Jewish peoples but rather of the Roman —or the combination of the Roman and the Grecian.

Hence when there is indicated that in certain periods there was the gathering of the peoples from every land, the entity was not only the interpreter but one that aided much in bringing about the better relationships between the varied activities of the apostles—as called, or those following soon after the periods when the organization became what is termed the Church.

For the entity was the one who pressed in the crowd and said, "Can I but touch the hem of His garment I *will* be healed." [1]

In the name then Eloise (or Lois), the entity was of the Grecian and Roman land, and among those who were with the mother at the Tomb, among those who were the closer to those of the own household of Joseph and Mary.

Much might be given of the entity's activities, for they then extended far and wide—as indicated by the associations of the entity with those peoples in the lands that politically ruled that portion of the world.

585-10   F.46   6/18/42

[Description of aura chart for 585]

. . . put the Master with the gray robe, the beard scant, the hair—not red nor yet golden, but as of reddish golden—blessing or healing the woman with the issue. This figure, of course, would be much more mature than the one indicated in the scenes below, but would be depicted as a very thin or pale individual, with very dark eyes and hair—and a robe of gray and purple, or the bands about same purple while the robe would be in the lighter gray. This would indicate the period, or the healing of the Master of the woman in the throng who touched the hem of the garment. Hence the figure should be kneeling upon one knee and reaching for the hem of the Master's robes—and He turned as to the left to encounter the figure kneeling, see? Other figures should be in the background, but this should be the main, central figure.

The Feeding of the Multitudes

1743-1   M.28   11/11/38

... the entity was in the land when the Master walked in the earth.

There we find, during the experience the entity was rather the child—and among those peoples or children present during the feeding of the five thousand [1]. ...

There we find the entity growing up under an environ in which there were many disputations, owing to the persecutions that arose in the experiences of the entity's surroundings, in the early portion of its life in that sojourn.

Hence we find a diffusion of ideas in relationships to spiritual teachings, or those that are of ethical activities in the various characters of treatments or applications for either physical or spiritual helpful forces in the lives of its associates, its environs, or the peoples at the present time.

But know, that which is material must have first had its inception in the spiritual—and has grown according to *mental* application respecting same to constructive forces in the lives of individuals, things, conditions, or from whatever phase it may be judged.

Hence in the application of self, forget not the *sources* of *all* power as may be manifested in the earth.

And as the purpose of each soul is to be a channel through which that as held as its ideal is to be made manifest, and that the glory of God be kept first and foremost—then so live, so act as to be consistent in thy thoughts, thy acts, thy expressions.

Not only in word but in deed. For being true to self will not make thee false to any . . .

Q-8. [*What was my association in other sojourns*] *with* [*1472*]?

A-8. This was an experience in which the entity looked toward that entity, Judy, as a teacher, a helper, an aid to the many—as a worshipfulness or worshipful experience in the Palestine sojourn . . .

1770-2   F.49   12/29/38

The entity was among those peoples in that Galilean land . . . and among those who were blessed by Him when feeding the five thousand upon the mountain and by the lake.

When there is then found within self that feeling of the supply, that feeling of the abilities through the application of self to meet whatever may be the needs, let this grow within thine inner being. For know, as ye live and move and have thy being in Him, so He is the supply—whether it be material, the mental, the spiritual.

For these are the representation within the awareness or consciousness of the individual of the Godhead—the Body, the Father; the Mind, the Christ, the Son; the Soul, the Holy Spirit through which all approach is made.

For even as the spirit moved, matter came into being. So as the Mind became the way, the truth, the light in materiality—as ye apply same in thy experiences day by day ye become aware.

Then as He hath given, and as ye heard so oft, "The kingdom is within." Turn ye within, for there in the temple of thine own body is the temple of the living God, where He hath promised to meet thee, to commune with thee, and to give thee the supply of *all* that may be needed within thine experience!

For as indeed He manifested, truth needs not justification but the glorification in the manner in which the love is dealt to thy fellow man.

As indeed ye heard as a child, indeed as ye heard as ye grew into active service through the experiences with many of those of the period, there *is* the way that may seem right to a man, but the end thereof may be death.

But if the heart is open, He will come and abide with thee.

And He in thee, as He in the Father, may know the truth that will make thee free indeed.

Throughout the activities in that experience the entity remained as one among those who grew into active service with the disciples and apostles, and the women of renown; the acquaintanceship with the holy family, the leaders. These then are not a mystery to the entity, yet as a thing a bit afar; yet may be made a material experience.

Look then again upon the light that shines within thine own heart, as ye read of how He called the lad. For the lad was thy brother—and thy associate that is close to thee through thy experiences in the present . . .

If ye would have friends, show thyself lovely. For the love He expressed in blessing and bringing abundance to others through thy own preparation in the hands of thy brother may bring again that to the thousands, as then—the awareness of the light of the life of the Christ.

1821-1   M.54   2/14/39

. . . the entity was in the Promised Land, and especially in that portion about the sea where the Master loved so well to be.

The entity was young in years, yet one of those—as the entity is in the present—ofttimes too careful as to preparations; yet this became in that particular experience that from which the entity never got away during that sojourn.

For the entity was the lad *from* whom Andrew obtained the loaves and fishes to feed the five thousand.

Hence the entity is under that influence of increase, yet *not* too great a gainer in the experience from the lesson there. Easy come, easy go became too great an influence in that particular sojourn.

Yet if there is the turning to that surety as was proclaimed that day to the many, as was experienced by all the hearers that day, the entity will realize that there are the needs each day for each soul to choose aright; that there is today, as every day, set before thee good and evil, life and death—choose thou!

Not in the choice of that which is so temporal as to blind self to the mental and spiritual needs. For unless the purpose, the ideal is founded in the spirituality, the increase and the growth — as ye experienced in seeing manifested to feed the *hordes* that day — *cannot,* will not be a part of the experience!

Yet ye may vision how that the words, yea the very feelings that ye may express may become as the loaves, fishes — yea, even as the manna in the wilderness that may sustain the physical, the mental and spiritual bodies of all.

For it, that purpose, is given power from on high.

2549-1   M.20   8/2/41   Ardoen

The appearance that may be given, then, was in the days when the Master walked in the earth; when there were those gatherings about the mount in the wilderness, and the call of the five thousand that they be sent not away in their weakness but the supplying of physical needs to the material man.

The entity then was the companion with that lad, whom *this* entity — as the son of Andrew — brought to his father that there might be supplied from that in hand sufficient of the material needs to feed that multitude, with the loaves and the few fishes.

That experience is the impelling influence for the entity in the present; so that in a social service should be those fields of activity in which the entity should apply self.

For, as ye then pointed the way through which material as well as the spiritual blessings came to many, so in the order of the day — when there is so much of doubt and fear, so much loss of that security — the entity may through such an activity aid the many to find their closer relationships to the Father-God — *through* the blessings of Him who gave, "Keep my commandments. Love one another."

The name then was Ardoen.

5346-1   M.53   7/15/44   Gardan

. . . the entity was in the Holy Land and among those of those periods when there was the preparation of a lunch for the entity's son, who sought to be among those seeking counsel from the Master. The entity prepared the loaves and fishes which fed the thousands, and as the entity gained from the message the son brought to the parent in that day, so may it gain in the material, in the mental, yea in the spiritual, to listen to the companion—who was the son in that particular sojourn . . .

The name then was Gardan.

3183-1   M.12   8/27/43   Thaddeus

. . . the entity was in the land when the Master walked in the earth during those periods when great throngs went to hear His teachings by the mountainside.

When there was the feeding of the four thousand, the entity supplied that from which the Master increased sufficient to feed the multitude.[2]

This then materially brought vast visions to the entity. Through the experiences these were used well for a while, and then its over-zealousness brought sudden cutting away, following those experiences when James was beheaded.[3] For these were friends of the entity through those experiences.

In the present walk ever closer with the Master. Let oft the deeds of thy hands be again multiplied by and through Him, and not of thyself. For, these are the manners in which ye may accomplish the most; letting that power—which ye *saw* so well demonstrated—flow through thee; by faith, yes; by works, yes; by the good will that is a part of thy whole being—but ever the power, the might in Him.

The entity in that experience was a teacher, a writer, for the few years of its sojourn. For, many of the notes that were a part of the entity's experience then, as Thaddeus, were a part of the records of Mark and Matthew; in Luke or John—though John, to be sure, was an acquaintance of the entity . . .

Q-3. Have I been related to any member of my family during a former incarnation?

A-3. . . . close to the mother [2946] in the period of the Master, for then the entity was also son of the present mother.

1532-1   F.18   2/10/38   Mariah

. . . the entity was in that land during the period when the Master walked in the earth; and when there were those gatherings of the many that came to hear the teachings as the Master taught by the sea and in the mountain.

And especially on those occasions when He blessed children, for the entity was among those children blessed by Him—also among those women and children when there was the feeding of the five thousand, also in that period of the feeding of the four thousand.

Hence to see the multiplying of things and experiences in the hand will always be a part of the entity. Hence while the entity is not stingy, it is not too easy either with that which is attained or gained by itself. Its desire to reach its goal, its desire to know and to have, to be, becomes rather the part of the entity.

Do not let these become a selfish thing. Let them be rather as He gave, when He blessed you — "Except ye become as little children, ye shall in no wise enter in"; unless ye are as forgiving, unless ye are as generous, unless ye are as dependent as little children — these become in their deeper sense the meaning, the influence that arises in the experience of the entity.[4]

The name then was Mariah.

In the experience the entity gained throughout; wedded then in early life to one among the followers and those dispersed during the first persecutions of the disciples and the Christians in the Jerusalem environ.

Hence the entity was among those that came in closer contact with the church in Laodicea, for the companion in that experience became what you would call in the present the deacon in the church there.

5002-1   F.24   4/1/44   Esther

... the entity was in the Holy Land when the Master walked in the earth, when the Master blessed the children on that mountainside when the thousands were fed as only the Master might feed, from the few loaves and fishes.

The entity caught something of the plenty, and this has ever been and may ever be manifested for the entity — sufficient unto the day is the good or evil thereof. If thy trust is put in the Lord of Lords, ye may indeed revel in that consciousness that "The Lord will take care of many, as I do His biddings."

The name then was Esther.

5398-1   M.10 wks.   8/24/44   Phailos

... the entity was in that land now known as the Holy Land, during the days when the Master walked in the earth, and during those periods when there was the establishing of churches or groups for the propagation and dissemination of the tenets and truths which were parts of the activity during those periods. The entity, young in years, was among the children in those groups at the feeding of the five thousand. Hence you will always find the entity ready to eat when it is time to eat, and he will expect it to be there, no matter where it comes from! This is innate, for—created from that which was a friend's little lunch for the multitudes—why shouldn't a divine Father supply those worthy, and unworthy as well?

Does mankind consider he is indeed his brother's keeper? This is the manner in which man may answer the question. There will be no want in bread for mankind when mankind eventually realizes he is indeed his brother's keeper. For the earth is the Lord's and the fullness thereof, and the bounty in one land is lent to man to give his brother. Who is his brother? "Our Father" (we say)—then each of every land, of every color, of every creed is brother of those who seek the Father-God. Instill this as you interpret. Be faithful to the trust given you.

The entity in that experience became a singer in the varied churches throughout the land. For the entity journeyed with Luke and Paul, Paul and Silas, Paul and Barnabas, and thus came in contact with those in many portions of the land; as a psalm-singer of real help, then, to all of the churches . . .

The name then was Phailos.

1681-1   M.33   9/7/38   Thurmel

. . . the entity was in the land now known as Palestine, during those periods of the development of the church idea.

The entity was very young during the sojourn of the Master in the earth, and was among the children *present* when there was the feeding of the five thousand in the wilderness.

Hence the dread of certain activities in the wilds; yet again the needs of individual searching in the entity's experience.

And the activities of the entity during that sojourn were as a keeper of an inn, in which there were the activities both of the Roman and the Jewish peoples, as well as the meetings of the various groups. All of such were active in the experience of the entity . . .

The name then was Thurmel, and of the Galilean land.

1614-2   F.41   12/18/40   Jaelorn

The entity was among the young, or children, blessed by the Master in those days, or that period, or that day when the five thousand were fed.

As we find, the entity's growth, development, mentally and materially through that experience, were oft determined by *material* circumstance. Yet there were those periods when the whole reliance upon the faith in those promises made manifest in Him held the entity to an experience of helpfulness to others.

The entity's acquaintance and association with many of the close followers of the Master brought periods of turmoil and persecutions from others; and these are the experiences in the present which at times bring the feeling of resentment towards others that were prompted to bring the turmoils physically by the activities in and through that sojourn . . .

The name then was Jaelorn . . .

He blessed thee in the flesh. He will bless thee again, if thou holdest to that purpose; putting away strife, jealousy, malice, condemnation. Condemn not, if ye would not be condemned.

2829-1   F.20   10/19/42   Cleo or Cleopas

. . . the entity was among those children blessed by the Master, especially upon that period when He fed the five thousand.

The stories, or the experiences told regarding the Master and His care for His disciples that the entity loved the most, and that have had the especial appeal in the present, are those of His walking on water, and of His bidding Peter to come to Him.[5]

While there were hardships physically in those experiences, the entity in the latter portion of its sojourn was an instructor to those in some of the churches—when the believers were scattered because of the persecutions in the Jerusalem church.

There the entity was in the name Cleo, or Cleopas; as an aid in establishing of homes, and in the care of the young throughout those experiences. Yes, a home of its own, though often under question because of its anxiety and activity.

5227-1   M.10   4/20/44   Jason

. . . entity was in the period when the Master was in the earth, being among the children who were with the crowds at the feeding of the five thousand. The entity was among those who witnessed those happenings. Thus there is seen the ability for the entity to easily pray, to see, to feel, to experience the presence of duty, of patience; those virtues which most every individual needs to be thoroughly acquainted with and able to apply in the experience of self.

There we find the entity was among those who were teachers and ministers when there was the spreading of the gospel following the activities on the day of Pentecost, though the entity was of those groups who came from both the teachings of the Samaritan as well as the orthodox Jewish relations.

The entity gained, in the name Jason; and it was in Jason's house that some of the activities took place which brought about questions; yet the abilities of the entity in its speaking, in its acting, brought great strength to others. And it may in this experience bring those understandings which will draw peoples to the knowledge of the relationships of man to the Creative Forces, or God.

2845-2   F.41   2/28/43   Matildah

. . . among those groups about Bethsaida where the Master oft dwelt and taught.

The entity was among those who saw many of the experiences that brought the awareness of the unusualness and the divinity of the Master; being present at the feeding of the five thousand, also when there were those wonderments at His joining His disciples without means of transportation in the ship; also present when there were the relatings of the happenings to the men when the evil forces were driven from same—and the destruction of the hogs.[6]

These made, then, those activities in which the entity gained. For, the entity was among those who might truly be called the holy women, yet not among those in the disturbance in Jerusalem—but was there on the day of Pentecost.

Those experiences make the life of the Master, His teachings, very real to the entity. And at times the entity is incapable of giving full expression as to what each of these happenings means.

The name then was Matildah . . .

2468-1   F.22   3/20/41   Durey

The entity knew of and knew the acquaintances of the Master, though very young in years. For the entity was among those blessed by the Master at that period of the feeding of the five thousand in the mount. But the entity followed oft rather those urges for the activities that were questioned by many of those of that period. Yet with the persecutions as arose, the entity rather made the greater contribution in aiding those who were of the faith to keep those periods that brought the helpful and hopeful influences into the experience of the individuals who were weak at times through that period of persecution.

Throughout that period, then, the entity gained; save during the periods of questionings. Yet we see latent urges from the Uranian sojourn, as well as Saturn, in its companionships, its relationships, its activities, its hopes, its desires, its purposes from the mental and material angles.

The name then was Durey.

2760-1   F.9   6/4/42   Marcella

The entity was among the children of that period of activities, coming in contact with same through associations with those closely associated in the Master's ministry. The entity was present during the period of the feeding of the five thousand; and in its teens—and through its life—the entity was a consistent (and this means much) follower in the teachings and the ways through that experience.

While among those peoples of the hill country, among those peoples where there were a great many questions as to the variation in the orthodox peoples of that day and the teachings as interpreted by those who followed in the footsteps of the Master, the entity was ever a student and a teacher—in its home and its surroundings—of those tenets and those truths . . .

The name then was Marcella. In the experience the entity gained throughout, though those activities were confined more to the home and to those of its own household; for the entity was able to live and to consistently manifest those principles and tenets that were as a light to many.

5089-2   F.50   5/15/44   Lydia

... the entity was in the Holy Land and among those who were present who had come with the groups of hundreds, yea when the five thousand were fed by the Master. This experience brought for the entity those activities which in the present make the entity as a teacher, as a healer, for the entity may, from those very activities as given, find that with the kind word, the patient word, the pressing of the hand upon the brow of those who are with fever, yea those who are troubled in heart there may be brought comfort by the words even as the entity heard through that period as it witnessed the great throng, not only being thrilled by the presence but by the words of the Master as He gave what ye call the Beatitudes.[7]

In the experience the entity learned patience. That keep. Don't lose patience with thy children, thy friends who become impatient. For He did not lose patience with His disciples when they said, "Should we go away to buy bread to feed this mob?" "What have we here?" "What have you here?" Did you ever hear this used to individuals? Try it! It is one of the most disturbing, yet one of the most quieting words which may be used, even to a mob. "What have we here?" And only a few loaves, a few fishes, yet in the hands of those who could realize as ye may, "Of myself, I can do nothing, but through His power," it may be multiplied into blessings. And remember, it can be multiplied in curses also, if ye use not thy abilities aright. In the name then Lydia.

The Teachings at Bethsaida

1877-1   F.44   5/9/39   Elcor

The entity was of the Galilean land, and closely associated with the activities about the sea.

Hence, as ye have experienced in thy listening—listening, and through the light, ye have heard the *meaning* of the word Galilee! as it rings in thy experience from thy sojourn there, when ye were blessed by Him—among the children that gathered about Him, as He entered into the teachings to His disciples as well as those gathered about![1]

As He gathered thee into His arms, materially, so is there—as ye abide in the presence of IIis love—that as may bring the security. For as goodness, as love lives on, so may thy body-soul realize that presence again, that blessing as ye magnify—in thy dealings with thy fellow men, "Inasmuch as ye do it unto the least of these, my little ones, ye do it unto me." [2]

Let that not *sink* into thy mind, but let it be ever as a *living* thing upon thy countenance with thy fellow man.

Ye gained throughout those experiences—in the name then Elcor.

1877-2   F.45   4/18/40   Elcor

During the experience the entity was among those peoples in that land because of the positions of those close to the entity as a helpful influence for the people of the land, as well as for the influences, forces or powers of other lands.

Hence it was a land of adoption for the entity, rather than merely by the birth there.

Thus we find that the developing of the mental, social and spiritual influences was twofold, through the experience of the entity.

When there was the voicing of groups and individuals as to that fact taking place in the land—of a new teacher, a new rabbi—at first this was considered by the entity merely as something of the same thing which had been as a report of those peoples for many, many years.

Yet, with the contact in a social manner, and in the manners in which needs were supplied in healings, and in the variations that were being considered among the Romans, the Grecians, the Parthians and the Jews of the experience, the entity began to consider those teachings and influences from a different angle, or from a different manner of thought.

Because of the character or manner of livelihood of many of those who were proclaimed as disciples or adherents to those teachings, the entity attempted to dismiss them.

However, again and again the entity was presented with those influences proclaimed by groups, as to the experience and life of the individual, and as to the followers being in that position of fulfilling the prophecies which had been a part of not only the teachings of those peculiar peoples, but also of the verse and the songs of many.³

Though many of those groups were oft questionable to the entity, these had again an altering influence in the entity's experience; sometimes doubting, sometimes fearing, sometimes dismissing. . .

As to the parentage, and the houshold environment—these had little to do with the things which made for the activities, owing to the associations, the social life, the variations in those groups and sects among the Jewish population, and the effect upon such population by the Romans who were in partial political power, and refrained from an active influence in the religious—or certain portions of the social life of individuals through the period. . .

Hence we find—as conditions developed in that experience, and as activities were brought about in the life of the man Jesus—there were periods of expectancy, periods of fear that there might be an uprising—as to undermine the very foundations of that upon which the entity and its associates, and its household, depended; not merely for the position, the political forces that brought the activities, but for the very *thoughts* of relationships with the material, mental and spiritual life, and the physical outlook upon same!

Then—during those periods when there were the activities which brought the relationships more with those in the religious authority, and as the death was brought about—again great changes came into the experience of the entity, as well as into the experience of groups—and those who had been in authority in high places of political influence, and those who were in authority among the various groups of the Jewish leaders.

Hence, with the questioning which arose as to the real divinity of Jesus—through and by the experience of those who saw and talked with those who knew the facts concerning what had taken place—the realization and the wonderment of it all dawned upon the entity; so that there was then the humbleness in the entity's activities for the time.

Then when there were the persecutions, and those being questioned as to their *intentions* in their dealings with their government, in their dealings with their beliefs in the *law* as had been a part of the experiences of so many—the entity again faltered in its willingness to stand without questioning; fearing what others might say.

Hence the entity heard again and again the consequences of self's own conscience, and these eventually became a physical experience of the entity.

Often in that sojourn, by the very nature of the entity's associations with those in political power and authority, there were changes to other lands.

Consequently, there was a knowledge of what took place in other lands—as in Alexandria, Cyrene, Silicia, Antioch, and even in Rome as the activities progressed.

Then eventually, in the latter portion of the sojourn, the entity determined to stand fast; when there were the activities and ministry of the leaders of the church—even Paul and Silas and their work; for the knowledge of their ministry brought the determining factors into the experience of the entity . . .

Hence we find that the entity throughout that sojourn was as one who would fear (to put in common parlance of the day), yet one who could not turn loose; one who denied, and yet conscientiously embraced; one who *feared,* yet who *gladly* aided others who showed the lack of fear—though they were of various castes, though they were of groups and peoples not the entity's equal in social, mental, or in any manners . . .

Q-1. *Of what race or nationality was the entity at that time?*
A-1. Of the peoples of the Palestine land that were not Jews, but were *among* the Jews; and the entity was wed to one of the Romans in authority but of the Grecian descent.

Q-2. *What contact did the entity have with Jesus during that period?*
A-2. *Oft* the entity was in the presence of the Master, and *especially* upon those occasions when He spoke in places where those in authority entertained.

When in the house of the "ruler" He was in the entity's own home; and when the woman of the street was questioned by one of the companions there, it brought confusion and yet determinations in the experience of the entity.

Also the entity was present when there were about five thousand who saw and heard the words of the Master after the resurrection; and as the entity thinks, dreams of or *feels* that experience, the *glory* of it warms the heart in the present.[4]

Q-5. What is the symbolic meaning of the name Elcor?

A-5. As may be found in Scripture itself—one who *joined* doubt with faith!

Q-6. Is there any way in which the entity at this time could serve her Father-God, as she has an intense desire to do so?

A-6. As indicated—it is not by might, nor by some great deed (as the entity saw illustrated in that experience), nor by something that may be spoken of by others, but as He has given so oft, it is here a little, there a little, line upon line, precept upon precept; *sowing* the fruits of the spirit, *leaving* the fruition of same to God!

So oft do individuals stumble over their own abilities, because of not seeing, not experiencing, great revolutions because of their attempts.

Remember, as it was told to those of old, as it was told to *thee* by those who answered when ye beheld Him enter the glory of the clouds, the sky—"Think not He has left thee, for His promise has been, Lo, I am with thee always, even unto the end of the world." [5]

So—all who open their hearts—all who keep their purpose in Him, are as under the protecting wing of that promise.

Faint not—but keep the faith.

2282-1   F.64   6/16/40   Hannah

. . . the entity was in the Promised Land, during that period when there were the establishments of the church in the various portions of the land.

The entity was young in years during the ministry of Jesus in the earth, and was among those who were blessed by His hands.

Thus the entity grew in grace, in knowledge, in understanding, under the tutelage of those of the faithful in that experience. And thus in the various churches in and about Jerusalem the entity found places of helpfulness for those who were doubtful, those who were often fearful . . .

Then in the name of Hannah, the entity was a companion

with Luke and Lucius in the experiences as they journeyed with the teachers of the experience; the entity aiding and helping in the various activities.

3667-2   F.43   2/17/44   Esther

. . . the entity was in the Promised Land, when the Master walked in the earth, then among the children who were blessed by the Master in the second period of the Master's activity in the southern portions of Galilee near unto the activities in the coast of the city itself or where the temples were to be erected.

The entity then was not exactly a soothsayer, yet one given to the study of the mysteries of the East, as well as to the application by the closer followers of the Master through the experience.

In the name then Esther, the entity gained, for it was acquainted with, and walked with many of those who heard of and who were active in those experiences in that land. The entity aided in compiling many of the letters written by the writers of the Gospels in that particular period.

3660-1   F.53   2/15/44   Jeseuel

. . . ye were in the land where the Master walked, when there were those gathered by the seashore who heard Him speak. At Bethsaida ye were among those who had heard, who looked for, who had come to expect that sometime, somewhere, God would hear the cry and answer those who were troubled by ills of body, turmoils of the struggles for life, for the meeting of the passions of the body of men, for the cries of the young for succor, for aid, yea for bread. And He spoke gentle words —the sower went forth to sow. What are ye casting into the soil of life for those ye meet? Upon what character of soil seek ye to prepare, even in thine own life and heart and body?

The name then was Jeseuel. Ye became strong by that simple trust in Jesus and again ye may find thy strength of thy mind and thy body in His purposes alone.

5373-1   F.48   7/22/44

. . . the entity was in the Holy Land and when there were the foregatherings at Bethsaida. Then the entity knew the Master. For it was one of the entity's children who was among those first blessed by the Master, when it became necessary to rebuke the disciples for their attempting to rebuke the peoples. Thus, as is indicated in the symbol, the cross, as well as Holy Writ. For as the Master gave Himself, "Search the scriptures, for in them ye think ye find eternal life and they are they that speak of me." [6]

1223-4   F.34   10/28/40   Morao

. . . the entity was in the Promised Land, during that period when the Master walked in the earth.

The entity was among those families in Bethsaida; in which the entity made the home His resting place. Hence the entity was close to and acquainted with Him; and gave self even in physical activities for the pleasure, the comfort, of a tired man —the Son of God.

We find that the entity became close in its activity with those who were the establishers of the church; among the holy women, and a helper oft. For, the entity was young in years during those periods of contact with Him in the physical manner; yet those periods, those activities, those conscious moments in His presence, with those happenings that to the entity were the loss not only of a friend but of a Savior, brought awe-inspiring experiences in the mental and the spiritual self that are a part of that consciousness experienced by many in the present who come into the very presence of the entity; though the entity is now not so oft conscious of such in the physical consciousness of the entity. But in moments of deep meditation and prayer, there comes oft that vision as of seeing His face—worn at times; at others that smile, that expression that brings the hope so necessary in the heart of the human—that there *is* the better way, there *is* safety in His presence, in the consciousness of the abiding faith in Him.

The name then was Morao. Too much might not be said as to the attainments of the entity through that experience, and as to the activities in a helpful manner that the entity brought into the experiences even of the closer disciples in their periods of disturbance because of physical conditions.

1223-9   F.37   5/22/44   Morao

Bethsaida was among the places often visited by the Master, as it was among the peoples of this place where the Master liked to rest.

The entity, as indicated, was in the teen-age years when first becoming acquainted with the tenets and teachings of the Master. The entity was an acquaintance of Peter, Andrew, James and John. Because of the entity's parent, the father being associated with those in their activities upon the sea in those relationships then, the entity was acquainted with Peter's mother-in-law who was healed in the early ministry of the Master. And during the Master's sojourning in Bethsaida in the periods when He preached by the seashore, as well as when He rested, the entity knew of and was acquainted personally with the Master. Oft the entity sought to make the things, the conditions, more comfortable for the Master; and thus may it be said that the entity became so closely associated with Jesus as to call Him by His name, Jesus, not Master until after His crucifixion.

In the experiences the entity not only then talked with but questioned the Master; and thus those tenets, the teachings that the Master gave as to friendships, associations, forgiveness, the lack of common gossip about others, were those warnings which were a portion of the experience with Jesus of Nazareth by the entity, Morao.

So, when there came about those periods when the disciples were scattered because of the happenings in Jerusalem after the resurrection, the entity was known as one who would aid, did aid in the ministering to the needs of the ministers, preachers or saints, as they are commonly termed, who were the active ones in the Christian ministry after His resurrection. Thus the entity became so imbued with those tenets, those teachings, that little may be said as to how great were the ideals, how great was the love of the entity for those ideals. How great the desire and purpose of the entity in telling the stories of, encouraging others by, those direct experiences the entity had with the Master.

These, then, applied in the present, come to that as has been indicated. If the entity will read or study or analyze how the Master treated children, young people, during His ministry in the earth, it will be seen how oft He used children, the young people, as the hope of the world, as to how unless each individual puts away those selfish desires which arise and becomes as little children, one may never quite understand the simplicity of Christ's faith; Christ-like faith, Christ-like simplicity, Christ-like forgiveness, Christ-like love, Christ-like helpfulness to others. For the entity gained these through those experiences.[7]

In the present, analyze these; and aid in ministering such to the young as a teacher, as an interpreter, as a helper for those of the young who seek to know, to interpret, to apply such in their experience.

Yes, even learn how to interpret to children as to how an individual may pass the collection plate in church on Sunday and swear like a sailor on Monday. Both are of God, one in the right direction, one in the opposite. These ye learned at the Master's feet. Keep that implicit faith which ye had through that experience.

The entity was known among the holy women, even to a great age. Married, yes, during those experiences, to one Turteltus of the Roman peoples.

3089-1   F.1   7/9/43   Dora

. . . the entity was in the Holy Land, during those periods when the Master walked in the earth—and with the activities in Bethsaida.

The entity was among the children of one of the disciples of the Master. The entity was blessed by the Master, being acquainted with many of those activities, and knew of those activities—as a child talking with the Way, the Truth and the Light.

This has brought the veracity of the *light* that may be seen, or even felt, by those that observe the entity when it is at play, or when it thinks or acts on its own intuitive forces, even in its early period of unfoldment.

From those experiences as the daughter of Andrew, we may find the entity harking to that which to the entity will be as the singing of the angels; yet it will bring sadness and joy, happiness and sorrow, when those stories are told. And these should be told often to the entity, as to what it meant to the children of that day to bask in the presence of the Master, and how it may be attained and felt in the present experience.

For His promises are sure, "If ye seek me, I stand at the door and knock." Not that this is to become a long-facedness, but the happiness—as well as the sorrow, the appreciation of correct emphasis upon all phases of the experience should be that outlined.

The name then was Dora.

1958-1   F.2 days   7/18/39   Martha

. . . the entity was in the Palestine land when the Master walked in the earth.

The entity was among the children of Bethsaida who were blessed by the Master.

There we find the entity had a great period of development in the spiritual things, and—as has been indicated—we will find periods when there will be extremes towards the desire to know, to learn, to have the stories and experiences of all of those who were active during that period told to the entity. For this was builded into the experience of the entity, though the entity was not acquainted with same save the experience as He passed through and there taught His disciples humility.

Again it may be said that those who would direct the experience of the entity are to teach the entity humility, as then was being taught by Him to those who would become teachers and ministers in the experiences and lives of others.

The name then was Martha, but of the peoples of Bethsaida —who were friends of Philip and Bartholomew.

In the experience the entity gained . . .

403-1   F.70   9/6/33   Marie

The entity then was among those of the household of Chloe when the Master blessed the little children. The entity then, in the name Marie, sat upon the Master's knee; was blessed by Him, and became throughout the experience a close follower of those lessons that were taught by Him during that experience. Being persecuted, yes; yet glorying in the fact that the blessings of Him, that provided for the way of understanding to all, had come in the experience of self in that sojourn.

702-1   F.47   10/20/34   Margie

. . . the entity was in that land now known as the Promised Land, or the Palestine land, when there were the turmoils and strifes arising there; when the Master of men, thy brother, thy Savior—yea, thine intercessor before the throne of grace, as man—walked in the earth.

And thou wert among those children that were blessed by Him in those days when He taught His followers, His beloved disciples, that humbleness of heart, singleness or centralness of purpose, with the very expression of same as the child; that hurts must be forgiven, that neglect must be overlooked, that dissension must be of short duration; that such, and of such, are those that are acceptable in His sight, and who will stand with Him and He with *them* before the throne of grace.

And as thou hast found, as thou wilt find in thine experiences day by day, "If the Lord be with me, *who* can be against me?" Hold *thou* to that thou hast gained in the study of these; for the entity then, in the name Margie, gained. Though finding in the material many things that brought dissensions and strife among even the very elect, for the satisfying of material desires, the entity has found in the very reading of those experiences of the young—and even has thought within self—how glorious to have been among those! Thou wert there, my child! Thou felt His hand upon thy brow; yea, ye saw the smile upon the Master's face; yea, ye felt within thine very soul that strength that so oft keeps thee—in thine trials—in this very day.

Keep that thou hast gained, and may gain, by the meditating upon those things in that experience; for where His promises have come, those that hold to same may find self safe in the arms of Him that held thee materially in His arms. For the day grows brighter, even for thee; as thou holdest to those things that He gave in the quiet of the hour, in the quietness of self may the strength—as is His promise to all—come to thee day by day.

1156-1   M.18   4/24/36

... the entity was in the land now called the Holy Land, during those periods when there were the turmoils, the strifes that arose in the persecutions of those that followed in the way of the Nazarene.

For the entity then was among the children that were blessed by Him in the way, of the house of Cleopas [?] [8] — he that walked in the way. And those activities that made for the interpretations to the developing mind, the developing body of the entity in that experience, made for one that was zealous as to good works — in the way of making rather *practical* application of spiritual law in the material world.

So few be they who become so zealous of an idea or ideal as this entity that make same as practical, living experiences of those tenets, those truths that were given in that experience!

The entity became an emissary from the peoples who were misunderstood, some on purpose, some for lack of understanding. But the entity represented those in the Roman land, and made for much that made for peace *between* those peoples for the period of the entity's sojourn, *as* an active person or individual during the experience.

2570-1   F.42   8/9/41   Jeanel

... the entity was in the Promised Land, during those periods when there were the activities especially of the Roman guards, the Roman rulers.

While still in the present sex, the entity's associations with the Roman forces brought much into the experiences of the centurions that made for preservation of the tenets and truths which have had, do have, and will have yet more to do with the purposes of man's relationships in the material world.

For, the entity came under those directions and influences of the Master as He walked in the earth; being of those of Bethsaida who cared for Him — for there the Master rested.

Throughout that activity the entity gained. Material hardships came from persecutions, as those changes came by the injection of the Roman influences, yet the entity mentally and spiritually unfolded; bringing assurance, hope to many — as the activities of the entity continued in the Roman force or power.

In the present experience, turn oft to those activities when there were the communications at Lazarus' resurrection, and the last of the teachings of the Master to the disciples on the night of the betrayal. For these ye learned well. Apply them today, in thine own experience. For His promises are sure today, as indicated through those periods of activity when— though separated from thine own peoples, from thine own land —ye made and brought hope to those who came in contact or in acquaintanceship with thee through that experience.

The name then was Jeanel.

665-1   F.8   9/20/34   Cleopatia

. . . the entity was during that period when the Master walked in the earth, when there were those that were gathered by the way when "A little child shall lead them" was given, and when those were called that He, the Master, might bless them.[9]

The entity was among those that were blessed in the wayside from Bethsaida; and was then in the household of the soldiery of Rome, yet in those activities—as it grew to active service in the material world—the efforts were given in behalf of those that followed in the way of the Nazarene.

And the healing influences that were manifested in the later experience were gained from that sojourn.

In the name Cleopatia, the entity gained throughout the sojourn in the earth, and made for those things, those experiences, that paved the way by the return of those of its own household to Rome for the carrying of the gospel of the Nazarene into that land. For while the entity remained among those that were persecuted by those that came into power, the family of same returning with the soldiery remembered what *this* entity had received through the blessings given by Him on the wayside. Those experiences of the entity are as the betterments, and the periods when consternation or distress of any nature arise, whether mental or physical in the present, the visions and dreams of those lessons given by Him as He spoke to the children in the childish *understanding* manner, and the lessons of the lamb and the lessons of the household pets that were given to those children there, have remained with the entity. And these may find expression when the entity even today visions these things, as they pertain to the activities of others. And the joy of such will bring much in the experience if they are applied in the artistic field of activity.

4065-1   F.60   4/3/44   Martha

... the entity lived when the Master walked in the earth, knowing of and hearing of much of His teachings. The greater experience, which has been and is a part of the dreams and visions of the entity, was in those periods when great numbers were gathered and He disappeared through the crowds.[10]

The entity was among those who heard the admonitions, who heard those things proclaimed by Him as to how He, in mercy, in grace, had overcome the world and how that it must indeed be that offenses come, but woe to those who would offend.[11]

Thus it may be said of this entity that no one, no, not even a little one has been offended by the activities of this entity in this experience.

The name then was Martha, being of those peoples from Galilee, of Bethsaida, in the household of one Simeon ...

Q-3. How have I been associated in the past with young Dr. [5776], whom I helped to educate in the present for the medical profession?

A-3. In the Holy Land experience the entity saw him healed by the Master. Then counseled him as to his keeping close to the promises of the Master, Jesus. In the early Holy Land experience, the entity saw him among those of the soldiery forced to do that which his whole being abhorred.

3209-2   F.51   12/31/43

... the entity was in the Holy Land when the Master walked in the earth, among the children once blessed by the Master at those periods in the teaching in Bethsaida by the sea.

The entity never forgot, yet never forgave those who brought strifes and turmoils into the experience because of those very crowning activities of the entity's experience.

Thus there are confusions at times in body, in mind, as to the relationships with others. These are parts of the entity's experience, though the entity through that sojourn was only sixteen years of age when it passed from that stage of activity through the persecutions brought and because of the activities necessary. For the entity in the attempt to preserve its life lost it.

526-1   F.24   4/4/34   Eloise

... the entity was in that land when the Master walked among men, and among the children that were blessed by Him as they came and were among those that were present when there were the teachings that were as lessons to His disciples —and those nearby when He blessed them.

The entity then, Eloise, was of the children of Chloe, the cousin of Elizabeth, and of the families then of the Levites, that were the brothers of those of Zebedee's family.

In that experience the entity suffered oft in body, yet in the mental and soul development it was that period when the "dreamer of dreams" (as seen in the present experience) was builded; when music and those things in color, in sound, have come to mean so much to the inmost forces of this entity. And in the awakening of these in the present experience may there be brought for the entity the greater development for the soul in this experience. For, as those tenets, truths, lessons of that experience and period made for building into the innate influences in the experience of that soul, so may the harkenings to same bring the arousing within self those answers from within to the beauties of those things that give expression in song, in words, in deeds, in the beauty in the canvas, in the beauty in the music, or in all nature that proclaims the beautiful year, the beautiful day, the beautiful experience of those that have named the name of Him. So may there come into the inmost recesses of the heart of this soul the awakening to the expressions of that which, and the abilities of the hands, may bring hope and peace and joy to the hearts of others. For, as He gave His life, His self, so may this soul give self in the manifesting, in the activities of the body, the mind, the soul, those joys in the life of Him in that sojourn . . .

Q-1. In what way can I best express the Government of God in the world?

A-1. In those things that may be opened to thee by the turning within to those things *thou hast* heard with thine mortal ear of those tenets that He gave thee in Galilee!

2571-1   F.14   8/10/41   Ruth

. . . the entity was in the Promised Land, during those periods when the Master walked in the earth, and in those lands where He was so active—as in Bethsaida.

The entity was among those children blessed by Him.

That experience makes for the basis of the home, the home-building that is the deeper influence in the present.

Then the entity was known as Ruth, but of the household that later became the household of faith—with the rulers in that land.

Throughout the experience the entity gained. For, there has remained—there will remain (if there is kept that purpose as then)—that blessing which was given by Him, who is the way, the truth and the light. For, these fade not. For as given, good lives on.

Use those, study those of His blessings to children. For, thou —through thy experience in this sojourn—should bless the earth with many.

3342-1   F.31   11/2/43   Samantha

. . . the entity was in the Palestine land, when the Master walked in the earth. The entity was among the children at Bethsaida blessed by Him. Thus the desire, ever active and latent since those experiences, to emulate His laughter, His care, His thoughtfulness of others. Hence the entity is a most gracious hostess, a most loving individual with those close and those apart. For as the entity applied itself through those periods when there were trials, then in the name Samantha the entity encouraged those that became weary and weak in the fleshly desires that arise in the experience of every human in materiality at times.

3003-1   F.61   5/16/43   Esta

The entity was among the children of Bethsaida whom the Master blessed. Thinkest thou it is naught that He has smiled upon thee, or touched thee? Just as thou hast felt in thy consciousness at times His presence near thee, for some thought ye have given for others to apply in the life of the young. These are the harkenings to those thoughts through thy experience there, as ye grew up under the stress of those persecutions and of the fearfulness, yet ever that peace that comes with knowing that He hath walked and talked with thee.

. . . as Esta (not Esther but Esta) in that period.

Later ye became associated with those activities, when persecutions caused thy peoples to be charged to the lands in and about Caesarea, and down to Antioch, where ye became acquainted with the centurion's household there.

There, again, much of that recorded was a part of thine effort in behalf of that thou believest.

1177-1   M.12   5/25/36   David

. . . the entity was among those who sojourned in the land when the Master walked in the earth, during those periods when there were the gatherings of many for the teachings of the lowly Nazarene.

The entity was among the children of one Bartellius (not Bartaemus), in the name David; and was blessed by the Master.

And the entity was among those that later in the experience suffered material hardships for the causes not only of those of its own peoples and its parentage but for those tenets as held by self.

2403-1   F.19   11/17/40   Lascha

. . . the entity was in the land now known as the Promised Land, during the early experiences of the Master, as He walked in the earth.

There we find the entity was among the children blessed by Him, by those activities in Bethsaida when there were the gatherings of the groups for the hearing of the messages of Him— who is the way, the truth, the light.

In those experiences the entity attained to great abilities in the *mental* activity of gathering spiritual truths, that brought into the lives of those who followed in *his* way that of *joy*— though in service; *joy*—though in trial; *joy*—though in persecutions for a cause and for a purpose.

In the latter portion of the experience the entity was closely associated with the activities and the establishings of the church in Laodicea.

The name then was Lascha. Throughout the experience there, the entity was the home builder; and many of that era called the entity blessed.

2960-1   F.20   4/12/43   Leah

The entity was then among those coming under the influence of the Master through those teachings especially in Bethsaida. Then the entity was associated with those activities about the disciples and their sojourns in that land, and later became one of the holy women that aided in the establishing of homes for those that were questioned as to their associations with the groups who came as rulers—or as the soldiery in that land.

Thus the entity became one upon whom many relied for counsel . . .

The name then was Leah.

5246-1   F.26   5/27/44   Estes

. . . the entity was in the land where the Master walked in the earth and in the activities among the children blessed at Bethsaida.

Thus the entity knew Him, and in the individuality of the entity, there is ever that hope of the blessing which was a portion of the experience, and the entity will never, never be far away; and yet there are, from even those experiences, as well as the one just given, that desire to be, to know, all sides of human experiences.

In the name then, the entity was known as Estes. There the entity contributed much to the aiding of the various groups following the establishing of church in varied communities and groups. Following the periods when there were persecutions, the entity was among those who went to Bethsaida, from Bethsaida to Laodicea to aid in the establishing of greater activities there.

Thus the entity entered into the social work in the church in Laodicea, being helpful influences to many.

3709-1   F.40   3/20/44   Celeste

. . . the entity was in the Holy Land among the mothers who gathered by the sea when the Master talked.

The entity was among those who sought for the blessings of the Master upon her children as well as those of the neighborhood.

Thus a purpose, a deep soul-purpose is a part of the entity's make-up. Whatever the entity promises it keeps, even though at times it hurts others or the entity finds it has been misunderstood in the causes or purposes. Yet this deep, innate experience of the entity as Celeste is that which gives this deeper purpose for others which may be applied in the present experience of the entity in its teachings.

Daughter of Syrophoenician Is Healed

2936-2   F.35   4/8/43   Istabuel

... the entity was in the Holy Land, or in the lands adjoining same, when the Master walked in the earth; when the activities of the Master brought Him to the outer coasts of the land, when there was the healing of the Syrophoenician.[1]

The entity then was one that had been a nurse to the entity who was made whole again. This brought to the entity, then, a wonderment that finds an answer in something and yet never quite able to be put into words by the entity, because of its surroundings. And yet, as is seen, most individuals are quieted, are bettered, are more useful — in *whatever* their activity may be — by being in companionship with the entity — even as in the experience of the entity as Istabuel.

1159-1   F.80   5/5/36   Armediee

... the entity was in the land now known as the Promised Land, or the Palestine land, during that period when those of that land knew the Master that walked in the earth.

The entity then was her to whom the Master gave, "Is it meet that I should take the bread and feed to the children —" and the answer, "Yea, Lord, but even the dogs eat of the crumbs from the master's table." And as was given, "I have not found so great a faith, no not in Israel."[2]

The entity was a Syrophoenician then, of those peoples of a

mixed race; those peoples that combined not only those things that became as the influences for the conveniences of individuals and groups but those things that also made for the associations and the connections and the expansions of the activity of the entity's peoples into other lands.

For of the entity's own peoples then were the first of the Syrophoenician groups extended off the borders of the Mediterranean; yea, even beyond the borders of what ye now term as the Canary Island, even into the Sargasso Sea—that into which the cauldrons of the earth were turned with the destructive forces in the Poseidian land in its last activity, and the embellishments that arose from those forces of the entity's experience among those peoples as well as that it gained by those periods of its association with the Teacher of teachers, the Lord of lords.

While those activities lasted in that experience, the entity was a leader, an interpreter, a director that spread the influences which are *still* being felt in and among the children of men.

Then the name was Armediee.

2364-1   F.27   9/2/31   Mirian

. . . in that land as was trod by the Holy One, in Mount Seir did the entity dwell, and a priestess of those that established the Mount and the worship in the temple there. That at the time being a combination of that taught in Dan and Beersheba by those that brought the dissolution of the kingdom and those that re-established in the land under the return of those of Zerubbabel, and with the establishing the entity became one of the priestesses of the temple in Mount Seir. *Then* in the name Mirian. The entity through this experience gained, for being true to those tenets as were taught, as were given, using that knowledge as was gained, and the entity—when it asked of the Master (and whose daughter was healed by same), and the answer as was given, that "Doth not the servants—even the dogs—eat at the master's table?" brought that that was said of her in that period, "I have found faith not so great even in Israel." In *this* new found faith came many blessings to many peoples, and the entity gained throughout *that* experience . . .

585-2   F.38   6/15/34   Anilen

. . . the entity was in the period when the Master of men, the son of Mary, walked in the earth; and during those periods when there were the gatherings of many that were healed by the Master.

The entity was the one to whom the Master said, "Must I give to those not of this household?" And with the healing of the body, with the following close, the entity gained much and gave much strength to those that were weak in those days when persecution came, through the political influences and the social strife . . .

The entity *blessed* many, for the Master put His hands upon the entity and *loved* the entity — Anilen.

In that experience the entity learned much to use the hands in the aid for others, in making things with the hands, in tending those that were weak and crippled.

585-6   F.43   10/11/39

Q-8. As Anilen in Palestine, was I the Syrophoenician who sought healing for her daughter, as recorded in the Bible, or some other?

A-8. Companion with the Syrophoenician, and a Syrophoenician herself.

105-2   F.Adult   1/31/28   Iaundia

The entity then was in the household of the Phoenician, as a maid servant, whom the Master blessed with the household. Entity in the name of Iaundia and the entity gained through this period, even though fear always remained over the entity's ability to express or mainfest that desire to be giving to others, the position, physical, the mental abilities of the entity did not coincide. In the present experience the urge is seen of that weightiness that is ever felt by the entity of the words spoken by that Holy One, and the manner in which same has been diverted by many of the writers of same, is as a thorn in the flesh often to the entity, yet would the entity bring that peace that passeth understanding, clinging close to those truths as is set in the words of that one: "He that believeth in me, or that cometh to me, I will in no wise cast out, for even as I am in the Father and ye in me, we are then one with the Father that doeth His will." [3]

An Example for the Disciples

3395-2   F.63   1/15/44   Armythar

... the entity was in the Holy Land when the Master walked in the earth, when there was the entering into Bethsaida on that occasion when there were the discussions about who would be the greatest in the kingdom of heaven. It was this entity's child who was set in the midst of the disciples, whom Jesus took upon His knee and gave "Except ye become as little children, ye shall in no wise enter in." [1] Unless you can be just as forgiving, unless you can find it just as easy to forget slights and slurs and things that would make afraid those who would judge others. For with what measure ye mete, it is measured to thee again. Even as He, the Master gave, the faults ye find in others are reflected in thine own mirror of life. And as He gave, "Cast the beam out of thine eye that ye may see to take the mote from thy brother's eye." [2]

The name then was Armythar. The entity was ever, from those periods, a follower of the teachings of the Master, and aided others by the recording in its own terms, in its own language, the sayings and doings of the Master when there were those things given to others.

As the days of the fulfilling of His journey in the earth were ended, the entity was among those even who assisted Peter, John, and the entity prompted Matthew to write his gospel. Thus it has appealed ever to the entity as the most authentic of all the records in this particular experience.

3395-3   F.63   4/17/44   Armythar

The entity in the period was not of that group called Essenes, yet was not wholly in accord with the teachings of the orthodox Jews. For in the land where the entity was born and brought up, Bethsaida, there were those tenets that made a division between the Samaritans and the orthodox Jews, as well as the Essenes.

These had not brought confusion but, as might be said, the entity felt rather that "Either one will do," and the activities were in accordance with the interpretation "Well, it's not necessary, and if I keep the faith within self, sometime, somewhere, somehow I will know." This is not very far wrong, if you don't do wrong yourself!

The entity kept in rather that attitude through its girlhood and early married life. The associates of the entity then were those who had to do with the teachings or the supplying materially of the means for transportation of activities in Bethsaida and the other countries or towns that looked to the particular area for the supply of foods for various groups.

For there were just as many cranks about what to eat on special days then as there are now! These are the nature, these are the human traits of man! Some want to do or be so and so because others are that way, while others want to be different — for they know they are different! It is the latent urge in many an individual entity.[3]

Thus this was rather the attitude of the entity, whether to be different or to do such and such because others did.

When the Master entered into those environs as a teacher, when there was the heralding of His teachings first by the associates who had first heard John in the wilderness, and especially those who had heard of the happenings when there had been the baptism of one Jesus of Nazareth, we find that such was the attitude and activity of the entity.

Then the entity had those opportunities of hearing the Master as He taught in Bethsaida and along the way, for it was along the way — that is, along the road — when they heard that He was coming, and the entity's child was set before the disciples for the lesson, "Who is the greatest in the kingdom of heaven?"[4] All will remember how He said, as He took the little child, "Unless ye become as a little child, ye shall in no wise enter in." Unless you become as open-minded, unless you can get mad and fight and then forgive and forget. For it is the nature of man to fight, while it is the nature of God to forgive.

Hence, as has been the injunction to the entity, "As ye forgive, so are ye forgiven." As ye treat thy fellow man ye are treating thy Maker.[5]

With the lesson gained there, we find that the entity changed entirely from the happy-go-lucky individual, or from that attitude of "what difference does it make?" For the time had come, the opportunity had arrived when the entity knew there was a work to do. The entity gained a real lesson from its own child, who didn't have a very good temper!

Then the entity became interested, because of the physical needs, when she met Matthew, who had been questioned by the Jews because he had accepted a civil position from Rome and collected tax—which every Jew and every individual in Bethsaida and Samaria, and all about, held to be a violation of the freedom of those who served a living God.

Individuals, as the entity, began to apply the lesson of forgiveness—and the lesson of correction that is part of the desire for forgiveness. Correction is part of the lesson of desire for forgiveness. Learn that well.

The entity then found that Matthew had been in about the same attitude as self. When there were the periods when the disciples were sent on their own mission, to tell the story of what they had seen, each individual being commissioned by the Master, Jesus Himself, the entity looked on; for Matthew was attracted to, as well as being sent to, those particular vicinities where the entity lived.[6]

Again the entity studied, trying to find out how one could be commissioned from the divine and not have the power without that commission; and it is still a mystery to the entity . . .

In those periods it may be said that the entity became the complement, the impelling influence that gave to Matthew that of confidence and help in self, with the happenings of the crucifixion and the persecution that followed with the beheading of James.

1401-1   F.9   7/6/37   Roselan

The entity was the one taken from among the children whom He used as an example when he gave, "Except ye become as little children, ye shall in no wise enter in."

Hence we will find that experience gradually making for the

advancement by the close adherence to those principles as He set; not as dogmatic influences of an orthodox activity—these He did not teach! For the whole gospel as He gave is, "Thou shalt love the Lord, thy God, with all thy heart, thy mind, thy body; and thy neighbor as thyself." [7]

This practiced, this applied, this lived in the experience of this entity will bring harmony and hope and the building of the home that may be blessed even by His presence not only with the entity but all those with whom the entity may journey or sojourn.

In the experience the entity was called Roselan, and gained; yet persecutions brought much disturbings to that developing entity during the experience.

1129-2   F.33   3/11/37   Eloise

. . . the entity was in the land now known as or called the Promised Land, or the Palestine land, or the Judean land.

For it was in those periods when the Master walked in the earth; and the entity then, though but a child, was among those who joined in pilgrimages during those periods to go upon the mountainside to listen to the words of the Master.

And the entity was blessed by Him in that day when, "And He took a little child and sat it in the midst of them and said, Lest ye become as a little child, ye shall in no wise enter in."

And as the entity has heard this again and again there has come rather that feeling even upon the spine that "It means me—It means me!" Yet there has not been the holding to that, for under those influences as has been indicated, there has been the feeling rather that "It couldn't be me—I am not worthy—It couldn't be me—I don't *feel* I am worthy!"

He that the Lord hath blessed shall never lose his hold upon that strength that His might gives to those who seek to know His way!

The name then was Eloise, and it was of those peoples that were kinsmen of Peter and Andrew—and close to those in Andrew's own household.

857-1   F.3 mos.   3/15/35   Clementina

. . . among those children that were blessed by Him on the way from Bethany.

The entity then beheld Him, knew Him, as one that drew children to Him and made of them and their lives an illustration of the manner in which people, men, women, everywhere, must accept those activities of their fellow associates. For if one would be forgiven as a child, one must forgive those that would —or do—err against self.

The entity heard that spoken by Him, "Lest ye become as little children ye will in no wise enter in."

Then the entity was of the household of Cleopas, in the name Clementina; and in the experience gained throughout, gained in the mental and the spiritual developments as attained through the experience. Being in the early teens when the incidents in the activities of those that had become the leaders and the teachers in those people that were tested, trained, taught by Him, the entity made for assistance especially to Mark and Luke in their activities as they accompanied those that made for the giving out of the tenets during that experience.

The entity became very closely associated with Mark in the activities that made for the preservation of those tenets, of those lessons as we find in the gospel recorded by Mark.

The Adulteress

295-1   F.26   12/23/29   Mary of Magdalene

. . . in that period when the Master walked among men. To her the Master said, "She hath chosen the better part." [1] In ministering to Him through that period, loved by Him in that experience, as the *sister* of Martha and of Lazarus, the entity gained through the experience—and little is the wonder to others that ever the song, or the wish, or the desire for help and succor and aid is paramount in the *entity's* soul; for only that others *might* be aided did the entity enter into another experience—for, as was said by Him, "Wherever my gospel is preached, her works will be spoken of." [2] What a heritage! In the present experience we find that His tenets, His truths, are easily taught, understood by the entity. Only be broader in the vision, condemning none—even as He condemned not even those who persecuted Him. Condemnation in the entity is *builded.* Blot *this* from *thine* experience, *through* Him who maketh all things possible.

. . . we find those tenets as were set in motion by that experience [Egypt] may be made compatible with that gained by the association with the Master, for *they* be one — even as has been given, they were the foundation of that as taught by the Master in *His* experience in the earth's period . . .

295-8   F.30   8/31/33   Mary of Magdalene

In giving a detailed account of the experience as Mary, the sister of Martha and Lazarus, indeed much might be given respecting the activities of the entity in that experience. For, as given in the Gospel account, this entity was then the Mary of Magdalene; or the courtesan that was active in the experiences both of those that were in the capacity of the Roman officers, Roman peoples, and those that were of the native lands and country.

When the body met first the Master, it was the woman brought before the council as taken in adultery; and the one whom the whole council or court at the time asked that, according to the law, the woman be stoned.[3]

With the cleansing of the body-mind, through the association and experience, the entity then joined again with those of the family from whom she had been separated in Bethany, and became then again of the household of those that dwelt there.

Hence the showing in the Gospel of the difference in attitude, in the manner of approach, with the various visits of the Master through the period.

The entity was the same to whom the Master first appeared upon the resurrection morn [4]; the same to whom many of the apostles and leaders during that experience went for counsel, in the ways and manners that are spoken of in the various accounts that are kept in the present.

As to the experiences before meeting the Master, these were more of the worldly nature; wherein there was the giving of self in body, in the indulgencies of the period, such that there was brought for the body and those associated with same the activities that brought condemnation, as well as the pomp, the power, the splendor, when considered from that angle, in the experience of the entity through the period.

In the activities, then, these should be—as we find—more dwelt upon in the activity after the cleansing in the temple.

Ready for questions.

Q-1. Is the account of Mary depicted in the book, "Under Pontius Pilate," a copy of which I hold in my hand, authentic?

A-1. In the main, authentic.

Q-2. Was the extraordinary reaction produced by reading this book caused by the soul-mind coming into the realization of the two being one?

A-2. That which brought the realization of the activities, and the forces that continue to war within self.

Q-3. Why is it not pointed out more clearly in the Gospels that they were one and the same?

A-3. It could hardly be pointed out more clearly than it is, when the references are read as one!

Q-4. Please describe the personal appearance of the body at that time.

A-4. This is well drawn by da Vinci, as well as in that by Blum [Blaum?]—The Magdalene. A body five feet four inches (5'4") in height, weight a hundred and twenty-one (121) pounds—in the general. Hair almost red. The eyes were blue. The features were those impelled both from the Grecian and Jewish ancestry.

Q-5. In what previous experience or experiences did Mary, the sister of Martha and Lazarus, contact the entity who became the Master of men in the Palestine experience?

A-5. Not in bodily form, or in what is termed earth experience, save in the *mental* associations through the experience in Egypt and in Persia.

Q-6. Please recall to the mind of the entity any scene or conversation which may be helpful and enlightening, as well as inspiring, in the present, between this entity or her associates and the Master, during the Master's ministry in the earth in the Palestine experience.

A-6. None greater than that given to the entity by the Master, that means for the entity an awakening: "Neither do I condemn thee—Neither do *I* condemn thee." That *has* awakened, *will* awaken within the soul of the entity, more of the love, the oneness of the force or power able to cleanse when condemnation is not in self.

Hence, as given then—and as has been given oft: Do not condemn self! And the condemnation of self is that to which the entity in self gives more of that repelling force than to any influence in the experience of the entity in the present.

Q-7. What did the Master write in the sand at the time of that experience?

A-7. That which condemned each individual, as each looked over His arm—or as He wrote.

Q-8. Have I learned to condemn less?

A-8. On the way!

Q-9. Did the entity repay any fraction of the debt owed the Master while He was in the earth?

A-9. That's impossible! For, as the entity and each soul learns, condemning self is condemning the abilities of the Master. As the Master has given, *God* is God of the *living—not* of the dead! For, the dead are separated from the living. As in the earth, so in the spiritual. Dead, or death, is separation. Death in the spiritual, then, is separation from life. Life, then, is God. The Master, the Christ, manifested life in the earth, through not only the material manifestations that were given in the ministry but in laying aside the life. As He gave, "I *give* my life —I give it of myself, and I take it of myself."

So, in any attempt to repay—there can be no repay! But when one lives the life that *manifests* the Christ life, love, joy, peace, harmony, grace, glory, the *joy* is in the life of the Master as He manifests—and manifested—life in the earth.

Q-10. How did the death of the Master affect the entity?

A-10. As visioned by that which is read, she thought He was the gardener.[5] This indicates all the hopelessness, all the sorrow that is possible to be indicated in hopelessness. Yet the *joy* should be the condition as would be thought on, rather than the separation at the time. This is going backward, even to be affected by the separation—when there is the joy as manifested in, "My Lord and my God."

Q-11. Was the entity present at the ascension?

A-11. To be sure.

Q-12. After the Master's death and resurrection, please give a brief biographical sketch of the remaining years of the lives of Mary, Martha and Lazarus. How long did each live, and what did each accomplish?

A-12. It would require volumes to give in detail as to what each may have been considered to have accomplished, or that each did accomplish.

Lazarus' life was only until the first of the rebellions arose; for, on *his* activity much of that which caused the dissension (from the first raising from the dead) was produced in the minds of the people and the experiences of the high priest at the time.

With the death and separation of the Master from the disciples (as it may be called), the home of Mary and Martha became —for the time—rather the center from which most of the activities of the disciples took place, who were of that activity; that is, who were not altogether Galileans, see?

Hence those associations that became the closest were with John, James, Matthew, Levi and Thaddeus. The others, of course, remained closer with the activities of the Galileans.

Hence we find, with the return from Galilee and the activities there upon the ascension (which was fifty days after the resurrection), Mary the mother of Christ became a dweller in the house or home of John—who joined with those in Bethany; for John, as may be well known, was the wealthiest of the disciples of the Christ. His estate would be counted in the present, in American money, as being near to a quarter of a million dollars; or to the estate where he was a power with those in the Roman and Jewish power at the period.

Hence the associations of Mary and John became the closest after this (we are speaking of Mary, the sister of Martha).

As to Martha's experience then, in this period: With the rebellions that arose (that is, the coming of the soldiery that made for the dissension), we find Martha joined with those that brought the rebellion of Saul [6]; and it was under *his* direction that the persecutions and banishments brought about the death of Martha.

With the joining of the mother of the Christ with John's household (which was composed then of Mary Magdalene and

Elois [?], or the sister of Mary that was the mother of James and John), these journeyed then to what would be called their *summer* home—or that portion on the lake of Gennesaret where the activities of those that came and went were supervised by those of the whole household.

The period of life of Mary (that is, of Mary the sister of Lazarus) was some twenty and two years; she being twenty-three years old when the Christ cleansed her from the seven devils: Avarice, hate, self-indulgence, and those of the kindred selfishnesses; hopelessness and blasphemy.[7]

Q-13. *Was there a special message to Mary after Christ arose that was not recorded?*

A-13. There [are] several Marys; which one is meant?

Q-14. *Mary, the sister of Martha.*

A-14. Wasn't it sufficient to have Him appear first? What more could be counted in earthly things, to be the first to meet Him?

Q-15. *Please give the lesson that should be learned from this experience by the entity.*

A-15. Subduing these very same conditions in the experience of self. *Ever* these are contending influences in the experience.

For, one should remember, even the cleansing power as in the raising of Lazarus—raised for the moment, but his own life to live! Forgiven, yes—entirely, by and through the blood of the Master, but the *own* life to live!

As the illustration, that has oft been given: Nails may be driven in a post and may be removed, but the holes cannot! Neither can the scars that remain, that touched the soul—as the devils do in their activity, be wholly erased; until self has passed through the whole cleansing in Him.

All those, then, that were cleansed by Him, have been called—are called—for special missions, for activities in each experience in and among men, that they—as souls, as portions of the life, as portions of the whole—may demonstrate, may give, the blessings to many.

Even as the body may, as Mary, give that in the experience of those; that ever stood as a monument, as a memorial, to the activity of the Christ life upon the life of a soul that was active in the earth during the Galilean or the Palestine experience.

EVENTS IN THE MINISTRY OF THE MASTER 257

And so may the entity in the experience in the earth in the present become the channel through which blessings may come to many that act as a manifestation of life in the earth for the bringing about of those things, in the hearts and minds and souls of men, that cause the recognition and the activity of the saving grace in the love of the Christ, the Savior of men.

1436-2   F.27   8/30/37   "one taken in adultery"
. . . the entity was in the land when the Master of masters walked in the earth, when there were those trials, those temptations, those activities and those desires for the ability of those in authority to trap Him.

The entity was that maid brought before the Master in the temple that was condemned as one taken in adultery; and because of the judgment passed upon that entity according to the law, the peoples or the high priest or those of the Sanhedrin declared that He must make a statement.

And He gave, "Let him that is without sin cast the first stone." [8] Let him that has been guiltless make the first move for the fulfilling of the *letter* of the law.

And lo, they all went their way! And as He wrote upon the ground, "Medi [?] Medici [?] Cui [?]" these meant—in the experience of they that looked on—that which showed the awakening in the heart of the entity of hope, and as the cry came, "Master, what sayest thou?" the answer came, "I condemn thee not, daughter—go and sin no more."

Is it any wonder, then, that those days that followed made for a remolding of the entity? though the entity kept afar, and not until after those periods when the persecutions began did she venture to come nigh unto those that were classed or called of the household of faith.

But to have had the words direct from the Master of masters, the Teacher of teachers, "I do not condemn thee," *has* meant, *must* mean, in the experience of the entity, that which words cannot portray; but only the deeds of the body, the desire of the mind to bring hope, faith, *in* that Lord, that Master, who is able to *save* unto the utmost, and who hath given to all, "My peace I leave *with* you, my peace I give *unto* you."

And when the entity has experienced and does experience

that consciousness by opening the door of its heart again to that voice that comes, "I condemn thee not—be thou merciful, even as I have shown and give thee mercy," then: In the life of intolerability in the experience, cannot the entity find in the heart of self to say, even as He, "They know not what they do"? and to give the cup of water, to give the healing in the hands, to give the cherishment to those that are sad?

To those that are joyous give them more joy in that the praise be given to Him who maketh life to all that seek to know His face.

How oft may the entity, if it will but cherish within the heart of self that experience, vision the experience when before those in penal law or authority, those with their pomp and glory—yet He in *all* His glory, His face shining as only from the Father-God itself!

Thus may the entity see and know that presence, "My daughter, I condemn thee not—My peace I give to thee."

Hold fast to that! For He will walk and talk with thee, if ye will but open thy mind, thy heart, to Him.

For He is nigh unto thee. For indeed in flesh, as ye will see, ye were a parent even unto Him.

[Old Testament incarnation: "Before that we find the entity was in that now known as or called the Palestine land, during those days when the sons of Jacob sought for companions; and to one of the sons of Judah (Er) the entity, Tamar, became the companion.

"Owing to the *willfulness* and the sin of Er, he was taken. There was the command or the seeking that there be the fulfullment of the law of the day; and Judah—in an unknown way—failing, yet the entity sought for that as would keep the issue of the body, and went in unto her own father-in-law; and bore two sons, one becoming then later the father of the fathers of Joseph and Mary—the parent of the Master." (See Genesis 38.)]

5749-9   10/21/37
[This reading taken to clarify seeming duplication of incidents of foregoing readings for 295 and 1436.]

In the interpretations, all the conditions that surrounded the period should be taken into consideration.

EVENTS IN THE MINISTRY OF THE MASTER 259

The variations in those particular incidents are apparently the same, yet the individuality is different in the two incidents.

Those were periods when there were those who questioned the Master as in the sect of the Pharisees. There were those who questioned when they were led by the Sadducees. There were others when questioned by those in the Roman authority.

There were, then, two individual experiences when He was questioned as to the law as related to that given by Moses respecting those taken in adultery.

The one about which the first information was given was the associate of John and James; while the last one was the associate of the Roman soldiery. And the questions in each instance were by the different sects of peoples.

These are overlapping in the records that are given (or that you have); though in the original they are given as two different experiences.[9]

Ready for questions.

Q-1. Which one was [1436]?
A-1. The one taken in the act with the Roman soldiery, and questioned by the Sadducee peoples; while the other [295] was the sister of Martha, and hence the associate (or cohort) of those that were the disciples or apostles later.

Q-2. In which instance did Jesus stoop and write?
A-2. In each; in each of these. In one that written was as given, "Medi [?] Medici [?] Cui [?]" or the expression of mercy and not sacrifice which showed to those that looked on the individual awakening of the entity. In the other that written was that which made the accusers recognize their *own* activities.

Q-3. Is there any other history of the period that we may have at this point?
A-3. Which portion is sought? We have most all of it here! Most any portion may be given!

The incident about which the last information was given, [1436] through this channel, occurred *after* there had been the re-uniting of Martha, Lazarus and Mary; while the first incident [295] occurred in the earlier portions of His ministry.

For as given, the incident of Magdala [295]—or Mary the

sister of Martha—occurred when the individual had set about what would be called now a home for, or a retreat for, those who sought to use and give their bodies to those activities for the indulgences and for the gaining of information of various sorts or natures through such activities of the individuals.

But the latter individual [1436], as we have indicated in that given, was only guilty of *self*-indulgence—and with the Romans and not those in authority in the various groups or activities.

5231-1   F.64   6/5/44   Marie

In giving the interpretations of the records, there is much from which to choose. Here we would minimize the faults, for so will the Christ if the body, mind and soul will but take Him as a guide. Remember, as that one taken in what men called a fault and the law demanded the life by stoning, yet the Master forgave, so may ye be forgiven.

We would then, as would He give: Magnify the abilities and, as He said, keep those abilities in the home, in the efforts for beautiful homes, that love may reign in the homes of those who are about the entity. Thus may ye, even as Marie [Mary Magdalene?] of old, become a shining light because ye have known how to forgive, because ye have been forgiven . . .

So the desire of thy heart to make a home for those who may have wandered, even may have erred in the eyes of man; yet God knows their hearts, and many of those whom ye would aid may come to know, too, the blessings of the Holy One, who honored woman that she might, too, be equal with man in the redemption of man from the wiles of the devil, or the wiles of him who would cause man or woman to err in any manner.

Lazarus Is Raised

295-2   F.27   11/10/30

Q-24. Are Martha and Lazarus in the earth plane?

A-24. . . . they are! . . . [Martha, 560; Lazarus, 1924; and their sister Mary, 295][1]

993-5   F.50   2/19/41   Ulai

In giving the interpretations of other appearances, or that which has been indicated for the entity as to its associations with the Master and those through that experience—this may be indicated in the present, if there will be the acceptance of it in that desire and purpose with which it may be given in the present.

For, through the experience all was not good; neither was all bad. Because of associations and activities through the present experience, this has been withheld; not because of that indicated but because of the needs for growth in that to be determined within the purposes of self as to the activities in the present material plane.

As may be indicated from that sojourn through those periods, it is not knowledge that is so important but the wisdom in application of that known. It is not what or how much one knows that counts, but what one does about that it knows, or experiences; or as to whether self and its attitudes are to be exalted or whether self-exaltation is to be renounced in that the activities are to induce or produce growth in spiritual determinations—such as to bring about attitudes, characteristics, manners of thinking and ways of determination through a given experience.

Then, in giving the biographical sketch of that indicated through the Palestine experience; the entrance, the varied activities, the applications, and that as may be manifested in the present from same:

It is well that something of those activities through the land be given here, that there may be the understanding of the background of the entity or the view of that taking place which caused the entity to act or react in those varying attitudes as assumed there.

There were those various groups that held to what might be called determining factors or principles. As would be termed in the present, there was the group that held to the orthodox Jewish belief—holding to the law and the prophets as the way of acceptance and grace in the spiritual sense. There was a mixed group—as the Samaritans—who, as for edification, were as well versed in the law as were those of the more orthodox belief in that particular period, but differed as to the manners in which there was the more oft the interpreting of the laws by the ministers and teachers in the synagogues of the day. Also the adherents to the Samaritanic law felt that they were just as well in keeping with the days, the seasons, the moons, the various activities, as were those of the more orthodox groups. The only factor dividing these was the differing as to place of worship; yet the orthodox had little of that in common with other groups. Then there were the divers groups, as well as the Essenes—that had set themselves as a channel through which there was expected to be the fulfilling in that particular period of those promises indicated from the first promise to Eve unto the last as had been recorded by Malachi. These were individuals who in their activities of daily life were in keeping with neither of the first indicated groups. Then there were those of the Grecian and Roman faiths, who held to that idea of glorifying the body itself as a channel through which there might be sought manifestation by the divine—if there was a choice made by the divine, or if there were the divine (according to their reasoning).

This entity then came into activity in that heterogeneous or conglomerate thought—in the name then Ulai. The parentage of the entity was one Archaus—a close adherent of the Essenes' thought yet of the orthodox group—and of one (the mother) who was a close associate of the mother of Martha, Mary and Lazarus, in the name Josada.

Then, the entity was brought up in the tenets or schools of thought that had attempted to be a reconstruction of the former activities established by Elijah in Mount Carmel.

Hence, coming under the influence of *all* of these tenets, the entity was greatly confused through its early experience. The entity had the greater teachings, or was acquainted with the greater teachings of the Carmelites—now the Essenes—and of the orthodox groups that held to the service in the temple and the close associations with these of the students and exponents of the Roman and Grecian people. It was to these latter mentioned teachings that the entity turned more, in its early years.

Thus when there were the first presentations to the entity

of the thought as to the teachings of the Nazarene, and the entity having rejected John as a disciple or even a forerunner, these appeared as mysteries to the entity.

Hence oft in its activities the entity grew cold, and again very enthusiastic as to the varying forms of activities—both as to the social and as to the more strict religious groups.

Thus we find that urge which eventually has become a part of the entity, from the experience there—the urge to adhere to a necessary form, the following of a chart or of a manner—as to posture or position, as well as to the other determining factors according to that taught. Yet, to the entity each must respond to something in the material nature.

This is not indicating that the entity is a materialist in the present; far from it! Rather that there are the needs for something that responds to the *material* application *from* the lesson taught, or the illustration given.

In those days of the Master's teachings when He journeyed oft in Bethany, and with the return of Mary after the conversion and the casting out of the demons—this brought even greater confusion to the entity.[2] For, to the entity, how *could* anyone who had been *such* a person—or who had so disregarded persons except for the material gains—become an honored one among those, or in association with a household of ones such as Lazarus and Martha.

Hence the entity withheld self from such associations, until there were the periods in which Lazarus was ill of a fever—what today would be called the slow fever, or typhoid—and there was the eventual death. Then the entity was among those of the mourners—not the hired mourners—and came in contact again with Mary and Martha during those periods of the Master's expressions regarding the activities among His disciples; not the apostles but the disciples.

And to the entity even today, the shortest verse recorded is that to which the entity responds the more oft, deepest within self.

For, with that concept of how He—the friend—wept with those of His friends in the face of criticism, in the company of the great and near great—there came a conviction to the entity that changed the whole concept of the entity as to the purposes, as to the whys and wherefores of that which had taken place in the mind and the heart of Mary; also as to why and how that Martha and Lazarus had again accepted this sister into their home, their company.

From that experience, and the raising of Lazarus, the entity became rather among those seeking then to know something of the heart and the experience of the mother. And the entity made that journey to notify the mother of that taking place in Jerusalem; missing the triumphal entry, but among those that saw and heard and spoke with the Master on the way to Calvary.

This brought the entity close into association then with those of the group later designated as the apostles.

The entity remained with or carried the mother, not to John's home but to her own. Later, when there were those periods of rejoicing over the knowledge of the resurrection, the meetings of the disciples and apostles in the upper room, the entity then went with the mother—Mary—to the home of John and saw her established there.

Later the entity became very active in the various meetings which took place until the completing of those days when Pentecost came.

The entity was among those who harkened to the speech, as it were, of Peter upon that day.

Then, becoming acquainted with the young converts of the Grecians as well as those in Laodicea, and with the separating of those when persecutions arose and Stephen was stoned, there was an aversion held by the entity as to the activities of Paul —or Saul during that particular period—such that it necessitated the entity withdrawing alone. For, Stephen was a close friend of Lucius, Luke, *and* those of the younger group that became the companions of the teachers.[3]

But with the spread of the teachings as brought about by the breaking up of the holy women (of which the entity was classed, though among the younger of that group), the entity joined in the church activities in Laodicea.

With what was termed by some the faithlessness of Lucius, and preached so even by Paul, the entity almost renounced all —and brought about what might be called the first separation in the church in Laodicea.

Because of the entity's activities, differences spread in many of the churches, not only in the local activities around Laodicea but in Antioch and in Pygarga, Jerusalem and in Patmos.

It was not until there was the report of Peter as to how the Gentiles had been and were having the out-pouring of the Holy Spirit [4] that there was again the unison, or the united activity of the entity, wholly, with those in the original of the group churches.

Hence we find that throughout the rest of the entity's experience—though as the companion of one who became a leader in the Antioch church, and eventually the head of the deacons of the church—one Pathaos—the entity made for the greater developments; never tiring of the instruction to the young— her own as well as those of the church, as well as the groups of the various faiths—concerning the happenings at Bethany, the speech of Stephen.

These were the great centers from which the entity drew through that experience, and may be those from which the entity in the present may oft gather deep within self that as is the safer course, that as is the assurance in the periods of distress, disappointments, aggravation.

But know—as ye understood—He *is* indeed the resurrection. He is indeed mindful of the sorrows as well as the joys of mankind.

The entity lived through those activities to a good old age, being eighty-seven; knowing through the period all of the apostles, as well as many of the teachers, ministers and interpreters of the various phases of differences which arose between Paul and Peter, Paul and Barnabas, Mark and Matthew, Thomas and all the rest—where there were differences and questions as to manner, as to form, and as to *who* was acceptable, and as to *who* might be trusted.

In the present, then, let not those of faults or failures make for questionings. It is not what one once did that counts, but what one *will* do about that it knows to do today!

Let that mind be in thy activities as ye found in self in His presence when He wept with Mary, Martha and that household.

Let that mind be in thee as was when ye listened to Stephen, as he brought about the explaining of the various influences which had brought about the different beliefs of the groups of which ye were a part in thy early experiences in that land.

Know that they all came to that conclusion as *He* gave—that he alone whom thou crucifiest may give that forgiveness as may bring one into the consciousness of the abiding presence of the Christ.

Be in that mind ye had as ye listened and saw those of all tongues, all faiths, hear the words of Peter as he sought for all to put away the thoughts of self and to accept, believe and be baptized.

In those thoughts remain steadfast—in that belief as so well expressed by one whom ye later learned to reverence, but who so oft brought disappointment and turmoil to thee—that "Others may believe this or that, but on Jesus the Christ do I stand, as the Savior, and him crucified." [5] That is the hope of man. That *is* thy hope.

Preach that. Practice that.

Crucify in self, then, that which might in any way hinder thee, or that might influence others to doubt or to fear. Or, as he expressed it, "Be ye all things to all men, that ye may thereby save the more."

Seek not to justify thyself in thought or belief. For, the glorifying of His tenets, His truths, is that necessary in thy own life day by day.

The spirit is willing, the flesh is weak—but hate not the flesh for its weakness; and know that in materiality they are one, that must coordinate as the body, the mind and the soul, if one would be creative in body, mind or spirit. For He, the Lord, in the Christ, is one; and His ways are not beyond approach. For He stands at the door and knocks, even as He did at the tomb as He called Lazarus to come forth.

For He overcame death, hell *and* the grave by His wholly trusting in the love of the Father.

So may *ye* in all things, in this time, come to know the manner in which ye may make His love known the better in the earth; by glorifying tears, by glorifying love, by glorifying joy. None of these are excuses, neither are they justifications in material things. It is only as ye apply that ye know that ye grow.

Ready for questions.

Q-1. Was I associated with Martha [560], the sister of Lazarus; if so, how?

A-1. Read that just given. A cousin, and—of course—closely associated after the death of Lazarus.

1924-1   M.55   1/8/31   Lazarus

. . . in that period when there were the many divisions in the land now known as Palestine, or the Promised Land, during that period when the Master walked in the land. The entity was then among those *to* whom the entity came, of Him, by Him, called again from the arms of that called death; being, then, the friend, the companion, of those who loved His name, who loved His manner, His way; hated of many peoples, the entity —yet set about to accomplish, under the various forces of the time, the period, the place, the circumstance, that which few accomplished that bore the name of those that *were* in the position of leaders of the peoples during the time. In this period the entity gained throughout the experience, in the associations, in the calls that were made upon the entity—either from those in places of power or those that were oppressed by those in power, or by those who would come and seek the entity's counsel, on account of the position even occupied by the entity. Over *this* entity, and the circumstances, did even He that walked in Galilee weep. Lazarus, then, was the entity, the brother to those whom the Lord loved. In his home, in the table, at the various functions, did the entity find the associations that have brought in the present experience those counsels, where —in places of high estate, in places of low degree, in the various sects, in the various conditions in individuals' lives—the entity has touched that which has made a change. Some are repelled; some are drawn to—yet that light, that love, as shed through that experience, brings to the entity those abilities to lay aside much that would beset many in various experiences and *give* them an understanding that is above *every* name; the abilities to heal in the hands, in the mind, in the activities—whether from within or without—is the entity blessed! *Keep* that committed unto thee, knowing He that called is able to keep that thou mayest commit unto Him against any experience that may come into the affairs of an individual, whether as individuals, groups, classes or masses. He is the way. He is the intercessor through which all approach the throne, whether of grace, of power, of love, of understanding, and *through* Him that may be accomplished that may *not* be accomplished through any other name.

1158-14   F.47   11/28/37
Q-5. If I believe that God within is capable of meeting my every need, how can I justify my going to an osteopath for treatments?
A-5. How did Jesus, the Son, the Christ, justify Himself in telling the man that was healed from leprosy to "Go, show thyself to the priest and offer the sacrifice as commanded by Moses"? [6]

Did the man remain healed because of the act or because God spoke and was sufficient?

Now: When Lazarus was dead, yea when Jairus' daughter lay dead, He spoke and they were aroused. Yet He took *her* by the hand and commanded that food and drink be given.[7]

For in the material world, material responses must apply to the material being.

To Lazarus we find He called, "Come forth!" yet he was not able to unbind himself.

560-1   F.45   9/30/31   Martha
The entity among those that were close *to* the Master, being then the sister to one of those that the Master raised from the dead, [Lazarus], living in Bethany in that experience. Hence those of that period are near and dear, and far *from* those things that hinder from *knowing* of those that would separate the entity from those experiences! Gaining, sure, through the experience, and giving much to many; though called by those that in the experience would bring censure for the parts chosen [as Martha], or those of the secular things of life, yet in the present—with the experience—brings that *practicability* of the entity, that in groups, in associations, has ever been called —while the dreamer, yet all *practical* thought must be in accord *with* the life lived, with the circumstances as surround, with the conditions in which people find themselves— *these* are the better part, as was in that experience. . .

Q-4. What was the name in Bethany?
A-4. The one, the sister to Mary — Martha.

2791-1   F.33   7/29/42   Ruth

The entity was very young through those periods when there was the last week of the Master's activity in and about Jerusalem; though the entity was among those close to that family in Bethany.

The entity knew the Master, the entity was blessed by Him; the entity was acquainted with those activities when Lazarus was called forth. The entity was acquainted with that activity when the great feast was made for Lazarus and the Master with His disciples [8]...

The entity in the experience was known as Ruth, and was of the associates and co-workers with Lazarus, Mary and Martha, in Bethany.

1179-2   F.7   7/28/36   Susane

... the entity was in the Palestine land, during that period when the Master walked in the earth, during those periods when there were great understandings and great turmoils about those especially of the city of Bethany when Lazarus was raised from the grave; when those of the followers, those of the sisters — Martha, Mary — made preparation for the supper, after the resurrection or the bringing to life of the brother.

The entity then as a neighbor child, and as a child of Cleopas, in the name Susane, saw those activities, saw also the fears created by those in authority who questioned the child and the parents and those about the feast.

Also the entity heard the words of the Teacher, the Master; and these especially then as indicated come to mean a great deal to the entity. Also if the entity is questioned, if there is given to the entity the experiences of the childhood of those nigh unto Him, it will be able to depict in its own, not imagination but in its own, experience by turning into the mirror of life and seeing those forces, those experiences that were had by them. As an experience, ask "What do you suppose was served at that supper?" and find *how* many things that are not known in the men of today will be recalled by the entity!

In those things then keep the balance for the entity, that they do not become as mysteries, as strange tales, but rather as the *living* Christ, as the living example for men and women. As a neighbor, as a brother, as a savior, show Him to *this* entity— in that light.

1179-7   F.12   11/24/40   Susane

[*Suggestion:*] *You will have before you the life existence in the earth plane of [1179] . . . as Susane, child of Cleopas . . .*

Yea—yea—Cleopas—one who walked on the road to Emmaus.[9]

We are given here the records of that entity now known as [1179]—as Susane.

In giving the biographical sketch . . . It is well that something be understood of the history or the background of the entity's environs or surroundings.

In the period there had been those appointed from Rome as collectors of the various forms of tax as imposed upon and collected from the people.

Cleopas was among those that were of the faith of the peoples at that time, as had been Matthew.[10]

Hence it was in that environ or that shadow, as may be termed, of one professing a faith in the teachings of the Scribes and Pharisees, yet *collecting* the tribute for a power over the peoples.

This brought condemnation to many of the household, then, from those who adhered more to the orthodox manner of living or activity. Yet the entity, Susane, was one that grew up during that period of the early life of the Master in the earth; acquainted with those of the household of Joseph and Mary. For, the entity was of the city of Capernaum at that time.

As to comparative ages, the entity then was near the age of the sister of the Master; and there were the close acquaintanceships and friendships, though there were the varied degrees of associations, owing to those questions as arose in the various groups that were of the synagogue activities. There were the close companionships, though, until there were the separations owing to the varied manners of education of the two.

Hence the entity knew a great deal about the happenings in that household. The acquaintanceship with Jude and James was also a part of the entity's experience; though the entity, more than most of the holy women—as they were eventually called years afterward—followed the teachings of the Master under the varied circumstances; being in the areas about Bethsaida in that period of the expression manifested when there was the feeding of the five thousand, and when there were the rebukings of the peoples that were especially about Judas at that time.

In the beginning the entity Susane rather favored the manner in which those groups about Judas sought to proclaim Jesus as the deliverer of the peoples from that bondage, that taxation.

This brought to the entity condemnation from her own groups of people. Then with those changes as came about by the shifting of the ministry of the Master to the area closer about Jerusalem, the entity joined with those activities at Bethany.

Thus the entity in the latter portion of His ministry was near to, and present at, those demonstrations of His power over death. And those activities of the entity with Mary, Martha, and the closer associations that later came with the mother of the Master, after the crucifixion and resurrection, brought the periods of the greater development.

For, after the Pentecost, when there were the establishings of the ministerings to the needs of the peoples far and near, the entity sought, felt, realized the real purposes in those tenets, those expressions of the Master through His periods of ministry in the earth.

Through the days of the teachings of those who followed Stephen, Philip, Barnabas, Paul—all of these were a portion of the entity's relationships.

The activities of the entity were the more constant in the ministry to the physical, the mental and spiritual needs of those throughout her sojourn in the land during those periods following the crucifixion, those periods of the construction and the applications of the early church.

The entity was not one that would in this day or period be termed a nun, but one ministering firsthand as nurse, as one working with the hands, as one giving counsel, as well as collecting and distributing from the sources of activities through that experience.

When there were the persecutions, and the dispersing of those who had gathered in Jerusalem, the entity was among those in the church in Laodicea, and under the association with Lucius, Mark, Luke, Paul. There the entity remained to be established as one of the first of the deaconesses of that church. There the entity remained throughout the period of its earthly experience, giving a great deal of self in the carrying on of the activities and the establishing of the ministry of the Holy One.

Throughout the period the entity gained, save in that period when there was the desire for material gains from the persecutions of the political natures. For, as indicated, with the full concept of the purposes, the hopes, the desires, the wishes—as it were—to be expressed by Him—who is the way, the truth, the light—the life was given as a minister to the needs of those who sought to know the truth that maketh men free indeed, though they may be under the shadow of a service to a higher power materially.

Much of those activities in the entity's service were through the ministering to those who were without the faith.

Thus in the present the entity's application may be in a ministering as a nurse, as one who by its own life may give itself and so live that others may take hope, may find the way, may enjoin others to a greater search for that attuning of the self with the creative forces as manifested in Him.

Ready for questions.

Q-1. Can you tell any conversation Jesus had with this child?
A-1. In those periods especially at the sea, when there was the feeding of the five thousand,[11] there was something of the rebuke; when the entity was reminded of its association in the household of the Master and the purposes for which His entrance into the world had been—as He gave, not for self, not for material gain, but that *all* should know the truth that would

make *all* men free under *every* circumstance in a material plane.

Q-6. Did the entity know in the Palestine experience her present father, [1151]?

A-6. Yes; for he was a companion of the entity's father then, on the walk to Emmaus.¹²

Q-9. What was the relationship in that period with the present mother, [1158]?

A-9. As indicated, oft in the household, acquainted with, and separated only when that period came for the education. For, it is not as so oft considered, that the family of the Master lacked material opportunities. For, from many sources there had come the opportunities for those in the household of the Master to have the greater training. For, that entity who is now the mother was educated not only in the best of the land but in other lands; and yet brought together with the companions of the entity in that experience.

Q-10. What was the experience, the thoughts of the entity when she witnessed the raising of Lazarus?

A-10. The thought that inspires each soul to determine within self to give itself in service to that ideal, that principle in Him.

Q-12. Did she have any other close contacts with Jesus?

A-12. As indicated, these were not only in the period when she was close with those in the household but also as she ministered; for she followed closely with these. Oft was she in the presence of and among the throngs that heard His ministry and His teachings to the peoples along the way.

2519-8   F.44   6/26/41   Juana

. . . the entity was in the Promised Land, when there were those activities which brought about the hope to the world; during those periods when the Master walked in the earth.

In the early portion of that experience the entity rejected those counsels for rather the activity of the old Mosaic expressions. Yet later, with the experiences about that home wherein there were the expressions of His ability to roll back death, even to defy same and to give to others a greater hope, the entity was that one who eventually aided Martha in the preparation of the feast of thanksgiving to those peoples from Jerusalem, as well as Bethany, when the supper was given to Lazarus.[13]

The entity, then, knew of the expressions of both the believers and those who questioned, and those who followed close with the interpretation of such experiences in the lives of individuals.

The entity was among those who on that first Lord's day went to view the place of the skull, who saw and heard the expressions from that individual who had first beheld the risen Lord [14] . . .

The name then was Juana.

3656-1   M.34   2/1/44   Thardal

There the entity was among those who carried messages back and forth to the various groups that were seeking to persecute the Master, as well as being in closer touch with those groups that were the closer in accord with the entity's activities and with the Master's activity.

Then the entity was among those who were personal friends to Lazarus, whom the Master raised from the dead. The entity then was inconsistent, until the experience of seeing his friend again return to his place in relationships not only with the family but with the friends roundabout.

The entity was among those who started the first stories as to the experiences of Lazarus during the four days in the tomb. But with the teachings that arose after the Master's resurrection, there came changes in the experience of the entity. . .

The name then was Thardal.

1775-1   F.18 days   12/31/38   "daughter of Zelot"

. . . among those children that were blessed by Him, especially when He taught His disciples humility—on the last journey to Jerusalem.

In and about Bethany—Martha, Mary, Lazarus, and those of that city—these were the acquaintances and the kinspeople of the entity during that sojourn.

Young in years, to be sure, through those early experiences;

yet a zealot, and one given to good works throughout that sojourn.

During the experience the entity was a weaver of cloth . . .

A knowledge then of all those surroundings; being a daughter of Zelot—Zelot being a nephew of Nicodemus, the one who went to the Master by night.

Hence, with the influence in the activities of the rulers during the experience, the entity was acquainted with the activities in the synagogue and the teachings.

1556-2   F.58   6/22/38   Elois

. . . the entity was in the land now called the Palestine land.

There we find the entity was quite young during that age when the Master walked in the earth. And during those activities that followed same, the entity then knew much of the various tenets as were proclaimed; the turmoils that arose in the mind and the experience of many.

For being nigh unto the place called Bethany, the entity was acquainted with many of those who were as figures in the activities that became a part of the experience.

Hence we find in the present there often comes to the entity a harkening to those tenets and teachings, yea and even the voices that come from those things which the entity experienced—as Elois.

In the experience the entity gained, the entity lost, the entity gained. Persecutions, hardships were a portion of the entity's experience. Yet with the spreading of the teachings and those things that came from the activities of the many, there came to the entity a satisfaction and a contentment in those periods of activity.

The entity then was blessed with the many children, that became a part of the activities to carry on with those teachings as were presented.

2466-1   F.63   10/29/31   Thessi

. . . during that period or experience when the Master walked in the land, in the flesh, and about that home the entity came to know *of* the service rendered; for the entity being a friend—or a neighbor—of the little house in Bethany, the entity knew much of that love shown in the experience to those peoples, wherever the *Master* walked. In the name Thessi . . .

307-1   F.51   7/18/29   Elois

The entity then among the friends of those that lived near Bethany, and *waited* with those upon the Master during that period. In the name Elois. The entity gained much through this experience, suffered much for the good given others in understanding, bore much of the troubles and sorrows of those about the cross when sorrowing was among the Master's friends . . .

966-1   F.35   7/31/35   Joda

The entity then was among those who were the associates and in the company of those to whom the Master went oft, as the rest place in Bethany.

Then in the name Joda, the entity gained much; for the entity came close to the understanding of Him as He taught, "Ye must love one another," and "Inasmuch as ye give of thyself, of thine abilities in making for harmonious influences in the experiences of others, ye establish within thyself thy *own* relationships to thy Maker."

Remember oft, as He taught thee, thou may see thy Redeemer face to face, if ye will but act in that way and manner in which He may ever be a guest in thine heart, thine surroundings, thine activities. For as by spirit, as by manner, as by truth, as by life He is the essence of these indeed, so may ye in thine expression and experience in thine ministry to others bring that to bear in thine *own* life that thou may walk with Him, thou may see Him face to face. For thy Redeemer liveth.

2787-1   F.49   7/25/42   Sobol

. . . the entity was in the Promised Land, during those periods when the Master walked in the earth; when there were those experiences in the city of Bethany.

The entity was among those of the acquaintances, though acted in the capacity as a hired mourner at the death and burial of Lazarus.

There the entity became acquainted with those two vital forces of such different natures—Mary and Martha, and Lazarus. Most of all the entity knew Jesus, and reminded even John that He wept as He spoke to Martha respecting the resurrection.

The entity witnessed the resurrection of Lazarus, the calling forth from the tomb, and was present and an aid at the great feast given to the friends and to Jesus and His disciples.

And from that day forth the entity was among those called the holy women; becoming only acquainted with the mother of Jesus after the day of the crucifixion, when there had been that injunction, "Behold thy son. Behold thy mother." [15]

These brought those experiences in the innate forces of this entity, so that mother and son—even the expression—brings a vibration to the entity not felt by many; brings a welling up of emotion as experienced only by those whose names are written in the book of life, or—as He called—in heaven . . .

The name then was Sobol.

3179-1   F.53   8/26/43   Ruhel

. . . during the period when the Master walked in the earth, the entity was a hired mourner. At those periods when Lazarus was raised from the tomb the entity came in contact with and knew the presence of the Master Himself.

Thus is the gift of the entity in preparation of the home; not so much of self as for others, in making a home for those on special missions in their experience in the earth.

The name then was Ruhel. The entity became acquainted with the holy women, during those periods preceding and following the crucifixion, when the entity was drawn closer to the mother of Zebedee's children and the other Mary.

5148-2   F.55   5/29/44   Jeauor

. . . the entity was in those periods when there were those building-ups and tearing-downs, just after the crucifixion of the Son of man, the Savior.

In those periods when there were those hired mourners, at that period when the brother of Mary and Martha had been raised, the entity heard and saw the throngs, the questions, the unusual activities, but was not touched until such had been the activity in the life, the experience of the Master Himself, not four days but after three days coming forth Himself from the tomb.[16]

These brought to the entity the desire to depict, to picture, to tell the story of what the entity had seen and something of what it had meant when she had heard Lazarus come forth. It carries with same a power that names imply, a power within themselves. These the entity did very well in keeping records then for those who became the ministers, those who became the teachers throughout the length and breadth of the land, though the entity itself was not wholly of the faith of the Jews. For the entity had spent much of its time in Samaria, but was of those known as the Essenes.

The name then was Jeauor.

2398-2   M.42   11/27/40   Agnosta

. . . the entity was in the land of the present nativity, during the early periods following the persecutions of those who had accepted the teachings of a Man—in the Holy Land.

The entity was in Thyatira, Thracia and portions of Greece, as an instructor in the schools for the molding in clay, and those activities as were a portion of those people's activity. Yet the entity attempted to first make or draw upon the walls of the meeting places of some of those groups the activities of that Teacher.

Hence the first one drawn was the raising of Lazarus. We find that still portions of this as drawn by the entity may be seen in the old Antioch church, in Silicia. It would be well for the entity one day to seek to see that, its first attempt to draw upon a flat surface.

There the entity gained throughout, for it gave to mankind a new concept of manners of expressing that not in words, not in forms, other than as might be interpreted in the mind and the experience of the beholder.

The name then was Agnosta.

2624-1   F.41   11/26/41   Susanna

. . . the entity was in the Promised Land, during those periods when the Master walked in the earth, during those activities in which many came to know Him in His personal activity.

For, the entity then was closely associated and identified with

Martha, in the city of Bethany. There the entity was as a helper, as a sister—not in the flesh, but in activity. Thus, through those conditions that arose from the associations, when this became a place for His footsteps, the entity was acquainted with Him. And there the entity learned *patience.* There the entity learned the manner in which the spirit of truth, as expressed in the seeds of virtue, of understanding, of acquaintanceship with brotherly love and kindness, may bring into the experience of others those things that make for harmony in the life.

When there were those periods of mourning for the death of the brother of Martha, the entity was among those that mourned.

When there were those preparations for the entertaining, after the resurrection of Lazarus, the entity aided there. And indeed in such preparations, few may be found who may equal the abilities, the virtues of the entity in those directions!

And remember, as He gave, "He that would be the greatest among you will minister to all." These are basic truths, then. Apply them in thy life.

The name then was Susanna, and the entity was among those of the holy women when there were the days of persecution. And there may be read much of the activities of the entity during those periods of trial.

3954-1   F.71   11/5/43   Martia

. . . the entity was in the earth when the Master walked in the land, among those that were of the holy women. In the beginning the entity was among that group of hired mourners at the passing of Lazarus. Becoming acquainted with the Master there, having the closer association with Mary, Martha, Lazarus, John, James, the other Mary, and Mary the mother after the crucifixion, brought the entity close to those activities that made the entity ever as one to whom many came for counsel. Many rely upon just being in the presence of the entity, that they might gain something from those activities, those words that the entity gives expression to. Yet the entity is active in many realms of activities, as it was in that experience—in the name Martia.

1747-3   F.34   7/13/39   Martha

. . . the entity was then born in that period when the earth trembled from the very happening upon Golgotha.

Hence those experiences of the entity as Martha, of the household of those who were akin to Martha and Mary and Lazarus, and those akin to the mother of John the Baptist as well as of other disciples.

Hence in that environment of awe the entity grew, and became the more fearful with those periods when in the younger years the persecutions arose and the cousin James was beheaded.[17]

5749-16   9/10/41

Just as experienced by those who stood about the grave of him, the brother of those whom the Lord loved—when He spoke, death itself gave up that it had claimed, even though the sister had warned that there had not been the embalming as had been the purposes of many. Instantly the activity brought life. For He *is* life. He *is* health, He *is* beauty, He *is*—not was, not will be, but *is!* For He having overcome death, hell and the grave, He is justified before God in giving to him who believes, who is in accord; that "If ye ask in my name, believing," doing, being that ye ask for, that shall be done unto thee.

Yet with the breaking of the bonds of death, the breaking of the material bonds—the binding about the head—must needs be done by others.[18]

There is ever, then—in thy material associations, in thy seeking for help, love, health, understanding for thy brother—*something,* some effort on their part as well as *thine.* But "Where two or three are gathered together in my name, there will I be in the midst of them."

These are the influences that all must realize, if they would understand, if they would comprehend, if they would contemplate, if they would seek—that ye cannot give that which ye do not possess. If ye have that love in the Christ, in the giving ye have the more; even as He demonstrated in the giving of life that ye might have life more abundantly, that there might be a closer walk with Him. And as ye walk, ye talk with Him, He talks with thee.

"Be not afraid, it is I." Has this come to thee? Has it not oft been thy experience and ye, in thy doubt, in thy fear of being in His presence, have turned away? "Inasmuch as ye do it unto the least of thy brethren ye do it unto me." This is for each of you. This is thy Lord, as He would approach thee, that ye in thy grace, in thy love, thy mercy as thou showest to thy brother, may find that love in Him.

The Rich Young Ruler

2677-1   M.21   1/27/42   Nicholas

. . . the entity was in that land when the Master walked in the earth.

. . . the entity was among those—yea, that one about whom much speculation has been in the minds of many, over what is written there in the records, concerning which many a verbose orator has proclaimed much about which he knew so little. For, the entity was the rich young ruler who declared, "These have I kept from my youth up. What lack I yet?" "Sell that thou hast, come and follow me." "And he went away sorrowing." [1]

But remember another line, "The Master loved the young man."

He whom the Master has favored, in mind or in purpose, may count his soul indeed fortunate. Remember one of those eternal laws, "He hath not willed that any soul should perish."

The entity then was in the name Nicholas, and the entity did just that—he came, later, and followed. Who prompted Nicodemus to seek the Lord? Who prompted those that cared for the body when it was placed in a new tomb yet unused?

These are the sources of that which is the greater virtue of the entity in the present—tolerance. This is the basis for patience, and in patience—my son—even as He gave, ye become aware of thy soul and its relationships to the purposes of infinity with the finite, and the ways of man seeking—seeking oft his own undoing, through the gratifying of the flesh and the glory of the own ego! . . .

In thy understandings, hold fast to that as ye gained through that experience. For, the entity then was a student of the law, which meant a student of the unwritten as well as that interpreted from the penal, the spiritual and the marital code. And these will be portions of thy experience in this sojourn.

1416-1   M.34   7/27/37   Jason

... the entity during that period when the Master walked in the earth.

And here we may find that question answered which has oft been asked by many in the last half century, "Who was—and what became of—the rich young ruler that came and asked 'How may I have eternal life?'" [2]

That was this entity. Hence the reason why again in the present experience the worldly goods are a portion of the entity's activities; and the abilities to distribute same as a helpful influence in the experiences of others are still a portion of the entity's activity.

Much might be said as to that period of sojourn, and as to the helpful forces that came into the lives and experiences of many owing to the activities of that entity, who would be termed in the present as Jason—if the interpretation were given of the experience or name in the sojourn.

The associations with those in authority, politically, then, as the activities of the persecutions of a local nature, and those activities of the entity in inducing the Roman authorities to become a part of that deciding factor in the experiences of the earthly sojourn of many, were a part of that whole experience.

But blessed indeed is the entity to whom or about whom it was said, "As the Master looked on him, He loved him."

Then the more necessity, the more reason, the more abilities for experiences in *any* sojourn may the entity find in making the material application of those things *He* gave: "Love the Lord with all thy heart, thy mind and thy body; thy neighbor as thyself." This is the whole law. This the entity has oft found in the experience brings the greatest of satisfaction, the greatest joy and happiness; making the opportunity for others to know *hope,* to know that there *is* Life and that there *are* those who really care, in the material as well as in the spiritual experiences of others...

Hold fast to that thou hast heard—"These have I kept from

my youth up"—but "Give that thou hast"—not all of thy worldly goods, but that thou hast attained, by bringing hope and help in the experiences of those who have lost their perspective, who have lost their way.

Blind Bartimaeus Is Healed

2124-3   M.54   10/2/31   Bartimaeus
. . . during that period when the Master walked in the earth. The entity then among those who came in close contact to that entity, and *receiving*—in the flesh—the benefits as were had by the acts of the Master. So is there builded in the warp and woof of the entity's being that of the desire to lift up, to aid, to succor, those in distress; yet mindful that those so aided are not those of spongers upon the good graces of those that would aid; being in the name then of Bartimaeus, as walked by the way [1]; being strong in body, yet lacking—through the activities of those with whom the body-entity then associated—in sight; being a worker then in those things as pertained to the metals, being a power to strengthen those that were weak. So may the entity in *this* experience bring that of the peace, of the understanding, of aid *to* those *who* would—*as* the entity sought—in *His* name bring the awakening of the inner man, to the abilities of that contact as may be made by the calling *on* His name. Also there is seen in the present experience, from that sojourn, the desire of the associations of those that have made for their heritage an association or study of *all* sources of knowledge as pertains to the mysteries of life, whether pertaining to the spiritual, the mental, or the material life . . .

688-2   F.61   10/17/34   Cleopas
. . . the entity was in those days when the Master of men walked in the earth, during those days of toil and strife among those that came under the messages that were given to the common peoples—yea, those that sought in His name.

The entity then was the mother of Bartimaeus, the blind that was healed even as a *strong* man; yet the entity in its seeking, in its faith, held to the tenets of the law of the land and of the period, in the name then Cleopas.

In the experience the entity gained and lost, and gained; for it was through the turmoils of the persecution that followed in those days when those in the earth that heard His words were made *strong* in determinations in the mind, in the bodies—yea, those who sought much during those periods to give of themselves in that service for a cause that reached into and awakened all those promises that have been set from the beginning, "I will meet thee in thine own activities toward thy fellow man." For with this judgment ye shall judge one another; not condemning any, for thine own self would condemn thee. Dost thou make for self's own aggrandizement through those relationships in this or that with thine fellow man, thou hast thine own reward—and so must meet that thou sowest. Thou must meet every word thou hast uttered in thine experience. Only in Him may the cleansing come; for, as He has given, "I go to prepare the place, that where I am there ye may be also." *These* words in those days meant much to the entity; brought to the entity the ability to suffer in body that the soul might be made alive in Him.[2] Do, my child, the same today; for His name is above *every* name, for through that name thou may approach the throne of grace itself in thy brethren, in thine brother, in thine neighbor, in thine *self*, in thine God thou dost worship.

688-4   F.61   5/5/36   Cleopas

Q-7. What was the association between us as Silas [707] and the mother of Bartimaeus [688], at the time of Christ?

A-7. These, as we find, as might be put in the common term: The mother of Bartimaeus was much older than Silas, see? and as one that cared for him.

As the mother makes for the necessary influences by making of self nothing that the young may grow, so did the mother of Bartimaeus make for those experiences in counseling, in advising. And yet as the power rose within the expressions of Silas, the gentleness, the kindness that was poured back into the mother heart made for *glory* to *God* for His love to the children of men. See?

As they each then found that within themselves which expressed the glory of the Father, so apply self in the present. For the lesson of the Teacher, the Christ, the Master is to look within *self;* "for of myself I can do *nothing,"* but it is the God that worketh within thee!

So did they find in all experiences that if credit is taken here, or if it is sought that others thank thee or bless thee or praise thee for the efforts that ye put forth, then ye are seeking *self-glory;* the ego of self is seeking expression!

In the application in the present, then, mind not high things; condescend rather to things of low estate. Humble thyself as one to another, as ye did through those experiences, and so manifest in Him—how that the King even of kings suffered with those that would betray even His fellow man.

So in these applications, hold fast to that love that He gave, and ye will find peace and harmony, much strength and much power that is gained only in *humbling* of self and self's own emotions, self's own self!

5277-1   F.65   7/1/44   Esthen

... the entity was in the Holy Land when the Master walked in the earth, and the entity was among those of the household of Bartimaeus when he was healed of his blindness by the Master.

The entity was a helper, but a resenter of those who would question the experiences that came to the entity through the administrations of Bartimaeus, of which little is told, and yet how great were the influences of his activities through those periods of development.

The entity was not always a spiritual helper, but ever a material helper through that experience, in the name then Esthen.

In the experience the entity, before the passing, gained the ability to heal; and in the present may apply, if self is put entirely aside, vibrations from even the hands, or magnetic forces, if they are used for good . . .

Q-4. Explain the phenomenon of the wildly beautiful face upon which is written recklessness, sorrow, pain and despair, which often fades in upon the canvas of my inner vision.

A-4. The experiences as in the companionship of one healed by the Master, should answer itself. Ye used it not too wisely. Don't make the same mistake again. No condemnation for the fact that ye are aware of yourself, and a student of the life that may set thee free indeed should make thee conscious that the Lord hath need of thee.

324-5   F.3   9/5/34   Eloin

. . . the entity was in that land now known as the Promised Land, or Palestine, during the periods when the Master walked in the earth, and when there were those relationships with the rulers and those that were in power of the *Jewish* peoples—or the Herods.

The entity then was among those of the household of Herod Antipas that made for such destructive influences in the minds of many as respecting those relationships with the activities of the Master. Yet when there had been those activities in which Eloin (the entity's name then) saw in person the healing of Bartimaeus and then the healing of the son of the Roman governor, the entity joined rather (with those that were of the royalty) with those people that aided in the distribution of the activities and in helping those people that made for the activities in many directions. While these activities were what would be called "under cover" in the period, the heart, the soul, the desire of the entity made for a period of contentment and peace, yet without turmoils and strife.

Zaccheus Entertains the Master

3377-1   F.46   11/23/43   Cerecea

The entity was among those of Laodicea that came to know of those activities in the periods of the Master's ministrations through the utmost portions of the country. The entity came in contact with those teachings at Jericho, and when there were those great throngs in the streets when Zaccheus was called from the tree, the entity was among those that ministered at that feast made by Zaccheus for the Master and His disciples.[1]

Thus groups of certain kinds have meant much to the entity, and especially when there is the breaking of bread, or where there are those that would speak and counsel together at such periods of activity.

The name then was Cerecea. The entity gained. For all those

activities throughout the periods were in relationships with the varied churches that were established later. Yet the entity did more in the personal labors and work.

307-4   F.54   10/19/32

... *but* remember—Zaccheus climbed higher that he might have the broader vision, and that day dined with Truth ...

254-54   3/4/31

As developments come through the channels that have been outlined for organization of, furtherance of the principles, policies, and efforts of a group, there will of necessity be many varied characters to deal with. Lose not thy patience because anxiousness is sought by many who do not wholly understand. Remember the enthusiasm of Zaccheus, and that day the Lord supped with him. Be not impatient with those who *become* anxious, and as conditions, circumstances progress, *ask* and ye *shall* receive ...

The Triumphal Entry

5749-10   4/5/39

Mrs. Cayce: You will have before you members of the Glad Helpers, and others, present in this room, desirous of a discourse to be given by the Master Jesus the Christ, Himself, on His last week, from the triumphal entry into Jerusalem and including the resurrection morn ...

Mr. Cayce: Yes, we have the members present here, and their desire.

This may be given by an observer of that period, in the present.

In considering that which materially passed through the minds of the followers of the Master, Jesus, and those experiences leading to the way of the cross: The decisive point in Peraea [Berea?] was the more trying even than the trial; and then those periods of taking leave after the establishing of the emblems as His body and blood, as a ritual for those who would honor and bring to remembrance those experiences through which each soul passes in putting on the whole armor of the Christ.

In those days preceding the entry into Jerusalem, we find those periods of much disturbance among the disciples who were of Galilee and those who were of the Judean ministry. These were in disputations as to what was to take place when He, Jesus, was to go to Jerusalem.[1]

Yet He chose to go, entering through the period of rest at Bethany with Mary, Martha, Lazarus; and *there* the triumphal entry and the message that was given to those throngs gathered there.

The next period we find in the upper chamber with the disciples, and the humbleness that was manifested.

Though He was their leader, their prophet, their Lord, their Master, He signified—through the humbleness of the act—the attitude to which each would come if he would know that true relationship with his God, his fellow man.

Those periods in the garden—these become that in which the great trial is shown, and the seeming indifference and the feeling of the loss of one in whom trust and hope had been given; and the fulfilling of all that had been in the purpose and the desire in the entrance into the world.

The trial—this was not with the pangs of pain as so oft indicated, but rather glorying in the opportunity of taking upon self that which would *right* man's relationship to the Father— in that man, through his free will, had brought sin into the activities of the children of God. Here *His Son* was bringing redemption through the shedding of blood that they might be free.

Here the law of love, of causation, of mercy, of justice, of all that makes for self becoming in the at-onement relationship, of filling the purposes for which one is called in materiality, becomes the activity of Him that is free indeed.

Thus in the hour of sacrifice, material, mental and spiritual relationships are attained and considered in His every word.

In those periods of transition from "It is finished," comes that which is to each heart the determination that it, too, may know the blessed hope that comes in seeing, knowing, experiencing the cross in the heart, the body, the mind.

The period of resurrection—here we find that in which ye *all* may glory. For without the fact of His overcoming death, the whole of the experience would have been as naught.

Then may ye as seekers of the way, may ye that have come seeking to know, to experience, to *feel* that presence of the Christ Consciousness within thine own breast, within thine own experience, *open* the door of thy heart!

For He stands ready to enter, to those who will bid Him enter.

He comes not unbidden, but as ye seek ye find; as ye knock it is opened. As ye live the life is the awareness of His closeness, of His presence, thine.

Then, again as He gave, "Love ye one another," thus fulfilling *all* that is in the purpose of His entrance into materiality; to replace hate and jealousy and those things that make one afraid, with love and hope and joy.

So be ye then as His children—those that show joy and gladness in the lives, the experiences, the hearts, the minds of those ye meet day by day; thus becoming indeed brethren with Him, in that He gave Himself as a ransom for all, that whosoever will may take *their* cross and *through* Him know the joy of entering into that realm of replacing jealousy and hate and selfishness with love and with joy and with gladness.

Be ye glad. Be ye joyous when those things come to be thy lot that should or would disturb the material-minded. Like Him, look up, lift up thy heart, thy mind unto the Giver of all good and perfect gifts; and cry aloud even as He, "My God, my God! Be Thou near unto me!"

In this, as ye raise then thy voice to Him, ye may be sure He will answer, "Here am I—be not afraid. For as the Father hath sent me, so come I into thy heart and life to bring gladness, that there may be life more abundant in thy experience."

Then, be ye *glad* in Him.

Ready for questions.

Q-1. Please explain John 19:34, "—forthwith came out blood and water."

A-1. The fulfilling of "Without the shedding of blood there is no remission of sins." Hence His blood was shed as the sacrifice of the just for the unjust, that ye all may stand in the same light with the Father.

Q-2. What changes had to take place in the physical body of Jesus to become a glorified spiritual body?

A-2. The passing of the material life into the spiritual life brought the *glorified* body; thus enabling the *perfect* body to be materialized in material life—a *glorified* body made perfect!

Q-3. What was the form that seemed to be made up of light, that appeared [to me, 993] in the room at the close of the meditation preceding this reading, and the meaning of same?

A-3. The attuning of self to the high vibrations of love and life and joy—and is but that which heals and keeps peace among men.

Q-4. Please explain: "He breathed on them, and saith unto them, Receive ye the Holy Ghost."

A-4. That change of doubt and fear which arose in the minds and hearts of those gathered in that room. For the fear of the interpreting of the phenomenon being experienced, He breathed. As the breath of life was breathed into the body of the man, see, so breathed He that of love and hope into the experience of those who were to become witnesses of Him in the material world.[2]

Q-5. John 21:25. Does this verse have reference to the beginning as Adam?

A-5. In the same manner of beginning, yes.

Q-6. Who were the women at the cross?

A-6. Many were there. Those of his own household, Mary Magdalene, the mother of John and James, and those who were of that whole group were among the women at the cross.[3]

Q-7. Are any of the women here (in this room) who were at the cross?

A-7. Two.

Q-8. Who is giving this discourse?

A-8. Are ye curious? Are ye serious? Look within self.

3615-1   F.53   1/2/44   Josie

. . . the entity was in the Holy Land, and the entity first came into personal contact with the Master, Jesus, on that day when there was the triumphal entry into the city.

Then in wonder the entity beheld the crowd of people, especially the little ones. For, though man would have most believe that there were great throngs, they were mostly women and children — and the entity was among the young women in that throng; then in the name Josie.

The entity also beheld from afar the cross, and beheld those visions and knew of the quaking of the earth, knew of those that arose from the tomb.

For the entity in that day became acquainted with Martha and Lazarus at Bethany, and those stories as preserved have meant, do mean much to the entity. For the entity was with that group when there came the proclamation by Peter, John and James that "the Master goeth before thee into Galilee." [4]

The entity was among the five hundred who beheld Him as He entered into glory and saw the angels, heard their announcement of the event that must one day come to pass — and will only be to those who believe, who have faith, who look for and who expect to see Him as He is.[5]

Keep that faith above all else. Let it be the prompting in the choice of thy associations, as it has been gradually builded in this experience in which you have put away doubt and fear, and have trusted in thy Lord, and in the doing right by the fellow men to bring right and peace and harmony into thine own life.

Forget not the life as Josie.

5257-1   F.12   6/13/44   Duors

... the entity was in that land when the Master walked in the earth, when there were those periods of activity in the Holy City. The entity knew the Master best on the day of triumphal entry. For it was in front of the entity's home that the ass, upon which the Master rode, was tied. Then to have been even associated with that which brought for the Son of God, the Savior of men, the hope of the world a physical comfort, a physical manifestation of kingship, of lordship, brought to the entity the opening of the light, of the light of the eyes of the Master.

Thus we find the entity one particularly interested in peoples' eyes and how they may affect or how they show the mood of an individual. These are portions of the consciousness of the entity.

The entity served with those who aided in preparations following the crucifixion. Not known with the holy women, but as a helper to the disciples and the apostles. The entity was well acquainted with Judas, Thomas and with John the Beloved. For the entity was then among those who gathered, as it were, help from the experiences of these apostles and disciples as they administered with the Master. In the name then Duors.

In the experience the entity gained, for it kept close to helpfulness to those who were in need from many of the activities, being among those who were later, by James and Peter, given charge, with Philip and Stephen, of the ministering to the needs of the visitors. And here again we find innate in the experience of this entity as to how careful it is to visitors wherever they may be, whether in home, in a party, in an activity wherever it may be, the entity looks out for others. Keep those as parts of thy consciousness, thy activity.

1301-1   F.40   12/1/36   Sylvia

. . . the entity was in the land now known as the Holy Land, or the Promised Land, during those periods when there were turmoils arising from the teachings of the Master; when there were those gatherings from all the lands nigh unto the Galilean, the Phoenician or Syrophoenician, Tyre and Sidon and all the peoples had come as *one* for the days that were counted as holy.

The entity then became acquainted, became in that position of *experiencing* that as had been told of the visit of that teacher to the land of Tyre and Sidon.[6]

Then the entity made overtures to not the holy women but rather to those who had been as companions to Him in Bethany, in Bethsaida, in Bethlehem and Capernaum, and questioned them.

Those confusions as to reports brought confusion to the entity. But when the eyes of the Master as He passed by on the road or the way to the city on that day of days were seen by the entity, when He gave that if it were not for the cry of the peoples the very hills and mountains would cry out, "Hosanna, Glory in the Highest—for the Prince of Peace comes to make those decisions whereunto man again has his closer, *closer* associations with his Maker, *then* the entity understood, *then* the entity realized that man as man may be far from God, but man as a god and acting godly may be close to the divine.[7]

And this was the lesson the entity gained. For though the turmoils and strifes arose, though the persecutions came about, and though the entity in the end was stoned for its very acceptance — it denied not.

Yet the thoughts of bodily suffering have brought in this experience the necessity of meeting same in the awakening to that fact that man as a *godly* man may be close to the divine.

Sylvia, then — the entity with Stephen was stoned. Thus we find those experiences of those words as given in that declaration by Stephen, among the first of the martyrs for a holy cause, become as ringing in the experience of the entity in those attempts to aid, " — until I see my Lord standing I fear; then I know His presence is near." [8]

In the experience the entity gained.

1456-1 F.29 10/8/37 Dienna, or Deunna

. . . the entity during that period when the Master walked in the earth, when there were the cries first — that the entity heard — of the triumphal march or entrance into the city.

For the entity was among those of the Parthians who came at that particular season for not *only* the service, not only the reckonings, but for the social and companionable activities during such feasts.

But hearing and seeing the influences that aroused the people to crying "Hosanna in the Highest — " there was aroused that which is innate in the entity in the present when there is the singing of such in unison by many; it raises as it were the vibrations along even the physical being to a worshipfulness that little else can do.

Just as the entity in its experiences in the days following heard the cries of the rabble, and the entity wondered *how* and *why* those in authority *could* override the people in such a manner.

Hence is there any wonder that disturbances have arisen and do arise in the experiences of the entity, even in the present, by the cry, "Lo, He is here — Lo, He is there"?

But rather know, as has been said by the psalmist, "Though I take the wings of the morning and fly unto the uttermost parts, He is there! Though I make my bed in hell, He is there! Though I fly unto the uttermost parts of the heavens, He is there!"

For the consciousness of His abiding presence is within, even as He gave, "The kingdom of heaven is within thee."

The entity then later was among those who came with Stephen and Philip, for the ministering and aiding to those activities that brought about the early associations in the church.

Then the entity was in the name Dienna, or Deunna.

In the experience the entity gained; and those influences that prompt the entity to seek in the religious or in the holiness of the individual activity arise from those experiences.

681-1   F.41   10/7/34   Phoebe

. . . the entity was during those periods when the Master of men walked in the earth, during the days when there were the gatherings of those from many lands when there was the procession or the triumphful entry into Jerusalem.

The entity then was among the Syrophoenician people that had heard, through the journeys into the land, of the activity of the individual or the man in that land; and came with many — and with those of the lands adjoining same — for that period when there was to be either the establishing of the material kingdom by that man, or there were to be the understandings of what those teachings were to bring into the experience of others.

Then in the name Phoebe, the entity gained through the experience in the material things. Much might be said about the entity's activities during that sojourn into the earth and those fields of activity that had to do with the teaching abilities of the entity with the young, and for the influence it had upon its associates in that period of material manifestation. Hence those things that pertain to colors, the modes of living of individuals, those things pertaining to not only the material life and its surroundings but the mental surroundings of individuals, arise from that experience of the entity in that, the Holy Land and the Syrophoenician land, and among those peoples that were the followers of same.

The Last Hours

The Betrayal

2067-7   F.53   6/25/41

Q-27. Was Judas Iscariot's idea in betraying Jesus to force Him to assert Himself as a king and bring in His kingdom then?

A-27. Rather the desire of the man to force same, and the fulfilling of that as Jesus spoke of same at the supper.[1]

137-125   M.31   11/15/29

Q-14. Is [the entity now known as 5770] Judas Iscariot?

A-14. "Judas Iscariot, betrayer of me."

Q-15. He is a fine man today.

A-15. A fine man and leans upon thee. Many have been the trials of this soul in the destruction of many places and cities. Yet, though today with much of what the world calls material bounty, he leans upon thee—yet, this soul leans on thee.

1265-2   M.62   10/5/36

Q-1. What is the explanation, for the belief held by the entity, that he was "Judas Iscariot" in a former incarnation?

A-1. As has been indicated, the entity is a "sensitive" in his present experience, and the associations during that period or sojourn were such that these influences as may be seen from that sojourn are of such a nature as to cause this "throw-back," as it were.

In the entity's activities during that experience, as a representative of those powers in order at that period, the entity came in contact with varied members of those known as the disciples of the Master. And among the closer associates, among those of the Roman forces that made for this delving into the activities of the period, were the entity *and* Judas.

The stories of Judas' experience had been told by those of a cult that was of interest, yet of a scoffing interest to the entity; that the entity, Judas, would become one that would betray his Lord, commit murder, incest and the like with those of his own household. And then to be accepted by one that others proclaimed as a teacher, a master, this was of special interest to the entity. And the entity followed the activities, the reports of Judas in such a manner that there was the *berating* of self when he, the entity, became closer associated with those of his friends in service there who had joined with those that were of the household and that were of the Master's family and kinsmen. The entity *berated* self.

Hence we find that in the experience of the entity in the present, when having been told in the present that the entity was Judas—this being the interpretation of that gained by the visions of some. Hence we find those urges, as it were, overshadow the entity at times. But as has been indicated, *never* belittle self! For know within that the Master, the Lord thy God, overlooks that thou hast done and has given, "Whosoever will may take the cup." Each soul is willing, the flesh *is* weak. The Lord hath not willed that any soul should perish for that berating of self, for any activity that may have, in the experience of an entity among its fellows, caused this or that to come to pass. Know, He hath willed that each soul should know the way, and hath prepared a way. Then look not back upon those associations, those environmental forces, nor thine own curiosity; but rather look up—to Him who may call thee that thou may know and see His face! . . .

But rather let that as may be given be that *each soul* must *know* its relationship to the Creative Forces or the Father. And in the application of same is the manner, the way, the *individual* treats or applies same to his brother—the lowliest of same!

For, as He gave, "He that is greatest among you will be the servant of all." Learn then *humbleness,* and *believe*—not only for that thou mayest experience thyself but for that as ye may see manifested in that love of thy fellow men in their activities day by day. For until each entity may see in the individual who is as his enemy, as that one he dislikes or whose ways he dislikes, such as is the image of that he would worship in the Father, he may not in deed and in truth know the way. *Learn* the lessons thou didst see portrayed, and that bear upon thine inner consciousness. For did He not commit the keeping of the worldly goods to Judas? ² Did He not give to him the power, the opportunity to meet himself?

Be willing then to meet thyself in that ye do, that ye say, day by day. For in so doing ye come to know thy relationship to thy Maker. And when ye call He will hear. And His promises are sure, "If ye will be my people, my son, I will be thy God."

The Last Supper

5749-1   6/14/32

Mr. Cayce: The Lord's Supper ¹—here with the Master—see what they had for supper—boiled fish, rice, with leeks, wine, and loaf. One of the pitchers in which it was served was broken —the handle was broken, as was the lip to same.

The whole robe of the Master was not white, but pearl gray —all combined into one—the gift of Nicodemus to the Lord.

The better looking of the twelve, of course, was Judas, while the younger was John—oval face, dark hair, smooth face— only one with the short hair. Peter, the rough and ready— always that of very short beard, rough, and not altogether clean; while Andrew's is just the opposite—very sparse, but inclined to be long more on the side and under the chin—long on the upper lip—his robe was always near gray or black, while his clouts or breeches were striped; while those of Philip and Bartholomew were red and brown.

The Master's hair is 'most red, inclined to be curly in portions, yet not feminine or weak—*strong*, with heavy piercing eyes that are blue or steel-gray.

His weight would be at least a hundred and seventy pounds. Long tapering fingers, nails well kept. Long nail, though, on the left little finger.

Merry—even in the hour of trial. Joke—even in the moment of betrayal.

The sack is empty. Judas departs.

The last is given of the wine and loaf, with which He gives the emblems that should be so dear to every follower of Him. Lays aside His robe, which is all of one piece—girds the towel about His waist, which is dressed with linen that is blue and white. Rolls back the folds, kneels first before John, James, then to Peter—who refuses.

Then the dissertation as to "He that would be the greatest would be servant of all." [2]

The basin is taken as without handle, and is made of wood. The water is from the gherkins, that are in the wide-mouth shibboleths that stand in the house of John's father, Zebedee.

And now comes "It is finished." [3]

They sing the ninety-first Psalm—"He that dwelleth in the secret place of the Most High shall abide under the shadow of the Almighty. I will say of the Lord, He is my refuge and my fortress: my God; in Him will I trust."

He is the musician as well, for He uses the harp.

They leave for the garden.

[This psychic reading given by Edgar Cayce at the end of reading 1315-3 after suggestion was given three times for him to wake up.]

2794-3   F.34   11/19/43   Elba

. . . the entity was in the land when the Master walked in the earth, when there were those activities that brought about the attending to the passover—which He kept with His disciples.

The entity was among those who aided in the preparation of that upper chamber where He spent the last supper with His beloved disciples.

It might be said that the entity was a maid or a helper in the household then of Zebedee, and very close to Mrs. Zebedee—being then a distant relative, in the name Elba.

In the experience, and especially in the even, as the entity heard those pronouncements "One among you will betray me," there was brought anger.[4] And such expressions often make the entity double its fists even in the present, when insincerity is indicated—by inference or by activity—in friendships or in purpose toward that to which the entity has given itself in any activity.

The entity will understand those periods in self, then, when there is caused—as from out of nowhere—those feelings of loneliness, of a longing to hear that voice again.

The entity aided through those periods of reconstruction, and when the church was begun on Pentecost, when the thousands were added to the groups and there were the needs for the ministering to the strangers that encompassed the city, and the needs for those that might instruct others.

Through that period the entity gained . . .

But know that thy body is indeed the temple of the living God. And He has promised to meet thee. Keep that body as the temple of God. Supply it with all the beauties as ye would a physical service to Him that ye would honor most—in thy heart, in thy body, in thy mind, in thy purpose. And let it ever be with that spirit of truth as manifested in Him, "I go unto the Father, that where I am ye may be also." It may be thine now if ye will accept it—as ye did in the upper room.

2778-2   F.30   9/15/42   Perseus

. . . the entity was in the Promised Land, when there were those periods of activity following the persecution of the followers of the Master; when there was the withdrawing of the Roman influence as to the activities related to the persecutions.

The entity then knew persecution, and want physically from same; yet caught a glimpse through those periods of that faith, that hope that brings into the present experience a *joy* in being of a service to others—from that lesson as gained then from the words He spoke at the Last Supper: "He that would be the greatest among you will be the minister, the servant; serving others." This was the entity's hold upon those experiences there.[5]

Again the entity did not grow to complete womanhood, but in the early teens passed to that activity in the spirit of guiding others through the shadows of that called death.

The name then was Perseus . . .

Q-1. What has been the past association with my mother that has brought about the antagonistic and resentful attitudes? Just how should I meet this situation for our mutual development?

A-1. In the experiences in the Promised Land ye held to thy faith, and thy mother wished then for thee to accede to the desires of thy persecutors. Ye would not. Hold *thy* attitude! For, every soul—not one for another—must give an account unto Him, in the same manner as He accounted unto His God, our God, your God.

The Trial

2934-1   F.42   3/1/43   "daughter of Caiaphas"
 . . . the entity was in the Holy City, when there were those exchanges of activities, when there were those conditions between the Roman and the Jewish rule, at the time the Master walked in the earth.

The entity then was the daughter of Caiaphas,[1] and thus the wife of the priest who first condemned the Master. These experiences, with the happenings that came later, brought fears into the experience of the entity. And the desire to have justification of the choices made brought those experiences through that sojourn that kept the entity in a state of doubt.

1251-1   M.57   8/18/36   Guldi
The entity then was among those of the soldiery that were garrisoned in Jerusalem during those periods when there were not only the trials of the disciples, as they became known, but of the Leader, the Teacher, the Master himself.[2]

Yet the entity was ever in that position as taking orders rather than giving expression of self, for home—as it has ever been and will ever be in the experience—was and is the more sacred even than the places of worship to the entity.

Hence those experiences through that sojourn brought for the entity many confusions, and many periods of turmoil within self.

Yet duty ever became the keynote not only as a true native of Rome as a soldier but as one representing rather the innate and true experience of service in a cause, an ideal.

The entity may be said to have gained, though not in those conditions or in those ways and manners in which many would consider as the activities during those periods; but rather did there come to the entity, through the associations of ideals within self as related to home and those expressions of the individuals that held to an ideal as related to the relationships to the fellow man, mental and spiritual development . . .

Then the entity was in the name Guldi.

1974-1   M.55   8/2/39   Mathias

. . . the entity was in the Roman lands when there were turmoils, when the entity was brought as one of those who would bear witness as to the activities of Pilate, during the trial of the man called Jesus.

There we find the entity was in that position of attempting to fulfill its own ideas as to the interpretation of the law, as well as the attempt to be upon the right terms with those who by force brought the entity to that activity.

Thus we find the entity was drawn between two fires—that as to whether to be true to its religion or to be true to that as *might* bring into the experience favor with those in authority.

The entity failed, yet the entity gained. For the desires—though the entity was brought into great trials—were counted as it were for the saving graces to the entity.

In the present experience we find the entity at times with a streak of religious fervor, and then—as indicated—this sours, becomes vinegar in the experience and activities or principles or associations with others.

In the business relations—again we find these becoming experiences in which the entity seeks favors, and yet rarely considering that it is the character of seed one sows that brings the result in one's experience.

Ye cannot sow selfishness and reap peace. Ye cannot sow selfishness or strife and reap that which brings harmony. Ye cannot be extravagant in thy words or thy activities and expect there to be always plenty in the activities or experiences of every nature.

Study, then, to show thyself approved, even as ye did in that experience as Mathias—to bring order out of chaos for *all.* Thus you will bring it for yourself also.

Thinkest thou that the love of the Father-God is for any individual above another? Be reminded that He is not a respecter of persons; and those who love Him keep His ways, and unto such will He be gracious.

2620-2   F.41   11/24/41   Amorela

. . . the entity was in the Holy Land, among the Roman peoples that were in high places during the sojourn of the Master in the earth.

And especially was the entity present (as has oft and may oft be a part of the present experience of the entity) during some of those periods when there were the trial, the crucifixion. And the entity joined with the holy women in those periods when He was seen again, in that period of manifestation.

The name then was Amorela, and associated with those that kept guard at the temple. There the entity, at the trial before Pilate, in the throng, saw the face of the Master. The entity heard those words, saw that tenderness with which He felt and experienced His aloneness when deserted by those who had been close to Him. The entity was spoken to by the Master when He gave, "Be not afraid, for me nor for thyself. All is *well* with thee."

Thus, when there were those reports of His resurrection, when there were the attempts of the Romans to put aside the questionings of the Jews, the entity sought to know. And these periods brought disturbance to the entity, when it wept much. And this still finds expression in its attempt for vision.

Know, then, that the healing is ever in Him, and that to Him goes the credit of the abilities as manifest through thy hands, through thy voice, through thy pronouncements. To Him the love, the honor must ever be given.

In the experience the entity gained throughout. And do not fail in the present to keep that as was the pronouncement to thee, "Be not afraid. All is well with thee." For, as He hath given, "If ye love me ye will keep my commandments, and my commandments are not grievous—only that ye love one another." These ye are manifesting. Keep them. Preserve them. Live them. Be them . . .

First, study to show thyself approved unto that ideal ye found and sought in Him, in the temple, or in the court at Pilate's condemnation period.

Hold to that as ye manifested in those experiences when ye saw Him bless those about Him, after the Resurrection.[3]

The Crucifixion

1463-2   F.58   11/8/37   Marlan

. . . the entity was in what is now known as the Promised Land, during those periods when there were the preparations for the coming of the teacher, the lowly one, yet the Great *I AM* into the experience of flesh—that man might again have an advocate with the divine that had grown so far away to the hearts of those that were lost in the toils of the day.

There the entity was among those peoples about the land of Bethany, during that period when Martha, Mary, and Lazarus, Jesus, the disciples, Peter, James, John, Andrew, Bartholomew, Philip, Thomas and the others made many pilgrimages to and from the various portions of the land.

The entity then was of those lands from which Bartholomew was drawn, was taken for his activities among the peoples.

Hence the entity was in association with Mary, the mother; with the daughter and sons of Joseph and Mary, that made for those influences which brought the beauties into the experiences of man during that sojourn.

The entity was active in the sect of the Essenes. Thus, as would be called, the entity was among the holy women—even at the days when they stood beneath the cross, the days when they waited on those who had been persecuted, stoned and beaten for a cause [1] . . .

In the experience the entity was called Sardenia [?], but the name was Marlan.

The activities of the entity made for the strength as of stone. For the entity gave much in self during the experience.

1929-1   F.41   10/4/32   Matildhen

. . . in that land or period when the Master walked in the earth, and especially about those lands when many peoples of many lands gathered at the feast when the way, the road to Jerusalem, was trod by Him. The entity then was among those who journeyed hither from the lower portion of the same land, then in the name Matildhen; being among those that came under the influence of those peoples and the experience of meeting Him in the way. In this experience the entity gained throughout; for being then of the household of those that sought to know more of the lessons given by the forerunner, the entity was among those that aided in bringing the attention of more and more individuals to these lessons that were being given. After the experience on the road, the entity then gave self in the greater service for bringing others to the knowledge and understanding of the teachings of this man of Galilee, throughout the experience in that particular portion of the sphere; being among those then that gathered with the peoples on that day when the sun was darkened and the cry went out to the world, "My Lord, my God, why hast thou forsaken me?" [2] The entity gave much in self and self's activities throughout this experience; hence the closer that the entity in *any* activity or experience draws nearer to those tenets, those truths as gained through this experience, the more will there be brought peace, harmony, joy, contentment that satisfies the inner man; the farther the entity leads from that experience the less does there come joy, harmony, peace or understanding.

333-2   M.50   5/15/33   Phlons

The entity then was among those of the soldiery of Pilate, that ruled in Judea and Jerusalem during the sojourn of the Prince of Peace in the earth.

Then the entity, coming under the influence of those surroundings, gained much in casting the lot of self with those peoples (and a whole history might be written here of the entity's presenting to Caesar the activities of Pilate at this trial, as well as those of the high priest in the condemning); for the entity, in the name Phlons, was among those who stood guard at the time of the crucifixion and *saw* the Prince of Peace die on the cross.

In the activities through this sojourn the entity, as Phlons, gained; for those peoples that later sojourned from Jerusalem to Rome were aided oft by the activities of the entity.

When in the present there has arisen those things in the authority of state as in controversy with the spiritual influences in men's lives, the entity has found a trembling within as of harking to a day when the sun was darkened and not by an eclipse alone, and when the earth shook and the temple veil was rent; for the entity *viewed* these experiences in the affairs of men. This should be written! ³

405-1   F.11   9/11/33   Marcellus
... the entity was in that land now known as the Roman, during those periods when there were the hardships brought to those peoples in the beliefs that were held by them from the teachings of those that came from the Palestine land, from meeting the soldiery that came back from the land.

The entity then was the companion of, the wife of, that soldier that stood by the cross when the Son of man was put thereon; in the name Marcellus.

Through this experience the entity gained and gained. While the positions in the social life of the entity made for associations with those of the royalty and with those that were persecuted, even that were given to the lions in that experience, the entity held self rather in that position as being able to give help both to those persecuted and strength to those whom duty demanded oft to act in the capacity of the persecutors.

518-1   F.24   2/20/34   Cleo
... the entity was in that land now known as the Roman, during those periods when there were the spreadings of the tenets from the soldiery, or through the soldiery that returned from the Palestine land during those periods when the earth was darkened and the foundations of the deep were broken up; for the Son of man, the Son of God, was suspended between earth and the sky.

In these experiences, from the lessons that were brought by word of mouth, the entity then—in the name Cleo—was the daughter of one that was sent later to fill those places, and coming with Felix and Agrippa into the land.⁴ This made for contacts that brought to the entity the understandings of how souls might gain a vision of the truths that make for life under any environ in the earth. Though the body may suffer, though the mind may be blanked, there is the remaining grace in the faith in Him that gave Himself as the ransom in the earth, despised of men yet without fault, showing forth His love in the manner of doing good among those that sought and that were of the household of faith.

The entity was among those that believed, yet with material persecution, with rebuke, with the sneers of those in power and those that were not of the faith, there was made for the *living* of an experience when the heart cried out from within for a turning to the knowledge that was known, and the feet walked in the ways of death.

This in the present experience makes for those periods when, looking upon the spiritual life, the entity becomes rather a recluse—and as to taking from the living experiences the joys and the pleasures of life; yet if there is the understanding there may be known there can be no joy, no happiness in a material plane, unless founded in truth and light as *poured* into the earth through those blessings that have come to the earth through the maker of the earth, the giver of life, the giver of hope, the giver of all that is good and perfect in a material plane. For, heaven and earth may pass away but His words pass *not* away. And He has given, "Be ye joyous in the service of the Lord." Do good to them thou may meet in the way, and especially to the household of faith. Thou art of that household. Keep thine heritage. Blot it not from thine memory. Make known; for, as He has given, "I will bring to thee remembrance of all that is necessary for thine understanding from the foundations of the earth, if ye will but keep my commandments." Love one another in Christ.

3006-1   F.63   5/17/43   Sopha

. . . the entity was in the Holy Land, when the Master walked in the earth.

There the entity was not among the holy women, as called in the periods just after the crucifixion, but rather among those groups who had authority, military authority in the land. But the entity's acquaintance with those who had been close to the Master brought the great change in the activities of the entity through that period.

The acquaintance with those activities near Jerusalem, at Bethany, and in the surrounding areas, made for a conviction that has ever—and ever will be a part of the experience of the entity; causing a deeper interest in the spiritual, the metaphysical, the occult activities, the expectancy of unusual things . . .

The entity in that experience was acquainted with Mary, Martha, the mother of the Master, "the other Mary," and those groups that saw the tomb empty.

The entity gave much of itself in those activities that brought what is not oft accredited to the proper source—the bringing of the Roman forces (of which the entity was a part, in association and in companionship during that period) to a greater interpretation of, and activity concerning, those tenets of the disciples in Rome.

For, with the recall of Pilate and the various groups about same, and about that area, the entity then returned to Rome; yet kept in close contact with not only those activities in Jerusalem but in other lands also . . .

The name then was Sopha—and the companion to the guard that was close to those activities at the time of the crucifixion, of which the entity knew much by hearsay.

2365-2   M.68   8/9/29   Romual

The entity then among those of the Roman guard who were struck by the sincerity of the *man* and of the followers of the man, as man, and *with* the breaking up of the general accepted rule on the last day, became a follower of those of the despised sect. In the name Romual, and the entity *waited* on those that bore the tree. In this experience the entity gained, and in the present the honor, the inspiring words of that as written of the Master always brings a tremble, a fear, a not wholly understanding of just why these make a trembling in the inner man.

5037-2   F.48   4/19/44   Ester

. . . the entity was in the Holy Land among those who looked on when there was the crucifying of the Master. The entity wept with those who wept, without the consciousness of why.

With the passing of days and the ministrations of the disciples on the day of Pentecost, the entity experienced the happenings that went on there.[5]

Thus the high emotional feeling of the entity in the present concerning some with whom the entity has been and has come in contact. These were associates, companions at those periods of great spiritual awakening, spiritual determinations.

Throughout that period of sojourn the entity was active in good deeds; that is, gentleness, patience, kindness, brotherly love, long-suffering. The name then was Ester.

1290-1   F.60   11/13/36   Larue

. . . the entity lived in the earth during those experiences when the Son, the Savior, walked therein.

The entity then was among those who were the mourners at Bethany when Lazarus was among those of the beloved of Him, who is life, light and immortality to the world today—ever. For He changeth not.

Then the entity came under the influence of those experiences not only of that household, of that home—Mary, Martha, but of the disciples; and then the Master.

The entity joined with those activities, and was among those who ministered not only at the burial of the Savior, Jesus, but ministered at those activities following same.[6]

Thus the experiences wherein the entity in its moments of greater distress, physically, or in those periods when the emotions arose by some influence that aroused in self the soul-experience of that when so close to the divine, has had visions that became as the help to the entity in those periods of trial, those periods of doubt, those periods of fear.

For He, as then, as in the call, casteth *out* fear—even to those that have slipped away from the consciousness of material environs.

In the application of self in that experience there came material disturbance, but the mental and spiritual gain—and those influences which if applied in the present experience may bring the greater harmony and joy in the activities of the entity in the present.

Then the name was Larue.

In the application of self to that to which it may attain in the present from those sojourns, we find—let the law of the Lord guide. For this became conscious in the activities of that experience in following those daily activities. For the entity began as a hired mourner but became as one nigh unto the ministering not only of the mental reactions of the Master but to those of the aged, to those that became fearful through the periods of strife that arose after His resurrection.

Hence thou may indeed resurrect in the minds of individuals that are *seekers, their* relationship to Creative Forces, or God, in their individual lives. And these be those experiences from which ye may gain the most.

Hence those expressions as are given in His conversation with his disciples, in portions of that recorded by the beloved of Him, may become to thee indeed as a lamp to thy feet, as a light to thy heart, as food to thy body in helping others to help themselves.

1058-1   F.23   11/15/35

Little did they of those days realize that the activities were but as He had given, "Ye will experience those days when ye shall be persecuted, and ye shall persecute in my name . . . yet I know you not." [7]

For he that would laud himself that the praise may be in His name has but lost the real purpose, the real cause. For there be only the name of Him that blessed and cursed not; that gave to those though they bruised His body, though they sought to do away with those principles. For the very activity made for the growth in the minds and the hearts and the souls of those who sought, and who do seek, to know His way. Not for self, but that the glory of the Father may be manifested through the Son in the earth.

1152-4   F.61   12/30/36

But to those who have chosen the more excellent way, ye have seen, ye have known, "As ye do it unto the least of these, my brethren, ye do it unto thy Maker."

And *again* ye have seen, when to man's estate alone upon the cross, yea into the grave, all hope seemed abandoned; yet even as the inn could not contain His birth, neither could the grave contain His body; because of *being purified,* in love, in service, in harmony to God's will. For "Not of myself," saith He, "but the Father that worketh in and through me do I bring thee health, do I bring thee hope, do I bring thee the living waters."

Did to any He ever give wealth or fame or fortune? Only in the fortunes of suffering, the fortunes of service, the fortunes of turning the other cheek—when thou art smitten by those that would despitefully use thee, that would use thee even for their own selfish purposes.

These are the fortunes that He gave, as the earth knows same —but to the heart and the soul He brought a light that faileth not, a water that is living, a home that is eternal, a bread that is *indeed* a staff of life!

For He *is* that life—that *life!*

5277-1   F.65   7/1/44

Q-7. Am I right in believing the real crucifixion of Jesus consisted in the suffering He was called upon to endure in meeting the tests involved in the initiation tactics to which He was subjected before He began His ministry?

A-7. No. The real test was in the garden when in the realization that He had met every test and yet must know the pang of death.[8]

2448-2   F.25   5/31/41

See the funny side—don't be too serious. Remember, He even made the joke as He walked to the garden to be betrayed. Remember, He looked with love upon His disciple that denied Him, even as He stood alone.

3003-1   F.61   5/16/43

For, remember—He laughed even on the way to Calvary; not as pictured so oft, but laughed even at those that tormented Him. This is what angered them most.

900-17   M.29   1/3/25

Q-2. It has also been given in these readings that Jesus lived a man and died a man. It has also been given that God so loved the world as to give His only begotten Son to act as an example, in the flesh, to man. Explain these things to us. How may we regard the truth regarding Jesus in relation to the Jewish and Christian religions, and to all the other religions of the world?

A-2. In that the man, Jesus, became the ensample of the flesh, manifest in the world, and the will one with the Father, He became the first to manifest same in the material world. Thus from man's viewpoint, becoming the only, the first, the begotten of the Father, and the ensample to the world, whether Jew, Gentile, or of any other religious forces. In this we find the true advocate with the Father, in that He, as man, manifest in the flesh the ability of flesh to make fleshly desires one with the will of the spirit, for God is spirit, and they who worship Him must worship in spirit and in truth, just as Jesus manifest in the flesh, and able to partake of the divine, for making all laws susceptible to the mandates, for the will was one with the Father, and in this we find He takes on all law, and a law unto Himself, for with the compliance, of even an earthly or material law, such a person *is* the law, and in that Jesus lived as man, and died as man, and in that became the ensample to all who *would* approach the throne of God.

As we see in all the religions of the world, we find all approaching those conditions where man may become as the law in his connection with the divine, the supreme, the oneness, of the world's manifestation. In Jesus we find the answer.

2533-8 M.39 5/3/44

Q-1. Is the transmutation of human flesh to flesh divine the real mystery of the crucifixion and resurrection? Explain this mystery.

A-1. There is no mystery to the transmutation of the body of the Christ. For having attained in the physical consciousness the at-onement with the Father-Mother-God, the completeness was such that with the disintegration of the body—as indicated in the manner in which the shroud, the robe, the napkin lay— there was then the taking of the body-physical form. This was the manner. It was not a transmutation, as of changing from one to another.

Just as indicated in the manner in which the body-physical entered the upper room with the doors closed, not by being a part of the wood through which the body passed but by forming from the ether waves that were within the room, because of a meeting prepared by faith. For as had been given, "Tarry ye in Jerusalem—in the upper chamber—until *ye* be endued with power from on high." [9]

As indicated in the spoken word to Mary in the garden, "Touch me not, for I have not yet ascended to my Father." The body (flesh) that formed that seen by the normal or carnal eye of Mary was such that it could not be handled until there had been the conscious union with the sources of all power, of all force.[10]

But afterward—when there had been the first, second, third, fourth and even the sixth meeting—He *then* said: "Put forth thy hand and touch the nail prints in my hands, in my feet. Thrust thy hand into my side and *believe*." This indicated the transformation.[11]

For as indicated when the soul departs from a body (this is not being spoken of the Christ, you see), it has all of the form of the body from which it has passed—yet it is not visible to the carnal mind unless that mind has been, and is, attuned to the infinite. Then it appears, in the infinite, as that which may be handled, with all the attributes of the physical being; with the appetites, until these have been accorded to a unit of activity with universal consciousness.

Just as it was with the Christ-body: "Children, have ye anything here to eat?" This indicated to the disciples and the apostles present that this was not transmutation but a regeneration, recreation of the atoms and cells of body that might, through desire, masticate material things—fish and honey (in the honeycomb) were given.[12]

As also indicated later, when He stood by the sea and the disciples and apostles who saw Him from the distance could not, in the early morning light, discern—but when He spoke, the voice made the impression upon the mind of the beloved disciple such that he spoke, "It is the Lord!"[13] The body had prepared fire upon the earth—fire, water, the elements that make for creation. For as the spirit is the beginning, water combined of elements is the mother of creation.

Not transmutation of flesh but creation, in the pattern indicated.

Just as when there are those various realms about the solar system in which each entity may find itself when absent from the body, it takes on in those other realms not an earthly form but a pattern — conforming to the same dimensional elements of that individual planet or space.

1504-1   F.48   12/30/37

For hope and faith are living — *living* — things! Thus hope springs anew with the growth and the knowledge and the understanding of the light on the way, and that life indeed is an eternal expression of the love of the Father; and that as it gives the expression through the individuality of each and every soul as it comes in material manifestation by the weaknesses, we find the strength in the Lord — and in the glories ever in His beauteous purpose with each soul; that purpose that ye might be the companions, one with Him.

Then indeed may there be a glimpse of the love the Father hath shown to the children of men, through the very gift of Him, thy brother, the Christ; that we may walk circumspectly one with another; and thus give, show forth, *His* activity in the earth till we be made as one with Him, in the glories that were His and that are as He has given for us. For we be joint heirs, as one with Him; not strangers, not aliens but joint heirs with the Christ to the kingdom of the Father — that is, that was, that ever shall be — even before the foundations of the earth were laid.

Hence we find to keep, to hold to those things as He gave in the beginning, "Subdue ye the earth — make ye then the laws thereof thy servants, not thy enemies" — this is saying only "Sin not; for ye that know sin and have fallen short must meet these in thyself." And only as He hath shown the way. Though He were in the world, He was not of the world; yet subject to the laws thereof, of materiality.

For His heart ached; yea His body was sore and weary; yea His body bled not only from the nail prints in His hands and feet but from the spear thrust into the heart of hearts! For the blood as of the perfect man was shed, not by reason of Himself but that there might be made an offering once for all; that then *ye* may know, ye in thine own self are not a burden to any.

For with thy mind, thy heart, ye may give much, much the more to those about thee in their ministry to thy physical weaknesses; that the very glory of Him may be manifested in their lives.

For if we do good only to those that would do good to us, what praise, what profit is there in same? For it was the unjustness of His trial, the persecutions of His body, that made the way for mankind, ye His brethren, ye thy own self, to *have* and know the way that leads to "That peace I leave with thee; not as the world knoweth peace, but my peace I give," in that:

Though ye be hindered, though ye be misunderstood, yea though ye be persecuted for those things that are not even thine own faults—how much greater is the manifestation of His glory for that which was a shortcoming in thee to be made right in ministering good unto others through the love He hath shown to thee?

1527-1   M.19   2/2/38

Thus the conditions become as a manifestation of that which was so well, so beautifully spoken of by Stephen as he pronounced—to those who would find fault with his adherence to the truth—that *Jesus,* the *man, was* the Son, *was* the Savior, *is* the manifestation of the God Consciousness in materiality! [14] Yet it must needs be that *He,* too, suffer through the trials of being buffeted, being tried by those who under the *law* (of man) were in authority but who under the spiritual law were His inferiors, His subjects; and die even the death on the cross!

649-1   F.17   9/4/34

Keep thine mind, thine body, thine purposes, in those things that He gave thee as He spoke to those gathered at the cross: "Peace I give; not as men count peace, but the purpose in the heart is sure in the Lord—I have shown thee the way."

877-29   M.48   7/31/39

For thy body is indeed the temple of the living God. There He has promised to meet thee. There He has promised to make Himself known to thee—His will, His purpose with thee.

That may *not* be supplied by another. If that were true, that it might be supplied by another, why the need of the Son to suffer the death on the cross, to offer Himself as a sacrifice? He offered it not alone for thyself, for the world, for the souls of men, but for His *own* being!

For, ye—too—are *His* son; and ye, too, are brethren one with another.

Seek and ye shall find, knock and it will be opened unto thee.

1499-1   F.50   12/14/37

For indeed He is the Creator, He indeed is the Maker of all that doth appear. For all power in heaven and in earth has been given unto His keeping through the faith He kept with His fellow man; by His advent into the earth, by His doing good in all ways, at all times, under every circumstance. Yet not railing, on any—though they demanded His life in the material, though they cuffed and buffeted Him, though they swore and spit upon him, though they crowned him with thorns, though they abased him in every manner, yet opened He not His mouth —though He were their Lord, their Master.[15]

5749-14   5/14/41

Hold fast to that ideal, and using Him ever as the ideal. And hold up that *necessity* for each to meet the same problems. And *do not* attempt to shed or to surpass or go around the cross. *This* is that upon which each and every soul *must* look and know it is to be borne in self *with* Him.

The Preparation of His Body

5122-1   F.43   5/17/44   Tilda

. . . the entity was in those periods when the holy women brought spices and those things to anoint the body. The entity was not able to bring spices because of the value, so brought flowers of the field which were just as acceptable as was the widow's mite, she of whom the Lord said, "She hath given more than them all." [1]

So in thy ministry to others through the beauties of nature, and that for God's companionship to those who love, those who are sick, to those who are happy, work thou with those things to bring new life and hope to the many. In the name then Tilda.

897-1   F.30   4/18/35   Cleopias

... the entity was in that experience when the Master walked among men, during those periods when there were the trials, the tribulations being brought in many of the peoples, when He gave, "I must go up that I may be offered as the living sacrifice."

The entity was among those that followed, as it were, afar off; during those periods or days when there were the hosannas in the triumphal entry in the city [2]; and again afar off when the day arose that He was lifted as between the earth and sky, so that those who looked, those who beheld, might know that they—themselves—must pass along that road, *crucifying* in their bodies that which would make for the gratifying of desires, that which would make for an exaltation of self rather than those tenets as He gave: "The new commandment I give, that ye love one another." [3]

Then the entity was of those people that came from Lycaonia, or in those portions of the cultures of the Grecians in the upper portions of the Samarian land; yet the entity embraced those tenets during those periods of activity, associating self with the holy women that made for the caring of the body during those periods of its preparation hurriedly—as it were; for the day was at an end when it was delivered to Joseph of Arimathea, and those that took care of same. Yet these were as friends to the entity in that experience.

And the entity, in the name Cleopias, in the latter part of that sojourn—as it returned to its own land—became of that place, that household, where there were many of the faithful that became as the ministers and the teachers for those activities that soon began in the land. And the entity made for those applications that brought to the entity the greater development during the sojourn in that land.

For, as the entity may experience in self throughout, that as was given, that as He the man represented in that taught was the Law of One; that each soul is a portion—its own portion— of that creative force that we may make manifest by the manner in which we minister to those whom we contact in every way, in every manner; whether they be those in high estate or those that are struggling along the road of fear and doubt, or those that have fallen by the wayside. For each soul is precious in His sight, and He hath not willed that any should perish but that all—through that *will* as was manifested in the man that the entity, Cleopias, saw hung upon the tree upon the hill—might have eternal life in Him.

1402-1   F.58   7/4/37   Josie

. . . the entity was in the land now known as the Promised Land, during those periods when the Master walked in the earth; and among those peoples that were influenced by those activities in that period was the entity's activity.

Though the entity was of those ruling powers or forces, its days, its associations, its conditions were bound with those peoples in that land.

When those periods arose when there were the persecutions and questionings as to whether that proclaimed by the fisherfolk, or that proclaimed by those in power or in authority, was to become the rule of the peoples, the entity was drawn between two influences, two forces.

And again that as has been given as a lesson: Learn—as was experienced there, as must be learned in the present—humbleness and patience. Not that the entity didn't gain mentally, not that the entity didn't build in its soul's experience, but you were neither hot nor cold! And the lesson from that experience has made much of that energy, much of that enthusiasm, much of that determination.

But know again, it must be guided aright. He without an ideal is sorry indeed; he with an ideal and lacking courage to live it is sorrier still.

Know that.

The name then was Josie, and the entity was of the household of those who made for the questionings at the trial of the Master; for it was of the household of one of the Sanhedrin—he who cared for the body when the burial time came: Nicodemus [4] . . .

Hold fast to those tenets that ye doubted oft. Know that Nicodemus *was* right; He had, He *has,* He *is* the words of Life; He is the Word that maketh all things anew!

1081-1   F.27   12/19/35   Beatrice

. . . the entity was in what is now known as or called the Holy Land, during those periods when there were the questionings as to the soldiery from the Roman rule, when there were the questionings of the teacher John.

The entity then was in the capacity of being among those who furnished entertainment, as a danseuse for Herod. And the entity was in close associations then with those under that individual's activity, and with those not only of Pilate's court but of the Roman associations; also with those that furnished the emperor's activities in the changes that were wrought.

Those experiences brought spectacular activities in the experience of the entity; though losing oft in the experiences, because of self-indulgences, self's gratifications.

With those periods when there was the harkening to those that joined in what was afterward termed in the records as the triumphal entry of the man of Galilee, a change came into the experience of the entity. And joining with many of those that were numbered among the holy women, the entity's activities then brought forth a service to many of many lands.

For as there were gathered those from all the lands for the periods of that particular feast when the entity became *overcome,* as it were, by the bodily abuses in many directions during the period, the *healing* that was accomplished not only by the words spoken but by the look, by the touch of the Holy One, brought joy and glory and understanding and knowledge and *wisdom* to the experience of the entity.

Then, as Beatrice, who helped in the preparations of the linens about the head of the Master when entombed by Josephus and the friends, the entity gained; for it gave of self, it brought aid and help.[5]

And from those deeper feelings, those deeper senses of purpose that arose during that experience, there come many things in the present having to do with the adornment of the body, the adornments of the head. And there are abilities in such directions whereby the entity may not only make the coiffure for the hair but may be as a designer of headdress, as one that may in such fields of activity show the *individuality* of the person for whom such may be made.

The Resurrection

1747-3   F.34   7/13/39

. . . "I *am* the resurrection, the life. I *told* thee to destroy the body and in three days I would raise it again." This must become a fact. Then it is understood how the emblem represents God, the way, the cross, self, the world—as to how there is the activity through same.¹

900-227   M.31   4/25/26

. . . to understand the resurrection,² we must first gain a concept of how spirit force entered into the body and man became a living soul; for we begin first as this:

The earth and the universe, as related to man, came into being through the *mind—mind—*of the Maker, and, as such, has its same being much as each atomic force multiplies in itself, or, as worlds are seen and being made in the present period, and as same became (earth we are speaking of) an abode for man, man entered as man, through the *mind* of the Maker, see? in the form of flesh *man;* that which carnally might die, decay, become dust, entering into material conditions. The spirit the gift of God, that man might be one with Him, with the concept of man's Creative Forces throughout the physical world. Man in Adam (as a group; not as an individual), entered into the world (for he entered in five places at once, we see—called Adam in one, see?), and as man's concept became to that point wherein man walked not after the ways of the spirit but after the desires of the flesh *sin* entered—that is, away from the face of the Maker, see? and death then became man's portion, *spiritually,* see? for the physical death existed from the beginning; for to create one must die, see?

In this, then, there is seen, as the body, in the flesh, of the Christ, became perfect in the flesh, in the world, and the body laid aside on the cross, in the tomb, the *physical* body moved away, through that as *man* will know as dimensions, and the spirit able then to take hold of that Being in the way as it enters again into the body, and as it presents itself to the world, to individuals at the time and to man at present.

1877-2   F.45   4/18/40

In the present, then, by keeping self reminded, the entity may remind others of the needs to live that life which was wholly, truly exemplified in the life of the man Jesus—who became the Christ through the things which He suffered, and through demonstrating in the earth the abilities to overcome *death,* the law of death.

5749-6   4/5/36

Mrs. Cayce: As we approach this Easter season our thoughts turn naturally toward the Biblical accounts of the resurrection of Jesus, the Christ. We seek at this time through this channel information dealing either with a completion of the historical account or interpretation and explanation of the full meaning of the resurrection which will help us to better understand and appreciate it.

Mr. Cayce: Yes. In seeking ye shall find. In the experience of each soul that has named the name of the Christ, this should be a season of rededication of self as being a true messenger of His in and among men.

In seeking, then, to know more of that, as to those here, much may be revealed to those that in their inner selves experienced that material period when *He,* Jesus, walked in the earth.

But for what purpose is this season observed, that caused or called for such a sacrifice that life might be made manifest? Is it not fitting that to those here, to those there in that land, it came at that particular season when life in its manifestations was being demonstrated in the material things about each soul?

How, why, was there the need for there to be a resurrection? Why came He into the earth to die the death, even on the cross? Has it been, then, the fulfillment of promise, the fulfillment of law, the fulfillment of man's estate? Else why did He put on flesh and come into the earth in the form of man, but to be one with the Father; to show to man *his* (man's) divinity, man's relationship to the Maker; to show man that indeed the Father meant it when He said, "If ye call I will hear. Even though ye be far away, even though ye be covered with sin, if ye be washed in the blood of the lamb ye may come back."

Then, though He were the first of man, the first of the sons of God in spirit, in flesh, it became necessary that He fulfill *all* those associations, those connections that were to wipe away in the experience of man that which separates him from his Maker.

Though man be far afield, then, though he may have erred, there is established that which makes for a closer, closer walk *with* Him, through that one who experienced all those turmoils, strifes, desires, urges that may be the lot of man in the earth. Yet He put on flesh, made *Himself* as naught — even as was promised throughout, to those who walked and talked with God.

In the history, then, of the resurrection as ye have recorded in part, may it be so interpreted that those here, now, that experienced (through that period of their advent) His suffering, may — as Andrew, Martha, Naomi, Loda[?], Elois[?], Phoenix[?] Phoebe[?] — again see those days. Though there were fears from the elements without, from the political powers that made for fears of body and mind, there were the rememberings that *He* had given, "Though ye destroy this temple, in three days it will rise again." [3]

And then as He hung upon the cross, He called to those that He loved and remembered not only their spiritual purposes but their material lives. For He indeed in suffering the death on the cross became the whole, the entire way; *the* way, *the* life, *the* understanding, that we who believe on Him may, too, have the everlasting life. For He committed unto those of His brethren not only the care of the spiritual life of the world but the material life of those that were of His own flesh, His own blood. Yea, as He gave His physical blood that doubt and fear might be banished, so He overcame death; not only in the physical body but in the *spirit* body — that it may become as *one* with Him, even as on that resurrection morn — that ye call thy Eastertide.

It is that breaking forth from the tomb, as exemplified in the bulb of the tree of nature itself breaking forth from the sleep that it may rise as He with healing in its very life, to bring all phases of man's experience to His consciousness—that indeed became then the fulfilling of the law.

On what wise, then, ye ask, did this happen in materiality? Not only was He dead in body, but the soul was separated from that body. As all phases of man in the earth are made manifest, the physical body, the mental body, the soul body became as each dependent upon their own experience. Is it any wonder that the man cried, "My God, my God, *why* hast thou forsaken me?" [4]

Each soul comes to stand as He before that throne of his Maker, with the deeds that have been done in the body, in the mind, presenting the body-spiritual before that throne of mercy, before that throne of the Maker, the Creator, the God.

Yet as He, the Father, hath given to each of you, "I have given my angels charge concerning thee, and they shall bear thee up, and thou shalt not know corruption."

This He demonstrated in the experience of thy brother, thy Savior, thy Jesus, thy Christ; that would come and dwell in the hearts and lives of you all—if you will but let Him, if you will but invite Him, if you will but open thy own heart, each of you, that He may enter and abide with you.

Hence when those of His loved ones and those of His brethren came on that glad morning when the tidings had come to them, those that stood guard heard a fearful noise and saw a light, and—"the stone has been rolled away!" Then they entered into the garden, and there Mary first saw her *risen* Lord.[5] Then came they of His brethren with the faithful women, those that loved His mother, those that were her companions in sorrow, those that were making preparations that the law might be kept that even there might be no desecration of the ground about His tomb. They, too, of His friends, His loved ones, His brethren, saw the angels.

How, why, took they on form? That there might be implanted into their hearts and souls that *fulfillment* of those promises.

What separates ye from seeing the glory even of Him that walks with thee oft in the touch of a loving hand, in the voice of those that would comfort and cheer? For He, thy Christ, is oft with thee.

Doubt, fear, unbelief; fear that thou art not worthy!

Open thine eyes and behold the glory, even of thy Christ present here, now, in thy midst! even as He appeared to them on that day!

What meaneth the story of the Christ, of His resurrection, of the man Jesus that walked in Galilee, without that resurrection morn?

Little, more than that of the man thou thinkest so little of, that though His body-physical touched the bones of Elisha He walked again among men! [6]

Dost thou believe that He has risen? How spoke Thomas? "Until I see, until I have put my hand in his side where I saw water and blood gush forth, until I have handled his body, I will *not* believe." [7]

Ye, too, oft doubt; ye, too, oft fear. Yet He is surely with thee. And when ye at this glad season rededicate thy life, thy body, thy mind to His service, ye—too—may know, as they, that He *lives*—and is at the right hand of God to make intercession for *you*—if ye will believe; if ye will believe that He is, ye may experience. For as many as have named the name, and that do unto their brethren the deeds that bring to them (to you) that closeness, oneness of purpose with Him, may know—ye, too—in body, in mind, that He *lives today,* and will come and receive you unto Himself, that where He is there ye may be also.

Crucify Him not in thy mind nor in thy bodily activities. Be not overcome by those things that are of the earth-earthy. Rather clothe thy body, thy mind, with the thoughts, the deeds, the privileges that His suffering as a man brought to thee, that He indeed might be the first of those that slept, the first of those that came in the flesh, that passed through all those periods of preparation in the flesh, even as thou.

But if ye would put on Him, ye must claim His promises as thine own. And how canst thou claim them unless ye in thine own knowledge, thine own consciousness, *have* done—do do from day to day—that thy heart has told and does tell thee is in keeping with what He has promised?

For thy Christ, thy Lord, thy Jesus, is nigh unto thee—just now!

5749-12   3/24/40

Mrs. Cayce: On this Easter day of 1940 we seek a discourse on the significance of the resurrection of Jesus, the Christ.

Mr. Cayce: In giving that as might be significant in the experiences of those present, it is well that there be considered those conditions which exist in the world of thought, as well as in the political and economic situations throughout the world—if there is to be a practical application of the significance of the resurrection of Jesus, the Christ.

The life, the death, the resurrection of Jesus are as facts, in the hearts and minds of those here. The resurrection of Jesus, the Christ, is a significant fact to each individual only according to how he applies same (as it is significant to him) in his daily life, experience and conversation with his fellow man.

Then, in a material world—a world of hate, of divided opinions—what is the course that you each will pursue, in relationships to your fellow men?

Is it the course outlined by the tenets, the principles which He, the Teacher of teachers gave as respecting the manner of life, of activity, that you each would give in your dealings and relationships with your fellow men?

We know, and only need to be reminded, that the whole law is in Him. For, as He gave that which is the basis, the principle, of the intent and desire and purpose which should prompt our activity, so we in our own world—as we live, as we speak, as we pray—are to let it be in that tempo, in that way and manner which was prompted by Him, as He taught His disciples how to pray.

Then, as we analyze this prayer in our experience, we see what the life, the death, the resurrection of Jesus, the Christ —who is the way, the truth, the light—must mean in this period in the experience of man.

Think not that He, God, will be mocked. For, whatsoever a man soweth, that must he also reap. This was truly exemplified in the life of the man of Galilee. For, in Him we all live, we all move, we all die. So, in Him we are all made alive.

Then:

Put away hate, malice, jealousy, or the taking sides with any that stir up strife.

Be ye rather on the Lord's side—knowing that no man is in any position of power or might save by the will of the Father, that there may be fulfilled that which has been promised of Him, by Him, and through that advent of the man Jesus into a material world.

Then, as ye meditate upon the meaning of the resurrection of this man of God—know that the way is open to thee to approach the throne of God; not as an excuse, not as a justification, but rather in love, in harmony, in that which brings hope for a sin-sick world.

Each individual, then, may act, may live, may pray—in his or her own little sphere of activity—in such a manner as to bring peace and harmony, even among those who *appear* to be at variance to the cause of the Christ in the material world.

Let not thy heart be troubled, then. Ye believe in God; believe also in Him—who came to bring peace, and the way to the Father, exemplifying same in the ability to take away death—that is as sin in the experience of man.

And thus may he (man) indeed love the Lord with all his heart, and his neighbor as himself.

5749-13   3/12/41

Mrs. Cayce: You will have before you the desire of those present here to secure at this time an Easter message which may be an inspiration and a help to those to whom it is presented. You will consider the intention of those present to pass this discourse on to others, and give that which will be most helpful now.

Mr. Cayce: In man's experience in the earth there come those periods of doubt and fear, and of the loss of hope. Then to all such there should be the reminding of that Easter Morn; and as to what it has meant and does mean in the hearts and minds of those who have and do put their trust in Jesus, the Christ.

There should be the reminding that—though He bowed under the burden of the cross, though His blood was shed, though He entered into the tomb—through that power, that ability, that love as manifested in Himself among His fellow men He broke the bonds of death; proclaiming in that act that *there is no death* when the individual, the soul, has and does put its trust in Him.

Thus in this hour of despair throughout the world, when those activities are such as to indicate hate, injustice, tyranny, desire to enslave or to impel others to submit to the dictates of this or that power—let all take heart and know that this, too, as the hour upon Calvary, must pass away; and that as upon the wings of the morning there comes that new hope, that new desire, to the hearts and minds of all who seek to know His face.

This must begin within thine own heart.

Then, let all so examine their hearts and minds as to put away doubt and fear; putting away hate and malice, jealousy and those things that cause man to err. Replace these with the desire to help, with hope, with the willingness to divide self and self's surroundings with those who are less fortunate; putting on the whole armor of God—in righteousness.

Magnify in the daily life the fruit of the spirit of truth, that all may take hold and make for that activity in their lives, knowing that as ye do it unto the least of thy brethren ye do it to thy Maker.

Meditate oft upon what it has meant, does mean today, to *crucify* the Lord thy God in thy daily experiences. Rather magnify, glorify Him in every word, every activity, in all thy dealings with thy fellow man. By thy very step, by thy very look, by thy word, create *hope* in the hearts, minds and lives of others.

Make it *sure* in thy *own* heart, for there—to thee—is the beginning and the end. For He is mindful of thee, and He has promised that whosoever will may come and take of the cup that He partook of; that through Him we may be *sure* in *our* hopes, *our* responses to the needs of the world at this sad changing hour.

Let that mind ever be in thee as was in Him as He offered Himself up: "Father, forgive them—they know not what they do. Father, it is finished—I come to thee. Give Thou Thy servant that glory which Thou hast promised." [8]

Live that in thy life, thy conversation, thy activity everywhere; and indeed then may each in that manner bear a real Easter message to others.

For He hath entrusted to thee—those that love Him—the redemption of the world, to make known His willingness, His care, His promises that may be the activity of each and every soul.

Then, let not your heart be troubled; ye believe in God—believe in Him, who has promised that "If ye will love me and keep my commandments, I will come and abide with thee—for, Lo, I am with thee always." [9]

His commandments are not grievous; just being kind, just being patient, just being long-suffering with thy problems, thy turmoils, thy strifes.

Through that ability to make Himself one with the Father, He has gained that right, that honor to declare Himself unto as many as will harken.

Let thy light, then, shine ever in the dark, in the light; in the sorrow, in the gladness of thy purpose, of thy desire; that He may be glorified even as He asks of the Father.

Ye—each of ye, as individuals—may do this. So ye, as ye come into His presence, may be given "Well done, thou good and faithful brother—enter into the joy of thy Lord." [10]

The Pentecost

3344-1   M.46   10/29/43   Philas

... the entity was in the Promised Land during those periods just following the Master's walk in the earth, when there were the mighty gatherings on the day of Pentecost when people of many nations, of many tongues, heard the message in their own tongue.[1] For as the body is the temple, so may indeed the spirit answer to thy spirit as to that as the sounding board of what ye may be, of what ye may do.

There the entity was among the acquaintances of Stephen, and among those set in order for the distribution of the needs of those that had set themselves and their only worldly goods to be used by those in authority in the church, when there were the first attempts for organized effort on the part of the teachers and ministers.

Hence many of the confusions that arose as to methods of activity. Yet we find the entity then, in the name Philas, was as a strengthening to the activities of many varied peoples. With the martyrdom of Stephen, the entity became a leader in that particular phase or area of the activities in the church.

3344-2   M.46   3/29/44   Philas

... [we have the records of 3344] and the earthly experience of the entity as Philas in the Holy Land ...

In giving the biographical outline ... it would be well to give something of an outline of conditions during those particular periods of activity.

We find that the entity Philas was of that group of people from Seleucia who came to Jerusalem during those days of the Pentecost when there was an outpouring of the Holy Spirit upon the apostles who had been warned to tarry in Jerusalem until that day.[2]

The entity was among those who were students of the law, those who were interested in the activities having to do with questionings pertaining to the law that had been interpreted from the priests and rabbis of the day pertaining to the Mosaic law, and the interesting facts and fancies that had come from the eastern lands, from which the Wise Men had come. These, as parts of the teachings, had become adopted by those groups of the Essenes of which John and Joseph and Mary had been a part before the entering of the Master, Jesus in the earth.

With Stephen, Philip and others, the entity was among those chosen, of the young men; Philas at the time being only a little past nineteen years of age.

Thus we find the entity was not acquainted directly with the individuals until this period who had been associated with the Master as disciples, now apostles, or those who had been very close in the activity.

As a student, though, the entity was aroused to the possibilities and probabilities of the activities to which the individuals might give themselves or contribute to, or gain something from, as to add to the interest in living.

Philas was of a group not wholly Jewish or Grecian but one interested in same because of the background genealogically of the things happening. The entity journeyed to Jerusalem because of the interest aroused by hearsay and the expectancy among the peoples, the great throngs. On the journey the entity became closely identified or associated with Stephen, who after the joining of so many to the efforts of the disciples or apostles on the day of Pentecost became the treasurer of the organization that became a necessity, in that record keepers had to be appointed because of the great amount of contributions of various natures to those peoples. Stephen and Philip and Philas, and others, had been chosen by the disciples or apostles to attend to the needs of the great throngs of people.

There were those chosen who were entirely of the circumcision. There were those chosen who were of the uncircumcised group, yet were identified with services in various forms, in that which had been adopted by the Samaritan Jews as well as Grecian Jews, who were only part Jews. Some of these facts became the problems (that were unnecessary in their particular activity or for their beliefs) in the teachings of Peter, John and James, who were the chief spokesmen during those periods following the outpouring of the Holy Spirit on the day of Pentecost.

With these activities there became for the entity questions, with some of the apostles, in that the entity, Philas, used the position to which he had been appointed, as a means for social relationships with the various groups of women, the girls that were a part of the activities through those particular periods. These brought questionings. They also brought into the experience of the entity some of those very conditions that are a part of the entity's present experience — as to the sincerity of purposes in the oaths taken and the living up to same, because of seeming negligence on the part of either or both concerned in the marital relationships.

Hence the entity is meeting its own self in the present.

In some groups there was not just the one factor but rather a questioning as there had been among many of those in the early church, in portions of the land from which the entity came; as in Laodicea, Thyatira, as in all of those where there were the mixed relationships of Greeks, Romans, Jews, Syrophoenicians or the followers of the eastern tenets of those peoples as to their relationship with the opposite sex.

These, then, are the problems to be met. These were the problems causing the questionings, rather than the honesty or sincerity in which the entity as Philas administered the contributions. The greater disturbance arose after the martyrdom of Stephen. This drew the entity closer and closer to the needs of the people, but because of the persecution many of the groups were scattered throughout the various lands and the entity returned to its own land; becoming engaged in those activities that brought about a greater contribution. For the entity was engaged in the tilling of the soil, the usage of teachings or tenets of both the old and new dispensations, as well as the legends of the East.

3253-2   F.44   10/31/43   Archar

. . . the entity was in the earth during those days when the church was established in Jerusalem, on the day of Pentecost when there were those quiet hours in which the Holy Spirit manifested in the activities of those that had been and had walked with Him; when the entity became attuned, as it were, to the voices of the universe—when nature itself spoke to the peoples that would listen.

Thus were there added to those groups such as would be saved. For it is the free gift of the Maker. Only self, then, may separate thee from the love of God. Through selfishness, lust or the like, ye may separate self from the love of the Maker.

The name then was Archar, and the entity aided in those activities, cared for those that were the strangers from many different lands.

2602-3   F.41   12/11/43   Rhea

. . . the entity was in the Holy Land when many were gathered from many points of interest to the feast at the day of Pentecost.

The entity was among those from Laodicea that journeyed with those groups for the edifying, because of those mysterious messages that had gone out from those gathered there.

The entity saw and heard the disciples, and heard Peter's sermon on that day.

The entity finds itself now not incredulous, but not too easily sold on any unusual or strange thing either. Very well balanced, then, but "show me and then I am with you" is the attitude of the entity.

These are those experiences gained by the entity then, as Rhea, and the entity was among those that saw disputations in the church in Laodicea with Paul, Barnabas, Mark, Luke, Lucius and those that were at disagreement regarding activities among the associations of individuals at that period.

Yet the entity learned much of politique and can be very politique in its applications or dealings with others in the present.

Q-5. [*When and where have I been associated in past experiences with*] *my son,* [*2780*]?

A-5. In the Palestine experience or in the land of Laodicea . . .

5055-1   F.44   5/5/44   Lydia

. . . the entity was in the Holy Land when the young were

in the throng and groups which came to Jerusalem upon the day of Pentecost, when there were those experiences of great throngs of peoples hearing and seeing the outpouring of the Holy Spirit as the disciples spoke to the throngs and were silenced by the very happenings of all the doubts which had been a part of many of the people's experiences.

The entity seeing these unusual things carried them away in her mind to a different land, a different clime. For the entity lived in the land beyond to the east of Damascus.

Thus we find the entity becoming as it were, a teacher, an emissary, an instructor in the manners in which there were the communications with the varied groups, and we find that in the environs were some of the disciples taken care of when there were those persecutions which began in Jerusalem.[3]

Thus we find those separations as being parts of the persecution, as in its own household, as being separate and apart in the present experience. In the name Lydia, the entity gained throughout those periods, and in same, there were associations with many who are a part of the own experience in the present. As with the sons, as well as with the companion, the father of the children of the entity.

3621-1   F.8   1/7/44   Ruth

. . . the entity was in those lands when the Master walked in the earth, when there were the disturbing forces by the Master's being offered up as the lamb of God; yet in these the entity found hope, also fear. For the entity followed in the wake of those who interpreted that expression of the promises of the Master on the day of Pentecost; dancing with others for joy, that the Lord had answered in sending the Holy Spirit to abide forever with man.

Forget not that promise in thyself. Learn this above every other, that the Holy Spirit abideth ever with those who seek the Lord.

Then the entity was known as Ruth, and was in the household of a sister of Peter's.

3654-1   F.65   1/22/44   Sachet

. . . the entity was in the Holy Land during those periods

when peoples gathered from many lands, when there were those activities in the city of Jerusalem on the day of Pentecost.

The entity was among those of the thousands added to the church, and if it is read correctly "added to the church, such as should be saved." [4] It didn't say that they were saved, but that they should be saved. These were those who, prompted by the activities of others, joined in to learn the law of the Lord.

The name then was Sachet. The entity gained through many a hardship. For personal application of those tenets and truths bespeaking of the unusual, rather the sensational was sought at times by the entity—and it confused the entity.

These ye have seen in the present sojourn. The law of the Lord, is such that he who runs may read. Even the fool may be taught in the way if he himself seeks, but none are so blind as those who will not see.

Open thy heart, thy mind, thy purpose "LORD, HERE AM I, THY SERVANT, USE ME IN SUCH A WAY THAT I MAY BE A CHANNEL OF BLESSING TO SOMEONE TODAY."

The principles, the purposes—not merely by the statement, but by the desire of applying self—will open for thee, from the experiences in that period, greater possibilities than the entity has been conscious of yet in this experience.

The ability to be a good cook arises from those activities, under whatever may be the environ, and you have recipes all your own. Keep them. And give them away if you would keep them. For, remember, you can never lose anything that really belongs to you, and you can't keep that which belongs to someone else. No matter if this is spiritual, mental or material, the law is the same.

Q-5. [*What has been the relationship with:*] *The entity known as [2880]?*

A-5. In the Holy Land especially, ye should follow those precepts closer.

5103-1   F.43   5/12/44

. . . the entity was in the Holy Land when there were those establishings of the care for the children of those who had viewed the disciples and apostles on the day of Pentecost.

The entity then was among those of Judah, Judah of the

coasts of Thessalonica, who came to Jerusalem. Young in years, yet faithful in purpose and in aiding in the distribution to those who were in need, were the activities. Thus the entity learned the stories, the tales of many who were in those varied positions by the overzealousness as well as the sincerity of others. These made for the abilities of the entity to talk and sometimes talk too much.

1647-1   M.5 mos.   7/27/38   Penuel

The entity was among those of the young who were among those gathered together following the ministry or teachings of the apostles on the day of Pentecost, and of the great numbers to whom much came as an active service.

There we find the entity, owing to the material things, as well as the material sufferings that were encountered or met by many in the environs of which the entity was a part, became rather inclined to fears and doubts.

Hence these in the present experience will make a great many questionings on the part of the entity as the lessons or tenets of any teaching become a part of the entity's experience.

The entity will be inclined to be rather in the nature of the doubter, until there are the actual experiences of the entity itself.

Throughout the experience the entity gained, the entity lost, and the entity gained. For as the entity found much of the service and activity as a duty rather than as a free-will offering, or the inclination to give of self in individual service for the good of all—these became stumbling blocks.

And only with the tenets that were later taken by those directly of the Master's household or family, there was brought for the entity a development—then in the name Penuel.

2982-1   F.34   4/27/43   Mercia

. . . the entity was in the Holy Land, when there were those activities especially following the persecution of the church.

For, the entity was rather young when the Master walked in the earth, and knew rather by hearsay of those that had seen and known Him in His ministry in the earth.

Yet those teachings of the Essenes were especially close to

the activities of the entity. Thus its embracing of same, as it aided in interpreting in the lives of others those tenets to which the teachers of the day had subscribed, brought the abilities of the entity to counsel with those in the various offices of the organizations through portions of the Holy Land.

Though the entity lived not in Jerusalem, it had visited there on feast days, and as a very young person had been impressed by the activities on the day of Pentecost—when there was the first speaking by the disciples in tongues.[5]

Those things of such natures still find a distant chord in the entity's consciousness.

As given, if ye live the way ye may know the way.

In the experience the entity aided many that faltered, in many various ways and manners, and in part was a teacher, rather as a helper to those put in authority in various places of the whole Holy Land.

Though the entity then was not Jewish, it knew the Jewish faith. The name then was Mercia.

5284-1   F.38   6/30/44   Dorcas

. . . the entity was in the Holy Land when the Master walked in the earth, when there were those hearings of, not personal experience of, how others were healed by the Master's only speaking to them and putting His hand upon the hand, the arm, the head of others.

The entity made fun of, yea, rebuked those who claimed such had come about; and eventually, when on the day of Pentecost the entity heard and saw the outpouring of the Holy Spirit, it believed and felt it was almost too late.

It is never too late to mend thy ways. For life is eternal and ye are today what ye are because of what ye have been. For ye are the co-creator with thy Maker, that ye may one day be present with all of those who love His coming.

The name then was Dorcas.

1825-1   F.54   2/19/39   Lydia

The entity was young in years during those periods when there were the gatherings of the many following the death of the Christ on the cross, or at Pentecost.

There we find the entity was among those gathered, and among the first to recognize that those teachings, those conversations of the followers on that day were being spoken in such manners as to be understood in the hearts and minds of those who spoke not the language of those Galileans.[6]

The entity was among those who came from the land about Thessalonica and hence spoke a different tongue from the Galileans; yet coming under the influence of the teachings of the holy women, as well as especially John and Philip, and again especially that one who first became the martyr for a cause—Stephen—being of that same land.

When there was the establishing then of the church in Thessalonica, the entity returned there, becoming then the helpmeet to one Cleopas who was the elder of the church to which Lucius *and* Paul ministered during those periods of the activities.

There we find the entity was especially given in the arts of the weaving, and in the manners of dress—especially the character of the plaids that were a part of the activities in that particular portion of the land during the entity's sojourn there.

Throughout its experience in that sojourn the entity gained, becoming a help to the minister's wife through those periods of interrupted activity in the church there; aiding in the contributing to the needs of those who were less fortunate, those who were persecuted, and those who depended upon the ministering.

Is it any wonder, then, that in the very hands of the entity in the present there is healing—as they minister to the needs, the activities of others?

Is there any wonder that there is particular emphasis in the present experience of the entity upon that message given by Stephen, or the teachings there that are especially recorded in Luke?

For the entity, as in that experience, may in the present best gain the insight into the revelations as come to those who love Him, through those ministrations in the conversation, in the gentle manner, in which those lessons may be given that the trust in Him brings that peace which is the promise of that

Master whom the entity served so well among its fellow men during that experience.

The name then was Lydia; giving then in the present greater and greater thought to those tenets, those lessons, those activities of those who ministered to the needs.

And the assurance that comes to the entity in such ministrations only makes for the *knowing* in whom ye have believed, and that *He is* able to keep that ye have committed to Him against that day.

The Followers and the Churches

816-3   M.51   2/17/35   Xercia

. . . the entity was in the land now known as or called Palestine, during those periods when the Master of men walked in the earth.

The entity then was among the Grecian peoples that represented their country in the Palestine land, or what would be termed in the present as a counselor, ambassador, or one in the capacity to see that his country was represented in that land—and dwelt there, though being a Grecian—in the lands about Bethsaida, and saw and heard much of those turmoils among those in power, of the various political factions that were represented among the Roman and the Jewish peoples in that particular land. Also the Pharisees, the Sadducees, the Essenes, those that would be called the Roman or the state, and those that would be called the conservatives and those that would be called the aggressives. Or those activities about the entity caused much of thought and of stir . . .

The entity from that experience, as Xercia, is naturally and *innately* a leader by proxy, or selects or gives the authority into the hands of others. And in the very nature of the experience and of the development the entity made for an advancement throughout that sojourn in that land. For when there became those activities of the followers of that teacher in the Grecian land, the entity became the defender of those that preached, "Peace on earth, good will to those that love His coming."

816-4   M.52   3/13/35   Xercia

The entity, according to time, entered the earthly experience one and one-half years B.C. Or the time of the entity's coming to the Palestine land as an ambassador (as would be termed in the present) was when the entity was thirty-four years of age.

The entrance, we find, was near that city (in the Grecian land) known as Macedonia. The entity was fair of hair, blue of eyes, ruddy of complexion. And in height at the period was (at the time of being appointed, or when going as the emissary) five feet, eleven and three-quarter inches, as would be measured in the measurements of this land, or in doneur [?] and xeres [?] we would have six or seven. The weight then was one fifty-six. (These, of course, are interpreted to the language of the present experience, as we find them.)

As to the activities during the early portion of the years, we find:

The entity entered in what would now be called the spring months, or the first of the year; what would be interpreted into the meaning of the present as March 19th. This was then two thousand three thirty from the deliverance in the land, or in the present two years seven months and two days B.C., before the birth of the Master then.

The entity was strong of body, alert of mind, and trained rather in the political way—as would be interpreted in the present. For the entity grew up under the trainings of one Demeutri, who was what would be termed today the master or teacher or companion. The entity was among those, of course, of the wealthier from those portions of the land; or among those that were well-livers of the day, living in that which was carved as the home and builded in an outer portion of the city—but would be called a house, in which the entity lived in the earlier portions of the experience.

It was trained in much by the teachers of the day, being well-versed; and with Demeutri [Demetrius?] and the associations the entity became among those that argued much of those teachings that had been given by the Grecians, and especially those of the periods just previous to the entity's entrance into the material plane.

In the thirty-fourth year of the entity's sojourn, then (and that which makes for the greater experience or the greater urges in the experience of the entity in the present), we find the entity was sent as an emissary or ambassador to the Palestine land, to make for the interchange of the commercial changes that came into Jerusalem and into the countries near to the seaports thereabout, as in Bethsaida and Joppa and the lands along the Great Sea.

The entity then, of course, was rather in sympathy with those in power—or the Roman rule at the time, for there was then the closer associations with the Caesars and the rulers by Demeutri or those in charge in the Grecian land of the entity's nativity.

Then the entity was wedded to the present wife [811], before coming to the land; and came into the Palestine land in what would be termed in the present the first years of the wedded life in that association. Not that the Grecians failed to have more than the one wife, but in that particular set or sect the entity—during those periods of the sojourns in the Grecian land and during the first years in the Palestine land—adhered to those tenets of monogamy instead of polygamy. And these made for the greater satisfactory activities to the entity, in those relationships as established among not only the Jewish faith but the Egyptian associations and also the Roman associations—of course.

During the experience when the entity came into contact with the teachings of the Master, these brought first the scorn; yet when the entity heard the reasonings—as the Master did with the young ruler, and later in the temple—there came a conviction to Xercia. And the news of this was carried to the mate, which—during that time and period—was ruled rather by command (and it's too much so in the present!).

So the entity came to know the associates, or what would be termed in the present the disciples that were close to the Master; *especially* with John, and Luke of Cyrenia—who was the young physician that never finished and never practiced, yet was known as the physician. For he, too, with Xercia was of the same land, being close to the brother-in-law of Pilate, and came to know much of those things that went on from those activities.

The entity was able to play both politics and society, as well as to engage in its own activities in what would be termed the artistic expression (he was a good drinker also during the experience!).

In those periods when the trial and the crucifixion came about, these brought those periods of the greater conviction by the entity, or of the entity, into those activities.

The entity then withdrew to what is now Crete, or the isle

in the sea. There began there the exchange through the navigations, or the boats that touched Alexandria, Joppa, the northern coast of Africa, into portions of now Turkey. The entity then became active in that portion of the commercial activities. But with those periods of the spreading of the tenets of the teacher, especially when Paul touched Cyrenius (and to Crete), the entity became as an emissary or a missionary aiding in those activities throughout the sojourn in Crete—as Xercia. There in the sixty-fourth year of the sojourn in the earth, through the bringing in of the fevers with the commerce, the entity passed on.

Ready for questions.

Q-1. Did the entity's wife live longer than the entity?
A-1. Ten years longer.
Q-2. Were there any children?
A-2. Not by this wife; but when the entity entered into Crete and had another wife, there was!
Q-3. Was the entity religious?
A-3. Religious from more than one angle. The entity would be termed today as one that was moral and one that professed religion, but didn't work at it very hard; yet was contributing to the activities of that which he felt to be the *necessary* things for the development in the spiritual light.
Q-4. Was the entity well educated?
A-4. *Well* educated.
Q-5. What character of food was eaten by the entity in that experience?
A-5. Grains. Grain and fruits. Little of meats. For it was a portion not only of the Grecian but the natural development of those of the period. [See brother's reading, 826-5, p. 345 indicating close association in Greece-Rome.]

811-2   F.39   2/14/35   Cleopiasis

. . . the entity was during those periods when the Master walked in the land, in the Palestine land when there were the questionings much among the peoples as to the Grecians that were acceptable in the fellowship of those that had accepted, did accept the activities in and during that experience.

The entity then was among the peoples of the Grecian land that lived in or had journeyed to that land in and about that known as Bethany, where there were many of the activities of that man of God, that lover of men, that Savior of a sin-sick world. Then in the name Cleopiasis, the entity gave much in not only precept but in example, and gained much in the early portion and in the activities in that land. When the persecutions began, when divisions arose, confusions were the experience of the entity, yet in its intent and purpose, in its heart, there were little or no changes; yet it brought the experiences when the outward life spoke but little of the real inner self . . .

. . . for the light that burns within thine inner self has been set as by Him who gave in thine inner presence and in thine sojourn in the Bethany land, "I am the resurrection and the life; he that taketh hold upon me shall *not* die." Let this, then, be as thy motto:

He *is* the life! He *is* the resurrection! And in Him is life, light and joy that maketh all else as but naught.

Q-2. *What was the former relationship between myself and my present husband [816]?*

A-2. In the Palestine and Grecian land, when the entity—as Cleopiasis—acted in the land, the relationships were the same as exist in the present. For both were Grecians, beautiful of body, high of mind; and represented the Grecian activity in the Palestine land. They were in those of crosses oft in the land, owing to the turmoils in both the political and the religious activities, yet they learned much; and again they are together, that their lives may be more and more founded in that which was heard by the entity in the experience, "I am the resurrection; I am the life." Then, in thy relationships, let thy yeas be yea, thy nays be nay in the present; but ye become a tonic one for another, if thy prayers are oft together, if thy purposes are as one.

1373-2   F.37   11/24/37   Jacobing

. . . the entity was in the land now known as the Promised Land, and in those activities especially in the associations with those who became sojourners from the Grecian and the Parthenian forces of what is now the Ukraine land.

For while of those peoples (birthly—or by birth) of the Palestine land, in and about even a portion of Damascus (in the lower portion), we find the entity's activities in the latter portion of its sojourn were among those peoples in part of the Grecian land; and closely associated with those who were the followers of the Nazarene—Jesus, the Master!

Hence the entity gained through those experiences in bringing hope to those who were troubled in body, in mind, as for their *own* safety in the material things. For the activities in bringing hope, by the cunning devices in which there were brought about those experiences for those who were troubled, as to the loving kindnesses, the gentlenesses, the patience, the long-suffering—these that are as the fruit of the spirit, were a portion of the entity's experience during those sojourns.

The entity was closely associated with those who were active in what ye would term those places that were out of the way, in those particular periods . . .

The name then was Jacobing. And in the experience the entity *gained* throughout. For though there were those experiences of sorrow from the physical, there were those lessons gained that brought *harmony* and joy in the inner self throughout the sojourn . . .

Know, as ye experienced through those periods in the Palestine or Holy Land, and in the southern portions of the Grecian land—holy, *holy* is His name!

954-1   F.37   7/18/35   Patricia

. . . the entity was in that period just after the Prince of Peace came into the land.

The entity was then of the Galilean land, of a Samaritan peoples that were misunderstood by their Jewish neighbors, by their associations in the theological experiences and the power of state in Rome.

Hence we find oft in the experience of the entity in the present it has been a disliker of some influences in the Jewish experiences of others; and yet holding to much that from a *spiritual* import has been and is the finer self of those peoples as a race.

Also there have been those experiences when communistic

thought has been a portion of the entity's urge latent within; and the study of the communistic thoughts and free experiences of others becomes a portion of the entity's inner urge. There is the dislike of those that show their pomp, their power, because of their position, either political, social or from money.

These come from that experience. Yet that innate urge has come from the quieting, by the closer communion with the inner self, from those lessons the entity—as Patricia in that experience—gained from those who had been in the company with Him who walked in Galilee. If *this* is magnified in the experience it may bring a *new* hope, a new purpose, a new experience in the inner self and the outward manifestation of same—to the entity.

Hold fast, then, to the faith that is latent within, and to that of thy *mother faith!*

826-2   M.33   2/21/35   Pluenon

. . . the entity was in that land now known as the Grecian, during the periods when there were the turmoils and the strifes which arose through the conquest of the Romans upon many of the eastern lands during those experiences.

The entity was among the recorders or those that kept the counsels with those who made the associations and activities in other lands. *Then* the entity was what would be termed today, in common parlance, a pacifist of no mean estate; in the name then Pluenon.

In the experience the entity gained throughout. Not merely because of the attempts to bring peace and harmony among the nations or the peoples that strove one with another, but rather in that the entity carried forward that which was innate in the experience from the previous development. That, unless that which is meted is for the greater good for the whole it must eventually fail. *This* was the message carried even into those lands where there were the turmoils and the strife for the Son of man who walked in the earth. And the entity then became in those experiences as one that had been sent to make for peace in the land. The entity coming under the influence of Joseph of Arimathea, and Nicodemus,[1] came to know much of those tenets that had made for the moving forces among those in powers of the Sanhedrin, of those that carried the influences in those activities in the Roman empire when the teachers were sent hither and yon by those who espoused the cause of the lowly Nazarene.

Hence those things that bespeak of proclaiming the acceptable day of the Lord must ever stand as the influences that would prompt the actings, the motivative influences of the entity in its associations, in its activities among its fellow man.

826-5   M.34   7/6/35   Pluenon

In the experience as Pluenon, we find the entrance of the entity in the earth then was in the Grecian reaction; entering at or near that period which would be termed in the present as 16 B.C., in those environs or sojourns of Carthage—just outside or near Athens.

And the activities were among the Athenians in the development of the mental experience during the sojourn.

The relations then were a family of three children, the entity being the second one.

As to the names of the parentage, they were of those people who made for the associations with the rulers and yet with those that tended toward rather what would be called the commercial or farming portion.

The parentage were of no mean estate, though those in the former portions of experience had been made freemen through the giving of themselves in service for the country.

The entity then made for advancements, as we have indicated, throughout that sojourn; through the ministering to the economic needs of the countries, also aiding later in the coalition of the activities of many of those smaller countries or kingdoms or houses or groups in the period with the Romans' activities in the Palestine, and in the Cretan land, in Cyrene, in portions of Persia, extending as far as Phoenicia (Palaetyrus) [early name for Tyre and Sidon] in Egypt and to the edges of what is now even the Moroccan governments.

The activities of the entity were in bringing to the attention of those in authority the activities of the various groups.

Hence the writing, the abilities to record facts as historical data making for the changes and for the necessities—even in those various spheres of activity—of meeting the needs towards keeping the purpose of those who had been or were subdued under the various activities of extending the Grecians' forces and the Romans' influence. Such correlations during the experience brought for the entity the advancement throughout its sojourn. And little were the aggrandizements of selfish interests as to bring retardments in the soul or spiritual development of the entity.

Hence, as we find, while the entity during the sojourn was not given power in a political way and manner, as it may be seen by drawing of comparisons in the present, those who are the counselors by and through the gathering of statistical data, or data of historical natures as respecting same, are in fact the powers behind those of authority.

Hence the entity in its sojourn made for the keeping of peace, bringing to the various groups then those experiences and necessary influences for the activities of the groups. And in relation to same those things that dealt with law and order in the economics of the various groups; those things that dealt with the activity or the influences of the associations of groups in sports—as would be called in the present, or the artistic reaction, or the exchange in the architectural reactions to meet the needs in the various sections and characters of the groups.

For it was at that time, as we find, that the entity (with two or three others of a like tendency) aided in making for those things pertaining to the pretentious edifices among the more humble peoples; and the exchange of ideas between the proletariats of the various sections.

Hence such giving of self has made, does and did make for a soul development throughout the experience. Yet in the latter portion, because there were those appearances as of unappreciativeness from those in authority for the great period of the entity's activities, for the active services of the entity in these directions, the entity—as it were—fell into that of sullenness. This brought for the last days, while not a period of loss in *soul* development, rather that which would and did make for the entity in the next sojourn being rather "hard-boiled," according to the common parlance in the present.

But the entity's activities of service ran from a period when the entity was twenty-two until it was eighty-two—when it withdrew from direct activity . . .

. . . from the experience of the entity in that sojourn, in Greece, Persia, Palestine or Judea, the entity supplied the necessary data for keeping peace in a religious manner, in a political manner, in an economic and social manner. Yet those in authority, gormandizing their bodies upon those things that made for the firing of the influences or forces within the natural or physical body, forgot what had been the promptings that had brought to their own land, their own peoples, the great powers that made for the ruling forces in that portion of the world in that experience . . .

Q-12. *Did I personally know Christ in my Grecian sojourn?*

A-12. Only as a *passing,* during the making up of the associations of the entity with the authorities in the Sanhedrin; then not as a *personal* acquaintance, but among those who saw and heard. The greater study of those conditions in that experience arose from the entity's associations with Joseph of Arimathea and (of course, coming from the same portion of the land as the entity, you see) Nicodemus.

Q-13. *How old did I live to be in that sojourn?*

A-13. Eighty-seven. Stopped work at eighty-two. Began work at twenty-two; had sixty years of active service; one or two years of grumbling.

633-2   M.24   7/26/35   Josepheush

. . . the entity was in that land known as the Roman, when there were the periods of much questioning as to *who* was to *represent* in the court or in the land of Rome those peoples of the Holy Land.

The entity was among the Sanhedrin [2] during that period when the Holy Land first came under the supervision or rule or power of the Roman peoples.

In the name then Josepheush, the entity made overtures for the representation of his peoples, of his activities, among those that were to rule. And through the very activities, through the very comings of those peoples, the entity gradually rose to one of power, one of affluence; yet always *questioned* as to the purposes of same. And being *fearful* of the power, the entity was reduced oft in rank owing to those conditions that arose as envy and strife among his own brethren.

967-1   F.42   8/2/35   Jabcobin

. . . the entity was during those periods when the Master walked in the land, in what is now known as the Holy Land or the Palestine land.

The entity then was again among those in authority, being of the household then of the second in charge in the Sanhedrin; in the name then Jabcobin.

In the experience the entity gained and lost, and gained; for during those periods when there was so much of the politic, and so much as related to the patriotic reactions through the Holy Land and its peoples, the entity—through the turmoils and strife in the latter portion—made for an adhering to those things that were of the more *convincing* nature to the doubters, as to the *principles* of the activities of Him who had come as an ensample, as a leader, as a teacher.

The very associations during that experience have brought into the present many questions of natures pertaining to law, order, the material or marital relationships, the social activities. And the *judgments* that must arise from those experiences oft bring in the present, from the very emotional portion of the entity itself, the necessity for definite stands to be taken as to the better manner of activity.

1497-1   M.46   12/10/37   Ardemetus

. . . the entity's earthly experience was in what is now called the Palestine land, or the Promised Land, or the Holy Land, during those periods when there were the activities that made for not only the religious changes but the activities of the Roman forces in the land of the entity's activity.

Then the entity was among those of the seventy elders, or the Sanhedrin; and among those that were close to the activities of him that came to the Master by night, and close to him who also begged that the physical body of Jesus be given to him that there might be the care and the protection.[3]

The entity was neither of those, but of that number that were in the heart and mind with Joseph of Arimathea and with the activities of him who came by night—but not openly did he proclaim his thoughts or activities.

Then the entity's name was Ardemetus, and the entity was acquainted much with the periods of activities among the Jewish as well as the Roman and the various sects, and the variations in property owners and the workmen.

So far as the worldly goods were concerned, the *entity* was *very* rich during that experience. The entity gained and lost, the entity gained and lost through the experience; and much of those indecisions, much of those abilities in its dealings with its fellow man in the present, arise from the experiences during that sojourn.

1497-2   M.46   2/8/38   Ardemetus

. . . the entity acted as the assistant in the experiences of the Romans with the law as propounded by the Lord of lords and the King of kings and the Prince of princes and the Son of man; yea the Son of God! Yet what did ye about same?

Thy great opportunities were before thee; they were not abased but they were not *used!* Yet it might be said to be the most outstanding, because of the great opportunities . . .

Q-1. During my sojourn on the earth in Palestine, did I know and was I in contact with the entity now known as [1151, my present brother], and under what conditions?

A-1. As indicated, you were; and under the circumstances where one was the supervisor, the other was one who sought to supervise over the *individual* in the various provinces and the various activities—and the other as a group supervisor.

693-3   M.11   3/13/35   Samaleuen

. . . the entity was in the land now known as the Palestine land, during the periods when the Master walked in the earth.

The entity then was among those that were the scoffers, among those of the Sanhedrin itself; for the entity then, in the name Samaleuen, represented the tribes of Reuben, and was of the household of those of that particular people. For it represented same in those experiences in the beginning of the separation of the house, for the entity was itself Reuben! [In this same reading the entity was told: "Before that we find the entity was among the firstborn of Jacob and Leah . . ."] [4]

In the experience there, we find the entity lost in many respects; gained somewhat in the latter portions, yet allowed self to be led away by that which seemed for the moment necessary for the satisfying of the material expressions and material beings in the activities of the individual.

1378-1   M.73   6/1/37   Artemas

. . . the entity was in the earth during the period when the Master walked in the earth.

Then the entity was among the elders, or of the Sanhedrin; in the name Artemas—a doubter, a questioner; oft in the capacity as one who would seek to give the interpretation to the rulers, to those in authority, as to the activities among the multitudes.

Hence a doubter during those periods of His material manifestation, yet with those experiences following not only the crucifixion but the resurrection morn, and that as related to the entity by Joseph of Arimathea and by Nicodemus, the entity became among the staunch defenders of the apostles, the disciples, during the days of persecution. And not until there was the demise of the entity in that experience was there any great amount of physical persecution to the first church.

As to the application in this experience—the entity has been a stickler for details; also the experiences of those who had experiences and visions, experiences in those activities that made for the closer associations with the unseen to many, have been and are a part of the whole experience of this entity.

1933-1   M.47   6/24/39   Elijah

. . . the entity was in the Palestine land, during those periods when there was the establishing of the Roman peoples in that land.

The entity was among those who were of the Pharisee group, and those who were in authority during those periods in which there were the needs for the consideration of not only the religious associations but the political affiliations as grew *by* the declaring of the needs for the means of exchange as well as the periods in which the activities of the tax were levied upon the peoples—and the means and necessity of those taxes being paid, or exchange being made into the country being represented by the manner or means of money.

Hence we find the entity was again associated or affiliated with those activities in which there were the needs for the consideration of such, and yet in those experiences we find the entity was able to make for the greater associations that brought less of the hardships by the attempts to correlate the needs of an activity in which the religious activities as well as the abilities of the entity's own peoples were to be considered.

The name then was Elijah. In the experience the entity gained, the entity lost. For there were periods in that experience when the entity sought to make for surety of material things for self, without the full, wholehearted thought of those who were dependent upon the entity for direction and counsel, owing to the position which the entity held.

Hence the warning that has been given—as to there being less of faultfinding and more of the magnifying of the helpful forces as may be derived from associations with any and *every* character or group.

For, know this—and that it applies to self: No man, no group is in authority save it is *allowed* by God! It may oft appear to be in conjunction with the forces of evil, yet all must be purged so as by fire, that we may indeed learn that each entity, each soul is his brother's keeper!

537-1   F.31   4/18/34   Marya

. . . the entity was in that period when the Master walked in the land, during those periods when there was the cleansing in the temple.

The entity then was among those who aided in the outer court, but being of that faith; for, being in the Gentile court, it was of the Hebraic faith.

Through coming in contact with those influences there was brought to the entity contentment in the inner self; though the outward appearances were oft as a turmoil and strife, for they were bickered about by the Roman influence in the land; and often there were rebukes received by those in charge because of its peculiar associations and adherence to this sect of the peoples that had been questioned—and that grew more and more to be questioned by those in authority; for indeed were those in authority sons of Belial.[5]

In that experience the entity gained much; for the experience was much that may be sought, to be in the hearing of life itself. He that was able to bring, and is able to bring into the hearts and souls of those that seek Him, the home, the hope for not only life eternal but the hopefulness in being able to be a channel of blessings to others—through the application of that experience in the life in the present sojourn.

Also abilities and lessons that may be taken from those experiences, or drawn upon by self in its application in the present, may make the greater background for the field of activity of the entity . . .

Q-2. *Just what have been the associations of myself and [295]?*

A-2. [Interrupting] They both knew the weaknesses of each in Galilee.

Q-4. *What was my name in Galilee?*

A-4. Marya.

2915-1   M.42   2/15/43   Eliazaer

. . . the entity was in that land when the Master walked in the earth; being among the Levites that cared for the building of the temple itself, in the repairs, in the making of moldings, in the repair of many of those things that had to do with that activity.

This gave the entity a sense of those purposes and ideals for which this edifice stood, and only in the latter portion of the entity's experience did there come the sense of the spiritual rather than the purely material application of the tenets and truths in the law of Moses.

Coordinating those with the teaching of the disciples and the followers of the Master became the problem of the entity through that period. And the entity saw the destruction of the temple of that day, but in the latter part of its sojourn in the earth—as Eliazaer.

1900-1   F.52   5/29/39   Polymus

. . . the entity was in the Roman rule and period when the natives were accepting the activities of the Christian principles and purposes of a strange people from a strange land. Yet those decided convictions as came to the entity then, as Polymus, made for those activities that aided every one of the groups that came into the Roman experience for the service in the establishing of church, in the establishing of a definite congregation, or the body politic for definite service and definite work in the varied directions.

1492-1   F.62   12/4/37   Ruthen

. . . the entity was in the Land of Promise, during those periods when the Master walked in the earth. When there were the activities following the crucifixion, the entity was among those who came into the city and joined with the apostles and the disciples in caring for those from other lands. And the entity then grew in grace; yea, in good favor with those that were given to the ministering to those peoples that had joined themselves and given of their worldly possessions for the care *of* the followers of the faithful for a cause.

There the entity gained through the experiences, lost through the attempts to make for rather personal association to rise to authority; gained again through the teachings that made for the greater *harmonious* experiences among those of many tongues, among those of many climes that had become then of a *one* desire and purpose . . .

Then the entity was in the name Ruthen.

4098-1   M.9 mos.   4/10/44   Sylvesta

. . . the entity was in the Holy Land when there were those activities in which there were the gatherings of those who sought to carry on the activities of the Master.

The entity was among those who added music to the service that brought the oneness of mind, not only in song but in the music of the instrument. For then the stringed instruments were used, but the piano—which should be used in the present—is by nature a stringed instrument.

The entity then added to that hope, that faith, that understanding, by keeping that touch which would span the varied realms of thought.

The name then was Sylvesta.

2308-1 F.4 7/13/40 Sister Duene

. . . the entity was in the Land of Promise, during those periods when there were the holy women set as the heads of the church, or as counselors; not as deaconesses, not as those today considered as sisters of mercy or sisters superior, but rather those who took the veil that there might be the better preparations of self to be offered *as* channels through which greater blessings might come, and greater abilities for teaching. They were those who separated themselves from their families, their homes, that they might become as channels of blessings to others.

The entity was known then as Sister Duene. In the experience the entity gained throughout, through the abilities as a nurse, as a teacher, as a reader, as a song-giver, as one who read poetry.

3379-2 F.49 11/27/43 Jacobeian

. . . the entity was in the Holy Land when there were those establishings of the church that brought people together who gave of all their substance for the furtherance of the teaching and ministering.

The entity then was one set in the same relationship to those groups as the first deacons, then in the same relationship as Stephen, as the rest of the deacons appointed to look after, to collect, to administer to the needs of the families and the children of those families.

Thus the entity came to be among those acting in the capacity of what today would be called a mother superior in any organized group for the care of mothers and children at that particular period of activity.

Then the name was Jacobeian. The entity again added much to judge the young, to judge its own sex and questioned men — even some of the disciples, as well as some of the deacons as to their manner of approach to others of their own activities in that experience.

Hence in the present experience we find a question mark after every man, for this entity. These bring about disturbances, at times.

2156-1   F.4½   3/30/40   Saint Cecilia
. . . the entity was among those who were given a special service in the early activities of the church, in the bringing of spiritual concepts into the minds of individuals through music.

Then the entity was Saint Cecilia—or as Celia the entity was first known, and then known for its abilities in the teaching and ministering to those in the various stages of man's expression and development there—in the Roman activity and experience of the early church; for the entity brought hope, patience, understanding.

Thus we will find hours in the present oft when music—that is of the nature that brings into association those forces of the celestial as well as the mental and spiritual—will be the greater channel in which the entity may enable, or be enabled, to give the expressions of those messages, those lessons that will be so much a help, and bring hope, in the minds of others.

Not by questioning, not by *any* of those things that are so oft as tortures to the entity. For, remember, as has been given, it is not in sacrifice but in a service of love—both within and from without—that the entity may give its best as the channel for aiding and assisting others.

For there will gradually come the growth of the abilities within the entity's experience to not only bring messages of hope and of light to others, but to bring aid—through the very laying on of hands—to those who are not only mentally but physically sick—to those who are ill at ease, rather than the diseased, throughout the entity's experience. In such a manner, with that tempering, with that training which has been indicated, may the entity be of the greater service.

Then, give particular attention to the music in the experience of the entity; not only as the channel, but as an outlet for itself in its desires for expressions in the mental and the spiritual. For, hath it not been said that only music may span that space between the finite and the infinite? The entity's music may be the means of arousing and awakening the best of hope, the best of desire, the best in the heart and soul of those who will and do listen. Is not music the universal language, both for those who would give praise and those who are sorry in their hearts and souls? Is it not a means, a manner of universal expression? Thus may the greater hope come.

1224-1   F.70   7/20/36   Susanna

. . . the entity was in the land now known as the Promised Land, during those periods when there were the teachings, the turmoils, the strifes between the Roman people, the natives, the people that used those conditions to exploit their activities and to present much of their teachings in the land.

The entity then was in a position of power, in a position of state, as it were; thus coming in *material* applications as to a knowledge of, as to an interpreting in her own experience of the activities of individuals in political, in economic, in ruling influences of state, in ruling influences of religious forces, and those forces that made for oppressions upon those that were already burdened with material taxation, with those that were beset by doubts and fears by the various teachings that were being presented by the various leaders or teachers during that sojourn.

For the entity then was in the household of those in authority as of the Roman soldiery, but of rather a Grecian descent; thus those teachings of Greece, the beauties in some expressions of same were a part of the entity. For during that period those things that made for conveniences in the home, those things that made for the rules and laws became a portion of the entity's activity; and thus under an environment of Roman taxation, aesthetic Jewish reaction, the rebellious forces as combined made for periods through which the entity—though as the period indicated—made for the woman power to rule in the home rather than in positions of power, that made for an activity that changed many of those influences as related to the authority of those that were of the Jewish faith.

The entity then in the name Susanna gained and lost, and gained and lost, from the spiritual and mental activity. Yet the help that was rendered to many during those experiences and the associations that made for those activities have brought into the experience of the entity many in its own household, in its own surroundings, that make for those periods to be met in the spiritual ideals to be set. And to the purposes and as to those influences, these are to be held as those that change not.

1874-1   F.65   5/6/39   Salome
. . . the entity was in the land now known as the Promised Land; during those periods when the Master walked in the earth.

There we find the entity came under those influences and activities of the Master Himself, as well as being among those who aided in the establishing of those who went about ministering—through the activities in those periods following the crucifixion, the resurrection, and the days of Pentecost.

For the entity was among those spoken of as the holy women, that attended those activities following the experiences; first the entity coming in contact with those activities at the death *and* the raising of Lazarus, and later with Elizabeth, Mary, Salome, Mary of Magda, Martha—all of those were a part of the experiences of the entity—as Salome.[6]

There we find the entity gaining the greater through the services and activities as a seamstress, or a maker of linen or tatting, or laces, during those experiences.

And through those activities the entity brought into the experiences of others assurances of help through confidences, through the activities that brought hope to those who were discouraged . . .

Hold to that as ye attained in that experience!

Hence again we find the life of Him, who is the Savior of *men*, becomes the more interesting—and especially the periods of His dwelling at Bethany, His aid to the sisters there, as well as those periods that were close to the days when He appeared so oft to His disciples and those who have kept alive His activities.

Do thou then likewise in the present—not only in thy conversation, in thy daily thoughts, but in thy dealings with thy fellow man. For these may be expressed even as He gave—they that give a kind word, that may become as a cup of water to a thirsty soul, shall in no wise lose their reward.

Gentleness, kindness, patience—as ye have had to learn—are not hard in *Him*—only when ye lose thy hold on His promises! . . .

Hold fast to that ye have determined in thy heart and mind, from those experiences in the Bethany land; and following in the making of experiences for others to know His love—not as obligations, but as a privilege to know His love.

2610-1   F.43   10/24/41   Pasquarl

. . . the entity was in the Promised Land, during the experiences when the Master walked in the earth. Acquaintanceships with those having to deal with the early life of the Master were a part of the entity's experience.

For, the entity then was among the women chosen as ministers to the sick, the distressed, the bereaved during those periods when there were the beginnings of the organized church as it is called today.

Hence the entity has those abilities of ferreting out data as may be related to a fact, to a condition.

Hence the entity is a good nurse, a good minister, a good bookkeeper, a good home builder. In any of these the entity may find the greater expression of self in the present.

The name then was Pasquarl.

5356-1   F.25   7/19/44   Judith

. . . the entity was in the Holy Land following the periods when the Master walked in the earth when there were those variations as to the position of the woman in the home. The entity was among those who were reared to follow closely in the precepts of the people who followed the Master. With persecutions, and the peoples in positions as the Romans, questions arose in the experience of the entity then, as Judith, as to the advisability of entertaining those in song, dance and the broader expressions of that which would be called free-love in relationships with groups. The entity gave way to self's own expression and yet, as has been given, the directions, the teachings from childhood brought the entity up short when there were questions which arose as to the morality of the entity. In the experience the entity suffered mentally and spiritually.

Beware, these are a part of thy consciousness, don't let it happen again!

3197-1   F.65   9/6/43   Lydia

... the entity was in the group of peoples active when there were the gatherings in the early church in Jerusalem.

The entity entered there from Thyatira, and had been active in the services in preparation for the application of home economics in a manner in which frugality was the principal theme of the home builders.

Then in the name Lydia, the entity aided in the preparations for the clothing, the making and weaving of same. Hence the necessity of the entity in the present being most careful as to its dress, as to its manners of approach—as we will see.

The entity gained and lost; gained when the application was for the greater activity, lost when fear as to the physical protection was allowed to enter to such an extent as to interfere with the spiritual things. Hence there were periods of disturbance for the entity.

3091-1   F.72   7/11/43

... the entity was in the Holy Land, though the entity was a visitor there from the northern and eastern lands.

Those experiences brought the ability as the searcher, as the mother to many that were less fortunate in the activities of that established as the church.

The entity did not come in personal contact with the Master in the earth, but with those closely associated with Him— especially Luke, Paul, Barnabas, John, and Lucius, in the activities in the church at Laodicea.

There the entity was among those who comforted those that were disturbed, and especially the young.

The entity has an interest, then, in children, and the unfortunate—especially from indifference on the part of others.

This again indicates that attained in the cross of gold, in the right side of the drawing illustrating the life's seal.

In the present experience hold fast to those tenets of the

truth, the light, the hope in Him. Though it may arise even from the muck, as the lily indicates, it in its beauty is clothed as with the glory of the Father Himself.

2803-2   F.23   9/11/42   Aquilasteben, called Amada

... the entity was in the Roman land, during those periods when there were those expansions in the land; when there were those activities in which varied groups of the soldiery were garrisoned in the Holy Land; during that period when the Master walked in the earth.

There the entity was one seeking for the knowledge of those activities carried on by the Master, as well as the disciples. We find the entity seeking out the Master, coming in contact with same through those offices of Mary, Martha, John and James.

Thus we find the entity contributing not only in the material needs and activities, but in the actual bringing of greater understanding to many of the peoples through those trials, through those persecutions that followed; aiding those who brought the tenets and truths to Rome.

For, because of this activity, the companion was recalled to Rome. Yet the entity was active even there, and thus became acquainted with Paul and Peter when they themselves became a part of those experiences that brought the establishing of the church in Rome.

The name then was Aquilasteben, called Amada. The entity gained. There were the greater activities then, in its associations, in its experiences, that brought about the greater unfoldment; save in those periods when the entity was the interpreter of the law—during those periods before that . . .

Q-2. What has been my past association with my mother that I feel the urge to protect her from hardships?

A-2. In the Palestine experience ye were in very close companionship, especially with the activities in the church. For, the mother then became the close friend who was brought from Palestine to Rome and eventually put in authority as the deaconess in the church there.

This should indicate those feelings for the mother in the present.

Q-3. What causes the resentment my brother . . . expresses when I attempt to help him and how may I bring about a better understanding?

A-3. So live that thine own life is a living example. Don't try to persuade him at all.

The associations were in the church in Rome, when there were disputations because of the servant being made deaconess.

1765-2   F.52   12/22/38   Media

. . . the entity was in the land now known as the Holy Land, or the Promised Land; during those periods just after the Master walked in the earth—when there were the greater settlings of a peoples, of which the entity was a part, in and about what is now known as the Palestine land.

There we find the entity was engaged in the serving of foods, or in what would be termed today a restaurant or wayside place for the rest; or an inn where those especially of milk and bread and the fruits of the land were served as a nourishment—rather than the providing of places of rest *as* only an inn.

In the experience we find the entity was continually in a wonderment; not only as to the stories heard, not only as to the experiences of those whom the entity met in the daily associations, but as to that which was aroused within self through those very associations . . .

The name then was Media—of the Parthenian peoples.

3578-1   F.37   12/30/43   Gassari

. . . the entity was in the Grecian land, when there were those teachers from the Holy Land who appeared through those periods when there was the building up of the teachings of the Holy One.

There the entity, in its ability as an artist, undertook the depicting for the young, and the groups gathered about the entity, those stories as related to the happenings in the life of the Master; as of Lazarus breaking the tomb, as of the Last Supper, as the healing of the man by the wayside, in the pool of Siloam, the driving of the exchangers from the temple. These the entity attempted to paint, and these the entity finds in self as the experience that answers to something deep within. They were flat in their colors, yes, but an execution worthy of an artist—that is still latent within self. The artistry of words as well as of color, the artistry of purpose in the hearts of the young and the old, the entity may weave into the souls and lives of men as to bring a new hope to many.

The name then was Gassari.

2922-1   M.3   2/8/43   Carvett

... the entity was in the Holy Land, during those periods when there were the teachings by the disciples and the apostles.

The entity while young in years attempted to picturalize the scenes as were told the entity of the Master's activities.

These, or any and all such drawings or pictures of the life of the Holy Child, will have an interesting effect upon the body. And watch how often he will tell you they left out this, or put in that—especially in the younger years!

Then, these are sources from which we will find an interest in various types of art, especially those descriptive of nature or of the activities of individuals in associations with such; as of battles or battle scenes, or those depicting the fireside—or peace at home.

The name then was Carvett. The entity held a position of power throughout that period of journeying through many lands, in its abilities as a cartoonist—or the beginning of that development, in certain definite schools of art.

1842-1   M.32   3/14/39

Q-5. How prominent was Peter in the life and work of the Christian church?

A-5. As has been indicated here, these variations and differences that arose in the establishing of the church by Philip and by others even rather than Paul (in the Roman church)—Peter stood first and foremost of those in the *established* organizations in and about Rome. *Paul* was rather among those that were in authority or power.

3258-1   M.17   10/3/43   Pheres

... the entity was in the Roman land during those periods when there was just the beginning of the persecution of the great numbers that had been drawn to those activities in which Peter spoke to great numbers or hordes as they were called in that particular period.

The applying of self in those tenets of that period will be well. And none may be found better than the Book itself, especially in the study of the admonitions first to that who was saved by the ark of the covenant.[7] Study these thoroughly and apply that thou findest to be good in the present. For these are well to live by as well as to die by.

But these have brought and do bring periods of seeking justification of that chosen to be done. Let thy yeas be yea, thy nays be nay in every activity; know, that you will meet these as ye apply yourself in the lessons taught in that particular period there in such a short time.

The name then was Pheres, and the entity was close to those that had the directions of the early church; not only in that particular phase of its service but throughout the whole activity of the life.

341-8   M.17   2/28/25   Andrew

In the one before this we find in this same land wherein the entity now has [then had] lost its earthly existence. Then in the fisherman on the Sea of Galilee, and became the follower of the Nazarene, the Gift to the world, and the entity sought this out and brought many to the sound of the living words as were given to the peoples roundabout, and the entity one of those [who] studied the lessons and had reached that point where the soul knew the awakening and the purpose for which it had set itself in earth's plane. The name then Andrew.[8]

341-19   M.18   1/30/26   Andrew

This experience then, especially in that physical body known as Andrew, we find the entity then the second brother in a family of four, and in the early childhood one willful in many ways, taking up the physical vocation of the parents and brother, and in the days when John began to teach in the wilderness, the entity, the body (physical), Andrew, became first an adherent and a disciple of that teacher, and remained close as an aide, from first conviction, until the appearance of Jesus to become the disciple of the entity's master. When pointed out by John as the one that should be greater, and increase as he decreased,[9] Andrew then followed the new leader into the wilderness, and was close with Him during the temptation, as is recorded by Matthew,[10] and when the return to the seashore, sought out the brother [Peter], telling of those ideas, ideals, as were propounded by Him who had been pointed out, and became the close disciple then of the Teacher and Master, following close throughout the whole physical career of the Master; not as the chosen three, yet one as is given often the greater physical conditions to do and to carry out. One often spoken to for the reference to others, and this is particularly seen, especially, upon two occasions: In the feeding of the multitudes [11] in the entrance to the city for the evening lodgement to keep the Passover. In the entering into the garden on the last evening.[12]

The entity, then among those who held the higher attitude towards the spiritual teachings of the Master, and to understand the full conception of that conception obtained, or that full consciousness obtained or gotten in this appearance, is then necessary to understand *why* the entity has chosen oft in the physical earth plane to manifest lessons gained, or, as is to be termed in slang parlance, often has the entity chosen to seek, to know, "why the wheels go round," from the physical action and the spiritual insight that impels same.

After the dispersing of the followers when persecutions came, the entity, Andrew, then went into Mesopotamia, and those countries where the entity felt that the learning of the Master was obtained, during the early education of the Master, and the travels of the Master, see?

Then, the entity remained true to that teaching, and brought *many* to the knowledge of God that *is* within every human physical being that seeks to know how same manifests through the individual.

There is seen, then, the urge as is given, as to how every measure of any truth is compared to that Master's teaching in the present, for, as is seen, when this is correlated with intent and purpose, and the first urge as is seen in a physical manifestation, this to the entity becomes the sine qua non of power, force, of manifesting forces in the physical, spiritual, mental world, and the application in the present is to ever weigh those experiences in the present, measuring them up to that standard as is seen and known, and felt, as is superior, and as high above all others as the heavens above the earth; as superior as the sun's light is to the moon's dull rays; as great as the winds are to the stench that rises from foul forces exumed from the low places; as great as the mountains above the plains; and as the entity keeps these ideals, these principles, applied in the teaching, the writings, the labors of the day, so may this lesson, this experience, gain for the entity that necessary to draw nigh unto that drawing force that gives the great impelling entity the effect of the Master.

2002-1   M.28   9/14/39   Cipio

. . . the entity was in the Promised Land, and in that particular vicinity of Caesarea—where there were those activities by the early workers in the church that was established in Jerusalem.

The entity was among those who became particularly interested in the activities of the disciples and apostles when Peter strengthened the church in Caesarea; especially being present when the rebuking of Simon brought such a change in that individual's activity as well as in the entity—then known as Cipio.[13]

Coming under those influences, with the studies as had been attained through the Egyptian as well as the East Indian legends, the entity made of himself that which became known as the physician in those experiences, but *not* in the dosing so much as in the applications of the external nature for the relief of disorders and disturbances to which man was especially heir to through that period of activity.

Disease has changed little—their names, their classifications, much!

In the experience the entity gained, the entity lost. A great opportunity for the embracing of the real source of truth and knowledge and understanding was partially passed by. Do not in the present sojourn make such an error again.

2480-1   M.17   10/3/27   Zioul

. . . in the land when the Master came in the land of Galilee. The entity then among those fishermen who heard, saw, and experienced much of the teaching and the ministering by the Master—for the entity, while not wholly accepting, never rejecting those teachings. Rather the fear of the position held preventing same from being in the life as the crowning experience in the earth's plane. Then in the name Zioul, and the entity in this experience *lost* rather than gained, for without applying those tenets, those lessons, with the experience, the entity lost in that experience. The urge, rather that of the innate desire to know what those teachings were by the Sea of Galilee, for this land, this teaching, this experience, holds the highest of urges for the entity. Cleave—cleave to same! . . .

In the abilities then of the entity lies that as the teacher, the minister, or the historian, for the entity needs first gain that full insight of that lost in the contact with the Master, and in this gain that understanding that the life lived must be the reflection of the entity's concept of the Creative Energy that the inner self must worship.

Then keep that of the Nazarene and Galilean history before self, and bring to others that knowledge that in the giving of self to service is the highest service to the Creative Energy, or God—for in Him is the light, and the light is the light of the world; for, as He became the Son through the manner of the experience in the earth's plane, so may we, as sons, become brothers and heirs to that kingdom.

3374-1   F.35   11/23/43   Mary

The entity was among those children who gathered first that day when He stood beside the sea and later spoke from Peter's boat. The entity was then a girl in the early teens who heard those words of the Master. When it allows itself in the present, these words can bring into the experience the greater realization of the beauties of water, the loveliness of clouds in the sky, of the storm, the snow, the sleet, the hail. All of these speak to the entity of the closeness, the loveliness of the Master's promises to the children of men.

Keep ever faithful to that, of the beauty that is wrought even from the contemplation. Again and again, read the different versions proclaimed by Matthew, Mark and John as to what those passages mean to man.[14]

THE FOLLOWERS AND THE CHURCHES 367

The entity was known as Mary; not of the holy women. For the entity later was among those very much in love with John Mark, until the questionings of Peter and Barnabas brought about dissuasions.

The entity later added to the helpers in the churches, in the various activities during the latter portion of the experience, even coming into the Grecian activities; almost being a missionary itself.

3054-4   F.50   2/16/44

[Aura chart reading] In the lower left-hand corner put the fishing boat wherein Jesus sat and spoke to the multitude on the seashore at Bethsaida, with Peter and John in the boat.[15] This picture would indicate the extreme ages of His followers. Peter would be about sixty, while John would only be about eighteen, and the Master thirty-two.

1935-2   F.39   8/13/42   Lacish

. . . the entity was in the Promised Land, or Palestine land, in those periods of activities of the followers or disciples of the Master in the earth.

The entity was among those given, by the very power given to the disciples or the apostles, to be a healer, an instructor, a teacher, both of the young and the old. This brought into the experience of the entity some periods of activity in which— while there were many persecutions and there were abilities necessarily used by the entity to be able to control crowds, groups, or individuals—there came understanding and aid to the entity, as well as its associates and activities, through the period.[16]

The name then was Lacish. In the experience the entity gained much.

5367-1   F.37   7/19/44   Elen

. . . the entity was in the Holy Land when there were those teachers who were following in the footsteps of the Son of man, even one Jesus of Nazareth.

The entity was one who in the period was used by others to interpret for men seeking material gain who were rebuked by Peter.[17] Thus the entity was healed from the body being used by other influences outside of self for gain. Thus the entity was purified for a purpose, and became one who supplied in the laying on of hands, healing forces to others . . .

The name then, as would be called in the present, was Elen.

870-1   M.15   3/28/35   Cleopas

The entity was among those that gathered with those of His followers, and was among those that became the closer disciples of the Master; remaining with those throughout the greater portion of the teachings of same, and was the brother-in-law of Peter, that one that became as the spokesman for those of the twelve that gathered as His material representatives in the earth.

Then the entity was in the name Cleopas, and the husband of Cleo—or the father of Mark. In the experience the entity gained throughout; for though the activities brought the entity into the close associations with those of the Jewish peoples and those of the Roman rulers, those of the various sets and sects of the period, the entity remained true to not only his duties— as those that were to represent the government in the land, as an appointed place—but also as a representative of those of the faith to which the entity's peoples had adhered and joined with those of the teachings.

963-1   M.15   7/26/35   Haniah

. . . during those periods when there was the establishing of those who followed close in the footsteps and teachings of the Nazarite, those who followed the Master in the day.

The entity came as a boy into that environ, being the son then of Simon Peter's sister, in the name then Haniah; young, but blessed by the Master when only a few months old, and grew to know much of those things that transpired *after* the crucifixion, and the persecution of those that followed in the way.

The entity then did not live long in that experience; only to early young manhood, or to the age of nineteen, when by choice the entity passed on to those activities in Venus.

In the application of that experience in the present, there is all the more need for the training; and especially in the insistence at first upon the entity reading of those happenings of that day. Then be sure these do not become as lodestones to the entity at that age of nineteen.

In the lessons gained, in the lessons that may be applied in the abilities which may be made manifest, much will be recalled by the entity; if these books are studied and those meditations are followed closely.

Let the meditation be oft, "FATHER, GOD, IN ME, OPEN THOU MY MIND, MY UNDERSTANDING, THAT I MAY SEE, MAY KNOW, THE TOUCH OF HIS HAND!". . .

Keep the body, the mind, *clean;* that there may be those reactions of the entity as the nephew of Peter.

3418-1   F.26   12/6/43   Rehbal

. . . the entity was in the Holy Land, during those periods when there were disappointments because the Son of man, the Savior, the Master, the Teacher had been crucified.

The entity while young in years took on much of those doubts and fears that arose in the hearts of people with whom the entity was associated. Yet, through the teachings of those close in the household of Peter, as well as the friends or the nephew of Peter (Mark), the entity came to know much of the beauty and the love and the joy that comes with finding peace in the knowledge of the risen Lord. For in same He becomes the resurrection, the symbol of life, and the fulfilling of that as He gave, "I came that ye might have life and that more abundant." What can be more abundant than more experiences of life in the earth, and these the manifestations through which opportunites of body, mind and soul may express self, in giving glory and praise ever to the sources of life, light and truth.

The name then was Rehbal.

1346-1   M.1 day   3/3/37   John Louis, or Louie

. . . the entity was in the land during those periods when the Master walked in the earth; and the entity was among those of the household of one of the apostles of the Master, being then a nephew of Peter—in the name then John Louis, or Louie—as the entity was called.

In the experience the entity was a leader, yet a weaver of nets and following in the ways of those who were the fishers; yet rather among those who prepared the means and manners than of those who were called the fishermen; what today would be called the wholesale dealing in same.

The entity was a follower of those disciples, and in a portion of the experience suffered through privations by reasons of being driven from place to place.

There the entity gained and lost, and gained. For material destruction and material persecution brought distraughtness.

Yet as was given, "Those that are strong, strengthen the weak" may have been well applied during those periods of activity; as the entity began to become a minister, a teacher, during that sojourn.

Then did the entity gain much, and become a leader and a strong fort to many that were troubled in those days.

2154-1   F.19   3/23/40   Cleo

The entity was among those who were later called the holy women—being among the daughters of those who were the leaders, the followers of the Master, Jesus, the Christ.

We find that the entity was a niece of Peter—a daughter of Andrew, one of the disciples; and was among those who were active following the crucifixion in caring for the upper chamber where the disciples and those first followers gathered.[18]

The entity then took care of that chamber, as it was then the wife of a brother of John and James, Zebedee's children; and the entity's activities brought blessings to the many, making that chamber as a home, a church, a meeting place, a hopeful experience for those throughout that period—even when the persecutions arose. For the entity then, as Cleo, made for those activities that brought hope to the persecuted. Disturbances that arose were counted rather by the entity as blessings, in that they enabled the entity to suffer for its faith.

Hence, as has been indicated, hold *fast* to that faith which has prompted thee, and which does prompt thee, in thy endeavors and relationships to that which has been and is thy ideal.

1742-2   F.47   9/2/31   Polias

. . . in that land, and during that period when there were the spreading of those teachings of the peoples from the Holy

Land into the Eternal City, as was then termed—as is oft considered in the present. The entity then among those of the womenfolk who followed those that were imprisoned during those periods, who were forced to give account of the activities before those in power, and the entity suffered in body and in mind, gained after there had been that suffering and that understanding coming in that there *be* the needs oft that those of the physical must be crucified that the *spiritual* life may be made alive. In the name then Polias, and a follower of him who taught in the catacombs of the city, he who was crucified with his head downward, and a member of his household, being then a *sister* of Peter's wife [19] . . .

1531-1   F.45   2/9/38   Salone
. . . the entity was in what is now called the Holy Land, during those periods that followed when there had been the crucifixion.

And the entity was among the children of those that were called of the household of faith.

For as the entity was closely associated with those in what would be termed the household of Peter, we find many of the younger ones—as Mark, Silas, John—were closely associated with the entity, as Salone, in the Jerusalem experiences.

And though those were periods of turmoil, periods of wonderment, periods of bodily suffering in many ways and manners, they brought for the entity soul-developments that make for the crying needs within the experience of the entity in the present experiences; wherein there are the desires to help not only the less fortunate but to make for ways and means in which those who have erred or wandered may find the way home.

528-14   F.29   12/30/37   Josia
. . . the entity was in the land now known as the Palestine land, or the land of promise—when there were those days following those when the Master had walked in the earth; and among those peoples who had gathered from many portions of the land during the latter days—or upon the day of Pentecost.

The entity was among those that were born in and during that period, and of the Galilean land; of those children that were close to Salome in the relationships to John Mark and of that household—kinsmen of Peter, Andrew.

Thus we find the entity growing under those periods of oppression, suppression; an activity in which there were the general conditions of oppression because of political rather than religious reasons—and later, in the early years, became the oppression because of the religious persecutions.

Thus the entity grew under those material environments during that sojourn . . .

And know that He in whom ye have believed is able to keep that ye may commit unto Him against any experience that may arise in thy conscious activity; whether in material things from the material causes or purposes or those in the mental achievements of the material or spiritual thoughts, or of the purely spiritual purposes and imports that become a part of the experience of every entity in its activity among material things.

The name then was Josia.

884-1   F.Adult   4/9/35   Anniaus

. . . the entity was in the land now known as the Roman, during those periods when there were those that were returning from other lands when the whole of the world—as it were—had been turned upside down by the teachings of those that had followed the lowly Nazarene.

The entity then was among those of the household of Cyrenius of the centurions that were in charge of some of those disciples and apostles that were entombed or jailed in the Roman periods just after those changes that were brought about by the new order of things under the Caesar that followed after Augustus.

And the entity listened oft to those psalms and songs of those that gathered for the making of praise; even for the bonds of the flesh, but for that which had released the spirit and soul of the speaker or the singer in the glorying of self being redeemed through those things that had been promised to Him and by Him that had opened the tomb and had spoken again to His fellows, to those of His brethren.

In the latter portion of its sojourn there, as Anniaus, the

entity accepted those teachings and gave out to others what became a portion of her own experience in those things that had made for an arousing of an awareness in the experience of the entity. For the visions came, and were seen; and the healing influences that came with those visions enabled the entity to quiet the fears of the little ones, to relieve the temperatures in the bodies of those that were aroused not only by passion but by the poisons of those influences from the impurities that were taken within. The fevers of certain types responded to the gentleness of Anniaus as she worked in and among those of her own people; suffering in body only when the greater persecutions came, yet her own household became one that many resorted to for the encouraging influences that were ever about the activities of the entity.

2988-2   F.37   5/6/43   Rhoda

. . . the entity then was a sister of John Mark. And it was at that house that there were the first consciousnesses of the attractiveness to men, as well as to the spiritual things—when Peter was released from prison.[20]

The name then was Rhoda; not the one that answered the door, but one present in that household at the time.

In that experience the entity suffered hardships, from a material angle; yet great were the helps the entity gave to strangers in the early church, and in the early meetings of those groups that worked as helpers to maintain the material things for those who contributed to the welfare of the apostles in that early period.

Yea, the Master knew the entity—and blessed the entity, among those children, though the entity was then in its early teen-age when blessed by the Master.

In the present, then—forget not thy God, nor all His benefits. Forget not those blessings that came from Him as an entity.

Ye are blessed, then, beyond many. Not that there is to be expressed a boastfulness, but make it rather the cause for thy unselfish devotion to the cause of Him in the way as ye go. Let others by thy smile, by thy speech, by thy kindness, take notice that thou hast walked, and dost daily walk, with Him.

2613-1   F.9   11/1/41   Mille

. . . the entity was the sister of Mark and Rhoda; hence acquainted with those persecutions that followed the activities in the Holy City; acquainted with and aroused the more by those experiences extolled by the church when Peter was released from prison . . .

In that experience the entity suffered bodily, yet in spirit, in purpose, in mind gained throughout. For, those principles, those tenets, those hopes aroused through those periods of consciousness and of awareness, remain as the guiding lights, the guiding influences in the present experience of the entity.

The name then was Mille.

2834-1   M.36   10/27/42   Partapathr

. . . the entity was in the Roman land, during those periods when there were the expansions being made in that empire; during the period when the Master walked in the earth.

As a keeper of the guard in those periods following the entrance into those activities of His followers, and the persecution of same, the entity came in contact with the leaders, the speakers, the ministers for the cause; and saw Peter released from prison.

And this brought that consternation, that awareness of a deeper purpose in the activities of the entity in that period of sojourn.

The embracing of the principles and the recall to activity in the Roman province, where again there were those contacts with the leaders, brought into the experience those influences that might sometimes confuse; yet the necessity of purposefulness becomes more apparent in the present experience of the entity.

Then the name was Partapathr.

1406-1   F.14   7/13/37   "household of Rhoda"

. . . the entity was in the Promised Land, or the Palestine period.

The entity was young in years during those experiences when the Master walked in the earth, but was known to many that endured many of the hardships.

For the entity was in the household of Rhoda [21] when there were the gatherings when the persecutions had begun, and when Peter was so miraculously released from prison.

Hence miracles, as ye would term them, to the entity are the things of the day. And true, the entity has the insight into those influences, that the so-called miraculous is a natural law; if there is the living, the thinking, the praying one and the same.

Hence these become to the entity, and those about the entity, wonderments to others as to the abilities; yet these become confusing at times to others and to the entity.

Then, think not on the things of the earth. Think not on those things that are as the passing fancy, but hold to that which is the innate influence from those very understandings as gained; that He *is* life—and to abide in that faith; that belief, that consciousness of His indwelling, is that experience that may bring the joy of living, the better experiences of life, and those things that make others conscious of the entity's presence whenever it is among others.

It would be impossible for the entity to go even among a group of a thousand and not all be conscious that the entity had entered. Why?

As the colors, as the vibrations are a portion of the entity, they also radiate from the entity. Hence many, many, *many* are influenced by the entity even as during that experience when she called to those that had heard, had known, and made for the strengthening influences in even the older of the apostles, even in the younger, and even those that were aged.

For the entity brings into the experience of others a helpful, hopeful influence.

Hence the admonition to never, *never*—though the earth may fall, though things may change—do that which would cause thy conscience to rebuke thee!

For these broken, then there will come too much of that which at times appears under the surface as of "Don't care." For these would lead to dismay, despair, and to disappointments that not only would injure, not only bring discouragement to others but to thyself in such measures that destruction would overshadow thee!

608-7   F.8   7/11/34   Junie

. . . the entity was in that now known as the Palestine land, or the Holy Land, during those periods when the Master walked in the earth.

The entity then was among the children of the household of Cleo, the wife of Peter and his peoples; or the one that was set *secondly* as the child blessed by the Master when He said, "Suffer little children to come unto me, and forbid them not, for of such is the kingdom of heaven." [22]

When a soul, then, has been blessed by Him, who *is* life, how may it ever *wholly* wander from that blessing as given by Life itself? How, when He—*life*—the *Christ*—has promised in thine own experience that ye are to fill a purpose in the experience of others? If ye will wholly trust in Him, He—and ye—will not fail.

The entity, then, in the name Junie, gained; though in the latter portion came suffering, yet the entity—when Peter came from prison—was among these that, with Rhoda, opened the door to let him in, though the prison door had opened to his touch.

In the experience the entity found that awakening that may be aroused in the present to the associations of that which is the ideal in every soul's experience, to be in the earth as a channel of blessings through Him that has blessed thee, that does bless thee, in the activities in a material world. Thus may the greater activity for the entity be aroused in the present.

1715-3   M.16   7/19/30   Clement

. . . during that period when the Master walked in the land. The entity then of the household of the brother of the Lord, in that of James the Less,[23] in the name Clement. In this period the entity gained, for when there was the call, when Peter knocked at the door, the entity opened, and was astonished, as the rest, at that beheld. In this experience the entity gained through the whole of the experience, and in the present that criterion, that trust, that hope as is ever builded, if held only in that same way and manner as *through* that experience, will the entity succeed in that as is asked for; for while physical suffering came *to* the entity during that experience, the lauding of that as is *builded* will be *reversed* in the present; but keep the faith in the way as held during that period. In the latter portion the entity also became the carpenter, even as the Master, and was held by many as the excellent one, especially in the building of the house in Antioch, and this holds a peculiar interest for the entity in the reading of same.

3902-2   M.40   3/25/44   Hedth

. . . the entity saw those activities in which there was either the compliance with or defiance of natural laws, in the period when the Master walked in the earth.

These are still the mysteries to the entity. But natural laws are God's laws. Everything in the earth is ruled by law. He said "Let there be light," and there was light—by law.

What law? Of the spirit of truth, of light itself moving into activity; thus becoming creative by law.

Learn ye then the spiritual law which ye attempted to understand, which ye studied then in the name Hedth.

The entity was an associate of Peter and John, eventually becoming a follower when the entity had been converted from the using of same as a material blessing.

For the universal blessing is, "As ye would that others should do to you, do you even so to them," not do others, lest they do thee; not to use brotherly love as something to build other than greater brotherly love or patience.

1431-1   F.15   8/27/37   Patience (or Ullen—Jhengo)

. . . the entity was in that land during the period when there were the changes being wrought in the activities of the social, the political and the religious world; by the activities of those who had been a part of that experience—or when the disciples and apostles were scattered abroad.

The entity then was among those of the Arab land, and to whose household Andrew and James came during those first periods of the activities. This was James the Less, *not* the brother of John but the brother of the Lord, that came in those activities—and the entity learned much of those from those experiences.

And also there came confusions by the very activities of the plain life, and that as experienced by the apostles when visions and dreams and the quieter moments became as a part of their teachings and their activities in their relationships and dealings with others.

The entity then was in the name Patience—or, as termed then, Ullen (Patience)—Jhengo.

In the experience the entity gained through the greater part of the activity, even though there were those disturbing forces by the variations in the teachings of the entity's peoples and those that were embraced by the entity from the teachings of those who were as companions as well as visitors and friends to the entity during the period.

After the departure and the changes, the entity sought to follow in the way; and only in the latter portion of the periods between twenty-five and thirty years of age did the entity journey to the city where the disciples' teachings were then a part of the activities.

Then the entity saw the persecutions, which it embraced; and very much more of terms and manners than that which had been of the nature where scorn had been a part of the entity's activity in its own surroundings.

Hence the entity came to be looked upon as one that from those without had embraced and manifested those teachings in its experiences, and its life was among those peoples in Jerusalem as an exemplary one to be followed and sought after in its dealings with its fellow man.

The culinary arts, the abilities with the needle, the activities of the household, the desires to minister to those as home building, arise from those experiences; though the entity only enjoyed it occasionally, for many changes were in the experiences of the dwelling of the entity during that sojourn. Yet much may be gained from the lessons innately and manifestedly as urges from the experience; particularly the innate urges for meditations that bring spiritual, inspirational activities in the experience of the entity.

2881-1   F.50   1/13/43   Sophia

. . . the entity was in the Holy Land, when there was the

spreading of those teachings that were a part of the experiences of many.

The entity then was among those of the household of faith, or those associated with the disciples and the teachers during that particular period.

While those persecutions brought periods of material hardships, the mental abilities as a teacher, as a leader, were manifested—as well as the greater universal consciousness as to the activity of spirit in its relationship to the mental and material bodies. These are the manifested abilities in the present.

Then in the name Sophia, the entity was associated with Peter, Andrew, and Matthew. The activities through that period were as a teacher, a minister to those who were carrying on the teachings during that particular sojourn.

4038-1   F.53   4/7/44   Paula

. . . the entity was in the Holy Land following the periods when the persecutions spread those who had come to a more perfect understanding from the teachings and tenets upon the day of Pentecost.

This portion of the activities or of the acts of some of the apostles has meant much to the entity. For there the entity was in close association with some of the apostles, becoming an associate or companion with the son of Andrew in the experience through that land.

Hence the entity was very close to Peter, Mark, as the companion to Andrew's son, and in those activities brought the establishing of helpful forces. For the entity was among the first proclaimed as a deaconess in a church, in its activities in Asia Minor.

The name then was Paula.

2483-2   M.56   12/15/27   Idoddxo

. . . in that land now known as Arabia. The entity then in the thirtieth year came under the influence of the teachings through a disciple of the Master—Andrew; and through this experience gained much. Being then in the time or period, as counted in the present, in the year forty-four. The entity gained, lost—lost, gained—through this appearance. Living to a great age, for the time and for the conditions surrounding the entity. First as the herdsman the entity gained, as the closeness to nature brought much retrospection for the entity. The surrounding conditions brought the keen insight into material conditions, and the association of the entity with the truths brought great power, great knowledge, great understanding. In the application, when these turned to those forces as are created by one being compatible with the law—bringing power, position, and the accompanying conditions with same—the entity *lost,* when this was turned into secular resources or secular purposes for the satisfaction of satisfying fleshly desires for self. In the persecutions that followed (for he became the teacher and the power in that region), the entity lost—and again in coming under the influence of self's own bodily preservation against those truths as set before others by the entity. In the release and the change again, when alone, the entity *gained* in attempting to adjust self and self's conditions to that force as awakened through the contact of one reflecting so much of the Master. In the name Idoddxo . . .

2775-1   M.49   7/1/42   Pebelus

. . . the entity was in the Palestine land, during those periods when there was the dispersing of the followers of the Nazarene; when there was the spreading of the teachings by the persecutions in Jerusalem when James was beheaded.[24]

The entity became especially affiliated or associated with those groups—as of Andrew and Bartholomew—who chose to go towards the east rather than the west. The entity became particularly associated with these two, in a part of the Persian land; then in the name Pebelus.

The entity was a teacher, a gatherer of groups. But with the attaining of those tenets and truths that were propounded to the entity, it became a follower of that sect of the Nazarenes in that land; bringing forth fruit worthy of acceptance before Him, the Maker.

In the experience the entity gained much.

78-1   M.17   5/23/25   Giovod

. . . in the plains country, where the entity became the follower of the Nazarene, under the tutelage of one close to the

Master. Then in the name of Giovod, and the entity became a missionary to the peoples in that land, and in the last days of earthly existence in that plane suffered martyrdom with the entity [Andrew?] whom he was then associated with in those labors. In the present we find the entity then, especially, gifted toward the study of the religion as was then deep-seated in the soul of the entity and remains a part of same, giving the ennobling influence in the life of the entity and becoming a part of same. Then, the abilities in the present plane lie in those relations as is sought in the inmost being of the entity in this sphere: As that of the teacher, lecturer or writer, to those seeking the knowledge of the spiritual indwelling in man of the principles of the Christ.

452-1   M.27   1/16/32   John Mark

. . . during that period when there were many turmoils among the peoples of which the entity then a part. While young in years in that experience, the entity saw much of the oppressions of peoples for the thought as held, and the first account as was written by anyone (that *remains* as an account) was written by the entity under the *direction* of him to whom was given the keys of the kingdom. In the name John Mark.[25] Be well were he to call himself John in the present! In this experience the entity suffered much in many ways, being afflicted in body and being questioned oft by superiors as one not well grounded in faith; yet the entity gained throughout the experience in the activities, in the service rendered to many. Then as a missionary . . .

Q-7. *What relation [was I] to Mary and Joseph?*

A-7. Mary and *Josie.* Rather a son of *Josie,* that was the sister *of* Mary.

452-5   M.28   11/25/32   John Mark

. . . the entity was born during that period which would be known as the sixteenth year of our Lord; his parents were Mary and Marcus, his sisters Rhoda and Mary. He was close to, and a relative of, Chloe and Lois, Josie; all relatives of Mary, the mother of the Lord, of the tribe of Judah; of the household of Marcus; hence sometimes referred to as Marcus, or son of Marcus. In his twelfth year he was healed from an infirmity by the associations with John, the cousin of the Lord, and the Lord. He was one at whose house Peter the apostle came when released from prison, and was a companion of Peter in travels. Later he was an associate and companion with Paul the apostle and Barnabas, and one that returned from the first missionary journey of these two, acting in the capacity of the secretary to Barnabas.[26] He was the first compiler of a letter that later became the gospel known as Mark, collaborating (as it would be termed in the present) with Peter and Barnabas. He became a helpmeet to many of the early martyrs, suffering martyrdom himself in the latter portion of his experience at that time; being, however, the martyrdom of expulsion and traveling in the latter portion of the experience (after the writings in Rome) to those eastern lands with Andrew, the brother of Peter, who had escaped from those same characters of martyrdoms as those that had been sent on to Rome; being sent by Peter *and* by Paul as an emissary to carry the messages of Paul and of Peter to those people whom Andrew was ministering to, rather in what is now called Persia, aiding oft in the *strengthening* of the brethren in the various centers where churches or established organizations had been builded by the efforts of Paul, Barnabas, Silas and the other ministers during that period. Oft he was a companion with Luke, who was an associate and companion of Paul oft in his travels. Luke being rather of those peoples that were free (as he was not of the Jewish descent), this aided John Mark in his abilities to go and come rather at ease; hence after becoming more stable (than as a young man) was of so much aid to the peoples during that period.

As yet there are little of the writings or letters of John Mark, or son of Marcus, other than that contained in the gospel known as Mark. This was written during the fifty-ninth year, or during the thirty-fourth year of the entity's experience in that plane.

He assisted Barnabas in the establishing of the church in northern Africa, or Alexandria, where so *much* persecution *later* was shown in the activities in that center. Much that was compiled by the entity in this land was destroyed in or during the second century. This had been compiled in the great library in Alexandria. There are still intact some writings that may

THE FOLLOWERS AND THE CHURCHES 383

yet be reclaimed, in some of the ruins about the place; as well as in some of those cities in Chaldea and Persia where the entity in the last days went in company with Andrew.

In poetry there was little, as we find, save the reconstruction of some of the psalms that were used in the dedicating of those places of meeting, and in the services at times in these various places.

As has been given regarding the entity that now manifests in the earth's plane, much of that in the stability of purpose and intent is gained by that experience of the entity in that sojourn; much of that which (as may be termed) rings true to the gospels that *were* given in word by those that were the companions of, the disciples of, the apostles of, the Lord — the Master.

Ready for questions.

Q-1. Was the whole Gospel of Mark written by him, or was the last part added on?

A-1. The whole Gospel was written rather in collaboration with Peter and Barnabas. This, as given, was the first of the *written* words respecting the acts, the life, the deeds of the Master; while it is shorter in words, there is more in body content of the acts than in most of the other writings. It is nearer in accord with that in Matthew, but not an abridged condition or abridged writing; for Matthew was written from the churches in Pamphylia, while Mark wrote from Rome. There had been some distribution, or a portion had been carried to many of the various groups before Mark's was accepted, and before Matthew's was given; for this was written some ten to eighteen years later.

Q-2. Did he associate with the Christ?

A-2. As a child.

Q-3. Was John Mark a cripple in boyhood, and how was he healed?

A-3. As given, he was lame in the left limb and healed by first the approaching of John, called the Baptist; later he was healed entirely by the Master during the first year of His ministry.

Q-4. Give any information that would be interesting historically.

A-4. These that have been given may be followed and found to be in accord with that which took place during those periods, when there was consternation among many. John Mark also in young manhood was among those that were fearful, gaining in stamina and strength as persecutions became the greater.

1637-1   M.31   7/12/38   Petros

. . . the entity was in the Holy Land, or Palestine land, during those periods following the life-experience of the Master in the earth.

The entity was very young during those periods, yet closely associated with the activities of many of those who gave their all in body, in purse, and in service toward bringing into the experiences of others the hope as created by the tenets of the Teacher during that sojourn.

Then in the name Petros, the entity was of the peoples that were close with Mark, John and the other John.

In those periods when persecutions and such activities arose, the entity was among those who went to the desert lands with a part of the activity of Andrew and Thomas and the influences that made for the building up in the oasis and the places about those lands in that particular area of a great hope and light in the experience of many.

There again we find the desires were to minister, physically and mentally, to the needs of the bodies of others; which might specially fit the entity in the present for the acts or in the capacities as a researcher in the field of preventative medicines, or those preventatives in relationship to activities or influences of those who become addicts in fields where these have been as yet little followed out.

In that sojourn we find the entity's activities were much in the open. Hence we find in the present that a restlessness comes over the entity often when there is too much of routine, or too much of dictatorial activity of those who are about the entity —no matter what their position or place may be.

3663-1   M.63   2/16/44   Schelmezadek

. . . the entity was in the Holy Land among those peoples of Rome given privilege as an entertainer, as a soothsayer, by the Roman guard, and by those peoples of the outer courts of the gentiles in the temple.

There the entity used what might be called the orange shell game—finding the pea under the shell, only the entity used as a pearl taken from the Persian Gulf.

The entity, as Schelmezadek, gained in power because of the teachings under which he gained when Peter healed those people in the land following the coming to Antioch to preach the gospel.[27]

Thus the entity became a power. He is spoken of there as being one who would buy the gift.

4087-1   M.6   4/15/44

For in the use of the power that has been a portion of the entity's consciousness there may come help to many.

For in the experience before this the entity attempted to buy same from Peter.[28] Hence that tendency, that realization that the misuse of same may bring destructive forces into the experience.

In that experience the entity being warned, as he asked "Pray that I may be forgiven for the thought that such might be purchased," he was forgiven. For as it was indicated, "What thou shalt bind on earth shall be bound in heaven, what thou shalt loose on earth shall be loosed in heaven." There we find that the entity through that experience used the ability granted through such for a greater understanding, a greater interpretation. For all of God that any individual may know is already within self. It is in the application and the practice of same within self, in its relations to its desires, its hopes, its fears, and to its fellow man. For as ye sow, ye must reap.

832-1   F.56   2/18/35   Irman

... the entity was in that period when there were those being persecuted in that land now known as the Galilean land, for the tenets that were being taught by those that had been the followers of that Teacher in Galilee.

In Antioch, not in Poseidia but in Antioch, did the entity then dwell; and the entity came under those influences of that leader among those teachers of the One Truth. And the entity was that one *cleansed* of a possession by Peter, who followed with Simeon the zealot.[29]

In the experience the entity came into the greater understanding that may be aroused in the experience of a soul in materiality. And if there will be the entering into the inner chambers of self there may be again experienced that which will not only bring for self an awakening but may bring help and aid to others.

In the name then Irman, the entity in the experience in the present from that sojourn may find the greater development. For as those tenets then, as those applications then brought the illuminations that set aside all those evil influences, so may the entity raise its own vibrations from within as to bring health, healing, harmony to those—if it will but enter into the holy of holies!

This, then, is that work, that labor, wherein the entity should enter more and more in the present . . .

Q-1. *I would like to know why I was led to St. Louis to meet a man I never heard of, whom I contacted in a spiritual way without any outside influence.*

A-1. As the associations of the entity were with Simeon, again ye met Simeon.

Q-2. *I didn't find out what I went there for?*

A-2. Read why ye left Simeon. Read why ye became among those of a different understanding and those activities in and about that experience when ye were led by him, and ye will find that it was rather the mental than the spiritual. Yet taking the lessons from same, as recorded even in Holy Writ and as is given in thine own understanding, ye will see. It was for a growth, for an understanding. A union of such forces and influences from the material activity would have made a change in the whole experience. The *truth* prevented this.

Q-3. *Can you give this so I will understand?*

A-3. Read the records!

Q-4. *Will I ever contact him again, or should I?*

A-4. Read the record and study for self! As has just been given, if it is for the material gains—well to contact. If it is for spiritual and mental gains, not so well. Read and understand!

1833-1   F.53   3/1/39   Cecelia

. . . the entity was in the Promised Land, during those periods when the Master walked in the earth—and especially during those activities of the apostles or disciples as related to the activities in Caesarea, when there were those questionings of those who became members and active in the church.

The entity was young in years during the period of the Master's sojourn, and was in the groups or crowds when there were those gatherings in the latter period of His sojourn in the material plane.

Hence the entity was acquainted with the activities of the arrest, the trial, the crucifixion, the resurrection; also acquainted with the activities of Simon, the sorcerer, or Simon Magus.[30]

There we find the entity was closely associated especially with that entity or body whom Simon used as one through whom information might come.

And there we find the entity was drawn between two confusing influences—the material things and those spiritual imports as were expressed by the teachers in that particular day.

Yet we find the entity gained throughout.

Then the name was Cecelia . . .

1210-1   M.54   6/29/36   Juohean

. . . the entity was in the land now known as the Roman, and a portion of the entity's experience was expended in the Grecian as well as the Roman. For as there came more and more of the hearsays of that influence that had made for an impressionable activity upon the people from the Judean ministry of that man called Jesus, the entity sought to know from whence the influence, whence the power came, and how it might be made a practical experience in the activities of individuals.

Hence it became as it were again to the entity "hide and seek," or once upon the track, again off, once understood, again losing sight. For the entity attempted to turn even as a correlator or worker with the entity, one Simon.[31]

The entity then, in the name Juohean, gained and lost. For that which is of a Creative Force, whether magnified in the activity of an individual or in the expressions that are given as emotions for the glorification of the relationship, is the *result* and not a cause—or an effect. It is the *result* of the relationship of the soul with Creative Forces and not to be used, not to be indulged, not to be classified or made to become as those forces that will supply only conveniences or ease from cares or duties or obligations!

For the earth is the Lord's and the fullness thereof, and they that partake of its glories for their own self-gratification become liars and thieves and murderers in purpose. But to use same for the glorification of the Creator is the purpose.

These the entity used, misused; yet those things are being met in thine experience. But *hold fast* to that thou knowest in thine inner self; *freedom* from those things that maketh afraid!

1848-1   M.57   3/25/39   Cornelius

One [incarnation], as we find—it stands out beyond the others; not merely because of its historical value in the experiences of man, but because of the changes and the activities wrought by the entity's taking such a stand in the face of oppositions that might have been a part of the experience.

And it would be well were the entity to have the history of that sojourn in its fullest extent—as Cornelius, the first of the Roman officials to take an open stand with the followers of the Nazarene [32]...

Before that we find the experience which is indicated as the outstanding activity of the entity—when the entity was the centurion, the keeper or the officer of the Roman forces stationed in Caesarea.

There the entity, through the associations with those who had come in personal contact with the man of Galilee, began his seeking—through prayer—to know what was man's relationship to his Maker.

Then there was the receiving of the vision as the warning that he, Cornelius, was to send for one that would acquaint him with those truths which had been proclaimed by that representative of the heavenly kingdom.[33]

And those activities of the entity in accepting, in experiencing the outpouring and the call through the activity of the spirit of truth, made for that *great* change which came in the governing of that land; and the modifying of the authority of those who were put in power through the activities of the authorities in Rome; making it possible, with those of its fellows, that there would come the great opportunities for man in every walk of life to become acquainted with those truths that are a part of man's heritage through the promises of the Creative Forces in man's experience.

Thus in the present may the entity, as one in authority, one in power, make for those activities in which there will be in the hearts of men and women *everywhere* the realization of the greater necessity, the greater need, the greater opportunity of the peoples becoming aware more and more of their need to turn again to those tenets, those truths; not because they are of that nature that would make men meek or lonely, but making them *strong* and meek *in* their *strength!* For *in* such comes the power and the ability of the entity from those experiences to not only lead and direct men of many a position or status, but to be a voice heard among the nations of the earth . . .

Q-4. Have I been associated in any previous life with the entity now known as [1151]? If so, what was the relationship and what are the urges to be met in the present?

A-4. These may be best drawn by the paralleling of the activities of the entities [1151], as now called, and [1848] as now called, in those experiences as representatives of the Roman government in the Palestine land—during that period just following and during the activities of the man of Galilee.

Q-6. Is there any advice that you can give me as to . . . my greatest life service . . . ?

A-6. Here is the greater service—even as ye rendered not only thy nation as the ruler in Caesarea as Cornelius, but to all of mankind—because of the stand ye took then!

2205-1   F.37   5/8/40   Celicene

. . . the entity was in the Promised Land during the period of the Roman activity there—during those periods when friendships in the household of Cornelius were a part of the entity's activity and associations.

The entity was a Roman in that land, and in the same sex as at present; being acquainted with much of the intrigue as well as religious activities, tendencies and trends.

These brought confusions to the entity—yet the entity held

to those things in which the entity became very much interested, but rather in the secret organizations.

Hence there is the tendency in the present for the entity to be acquainted or affiliated with, or to search out those activities of groups who organize themselves for certain activities or divisions of activities.

We find that the entity gained and lost. It gained when those influences were turned into activities which brought individuals' minds towards universal peace; lost when they were turned into those channels for self-aggrandizement or self-indulgence . . .

And in whatever field of service the entity chooses, great relationships, great activities might be accomplished by the entity—especially if it would tend to writing as a part of the entity's experience.

The name then was Celicene.

2205-3   F.37   8/22/40   Celicene

. . . the position of the entity was as the elder daughter of the ruler or judge, or proconsul of the actions connected with the Roman soldiery—for, Cornelius was in the office of all of these in Caesarea.

Though born in Rome, the entity came into that environ early in the life; in which the surroundings were such as to make for the understanding that differences existed in the lives of the individuals about the entity.

Hence the early life brought those conditions in which there was the feeling in the experience of the entity of being *above* most of those about the entity, or that they were somewhat inferior. This is not given in the nature of criticism, for the environs and conditions which existed caused such a feeling.

Then with the changes which came about because of the conversion of Cornelius, and the association of his household with the disciples, the change in the entity was not so quick. Neither was there the absorbing wholly of the ideas presented by those teachers, who to the entity—in the most part—appeared to be rather uncouth, or men who were not of the same estate or class or group as the entity. Yet the entity sought and desired—because of the sincerity of those of the household—

to be in accord with that being practiced as a part of the experience of the household.

Hence no wonder that there were turmoils in the inner feelings, the inner emotions of the entity. For, there were the social and economic changes which were naturally wrought by those of the household becoming so absorbed as to make the home a place where there were the meetings of various groups.

And remember, as indicated here in the experience of the entity, the followers and disciples and teachers or ministers did not always hold the same tenets as the ones who were in the position of the Roman citizens and those of the household of the Jews. Remember, there was a vast difference in the teachings even of the leaders!

No wonder, then, that the entity in the present finds the writings of some of those hard to correlate, who attempted to present their understanding; and a variation as to just what Peter meant as expressed in Mark, in Luke, or by Paul. Luke and Lucius were very good friends of the entity during those experiences. Paul became rather that one, to the entity, who brought those turmoils, because of his manner of presentation to the various groups.

And as indicated here, we find there was a great variation which arose in the experience during that particular sojourn, in the attempt of the entity to unify the teachings of Paul and the teachings of Peter (who was to the entity's parent the confessor). There was a great variation. One held that the body must be under surveillance at all times. The other held that the use of the offices of the body, whether physical, social or material, were not to be considered so much — just so the mind was kept in accord.

Thus we find much of the same turmoils arising within the experiences of the entity in the present. Yet these as we find may be met in those manners as we have indicated for the entity — in that each phase of the entity's personality, individuality, has of itself its own questions, its own problems; yet they are all answered in that *oneness* of purpose, oneness of desire that the body, the mind, the soul be in accord, in attune, with that as *he* would have thee be!

He never condemned any. Peter, Paul, Luke, Mark, Lucius,

all were men; with appetites, desires that sought their own indulgence oft, and gave expressions to same—and these, with the various groups, produced the turmoils.

Yet later in the experience when the activities brought about the greater associations with those of her own peoples in the Roman land, the entity found that answer as has been indicated; and thus brought constructive experiences through her activities throughout the sojourn there of many years, and brought the greater blessings to those with whom the entity came in contact through that sojourn . . .

Ye saw phenomena in the household of Cornelius, in the servants, in thine own parents—which ye sought and yet never fully experienced. Ye learned later it was not necessary that ye speak with tongues, but with that tongue of love—which is the language of all who seek His face.[34]

3250-1   F.55   9/29/43   Leoda

The entity was not of the Jewish peoples but rather of the Romans that were in authority in the various centers. Thus the entity came into those places of activities pertaining to the penal law as well as the moral and religious laws. For the entity then was in the household of Cornelius as the daughter; knew the disciples; especially Peter—and all of those activities that followed through the experiences.

Thus throughout the present experience of the entity the activities of Peter in all of their varied manners in which they may be presented have not been quite up to the standard that the entity has held for that power, that influence in the earth through that period.

Embracing the tenets and truths presented, and with the outpouring of the Holy Ghost in that period when there was the conversion of the household, has brought and does bring for the entity a reverence of holy experiences that may not be interpreted in any other manner—save by experiencing same one's self.

The entity gained throughout that experience. Though there was the eventual returning to the Roman land, the activity of the entity's household and those influences brought to bear has contributed, may still contribute—through that which the entity has been and is a part of to the world's knowledge of the one and only way through which man may know the closer relationships to the Maker.

Again, be faithful to the trust. Be not weary in well-doing. The name then was Leoda.

5040-1   F.45   5/4/44   Ava

. . . the entity was in the land now known as the Roman, following those periods of presentation or teaching of the Nazarene, from those of other lands.

And as groups were made, the entity sought knowledge. Yea, the entity was a keeper of records for those groups, and hence finds within itself latent and manifested the abilities to keep quiet when necessary and to talk when necessary. These are judgments to be meted, for silence is oft golden, and a boastfulness may bring its own house tumbling on itself.

In that experience the entity gained much in its ministry in the household of faith, for friendship begets friendship and love begets love, and if these are made manifest, these are of the spiritual forces of the entity.

The name then was Ava. Keep in self much of that which was gained through that experience with the daughters of Cornelius of that period.

1757-2   M.63   10/17/41   Pharsen

The entity was among the soldiery stationed in portions of the land, and especially in the household of Cornelius; one that knew of, had acquaintance with, had knowledge of the teachings of the apostle Peter; though the entity itself had been acquainted with the activities of the Master Himself. A part of the entity's experience was in bringing these activities to the awareness of Cornelius, for a greater interpreting of the tenets and principles and teachings through that period.

Hence in the activities of the present sojourn, that as may be sought of interest and help might be through the associations or connections with that entity Cornelius in the present —whether it be political activities or those having to do with the acquaintanceships in varied forms of activities in the land.

The name then was Pharsen. The entity gained through the

greater portion, though there were sorrows that brought about the determining factors in relationships to the teachings. For the duties as a soldier and as pertaining to the heart, and as related to the spiritual things, *eventually* brought a unison of purpose with the determining factors—by the changes wrought in the activities in Antioch.[35]

4047-2   M.36   4/1/44   Ederle

The entity was among those of the soldiery under Cornelius, being of that company who heard, who saw Peter speak, who heard of that which prompted Peter's activities in the earth.[36]

The entity was the gainer through those experiences, for these have been and are shadows, as it were, in the consciousness of the entity ever. Cultivate them, bring them out of the darkness of the mind. Use them in the daily relationships with others, and thy life experience here will grow to be more worthwhile. Greater and easier will be thy choices in the activities.

The name then was Ederle.

2559-1   F.40   5/7/41   Chardee

The entity was among the offspring of a companionship between a Roman and one of the Palestine land. Hence the entity through that experience was in the position of questioning self, questioning others, because of the variation produced in some places, some sections, by class distinction.

Yet those truths, those tenets gained there—under the tutelage of that parent of the faith in the household of Cornelius—brought hope, understanding, the ability to judge only as ye would desire to be judged by others.

Thus, the entity was not only one whose parentage in authority brought helpful forces through the experience, but the entity in its application of its abilities was as a teacher—especially of economic and political science, political economy, political affability, and language. All of these were a part of the entity's experience in that sojourn . . .

The name then was Chardee.

1710-3   M.24   4/12/39   Philon

. . . the entity was in the land now known as the Promised Land, during those experiences when there was the choosing of those who were to be the representatives of the Roman government in that land.

The entity then was stationed in what might be called the port of entry in the land—a native of the land in Caesarea.

There the entity was first associated with the activity of the centurion set in charge there, as well as the experiences and the expressions that became a part of the activities throughout the period of the entity's sojourn there.

The entity was not a collector of customs, but rather as a director of those who collected same under the supervision of the Roman government. Hence the entity was liked and disliked by those peoples of its own land—and yet through those offices and activities of the centurion there, under which the entity was directed, who became active in the service of those followers of the Nazarene, we find the entity gained through its abilities to apply those tenets and truths of "As ye would that men should do to you, do ye even so to them"...

The name then was Philon.

2460-1   M.40   3/8/41   Pollos

... the entity was in the Roman land, during those activities of the soldiers in the Palestine land; the entity being among the legions that were stationed through the various portions of Palestine—during and following the persecution of those who sought to become more closely affiliated with the teachings of the Master.

There the entity was not only among the guard of Cornelius but also of Archippus in Laodicea.[37] For, there the entity first came under the direct activities of the church established by Lucius and his followers and associates.

Through the greater portion of its experience and sojourn in the land, the entity was an active member in keeping down even the disputes that arose among the Jews as well as the centurion or Roman guard.

In the experience the entity gained the more. For, as indicated, there lies in the entity at present the ability to keep peace among those who labor daily and those who are as the keepers of the activities of those who thus labor.

The entity through that experience, then, gained in its abilities; bringing into this present experience the urges not only in those directions of church and social activities but also in regard to material gains or relations.

Then the name was Pollos.

956-1   M.23   7/20/35   Pamphylus

. . . during those periods when Pontius Pilate, when Herod, and when those ruled in that land during the period when the Master of men walked in the earth.

The entity then was among those stationed in the land, not in Jerusalem during the trial but in Caesarea, when there were the turmoils; and much that transpired among the questionings of the soldiery in Rome following same did the entity hear and harken to, which made for an activity in the experience of the entity then, as Pamphylus.

For there has been innate and manifested in the experience of the entity in the present a special interest in the happenings of that land during that day. And as the entity has read, and as the entity has heard, and as the entity has experienced in its contemplations of the activities, much has not rung true to that as has been thought in the experience. Yet there is a drawing to those lessons that may be gained by the adherence to that as He gave, "The meek shall inherit the earth—As ye would that men should do to you, do ye even so to them—I go to the Father, and ye abiding in me, ye abide in me and I in the Father, we will abide in you also." These and such have become and do become as *real* experiences to the entity from those activities during that sojourn then in the Palestine land.

Much might be given as respecting the entity's activities during that entire sojourn.

In the experience the entity gained almost throughout; for in the present the orderliness, obeying orders, giving commands and having same obeyed, arise from much of the entity's experience physically and materially during that sojourn.

In the latter days of the entity's experience in that activity great disturbances arose, yet the entity became one to whom many came for counsel during the latter experience.

2612-1   F.64   10/31/41   Pharlos

. . . the entity was in the Roman land, when individuals

were being chosen to act in various capacities as representatives of the government.

The entity then, in the opposite sex, was chosen as a representative, or as a judge, in portions of the land now known as the Holy Land or the Promised Land; not as a soldier, but rather as a judge to and through which there was the administering of the law as related to relationships, as well as the collecting of customs. And through the entity's office or hands much of same passed.

Thus we find that the activities brought the entity into the associations with all classes, as well as the political and religious groups of that particular period.

The entity then was later associated with Cornelius, for the entity then — in the name Pharlos — became the greater active in its homeland. For, with the recall and with the changes brought by the advancement of the entity during the periods when there was the change in the emperors, the entity became active in the home office — as the greater activities of the new sect began.

2786-1   F.45   7/24/42   Pergola

. . . the entity was in the Roman land, when there were those periods in which groups of individuals were appointed as leaders or directors in the Palestine land.

The entity, coming under the influence of those who had been in authority as to the teachings of the Nazarene, sought counsel respecting same from those — or especially that entity then known as Cornelius.

Thus we find the entity embraced those tenets and teachings; and interest was indicated in the activities in Rome, even during those periods before there were the persecutions of the followers of the disciples that became a part of the activity there . . .

The name then was Pergola. It may be said that it was the greater period of development for the entity through the material experiences. Not only was the entity considered as among those of the faith, as a help, as an aid; yet was able to keep in associations with those in political powers and places so as to keep much intact for those who would become as spreaders of the faith through that period . . .

... spread that gospel as ye learned at the behest of Cornelius.

2034-1   F.22   11/2/39

... the entity was in the Roman land. There we find the entity was a servant—yet not a servant in the way of being a menial servant, but rather what would be called in the present the companion and teacher of the young of the household which the entity joined then, of the Roman director in the Palestine land.

For the entity was a companion then of the wife of Cornelius; and in Caesarea, as well as in Joppa and Jerusalem, the entity gained much through that experience.

1921-1   F.52   6/19/39   Justine

... the entity was among those of the women of that land who became companions to, or closely associated with, the Roman peoples.

Through the instrumentality or activity of the entity, many of those that were in power or authority came to understand those principles for which the entity as well as its peoples stood—in the teachings and the ministry of the Master.

Hence security for many was wrought in their material lives by the intercession of the entity, through its companions and associates of that experience.

Only in the latter portion of the entity's sojourn in the land did the entity become a resident of the Roman empire, or in the Roman land; though it was a portion of the Roman rule through its associations.

There the entity gained throughout because of its consistency, because of its activities in such ways and manners as to bring a great assistance and help to all of those with whom it came in contact.

Beautiful in body was the entity—beautiful in mind, beautiful in purpose—that made for and produced through the experience the surety for the entity in its activities and associations ...

The name then was Justine, and it was *of* those who were close to Cornelius in Caesarea and the entrance ports to the Promised Land.

The entity was acquainted with many of those who were of the household of the Master, as well as those of His disciples, and those who aided in the early portion of the ministry.

2998-2   M.36   5/11/43
. . . the entity was in the Roman land, during those periods when there were those combinations of groups and individuals put in authority through the various portions of the lands that were paying tribute to the Roman land.

The entity spent portions of the time in what is now North Africa, and other portions in the Holy Land; coming in contact with some of those problems that were a portion of the Jewish problem as well as the Roman, as well as those problems that arose in the church . . .

There the entity was closely affiliated with some of those activities that were a part of Cornelius in Caesarea, and the entity then may become associated or affiliated, directly or indirectly under the same activities in the present of that entity [1848]—through the political interests and those having to do with certain organizations or certain groups.

3202-1   M.7   9/9/43   Pecbo
. . . the entity was in the periods when the Master walked in the earth, among those of the household of Cornelius that were brought under the directions and teachings especially of Peter.

Hence the entity in the present is interested in those things of an unusual and of a mysterious nature. Yet there is ever the semblance of a good story well told, as well as the principles pertaining to Christian living. Reading, a little outside games —these are the most interesting to the entity, as from those experiences then—in the name Pecbo . . .

Q-1. *When, where and how has the entity been associated in the past with his present grandmother, [3006]?*
A-1. In the Holy Land we find there was an acquaintance, the entity receiving teaching from the one who is now the grandmother. And in the Egyptian land the entity was very close, being an offspring of the one who is present grandmother.

400   EARLY CHRISTIAN EPOCH

1849-2   F.37   7/3/39   Ex-elor

. . . the entity was in that period when there were the activities of the Roman land in the Land of Promise.

There we find the entity was among those who were the companions and the entity being the associate of one in authority, in power, in that land.

There we find the entity was among those peoples who embraced the teachings not only of the Master but of His followers, and among those who were of the *first* in authority and power to do so—not only in the Caesarean land or in Palestine but also in Rome.

Hence, as has been indicated, the emblems of Rome—*not* of Italy, but as to what Rome itself stood for—in might, in power, and yet as dealing might and power in creating hope, creating patience, creating passion, creating brotherly love, creating kindness, creating gentleness, *as* is indicated by the very *fact* of the church being Roman in its purpose, in its *intuitive* reaction.

Hence we find the entity, then, was as the companion of Cornelius. No, the entity has not been in association with that one in the present save as afar, yet through the *associates* and companions of that one in the present—who is among the rulers in the present land—may the entity find a means, a channel for an outlet of its purposes in this material plane.

The name then was Ex-elor.

2891-1   M.18   1/27/43   Philcholos

. . . the entity was then among the soldiery of the Romans. But the entity came under the influence of the teachings of those peoples during the period when there was the spreading of the teachings of the Master.

Then the entity, through its associations with the ruler or director was active in that capacity as the orderly—as might be called—under Cornelius; who kept the records of the various activities of the peoples in the forts in Antioch, as well as carrying messages to those in authority in Rome . . .

In that sojourn the entity gained; and deep latent spiritual influences arise from that activity, as well as the abilities as a speaker, as a writer, as a record keeper . . .

The name then was Philcholos.

3420-1   F.57   12/17/43   Rebba

. . . the entity was in the Holy Land during those periods when there were upheavals from the persecutions of the church by those not only in high places but those who would seek to use such as a political way of attaining notoriety.

The entity was among those persecuted in Antioch.[38] But when there was the appealing to the group to which the entity had affiliated itself, to those who had been in authority there, the entity knew Rome and the varied groups in authority. For the entity had embraced the tenets or teachings of the household of Cornelius, for it was his activities in Rome that enabled the entity to be raised to a place wherein there was less persecutions and more of that hope which the entity may apply in its experience today—in just kindness, just patience, just love.

Then the entity became a good reporter to those varied groups and peoples there.

The name then was Rebba.

5142-1   M.44   4/21/44   Shugard

. . . the entity was in the Roman land during those periods when there were the teachers from the Holy Land coming into Rome with those who had been in authority in the various portions of the land.

The entity was among the Romans who did not altogether hold to the tenets which had been a part of the activities of Cornelius or of the ruler who, under the entity, had built a synagogue for the people in Antioch.

These activities to the entity appeared to be unpatriotic to the cause of Rome, and yet with those associations there came a softening, and finally an acceptance.

Be as sincere in the present in thy activities as ye were through those periods; as Shugard.

In that period the entity gained, and it would do well in the present to apply self in the greater principles which were then a portion of the entity's experience through that land or that period of sojourn.

1151-1   M.47   4/22/36   Philoas

. . . the entity was in that land and period when the Master walked in the earth, when there were the teachings in the temple and the journeys through those portions of the land in and about Jerusalem.

The entity then was among the Roman peoples; not as a soldier, not as a lord or a king; *rather* as one that *represented* the Roman peoples. Not as a tax gatherer, but as to the *abilities* of the peoples to contribute, not only of the fruits of their labors but of their activities in the various fields of service.

During those periods of the last journey or the *triumphal* journey into Jerusalem,[39] the entity then became the more closely associated with, having the better understanding of, that being presented to a stiff-necked people; that as touched the hearts, the minds, the lives of those peoples during that experience.

And the entity was with those proclaiming the resurrection, and those that heard the teachings. For the entity was present in the inn when He walked to Emmaus [40]; present when there was the arising to call to meet those that would come after Him and learn of Him.

Hence in the experience of the entity there has come in the present that coming again of Him into the presence of the entity, making sure, making secure in the inmost feelings and experiences of the entity; not only His thought of men but the fulfilling of those promises that have been and are a portion of man's heritage, that "If ye abide in me, I in thee, ask and it shall be given thee—for through such may the Father be glorified in you through me."

These are a portion of the experiences of the entity. Hold fast to that thou hast gained in those experiences as thou didst gain in that experience as ye followed with those of His disciples into that hill from which He ascended to those glories that had been prepared by Him, for Him,[41] in *that* land, in that experience, where—as He gave—"I go to prepare a place, that where I am there ye may be also. The place ye know, the way ye know." [42]

Then in the name Philoas, and of the Roman city, yet the entity made for those experiences, those developments during that sojourn that brought help, aid to many.

Thus may be the experiences of the entity in the present. For as the Master gave, not in some great deed that ye may do, but just being kind, just being gentle, just being faithful, just being true does the life of an individual, of a person—as in thine self—become as a living example known among men.

For it is here a little, there a little, line upon line, precept upon precept, but *living* the love—the law. For this indeed is the way, the manner that those things that have been prepared for those who love His coming, His presence, may be known—that He abides forever.

1151-3   M.47   5/30/36   Philoas

In interpreting that as is the experience of the entity in the present, and those experiences through the activity during the periods of the sojourn in the Palestine and Roman experience, we find these are in accord with or nearer to repeating themselves in the experience and activity of the entity in the present sojourn. For the environs under which the entity was activating then and those experiences through which there may be actions in the present, are of a period in the experiences of many that *then* sojourned in the earth and are active in the affairs of a nation, a people. And it is an experience in the present that may be shaped, as then, by the very activities of the entity, as the entity shaped those then.

For through whose activity came those requirements by those in authority in the experience that Pilate must make a personal report of what took place in that period when a prophet—yea, more than a prophet—was condemned, when one that—by the very voice of many—was known to be of unsavory repute was loosed again in the earth?

And these are again making for an activity in which the entity may through its associations become one who may call many of those who gave voice for that happening in that experience.

For as the representative of the government, the entity then was acting in the capacity of one who was *not* one that looked upon the abilities of groups, of individuals, as a spy, but rather as an analyst of their relationship under a divided spiritual guidance for not only their patriotism—as would be termed today—to the Roman land but as one that looked to the interests of the *people*. Not as one that considered only those in authority, of high estate, but rather as man to man were the real purposes of the Roman rule in those experiences; and that they were to be carried not to the extremes but as considered by those in power, in position, these made for the activity of the entity as one in authority higher than the local government or the protectorate, or any other influence. And these then were the background as shown by the entity's report to Caesar:

Those activities of Herod, that was as the local representative of the peoples in their religious thought, their religious intent, their religious claim as may be said.

Then the authority as given to the protectorate, or proletariat—as would be termed; for the civil government, law, order. And that condition which existed *between* the two, as the entity set in motion; that not only was tribute collected by the Roman citizenry but rather was there to be kept, to be created, to be made, the more perfect understanding—not *only* of the protectorate as to their religious forces but also as to their political forces and influence. And yet these built many experiences that made for the condemning of same because of the differences that arose in the powers that were altered much in their operative forces.

These were the conditions when this man, this prophet, this master, was presented to those in authority for civil consideration; *claiming* by the ones in authority that there had been a neglect to pay tribute, or that there had been first that attempt upon the part of those that were as the followers of same to prevent the tax, the levies to be paid. *This* was the manner of presentation rather than much of that as ye have recorded even in Holy Writ.[43]

In these conditions did the entity come under this influence of peace, the Prince of Peace, the teachings of the Nazarene. Not as one ever that acted in those capacities of the service to the people, to the nation, to the world, as one in a passive manner; but rather ever as the *positive,* as the active influence in the experiences of those that came under the visions, the experiences of the Man *as* a teacher, as a healer. These were the conditions the entity then saw.

These are the conditions or the shadows of same, or those that present themselves as conditions in the affairs, in the experiences of man in this land in the present. Yea, there is a form of religious freedom; yea, there is an application in part of that moral duty, of that economic duty to those influences and forces that are to guide a nation, a peoples; by that which has been handed down from those that in faith to their Maker, in their belief in their fellow man, established a *freedom* of speech, a freedom of press, a freedom of worship of the Maker according to the dictates of their conscience.

And as the entity upheld these and all of their kindred influences and forces in that experience, in the land as a representative of the Roman land, so must he indeed as the soldier of the cross, of the lamb, of those forces, represent *his* Master, *his* Lord, in the present.

For as given, hath he not been called? Hath he not seen Him entering there and giving that command, "Ye must stand in my and thy brothers' stead, for as they do it unto thy brethren they do it unto me."

In those experiences also, there came the time when there was the report to be made by the entity upon those happenings there upon the hill of shame, upon the cross—yet of glory. There was the command that there be a report of the civil ruler, Pilate, before the emperor, the physical king.

The entity then may be said to have been the influence, even greater than the apostle Paul, in bringing to the Roman conscience a correct report of what happened in Jerusalem; yea, in Galilee and Samaria.

For those that made for that accounting for what happened brought to the peoples a *physical* activity, yet—as known of those who seek to know His ways—not of self but rather an appointment, a judgment, a *call*ment of the Father.

Hence the entity then in those activities at this period in the history of his own land stands as in the balance for those influences and forces that will bring to fore, to judgment, the conditions that exist in this his native land today.

In these experiences oft, the more oft, yea again and again, call ye then upon that promise, upon that influence which has prompted from within; that ye be guided aright, that ye be led by Him even as the Prince of Peace. For the burdens of those that would again crucify the truths of Him that *is* the Prince of Peace have been delivered, as it were, to a peoples — and make again slaves of those that would come under the tyranny rather of the money changers and those that have let position, fame or fortune become as their god rather than Him that guided those in the establishing of the land.

This is thy message then:

Hold fast to that thou hast purposed in thine heart as to the dealings between those that are in authority and those that labor for their home, their loved ones, their friends; they that would be at peace with their fellow man, they that would know the ways of the Father among His children, rather than those that only seek for the satisfying, the gratifying of their own selfish motives, their own selfish minds. For again the judgments are at hand . . .

Q-4. Would my life indicate talent in respect to transportation and distribution of the products of nature?

A-4. This is a *natural*, NATURAL, experience from the activities of the entity throughout the sojourns in the earth. For these have been not only in that experience as we are giving concerning now, but [in other incarnations] . . .

Q-5. Did I travel along the road to Emmaus with the Master or did I meet Him at the end?

A-5. Traveled along the road.[44]

Q-6. Then I knew the Master and understood Him well?

A-6. Knew the Master; not understanding wholly, even as the conversation would indicate: "Hast thou heard the happenings of the day? Hast thou known the considerations upon or of this man, both from the religious and the economic standpoint, also the civil experiences of same?" And yet only in the breaking of the bread did the consciousness come of that He had said.[45]

Then it cannot be said that the entity fully understood Him, from the *material* or *physical* angle; yet the inner consciousness did understand — else *how* would there have been that call again, and again?

Q-7. Was I condemned at that particular time in Rome for the report I made?

A-7. Not condemned by those that knew; condemned rather by those who became fearful of the change in the social order of the day—only in that; not by those in authority civilly, not by those in authority from the religious point of view, but rather the social.

Q-8. Did I pass on naturally then in the body?

A-8. Passed on naturally, yet losing much in the strength through privations of self that there might be help to those condemned later.

Do not confuse the condemning that arose in the years later with that character of condemning in the period of the entity's sojourn. For some sixty, some ninety years later the entity's activities became as very much evilspoken of. Only in the latter days of those experiences some two hundred years later were they lauded or put in their proper place.

Let His light, of love, of service, of mercy, of peace, of judgment, rest upon thee. Let His love so fire thy heart, thy being, that He may say, "Come, I will keep the faith with thee."

1151-4   M.47   11/21/36   Philoas

Q-4. Am I in accord with R.R. labor sufficiently to establish greater harmony in labor management relations on the railroads?

A-4. These, to be sure, offer problems, even in the greatest of ideals or purposes, to leaders in the various groups.

But as we find, this is an indication of that just given as to how the entity in those periods of activity from the Roman and Palestine experience made for such associations where turmoils, strifes of every nature were under the influence of the entity's own convictions within himself of a peaceful, harmonious activity among the laymen, the workmen, the official, those in the higher financial circles.

So as we find, so long as the entity holds to those purposes, those policies, those ideals as were maintained in those experiences, in the present, we will find the entity not only efficient but sufficient to meet the greater demands of those who are *not entirely* so erratic as to seek for self without consideration to the whole.

Hence we would give that the entity is efficient, so long as there is remembered that walk to Emmaus! . . .

Q-8. Would you give to me more details concerning the walk with the Master to Emmaus?

A-8. As has been indicated, during the actual period of crucifixion the entity was in Rome—or upon the way from Rome to Palestine.

Hence those three days and those activities that brought about this were the natural associations of the entity, now called [1151], with those that were in close association and of the family of the companion that was so disturbed by the reports. And the natural, the *human* relationships *drew* the companions—not the apostles or disciples but the *companions*. And as this was a portion of the entity's activity for its government, to inspect the activities about Emmaus, this became then a natural thing.

And as there had been created in the heart and the mind of the entity, there was—as has been the promise ever—"Draw nigh to me and I, thy Lord, will draw nigh to thee." And He came, and walked, and talked. And as the questions arose as to the discussions, their natural tendencies were, upon the part of the entity now [1151], to question not only the Master but the companion as to what had been the happenings, what part the Romans, what part the Jews, what part those of others had taken in this deed that had brought *so much* to the activities and thoughts and the very conditions surrounding all of the conditions that arose—as to the opening of graves, the rending of the veil of the temple, and the like.

Then as they sat at meat, as He brake the bread (that represents His broken body), there came the knowledge that they spoke with the Master!

Hence an experience which may draw this very near to the entity in the present: How oft in thine experience has there come to thy inmost knowledge the *real, REAL* purpose of individuals as ye broke bread with them!

Not that this then becomes as an omen. It is a *reality;* for ye broke bread with *life* itself! And as it represents the staff of life, as it represents His body, how *much,* how oft, how great is the influence in thine experience of those ye break bread with!

Q-9. Was the period between the crucifixion and the walk to Emmaus a period of several weeks, or months?

A-9. Rather days; for it was still fresh, still the topic not only of those of his followers (that were so bewildered) but the *wonderment* of those that had been touched, the *seeking* of knowledge concerning the happenings by those that were in authority.

1151-9   M.48   11/7/37   Philoas

A great light appears to shine upon much of that record [of the entity], in the efforts that are being made in the present as related to those that become such a part of the experience in the present—prompting again that counsel as taken one with another from the walk to Emmaus, as well as that which came from the counsel of those with the entity's report.

Q-1. Was I once incarnated as Agrippa, assisting Augustus Caesar in governing the Roman Empire?

A-1. That incarnation, as we have indicated, was not as Agrippa but rather as that emissary—not as one that was almost but *altogether* persuaded during those experiences. Assisted in the government, to be sure, but not as Agrippa.

1151-10   M.48   11/21/37   Philoas

In giving that as we find the interpretation of [the Roman-Palestine sojourn]:

It was in those years when there was the establishing of the Julian calendar, and when changes were wrought as to times. Hence the record will be measured here from that in which time was counted later.

In that portion of the land now called Rome, then a portion of Heliopolis, the entity was the son then of one Antonius [?] and Josie [?], that came in the activities of the Roman experience; educated in the ways of those peoples that were both for the Roman and the Grecian forces.

And those things that became a part of the experiences were the lessons which had been taught by the Grecian soldier that later fed the hemlock.

Thus the entity grew into grace with those in authority, through the activities as came under the influences of Caesar

Augustus, later Claudius and those that ruled over the varied lands that had become a portion of the experiences — or under the direction of the Romans.

The entity, as has been indicated, was one who traveled through those lands, making those associations, those recommendations for the manners in which the peoples under the various schools would be taxed, according to their *spiritual* counsel — or according to what ye would call the religious influences and the judging of these.

Hence we find the man, then, at thirty, coming into associations during those periods when the Master walked in the earth — as the young man just beginning the ministry.

In these associations the entity came in close contact with those of the household from which the Master had gone out; becoming associated with, later married to (and by the Master), the *sister* of the Master — the *only* sister, who had received education in Greece *and* Rome, through the associations of the family with the sects of the Jews and a portion that favored the Romans.[46]

Hence much of that which had been a portion of the experience of the household of Mary and Joseph was known to the entity.

And when the Master was called home, owing to the death of Joseph, the husband of Mary, the entity then — that ye now call [1151] — first became the closer associated with Jesus, the Master.

For owing to the visitations of Jesus the man in other lands, and because of the Roman rule, and the changes wrought the entity then — Romacio [?] — found it necessary to make for the activities that brought a closer understanding.

During those periods the activities were in keeping the Jewish masters or the Jewish rulers *coordinating* with the activities of the Roman rulers — as in that particular province in which the greater activities were under Pontius Pilate.

Hence we find, as would be applied in the present, as is the experience of the entity ever in the present experience, the entity became as one associated with the producer and that produced — or with the capital and the labor, or the activities as related to same.

These become a natural activity from same; as then many of not only the tax assessors, the tax gatherers, but those who judged in the various provinces as to the amounts, as to the abilities came under the supervision of the entity during those experiences.

Hence we find there were many of those that were the followers, yea the disciples, later called apostles, who became close friends then in one manner or another—of the entity.

It is sometimes judged that most of the disciples were poor; and this was not true. For Zebedee and his sons, Matthew the publican, all who were closely associated were rather well-to-do. Peter and Andrew, of course, were servants or laborers with the sons of Zebedee; but Zebedee was among the wealthy—and among those closely associated with those in authority.[47]

For as these were a portion of the family of which John, James, Jude, Ruth and all became a part, these were kinsmen and people that were in authority so far as capital is concerned —as ye would term in the present; and were not poor!

While Peter, Andrew, Thomas, Alphaeus were not of the wealthy, all of these were known to the entity; as also was Matthew, as just given, who had been one appointed by an aide of the entity in the experience.

Thus came the closer understanding. For the entity then studied, as it were, those things that *prompted* the activity of the various sets and sects; as the Pharisees, the Saducees, the Essenes, the influence upon the Roman soldiery as well as the Roman rule, as well as upon the individuals who were set in authority in the varied provinces.

Then, the period arrives when the entity is just called to Rome, during that period of the trial—or just before the trial, during the crucifixion; returning to Jerusalem or to those environs of same just the day *after* this had occurred.

Thus we find the walk to Emmaus with the disciples, one Luke the beloved physician who was both a Roman and a Jew —and *of* those same provinces in the Grecian rule that were under the Roman authorities.

Thus we find the entity again *physically* in association, in touch with the influence of the Master, Jesus, who became the Christ in the life lived.

Thus we find the entity later, when there was the recall of Pilate for that which had been brought about, returned to Rome as one who counseled with the Caesars for those very activities, and making the changes that brought Philip and Agrippa and the judges that were to judge later when those periods in which Paul, Peter, John, Philip and Stephen were active. These all became a portion of the experiences of the entity.

Though remaining a Roman, the entity was in sympathy with those activities; lending counsel and giving those influences that prevented the full destruction of the disciples — during those periods of experience.

Is there any wonderment then that the entity in the present experience finds the urge for service? For it was gained by those close walks with the entity, the man, Jesus; who had given, "He that would be the greatest among you, he is the servant of all."

These became then as it were the sign, the guide, the directing influence in the experience of the entity.

And we find little in that sojourn, that activity, that may be said to have been even a tendency towards retardment.

For *all* was in purpose, in desire, to be even as He had taught, that they who for any cause lord over their fellow man become that as must sooner or later become a stumbling stone.

And as He gave also, each and every individual is in that position, that phase, that state of development, or *unfoldment,* that they have builded in their application of that as He gave *is* the whole law; to love the Lord thy God with all thy body, thy mind, thy soul, and thy neighbor as thyself.

This is the whole law. May all learn, as the entity strove then to apply those tenets, those truths in the *experiences* of those that were put in authority — by man, yea, but that they might have, they might show in their opportunity, that the love of the Father surpasses the *glory* of man.

In those periods of activity following those persecutions and the changes that came about in the individual authorities in the various provinces, the entity returned again and again to those lands, associations and activities; meeting with those who had been keepers of the records here or there, those who had been in authority for the levying of taxes, the manners of the levying, etc.

THE FOLLOWERS AND THE CHURCHES

Thus we find throughout the entity's experience and the entity's associations with those of what ye call or term the Palestine experience, there was *no rebellion of* those peoples of the land agains *Roman* authority—only after those periods when the entity was recalled, or attempted to keep closer in touch with those who had been called to Rome, when Paul—by his own *self*—brought misinterpreting, misunderstanding; and when Peter, and the Church—as John—and here the entity, in the last acts of his intervention, *saved* that entity—for the followers, for the world—from that death as the others had drawn or had come to.

Hence the banishment of John [48] was by the very *direct* intervention of the entity with those in authority, and the taking away from the churches that had been established in the various places that there might be preserved the records for same —became a portion of the entity's experience.

There was the passing then from the physical activity in Rome during that period when there were just the beginnings of the attempts for the unification of the religious as well as the penal laws, or the laws in the other lands ruled by the Roman empire.

The entity once, just before the interventions, went to the libraries in Alexandria—and there were the attempts to placate any of the destructions that later became the loss to what is now called the Christian world.

It was at that age or period some sixty years *after* the crucifixion—then ninety years or ninety-three years of age—at the passing.

Q-1. I would like to know a more detailed account of the report I made to Rome concerning the Christian movement in Palestine.

A-1. These were of such varied characters, we find it is necessary that all of these be taken as what may be termed individual reports, see?

At the time when there was the recalling of Pilate, and the reports that had been made as to the activities of the wife of Pilate as related to the healing that had been accomplished in the household, then we find a very *favorable* report to the Christians—though the entity was questioned much by those who were directly under the supervision of the entity. But the report was accepted by the Roman emperor and acted upon according to the directions of the entity; that Pilate be removed, and one closer in association or in sympathy with the Christian movement be appointed in the stead—as is seen or is recorded by profane history as well as by intimation in sacred history.

During those periods when there were the uprisings, as in some places and positions, we find the reports then were not so severe against the individual activities of the Romans in authority; for never again do we find, as has just been given, any of the Roman *rulers* of the various provinces acting *without* the direction from Rome through the activities of the entity. While these reports were not that Rome should just *accept* the authority, but that there be the *reasoning together*. For he gave then, even as did the great teacher from the Sanhedrin—Gamaliel—let not ye find thyselves fighting against God.[49] This might be said then to be the whole of the report. Not be in that attitude of condemning, but do not act in such measures as to find thyself fighting against providence and God.

Q-2. Did I secure information from the entity now known as [1472]?

A-2. Information respecting the activities of the Essenes as to whether they were averse to the authority of the Jewish rulers, as well as the Romans. The activities or lessons, or information gained from the keeper of the records of the Essenes—or Judy—were those things that prompted the entity later to investigate for self those records that were reported to have been made, and that were in the library of Alexandria, of the Wise Men that came from the other lands just before the birth, and at the time of the birth presented themselves—or a few days later—in the town of Bethlehem.

Yes, the entity gained, or obtained, a record of that as had been gathered by the keeper of records from Carmel.

Q-3. How close a relationship had I with the entity now known as [1472]?

A-3. Just as would be intimated—as here the entity Judy was held in reverence by all of the followers of Jesus, though persecuted oft by the Jews—or the sects of the Jews—under various circumstances. But not as an informer was the entity con-

THE FOLLOWERS AND THE CHURCHES 415

sidered by the entity now known as [1151], but as one that would and that did give the facts of the activities of various groups in respect to not only the Essenes but the other portions of the various groups in the land.

The association then was quite close at times; at others not so closely associated yet keeping in touch with the activities.

Q-4. How close was I to the entity now known as [1470]?

A-4. As has been indicated, or may be gathered from that which has been given, the entity now called [1470], was what would be called a deputy—or one who was given certain portions of the province from which to make the levy. Then, what ye would term in the present as a clerk, or as an agent, or as an associate—but rather a subordinate associate.

Q-5. Does my expereince from that period justify now my approaching Foundations for financing my activities in relation to labor policies?

A-5. The activities of the entity, as just indicated, were such as to lend to self not only the motives but the impetus, the feelings of necessities for this understanding to ever be between the supply, the demand; the one who labors—those that receive not only the benefits materially but physically and mentally from such.

Hence this would make for that ability in which there may be made overtures in such ways and manners as to receive the greatest and the wholehearted cooperation from Foundations, from groups.

Q-6. Did I know the entity, [1486], in the Palestine period?

A-6. We don't find quite the association, yet we get the vibration. Hold it. [Pause]

Yes, the entity as we find, [1486], was put in authority as a special judge during that experience by the entity; when there were those disturbances in that portion of the province—or activities in Galilee.

Q-7. Any other advice that may be given at this time that will be of benefit and help?

A-7. Hold to that purpose that has prompted thee, not only in thy activities then but in those that ye are repeating in this experience—from those great awakenings and unfoldments that came to thee when thou had indeed learned, thou had experienced indeed, "I am my brother's keeper!" even as the Master gave of His whole self—body and mind—risking even the spirit, that man might know there is an advocate with the Father.

So can ye bring into the hearts and minds of those in authority, here or there, whether it be those that labor day by day, or those that work in the office or where, the realization that *all* must work as the cog, the wheel, that must bring together all for *one* purpose— *service,* that the Father may be manifested through the love each soul shows for the other!

1151-12   M.48   2/9/38   Philoas

In giving advice or counsel, from what has been given and intimated from and through the activities of the entity now called [1151] in the Roman and Palestine period:

As is seen and indicated, the effects of the activities were far-reaching in the Roman land, and in what ye term in the present as the Christian way of thinking.

Then, the activities and the desires were not that self might be exalted in any way or manner; not even *known* in the help, the aid given to those that were giving their all in the bringing to the minds and the hearts and the consciousnesses of men the teachings of the Nazarene.

Not that the entity *then* attempted to keep self as a blind, or was even fearful of what might be done or said by those in political authority—and as is seen by the activities among those in power, even with the changes wrought by the very nature of the changing of the Caesars during that experience.

And with all of the varying forces that may well be signified in those conditions that in the activities of the entity in the present are indicated in political powers, or political followings, the entity remained true to the ideals, the principles from within.

And as that period in the experience in the outstanding, and a parallel to the work, the efforts of the entity in the present — *this*— *this* must be the criterion for the entity in the dealings with the problems in its efforts in the present that have to do with its fellow man; that:

There must be the *answer within* as to whether the choices

to be made are in keeping with that as thy Lord—in spirit, in mind, in soul—would have thee to do; in determining the time and the place, and the factors that have to do with the problems, the situations that are to be brought into the lives and the experiences of whose whom the entity in the present would aid with their problems.

1151-23   M.50   7/9/39   Philoas

There are those efforts upon the part of the entity, then, not only to assist individuals and groups to adjust themselves to the new order of activities in progress, but the purpose, the desire to fulfill those same activities that were a part of that experience on the walk to Emmaus.

For, these continue to become a part of that hope, that desire, that purpose of the soul—to see not only in the hearts and lives of men the fulfilling of that which was the prompting of that day, but that all men everywhere become more and more aware of their part, their place in such an awakening, such a return to that of giving God a chance in *their* lives, *their* associations —and that each, in whatever place he is, is responsible for what others—because of his activity—think or conceive as the love of the Christ, the love of God in the lives of individuals . . .

*Q-7. Shall I continue to remain in the background in the effort to advance [1848]? * Please discuss.   *[Cornelius]*

A-7. As we find, as was even in that period where "the other disciple" was named—yet self remained in the background— by choice. In the household of that entity now called [1848], ye made it possible for not only the acceptance of but the abilities for that entity to become the power through its authority to establish the first church in Rome—through a great deal of thy efforts. This, too, has been, was kept in the background . . .

1151-24   M.50   11/26/39   Philoas

In giving that as may be helpful and constructive in the experience of this entity in the present, again we would refer the entity to those activities, those principles which were shown or manifested through those experiences when such turmoils were in the land—and as to how, and as toward what, the entity gave his strength and purpose—and that these same principles and tenets be a part of the experience in the present.

While, to be sure, they may appear to be under different circumstances, different environs, know that they—as then—are principles that change not.

> Note: [1158]—present wife and wife in Palestine.
> [1188]—present son and associate in Palestine.
> [1206]—present daughter and close associate in Palestine.
> [1265]—associate in Rome.
> [1341]—associate in Rome.
> [1179]—present daughter; daughter of Cleopas in Palestine who walked on road to Emmaus with [1151].
> [1497]—present brother, associate in Palestine.

2489-1   M.48   4/23/41   Philas

The entity was not among those who levied the tax, but was of the Romans in the Palestine land close to those days when the Master walked in the earth.

The entity aided in judging the abilities of groups, cities or counties, to pay tax, and also in seeing that those who gathered the tax made their reports properly through the regular channels.

Hence, again, we find those present abilities of the entity to pass judgments, as it were, either through the letter of the law or the spirit of the law; not only from the material but from the mental and spiritual angle.

And, as the entity has learned long since, unless a loan is a good moral loan it isn't a very good loan in any sense!

The entity gained throughout that sojourn. For, as in the present, while the political and religious forces do not always act or appear compatible, they must be practical in their relationships one to another. For, the divine law remains, ever—know that all life is one before Him (or all lives, if ye choose to term it so), even as thy Lord, thy God is one.

Thus each experience builds the ability of the individual, either mentally, spiritually or physically, to make application in whatever may be the next experience.

And in this relationship, remember that opportunity arises with each meeting, each association. Each problem has its opportunity for choice of spiritual, mental, material opportunities. They are one in their greater, their better sense.

The name then was Philas; and the entity was of those first appointed to such offices under the one who was the companion of Cleopas in the walk to Emmaus . . .

Be patient; and ye will find greater and greater His walks with thee—even as ye learned from thy associate of his walk with Him.

3212-1   F.46   9/14/43   Jeuel

. . . the entity was in the land when the Master walked in the earth. The entity was among those who heard Him gladly, and who with the associations and the companions at the time kept rather close in the activities, especially when there was the establishing of the church in the Holy City.

The entity was among those chosen to administer the bread after there had been the instituting of same as the body and the blood of the Master [50]; who felt equal to it in self, to miss the way of the cross, yet as He prayed, "Let not this cup pass from me unless I be glorified in Thee through Him."

So, as in the experience of the entity then, as Jeuel, the activities are ever dependent upon changes, although rote is a part of the experience needing discipline; that you more and more may become a reflection of that you would desire in thy purposes and thy ideals.

5096-1   M.52   5/18/44   Pleney

. . . the entity was in the Holy Land following the activities when the disciples, the apostles, were instructing and leading individuals through a period of turmoils; following the advent of the Master in the earth.

The entity acted in the capacity of supplying propaganda for the various activities in attempting to unite those of various groups into one perfect cause, where there were people who had been brought up under different leadership and different environ entirely.

Hence the entity in the present may be called something of

a propagandist, but if the activities are in that direction of presenting purposes and ideals that are creative, it will be well.

The name then was Pleney. The entity applied self, the entity gained; and yet paid materially many prices, or the supreme physical price.

Thus we find latent a little fear creeps into the entity as concerning its material or social safety.

3027-2   F.34   6/28/43   Jeseuha

... the entity was in the Holy Land, during those periods when the Master walked in the earth.

The entity was among the women of Bethsaida that heard Him gladly. Yet persecutions, in those days when there were the activities following the crucifixion, brought the entity's choosing rather to flee from the environs. But attempting to hold to its activity, then in the name Jeseuha.

The entity then became the wife of one that became a martyr, when there was the establishing of the first of the deacons in the church at Jerusalem. With that persecution the entity fled. Coming in contact, in the latter part of the life, with the problems of Paul, Peter and Lucius, and Luke, in Laodicea, the entity there gained much.

The children of the entity in that experience came to be the leaders in that church, when Lucius left the activities there.

Hence we find an interest not only in the mysteries of the Master's teachings, but the interest in the intrigues of political and social natures; the abilities to ferret out or detect the little, undermining things others would do, are a part of the entity's consciousness or awareness.

If those associated with the entity want to prevent the entity from knowing all about them, they had better keep their mouth shut! For the entity can piece, bit by bit, a little here, a little there, to know almost the thoughts of others.

The interest in, and the abilities in spiritual things may be aroused from that experience. The ability as a writer may be indicated from those experiences there. These the entity should know much more about ...

Then study to show thyself approved unto that ideal, and know ye chose wisely in Laodicea ...

THE FOLLOWERS AND THE CHURCHES 421

1367-1   F.18   4/28/37   Helene

. . . the entity was in the land now called the Holy Land, just after there had been those experiences of the personal teachings of the Master—when there was builded in the hearts and minds of many the attitude that material rebellion meant spiritual separation, and that spiritual separation meant material rebellion; or during those days when the church in Jerusalem and in Caesarea Philippi was being persecuted because of those activities on the part of those who were adherents to same.

The entity was young in years when it lost its life by those exposures in fleeing from the persecutions.

Hence there is an innate tendency, when there are disturbances, for the entity to desire to change, to "forget it," to get away from it. Yet these must ever be met.

In each experience the activity of a soul is for its closer walk, closer communion with the Creative Forces or God in its dealings with the fellow man.

Running away from same only prolongs the mental and material torture, and does not aid the mental and spiritual-mental self towards development, but creates fear—and that activity that finds expression in sarcasm and irony; that finds expression at times in the entity as regarding conditions, experiences in even individuals . . .

The name then was Helene, and the entity gained and lost and gained.

281-16   3/13/33

In making this worthwhile in the experience of individuals who are seeking for the light, for the revelation that may be theirs as promised in the promises of same, it would be well that there be considered first the conditions which surrounded the writer, the apostle, the beloved, the last of those chosen; writing to a persecuted people, many despairing, many fallen away, yet, many seeking to hold to that which had been delivered to them through the efforts and activities of those upon whom the spirit had fallen by the very indwelling and the manifestations that had become the common knowledge of all.

Remember, then, that Peter—chosen as the rock, chosen to

open the doors of that known today as the church—had said to this companion, "I will endeavor to keep thee in remembrance; even after my demise I will return to you."

The beloved, then, was banished to the isle, and was in meditation, in prayer, in communion with those saints who were in that position to see, to comprehend the greater needs of those that would carry on.[51]

3037-1   F.35   6/9/43   Jueneta

. . . the entity was in the Holy Land, during those periods when there were the activities following the life of the Master in the earth.

The entity as a child knew John the beloved. The entity heard John's exhortation to little children. The entity heard and knew of the persecutions of those who had been close with the Master.[52]

The entity made application of those tenets and truths among the peoples especially in those lands about Gennesareth. In the experience the entity gained. For, the entity became—though far from the cloisters that are made today—a sister superior in a school in that land, under the aid even from the Romans.

Thus we find the entity capable of meeting many hard problems where others may fail. When it touches the political or social life the entity is capable of meeting those problems and of arousing an interst in those that are in political or economic authority.

Use such, do not abuse such—just as ye did in the experience then, as Jueneta . . .

Let that mind be in thee ever as ye sought the teachings of the lawgiver, as ye found in the way, the truth, the light, as ye heard from John the beloved. And thy vision of the light will come stronger and stronger to thee.

1703-3   F.52   3/8/39   Cleopus

. . . the entity was in the Holy Land, during those periods when there was the interpreting and the attempt to write or correlate those teachings of the Master, as well as of those who were in such close companionship to Him.

The entity was close to the younger of the disciples, John; and it was to the entity that one of his last letters was addressed—to the lady. For to that entity, John, who should come again soon into material experience, seeks a means, a plane of expression.[53]

Through those periods the entity gained in attempting to give to the various groups in the many divisions of the church, as it might be called; though not considered such in that period.

The name then was Cleopus.

From the activities in that sojourn much might be gained, if there would be the turning to the inner self for recognition of that which is the impelling force that motivated the activities of John through that experience—of which the entity caught a glimpse oft—and yet was hardened in the experience through the disappointments not only of those in authority in the various groups or congregations but through the intent in self to impress others with the feeling of superiority owing to its close affiliation with one known and spoken of as the Beloved.

Understand, this is not the John, author of that called the Gospel, but rather the Epistles, the letters—the elderly man then—the last of those in his period *personally* in association with Jesus of Nazareth.

Study those letters, then, for in them ye may find much that may give thee an insight into that ye have sought so often through this experience. For know, as he gave to thee in those periods of counsel, in those periods of direction, there is *no name* given under heaven whereby men may be saved but He, the begotten of the Father—even Jesus, the Christ!

3615-1   F.53   1/2/44

Then know, as ye walk in the presence of the Master it will be as leaning on the arm of someone to whom ye have pointed the way to the Christ-life—just as the beloved in the hour that there was set forth the emblem of the broken body and the shed blood, in order that man might ever be mindful of same—the beloved leaned upon the arm and the breast of His Lord.

3282-1   F.42   10/11/43   Micah

. . . the entity was in the Holy Land during those days when the Master walked in the earth, when the Master taught in Bethsaida.

There the entity, in the name Micah, was among the children blessed by the Master and among those that later became helpers in the church first established in Jerusalem, dissipated by the orders and by the persecutions when James was beheaded, when Philip and Stephen were stoned. All of these as martyrs were friends of the entity.[54]

Thus the abilities as a nurse, as an aid, as a helper for children, as one lending hand in every manner.

And those that may know the entity may indeed count themselves fortunate . . .

Q-4. How have I been associated in the past with my present brother, [3158] . . . ?

A-4. The experience in the Holy Land, when he was among those healed of the unclean spirit . . . [3158 had physical readings. Subject to possession this time.]

2990-2   F.44   8/15/43   Cerle

. . . the entity was in the Holy Land or Promised Land, following the periods of the Master's sojourn in the earth.

The entity was associated and acquainted with many of those that were of the household of faith, or those that were disciples or apostles of the Master.

But during those days of persecution much that might have been gained by the entity in spiritual lessons was denied, for fear of material hardships. For, it is ever—"Today there is set before thee—choose thou."

The entity then was known as Cerle; among those that knew of the disturbances between Peter and Paul, especially in the disputation brought about in the early church at Jerusalem.

The entity moved with that household to which it had joined during those periods when James was beheaded at Jerusalem to portions of Macedonia where the disturbances arose.

3635-1   F.24   1/13/44   Isalen

. . . the entity was in the Holy Land, among the children of the first of the martyrs for a cause.

The entity then was a daughter of James, the brother of John [55]; in the name then Isalen. The entity was a power and a might in the supplying of help to those who were persecuted throughout the period of the entity's sojourn in the earth.

The entity then learned detail, learned how to meet people and to show itself friendly . . .

2346-1   F.44   9/16/40   Suphor

. . . the entity was in the Promised Land, during those periods when the Master walked in the earth.

The entity was among the children about the land where the Master dwelt. The entity came directly under the influences of the Master through those periods when there were the gatherings of the children for His blessings, as He walked by the wayside.

The entity held to those tenets, those truths; which are the principles of His teachings even in the present—the beauty of a smile, the beauty of speech, the beauty of companionship; for the helpful, improving influences in the experience of others were as the watchword of the entity throughout that sojourn.

The entity was acquainted with some closely, others as afar, of those of the twelve that followed with Him; and was blessed by them because of the care the entity made for the Master's household after the crucifixion.

The name then was Suphor. The entity *gained* throughout the experience. The entity brought to James, the brother of the Lord, the helpful influences through the aiding in the activities in the first church.

3605-1   M.31   1/21/44   James

. . . the entity was in the Holy Land during the days when there were many questionings as to the activities of the Master as He walked in the earth.

The entity was among those who labored a part of the time with the fishermen of Galilee, being one who had more to do with the carrying of the products to other places for distribution . . .

The name then was James, an acquaintance with Peter, Andrew, James and John, the fishermen of that period who were companions with the Master. The entity was not particularly interested in those things, save in the influence such association had upon the individuals with whom he came in contact —this was of particular interest to the entity.

Yet in the latter days of the entity's experience, especially after the martyrdom of James the son of Zebedee, this entity —James—became a zealous individual for the activities of the disciples.

1211-1   M.36   7/3/36   Barsaboi

. . . the entity was in that now known as the Promised Land, during those periods when the Master walked in the earth, during those periods when there were choices being made by those of the brotherhood to whom the entity had belonged, and the activities as set about by those who had become a portion of the gathering about the Teacher.

For the entity then was among those that were *given* authority to become as representatives and teachers, during that first portion of the entity's activity in the ministry of the Teacher.

Not until those periods when there arose the questionings by the authorities—as the Pharisees and the Sadducees, the Romans, that had become in a turmoil through the advancing forces of the Essenes—did the entity then withdraw as an *active* teacher; not until the latter portions of those influences in that land.

And when the rebellions and forces arose after the death of James, then the entity again became as a figure, as an active one in the influences that had been presented by the Teacher in that experience.

Then in the name Barsaboi, the entity gained, the entity lost, the entity gained.

2970-1   F.48   4/22/43   Lydia

. . . the entity was in the Promised Land, in that portion where the Master oft walked—in Galilee. Hence the entity came under that direction, that teaching, but because of fear of oppression, because of those things which came about in the experience with the beheading of James, the entity became unstable in itself.

Know, as given, thy body, thy mind and thy soul are *one*. Where ye have fallen short is in the recognition of that, even as the Father, the Son and the Holy Spirit are *one!* In what? Not body, not mind, but in purpose, in hope, in desire; those things that are invisible yet are the ruling influences in the application of the relationships of individuals one to another. Individualized, they are not one; spiritualized, they are one.

Keep the faith.

In that sojourn, as Lydia, ye knew sorrow, ye knew joy. Ye were pulled from one place to another. *There,* thine own companion in the present was then thy companion. He sought not to make a home, neither did ye; but ye added much to the good of the activities of the church later in that experience.

For ye kept the letters, the communications with many of the disciples and apostles.

420-6   M.62   1/24/42   Zebedee

. . . in the period when the Master walked in the house, in that home from whom there were the selecting of the two outstanding disciples in that group, the entity was then the father of James and John—and in the name Zebedee.[56]

The entity then was given to the obtaining and leasing of privileges to others, and was engaged—as were the sons—in the fleets, or fishing; though these were only a small part of the entity's activities itself.

Coming under those influences, at first the entity was averse to the interest shown by James and John. Then, with the better acquaintance, the entity grew into that attitude which is exhibited in the present—a greater advocate of the "all out" administration of self and of self's abilities, and of self's physical, mental and material abilities, for the welfare of those in spiritual truth.

As was manifested or maintained by the entity in that experience, as maintained and growing in the present—a stickler for a set rule of formality, yet that also of the perfect—or more perfect—understanding of the true meaning of those abilities for one to be tolerant with others.

This is thy greater virtue, then, in the present. That needed for greater manifestation is also akin—patience. In these the entity grows. Keep that growth.

Throughout that experience it may be said that the entity gained, though there were many periods when that activity was considered—and has been in the present considered by others —indifferent.

It is well to remember these facts in thy study of ways, means or manners of being the manifestation of a channel for a definite service: God and Godlikeness alone shows or manifests true appreciation, yet judgments in the material world are the office that man chooses to do. "Judge not, then, that ye be not judged" was that tenet which became as the watchword for the entity throughout that activity.

More and more there have been those appreciations manifested by the entity's associations in various groups. Stress that lesson as given here—God judges not. He gives and gives and blesses and blesses. The *law* is set. Ye become thy judge. And with the judgment ye mete to others, ye mete to thyself . . .

Q-3. Was I in the Essene temple at Carmel, or orthodox at Jerusalem?

A-3. First in the Essene, and then you had a fuss with Judy [1472]! Then closer in the ones in Jerusalem, but *not* strictly orthodox—as indicated by being both a landowner and a fisherman.

1089-3   M.20   1/23/36   Zebedee

. . . the entity was in that experience when the Master walked in the earth, and was among those who were drawn to the Master—not only through the teachings but through the necessities from the material persecutions during those days when there were the interpretations of the material laws as controlled by the proletariat and the Roman and the Jewish and the Parthenian and the Scythian.

The entity then was among the disciples that walked with Him, and yet *not* of the chosen twelve—but among those that labored with Peter, Andrew, John and James; for the entity then was the father, [of?] Zebedee, that made for the encouragements to the young—and gave of self, gave of those activities, yet keeping self partially aloof.

Yet when there came the periods that there was the dispersing of the disciples, the twelve, the seventy, to *this* entity many, many came oft for counsel and to reason with, and to talk with as concerning manners and means and ways, and as to whether this indeed be the *true* prophet, the true teacher.

For Zebedee first was a follower of John, then of those that had separated themselves from the Jewish Sanhedrin, the Jewish law, and of the head of the Essenes in those studies to which *both* John the Baptist and the Master came first as teachers, and as instructors.

The entity gained through the experience, yet reserving the body, reserving the self oft when there might have been the greater understanding. Yet there arises now, within, the abilities to which the entity may attain in the present; of becoming a channel to all those that seek the counsel of Him who became the Son of man; yea, the son of Mary, becoming the Son of God!

In these manners, then, may the entity in the present become of the greater service; the greater master of self first, then—as thou has received—*give* unto thy fellow man.

Remember ever the admonition that the Master gave, "Feed my sheep. Feed my lambs."

Thus there may come not only to self the joy and happiness, the peace and understanding, but ye may *indeed* know whereunto thou hast been called.

How—ye ask—may the preparation be in the present?

Study to show thyself approved unto that *ideal,* rightly divining the words of truth. For remember *He* is the Word; He *is* that which may not be divided—but *divined* in each word that makes for the correlating, the coordinating, the understanding of those motivative forces of thy activities in the earth.

Meditate, oft. Separate thyself for a season from the cares of the world. Get close to nature and *learn* from the lowliest of that which manifests in nature, in the earth; in the birds, in the trees, in the grass, in the flowers, in the bees; that the life of each is a manifesting, is a song of glory to its Maker. And do thou *likewise!*

Make thy *heart,* thy *mind,* thy *body, ONE* with Him; and ye *may*—by the laying on of hands, by the counseling with those that be weak in body, disturbed in the mind—be a channel through which the message of the *Master* may come!

5369-2   M.63   7/19/44   Reruhel

. . . the entity was in the land when the Master walked in the earth and the entity was among those who were of the "seventy" who were chosen as messengers for the Master. The entity was among those who were of the households of those who were in the activities as the apostles, and yet not numbered among the apostles but the entity was a brother of Zebedee, the father of James and John, who were so close to the Master.[57]

The entity contributed of its material means as well as its physical activities through the experience. The entity was then in the name Reruhel. The entity gained through the experience and may there be that counsel. Keep that faith which prompted thee. Let nothing take it from thee. For as you have known, there is nothing in heaven or in hell that may separate thee from the love of God, but thine own self, thine own denial of self in relationships to Him, who blessed thee in person.

1744-1   F.28   11/12/38

. . . the entity was in the land where the Master walked, and among those that were well acquainted with the disciples as well as His teachings; and of those that were the forerunners —or John as well as Zacheus. All of those were a part of the entity's knowledge and experience.

Hence those things that pertain to religious thought are *very* sacred to the entity. Yet again we find the entity in such environs or surroundings tending towards being more tolerant with others than with self respecting its duties or obligations or its relationships to that manner through which the entity may attempt to give expression of its purposes in the spiritual life.

But hold fast to that thou has gained in the knowledge that He is thy elder brother; that He is the way, the truth, the light; He is the law. And if we as individuals walk in that way, there will be no faltering. Condemn not, as He condemned not. For in the manner as He taught, so it is ever, "As ye do it unto the least of thy brethren, of thy acquaintances—yea, thy enemies—ye do it unto Him."

The entity then was in close association with the sons of Zebedee; and the peoples about the lake.

Hence we find waters that are quiet, waters that are as of the ripple in the brook and the falls have a great drawing for the entity, at times.

540-1   F.30   4/26/34   Naomi

... the entity was in that known as the Promised Land, during those periods when the Master walked in the earth.

The entity then was among those that came under those influences in the sojourns of the Master in that land of Galilee; for the entity was then a daughter of Zebedee and a sister to those that were close in the activities of the Master in that land.

Through that experience the entity gained in soul development. While fears and doubts arose at times from the activities through the periods of persecution, that sojourn has builded and does make for those abilities to arouse in others those things that may be helpful in their mental and physical self; also that purposefulness in the inmost self that may bring to the entity those satisfying things that bring joy, peace and harmony. And oft in the visions have there come periods when the entity has walked close with those during that sojourn. . . .

Q-5. *Have I ever been associated with my husband [555] before; if so, where and under what conditions?*

A-5. In Persia, in Palestine, in America.

Q-6. *What are the objects that I almost constantly see?*

A-6. The boats that carried the brother, the Master, away upon the sea, as the self belabored with those turmoils at the feeding of the five thousand. The baskets that the self helped to fill. These are often almost visioned in the life [58]. . .

540-4   F.32   2/20/36   Naomi

... the entity was the daughter of Zebedee and the other Mary. These individuals were not of the rabble, not of the political, not of great *spiritual* influence or force among the associates of the group. While both were of the Jewish faith, as would be termed today, or the Hebraic faith, they were in that position socially which was above that of the ordinary individuals.

For, as we find, these (Mary and Zebedee) were one of the house of Judah, the other of the house or lineage of Levi. Hence the close associations with those of the priesthood. Yet, by and through the associations of Zebedee, there were the contacts with the Essenes and those groups that held rather to a more universality of application of the tenets and teachings of the peoples during the period.

Hence in such an environment we find that the entity entered, during that period just *after* the birth of the Master to Joseph and Mary—of the household of Judah.

The entity was between James and John. Hence during that period when the Master, Jesus, was in Egypt; the place being outside of Jerusalem nigh unto Bethany. Hence we see how that the environs for Naomi in the early portion of its experience in that land were under a *varied* effect.

Here we find *something* of the conditions that surrounded the activities of those about the entity:

Owing to the circumstances of the group to which Zebedee, the father, belonged, this necessitated the choosing of a following or vocation somewhat in keeping with the forefathers—as the *custom* ran. Yet the very location of the home or the dwelling belied or was at variance to the general customs, owing to the political situations not only as to the Roman rule but because of the edicts that had become rather contrariwise or at variance with—or at cross-purposes with Herod's ruling then of the portions of Judea that later became known as the Galilean or the Samaritan or a questioned peoples.

The activities of Zebedee required that the purposes and aims be rather carried on through or by agents. Or, to put in the parlance of the present, the entity was rather in the fishing business as a wholesaler, than being in active service himself. As indicated or given, that as He passed by He saw James and John with their father Zebedee *mending* their nets,[59] rather were the brothers of Naomi and the father *supervising* and reasoning with the employees as to their activities. For, remember the situations:

Mary, the mother, was of the priesthood that was renounced by the cousin, John the Baptist, as known; yet the activities with the Essenes demanded (as would be termed in the present) the keeping secret the meetings of the peoples or the adherents during those cross-purposed edicts of the Roman ruler and Herod. But after the death of Herod the Great,[60] when Herod the Less became in power in the political forces, more consideration was brought or given to those who called their meetings in those various manners. These activities came about, then, when Naomi was nigh unto thirty years of age.

When did the entity first consider its harkening to an echo of itself? Nigh unto its thirtieth year of age.

As to the surroundings, we find that the entity's home life was out of the ordinary—even in that period of experience. For it was pulled, as it were, *between* the teachings or the training of the mother and the activities of the father and the brother; yet it had associations in the Roman activities, as *well* as a position in the Jewish faith or Jewish activity.

Hence we find this as a description of the body:

One educated in the schools of those that were the teachers from Carmel, yet associated with those activities of the people about the temple—and those who dedicated themselves to the service that was to bring those activities which to the world today find themselves exemplified in many ways; in one the sisters of the orders known as the Catholic—or the Church—in the present; in the other the orthodox activities of the sisters of mercy among certain Jewish sects.

These, then, may give the *conditions*—of the activity in which the entity, Naomi, in its teen years, found itself; pulled between whether the holy activities of the Essenes or the dedicating of self to the faith of the fathers.

When there first began those activities among John's teachings, we find the entity then joined rather with those of the Essene group. For John first taught that the women who *chose* might dedicate their lives to a specific service.

Hence not only the brothers but those employed by the brothers (Peter, Andrew and Judas—not Iscariot) joined in the activities. These were of the fisherfolk who aided in establishing the teachings in and among the people, that held to *both* the old and the new environs.

The body then was fair, with gray eyes—and dark hair, but

brown in its tinge. In mien the body was gentle, and a good cook — a good housekeeper; a *wonderful* singer, and given to meditations.

Not until *after* those teachings of the Master, that made for the establishing more of what would be in the present called the home altars, did the entity wed; being then thirty and four years of age. And it was among the groups in Cana when the wedding feast was held that the associations were made which culminated in the home ties for the entity; making for the reconciliation between Mary and Martha and Lazarus also, and the closer association with Elizabeth, the mother of John.

In the entity's home, then, did Elizabeth — of its own kinspeople — dwell; during those portions of its activity among the *holy* women who had dedicated their lives, their bodies, their purposes, their aims, to those changed teachings between John the forerunner and the Master, Jesus.

The entity in those environs, then, made for its development during those experiences in the earth during that period.

As to the various activities to which the entity was joined during the period, that make for or give experiences in the present activity as to the entity's purpose, we find:

There is exhibited much of that which was experienced in those days; of oft being seen and not heard, yet keeping that which was given as an ensample of the women of the period; "pondering oft in the heart" that they had seen and heard.

555-1   M.36   5/19/34   Cephas

Q-2. Who was I in the Galilean experience?

A-2. One that was healed by the Master, in the name then Cephas.

Q-6. Please give my relations with my wife, [540], during the Palestine incarnation.

A-6. During that sojourn, as is found, the relations then were much as in the present; for was not the self brought under the voice and aid of Him that healed thee by the way?

Q-7. Have I been associated with my child, [665], in other incarnations? If so, under what conditions and relations?

A-7. . . . In the Galilean ministry, or the activity of self as the carpet maker in Galilee; or tent and carpet maker . . .

2799-1   F.40   8/26/42   Ersa

. . . the entity was not only acquainted with but in touch with those periods when the Master taught the multitudes; being of those peoples that were in relationships with several of the disciples.

The entity then was a daughter of Zebedee's sister, and thus was related to James and John; acquainted with Peter and Andrew, Mathias or Matthew, and Thomas.

Though not always adhered to, those teachings meant much. As with most of those people of that particular period, there was not the complete awareness of what had happened until He was taken from them—when there began to be the appearances or experiences which He had promised would come about.

The entity was in those circles in which some of the family were acquainted with those in political as well as religious authority; bringing about experiences in which there was something of the social ideals.

But becoming acquainted with Luke, after the crucifixion, the naturalness of the ability to report a happening or an experience, a lecture, a teacher's thought, as a fact, makes for those abilities as a speaker, as a teacher, as a reporter, as a writer . . .

The name then was Ersa.

1424-3   M.50   8/31/37   Simeon

. . . the entity was in the period when the Master walked in the land.

The entity was among the followers of the Essenes that made for the preparations, the activities that made so much of those experiences possible for that particular period, for the entering of the Master at that time.

And though lame in limb during the experience, through its activities in that period—if these are held to—there may be brought those things that may bring to the heart of many a greater concept of the love, the mercy, yet the *strength*, the power, the might, in the Master—during His sojourn in the earth.

In the abilities then of the entity in the artistic realm, the pastoral scenes should be depicted but with the concept of the religious subjects; those depicting the life of the Christ with the disciples and *more* so those chosen as special messengers or servants.

Hence the great portrait of the entity should be not only that of the Master but of Stephen; not as the martyr but Stephen the speaker to the people before his martyrdom.

Here we will find the entity (for to the entity this was a part of the entity's experience) listening to that address of Stephen before those that would take his life.[61]

And the entity may depict this in such a way and manner as to bring to the mind of every one what that activity meant, not only during that particular experience but to make same as a personal experience for the eyes and mind of the beholders of same.

In the portrait of the Master, depict again the leaving of the upper chamber, when there will be little seen in the faces of the eleven about Him of that fear that was created by the leaving of Judas; but rather that as was experienced in the heart and mind of all when He gave, "My peace I leave with you—in my Father's house are many mansions—if it were not so I would have told you—I go to prepare a place, that where I am there ye may be also." [62]

In this much may be given (if this appeals to the entity) of the color, of the position, of that which will carry upon the canvas the colors for the expressing of that moment, that *hour*, in the hearts of the beholders, those experiencing it, and that will carry that message to those that may behold same as to the eternal oneness of the Christ-life and hope into the hearts of men.

The name then was Simeon; the one-legged man.

1522-1   F.54   1/26/38   Sara

. . . the entity was in that now known as the Holy Land; during those periods and trying times following the crucifixion.

While the entity was young in years, as would be termed from today, it knew much of the application of self in the care of the household under those periods and those activities of the day when there were those who were the toilers of the land and those who were active in what would be called gardening (and not gardening then as would be termed today as "all roses," for it was not!).

Yet the entity came under the influence of the teachings of the disciples; *especially* of Stephen and Philip. This was then in the latter portion of the activities of those in the city where the entity came with the throngs, following the feast of the Pentecost.

In the experience the entity gained, for the entity saw the application of the tenets that were the message, that were the interpretations of the experiences that had come into the lives of those that had known and had followed closely with the man Jesus. The entity saw these applied in the ways and manners in which they become a part of the living experience of the individual—as they did during that sojourn . . .

The name then was Sara, and it was of those peoples that came from the Galilean land.

2402-2   F.56   11/16/40   Lieoth

. . . the entity was in the Palestine land, in that period from which the entity has so oft found a consciousness of a rhythm, a song from without.

It was during that period when Stephen was stoned for his beliefs, because of the visions that had been a part of his experience; and the entity heard the voice of the mob as well as of the brethren who listened with that awe as brought to the hearts and minds of the people of that experience the awareness that man—within his own power—had the ability to refuse, to reject even, the presence of God among men; to so raise his own ego as to defy even God in His dealings with, in His seeking to be a loving Father to the children of men! [63]

The entity then was in the name of Lieoth, and the entity gained, the entity lost, the entity gained. For, there were those periods when the entity felt resentment and hate because they mistreated that source *through* which the entity today oft hears the voice as of the brethren—to awake to that awareness of the indwelling of the spirit of peace and harmony, which alone comes from the Prince of Peace, the *Son* of light, the way of hope, the voice of God in the earth!

2067-7 F.53 6/25/41

Q-25. A reading gives Sylvia as a man stoned with Stephen, and Anniaus as a woman of the household of Cyrenus—are these names correct?

A-25. Correct.

315-4 M.27 6/18/34 Euendi

... the entity was in that period when there were the teachings being spread abroad in the now called Promised Land of Him who had suffered in body, had been despised of men, had been cruelly put on the cross, who had risen and had appeared not only to those that were of the lowly band but to many another.

The entity then was a ruler in the Ethiopian land, and an emissary to these people of the Queen of Candace, and came for political reasons that there might be the activity when he came directly under the influence of Philip,[64] that teacher during those experiences. And the entity hearing, reading in the present much of that which pertained not to the history of its *own* land but of those peoples to the land to which he had gone; and being convicted in self of the purposefulness of an all-wise Creator in making for the associations of souls with the Word itself that had come into the earth to fulfill those things that had been promised to a people.

The entity then, in the name Euendi, made the confession and accepted those teachings, and when the return was made to that land much of accomplishings in bringing self to power were used through those associations, those abilities in that sojourn, and that experience by the way.

The entity gained and lost through that sojourn; yet the inner man was grounded much in the latter portion through the visions that were brought into the land. And there may yet be, there recently has been uncovered in the Ethiopian land the *records* made by this entity of the teachings of Philip and of Simon in that land. For, these are among the purest records; for they were written not only on the papyrus that is of the better character but in the Ethiopian land it still remains intact, this experience of the entity meeting Philip and as to what were the words and teachings of Jesus of Nazareth.

289-9   M.56   1/30/43   Pontitutulus

. . . the entity was in the Promised Land, during those periods when the Master walked in the earth; though the entity was among the Romans rather than the Jews. And he doesn't like the Jews any too well! This is a part of the experiences from that sojourn.

The entity then was not as one in authority, but rather as one who was in the position as the judge; and thus able, and in the position, to exercise the authority the entity represented in that land.

Thus we find the entity was in that capacity as a judge, as would be called in the present.

In that sojourn the entity became aware of the tenets of the teachers, or the apostles, through the associations and activities of those individuals who became acquainted with them. Though the entity was not acquainted with the activities of the Master, he was acquainted with many—or several of the apostles; Peter, John, Philip—Philip the entity knew the better. These were those activities for the entity then, in the Antioch area—as the judge, or as the procurator in that period of activity.

The name then was Pontitutulus. The entity gained, the entity lost. The entity found those activities of the race, or groups that represented the followers, as not true to their own activities. Thus the questioning that still remains with the entity as respecting that particular group, or race.

In the latter portion the entity became acquainted with Timothy, and thus found those activities in keeping with many of those tenets, as may be found especially in the letters to Timothy by Paul; for Timothy was not all a Jew.

2329-1   F.41   8/23/40   Lydias

. . . the entity was in the Promised Land, but *not* of those peoples ordinarily thought of or determined as being the natives of the land during that particular sojourn. For, the entity was among those of the Grecian land who journeyed there with those who were of the faith and sect known as the Nazarenes. Not those who later became followers of Jesus of Nazareth, but those that held to the needs for the *gratifying* of the bodily forces that there might be the greater expression in the material as well as the spiritual relationships. For, literal were the concepts of that sect as to doing to others as others would do to you; not as ye would that men should do to you, do ye even so to them. It was a confusion of the same.

In the experience the entity gained when coming under the teachings of Philip and some of the rest of those who had been put in charge of the visitors to the Holy City.

Hence the entity rose to one thought of, as it might be said, as the head of the early churches, or the counselor for many of those groups who were the heads of the early churches; being *especially* active in Laodicea.

Then the name was Lydias.

1440-1   F.44   9/1/37   Thessile

. . . the entity was in what is now called the Promised Land, during those periods when the Master walked in the earth, and there were those that came from many portions of the land to hear of those strange happenings that had come to pass.

While the entity only came in contact with the Master during the sojourns or travels of the Master through the lands of the upper Palestine coast, and the entity only heard—during the activities of the Master—those admonitions given to the lady that sought for aid for her own household, the entity was a friend of that entity—and from same came in contact during those periods when the disciples stood and there were heard in all tongues those teachings of that one that had been given, as it were, the keys of the kingdom—or the leader.[65]

Then the entity joined with those that were from the lands over which Philip was put as the particular ministering to their needs, and for the care; also Stephen that came close into the experience of the entity.

The entity was not of the Jewish peoples but among them, aiding, ministering not only to those that were in need for material things but that were in need for the mental and spiritual understandings; in the name then Thessile.

In the experience the entity gained throughout the greater portion.

The abilities to be a nurse, the abilities to make a home, the abilities to find all of these hard to be carried on in the experience, arise from the very activities and the thoughts during that experience.

Yet if the lessons, if the tenets, if the life's activities are guided by those very things that were heard, and that have been pondered oft in the experience, and they are kept as the watchword, as the guiding light, as the standard of its ideal, there will come a greater harmony and peace into the experience with which it now deals.

For as is the purpose of the entity's experience in the present, as to others, that their lessons may be learned. For it is continually self being met, and what ye have done about it, and only the promises, the faith, the activity in those things for whom and from whom there has been obtained an advocate with the Father may mercies be shown. For only as ye show mercy may it be shown to thee. Only as ye show patience, long-suffering, brotherly kindness, may these be shown to thee. For thou art indeed a god in its making, for He would have thee as one with Him; yet the choices must be made by thee, or else ye become only as an automaton, only capable of doing that to which ye have been set as unchangeable. For while the law of the Lord is ever the same, the abilities to show forth same are according to the individual application. Good is good. There is not better good than *good*.

Be not then merely good, but be good for something—in *His* name! . . .

Q-5. *What was my relation with my present husband in former experiences?*

A-5. Very close relationship, and in the latter portion of the experience in Palestine was a keeper of the home for Simeon.[66]

958-3   F.31   6/28/40   Lydias

. . . the entity was in the uppermost portion of the Promised Land, when there was the establishing of the Greek church—following the dispersing of the followers of the Nazarene.

The entity was of the Greek faith, and thus worshiped rather more the abilities to bring beautiful activities into the experiences of the individuals, as well as the determined groups.

. . . yet the entity through that sojourn—when coming in

contact with the church at Thessalonica—became an ardent supporter of those teachings. However, the disputations which arose caused some concern to the entity in that experience.

The name then was Lydias; and the entity gained throughout; though there were periods of disturbances and discouraging thoughts momentarily, in the main there were developments through that experience, physically, mentally and spiritually.

2246-1   M.70   6/11/41   Philen

. . . the entity was in the Holy Land, or the Promised Land, yet the entity was a Roman; being among those of the procurators or judges—not among those stationed in the various cities as soldiers, but rather among those who gathered the statistical activities under the rulers as for the abilities of individuals or groups to contribute in this or that form to the betterment of the empire.

Thus the interest of the entity in those things of an agricultural and of a mineral nature, that supplies man from nature's storehouse, also became a part of the entity's experience then; as well as those tenets of the mental and spiritual realm through which the entity spoke and acted.

The entity then was acquainted especially with those of the early church, as some of the disciples and teachers—Barnabas, Lucius, and especially Niger [?] [Nylen?] the cousin of Herod; for she was a close friend of the entity through that experience.

Then the entity was associated with those activities in Antioch and in Syria.

Thus all of the land, as well as the teachings, are and have been of special interest to the entity; and the entity wrote through that period of those things and of the activity of the earlier disciples. Some of the writings may yet be found there. Some of them are even preserved in the Vatican—then being in the name Philen—not Philos, but Philen.

The entity made the greater advancements through those periods of activity. For, while the activities were more and more for the land and its people, more and more of the mental and spiritual teachings were also given out by the entity—not only in Rome and in Alexandria but throughout all the lands that

THE FOLLOWERS AND THE CHURCHES   443

the entity visited—in those capacities of recording the determining factors in the rule of people.

There may be little fear, then, that the entity will ever be an advocate of, or one to assist in, those things that would make men other than *free*—in thought, in expression, in their search for God . . .

Keep the faith that ye attained in those activities in Antioch . . .

2716-1   F.32   3/30/42   Vashti Cleo

. . . the entity was in the Promised Land; not at the time but during those periods following the walk of the Master in the earth.

The entity was born during that period, but its years of activity came during the changing periods of the first few years of acceptance—and then persecutions. These brought fear, the desire to hold to but fear of authority.

Thus an innate fear oft in its visions, in its experiences, of hidden things that the entity understands not. The fear of that it doesn't understand arises in the experience.

Yet we find the entity gained, with the periods of application, the periods of tempering self to those principles of making the life practical. For, true Christian principle is a life of *practical* application of brotherly love, and in the application of the fruits of the spirit of truth; long-suffering, kindness, gentleness, patience. Against these there is no law; they *are* the law—love, and life.

In the experience the entity was known first as Vashti, then Cleo—as an associate of those that were of the Antioch church.

2938-1   F.60   3/17/43   Lystra

. . . the entity was in the Promised Land, during those periods when there were those activities that were as judgments upon the peoples of the day; following the crucifixion and the turmoils as brought into the land through those differences of opinions in many groups that were a part of the political, the religious and the social life of those centers in which the entity dwelt; especially about the city of Caesarea.

There the entity was engaged in those activities as a director of customs as related to those things pertaining to the spiritual and mental life of groups. The entity gained, being a leader or teacher; assisting in the directing of those who chose to establish the centers in varied lands.

The name then was Lystra. In the experience the entity applied self well, and the love of home arose from some of those experiences there. The entity was closely associated with those of its own present household, in the varied capacities, as the entity did advise or counsel with those of the various groups who united in efforts; in clarifying the relations of groups and peoples through those particular political and religious periods of strivings.

361-4   M.15   8/10/34   Thaddues

. . . the entity was during that sojourn of the Prince of Peace in the earth, when men were called unto an activity in that land now known as the Promised Land, or Palestine; during those periods when there was the ministry in Galilee, even in the Holy City, even unto Tyre and Sidon.

The entity followed with the Master in those activities, in the name then Thaddues, among those that were chosen as a light bearer to a people that had been shown a light as shining into the darkness of those periods.

Through that experience the entity gained, though oft was among those that were weighing well the material gains to be had; yet gaining throughout the sojourn, for it was among those who came under the sound of the Voice and heard, "Believe ye not for my words, for the very works' sake believe ye!" [67]

Then, from that experience in the present, those things whether of the mystic forces, the material world or of the spiritual import that come to the entity should ever be weighed well with—and bear the mark of—the judgment set by Him: "As ye do it unto the least of these, my brethren, ye do it unto me." These *are* innately, manifestedly, the judgments of the body. Hold fast to that thou hast gained in this judgment of the world, for the judge of this world cometh and there will be light again found in Him, and thou may be in that position as thou wert in that land—as a light, as a guide, to him that may be the messenger of the King coming to His own!

428-5   F.48   2/23/32

... the entity then was the sister to the one who called the people from the village near the well, and who with those that headed the lessons that were gained through that meeting—established the church that later was ministered to by many of those who were His apostles and teachers; and particularly by Philip, Stephen, Peter, Paul, Apollos. Later, in the latter portion of the entity's experience, the entity was the *mother,* as it were, of the church—known as Pisillia [?] [Pisidia?], the church ...

As for those of the household—the ruler then was Pagosius [?], as *of* the kingdoms of those of Syria *to whom* Samaria had paid tribute. In the general, under the rule of the Romans, to whom *all* Palestine paid tribute in that day.

That accomplished then by the entity, of the twofold nature; overcoming not only that of the hatred of those of another race, but also overcoming of self in its exultant, exalted opinions—on account of birth and of position.

3271-1   F.55   10/7/43   Corine

... the entity was in the Holy Land, during those periods when the Master walked in the earth.

The entity was among those who became close to those activities in the latter portion of that ministry; being among those who journeyed into the land and then remained to carry on afterward.

The entity became among those ministered to, and who ministered for the efforts of the church after the days of waiting for the coming of the Holy Spirit.

The entity was among that group or throng, though it had already been admitted or accepted into the group; and the entity contributed much to the welfare during those periods just before the beginning of the persecutions.

With the persecutions the entity withdrew in such an outward activity, yet in sincerity of purpose carried on with those contributions to the labors; not only to the ministers and teachers, but to those that came from far and near.

The name then was Corine.

1688-6   F.30   2/14/41   Josida

. . . the entity was in the Holy Land, or Promised Land; during those periods when there was the establishing of the church as a permanent place of activity.

Many have not oft considered such, as this entity has (which may be proof in self)—as to how the church took the place of the synagogues or the temple worship.

The entity was among the young of that group who heard Peter on the day of Pentecost. Later, when Peter established the church in Antioch; the entity was present when there were those activities in Laodicea, and the entity saw these scattered—with the early persecutions by the Romans who were sent to replace the centurion in Antioch. Thus the entity became a follower of Paul and Barnabas into Laodicea, and became an active influence there; being the lady superior or mother of the church there (as would be called today), growing under the activities of the various disputes as arose with the bishops as well as the members of what later was called the Presbytery of that particular group of individuals.

The name then was Josida. Throughout the experience the entity gained, yet suffered at times through those periods of turmoils among the leaders—as the disputes with Lucius and Paul, the disputes there of Paul, Barnabas and Mark. All of these became as portions of the records kept by the entity. Thus the entity was kept, as it were, between the fires of disputation.

In the present application of self respecting the urges that arise from that sojourn, remember those influences that are to *fill* the spokes of thy wheel, and that are to reach to the outward activity among thy fellow men.

3273-1   M.49   10/7/43   Smithene

. . . the entity was in the Holy Land, when there were those divisions in the church following the spreading of the apostles and teachers, after the persecution by those that were called to activities in Rome; when there had been the administering of the death sentence to the Prince of Peace.

The entity became a power, until it attempted to use it for its own satisfaction. Yet the entity's activity led a great many of those peoples to become active so as to bring about the building up of that people as a nation.

The name then was Smithene, there the entity gained.

2533-1   M.36   7/8/41   Belden

. . . the entity was in the Aryan land, in the periods when there was the spreading of the church through Laodicea; during those activities of the part Grecian and part Roman experience, of which the entity was a part.

Then the entity was among those who heard of, who analyzed, and then eventually accepted, the teachings of the early church in Laodicea. Then, though, the entity was of the Romans who made an analysis of the people's activities as related to the home and the government activities in the land.

The entity was not a soldier, but rather as a political guide; yet gave expression of its activities among its fellow men by being a part of them—not as a spy upon those of other faiths, but rather as one that would give counsel and advice to aid those who were put in authority, or the natives who were put into their place of activity because of their abilities.

The entity's training brought the experiences of a mind analytical, as to activities, in the analysis of purposes and causes—both as to individual and group activities . . .

The name then was Belden . . .

Q-7. When, where and how in the past, and under what circumstances, have I been associated with my present wife, [2390]?

A-7. In the experience through the Laodicea period, the entity eventually became the very close companion and associate with the present wife.

2953-1   M.49   3/28/43   Terteleus

. . . the entity was active during the Roman expansion; when those activities had to do with bringing other lands under a coordinant activity, as provinces or groups or whole nations or lands.

The entity was among those chosen to pronounce the ability of certain groups to pay tax or tribute to the Roman influence.

There the entity, though, came under the influence of the

experience of the Nazarene; and this brought to the entity a period of unfoldment where there was the greater consideration given, and the consideration of those things which had been given as to how certain periods, certain years, were to be the free years, free periods for the activity. This activity of the entity, especially in Laodicea, brought the entity—because of the closer contact with one Lucius—into an experience that made for the greater activity; when the entity began the brotherhood groups that were a part of the experience of men, and yet not being limited to any one of the religious groups of the period.

In that experience the entity excelled the more . . .

The name then was Terteleus. In the experience the entity gained . . .

3479-2   F.28   3/21/44   Lucei

. . . the entity was in the Holy Land when there were those separations as persecutions began around Jerusalem.

The entity was among those people who had come from Laodicea who were again, with the separations, among those groups seeking shelter in the lands thereabout. Coming in contact with the teachers and ministers in the activities there, the entity—in the name Lucei—became a helpful force in the activities of the church in Laodicea.

. . . During those experiences there were questions regarding those in authority or the leaders, but ye remained in true fellowship. Keep those ideals in the present.

1695-1   F.32   9/29/38   Theresa

. . . the entity was in portions of Turkey, or during the periods when they were known as the land of Laodicea; when there were the activities and the ministering and preaching of those individuals who had been a part of the movement known as the Christian.

The entity then was one in the land of Laodicea, and a worker in the church established there. For a part of those activities were in the household of the entity who then was in the capacity as a weaver of the linens and the brocades that were a part of each household's activities, or the family dress.

Then in the name Theresa, the entity gained through the experience; by the abilities of the counsel gained by the entity's activities and associations with the leaders—or the bishops, or bishop of the church there.

And the counsel the entity gave to those in those activities for their continuance in the purposes to which each and every soul was called, was the influence that made for the development during that sojourn . . .

In music, in art, ye may find an outlet for the expressions of the abilities of self, and through same ye may draw closer to that realm of the inter-between wherein the love of the Father as shown to the children of men may find a way and manner of expressing self—whether in color or in chords. As such ye may gain the abilities to direct again even as Theresa in Laodicea!

2753-2   F.20   7/14/42   Erbert

. . . the entity was in the Roman experience when there were those activities so closely following the period of the Master.

Then in the name Erbert, the entity as the wife of Ersebus [?], a companion of Lucius in the activities in Laodicea and in Rome, was closely associated in those activities there and brought about in a strange land much that was of a practical nature in the application of the tenets of "Love thy neighbor as thyself."

There the entity Ersebus, as the entity's present companion or husband, was in that same relationship in that experience —and he was healed by Lucius as there were those periods when there was that necessity for the entity Ersebus to fight with the beasts in the arena.

These bring at times in the experience of the entity the fear especially of wild animals, as well as the fear of open spaces alone—but companionships, and the ability to give encouragement to others in groups is a part of the entity's experience in the present . . .

Q-1. When, where and how have I been formerly associated with the following: First, my husband, [533]?

A-1. He was Ersebus. Ye were the wife of Ersebus . . .

Before that the entity was among the children that were blessed by the Master. And while the entity was among those who suffered in that of physical persecution, and died in the early years in that experience, the awareness makes for the practical application of those tenets of His blessings in the present sojourn. And these may be counted as blessings to the entity.

2581-2   F.50   10/23/41   Matildah

. . . the entity was in the Promised Land, among those peoples who became aware of spiritual things through the adherence to form, being convicted [convinced] of the need to keep that as had been handed down from generation to generation as to their appearance at certain seasons for a unison of offering to an unknown, an all-wise influence, that had power to direct —through man's latent and manifested abilities—for good or for judgments.

The entity came in contact with voices of those who told of happenings that to the entity were as a distant voice of something heard, expected, longed for, yet never quite attained. And in the present it has made that feeling that something has almost passed the entity by.

Hence we find the entity was among those in the northernmost portion of that Promised Land about the regions of Laodicea. With the new messages, with the new activities that found an answer to something that had been as but just behind the veil in the consciousness of the entity—then as Matildah— there came a sudden desire for doing something about same. The entity sought out those of its own kind, and questioned as to what manner of relationships these speakers, these men bore to conditions, and whereof they did speak such weird words that answered to that call within.

The entity carried much of this home to its own group, later becoming almost too officious in the activity established by teachers and leaders from the church in Jerusalem.

In the present from that sojourn we find the inability to accept altogether certain orthodox views, or certain rites, certain ceremonies that are the basis of organized activity in some directions. They do not always answer to the entity, because of the turmoils with some of those teachers through that experience.

3257-1   F.36   10/3/43   Cleo

. . . the entity was in the Holy Land during those periods just following the ministry of the Christ.

The entity was among those peoples who on the day of Pentecost became so enthused with the experiences through which each one passed that heard the speaker of the day in their own tongue or in their own language.[68]

. . . the entity became as a green fir tree, offering to all not only comfort but direction, an increasing in the evaluation of experiences of others in their relationships with individual activities, as well as the concerted efforts in the various churches or various groups.

For we find the entity was an aid in carrying the messages to the various groups that became organized in their efforts. Thus in the associations in the church of Laodicea the entity brought a helpful influence. For the entity became as the lady elect or the select lady in the ministering to the needs of the saints as well as the young, the afflicted, the indigent . . .

Then the name was Cleo. The entity gained throughout the experience . . .

Let the law of the Lord be ever before thee, keeping the faith —as ye grew in those experiences as Cleo that made for such a branching out of the service to many.

2780-3   M.10   12/11/43   Juhel

. . . the entity was in the Promised Land when there were those changes wrought by the happenings on the day of Pentecost.

The entity was present, among those from Laodicea, that joined with the activities; becoming one that helped in the organization to which Lucius ministered, when all was converted in the tenets and teachings of Barnabas.

In the experience, the entity gained, he was active in those things having to do with weaving . . .

The name then was Juhel.

2300-1   F.36   7/5/40   Dorcohen

... the entity was in the land where there was the distributing or dispersing of the followers of the Nazarene, during those early days when there were the persecutions in the Palestine land.

The entity then was in the land of its present nativity, especially Laodicea; and the entity then under the directions of the church was instrumental in establishing the bishopric activities in the various sections where there was the distributing of goods to the poor and needy, and the aid in the various groups.

Hence the entity was one in authority in that church established there—in the name then Dorcohen.

5163-1   M.33   5/27/44   Jesua

... the entity was in the Holy Land when there were those activities in which many peoples joined following the meetings on the day of Pentecost. The entity was then from that area, which later became known, particularly then, as Laodicea; and with the establishing of the church there and the activities of Paul, Lucius, Barnabas and John, the entity joined in the work. With the disputations which arose between some of those in the order of the church, the entity became disturbed and chose rather the Perean ideas respecting some of those in, and kept in, authority. Later the entity became reconciled, when there had been changes made in relationships of the leaders.

These are innate and manifested in the entity in the present. It forms its ideas of the leaders; though, as then, learns to keep his own counsel; but you don't change his thoughts much about whether they are leaders or whether they are jerkers or shirkers!

In the activities the entity gained mentally and spiritually, in the name then Jesua . . .

Q-7. *What have been my past associations with my wife [2823]?*

A-7. In Palestine or Laodicea, as well as in the Egyptian experience.

2185-1   F.56   5/4/40   Josephine

... the entity was in what is now known as the Promised

Land, especially in Laodicea and Greece and the lands nigh unto the place where the church activities were first established in those lands—following the activities of the disciples and the apostles of the Master.

The entity was among the women of the church in that particular land which was a part of the activity of Mariaerh and Lucius during that particular experience—being of the household in which that minister was active, through the influences of the entity.

We find that the entity changed much in its activity because of some of the teachers; bringing disturbing forces in the church at times, and disputations which caused the activities that brought changes in the lives and experiences of individuals.

Hence we find in the present those conditions arising in which the entity is not very orthodox in its relationships—whether they be of the marital nature, or as to friends, or as to the social order or as to church affiliations, or the spiritual activities.

Consequently, there is the need for analyzing the own self and its soul relationships.

Then the entity was in the name of Josephine; and the entity gained and lost and gained. And those experiences that brought so much of the changes need to be analyzed again in the present activities of the entity.

5070-1   F.23   5/6/44

. . . the entity was in the land joining the Holy Land, in the disturbing factors. In the church in Laodicea were the activities of the entity. While among those who only heard of the disturbances there, yet into these were the abilities of the entity cast as one who attempted to hold together the church by psalm singing.

And this should be the character of helpfulness in which the entity may administer the greater in its music and its song; distasteful in the beginning, yes, but in applying self, ye may find that these may bring the greater attunement to the influences that are creative, not merely in church, but in the daily living. And you'll need it in the home to keep harmony!

In the activities the entity gained throughout the greater

portion of that experience, bringing helpfulness to the spreading of the work of the church through those areas in those periods . . .

Q-4. [What was my relationship with] my mother-in-law, [2946]?

A-4. In the activities in the Holy Land. These were quite close in that activity. And yet fell out one with the other.

Q-6. My friend, [1523]?

A-6. . . . Trusted her in the experience in Laodicea.

5091-2   F.43   5/13/44   Eloise

. . . the entity was in Laodicea when there were those disputations in the church with Lucius, Paul, Barnabas and Mark. These brought questionings to the entity as to the manner in which varied individuals made use of that called the power of God, to self, in such measures as to become their own undoing.

These make for the sincerity of experiences of the entity in the present.

In that activity the entity was known as Eloise.

3292-1   F.47   10/15/43   Eloirn

. . . the entity was in the Holy Land, during those periods when there were many convinced in their minds on the day of Pentecost.

The entity later was among those that were as messengers to the church in Laodicea. Being among those caught in the disputations that arose with Paul, Barnabas, Lucius, Luke, the entity became as one adrift because of the circumstance, because of strife—and turned again to the world experience.

Then in the name Eloirn, the entity gained and lost, and gained again through the latter days when the entity became the minister unto those ill, those unfortunate . . .

In the activities, much may be gained from the lessons of that experience. Let not strifes nor differences of opinions concerning morality, those activities that may direct such, enter into thy experience. Who made thee a judge of thy brother?

As has been indicated, nothing in heaven or hell may separate a soul from the knowledge of God save self. For ye are, ye have been—as ye learned in the experiences in the earth before and in the present—a co-creator with God, in being a channel for souls to manifest in the earth.

3051-2   F.45   6/17/43

... the entity was in the Promised Land, during those periods when there were persecutions, those activities that brought about disturbances among many peoples.

There the entity was associated in those activities in the church at Laodicea, when there were those disputations with Paul and Lucius, the questionings of Peter and Andrew and Bartholomew. All of these were a part of the entity's experience, in which it was torn, as it were, between two opinions. And later, when there were those reestablishings of the activities with Lucius as the elder, the minister, those overtures were made that brought the entity to that interpreting of the activities according to the *Christ* Consciousness, rather than as to an individual man. These brought harmony and peace, and the entity in the latter part of that sojourn was a deaconess in the church at Laodicea.

3298-1   F.38   10/17/43   Anna

... the entity was in Laodicea, when there were the activities in the church that caused turmoils between the leaders as well as the associates in the area.

The entity was among those that were against all of the activities propounded by Paul, and favored Lucius in the activity in the church. For the entity then acted in the capacity as a deaconess, and contributed to the welfare work in all the churches throughout Asia, as well as in Palestine and the northernmost portion of Africa, and Rome.

The entity then was known for its good works, in the name Anna.

1661-2   F.60   3/28/41   Jessica

... the entity was in the Macedonian land, during those periods when there were turmoils arising from the Roman activities as well as the thought in the spiritual life from the teachings of the disciples and apostles of the Master.

The entity was in those groups of the church in Laodicea, during those periods when the church was near to those activities of being divided; and the entity aided the sister of the minister or leader there to bring order in the church's ministry . . .

The entity then was known as Jessica.

262-126   1/19/41

To be sure, many are active as illustrated in that pronouncement of Paul, "I did in all good consciousness persecute the church." [69] This to him was sin, yet—according to the consciousness—righteous sinning; for when he was aware of his error, through the call to service, he became as active in the defense of that *as* he had persecuted in all good consciousness . . .

When there had been fulfilled that preparation, or a part preparation of material knowledge of Moses, he set about to put into activity that purpose for which he had come into the earth. Yet materially he chose an error, a sin, in establishing the righteousness of his fellow men. Thus a full period was required —as of earthly righteousness or earthly knowledge—to undo or to coordinate that as was to be a working principle of righteousness versus sin. *Then* he was *called;* as was Paul in his persecution of the church, conscious of a purpose, but *active, doing* something *toward* an activity which by education to him (physically) was correct, yet sin.

3545-1   M.22   12/20/43   Justin

. . . the entity was in the Holy Land, when there were those activities in portions of the land where Paul, Silas, Barnabas, John and the disciples had opened the way through the lands roundabout, in Caesarea, in Thyatira.

And as Paul practiced the healing as well as ministering, the entity—because of its belief—attempted to apply those same tenets; and was that entity rebuked by the Holy Spirit when it gave, "Paul we know, Jesus we know, but who art thou?" [70]

The name then was Justin.

So may the entity in the present take that rebuke as a personal one. Know in whom ye believe, and why. Know thyself to be thyself, and thy relationships to thy Creator, and ye will walk closer in accord with Him.

3019-1   F.49   5/24/43

As recorded when individuals saw Paul heal those individuals at Laodicea, even by the sending of a kerchief or by the laying on of hands—and there was the attempt of others to apply the same character, or to produce the same manifestation—there was the speaking out of those forces that would be hindered, in saying: "Jesus we know. Paul we know. But *who* art thou?" [71]

1230-1   F.30   7/23/36   Pondus

. . . the entity lived in the earth during those periods when there were the influences in the Roman activity from the journeyings of many from a land where the teachings of the Nazarene had become a portion of those influences about which the entity made for many changes in her surroundings.

For coming under the influence of Paul, coming under the influence of Titus, knowing of or having the knowledge of Timothy's activities, these brought a strength in individuals that made for a caring of those forces that produced in the experiences of the lowly a strength, that produced in the experiences of those in high estate or authority or social prestige the love and the knowledge of all being of one purpose before a creative force.

The entity then in the name Pondus was among those in the Roman rule who first induced the rulers to *consider* that those teachings were becoming a part of that empire.

2656-1   M.72   4/1/27   Isabodd

. . . that period when there was the persecution of that sect then in the Roman rule. The entity then among those who would shield that minister as came to that peoples, and then in the name Isabodd, and the entity being then in that of the tentmaker, and in the service of those that were in power, yet brought much of the comforts to the teacher, Paul, and the entity finds in every experience in the present life that peace, that hope, in the message as was left by that individual in the earth's plane. Hence there is seen in the urge that of the love for that ministry to others, yet that temperamental condition as has been presented has made the entity—even in this at times—sometimes cold and sometimes hot.

... Remain, then, true to that calling as has been set in Him —for those words are true as are loved by the entity (those of Paul), in that "My course is run. I have fought the good fight. There is henceforth laid up for me the crown of righteousness, for in Him is the light, and the light shineth unto the dark places." [72]

694-2   F.45   10/16/34   daughter of Aquila

... the entity was in the earth during those days when there were the persecutions of those that had chosen to follow the tenets of those of the Promised Land, or that Teacher that had come into the earth and whose followers were little fearful of those things that partook of the aggrandizing of thoughts and things of the body.

The *entity* then was among the daughters of Priscilla, to whom Paul came, who with Priscilla and with those activities rendered such a service to those in that experience; suffering in body yet glorying in the ability of giving of self in those things that would bespeak that gentleness of purpose that was exemplified in the life of Priscilla and Aquila (the father) in that experience.[73]

In the spiritual and mental life the entity *gained,* though lost in material things—yet counted it all as gain, that there might be given of the body for those tenets and truths that were embraced in the experiences during that sojourn.

And this makes for the experiences in the present where there are the attempts so often to atone, or to make drudges for self for those things. *Rather* know ye that the Lord loveth rather that of love than sacrifice; rather the purposes, the aims, the desires! *What* is thy desire toward thy fellow man? What is that motivating thy activities? Let the love of the Father *constrain* thee!

1460-2   M.18   11/7/42   Petromus

... the entity was in the Promised Land, during those periods when the Master walked in the earth; though the entity was among those of the Roman peoples in charge of the varied activities for the distribution of the varied groups through the land.

Thus the entity was given to sea service, yet came under those influences of the activities that later were a part of Paul's relationship, and others of the disciples that were travelers in the later periods of that experience.

Thus the entity learned of spiritual imports. The abilities as manifested by Paul, by Peter, came under the entity's sojourn in the latter part of the experience, when there was the full acceptance, because of the wreck of the entity's crew, when there came the knowledge that these were inner forces of the soul, of the mind-soul.

Then in the name Petromus, the entity gained in the latter portion, and aided much in the dissemination of truth, of understanding, of the bettering of the conditions materially, spiritually, of many peoples through that era.

As to the present application from those latent urges—study more and more those periods recorded in the Book, and they will become more and more a part of self, if there is the giving of self to same; not materializing, other than living, living self in the truth and the way.

427-3   M.16   9/29/27   Agial

. . . in that land when the Roman rule brought much persecution to the peoples that accepted the teaching of the Master. The entity then the companion of the teacher [Paul] who came to Rome as the prisoner bound to Caesar.[74] The entity coming under this teacher became the follower and the teacher in the secluded way, yet gaining much through this experience, yet fearful of physical violence through public announcements of self's position . . .

. . . In that experience known as Agial. In the urge is seen the love of those teachings, and especially of the experiences of Saul [Paul] the teacher.

3478-2   F.66   12/22/43   Juliah

. . . the entity was in the Holy Land during those periods when healings were being attempted and practiced by the disciples or apostles, during and after the activities of the Master in the earth.

The entity then was among those of the household of the

jailor whom Paul aided when he was released from prison.[75] Following the experience the entity then, as the wife of the jailor, made profession of the faith and became active as a healer . . .

The name then was Juliah.

2137-1   M.17   5/23/31

. . . in that land then known as the City in the Hills, where there were those of the new peoples, or new truths being given. Then, when there was the persecution of those as had accepted, or did accept or teach this new teaching. The entity was then among those who heard, who accepted, who became among those followers, later among those *persecuted* for the undertakings in that experience. In this the entity gained. In the first *portion* of the experience the entity lost, but with the new understanding, the new application of that as had been gained, the entity builded in the application of self for those whom the entity would serve . . .

In the name then, that may be seen—as the one that returned the cloak to the Master.

. . . live that the soul may grow, and the successes that come *through material* forces will be the outcome of same; remembering that as in the return of the cloak taken from the Master, when under the influence of the teacher Paul, the entity gained that insight that that sowed *must* bring the kind of harvest that the cultivation brings of the seed sown; for we cultivate by nature those deeds, those seeds of life, as we sow them. What *will* the harvest be? For as ye sow, as ye cultivate that sown, as ye apply in the mental body, so *must* that seed be that the entity presents to *its* Maker. Keep thine body, thine mind, pure, that the soul may expand into the knowledge and understanding of *its* Maker; for *God* gives the increase.

3053-3   F.11   11/11/43   Melia

. . . the entity was in the Grecian land, in that period when the activities of the people extended more from Rome to Greece —than in those periods when Greece brought the activities of drama or art to Rome.

This was in the early days of the church, when the Roman

rule had brought the church to Rome through the arrest of Paul, Peter and some of the other apostles that caused the establishing of those activities; and then those activities first came to Greece—through those periods when Paul, Barnabas, Silas and others of the ministry had brought a message to portions of that land.[76]

The entity then came close to those activities, being in the home of Dorcas. There the entity acted as a helper in those periods when it became necessary that the activities be kept at late hours.

The entity likes to keep late hours yet! It's not very good in the beginnings but later such may be a part of thy experience—as ye are enabled to give thy music to others.

There ye aided in the singing of psalms, in the care of the children.

Hence in the beginning here, we find that the activities should often be measured by or tempered with the thought of children.

The name then was Melia.

620-1   F.35   7/30/34   Lilean Jueanu

. . . the entity was in that land known as the Roman, during those periods when there were the persecutions of those that had given of themselves in body and mind to the understandings of the teachings that were being presented by those who had been the emissaries and soldiers in the Land of Promise.

The entity then was among those who followed close in the way of one of the ministers to that teacher known as Paul, or Saul of Tarsus; then among those that were of the households of those that were in rule and in power; and, joining self with these people, suffered in body and in mind, yet—through the spiritual and mental development—gained throughout.

Hence in the present we find much of that pertaining to the mystical forces, the ideas of numbers, crosses, marks, and those things ordinarily termed superstitious; yet these are not, to those that give credit to same, for to them they bring a better understanding of that in the material world being a shadow of the spiritual forces—and thus such a shadow may bring forth or keep within the mental activities of individuals and souls a picture of those things that will bring peace and harmony and joy; just as does the expectant mother keep in her heart of hearts the image of that offspring desired, thus moulding much of the physiognomy of those that would bring forth into material things from the unseen.

For, as the body during that sojourn—in the name of Lilean Jueanu—gained in physical and material development, it brought to many of those, as they suffered under the persecutions, that which built in themselves and in herself the *spiritual* harmony that made the suffering rather the joy; that should be counted by all that would make themselves a channel for the blessings of those that are to come to bring peace and joy to others. Count that thou sufferest at the hands even of others as *joy* in a service for thy Son, for thy Maker!

2457-2   F.35   7/15/26   Lystra

. . . in the days when the first establishing of the church in Rome. The entity among those who administered to Paul, the apostle, and this entity has ever held the highest reverence within the present earth's plane for the words, the teachings, of this apostle. Then the entity gained and lost, for in the persecution that followed the burning and the sacking of those quarters held by those followers of the teacher, the entity submitted to the questions of those who would persecute to gain life for companions, and in this lost both self's sustenance and life, and lost in purpose. In the urge as is seen—the love of the teaching, and the dislike of any conversation concerning persecution for the Master's sake. In the name then of Lystra . . .

406-1   M.14   9/11/33

. . . the entity was in the Roman land when there were persecutions being made to those of the Christian faith.

The entity then was among those converted to those teachings through the preaching and ministry of Paul during that period; and, being young in years, was attempted to be used by the soldiery, yet tortured for the activities in protecting those of the faith.

Through the experience the entity gained, though the sojourn in the land was of only a few years; yet many were the

THE FOLLOWERS AND THE CHURCHES 463

contacts the entity made that will be contacted in the present; and the opportunity for aid to many that passed through those experiences may be in the present.

Hence, those influences through the mystical and occult forces weighed with the activity of the Christian principles in the mind and experience of the entity, will make for a *peculiar* activity of the entity in these relations in the present. Yet, if the entity will make a close study of the doings and activities of the early churches, there will arise within the experience the abilities to draw upon the imaginations (as termed by many) and come closer to the actual happenings to many during the experience, than much recorded without the text of the Scripture itself—and much that is written there.

2310-2   F.37   7/23/40   Constantine Tupela

. . . the entity was in the Grecian land, during those periods just close to the activities in the Promised Land when the Master walked in the earth.

The entity then came under the influence of those who had been close followers of the Nazarene. The entity became filled with that desire to depict for others the characters and characterizations, the love and the love light as was told by those teachers of the day.

Hence we find the entity came under the influence of the followers of Paul, Silas, Philip, and the early fathers of the church; in the name then Constantine Tupela—and among the first to attempt to depict upon the meeting place of the Grecians in Athens the raising of Lazarus—as among the first of the pictures painted upon the walls of meeting places as to those who accepted or heard the calls of those teachers in that experience.

There we find that the entity abused, yet gained through the experience; for the entity became rather secular and one who withdrew from the activities of those peoples unless they adhered to or thought much as the entity did.

1716-1   F.63   7/3/30   Lydias

. . . in that land known as the Roman land, and in that period when there was the new teaching being brought in, and when the prisoner was bound and brought in.[77] The entity among those to whom this one ministered, especially in the gardens through which the body went as a seller of linens, and the entity gained during that experience—in the name Lydias, and the daughter of that one who made fine linen in Tyre and Sidon, and who brought many under the influence of Paul, the minister. The entity in that experience suffered physically, yet mentally grew to be one to be reckoned with among the peoples of that day. In the present experience, hard has it been for the entity to judge other than by the criterions as set down by, even the "old bachelor"—as has oft been termed by many . . .

. . . remembering, much that has been gained came from that in the hill country about Rome, and in the isles thereabout, and is of the Word. Keep inviolate that committed unto self *through* introspection, yet write about same.

2110-1   F.60   8/30/32   Lydiaus

. . . during that period when the dissemination of the truths were among those peoples of the Grecian period and land, when that minister from Tarsus entered into the land of the Lystrians.[78] In the city of Macedonia did the entity then reside, and —coming under the influences of that experience—gained and lost, and gained, through the experience; for the entity was among those that heard readily, and when the hardships and physical persecutions arose the entity faltered—for the pain to the body-mind, the pain to the physical associations, brought fear that was not easily overcome; yet when the final tests came, through the persecutions, there arose those that aided in strengthening the entity, through the associations from those peoples that had once dwelt in the Arabian land, and the entity gained—in the name Lydiaus . . .

5075-1   F.40   5/8/44   Susana

. . . the entity was in the Holy Land when there were those teachings which were being a part of the ministers and the apostles of the Master. The entity taught the young, being all things to all men and yet forgot the appetites and that of habit. The entity was questioned through its associations and activities, and yet brought many to the more perfect understanding, and was a close associate with the companions of, and the close activities with Paul the apostle, or Saul of Tarsus.

The entity's activities then were in Lystra. The name then was Susana.

2654-1   F.23   2/6/30   Aiel

... in that land when persecutions arose from the religious cult, as was called in that period, during that reign of the one called contemptible, or in the latter portion of Nero's reign. The entity then among those who accepted the new teachings, becoming a disciple of Paul in that period—and oft has the entity in discussion unconsciously quoted many of that writer's sayings. In the period the entity gained, even in the sacrifices made —physical and mental, and bodily. In the name Aiel ...

1530-1   F.50   2/5/38   Elizeboth Mae

... the entity was in the Roman land, during those periods when there were the persecutions of those of the land who believed in or accepted the new tenets that were being brought to the land by not only the natives but those that were brought either in bondage or as teachers and ministers from the Palestine land.

The entity then was among those peoples that would be called in the present the artisans or laborers in the niceties for conveniences in the homes, and in the application of those things that would bring more or less of the associations with the means, source or manners for worship in the various forms.

Then the entity *accepted* the teachings by Paul, and the close followers, and received persecutions and activities that brought disturbances in the experience of the entity during that sojourn.

The name then was what would be termed Elizeboth Mae. In the experience the entity gained.

2138-1   F.59   8/1/31   Eunice

... in that land known as the Promised Land, and yet the entity again a sojourner from a northern and western country. The entity then a worker in linens, and an embroiderer of no mean estate, coming in the latter period of the experience under the influence of the teacher as became the *leader,* of the chief of the *speaking* exponents of the new set, or sect. The entity gaining through this experience, for — as was said of the follower of Paul — "so in that graciousness of thine grandmother Eunice." The entity Eunice through this experience, the name being changed from that of the combined — or the Grecian and the Hebrew name also, Amon-Dekar. In this experience those truths, though they find a different meaning to the entity from many, find an answer within that is oft not explainable by the entity, and the holding to those tenets will bring *to* the entity that of the greatest faith, the greatest satisfaction, the greatest understanding; for though there be those things that would attempt to make one afraid that are of the earthly making, and those things that would bring those bindings from material things, in *Him* — as taught by Paul — *is* the light, and there *is* no variableness in His understanding. When one once gains that consciousness of that presence as was gained by the entity in that experience, nothing in the heavens above, in the seas beneath, neither far or near, can shake or change *that* understanding; for He *is* the light, and the way man *and* woman may approach the *Throne* of Grace [79] . . .

2283-1   F.35   6/14/40   Marcia

. . . the entity was in the Promised Land, during those periods when the Master walked in the earth.

The entity was among those peoples of Bethsaida with whom the Lord walked and talked and worked. The entity became a companion of those known as the keepers of the faith, and aided especially the teacher who helped Paul in his ministrations — Barnabas.

Hence the entity was closely associated with the activities, teachings and writings of many of those things which were a part of the early experiences of the peoples in that period of activity.

The entity was beautiful in body, in mind; the entity wrought much disturbance among some of those early activities in the church in Antioch. Yet, as an associate and a companion of Barnabas, with the persecutions which came with Paul, the entity aided in all of the activities of the early church; the entity losing its life only in those periods when carried to Rome as an example for those of that era and period.

The name then was Marcia. In the present the entity may gain its concepts, its hopes, its activities, from the teachings of that period.

Study, then, the 14th, 15th, 16th and 17th of St. John, with all of that which thou helped to write, in those activities that brought to those people much that is not given in other portions, even of the New or the Old Testament; as: "Faith is the substance of things hoped for, the evidence of things not seen —by it, through it, were the worlds brought into being." [80] Also, "yet we have a high priest after the order of Melchizedek." [81] For, the entity then bore the marks as the children made, as the followers of Melchizedek, the priest, as manifested in Him who gave, "In my father's house are many mansions; if it were not so I would have told you."

These and such have been and are the things which the entity may "bring home" to others, as it did to all those whom it met . . .

Find first what is thy ideal. Is it bound up in Him, even as in those ministerings in Antioch, in Rome and in Laodicea and other lands? Or is it such that ye are confused with those things that partake of others' activities?

2615-1   M.47   11/10/41   Paulos

. . . the entity was in the Holy Land, during those periods following the Master's walk in the earth.

The entity knew of, was acquainted with those activities during that period; seeing the greater application, however, as a man, during part of the experience of the teachings or establishments of organized activity under the leadership of the various apostles.

The entity was acquainted with the activities of some of these; Andrew, Paul, Silas, and especially Barnabas. And while the activities were not as a teacher or minister, as termed in that period or today in some quarters, we find that the manners in which the entity encouraged those who accepted those tenets and made of them a part of their daily experience, were the work of the entity, in making same practical in many of the communities in which there were activities not only of persecution but of greater knowledge as to the purposes of that experience in the earth.

So in the present, there are the doubts—latent and manifested in the entity—of organized effort in spiritual things. Thus it may be said that the entity is very orthodox, and—as indicated in Uranus—very *un*orthodox in the *applications* of the tenets of that which is the hope, ever was, ever will be, of the world and of man's being at peace with his fellow man . . .

The name then was Paulos, known and acquainted with the activities having to do with the taxation by the Roman peoples. Thus these as of rules, as of taxation, as of body principles, are still latent and manifested as a part of the body.

2560-1   F.65   5/8/41   Cilcia

. . . the entity was in the Roman land, during those periods when authority was usurped in other lands; at that period when the early church was being formed in Laodicea.

There the entity was the companion of one in the Roman authority, yet one who was a most helpful influence in bringing the activities to a more unified effort—even when divisions arose between the leaders of that particular church.

The entity was acquainted with Paul and Barnabas at that period; siding with the teachings of Barnabas in preference to some of Paul's. In the experience the entity gained throughout its activity. For, there was the application of that principle that indeed the spirit of truth is manifested in just being kind, just being patient, just being long-suffering; showing brotherly love, forgiving to those who are easily beset by the weaknesses of appetite or of the flesh.

For, the entity aided much in those periods, not only that group in authority from Rome but the weaker vessels in the church activity.

The name then was Cilcia.

1613-1   M.68   6/10/38   Cyprus

. . . the entity was in the Grecian land, or the Parthenian-Grecian land, during those periods following the activities when there had been the putting away by man of his association with creation and God, in the crucifixion.

And the entity heard of same when those of that land had begun to tell the story of Him who had given, "Come unto me, all ye that are weak and heavy laden, and ye shall find rest unto your souls." [82]

This to many had become as a message of hope, under the burdens of those who were in power for the satisfying of their own material desires in riotous living and in the pleasures of the moment.

And the entity then, hearing, heard as it were a call to those things that had been a part of the entity in an experience before; and it brought hope and a new experience!

And the entity became a messenger, yea a healing messenger, through the awakening that had come to the entity from the teachings of Paul and Barnabas as they had journeyed through that land.

Then the entity was in the name Cyprus, and gained throughout.

And oft in the present the entity has again and again caught a glimpse of those experiences; from a word here, or an act there, which has called forth those visions of old.

Hold fast to these, for as ye measure to thy fellow man, so measure ye to thy Maker.

For ye must stand before Him, thy Maker, with the deeds done in the body as a witness of thy purposes, of thy desires.

707-1   M.57   10/23/34   Silas

. . . the entity was in that land now known as the Roman and the Grecian, in those periods when there were the gatherings of those that partook of those understandings, tenets and teachings of the man of Galilee.

The entity was among those that were His close followers, among those that knew the powers and the might of those influences in the experience; for the entity—with Paul, with Barnabas—learned of those manifestations that had come to the sons of men; suffering in body—as Silas,[83] that ye have read of, that ye have loved as ye read, that ye have understood better than ye have many of those. For thou wert the companion of Luke, and Mark—who was the recorder of the first of those things that were dictated by his own uncle, Peter, who gave to thee strength. Though in bonds, thou hast seen them fall away. Though in poverty, thou hast seen all the good things of the earth, all good things of the spirit, poured out upon the sons of men! Hold thou, mine brother, mine friend, to those things that thou gavest to thy fellow man in that day! Let him that was thy guide, let him that was thy teacher, *still* come to thee. Open again the doors that thou may see the glories of the Lord as thou usest thy voice, as thou raisest that night in the prison when the doors were opened, as thou sawest the Romans made afraid.[84] Then may thou feel within thine inner self those bonds of doubt and fear, that have at times taken possession of thee, fade even as the darkness from those prison walls faded—as there was the light of the countenance of the Son of man that makes men free indeed shed abroad in thine self in that body thou wore during that experience. *Such glory* that the bars were severed, the doors were opened, and all spoke the *glory* of God! Thou may make manifest such in this material world, wilt thou *hold fast* to that thou hast gained in that experience as Silas, the helpmeet of him to whom was given the keys of the kingdom in the earth, who made that declaration of all declarations to his brethren as they walked, "Thou art Him who has been sent from God that we might know that His love may sustain men in their trials, in their tribulations, in their joys, in their sorrows, in their weakness; yea, even in their might. Thou, O God, *art* the Giver of life, and light, and understanding!" *Hold* to that, my friend, my brother [85] . . .

Study, *study*—as thou didst in the Macedonian land, as thou did in those periods when ye sought to know the man acquainted with grief, yet a *power* of might, a man among men —Him that walked in Galilee, Him that defied all the Romans' influence, He that defied even His brethren in the Sanhedrin, He that aided in making the paths straight that they that walked therein might know the light and the truth! *Thou,* in thine self, then, may help thy fellow man. The soul's awakening, whether from the body or the body from without, must *find* expression from *within.* For *there* has He promised to meet thee, in the mount of thine *own* self! Hence give—*give*—give of self's strength that thou may have life, and having life have it more abundantly in Him. For thy abilities are many. Make of them that which is more and more the manifestation of thy Lord.

417-1   M.35   9/10/29   Matthew

. . . the entity was called by the Master, in the place of collector of custom, and much has been given to the world through the attempt of the entity to explain the position of his *peoples* to the Master. The entity then was in the name Matthew.[86] In this experience the entity gained. Gained through the association, through the intent and purport, through the desire to set others aright. In the present we find that innate which is truth to the entity, that the entity desires to give to another in the *manner* as received by self.

279-4   M.31   7/14/31   Judah

. . . in those days when those peoples in the Promised Land gathered about to hear the new teacher, the new minister. The entity then was a keeper of custom under the Roman rule, and a brother of Levi, or Matthew, in this experience; rejecting much that was accepted by the older brother, yet coming under the influence that brought *to* the entity a development in that of being gentle in nature, as well as masculine in body and mind, *kind,* affectionate, kind-hearted, tender-hearted, true, pure in mind — *this* brought development, even under stress, to this entity, Judah.

In the present there is that innate awe of any religious service, of any cult. Any purport of a service brings awe and a respect of the one so serving, unless there is seen that same is a sham — *then* abhorrence comes to the entity. Then, as an innate experience in the present, the entity may be trusted as to word given, often to its own *undoing,* if governed or judged by the material-*minded* body, but remain true to that though the heavens fall! For being true to self brings that satisfaction that does not breed contempt, nor does it bring dishonor or shame . . .

As to the abilities of the entity, these being many — may be hedged only by self . . . As one *wielding* [yielding] to those influences *as* the entity had upon the shaping of the earth's influence *in* that of Galilee, that about the mound city, so may same be in the present . . .

1213-1   M.28   7/16/36   Celopas

. . . the entity was in that now known as the Holy Land, or

the Promised Land, during those periods when there were those establishings of the protectorates, the establishing of religious thought as a protection for a peculiar people—the divisions as arose.

The entity then was among those peoples of that land but of the Roman land, and acted in the capacity of that one that made for the accountings to those of the Roman land in authority.

In these the entity made for activities, then, in and during those periods when the Master came into the earth.

The entity then knew, the entity then was acquainted with many of those that were of His *own* associations; being a close friend to James and John, and an overseer to Matthew.

In those associations the entity gained much, yet when there was seen those divisions, those disputes even among those that were the closest to the Master, the entity doubted all men, the entity became fearful of those teachings. Yet as they became in the years that followed experiences in the daily life of those things that he had heard, of those things that he had counseled with and heard as hearsay, *then* they became as much in the experience.

Then in the name Celopas, in the experience as a whole the entity gained, in the experience the entity had much of those forces that made for doubts and fears to arise. But as he found then those that made for answering within, so may he in the present holding fast to those forces, to those truths, to those tenets as He gave, meet the issues of life, of experience, the criticism in mind, the unkindness in the activities of those that the entity even had befriended. But remembering that the fruits of the spirit bear witness even in that it brings as the fruition in the life, if adhered to.

Hold then not to those things that create malice, that create misunderstandings, misinterpretations. Choose rather to do good to all.

2697-1   M.48   3/11/42   Pebelus

. . . the entity was in the Promised Land, during those days when there were the activities after the Prince of Peace had walked in the earth.

The entity was among the Romans who were set as those that garrisoned the land, as well as in military rule. The entity acted rather in those capacities of supervising the collecting of customs, or the setting in order of the natives as well as those of its own peoples.

Thus the entity was acquainted with the teachings of the Master as hearsay; later becoming acquainted with Matthew. These brought about changes in the entity's faith or belief, and activity.

Thus, as it were, set in a purposefulness in relationships to those in military authority, to aid in bringing messages of the activities that had been the experience of man to the Roman land.

The entity thus was acquainted with the variations as to the acceptance of same by peoples in the varied positions through that experience.

The name then was Pebelus . . .

Q-4. Has he had any other association before in any plane with Edgar Cayce?

A-4. In the Palestine as well as in the Egyptian land.

2476-1   M.33   3/29/41   Lectus

. . . the entity was in the Promised Land during the periods when the Master walked in the earth.

The entity was aware of those activities, and yet questioned self throughout the experience—as to whether it were the most expedient thing for self to accept or to reject same; though the entity was convinced in self that there was that worthwhile in same, because of that produced in the experience of its associates and many of its friends.

There the entity lost its greater opportunity for embracing, or for fully comprehending, knowing the meaning of what indeed is truth in the experience of an individual, in its relationships to its fellow man.

For, the entity then was a tax gatherer, but of those peoples who were of the faith in that land; and especially was the entity acquainted with Levi and Matthew . . .

There are the needs for the having of an *ideal*—mentally, physically, spiritually; and to realize that only the spiritual values continue. Good lives on. God is Spirit. Man in his creative abilities, in his inner self or soul, is also spirit. Then individually, wherever thy purpose is set, there is thy god. If it is set in self-indulgence, self-glorification, attainment, fame, fortune or whatnot, it perishes with the passing thereof. Only good continues.

The name then was Lectus.

1842-1   M.32   3/14/39   Titus

. . . the entity in those days when the Master walked in the earth.

The entity was a youth, and of Grecian parentage; coming under the ministry of Paul. And if there will be studied—alone —those epistles or letters written to the entity, as Titus,[87] ye will find much of that admonition that at times becomes as living fires within the emotions of the inner self, and at others a rebellious force or not fully understood.

The entity knew of, rather than being closely associated with the Master; yet whose disciples or apostles who came through that portion of the land—Andrew, James, Thaddeus, Thomas —all of those were not merely acquaintances but associates of the entity during that early portion of its experience.

Yet those activities of the entity—especially in the churches of Asia Minor and the activities in Rome, when—in the latter portion of Paul's sojourn there—the acquaintance with Peter *and* Paul brought to the entity a *conviction* that will *ever* be that which causes it to proclaim, "There *can* be, there *is* only one church—even Jesus, the Christ!"

Hold fast to that! Let not those disturbances as caused thee through those experiences in Pamphylia and Laodicea, bring about such disturbances as arose between thee and Lucius as a part of the activity in the church there; but rather hold to that which *is* the criterion—"I am determined to know nothing among men save Jesus, the Christ, and him crucified!"[88] Not the man Jesus, but that which would keep men from knowing of that consciousness and promise that has been and is a part of every soul that seeks to know Him.

For He indeed stands at the door of every consciousness of man that seeks to know; and will enter if man will but open.

Let thy activity, then—whether in that capacity as the minister of the Gospel or as the minister of the gospel of the law—be in that attitude of loving and making for that intercession for the wish in the experiences of every soul that is seeking to know more of its relationships to its Maker . . .

Q-2. *What was my relationship with my son, what urges have arisen from association with him, and what ought I to do about these with reference to his training?*

A-2. The close association here was through the ministry or the activity as Titus in the Grecian land. As to what may be the better manner of *determining* the relationships, or what to do about same—this may be best drawn from the paralleling. For, as will be the experience, these were not always easy through that sojourn! As to the relationships, very close—or what ye would term cousins.

509-1   F.65   2/5/34

. . . the entity was during those periods when there were the turmoils in that land now known as the Roman, during the periods when individuals were used as pawns to bring to the activities and light of others the physical sufferings for the truths that were implanted in those individuals that had accepted the tenets of the lessons that had been brought and were being brought to the peoples by not only the soldiery but by those that were acting in the capacity of teachers and ministers to those peoples.

The entity came directly under the influence of one Saul of Tarsus, or Paul,[89] through the ministrations of Titus, the beloved friend of Paul, and this made for those activities in the experience of the entity; though young and tender in years, as would be termed in the present, the entity was offered as a sacrifice to the aggrandizement of interests or feelings or activities of others—only sixteen years of age when the entity left that sojourn; yet that implanted in the soul of the entity from that experience will remain and has remained in the activities of the entity in such ways and measures and manners as to be part and parcel of the soul itself.

In material things it has given those influences as of *rote;* that is, when there are the orders in self that activities must be performed in such a way and manner, it becomes the very part and parcel of the activities of the physical body without respect as to results or effects—yet that it is as a duty bound. And has made for experiences in the present sojourn of the entity when the entity is often misunderstood, from those very things. Yet the deeper concept has been in the soul as to the oneness of God, the Father, that was presented by Titus during the experience, and emphasized through those associations with Paul; yet has made for those feelings of dependence upon the influences of that creative force in the heart and soul and fibre of the body-life itself.

[See page 88 for incarnation at time of the birth of Jesus.]

683-1   F.43   10/8/34   Sylvia

. . . the entity was during those periods when there were the activities being carried on in the city of many hills (or Seven Hills), when the persecutions arose, and when those that had espoused the cause of the teachers from the Holy Land were taken rather from place to place and were *hounded*—as it were —for their beliefs.

The entity then was a keeper of goats in the hills beyond the city; beautiful in body, clearness of voice, of vision; hearing only through the passersby that message that had been carried by Peter, Paul and the other disciples that had come to strengthen those. Yet when Titus and Philemon came (for the entity was then among the daughters of Philemon, the keeper, that sent his servant to Paul to strengthen him while in the house),[90] Titus then became as the teacher for the entity—who was then in the name Sylvia. The entity harkened to the teachings, yet kept an even balance; and those things that pertained to the music of the reeds were in the hands of the entity during that sojourn.

And the entity might have in the present made of itself a musician on the flute or clarinet, or the reeded instruments that would bespeak of the sylvan dells, the great outdoors, the dance of the nymphs and of the gods and of the beautiful things that are awakened with the touch of the sun upon the hilltop, the gambol of the lamb, the goat, and those in the earth or in the dell as they bespeak of the glories of the activities of the

Spirit of the one God upon those things in the earth. For these were the dreams of the entity, and the fantasies to which it turned its abilities and activities during those periods of its greater development. Yet when those hours came that there were the needs of strengthening those that were kept in the caves for the days when their cries might be heard by those who had defied the living God in bringing destructive forces by having them called into the arena, the strength to many was given by Sylvia as she came to encourage, to raise the hopes again in that there had been the promise in those things that had been seen by the entity through its activities in the lessons it had gained by its closeness to nature, its closeness to the spiritual things that through the earthly expressions may find the way to manifest their glory. For, as it had been given by Him as He walked into the city, "Were the voices of the people to be stopped, the very stones and the hills would cry in their glory to the Father, the God." [91] The entity had experienced this in those moments when there had been the pondering of those messages, those promises that Titus had given to the entity in the walks and talks there.

Again in the expression in the present the entity has found many of these confusing at times, for when there has been the application to the material things in the present many have called the entity impractical. And the lack of the patience that was attained in that experience makes for periods when doubts and confusions arise in the experience of the entity in the present. Yet, as has been indicated, if the entity will turn within it may gain the lessons again that were given by that Teacher among men, learn again those messages with which it strengthened those when the fear of death was upon those that were young and strong in body, those that were old and were being separated from those they loved the most in the earth, and how that strengthening cry went up; "Lo, I am with thee always, even unto the end of the world! Put thine trust in me and thou wilt know that thy Redeemer liveth, and thou shalt see Him as He is." [92] For He has promised that He will comfort and strengthen and sustain those that to their fellow man show forth the love of the Father. And he that doeth those kindnesses to his fellow man lendeth to the Lord, and He has

478   EARLY CHRISTIAN EPOCH

prepared those mansions — even as He has given, "I prepare a place and where I am there ye may be also." [93] If the entity will ponder upon these messages that the entity gave in those experiences as Sylvia, the shepherdess, the one that strengthened so many in those days, there will come a strength, a glory, a vision, an understanding that will raise thee up above. But "He that is the servant of all is the greatest among thee!" [94]

891-1   F.21   4/13/35   Iola

... was in the Roman land, during those periods when many of those that were in authority, in power, were of the soldiery.

The entity then was in the household of those that had come under the teachings of some of the hated peoples. And the entity embraced then the teachings of one that was taught by Paul when in bondage — Titus.

Then the entity was of stature beautiful, and expressed in the Roman game activities that were beset or touched upon by ladies of the court. For the entity then was of the household of one Philemon, among those that counseled with the rulers during those experiences; the second, yea the third Caesars.

In the name then of Iola, the entity made for the greater spiritual development in that experience; for the gentleness of manner, the ability to use the personality, through the individual forces of the entity, was at a period of great activity; making for those gentlenesses, for those kindnesses, of those that were oppressed even by the rulers; yet keeping self ever in a position of not being questioned by any.

The entity will find in the present the greater blessings in soul development and in the real activities in a mental and material world from the promptings of the spiritual self may be had from those same lessons as were gathered from that presented by Paul and Titus during that sojourn. Well that the entity tarry long and oft in meditation upon those things necessary for the establishing of self as in relation to those things that make for peace and harmony and understanding, and the harmony and peace being not in inactivity or in quietness but rather in filling that purpose for which the entity came into being, as a channel of blessing to others. In making manifest the fruits of the spirit that make individuals not afraid; that as given in even those letters recorded (which are only a few). But study to show thyself approved unto God, a workman not ashamed; but presenting thy body as a *living* sacrifice, holy, acceptable unto Him, for it is but a reasonable service; keeping thine mind, thine body, unspotted from the world.

818-1   F.49   2/8/35   Cleoprates

... the entity was in the now known Roman land, during those periods when there were the questioning of many of those of the armies, the people that were as the potentates and the active forces in those lands where the world, as it were, had been turned by the teachings of those lowly fishermen that followed Him that walked in Bethsaida and by the sea as He called to those that would become fishers of men, as He walked in the hills of Judea.

The entity then was among the peoples in the Roman land that were of the rich, those blessed with this world's possessions that seemed to be in jeopardy if there were to be the acceptance of that which came to the entity, that "they sold *all* and divided it among the leaders of that sect." This brought turmoils, distresses, the attempts to justify self in enjoying rather the pleasures of the flesh for a season, and made for the recklessness of the entity's activities—in the name Cleoprates. Coming under the influences of Titus, Philemon (for the entity was in the household where Philemon was the servant), as the changes were brought about the entity through the acceptance of those teachings by the leader of the household, there were brought questionings to the social life, to the activities in the various experiences; and turmoils and reckless extravagance of body and mind followed Cleo in that experience. So the entity lost and gained, lost and gained; for the entity was pulled by the desires of the body and the promptings of the inner self.

1043-1   F.17   10/20/35   Claudiuss

... the entity was in the land now known as the Roman, during those periods when there were the presentations to the people in authority through the reports by the soldiery and those in command of soldiery from other lands; pagan or religious, Grecian or Jewish or Egyptian.

All of those became a portion of the entity's thought during the sojourn in the Roman period, when the first and second of the Caesars were in command in that *now* known as Rome.

There were those things that brought fear, until—in the latter portion of the experience—there were those teachings or tenets that had been presented by one Tutilius [?] [Tertullianus?], an officer and a kinsman of the ruling forces. The acceptance through the teachings of Titus, or those that had followed in the way, brought for the entity an awakening; and an application of those experiences.

Thus there were the abilities of the entity innately and actively during the period, to become as an instructress to the young—and to those that were seeking for knowledge as to practical application of the tenets taught by those teachers or leaders during the day. Then the entity was in the name Claudiuss.

4041-1   F.51   3/31/44   Lidio

. . . the entity was in the Roman land in those periods when there was the acceptance in many quarters of the teachings of the Nazarene, when even there was the returning of the Roman officials in various positions or places, or when there were the visitations of those groups to such.

The entity became impressed with these, through hearing of same, and when coming in contact with Titus—who eventually became an emissary or teacher—the entity aided in such work. Thus we find that particular phase or portion of the book of Acts is the more interesting to the entity.

Then in the name Lidio, the entity joined with those groups. This called for the necessity of the entity keeping secrets during portions of the experience, for there were secret meetings—until there was sufficient strength among groups, yet the entity in the latter portion suffered persecutions.

Hence the fears in the present and yet, as indicated, a sincerity in the entity that would be almost beyond description, other than what is given by the entity as the word is the word to the entity.

390-2   F.35   8/15/33   Veldejui

. . . the entity was in that period when there were the gatherings of many in the "city on the hills," when there were those that were persecuted for their beliefs in the tenets of the Galilean.

The entity then was among those of the court who made jeers and, as it were, made light and sport of those for their beliefs. Yet, with the sincerities that were shown, the entity came to the point of one halting between those that would join with these of the hated class; yet faltered and gained, faltered and lost—and gained. Yet, the entity suffered much in the disappointments of those that made sport and light of the determinations that were set in the activities of the entity in that experience, in the name Veldejui.

And the entity was among those that came to know Titus, as the emissary or instructor for those that were or had been under the teachings of both Peter and Paul.

Hence the entity found contentment and peace in the latter portion of the experience.

Hence, the more easily will the entity find in the present that which will bring joy, comfort, peace and understanding, especially when reading the letters to the Romans—and those of John and James in the latter portions of their chapters or books.

3411-1   M.45   12/15/43   Robolus

. . . the entity was in the Holy Land during those periods when there was much talk of what had taken place in Jerusalem when the Nazarene had been crucified with the thieves.

The entity was among the Romans who had taken little thought or stock of such happenings. But when the persecutions of the church began and there was the turning to the entity for a verification as to whether the authority to do such things was vested in Rome or in the people in authority, the entity listened and became interested—and sought to know more of the background.

Thus the entity came to know a great deal of what the prophets had said concerning this man. Thus in the present when the entity would present Jesus it turns to Isaiah, Jeremiah, Joel,

Habakkuk, or Malachi or Daniel. These appear as reasons to the entity, and they are good ones, for they apply to the daily life of the individual. These are things to be studied.

The entity gained throughout that application, yet was never quite satisfied until the latter days of its activity and it came into contact with one Titus in the offices in Rome. Then the entity gave himself wholly into being a minister unto those people who sat in high places, those people who were in authority. Thus much of those things that had to do with the changing into organizations throughout the Roman empire came from the entity.

The name was Robolus.

357-2 F.31 6/20/33 Amelia

. . . the entity was in that land now known as the Roman, during those periods when there was the changing of the peoples in their ideas of associations and relations that were being affected by the teachings from the hated people in the Judean land.

The entity then was among those peoples that accepted the tenets of the new teachings, and became particularly associated with Titus in his activity in that period and in that land.

As Amelia, the entity suffered even martyrdom in the experience, yet gained throughout.

2272-1 F.55 6/7/40 Julia

. . . the entity was in the earth when the Master walked in the land.

The entity was among the holy women, not only during that period of activity in which there was the lauding of the actions of the man of Galilee, but during the periods of dissension and railing, of sorrow because of separations.

Yet, the entity was among those who knew of—yea, experienced—that day upon the mount when the last benediction was given.[95]

Thus the beliefs in those promises of others have held and do hold for the entity something that bespeaks of something hoped for. Though the entity has oft been deceived in the promises of some of its friends, associates, even of its own household, this never causes the entity to waver. For, the entity's belief in those promises is sure. Hold fast to that purpose that ye understood then—as Julia, of the household even of the doubter, Thomas.

The entity brought into the experience of many the hope and faith which had been and was a part of the experience. So may it even in the present, under the very shadow of doubts and fears, create within the hearts and minds of others who seek to know His way that of hope which springs eternally anew within the human breast—by those influences which He, the man of Galilee, brought into the experience of those gathered about Him there.

For, the entity was a part of same—and so may the entity in the present in its efforts, in the formations of activities for those studies, those purposeful organizations of one nature or another, bring that of hope.

For, it isn't those who do the great deed who are written the highest. For even as He gave, he that is the greatest among you is the servant of all.

So, as ye have found, so as ye may find in thy experiences in the present, doubt and fear are cast away when the thoughts are lifted to the hope that comes in the cross, even in the cross of Jesus!

2650-1   F.34   1/16/42   Eleiza

. . . the entity was in the Promised Land, during those periods when the Master walked in the earth—when there were trials and tribulations for those who believed, and who walked in the straight and narrow way. Yet the entity, even as He, learned obedience through the things which she suffered.

Though the entity knew material hardships, though the entity engaged in those activities that were questioned by many, the entity aided especially some of those that had been closely associated with the Master.

For the entity then, as the sister of Bartholomew, the companion of Thomas, brought those periods of doubts and fears, and yet those activities and abilities to contribute to the mental and physical awarenesses of those that suffer in body and mind.[96]

And the entity became then, as would be called today, a practical nurse.

Thus those abilities to adjust itself to the varied environs—to minister to those who are ill in body and mind—were portions of the activities of the entity through that experience.

Hence such opportunities will be manifested in the present experience. Be thou mindful of that lesson learned, and be thou faithful to the hope ye learned in that sojourn.

The name then was Eleiza.

5359-1   F.14   7/22/44   Ishneth

. . . the entity was in the lands to which the apostles went when they were driven because of persecutions to the Holy Land, and those parts of what is Asia Minor or the old portions and to Persia; and we find the entity, not as a "hanger-on" but as one who aided the disciples, who followed through in these directions with John in one portion of the land, and then with the descriptions of Bartholomew. The entity was closely associated with these in singing psalms and in the alms and good deeds for those attracted to same for the material as well as spiritual portion of their lives. In the experience the entity was then known as Ishneth.

294-192   M.60   2/11/38   Lucius

Mr. Cayce: Yes, we have the records of that entity now called [294]; and those experiences in the earth's plane known as Lucius of Cyrene—or known in the early portion of the experience as Lucius Ceptulus, of Grecian and Roman parentage, and of the city of Cyrene.

As a developing youth and young man, Lucius was known rather as a ne'er-do-well; or one that wandered from pillar to post; or became—as would be termed in the present day parlance—a soldier of fortune.

When there were those activities in and about Jerusalem and Galilee of the ministry of the man Jesus, Lucius came into those environs.

Being impelled by the experiences with the followers, and the great lessons as given by the Teacher, he became rather as one that was a hanger-on, and of the very intent and purpose that

THE FOLLOWERS AND THE CHURCHES   485

this was to be the time when there was to be a rebellion against the Roman legions, the Romans in the authority.

And the entity Lucius looked forward to same; acting rather in the capacity of not an informant but rather as one attempting to keep in touch with the edicts of the various natures between the political forces in Rome and the political forces among the Jews.

The entity was disregarded and questioned by those who were of the Jewish faith who were the close followers of the Master; yet it was among those that were sent *as* those who were to be as teachers—or among the seventy.[97]

With the arousing, and the demanding that there be more and more of the closer association with the Teacher, Lucius being of the foreign group was rejected as one of the apostles; yet was questioned mostly by John, Peter, Andrew, James and those of the closer following—as Matthew, Bartholomew; and was the closer affiliated or associated with Thomas.

In those activities then that followed the crucifixion, and the days of the Pentecost, and the sermon or teachings—and when there was beheld by Lucius the outpouring of the Holy Spirit, when Peter spoke in tongues—or as he spoke in his *own* tongue, it, the message was *heard* by those of *every* nation in their *own* tongue—this so impressed Lucius that there came a rededicating, and the determination within self to become the closer associated, the closer affiliated with the disciples or apostles.[98]

But when the persecutions arose, and there was the choice of those that were to act as those called the deacons—as Philip and Stephen and the others—again he was rejected because of his close associations with one later called Paul, or Saul; he being also of Tarsus or of the country, and a Roman, and questioned as to his Jewish ancestry—though claimed by Paul (or Saul) that he was a Jew. His mother was indeed, and of the tribe of Benjamin, though his father was not.

Hence we find the questions arose as to the advisability of putting those in position, either as teachers, ministers or those in active service, that were questioned as to their lineal descent.

And again the old question as to whether *any* were to receive the word but those of the household of faith, or of the Jews.

During the sojourn in Jerusalem, though, before the greater persecutions—that is, before the beheading of James the brother of John and the stoning of Stephen—here again we had a great question arise.⁹⁹ For Lucius, through the associations with the one who became his companion or wife as ye would call, was entertained and kept by Mary and Martha and Lazarus—thus we find these again made questions.

And there is often the confusing of Lucius and Luke, for these were kinsmen; and Lucius and Luke were drawn or thrown together, and with the conversion of Saul ¹⁰⁰ (or Paul) (as he became) they followed closer and closer with the activities of Paul.

With the acceptance of Lucius by Paul, and part of those in the Caesarean church, Lucius determined—with his companion—to return to the portion of his own land, owing to the persecutions, and to there attempt to establish a church; to be the minister, to be the active force in those portions of the land.

Thus we find in those latter portions of the experience he became the bishop or the director or the president of the Presbytery; or what ye would call the priest or the father or the high counselor as given to those in the early periods of the Church; that is, the one to whom *all questions* were taken respecting what ye would term in the present as theology, or questions pertaining to the laws.

In such the entity as the bishop was the last word, other than that there might be the appeal from such a verdict to the church in Jerusalem—or the apostles themselves.

Such disputes brought disturbances at times, when there were the questionings especially as Paul brought into that region as to whether it was well for those in such positions to be married or not.¹⁰¹

And the declarations as made through the Corinthian and the Ephesian leaders indicate what disturbances there were; because differences arose between Lucius and Paul as well as between Silas and Paul and Barnabas and those that had become the leaders or the real ministers or the missionaries for the Church.¹⁰²

Hence this brought into the experience of the entity Lucius

disturbance between himself and his companion, because—in the first, the companion was younger in years than Lucius and to them there had been no offspring—no child.

This confusion made for periods when there was the withdrawing of the companion, and the closer association of the companion with the teacher that had been the proclaimer and the director in the early experience of the Master's life Himself —or with Judy [1472]; and with Elizabeth and with Mary the mother of the Lord.

With those experiences, and with Paul's being carried on in his second and even his third missionary journey, and with *many* of the things propounded by him that Lucius had declared as things that were unstable, there again—with the teachings to the companion by Judy, by the mother of the Lord and Elizabeth in their years of maturity teaching this younger person—was brought to Lucius that which later John proclaimed; that there *is* in this church of Laodicea no fault, yet it is neither hot nor cold—and that for the lack of its very stand it would find condemning.[103]

Those became periods when Lucius then was thrown the closer, or drawn the closer to the companion; and with the birth of the child there were brought those periods of the greater contentment and peace in the latter days of the entity called Lucius, and a seeing of the development of those experiences.

It may be questioned by some as to why such an *outstanding* experience of the entity now called [294] should not have been given in the first.

As has been indicated, each entity, each individual *grows* or applies, or is meeting self in the varied experiences—as the tenets of an individual experience are applied in this present sojourn or activity.

If this had been given in the first, there would have been a puffing up—but the very unstableness as was indicated throughout the experience, until there were the lessons to be gained from the companion, may be seen.

Then meeting that companion in the present experience brings about that as may be given—that is the *humbleness* as was gained, *still held.*

Then these may become experiences in counseling, in giving

to others what may become lessons—from questions of every nature that may arise from *every* phase of the human experience.

And indeed the entity as Lucius *in* the activities of the entity called [294] may become an influence and a power for good in this present portion of this sojourn.

Ready for questions.

Q-1. How closely was the entity associated with Andrew in that experience?

A-1. Rather there was still questioning, for with Peter the speaker, Andrew the listener, there were disputes as to the advisability of Lucius being put into power; though in the latter portion of the experience we find—as has been indicated in Andrew's experience—they were rather close associated, and Andrew was a defender of Lucius—*after* there was the settling between the companion and Lucius, after their separation and then reuniting.

Q-2. Please explain how all heard in their various tongues the message that was given by Peter in the one tongue.[104]

A-2. This was the activity of the spirit, and what the spirit indeed meant and means in the experiences of the individuals during that period.

For one that was of Cyrene heard a mixture of the Greek and Aryan tongue; while—though Peter spoke in the Arabic—those that were of the Hebrews heard in the Hebrew language; those in Greek heard in Greek, see?

1468-1   F.47   11/2/37   Mariaerh

For as in the experiences of the entity in those sojourns, and especially that individual one that stands out beyond or above the others, from that which has brought into the experience those forces and influences of love and love's influence, there comes that longing for that cry—yea, for that voice that was an experience, "Behold, He passeth by!". . .

. . . the entity was in that land or experience from which the greater knowledge, the greater joy has been or may be the influence to make for the weal or the woe in the experience ever.

THE FOLLOWERS AND THE CHURCHES 489

For it was during those periods when the Master walked in the earth, and during those periods when the Master was seen and heard by many in the triumphal entry into Jerusalem.

During those sojourns of the individuals from many portions of the Judean land, the entity was then among those peoples of the hill country that came to the city during those periods of the feast—when there was the triumphal entry into Jerusalem.[105]

The entity for the first time then saw (though it had heard of) the activities of the man called Jesu, or Jesus, in those experiences.

And when there were the cries of "Hosanna!" and there were the processions, these brought strange feelings to the entity, as a harking to something that had lain dormant within the experiences of self—and the wonder became rather that of a worshipfulness.[106]

Then the entity, as Mariaerh, made overtures; joining with those for the searching out of those activities of that strange new experience of self.

And the entity in those periods became among those that ministered to the needs of those that were supplied by the gifts of those during the days following the persecutions and the establishing of the church, or the groups in the various portions of the city.

The entity grew in years and joined with the activities, for it was only in its teens when these began; and the entity was from the upper portion of the Judean land.

Hence we will find in the present that which was held to, in the giving of service to those that may minister in the various fields of activity, becomes an innate longing within the soul; the searching out of those that are the promptings becomes an innate and a manifested portion of the entity's activities.

Thus again we may find the arousing within the entity's inner self of that which becomes the motivative force for the experiences in a material plane. Though it may come oft under the guise of servitude or service, or activities in the various spheres, with those experiences as the promptings—time passeth; and in time and in space and in patience man becomes aware of his relationship to that we worship as God.

These are the days when the paths must be made straight, that indeed there may be peace on earth, good will to men.

For, even as He gave on that memorial day, if the people do not proclaim Him—or if the people had not cried "Hosanna!" —the very rocks, the very trees, the very nature about, would cry out *against* those opportunities lost by the children of men —to proclaim the great day of the Lord! [107]

Hence in the experience of the entity, as He—these do not become as tenets, do not become as edicts, but as *opportunities* in the experience of self to make each association, each contact, more and more aware of the love the Father hath shown to the children of men—if they seek to know His face . . .

May that love, that peace, as ye find in the cry of "Hosanna to the king!" ever be the promptings of thy heart in this experience; that the beauty, the joys as He hath promised may be fulfilled in thee; that "they may be where I am, that they may behold the glory I had with thee before the world was!". . .

Q-5. What are the lights which I see coming and going, like twinkling stars?

A-5. As there were those varying lights that appeared when ye first beheld the company following the Master, they are as the ways being pointed for the greater awakening, the greater understanding in thy spiritual and mental experiences in the earth.

These are *as* the influences such as we have given in regard to the urges from astrological sojourns and from experiences in the earth; they are signs, omens. Not to be worshiped *as* such; but as He gave the light of the rainbow to those of old, they are as but the keeping of the promise to thee, that thy ways, thy works, thy activities are not forgotten before Him. They are assurances, then, of His love, of His care.

Then with *Him* ye can never, no never, feel or be alone.

Q-6. Would my life work be writing?

A-6. These are as experiences that applied in giving the beauties of love, not in the material alone but as to how the divine love overcomes, may bring help, aid and hope. And he that saves a soul through hope renewed hath covered a multitude of shortcomings.

These would be well—but as in cards, in verse, in the stories of the way to Jerusalem—from Bethany to Jerusalem, from the temple to the cross—these would be well.

Q-7. Is there anything I can do to help it come through?

A-7. Look within—these will aid. *Begin* it! As ye use that ye have in hand, more and more will be given thee.

But, as has been depicted for thee, can ye not see the place, the little town in the hills from which ye journeyed to the city of the many strange noises, the many strange lights, the many unusual customs to *thine* own tenets? and then this new experience of He that brought hope and cheer to those that were ill in body, those that had lost hope through the holding to material things and to the old tenets of tradition? And can you not see the great throng as they spread their garments—yea, those of high and low estate or position—and all the wonderment and loveliness of companionship sought in the material ways? These became a vision. Build upon it, carrying—as it were—thine own part in same. And it may be brought through to a *beautiful,* helpful experience—from Bethany to Jerusalem! . . .

. . . Hold to that thought—The way from Bethany to the temple—to Jerusalem!

1468-2   F.47   12/15/37

Mr. Cayce: Yes—again we have the records here of that entity now called [1468]; and those experiences of the entity as Mariaerh, in the hill country, and in and about Jerusalem and the activities during that sojourn.

We find that the entering, or the growing up of the entity was during that period of the ministry and that life experience of the Master in the earth.

The entity then entered during those experiences—as would be called in the variations of the records—some period before time was recorded from the calendar as established by first those in Carmel, and then in Caesarea and Jerusalem and the ages or eras of the first, second and fourth century were gradually accepted by the many—and now as the records in the earth.

Then we find the entity grew up in the hill country of Judea, nigh unto those places where Elizabeth and Zacharias had lived; Zacharias becoming as it were the first of the martyrs, Elizabeth remaining in the land of the hill country.

There the entity was brought up and taught, and the entity was acquainted in its very early years with the visiting of John by the young man—just before the ministry began—who in His return was called Jesus.

The entity's parentage were of the Jewish peoples and those that were disturbed or had been a remnant or a portion of the Galilean peoples.

Hence in the entity's experience there was not a great deal of the strictly orthodox Jewish activity, nor strictly orthodox activity of those that were of that separate people—or the Samaritans.

Hence we find the entity only came to Jerusalem, at the age of accountability, according to women, in about its fourteenth year; to be recorded, or polled, as to those that were of marriageable age, or taxable, or for the whole consideration both from the Jewish and the Roman associations or requirements for the poll or taxation.

Hence it was during the entity's first visit with its own parentage and Elizabeth and the older peoples that the entity was in Jerusalem, or came to Jerusalem, when the Master—Jesus —came for that period when there was the triumphal entry from Bethany into Jerusalem.

That was the period when the entity first heard of or was fully acquainted with the happenings in Bethany, or the raising of Lazarus and the activities, influences and associations associated with same.[108]

Hence we find the entity was an early acquaintance with many of those that were associated during those periods, as were later called the holy women—that stood about the sepulchre, about the cross, that made preparations for the burial or the activities regarding same.

And all of these became as parts of the experiences of the entity.

And in the application of same, as has been indicated, if the entity will meditate deeply there may be brought into the experience much of that vision—as may be written as a description by the entity—of the road from Bethany to the temple, or to Jerusalem.

For as it was an experience in the entity's activities during that sojourn in which there was first the hearing, then the experiencing, then the conversion and activity, these are innate, these are a portion, these may become full experiences of the entity.

If there is the attempt upon the part of the entity to make application of that in the experience which brought about the same experiences during the latter portions of its activities, there may be aroused those feelings in which the entity may picture, may depict, may paint in words, not merely the triumphal entry but the humbleness—yet the graciousness, the glory, the dignity of the Man, who—with His disciples—waited among friends that from the material angle sought that He not expose the physical man to danger. And yet as He preached, or as He counseled, He gave that indeed for that purpose came He into the world, and as a man must stand forth for what had been the purposes for His entrance.

And the entity, Mariaerh, caught that concept of how each soul must in each experience live as the grain of wheat, as the grain of mustard, as the seeds of every nature; fulfilling that purpose for which it enters into an experience in a sojourn irrespective of self's individual or personal desires, letting the personality of self be lost in the individuality of the Christ-purpose as He so magnificently gave in that way from Bethany to Jerusalem!

As to the entity's experience after same, we find there soon followed the historical events of the arrest, the trial and the crucifixion; and those days followed—and then those periods when the entity remained in and about Bethany and the areas about same.[109]

Then, fifty days later when there was again the Pentecostal activity, when all of the gatherings were in Jerusalem and there were the many of many lands and of many tongues that were brought to conviction by the teachings of the disciples or apostles, and especially in that memorial one of Peter's on the day of Pentecost, we find the entity was among the first *ten* that were baptized on that day.[110]

Then when there was the selection of those that were to act in the capacity of the ministers, or the deacons for the ministering to the peoples, when all their material belongings had become as a part of the disciples' or apostles' and they were all with one accord together, the entity heard much of those activities of Philip and Peter, but became closer associated with one Lucius—a kinsman of Luke. And Lucius is the entity now [294] through whom this information is being given.

Hence the activities and associations of the entity with Lucius became as those close activities for the founding of the ministry, the missionary activities, the influences that brought about the establishing of many portions of the Church during that early ministry of not only the disciples or apostles but those early ministers of the Church; as Mark and Luke and Lucius and all of those—Thaddeus and Saul or Paul and Barnabas, and those of Laodicea.

For it was there that the entity went with Lucius when there was the establishings of the Church there; when Paul preached in Laodicea.

For these were a portion of the kinsmen of the people from the Roman land. And there the entity ministered as the helpmeet or the wife of Lucius for those early peoples of the church there.

There the entity spent the rest of its days, living to those periods when there were the—[Here Mr. Cayce sneezed and stopped. The reading is continued in 1468-3.]

We are through for the present.

1468-3   F.47   1/6/38   Mariaerh
[Continuation of reading 1468-2 which stopped abruptly.]

Mr. Cayce: (In undertone—"Mariaerh of the Samaritans, Judean hill country—triumphal entry—associations with the women—affiliation with those during the Pentecost—companion or wedded to Lucius of Cyrene, the bishop of the church in Laodicea.")

Yes—with the activities in the ministry, when the entity was with its companion Lucius in Laodicea, when Lucius was made —by Paul, and Barnabas—head of the church; there came some hardships to the entity owing to the teachings of Paul concerning the interests of those who were as leaders or the head of the churches, and from which grew in many quarters the commanding or demanding of celibacy as a prerequisite for the activities as a bishop or leader.

This caused the entity, Mariaerh, owing to the fact that there were no children, to feel that most of those teachings of Paul —or many—were directed at her.[111]

Owing then to the close friendships that grew between John Mark and Mariaerh, again questions arose in the minds of many—owing to the differences in the ages of Lucius and Mariaerh.

These caused many disturbing conditions with the entity in that experience.

Only when there had been, with Luke and Barnabas, the greater and better understanding, did there come to be a greater activity by Mariaerh in these activities and surroundings.

In the latter portion of the activities—before the persecutions of the church arose, through the activities of the enmity as aroused against Paul and his disputes with the mother church; or the first church in Antioch and the first church in Jerusalem headed by the brother of the Lord, James, and Peter and Andrew and the others that from time to time made those visitations there—there was a son born to the entity, that grew in grace and in favor with all of those not only in the first church but those that had been closely associated with the activities that preceded the coming of the Master, and the teachings of the Essenes.

These made for greater and better activities by the entity during the experience.

The entity then lived to those ages of sixty-nine, seeing then that the son—Sylvius—came to be reckoned by the leaders as one chosen for service in the name of the Master.

While there were many disturbances from the material, the entity's experience throughout was for a growth in the mental and spiritual.

As to the applications in the present from the experience:

The abilities of the entity to write; especially Bethany to the temple, or from the experiences of self as associated with Lucius

—as the love story in same; and the cry of the multitudes, the words and the messages of the Master on the way.

These may become in the experience an awakening to the greater abilities.

Ready for questions.

Q-1. Can you give me the names of my parents in that experience?

A-1. Jochim, the father. Marh, the mother; of the Judean or the Samaritan peoples, or those of the country—as indicated in the northernmost portion, or close to the Galilean activity.

Q-2. Did I have brothers or sisters, or both?

A-2. Two brothers and a sister.

Q-5. Were my human mother and father . . . associated with me in that sojourn and how?

A-5. A brother and a sister, in that particular experience.

Q-7. Was I associated with the entity in that sojourn now known as [1472]?

A-7. In a portion there was an acquaintance, and especially in the latter years of the entity now called . . . —or [1472], then Judy—when there was a reviving of the teachings for the son Sylvius as related to the prophecies that had been made by the leader or teacher or prophetess of the Essenes; in the latter portion of the experiences of the entity Judy, were the closer associations then more as the advisor or counselor.

Q-8. Was Sylvius the only child born to Mariaerh and Lucius?

A-8. The only child.

1986-1   F.39   8/27/39   Thelda

. . . the entity was in the Palestine land, when the Master walked in the earth.

There we find the entity was among those who were the acquaintances of Martha and Mary, to whom the Master came oft. The entity was among those who were the hired ones as a mourner at the time of Lazarus' death; and became a believer —seeing the activities, experiencing the influence of the Master's life on the friends, associates and acquaintances of that group there.

And from henceforth the entity was known as one among those of the holy women.

Then the name was Thelda, and in the experience the entity gained. While it was late in years (according to the years of many of those women of that experience) when the entity became acquainted with all of the activities of the disciples, all of the apostles, all of the influences brought about during those periods just before and after the crucifixion were experienced by the entity.

The entity also saw that experience of the crucifixion — the darkening of the day, the rending of the veil of the temple, the noises that were experienced — as well as those periods that followed same, in the upper room, when the entity with the followers of the Master was made aware of His resurrection. For those things that happened to the peoples and children of the entity's acquaintances were witnessed, as well as to the heathen — or especially the Romans.[112]

There we find the entity was closely associated with Mariaerh [1468], who was the companion of Lucius in the activities in Laodicea.

For the entity then was the aunt of that entity, bringing her into close associations with the activities of the people in that experience.

Throughout the entity gained, for those tenets — as well as desires and purposes and intents — became deep-seated within the soul of the entity; and these oft rise within the experience.

Thus, as the entity finds in its associations and activities, those things that bespeak of those influences that bore upon the lives of individuals during that period become more and more as the more important; for the entity learned well that lesson, as she heard given to Martha and Mary by the Master — "These things are not to be left undone, but she, my daughter, hath chosen the greater part" [113] — listening to the voice as may come within, as directs the activities of the individual in not only its associations with individuals here and now, but that as *prompts* the heart as *to* those relationships with others.

There may yet be much of that finished as was undertaken then, in bringing to the minds and hearts of those who seek to know His way the greater understanding.

And the entity might indeed write that story of His dwelling, His visit to Bethany. For as there comes into the experience the knowledge of the various influences and forces, an individual life history of the entity during that sojourn might bring the interpretations of such in such a way and manner that the entity—*now*—might make that as a book, as a leaflet, as a tract, something to be treasured by many.[114]

While much has been said as to His visits, His friendship with Mary, Martha and Lazarus, we find that much more remains to be said as to how indeed that friendship with those brought so much into the hearts of men at that experience, many who never followed save as afar; and as to how closely this may illustrate how His being may be to the children of men even in this experience . . .

And in those channels as indicated may come the greater awakening to the fulfilling of that purpose. For, as indicated, ye held to thy purpose under stress and strain in the Egyptian land, as As-Ma; and in the land where the Lord made Himself known to the children of men ye *blessed* many; and ye sought there to fulfill that to which ye were aroused by His coming. Then in the land of thy present nativity ye brought ways, means and manners for the application of these same tenets.

1523-4   F.29   4/12/38   Vesta

. . . the entity was in the Roman and the Grecian experience. This, however, was during those periods when there were the establishings of the Church in the land of the Romans.

The entity then was of royal power, being not of the Caesars that were in power or authority but of the household of the cousins—as ye would term it; and in the position to draw upon the influences of the court as well as the established places of activity of the empire then through Macedonia, through Greece, through Palestine, through the North African land.

There the entity's greater experience or influence came in the contact with those who were as the missionaries, or those who had been set in authority over the churches or places of activity.

Though through its secular forces the entity was averse to

such affairs, the entity acted rather in the capacity of one who looked upon the activities of those for the reporting; or—as ye would term such an activity in the present—the entity was in a diplomatic service or activity.

However, the entity was in the same sex as in the present; and became associated especially with one Lucius [294] who drew from those activities in Macedonia, in Mesopotamia, and the northern portions of the Palestine land.

The entity was greatly influenced by that association, but when faced with the teachings of Paul—and the activities in which the entity had been the means for *separating* Lucius and his companion [1468] during that experience—such influences caused the entity to withdraw, into its activities in the Roman rule.

Hence we find the entity in the present oft has those periods when it becomes confused materially or mentally, and it draws then within itself and becomes moody for a period. Yet it is able and capable to put, as it would be proverbially said, the best foot foremost when the occasion arises. Yet this subjugating of the feelings brings on those periods when questions arise as to the motive of the entity's activities during such periods in its associations with others.

The name then was Vesta, and of the royal families. Hence the entity may in the present bedeck itself in the very royal robes or in the garments of the ash girl or goose girl and still be queenly in either!

1523-16   F.33   10/14/42   Vesta

Mr. Cayce: Yes, we have the records here of that entity now known as [1523] . . . and those experiences of this entity in the Roman period.

In giving an interpretation of the records as we find them, it is well that the background of the place or period be given, in regard to the religious and political conditions; that there may be the correct interpretation of the activities and associations of the entity through that experience.

As may be found in the records—there had been those journeyings of the peoples of the families of the Caesars to what was then the area around Laodicea—which was peopled with those combinations of Grecians, Romans and Jews that had been expelled from portions of Galilee.

Hence this background of the activities was a part of the entity's experience. The land or country was under the direct rulership of the Romans, not as in those areas of Palestine where there were the Jewish rulers overseeing or being superseded by the Jewish religious groups or sects of peoples.

Thus those variations of the customs that were a part of those peoples; both the Grecian and the Roman, according to the dictates or tenets of the peoples of the time, yet shaded by those customs which had become a part of the people's activity as the influence of the Christian faith began to be noted in the land.

It was under such conditions that the entity, Vesta, then came into the consciousness of activity; of the background of those who were part Grecian and part Roman. As the entity's father, Xeren, was a Roman citizen, the entity was known as or called a Roman.

In the early developing of the entity the associations were with the people of the Roman influence, though—as indicated —shaded by the Grecian.

Thus those activities in the abilities as an athlete, or as one oft engaged in the games that were a part of the experience; also dancing was a portion of the entity's experience.

With the meeting of the one who later became the head of the church in that area, there began the greater period of unfoldment or development of the entity.

As there were the associations with individuals who had in a manner adopted the Christian or the Jewish and Christian faith, these brought entanglements.

As the companionship was with Lucius [294] through that particular sojourn, there came the adopting of some of the customs of these. And yet there had been the making of the agreements, or the marriage contract for Lucius. Yet this had little to do with the associations of these two, or their companionship. For, there were children born to these through those associations in the early part of that activity in the experiences.

When there were those acceptances by Lucius, Luke and the

Laodiceans or Grecians and Romans, to journey to the Holy Land, or to Jerusalem, these brought disputations.

During that experience the marriage took place between the contracting parties—the entity who had been Vesta's companion [294], and Mariaerh [1468].

These, of course, brought questionings, as well as questionings as to the experience of Vesta; and the disputations that arose later as to the associations of the entity with those of her own household, as well as the associations with those in the church—that later became established, with the journeys of Barnabas, Paul, Mark, and those of the early church.

The disputations arose especially with Paul. For, Paul sided with Vesta, in the periods when, for the eighteen months, he remained in Laodicea to build up or strengthen the church. Yet Barnabas, who had been of the combinations that guided the offices of the church, had sided with those of Lucius' household. These brought about those periods of questionings.

Thus, in the application of this part of the entity's experience, is there any wonder that there has been the questioning regarding the church and those who officiate in various capacities as directors in the affairs of same?

Innately within the entity there has ever been and is the questioning, as to the lives of those put in authority as the directors, ministers, deacons, elders, teachers. This is then the natural consequence of the entity's experience through that particular sojourn.

With the settling of those conditions, the entity began its active work among the peoples in that particular area or land. The activities that had been a part of the entity's experience in its early childhood then began to show expression. Thus the entity's influence with the young, its special interest and feeling for children, and especially of the young—as these were a part of the entity's activity then, in the directing of same, because of the great diffusion of tongues, as it might be termed, or because of the customs from the various influences of the religion of the Grecians, the Romans, the Parthenians and the Jews. These naturally caused confusions.

Yet the entity in its activity through the experience, it may be said, was given to the directing of the activities of the youth in every form; as of weaving, knitting, dancing, basket weaving, applique work, tentmaking—all of these were a part of the entity's experience.

The entity did not wed after that experience, and brought—through the experience—the greater unfoldment in the adapting of varied groups to religious purposes in and through the experience.

The entity lived to be a deaconess in the church in Laodicea, and lived to a ripe old age.

This was the experience of the entity, as we find, in the Roman sojourn.

Ready for questions.

Q-1. Did I come in contact with Jesus; if so, in what activity and under what circumstances?

A-1. Only as the experience through the visions and through the close associations with those who *had* been with Him. These had been explained, these had been developed, so that the visions became realities.

Q-2. Have I met or been associated in the present with the father of Pebilus, my child in Palestine (now my nephew, [1990]); if so, what association and name?

A-2. This was Lucius.

Q-3. What was the association and activity with my present husband [1650] who was then Pitmumus; how may I further bring about a oneness of purpose between us?

A-3. In keeping to the unifying of purposes in those that are the ordained activities in the church. A very good friend, and eventually bringing him into the activities in the church. He was a fisherman then!

Q-4. As given, there was a close activity with Luke; what was the type of activity, and what are the urges in the present?

A-4. In aiding in the writing, and what might be called the reporting of the activities of the church to Luke, and also to John. For the entity then was associated with John, the beloved, in the periods before he was sent to Patmos as an old man; and it was under his influence and direction that the entity was made the deaconess in the church.

The associations with Luke were those because of the close

friendship between Lucius and Luke, whom the entity never lost association or contact with through the experience in the Roman or Laodicean period.

Q-5. Was there a close association with Andrew; if so, in what type of activity?

A-5. Only as a part of the directing of the journeys of Andrew, as he passed through that portion of the land.

2824-1   M.4 hrs.   10/7/42

Q-4. Can any more be given at this time regarding the appearances in the earth?

A-4. These should be sufficient for knowing what you have to deal with for the present. Let the entity seek that as indicates other activities.

To be sure, it was a physician in the period of the Master —and the writer . . .

3188-1   M.23   8/31/43   Thaddeus

Of these take thought. For they take hold upon those things ye preached, as Thaddeus, in those periods in Laodicea, when ye—as one of the sons of Lucius [and 1523?]—came into associations with those activities of the church in that day and period; when ye made for the establishings of truth and understanding, even in those periods of turmoils—and yet remained strong throughout.

Ye knew of and talked at times with many of those that had been with the Master. Thus ye find that deep longing within to fulfill, to see finished again those abilities that were a part of the apostleship to those upon whom the Holy Spirit had descended.

What is the Godhead? Father, Son and Holy Spirit. There is the outpouring of the spirit on thee as ye pour it out upon thy fellow man. For, as ye do it unto the least of thy brethren, ye do it unto thy Maker. For, until ye have seen in the purpose of each soul—though in error he may be, that ye would worship in thy Maker, ye have not begun to think straight. For, God is one Lord, one law, that abideth aright in the hearts of those that seek to do and to know His biddings. Then, empty self—as ye did of old—of self. For ye must come before the throne empty-handed if ye would have thy hands, thy heart, thy mind filled with the goodness of the Lord . . .

Q-9. Whom of those now relatives or associates were close to me in past incarnations?

A-9. Many. Closest to the mother [2946] in the Laodicea period as Thaddeus, or with Lucius in Laodicea and the church in Jerusalem, and the various experiences as befell the entity in Rome and other places.

1990-3   M.2   12/2/39   Pebilus

. . . the entity was in the Promised Land, during those periods when there was the greater expression of the God-love in the earth.

The entity was among those of the children of the household of those who became the leaders in Laodicea, or of those peoples of Lycia. And the entity was among those who were blessed as a child by the Master, on the way to the upper coasts of Galilee.[115]

These the entity held to, in the activities in the early church in Perga and Pamphylia, and Laodicea; for the entity was a companion of Luke and Paul and Lucius, through portions of those periods of activity in all of that part of the Holy Land.

The entity was among those who were sent to the Roman experience for that activity in the church there; *chosen* by those of the Romans who became converted to the doctrines of the church in Caesarea, Jerusalem and other lands.

Hence in portions of the activity there the entity ministered to the needs of the saints who were imprisoned before their demise in the experience.

As to the activities in the present from that sojourn, we will find the abilities of the entity as a statistician, or as a keeper of records for activities whether in a commercial or an ecclesiastical field; or any form of records being kept will be a channel through which the entity may find the greater expression in this experience.

The name then was Pebilus. In the experience the entity gained throughout; and much of same may be needed in the present to direct the entity in those activities in which the greater influences may find their expression . . .

Q-9. What have been the entity's past associations with his present aunt, [1523]?

A-9. The child in the Laodicea experience!

Q-10. What are the urges brought forward in the present, and how may they be best used for their mutual development?

A-10. As may be indicated from the activity of each of these, they may be a prop one to the other.

3685-1   F.29   2/20/44   Susana

. . . entity was in the Holy Land following those periods when the Master walked in the earth.

The entity then was among those of the household of faith, for the entity then was the offspring of one chosen as the minister and teacher in the church at Laodicea. There the entity was the bone of contention between some of those of the church and some of those peoples, in that period of disturbance between Paul, Barnabas, Lucius and his household. For the entity then was of the household of Lucius; knowing of and yet not wholly aware of those contentions that arose.

And the questioning of the purpose of men arose from that experience. For the way of a man with a maid, as the preacher gave, is not understood by others; only by the individual, according to the purpose within.

The name then was Susana. . .

Q-8. [What have been my past associations with the following]: [294]?

A-8. The father in the Holy Land experience.

2574-1   F.53   8/14/41   Merceden

. . . the entity was in the Holy Land, among those acquainted with the early experiences of the Master as He walked in the earth.

During those periods of the preparation, the entity journeyed to those lands that partook of a portion of the Grecian activities; but with the beginnings of the ministry, the offspring of the entity were brought under those influences of the teachings not only of the Master but of the disciples.

The entity then was the mother of Lucius, having companionship with, or being the sister of Luke; and this brought those experiences and activities with the holy women.

And with those turmoils that eventually arose between the followers of Paul and Peter and Barnabas in the church, the entity aided in bringing harmony out of those periods of turmoil with Lucius as the bishop of the church.

A whole book might be written of the activities of the entity in the experience. For, many of the activities were begun by the entity that later became proclaimed by many of the teachers in the early church; especially in Laodicea, in Achaia, in Corinth and in the various portions. For, the entity was acquainted with most of the leaders and strengthened the activity through that portion of the land.

The name then was Merceden.

Too much might not be said as to the abilities that arise in the present, as to the interest in and the work with those who seek to know the way as proclaimed by Him of Galilee.

In seeking—seek to know much more of that experience . . .

One need never attempt to justify, but needs only to glorify Him; as ye so well proclaimed through Laodicea, as ye so well put Paul in his place, as ye so well comforted Timothy as well as Peter, Andrew, and brought Lucius to his senses. These manifest again in thy labor of love, of service to thy fellow man . . .

Q-3. *How many times have my husband . . . and I been associated together? . . .*

A-3. . . . In the Palestine experience, husband and wife.

Q-6. *How have I been associated in the past with . . . [993], and how may we be of the greatest assistance to one another at present?*

A-6. In the church in Laodicea. Good "spatters" and yet good friends. These brought about differences, yet they may be united in a common cause and a common effort in the present.

2823-1   F.32   9/26/42   Lucia or Lucy

. . . the entity was in the Promised Land, especially in those periods of the early church in Laodicea; for the founders and teachers there were a part of the entity's experience, as well as the disputations that arose between Paul and Lucius, and the associates there.

The entity then was a sister, or the elder sister of Lucius the head of the church there during a part of those experiences.

This brought about periods of turmoils for the entity. Yet with the stand taken by a part of that same group or family, there came the greater experiences for all.

There the entity was the home builder, the weaver, or one who taught the young—or groups—to weave and to make for such activities in the home, and in the church.

Then in the name Lucia, or Lucy (as would be called in the present), the entity gained; though there were hardships of great numbers in the entity's own family, for there were eleven children in that experience . . .

Q-7. *What have been my past associations with: My son, [2869]?*

A-7. In the experiences in Laodicea ye disputed with him . . .

Q-10. *[2390]?*

A-10. Sister in the Laodicea experience . . .

Q-12. *[1523]?*

A-12. In Laodicea . . .

2390-1 F.30 11/2/40 Nimmuo

. . . the entity was in the Promised Land, in that activity of the church in Laodicea when Lucius was bishop of the church.

The entity was then the sister of Lucius, and active in those influences; yet disputing with Paul, siding—because of Barnabas—with those activities of the brother in relationships to his companions in the experience.

Thus the determination to become the more practical in those things of the world, yet holding to those principles that were once heard by the elders of the church; when the entity upon the day of Pentecost saw and heard that which was as the wonderment of that period—each hearing the speech in his own language, his own tongue! [116]

Is it any wonder then that all phases of phenomena (as called in the present) are of interest to the entity? Yet none are mysterious to the entity; for it catches a glimpse of the meaning of same—as from that experience.

The name then was Nimmuo.

2390-3 F.30 3/8/41 Nimmuo

This particular experience of the entity in the earth plane is so filled with those happenings that dealt with the conditions existing among the early adherents to the Christian principles — it is well that much of a history be given — from the view of those studying or analyzing same — that there may be a more perfect understanding, and to make those lessons gained the more effective in their present application.

First — that particular portion of Asia of which Lucius and Nimmuo were a part had long been under the supervision of the Roman empire.

There had been the attempts of many of those put in authority from the Roman empire to give every advantage to those who offered promise of being in sympathy with those rulings, or who were in the position to be conducive to making for activities in accord with such rulings.

Thus we find that all the family of Lucius and Nimmuo were among those having the greater advantages of the educational facilities of the time. For, much of the lewdness of that period had come from the Grecian and Roman peoples that had become a part of that portion of the land.

With those activities that eventually arose in Palestine, and the ministry that had been in the northernmost portions of the land during the teachings and travelings of the Master — those very close in the family had come under the direction of those teachings.

Then with the changes wrought during the periods of the trial, the crucifixion, and then the happenings which had come about from the reports spread abroad as to what were the actual conditions existent when the hour of crucifixion had come; then the third day and the reports of His rising again and of His meeting with the disciples at the Sea of Tiberius, and then the ascension upon or from the holy mount — these had brought to that family wonderment, and interest.

So with the repeating of that as had been the experience of the brother, little wonder that the sister — Nimmuo — was desirous of knowing more of those happenings; desirous of seeing, experiencing, being in contact with individuals who had actually seen and heard the words of the Master; desirous of meeting those who had been healed by the laying on of hands or by merely the word spoken; desirous of hearing those who had eaten of bread created by the word of that Teacher.

Thus—though young in years, being around sixteen years of age—the entity with the brother journeyed to those environs in which those things, those experiences, had been an actual, living part of the experience of those many individuals.

Being in the position of not only being countenanced by but friends of those in authority, there were questionings; yet there was honor shown these two through their activities in that journey through the Holy Land, across the Sea of Galilee, down those portions of Jordan, through Perea to Bethany, the house of Martha and Mary and Lazarus, into the city itself; the acquaintance of the mother Mary and the rest of the family that had been gathered by John—then—as in keeping with that command from the Cross.[117]

Each of these individuals heard again and again much of that which has been lost by the attempt of individuals to interpret it in the varied tongues.

And then there came the day of Pentecost, when the entity heard that speech of Peter; saw John, James and the other apostles as they sat—as it were—in awe; when the Spirit had descended as in tongues of fire and sat upon that body of the Twelve.

It is little wonder then, as has been indicated, that deep in the consciousness of this entity there is felt the reverence for all forms of spiritual—not spiritualistic but spiritual—phenomena.

There is oft that desire to be alone, to listen to the consciousness within, to hear again—as it were—that story, that experience of those who had known, those who themselves may know that feeling, that awareness of His peace, His presence abiding near.

All of these—and much, much more—were the experiences of this entity, this individual, as she came in contact with those activities which later made the entity a power in the environs of Laodicea, Thyatira, Pamphylia, Philadelphia, and those churches through those portions of the activities in the home land.

With the establishing of the church at Jerusalem, the entity was present when James—the brother of the Lord—was raised to that position or place as the head of the church, through the direct affluence of James and John, the sons of Zebedee. *This* brought about that first of the authorities putting forth their hand and slaying James by the sword. This happened not by that of trial, but by that as would be called a riot; and not incorrectly were James and John called the sons of thunder.[118]

All of those happenings were a portion of the experience of this entity. Most of the periods there were spent either in the direct companionship of the brother or of the holy women and their associates, their friends, in and around Jerusalem.

Oft the entity heard, again and again, the stories of what happened at Bethany; as to when and how Mary had been cleansed from those activities and experiences, little of which until then had even been spoken of in the presence of the entity. Also the entity heard much of Martha, the one sedate, calm, never even venturing to offer her body *ever* in those activities that had made Mary the byword of so many; also those stories as to how word had been sent to the Master as to the illness of Lazarus, His visits, and the eventual bringing forth — after four days in the tomb. Then the entity also heard of the happening and the experiences as Lazarus himself had given, as to his experience or consciousness in that period of the inter-between; as to what had happened, as to how there had arisen that consciousness, that movement within, when that Voice had called, "Lazarus — come forth!" [119]

All of those brought an awareness that was to be a part of the entity's experience during those questionings which arose later in the church at Laodicea.

With the scattering of the disciples, the friends, the entity then returned to the home in Laodicea; where the entity was one of four children, in a home that had been of the faith of the Samaritan Jews, but tempered with the teachings of the Grecians and Romans; later, with the teachings of the Master, who had given so full and complete an interpretation of God as the Father, and as love, God as patience, God as long-suffering.

Thus the entity, for the time, became an enigma to the mother Sophia and to the father Philippi, who not until the teachings or the ministry of Paul understood or interpreted aright the entity's attempt to give the better or greater impressions of what had been received by the visit to Jerusalem and those happenings there. Much of this, of course, was owing to the circumstances — as might be said — of that day or period.

Yet with the coming of Paul and Barnabas, there was in the house of Philippi a great awakening to those possibilities, those probabilities as being presented by the whole acceptance of those teachings.

Then more and more were the other disciples frequenting those portions of the land, as they were scattered more and more by the edicts that had been brought about in the church in Jerusalem.

When there was the establishing of the church, and thus the choice of Peter and of James the brother — or the head of the church, and of Lucius as the elder or as the bishop of the church — *then* the brother returned to the place in Laodicea.[120]

With him came Mariaerh as the companion or wife, who had been a part of the activities in a portion of the Jerusalem experience, and who — though much younger even then in years than Nimmuo — became acquainted with, and associated with, the activities in Laodicea.

Then the activities with the royal family and the companionship with Vesta — these overpowered Mariaerh, as it were; as to the meanings of the associations and activities there.

For, many — *many* — questioned the purposes of Vesta with Lucius.

Yet Nimmuo — having known, having heard much of what had been given by Martha, by Mary, by Lazarus, by John and the other disciples — felt for and sided with that royal personage, even against Paul who had espoused the part of Mariaerh.

Thus the entity was thrown or drawn into a disturbance that made for those conditions in which *another* (Ulai) brought about what was almost the dividing of the church in Laodicea, and caused that saint in Patmos to declare "I will spue thee out." [121]

Eventually the entity brought about order, discipline; even treading where others would have feared to undertake to admonish those who were the superiors as to positions in the church. For the entity admonished those also who were many years the senior. But having received that conviction, that purpose, that ideal from those experiences in Bethany, in the home of the mother of the Lord—in John's home as well as in that experience on the day of Pentecost—the entity stood as a mighty power—alone with the *truth* in the lack of condemnation to any!

These again bring into the experience of the present entity a concept of truth, right, justice, mercy, love, as few may know. And though the entity itself may not always be able to put same into words, if those who are seeking—really seeking—will watch, listen, there may be brought to them oft that counsel, that admonishment, that force and power from the very presence of the entity: that will bring strength to the failing, the doubting ones.

Hence again it may be indicated that the entity itself is good for those of younger, tender years; for those in trouble, for those in joy, for those expectant, for those disappointed; for those preparing for the great adventure; for those expecting the greater expectancy of all; for those in sorrow from death; for those in joy at birth.

All may gain much from the *truth,* the deep conviction that lies with *this* entity from its activities, in its search itself for truth, and its application of same in those troubled periods in Laodicea.

At the age of twenty-four the entity was wed with one of the newer converts that were a portion of the activities with Barnabas.

For, with those disputes that arose in those vicinities, the entity went with many of those teachers to the various groups. For, as indicated, the entity—in its preparation—spoke many of the dialects as well as the languages of the varied groups.

In that companionship there grew three offspring, that later were known as the strengths in the various activities through Rome and Spain, as well as the other lands.

The entity lived to a very ripe old age, as would be called today; eighty-four.

And throughout the experience the entity brought the greater interpretations of the power of the "word" in the hearts of those who would live—*live*—His life.

Ready for questions.

Q-1. Did I at any time see the Christ and recognize Him as the Christ?

A-1. In those meetings just before the Ascension, yes.

Q-2. What is the meaning of the name Nimmuo, that I had then?

A-2. One sent.

Q-3. What part of my life seal comes from that period?

A-3. The ever springing anew of those blossoms in the foreground, see?

Q-4. Was I associated with Posnell, now [845] of the ruler's household in Rome?

A-4. Acquainted with, but not a close associate of.

Keep — in the present — ever close to that as ye so oft sought through that experience; to go aside and to put self — as it were — in the place of those from whom ye heard, and by and through whom ye experienced that ability to bring harmony into the hearts and minds of those disturbed from any cause.

And hold fast to that faith as ye expressed oft — so much good in all, none may bear to speak evil of any!

1598-2   M.67   5/29/38

Q-8. I am writing a book. Can you help me, from the hall of records? Who actually wrote the four Gospels? In what order? And when were they written?

A-8. These as we find may *best* be determined by the investigations of the records as related to same; that is, to satisfy self as to its claim — or a physical record — in the Vatican's own libraries. These will be accessible, or made accessible, if there is the seeking, during this present year.

As we find, this will be the manner in which these are indicated; but *verify* same for self's *own* understanding, as well as self's satisfaction:

Mark was first dictated, greatly by Peter, and this in those periods just before Peter was carried to Rome.

The next was *Matthew,* written by the one whose name it bears — *as* for the *specific* reasons — to those who were scattered into the upper portions of Palestine and through Laodicea. This was written something like thirty-three to -four years later than *Mark;* and while this body — that wrote same — was in exile.

Luke was written by Lucius, rather than Luke; though a companion with Luke during those activities of Paul; and written, of course, unto those of the faith under the Roman *influence*—not to the Roman peoples but to the provinces ruled *by* the Romans! And it was from those sources that the very changes were made, as to the differences in that given by *Mark* and *Matthew*.

John was written by several; not by the John who was the beloved, but the John who *represented* or who was the scribe *for* John the beloved; and—as much of same—was written much later. Portions of it were written at different times and combined some fifty years after the crucifixion.

5749-14   5/14/41

Q-21. *The eleventh problem concerns a parallel with Christianity. Is Gnosticism the closest type of Christianity to that which is given through this source?*

A-21. This is a parallel, and was the commonly accepted one until there began to be set rules in which there were the attempts to take short cuts. And there are none in Christianity!

Q-22. *What action of the early church, or council, can be mentioned as that which ruled reincarnation from Christian theology?*

A-22. Just as indicated—the attempts of individuals to accept or take advantage of, because of this knowledge, see?

452-7   M.29   11/22/33

Q-7. *Is the Roman Catholic Church the true Church founded by Jesus Christ through the apostles?*

A-7. This would depend upon who was asking for such. As we would give here, the *church* as founded by Jesus Christ was, is, the Catholic Church [catholic church?]; but *not* the *Roman* Catholic Church! This has rather been added, as have most of those—in their activities—that call or classify themselves as churches. For, the true church is within you, as the Master, as the Christ gave Himself: "I to *you* am the bridegroom—I to *you* am the church. The kingdom is within *you!*" Hence that which has been coordinated into bodies in any activity is a representation *of* that which has gathered together for coordinating activity in whatever field; but are most man-made.

1561-18   M.60   10/22/40

Q-10. How should I go about such a task [the task of setting up a retreat for earnest seekers], along practical lines?

A-10. As each is proven, then that which has been and is the *outcome* of the help attained is the manner, see?

Consider, for the moment, that the Master was the Creator, the Maker of all that was; and yet in establishing the church did He ask any? Rather He gave His blood, His body, as the memorial. As this crystallized in the mind and the desire of those with the means materially, from same arose spires, cathedrals, church buildings and schools.

Do thou likewise.

5322-1   F.47   7/3/44

Isn't it a scientific fact that He is the Savior of the world? Or have ye thought of it in that manner? It is true. For from the very first of the Old Testament to the very last even of Revelation, He is not merely the subject of the book, He is the author in the greater part, having given to man the mind and the purpose for its having been put in print. For it is in Him ye live and move and have thy being and as He gave, "Search ye the scriptures, for they be they that testify of me, and in them ye *think* ye have eternal life." [122]

If you know Him, ye know that in Him ye have eternal life. For He is the beginning and the end of all things.

851-2   F.72   1/31/35   Anneuel

... the entity was in that land now known as the Roman, during those periods when there were the first oppressions of those that followed in the teachings of the Nazarene, as there was the return of the soldiery, as there was the ministering or preaching or teaching of the disciples who set about to bring the message or the gospel as understood by them to other lands.

The entity was among the associates of the soldiery that had returned from the Holy Land, or Palestine, or Judea as called then. At the first of the return there was rather the indifference, yet spoken of rather as in awe; but as the activities began to become more and more spoken of, greater became the interest of the entity. And when the days arose when there was the necessity of taking their individual stands, the *entity* was among those who became—from the social portion of the experience, which the entity enjoyed—the outcasts. Yet many of those in power or authority were enjoined by the life, the teachings, the ministry of the entity as Anneuel, made towards not only the friends but the acquaintances and associations. Again we find the entity gained through the experience, yet suffering oft in the material things and in the wonderments for the stands as taken in the mental attitudes of the entity and body itself; yet bringing in the latter portion of the experience joy, happiness, for that of a life well spent. And there may still be found among the ruins in the grounds where the meetings were held, that are being opened, something of Anneuel's teachings. For being of the soldiery, the entity was among the first of those in the Roman land to make the records of the happenings, the teachings of the ministers—even of the apostles that came as teachers to the land.

1608-1 F.35 6/4/38 Marga

. . . the entity was in the land now known as the Promised Land, when the Master walked in the earth.

The entity was among those who were called of the household of faith. And with the messages, the tenets that were proclaimed by many during the entity's experience then, as Marga, the entity gained, the entity misunderstood; yet the entity gained.

For as has been indicated, as is the promise to each soul, the Lord looketh on the purpose, on the heart of *every* soul, rather than the outward experiences.

Be ye up, then and *doing;* ever in the name of that as ye held during those experiences when the turmoils came by the persecution of the church, by those activities not only of the secular forces from the political disputes among the Jews of the period but the activities of those from without.

For rather the Romans of the period were and *are* condemned, when they were rather the preservers of what ye call your Jewish records!

The Romans

1266-1   M.76   9/28/36   Caesar Augustus

. . . the entity was as Caesar Augustus, who made for the great expansions of the Roman land not only for power but for the gratifying of the ego of self; and those periods when the great expansions of that land arose.

The entity then was that one who builded for that empire.

And there is felt innately in every move that those peoples of that land, that are of the *Roman* and not the Italian mixture, are superior in some manner or way. This is *innate,* and yet there is known and must be known within self that the spiritual purposes, the spiritual desires *must* be those that make for the greater forces that manifest in and among men.

1265-1   M.62   9/26/36   Puburus

. . . the entity was in the Roman experience, when there were the expansions of many in the varied lands, and especially in those periods when there were those supervisions of the activities in what is now known as the Palestine or the Promised Land; during those periods when the Master walked in the earth.

The entity then was among those that were sent from what would be termed in the present as a portion of the governmental forces as to resources of the land for use in the Roman land.

The entity was of the Roman peoples and of those that made for the overlooking of those influences where there were the conservations of the wheat, the conservations of the corn, the conserving of the products of the soil, of the storehouses of nature, of the abilities in the manufacture of wood, of ships.

Hence all of these have their influence in the experience of the entity. But from that experience the coldness, the aloofness that at times finds its expression in the present experience of the entity arises.

Not that there is not to be what is termed today as business in its business way, but as ye would find love and hope and patience and joy—show these in thy dealings with thy fellow man.

The name then was Puburus, and the entity was close to those in authority that levied the taxes or made the arrangements for same. For one worked towards the abilities to pay and the other towards assisting or finding that wherein there were those resources for the developments of the land as well as the supplying of those things needed in the Roman experience . . .

Q-1. Did I have any contact with the entity [1266], now resident in . . . Ohio, in any previous existence?

A-1. In the Roman period, for then [1266] was one in authority—a Caesar.

Q-2. What was the nature of such connection?

A-2. The entity then acted in the capacity of making preparations of the lands of the ruler for greater undertakings—or as the agent for same.

Q-4. Can anything be done by me to help me cooperate and assist soundly at the present time in my dealings with the entity, [1266]?

A-4. In keeping the same character of associations as in the Roman experience. *Ferret* out the abilities of the lands in which all are interested and associated, and as to how these may bring to those of the peoples of the land, as well as to others, the material benefits from the conserving of the values in those lands.

1265-3   M.62   10/14/36   Puburus

Q-5. . . . What was the relation between the entity, [1265], and the entity [1266], in the Roman experience, which you suggest should be followed out in the present experience?

A-5. As has been given, [1266] was the emperor, [1265] was an authority over those of that land of which the entity was a part—to determine as to the abilities, as to the character of the products of the land.

Hence their co-relationship in that experience. Not equal to but one with the emperor, see? And the associations then brought to the entity—[1265] now—with [1151] as a co-worker; one as the overseer, the other as the gatherer of data as indicated—relationships that should cement in the experiences of the present. If their purposes are one, then their union of efforts in bringing understanding and comprehension to their fellow man becomes the more effective.

For in union there is strength. Unity, as has ever been; for "Where two or three are gathered in my name—" And one purpose, one desire to be a channel, is in that name. And in that name alone is there hope for the world, for the country, for the state, for the home, for the individual. For without Him, without that Name, it is oblivion . . .

Q-7. Was the entity, [1265] connected with any relatives of the Master's family in the Palestine Roman experience?

A-7. Only the associations that have been indicated. And when these associations came about, and the greater understandings came, then there was self-condemnation in the experience.

Acquaintanceships and friendships that grew.

Q-9. What relationship did the entity, [1265], have with the entity [1151] in the Palestine Roman experience?

A-9. As has been given.

As the emperor was in authority over the inspector, so the inspector (if it be termed so) was over he that gathered the data for the levying of the tax.

877-1   M.43   4/3/35   Cercel

. . . the entity was in the Roman land, during those periods when there were the activities in the land as pertaining to the various countries that paid tribute then to the Roman.

The entity was among those that were in charge of those in the collecting of the customs in the various ports, and as an active influence in making for the accounting of those that were set in authority.

Then, in the name Cercel, the entity made trips—as it were —to Alexandria, to Jerusalem, to Antioch, to those places where there were the messages and the hearing of the tenets of Him that—during the entity's sojourn in the land—became as the sacrifice to the peoples in that experience.

The entity did not contact in person the Son of man in the experience, but many of those that were of the household of faith; for the entity was acquainted with John, with Luke, with

Pylemus [?]—the brother-in-law of Pilate. For to Pilate the entity went for the customs after that experience of the crucifixion or condemnation of Pilate in that experience.

In the mental forces the entity may be said to have gained, but as to the spiritual influences during the sojourns—these were not awakened until the latter portion. When the entity saw those activities and persecutions in the own city and in the own lands, these made for changes and brought to the entity in the last days of the experience greater joy of service because of those activities in that sojourn.

There have been those things in the present that particularly pertain to the librarians of Alexandria, the hidden influences in Rome, the activities of those peoples in the Holy Land that have at different periods been of particular interest to the entity. And there have been visions of same even in the dreams; for the entity is psychic from the experience there, as Cercel.

877-27   M.46   5/24/38   Cercel

In giving the interpretation of the records, we would give something of the background—to be combined with that which has been written respecting the activities of individuals during that period of earthly experience.

There were the periods of rule by individuals called Caesars —Caesar being a name, a cognomen given or chosen by a family, those that were of lineal descent or those who had been adopted or who had acquired the position in the Roman rule.

It was during that period when Rome governed much of that adjacent to the Mediterranean; Rome, Sicily, Mesopotamia or Turkey or Greece, Palestine, and all of northern Africa and southern Europe—as called in the present.

During those periods of Claudius and Tiberius Caesar [1] do we find the activities of the entity known as Cercel. The entity was not of the household of the Caesars, but of those who were in the relative relationships—as would be termed—by those who had been given authority by those in office or in power at the period.

The entity was chosen because of his executive and physical abilities, as well as because of favors bestowed by the parents.

In his activities the entity visited many of the lands from

which there were customs to be gathered; and counseled not only with those who were set in authority as the judges or the political representatives of the land but also with those who actually gathered or collected the tribute or tax and whose activities, in coordination or cooperation with the entity Cercel, were to *carry* that collected *to* those in authority at Rome . . .

 . . . from the information obtained or contacts made, especially in the studies made by the entity in the great library that was a part of the entity's experience during the sojourn in what is now known as Alexandria—where there had been the gatherings of data from or by the sages of old. For all of those influences and forces of not only the Egyptians and the Persians and the lands beyond the seas, but the activities in the many other lands, were included in the records there.

Those became a part of the entity's study.

Then there were the experiences that arose when the entity journeyed into the Palestine land, just after the crucifixion of the Master; because of the cries from some of the individuals who were associated with the entity Cercel in the collecting of taxes, and the demands by some that there be a questioning of Pilate by Caesar as related to those things which had come about . . .

Consider all of those things given of old in comparison to that taught by the Master, which is that to be gained by each and every entity in the present; that it is not from without where there may be visions, voices or whatnot, but it is the light that comes from within.

This He taught, this He manifested; that it is *not* a dependence upon the powers without! Remember the great lesson taught in that record given or indicated to those who were with Him; that "there be those standing here who shall not taste death until they have seen the Son of man coming in his glory."

Then, what were the purposes of the lesson to *you*—and *you* —and *you*—as an individual, from the transfiguration?

Did Moses and Elias give strength to Him, or gain strength from Him?

This is an important lesson in thy experience!

It is *within* that there is the kingdom of heaven! The kingdom of *God* is without, but is manifested in how it is reacting upon *thee*—by the manner in which ye mete to thy associates day by day that concept of that light which rises within!

Not that the light, then, is other than to bring encouragement. And ye may *indeed* say, then, even as they, "Let us make here a tabernacle." What indeed is thy tabernacle? It is thy body, thy mind, thy soul! Present them, therefore, as things holy, acceptable unto Him who *is* the Giver of all good and perfect gifts!

He *is* giving Himself in power to those who, as many as use that they have in hand to the *glory* of Him who thought it not robbery to be equal with God yet made Himself of *no* estate that He might enter into the holy of holies with thee in thy *own* tabernacle!

Study then to show thyself approved unto God, a workman not ashamed; keeping self from condemnation by not condemning thy neighbor—yet showing a more excellent way by the very glory of the Lord in thy dealings with thy fellow man day by day!

2940-1   M.26   3/21/43   Margill

. . . the entity was in the period of Augustus Caesar, when there was the recording of the activities of the various groups, or individuals put in authority in varied lands.

The entity then was an historian, as might be called today, yet the activities of the entity went much farther. For, there are yet those manuscripts in the Vatican that Margill [?] recorded as to the activities of those in political authority in the Holy Land, as well as those in authority in northern Africa, in Alexandria, in Macedonia and in Mesopotamia . . .

It may be said that the entity through that period made the greater contribution to what became the relationship of individuals in political authority upon the religious world of that period. For, the entity's experience covered other activities and was for many years the leading influence in those lives that were set in the political forces.

Yet the entity has such a slight interest in politics, save as it deals with the spiritual life of groups and individuals . . .

First, as indicated—study self and self's purposes. Know thy ideals—spiritual, mental, material. Study to show self approved unto such ideals. For, as was demonstrated, as was testified of in thy activities in Rome, in Jerusalem, in Caesarea, in Troy, in Philippi, thine own body is the temple of the living God. There He has promised to meet thee.

2890-2   M.10   2/6/43   Perlesus

. . . the entity was in the Roman and Palestine land, during those periods of Augustus Caesar's rule.[2]

The entity was among those set as judges, or those that were to pass upon the activities not only of the Romans in other lands but upon the application of the Roman rule in Palestine, as well as in the neighboring lands.

Thus the entity journeyed much. And those particular areas of North Africa, Palestine, Syria and Turkey, have a particular interest—as to history, as to geography, as to the religious as well as political influences that affect other lands.

Such were the activities of the entity then, as Perlesus. For, the entity made many changes in relationships with the various peoples that represented the political as well as the religious factors in those lands.

Thus, as indicated, as the entity through that experience learned or gained the concept of the letter of the law, he should —as he did in the latter portion of that sojourn—gain the interpreting and the understanding of the spirit of the law, the spirit of control in all phases of individual and group and national experience, before the letter of the law.

2627-1   M.26   11/20/41   Philo

. . . the entity was in the Roman, Palestine, Grecian and Archean [?] land; that one who truly, it may be said, gave the emphasis to the statement: He that serves Rome the better is the greater Roman of all.

It was during those activities in that period of the expansion, when Caesar Augustus made those attempts to *unify* the service for peoples in every land; following closely in purpose that as had been the ideal materially of the emperor Xerxes and Midias [?].

This was that there was innate in the soul of man the ability to rule himself and his household, either for weal or woe, but the privilege of such, of doing such, should be the privilege of groups, of masses—yea, of the individual.

Thus the entity in its service, in its activity, made those expansions in the correct directions. However, these brought disturbing to many—for some groups, whose purpose, whose ideals were self-indulgence, self-laudation, that it might be the better spoken of, or considered the greater influence for those activities that made their impressions upon groups. These brought some disturbing factors in the lives of many.

The entity served as that counselor to those placed in authority in the varied lands, for the gathering of taxes; not as taxes, according to the entity's purpose, but that the various groups might contribute to that purpose that was the prompting of the entity's emperor.

The name then was Philo, and the entity brought great advancements; yet, as indicated by the next appearance, fell—by circumstance—into that very slough of despair that it attempted to point a great empire away from.

478-1   M.43   1/5/34   Phylos

... the entity was in that experience in the Roman land when there were those that were teaching in the city of the activities in the Promised Land.

The entity then was among the soldiery of the peoples; hence making a voyage or visit to the protectorate at the time that those peoples had condemned the Prince of Peace to death—or Pilate. And the entity aided in bringing him, or seeing that Pilate was brought, before Caesar at that time. The name then was Phylos.[3]

In the experience the entity gained and lost. While in the service of the ruler the entity gained. In the periods when persecutions were heaped upon the peoples in the land, the entity lost. When the entity returned and came under the influences of the teachers that later came, the entity lost materially but gained much in soul and spiritual development. For, with the teachings of Timothy of Ephesus and John (Mark) that came as ministers to those people while those rested in the bonds, the entity—joining in the activities—renounced the associations with the soldiery and cast the lot with those peoples.

Hence ever has been a particular interest in the present in (and will harken almost to hearing the voices of) not only the teachers but also Pilate and Caesar and those in that particular experience . . .

603-1   F.31   1/3/34   Agatha

. . . the entity was during those periods when there were in the Roman land the oppressions of those first from the soldiery teaching, later from those that came as emissaries or missionaries or teachers from the hated land by many.

The entity was among what would be termed today the gentry; for it was in the household of one that was a counselor to Caesar, and especially that one that had been a procurator in the Land of Promise.

Then in the name Agatha, the entity gained and lost and gained mightily through that experience, and was changed particularly through the dream that was had of the man that was tried before the procurator.

The entity then joined in the service of that teaching, and with the return to the Roman land gave not only of the material means but of self in the services that were rendered to these people who—for a cause—had brought and brought, and bring to all mankind, the closer knowledge of the walks of God with man . . .

Q-8. Have I ever been associated with the Master personally during any of His sojourns in the earth; if so, where and how?

A-8. When He healed thine own son of the possession, in the court in Jerusalem.

Q-9. Have I ever known before the boy, [4917], who is now in my care? If so, where and how?

A-9. That son.

Q-10. That was healed?

A-10. That was healed.

Q-11. Has [857's father] ever known this body, [4917]?

A-11. During the same experience.

603-2   F.32   5/30/35   Agatha

In the experience in the earth during the Galilean (or the Palestine) experience, the entity then was born in the earth during those periods when there was the establishing of the proletariat over this portion. Herod Antipas coming to the throne made for the checking up on the numbers of children destroyed by Herod the Great.[4] And the entity, Agatha, was then numbered among those that in Galilee had been spared. For the entity then was of those people who lived in the Nazareth and Capernaum vicinity, being of those whose experience was as the tradesmen as well as of the sea.

Hence the entity Agatha, as it grew to maturity in years, became not as a servant (as would be termed in the present) but rather as an instructress, a teacher, in the garrisons of the Roman *and* the Galilean peoples; to interpret for the wives, the companions of the Romans, the customs of the Samaritans and their relationships with the Jewish portion of their acceptance.

The entity then was in the household of Samantha, that was in the *Jewish* portion of the Roman rule; aiding rather in the collecting—or recording of the collecting—of the tribute for the Roman people.

With the ministry of John near the lower waters of the Jordan, with the ministry later of Jesus of Nazareth, the entity became more and more outspoken as to the acceptance of the various teachings. And, as would be called in the present, this caused rebuffs from the soldiery or those of the garrison; for it was considered among those that would assist in a rebellious activity. For the entity with its training and learning, both in the activities of the Samaritans and the Jewish people—and also the Romans, rose to power in the position as one of its sex could or would during those periods.

Then began the closer associations with those of the soldiery, and this became at a time a part of the undoing—or the losing of favor of the entity with a portion of the associations in the Samaritan portion of the acquaintanceship.

Then there was more and more the acceptance of the Jewish and then the Roman activity, until the entity came in contact with the Master—of Jesus—in His ministry through that portion of the land.

The entity then joined with those that moved from place to place, ministering, teaching; and general activity as would be called in the present as missionary associations.

In those periods when there were the persecutions of the Herodians, that during that portion had held to the mixing of the blood of the human with those of the sacrifice, the entity then again rebelled with those people who held *closer* to the teachings of the Master. It joined *then* with those in Caesarea who made for the establishing of a definite organization; and in the latter portion of the sojourn became rather as one to whom many went for counsel in their problems of the social, political or religious experiences in that period; passing from that sojourn or experience at the age of ninety-six . . .

Q-1. *Where and in how many appearances have I known [857's father]?*

A-1. In many. In the Palestine association was there the greater or closer associations, for the entity then was the cause of . . . (as called in the present) starting many of the questionings as to the activities of the entity, owing to the rebuffs the entity gave to the soldiery for those activities during that experience.

Q-2. *What were the relationships during the Galilean period?*

A-2. What might be called friend and foe.

Q-3. *What is the cause of my suffering in the present so much from the association of this individual?*

A-3. The same as caused in that experience the inability to hold to the *one* purpose.

Q-8. *What was the relationship with Pontius Pilate?*

A-8. A very close associate in the relationships of the household, and with the wife of same.

2513-1   F.70   6/12/41

. . . the entity was in the Roman land, yet the activities in the greater part were in the Promised Land, during those periods when there were those activities following the crucifixion; when the Romans became those influences that protected the ideals of the teachings, or prevented their destruction by the Jews who rejected same.

Hence we find the abilities of the entity again indicated in the judgment of peoples, as to why individuals do this, that or the other, and as to whether they are "for" the common good or egotistical in their own desires and purposes.

For, the entity was the companion to one of the procurators in that experience, which brought about those activities that made for developments, advancements, and the interest in occult as well as mystical forces.

The entity then was a companion in the household of Pilate, knowing both the good and the bad, and was that companion who persuaded Pilate's wife to seek help in those periods just before the time of the crucifixion.[5]

Hence the entity knew not so much of the activities of the Master as of the disciples and apostles.

1754-1   F.20   11/25/38   Teleman

. . . the entity was in the land known as the Roman, during that time when there were the words, when there were those being influenced by the teachings of Him who had walked in Galilee—He that is thy Lord!

There ye heard much from those of that land. For thy associations, thy environs during the experience brought thee in close associations with many of those of both sexes in authority in that land. For ye heard from the lips of Pilate's wife of how He healed her son that was a lunatic, an epileptic as ye would call. These made impressions upon thy mind during that experience, that sojourn. And ye wavered oft as to what would be thy choice, as to which group ye would join thyself when there were those as Paul, as Peter, who came—Titus, Philemon. For ye were in the household of that family in which Philemon was a servant.

The name then was Teleman—*beautiful* in body, in mind, in purpose; but the ways of the world drew hard upon thine environs, thine experience. Yet with the knowledge of the teachings of Titus, ye became a supporter, not only with thy material but with thy mind, thyself.

Then study, read carefully the messages sent to Titus and Philemon by Paul; and ye will learn—if ye will meditate upon same—much that has escaped thy understanding. For in such ye may find joy and happiness—not longfacedness but *joy*—in knowing that thy life, thy self is spent in being a channel through which blessings may come to those ye meet day by day.

Let no day then pass that ye do not speak a *cheery* and an

encouraging word to someone! And ye will find thine own heart uplifted, thine own life opened, thy love appreciated, thy purposes understood!

1444-1   F.34   9/15/37   Mara

... the entity was in that period which is among the outstanding experiences of the entity, that would have much to do with its activities and influences in the present; for it was when the Master walked in the earth.

Though the entity was not of those peoples, though the entity was not of those dwellers in that particular land, owing to the activities of the companions (though not the mate of the entity, as a Roman), the entity was in the Holy Land during those periods when the activities brought to the wife of Pilate the knowledge of the Master, through the healing of those of Pilate's own household.

The entity was not a servant; the entity was rather as an instructress, as a teacher, because it made itself so, and *not* because of necessity.

And as a Roman, the entity accepted the teachings of John and James and especially those presented by Philip and the Master Himself—though not in person.

The entity brought to those that were persecuted, by those that were of the rabble of the rulers, much easing as to the activities during the periods of persecution.

And the entity then, in the name Mara, made for great development; for she gained that understanding, "As ye do it to the least of these, thy brethren, ye do it unto me."

Hence that ability in the entity to bring ease or comfort, or for those whom the entity may meet only in passing to feel that ease and understanding has come their way, arises from those innate influences of the entity during that experience; though the times were stirring, though the periods of intrigue and of political influences were in vogue, though there were those in authority in a military way, as in the church, as in the synagogue, as in the varied sets or sects of individuals and groups.

Yet the entity gained much from them all, and *all* were afraid by the very ability of the entity to dispute that the entity put into practice.

793-2   F.53   8/27/36   Saparah

. . . the entity was in the Roman land when the understandings of the teachings of the Master were being spread abroad.

The entity then was of the household of the cousin of Pilate, but abiding in the city from which those forces, edicts and orders for persecutions arose.

There the entity saw and experienced much that brought disturbance to the physical experiences of many.

Thus there became builded much that arises in the present of the feelings of "Something must be done about this and that; something must be accomplished. I must raise my voice and hear in the defense of that, or in the putting down of this or that."

These became or become urges from those experiences as Saparah, that was so close to Titus, Timothy, Paul.

And as these characters and their activities are re-enacted as it were in the experience of the entity in reading same, there is the welling up within "not all is told." And indeed it is not, in thy records. But much of these ye may know. For what is His promise? "As ye live, I will bring to thy remembrance all those things that may aid thee." For He hath not willed that any soul should perish but hath with each temptation prepared a way of escape and brings and bears with each all each soul will give to Him; for that ye give ye possess.

1217-1   M.60   7/10/36   Romoluen

The entity lived in the earth during those days when the Master walked in the land, when there was the ministry and when there were the teachings and activities of a political nature as well as of a rabbinistical nature in many lands.

The entity then was a subject of the Roman experience but among those of the soldiery that came in close contact with the teachings of the Nazarene.

For the entity then was of Pilate's own guard. The entity was given the privilege of being the companion or guard for Pilate's wife that brought their afflicted or epileptic son to the Master for healing.

Then in the name Romoluen, the entity gained; while in the material things, social things, the entity was often questioned.

For there arose those periods when there were the temptations owing to being as one in authority, and for the rulings against those that followed in the religious thought these made for turmoils and strife as they have in the experience. And yet may the entity as in those last days in that experience turn to *not* as a preacher, not as a teacher alone; rather as one that may counsel with those pertaining to combinations or duty with privilege, opportunity with authority.

2144-1   F.41   3/11/40   Cassius

. . . the entity was in the Roman land, during those periods just following the sojourn of Him who is the way, the truth and the light in the earth.

The entity was a companion of one who was an emissary, or a teacher or a lawmaker in that Land of Promise; then in the name of Cassius, and the companion or wife of one Claudius—a follower of that procurator who sentenced the Master.

In the experience much of the turmoils created between the political and religious thought of those periods became a part of the entity's experience. . .

The entity gained mentally throughout that experience, for it studied much, it wrote much, that was helpful, enlightening, encouraging to those of the faith in those periods of activity.

830-1   M.18   2/17/35   Philolos

The entity was among the Romans that dwelt in that land now known as a portion of Bethsaida, or about that town; being garrisoned there, as would be termed in the present. The entity noted much of those activities in and during those periods when there was so much concern from the teachings of the Master, or Him who walked in Galilee, Him who made for the strifes among the sects of the Pharisees, the Sadducees, the Essenes. At first the entity looked on in wonderment, and then—with the peoples of the Parcaenia [?], the peoples from Greece, the peoples from the other lands that were interested in the commercial associations—became rather as an influential activity; and with the return of the entity during that sojourn to the Roman land became the teachings that made for *first*—by the Roman Emperor—the demand of Pilate's return and to give an account for those activities that had brought about such a turmoil and strife in that Palestine land.

Then in the name Philolos, the entity gained. The greater activities, the greater spiritual development arose under those experiences when there were the necessities of the *training* of the Roman soldiery, yet the ability through that activity to know the needs and the motivative influences in the experiences of individuals in their relationships to nation and people, to an individual and to a cult, to an activity that has made for, may make for in the present experience of the entity, those forces that are as ideals raised above the mere success in material things. It may bring the greater joy, the greater happiness, the greater spiritual and soul development of an entity or being in *any* environ.

2021-1   M.23   10/7/39   Zebra

. . . the entity was among the Roman soldiery who were in that land during those periods following the crucifixion, the questionings, when Pilate was recalled. And the entity was acquainted with, and knew much of those activities; coming under the influence of those who were persuaded, or who were in the way of Him, who accepted that teaching as the principle.

There again we find the entity acted in the capacity of a recorder, one who made records not only of its own company but of many of those things in the land . . .

The name then was Zebra.

557-2   F.52   5/23/34   Sheliah

. . . the entity was in that land now known as the Holy Land, during those periods when there were the teachings in that land of Him who walked by the sea, and He who taught in Galilee.

The entity then was among those to whom the teachings often came, not direct but by the words of those who had gathered with the Master and His followers as they oft dwelt in Bethany; for the entity then was in that land not by choice but rather by the influences of those to whom the entity belonged—being of the Roman people and those that were in possession or in the active service of keeping the land in order.

In the name Sheliah, the entity then was the wife of a ruler under the Pilate regime—and next to Pilate in command, but an officer of the guard.

During those periods when there were many of the turmoils and strifes that arose from the activities then, the entity came under the influence of those teachings and accepted same.

Yet in the present from that sojourn we find order in the self, in the relationships about same, and those tendencies for the listening, the harkening to those in places of experience or in power that influence the affairs of individuals and their particular associations in the inner self. From that experience also we find a very *definite* condition in the present; that when there is reference made to the character of execution, there is a tendency of a shudder in the body that responds to that heard in that experience.[6]

In that experience the entity gained through the soul development, through the physical activities, through the social experiences; for the entity, though under stress and strain mentally often, kept self in an attitude of taking advantage of all experiences through the sojourn for its mental, physical and material development.

961-1   M.55   7/25/35   Ponticalos

. . . the entity was a Roman soldier in the services of one Pontius; *not* Pilate, but under the *supervision* of Pilate during those periods of the sojourn of the Son of man or Jesus of Nazareth (so called; should be Nazarite!), in that experience in Galilee, Judea, and the lands thereabout.

The entity came under the activities wherein much was experienced by the entity because of those activities of that man during the sojourn there.

Thus in the present the entity may do well, may find the greater aid and help, to harken to those promptings that were the experience of the entity during that sojourn, as Ponticalos.

In the experience the entity may be said to have gained in the material, the mental and the spiritual aspects of its sojourn through those activities.

While the entity was in the capacity of a soldier that took orders, that gave commands, that made for the keeping of peace in the *physical* sense; yet those things that pertain to the varied forms of law as under the various types or characters of activities, penal law, moral law, religious law or the theological understanding (which arose as turmoils during that experience), are experiences in the present sojourn by the very associations of ideas and the relations they have from that which prompts individuals' activity.

If through the activities of the entity there is first set *not* a material ideal, but rather a spiritual ideal, there will be found —with the mental capacities and mental abilities—that the entity may turn within oft for that which will become more and more the ruling influence in the present experience of the entity.

And as more and more of this is correlated with the various facts that were gained by the entity during that contact and that experience with the Son of man, Jesus the Nazarite, ye may come more and more to understand what may be the promptings of each and every individual who in a service to his fellow man may be as He; not regarding self but being of a service to his fellow man.

For as He gave, "As ye do it unto the least of these, thy brethren, ye do it unto thy God."

For that creative force, that spirit that *prompts* the activities in a material world, arises within the heart, the soul of each individual in meting out to its fellow man. For one may not hate his brother and love his God; one may not worship his God and hold malice or envy against his brother. For these are of *One*, and the Law of One must carry through.

As ye sow in spirit, so may the mind build that ye reap in materiality. As ye sow in materiality, so may that mind build to make for dissension or a paralleling of an activity in the spiritual import. They are interchangeable.

Keep the faith that thou didst make in thine experience in that sojourn.

1037-1   F.49   10/28/35   Charlene

The entity was among those that were born of the peoples in control of the Holy Land, or Palestine, during the periods when the Master walked in the earth.

Those experiences made for that which grew to be a barrier in the experience of the entity from the material angle, yet the soul, the mental forces grew through the associations that came about during that sojourn.

Then the entity was among the ruling forces, and the daughter of the leader of the soldiers under Pilate—one Pontifus [?].

The entity then, in the name Charlene, through the soul and spirit *gained* throughout. The pomp and glory in the earlier portion of the experience came to mean much, and these find in the present experience of the entity their place and their usages; yet in the latter days—when the entity renounced positions in the social life—there were periods of the dread of same.

Hence the rattle of armament, the blaze of the trumpet, the beat of the drums in certain conditions make even in the present a tingling that runs through the system as a dread.

Then, those experiences make in the present for the love of that for which the Master, in the Sermon on the Mount, stood. And those words make for the same tingle, but it arises to *expression;* while the dread makes for the oppressions within self.

Hold *fast* to that thou hast gained in that thou didst learn there, "The righteous *shall* inherit the earth." This was that upon which the entity builded its experience during that sojourn. Then, in the present hold to that understanding that righteousness is not goodness as man counts goodness, but goodness as the Giver of life has given unto the sons of man. That thou hast purposed in the *heart,* that thou dost hold in the inner recesses of thy mind—*these* be righteousness before the Father . . .

Q-9. [*What was my relationship*] With Mrs. [*509*]?

A-9. Here again we find the closer associations of these (in the Palestine land). For as they came to know the messages, they came to know more and more of His *freedom* from those things that *bound* men in superstition.

1302-2   F.63   12/22/36   Charteuce

. . . the entity was in the Promised Land, or Palestine, during those periods when there were those turmoils arising from the activities and the persecutions of those called Christians.

The entity then was among the Romans that lived in the land.

The entity saw much persecution of those of a faith. The entity partook of those activities, but as one that would protect in terms and ways and manners that would be called—and was classed at the time one as neither a very good Christian nor a very good Roman. Yet in the deeper self the entity gained, for the entity's purposes and desires were kindled by sympathy for the overtrodden or the "underdog" as would be termed in common parlance, that made for an experience in the entity.

Then as Charteuce, the associate of the ruler who succeeded Pilate in those activities, the entity knew much of those activities.

Thus in this experience from those activities the entity finds things that are old, things that are new, music that is strange, psychic forces and their interests and those things as pertain to spiritual aspects and the influence of spiritual things and conditions in the lives of individuals, become as a part of the entity's experience.

And yet, even as then, the entity holds most of same to be performed or acted upon by others, and acts as an observer rather than one partaking of same.

Yet the Lord, the Law, Love—and all that pertains to the real of Life; whether in the material concepts or its spiritual perfection or its mental building—is for *all* alike.

And to experience Life one must *live* it, and be equal to and know that in no wise is the Creator respecter of persons—as man!

1472-6   F.58   6/19/38

. . . how did He give to Pilate? that no one hath power of *any* nature except it is allowed by or of God! [7]. . .

809-1   F.47   2/2/35

. . . the entity was during the period now known as the Roman oppression to the teachings of the Galilean who had, as the Son of man, walked in the earth and given those tenets, those understandings, those hopes, those faiths, to those that knew that the *Lord lives!*

The entity then was among the Roman people in authority during the sojourns of Augustus Caesar,[8] when many lands were disturbed through the activity of the material powers in that particular land; yet the entity came the closer in touch with those that had been in authority in the Palestine or Holy Land, or the land of those wanderings of that man of God.

And as those tenets began to find their activity among the peoples, the entity first scoffed, then listened, then accepted. This brought through the material activities, the material surroundings, periods of fear, doubt, consternation; yea, periods of joy to be counted worthy as one that might in a small measure or large give not only of her means but of herself that others might know that the *Redeemer lives,* and is at the right hand of the Father to make intercession for those who in their ignorance and in their willfulness turn their faces against Him!

729-1   F.44   11/12/34

. . . the entity's activities were in the Roman land, during the periods when there were the expressions of expansion—or their taking in the various lands. And these were first sent by the entity, in one of the Caesars—in the first; and the entity then (in the man) made for the expansion, not by might alone but by the power of right which made for the standard set by those who were sent to the various lands, that made for a power which stood for those things that have ever made a great influence upon the human activities in the material things.

In the mental and material the entity gained. In the spiritual the high ideals were abased in the latter portion of the experience, yet these are being met in the present in the creating in the minds and hearts and souls of those whom the entity contacts that which is *creative* and helpful and hopeful in their own experience. Just as in that sojourn, when the entity made for a power—yea, upon all those influences in the earth in that experience, so may the entity in the present—with its sojourn of tempering of justice, in the matter of making for an expression or manifestation of mercy—find such activities bringing to the inner self a satisfaction, and the peace that passeth understanding.

1206-3   F.11   12/16/36   Garcia

. . . the entity was in the land or country now known as the Roman, and in the city of Rome; during those periods when there were the activities of those that made for the expressions of entertainment for those in authority.

And during those latter portions of the experiences under a Roman ruler, Tiberius,[9] when were those fraught with fear for the expressions coming from those activities of the peoples from another land.

The entity was among those that were of what would be termed royalty, or in the household of those closely associated with that as had been of the household of Claudius,[10] as well as Tiberius when those changes came.

Then the entity was in those positions where the very position brought disturbing conditions. For there were those things and experiences that brought changes in the affairs of those with whom the entity was associated. Yet when there came into the experience those associations and activities that brought the first hearings of the tenets and truths, a strange experience came.

Thus as may be seen, those effects upon the entity of too deep a relationship in the experiences of a religious life without purpose may bring—as in that sojourn—disturbing of peace of mind of the entity.

Yet when there were those associations of the entity with Ruth and those who had been so close with those activities in the Palestine land, the entity came to be a power among those groups that even gave their bodies for sacrifices for a cause, a purpose, an ideal.

Hence these will become as the entity's experience in that sojourn; it may become welded with that inducement of good for an ideal's activity, good in the experience not for that of "just because" but for a purpose wherein the self may be the channel of expressions of ideals to others . . .

Q-1. Was this entity known to her present parents, [1158] and [1151] in other lives?

A-1. As indicated, especially in the Roman experience. There we find their associations meant the most, as they may in the present. And it is in the environ for those very expressions and manifestations of that indicated. In the name then Garcia, of the household of the Caesars but of those portions that were of the stepchildren of Claudius.

1341-1   M.54   2/25/37   Tultimustouen or Timous

. . . the entity was in the land now called the Roman, during those periods when there were the greater expansions under Claudius Caesar for an empire that was to rule not only most of the activities of the world in military and economic life but in the moral life.

The entity then was among those of the emissaries who represented the reporting to those in authority under that Caesar, especially in the Grecian land, the Mesopotamian land, and a portion of the Palestine land.

There the entity gained, there the entity lost. For with the taking on of the entity's experiences with the teachings of Paul in portions of the land, in the acceptance of same, the entity gained; yet with being laughed at for his tender-heartedness, his chicken-heartedness even as called then, it became the downfall or the losing portion of that experience—as Tultimustouen, or Timous as was generally termed in the experience.

From that experience and those activities, we find in the present those inclinations for the questioning of those who rely too much (as judged by the entity) upon their religious affiliations or associations; and yet not tolerant enough is the fault in these directions. Though there is the holding to tenets, the entity makes them as mental abilities rather than giving their proper evaluation in the affairs and in the lives and in the promptings of the fellow men. This became—and is yet—a condition, an experience, to be met.

Do it *now!*

For without the Lord guide, indeed may the greater mind fail—for it must! . . .

Q-1. Was the entity [1341] connected with or related to the entity [1151] in any previous life?

A-1. In the Roman experience. They were then as co-laborers for a purpose.

852-12   F.18   11/15/35

. . . the entity was in that period when there was the expanding of the Roman land, when settlements were being made in what is now northern Africa, the Holy Land, and the isles of the sea.

The entity then was one in authority, as one who gave the necessity of those groups or those peoples to make their report to Caesar in the Latin tongue.

Hence in the experience the entity created or made for itself many of those things that brought to the entity condemnations from those in authority in some of those lands, yet the entity's contribution to its own people—as well as to the world in general—was in writing into the Roman tongue the teachings of Paul, Peter and Titus.

These brought to the entity not only a self-satisfying experience, but the knowledge innate within self that the abilities within self were of the nature that its own contribution would remain as lasting experiences in the minds and the hearts of those that were to pass that way.

Then, hold within self ever those ideals, those purposes, that were purported during that experience. For *then* did the entity gain, though under stress and strain from the material angles, the greater soul expressions. For those teachings of Him, who is and who ever will be the Savior of men, brought harmony, peace and understanding in the expressions of the entity.

And oft, if the entity will read those expressions in Romans, Philemon, Timothy, there will be brought the awakening from within that will arouse to activity.

Judge not others that have not awakened so, but let thine own life, thine own example, thine own expression, become as then—a *living* way; that others may see the light and be encouraged, that they—too—may *renew* their faith, their hope.

For, as thou hast given in thine manner of interpretation and expression; He *is* the light, He *is* the way, and no man approaches the Father save through that *living* way, "As ye do it unto the least of these, my brethren, ye do it unto me."

Would that all would but write that upon their hearts, their souls, and know it *is* the living way!

2340-1   M.16   9/6/40   Lermarn

. . . the entity was in the Roman land, though the entity was active most in that now called the Palestine or Promised Land; for the entity was stationed in the garrisons of Caesarea, Jerusalem and Damascus, and the various places to which various groups were sent—and called a centurion of no mean order!

The name then was Lermarn. In the experience the entity gained much of that pertaining to things regarding religious tolerance, or the beliefs of various peoples and their effect, and the activities as related to same.

Oft the entity acted as a counselor through the latter part of that sojourn, as there were the changes brought about.

1347-1   M.21   3/10/37   Polyneus

... the entity was in the land now known as the Roman, during those periods when there was the special activity in the foreign lands; when there was the establishing of the procuratorship in other lands—as in Egypt, Greece, Palestine and other lands.

The entity then was a representative of that ruler who began that period of activity in the beginning of the first Christian era; or during the days when the Master walked in the earth.

Then the entity established its representation in the Grecian land, or that which is a portion now of the Turkish land.

The entity gained and lost, for during those experiences there were those in the entity's own association—among its own associates—who made for the ruling of influences, or the denying of much of the reports.

Hence confusions and activities that brought about a great deal of discussions arose.

So not until the very latter portion of the entity's sojourn, again back in Rome, do we find the entity—as Polyneus—making for that which may be termed as mental or soul development during the experience; though the material experiences were in that of a gradual rise to power—but after there had been a change in the rulers in Rome.

From that experience or sojourn we find in the present, from the emotional self, not only that as represented from the Martian astrological influence but the anger from being crossed in purposes.

And much of the timidity arises from those experiences also; yet much of that strength as was gained in the study of those things that were experienced in the latter days of the entity's experience in that land—the lessons of the Master.

These became a part of the experience of the mental forces of self, and becoming expressed in the present may be as the bulwarks of faith; that upon which the body mentally, the body spiritually, yea the body physically, may rely for strength.

For the power of His might remains within those places in self where He has promised to meet thee oft, and He will not leave thy soul desolate but will come to give strength within self to as many as call upon His name and *do* His biddings towards their fellow men.

Be *consistent* in all thy dealings.

2572-1   F.11   8/10/41   Philoas

. . . the entity was in the Promised Land, during those periods when there were the activities following and during the walk of the Master in the earth.

The entity then was a Roman, and one who today would be called a spy—or a recorder of the activities of those who were sent as emissaries, or individuals who were to act in the various capacities as instructors, collectors of custom, as to the forming of activities in the administering of law, and the varied periods of activity.

Yet the entity *used* its abilities not in a self-advantageous manner but to a credit to itself, to the land it represented, and gained much through the period—in its activities from its associations with those who had been as companions or workers with those in that period of man's opportunity.

The name then was Philoas, and the entity gained throughout. Hence much of those abilities in making itself felt by its affability may be experienced in the present . . .

Q-6. How have I been associated in the past with the following members of my family, and how may I best help them in the present: My mother, [2570]?

A-6. In the experience before this, and especially through the Palestine sojourn. Helpfulness may be most shown in not only taking the counsel of the mother, but in *proving* to be helpfulness in every phase of thy endeavors.

Q-7. My father, [2489]?

A-7. The special association here was in the Roman and Palestine land, for the entity then "checked up" oft on the father's activities. Close friends, but questioned one another —as they do today. But keep those abilities to see the funny side of everything, especially in the relationships here.

2523-1   F.73   7/1/41   Armelia

. . . the entity was in the Promised Land, during those periods when there had been the preparations made for the coming of the forerunner as well as the Lord, the Master.

The entity was among the Roman peoples—a companion to one in authority, who became acquainted with those who were so zealous as to the promises which had been made by Him in His service and ministry in the earth.

Then the entity was close to those in authority through a military rule, especially about Jerusalem. Though the entity found a great deal of excitement, it also found a great deal of hope.

Thus we find in the present, latent and manifested, a streak of religious fervor that at times almost becomes a ruling force in the experience—until some call the entity fanatical upon some subjects, or some phases pertaining to religious beliefs.

The freedom of thought has kept the entity well balanced in its judgments. For, He *is* Lord of all. And remember, there was nothing made that was made—materially, mentally or spiritually—of which man in flesh may know—that was not made or experienced by Him. This ye have gained from that experience.

The entity then was the companion of one of the Roman guards, or the Romans in authority under the procurator.

Then in the name Armelia, the entity gained.

2850-1   M.18   11/14/42   Margii

. . . the entity was in the Roman land, and the Holy Land. The entity then was a scientist, or an interpreter of the law of the Romans to a people so imbibed with a spiritual law, attempted to be materially applied, that it brought periods of disturbance to the entity.

Yet the abilities to judge peoples, to interpret the emotions of groups as related to their spiritual, social or religious environs, made for a period of unusual activities—as the entity attempted to aid a people disturbed by a rule or order that embraced materiality as well as threads of might and power, yet not unmindful of spiritual values.

Hence the entity's activities as an interpreter of group influence in the Holy Land brought the entity in touch with many of those who were leaders in the varied groups; the leaders in the Essenes, the interpreters in the Temple—or the high priests. And the knowledge of the manners in which other groups were used by these interpreters of the impelling forces in the groups brought disturbing forces, and finds expression in the present as to economic and social relationships that are portions of man's experience in varied groups and climes.

The name then was Margii. It may be said that the entity gained, the entity stumbled oft but gained—in comparison to some other experiences in the earth plane.

In the present from that experience there may be applied the knowledge or awareness of an influence in the material plane through the manner of life of the Nazarene. For the entity in that period was *almost* but not quite persuaded, even as Felix [11]—who was an uncle of the entity. For, what brought such save sacrifice? And this has ever, and innately in the present, has found soil for an unfoldment in the being—*why* sacrifice? *If* man in his eternal seeking be of the Creative Force, *why* sacrifice? Yet it is that necessary to be interpreted in self; if in no other manner, in that necessary in self of the application of the law of cause and effect, of spiritual law in its interpreting through material manifestation, occult law as may be *only* interpreted in the law of the soul—or the psychic power, or soul power, the ability given by the First Cause for reproducing its own kind; yet the altering of kind manifestedly by application to universal consciousness or self-indulgence.

1486-1   M.55   11/26/37   Philos

... the entity was in the experience during that period when the Master walked in the earth, during those periods also when there were the turmoils and the strifes that arose among those sects that were as the political factors during that experience.

The entity was among those natives of the Grecian land that made for activities through the Roman rule in those portions about the capitals or the larger cities of the provinces of the Palestine land.

During that particular experience the entity, as Philos, was active in inducing those *political* lands to accept a single standard, especially as related to the calendar, the judgment of time and activities.

For there had been through the Jewish peoples the reckoning of time from the Exodus, while through the Romans it had been counted from the establishing of Roman rule and power. Thus in each generation there had been many varied experiences in the rulers to have time reckoned by, or from, some definite activity of the ruler—as of themselves or those just preceding them in rule or generations.

Hence the entity joined with the Romans in sympathy with the reckoning from the Christian era.

Hence the entity had much to do in aiding those in the church, first in those about the Essene associations in Carmel, where such data began to be set—as from the birth. Hence A.D. and B.C. were begun as a part of the activity of the entity during those experiences ...

Q-1. Did I have personal contact with Jesus, the Master?

A-1. Personal contact, especially as Jesus the Child taught or reasoned with the rulers in the temple.[12] Later when there were those activities as a teacher, and the entity then—associated with the Roman as well as the Jewish leaders—taught or heard taught those things the Master gave just before the period of crucifixion.

Hence these two definite periods have been and are a portion of the entity's *inner* consciousness.

Q-2. Was I among the "Faithisto" of Jesus during His incarnation in the earth?

A-2. Among those that watched rather on that period when from the mount He took the ways towards the heavenly hosts.[13]

1911-1   F.7   1/27/31   Pomtplema

. . . during that period known as the troublesome one in the Roman land, when there were the changes in the ideals of the peoples that were being proclaimed by those that came from the Judean land. The entity was among those who became the followers during the early period, yet in the household of the ruler Caius [?]. In the name Pomtplema, the entity gained throughout this experience. Beautiful in body, beautiful in mind, glorious in the life as lived; suffering in intense pains at times, yet ministering to those of the saints, those of the common people, bringing many an one of the household of this ruler (in a lesser degree) to the understanding of those tenets as taught by Paul and Peter in this land. Hence the innate expressions of the entity of the beauty of those who serve in an ideal, and oft does the entity see innately in self many of the experiences of *this* experience. Do not *build* these, but rather let these be as guiding points for the entity's development to the spiritual side of life, and that builded in that experience may be the basis upon which that in this and others may be builded. Keeping the beauty of the Christ life as depicted by those in that period will be that as will be the bulwark of the entity's experience through this sojourn.

1173-4   M.28   7/8/36   Puliduon

. . . the entity then was among those of the soldiery during those periods when there were the establishings of rulers or tetrarchs over the lands, or those who supervised the activities.

And during that period the entity was among those that came—when there was the trial of those that were persecuted by the *Jews* for *their* activity in a religious reaction from those experiences of the Master in the land—when there was the recall of the ruler Herod, the ruler that made *for* those activities when there were the persecutions of the Master and His disciples—or in those forces that made for the reconstruction of the activities in that land.[14]

Then in the name Puliduon, the entity—it may be said—

gained and lost, lost and gained. For as more and more the experiences of those that were persecuted came to be a portion of the entity's experience, more and more there came to be an understanding of those relationships between individuals as compared with the relationships of individuals to Creative Forces.

And these phases of man's experience form differences between religious influences in most of the cults or most of the groups or most of the philosophies of the various teachers and leaders.

Hence the entity in the latter portion gained in those experiences in the applying of the tenets that were gathered from the soldiery; for the entity *tended* as one *with* Paul when there was the first of the journeys to Rome, upon the ship—yes, that was shipwrecked [15]; but among those—as indicated in the accounts by some—that arrived in Rome.

1610-2   M.34   6/29/38   Pelostos

. . . the entity was in the now called Roman period, during those experiences when there was a great deal of the practices and the games that had become so much a part of the Grecian activities—in the developments of the body, the developing of the gladiators, the ones that might show their strength or such.

There we find the entity was among those Romans who were chosen not only for the physical prowess, not only for the beauties of the body, the symmetrical activity of the figure, not only because of those activities for which many an artist or sculptor sought the entity as an example or as a model, but because of the abilities of the entity to teach or instruct or direct.

For there were the attempts of the entity to bring same into a part of the training of those ye would term today the diplomats, as well as the soldiery or the defenders of the home, or the environs—as ye would call the police, or the like.

But all of those brought much temptation as well as great material developments for the entity.

During the latter portion of the entity's experience, when there was the overcoming of the Palestine land—or the sending of the Roman soldiery into Palestine; from the social and the spiritual angle it was not so well an experience for the entity.

For the rivalry, the revelries in drink and meat and the like became that which became the stumbling stone for the entity during that portion of its sojourn. For he came close unto the knowledge of those things that were a part of poor old Herod, or the environs about same—so that wine, women and song became the undoing of the entity during that part of its sojourn.

With the purposes as had been set, these brought dismay and disappointments to the entity. But with the recall, and with a friendship shown by one of the Roman tax legislators, there came to the entity a new awakening. For he learned the lessons of the Cross from a Roman superior!

In the latter portion the entity gathered the activities of Paul, when the greater freedom was given him in the Roman sojourn. There the entity came under a still greater influence.

Then in the name Pelostos, the entity gained and lost . . .

1233-1   M.22   7/31/36   Felix

. . . the entity was in the Holy Land, during those periods when there was what is called the period of preparation, or those activities were in order not only from the Roman but from the Jewish and the Grecian lands.

For the entity then was among those of the Roman soldiery that were among the first to be as the supervisors over that land previous to those days when there was the activity among the Essenes for the coming of the Master.

The entity then was a soldier in authority, one to whom reports were given for the abilities of this or that city, this or that district for the gathering of taxes, for the preparations for those influences that made for the abilities for that land to pay tribute to the Roman forces.

Hence we will find in the experience of the entity those inclinations towards a political rule. And this in the latter portion of the experience in this sojourn may be applied, if there are the purposes, the aims, the desires for a helpfulness to the fellow man rather than for the satisfying of a selfish purpose in self.

Then the name was Felix.

1724-4   M.40   2/9/39   Zebuden

. . . the experience was in quite a varied activity; during those periods in the Roman land when there was the distribution of the activities, or when there was the gathering of many lines of activities through the early Caesars—and especially in those periods covering the Palestine sojourn of the Master and the early portion of the same activities in the Alexandrian experience.

The entity was rather in the capacity of what would be termed now the recorder for those in the high authority; keeping the tab or the tabulation on the amounts—not in the capacity of what would be called today a bookkeeper, but rather the supervisor of those who kept the amounts in weight of the various commodities that were sent into the lands—as to the various taxes gathered from the lands—as to the various sources and means of exchange.

There we find the entity was closely associated with those in authority *under* the ruler of the day; where pomp and show were a part of the entity's experience.

And through same the entity lost, yet there were the abilities to meet the influences through those things which befell the entity during the experience. For the entity was raised to authority by those who were in the capacity of the gatherers of data for the king or the emperor *in* other lands.

The entity then became much acquainted with the influence in the Alexandrian land, and there we find the activities or interests were in the unusual, the mysteries, those things which delved into the abilities of individuals to use the unseen forces; or to work in what would be called by some *magic,* by others those influences in which the elementals were used for activities upon the higher tension of the mental forces of individuals.

Again we find the entity slipped into those things in which self-indulgence and self-aggrandizement brought disappointing forces to the entity. And the entity was raised only by its associations with those in authority to the better activities during the experience.

The abilities then as a writer, the abilities as a musician, the abilities as a delver into the mysterious forces, arise in the present experience *innately* and manifestedly according to the harkening within from those experiences through the Roman, the Palestine and the Alexandrian lands; in the name then of Zebuden.

1470-1 M.29 11/4/37 Polyneius
. . . the entity was in the land now known as the Roman, during those periods when there were those questionings of those teachings that had been given by Him who had set the whole of the Palestine land in disturbance.

The entity was a Roman, yet was in a position of authority in that Palestine land, and made for the gathering of data as to the activities of those that were the tax gatherers for the Roman peoples.

Thus the entity came into contact with all the periods, all the activities of unrest among those that were of the various sects and sets and classes of that particular land—yet in close association with those in authority in all the various forms.

There the entity lost and gained; gained when those convictions of that which had been given became a part of the entity's experience, in that "As ye would that men should do to you, do ye even so to them."

For it brings harmony and peace and understanding into the heart and soul of the entity, as experienced by the entity during those activities—as Polyneius. Though the turmoils of every nature may be about one, knowing there is no condemnation in self brings harmony, and a *purposeful* life—making for developments through the experiences.

In the present we find more and more there have been those periods when activities as related to same have become necessary; yea, will become more and more necessary in dealings with the many . . .

Hold *fast* to those principles that have directed thee from thy sojourn in the Palestine land— *these* be the ways of life! . . .

Q-1. *In any past experience have I known the entity now called in this experience* [1472]?

A-1. In that Roman experience, or as the dweller rather in the Palestine land. The associations then were as helpmeets, *after* there had come the better understanding—but as a tormenter before same.

1472-1   F.57   11/6/37   Judy

Q-2. Where, when and what was my relationship to the entity now known as [1470], in any past incarnation, and what does he mean to my present life pattern?

A-2. In the Palestine period the self was as Judy, the entity [1470] was as the Roman that made light much, and later came to seek.

And thus in authority in self doth he find that those activities in the present will become much in the same way and manner. For not as one dependent upon the other, but one as bolstering as it were the purposes that may be held aright.

781-5   M.18   9/14/36   Juahn

. . . the entity was in the land now known as the Promised Land, or in those periods about the Palestine land when there were the Romans that were of the soldiery, of the guards, of the various activities that made that land as a protectorate for the Roman experience.

The entity was of the natives of the land that were among the tax gatherers of the land for the Roman peoples.

Hence the entity stood at times in a position of authority over those who disliked the authority exercised by the individual; also in those positions at times of authority for those lands and groups whom the entity represented, yet because of the nativity of the entity *not* in good standing with those that were of a sect or group among those peoples.

Then in the name of Juahn, and of a Grecian and a Roman-Grecian descent, but active in the lands or the surrounding lands of Jerusalem and Bethany and Nazareth and Capernaum—all of these were portions of the entity's sojourn.

Hence the study of those even of those periods when the Master walked in the earth become of a peculiar interest, and oft has the entity visioned some of those experiences where there are given as the journeys from the upper to the lower portions of the land, to the mountains or about the sea; for these were related to the entity during those experiences, though the entity came not in actual or physical contact with the Master *as* an individual then, but the teachers, the disciples, the apostles, many of these the entity knew. Not wholly did the entity embrace the tenets during those experiences, nor was there the giving of the whole self towards the Jewish faith nor those activities among the own peoples, the Grecians; yet these in themselves made for turmoils. And as will be experienced in the entity in the present, there will come those periods when as to ideals in relationship to spiritual forces and influences will become as entanglements in the experience of the entity.

Hence the necessity of the entity finding its own ideal, its own application of itself to that as is its own moral standard, in relationship to that chosen as its spiritual guide and activity. Hence the study especially of those portions, of the gospel of John and Luke, especially in those portions where there are the descriptions of the purposes, as also in Jude and in Revelations, in such may the entity find those ideals. Set them down in black and white, but bind them upon thine heart-purposes. For the religion of Christ is a practical, everyday living, and not a tenet or a thing to be taken lightly but is to bring life, purpose, peace and harmony by its application in its relationships to the fellow man . . .

Q-1. What important lessons have I learned from past incarnations?

A-1. . . . In the Palestine, that there cannot be carried water on the both shoulders — or the attempt to be something and to live another life. Neither can there be oppression to make for understanding. For it's not by might nor by power but by the Spirit of Truth, which is of God. These the entity has learned, the entity now *must* apply.

1751-1   M.33   11/18/38   Poppipano

. . . the experience in the earth was in those periods when the Master walked in the land.

There we find the entity was a Roman, and a keeper of the amounts as it were of the custom paid, of the tax assessed, of the returns from the provinces about which during the period there was the ministry of the Master; as well as the ministry of many of the apostles or disciples during those days just after His resurrection.

We find the entity was oft in a state of awe and wonderment.

From those experiences of looking on and watching the activities of those during holy days and holy periods, and the establishing of the new order of days or periods when there were the special dedications or settings aside of self and the followers of Him—is it any wonder that these mean so much?

Yet innately in the experience of the entity, remember well —as He gave regarding the Sabbath—days were made for man, not man *for* the day!

For the more often there is the indwelling, the meditating, the pondering over those things that are the periods of contact with the spiritual influences and forces, greater becomes the ability of understanding to the individual who will mentally and spiritually and truthfully indulge in such.

And as the material plane is a channel, a way and manner through and in which each soul, all souls may grow in grace and knowledge and in understanding—thus it behooves all souls that they be oft in prayer, oft in those periods when there *is* an entering into the holy of holies as within, and the rededicating of self for that of being a channel through which the knowledge of God's love for His children may flow to others.

Know then in what ye have believed, as ye so oft quoted in those experiences as Poppipano—*who* is thy authority, *who is* the source of thy claims, mentally and materially?

A good recorder wert thou, and in holy esteem before all the peoples in all of thy phases of activity during that sojourn— both those who were in the position of paying the custom or tax and those to whom it was rendered materially.

459-12   F.44   1/30/41   Endoren

. . . the entity was in the Roman and the Palestine land, during those periods when there were the activities in which the Holy Land was being subjugated or ruled by the *purposeful* taxing of the land for the support of the Roman empire.

There the entity was used by its own people, as well as in the latter portion determining of itself, to break the rule of those peoples upon the land. For, the entity became the companion of a Roman guard—that to the entity, and its associates and family, was as an unbeliever.

Hence the entity knew of those activities in Rome, for it went back and forth from the garrisons that had been established in the various portions of the Holy Land.

But when the entity became closely associated with the activities in the *temple,* there came the determinations to *renounce* those things that had been a part of the social or material life.

Thus we find in the present experience of the entity a desire to hold to that of ritual, rote, as pertaining to such a service; yet a hope for an affiliation or association with those of other interpretations of spiritual life.

Such were a part of the entity's experience throughout that sojourn, with the vision oft of those things that had been a part of the entity's activity before that.

Then the name was Endoren.

3630-2   F.53   5/11/44   Phoebe

. . . the entity was in that now known as the Holy Land during those periods when the Master walked in the earth.

The entity was among those who questioned the associations of the Master with questionable morality, and because of the position of the entity as a social activity in the temple service as the wife of one of the priests, Phoebe, for that was the name in the experience. The entity showed those characteristics which are at times the questionings, or have been within self as well as from others.

1003-2   M.25   3/6/37   Leveudus

. . . the entity was in the experience when changes were being wrought in that land now known as the Holy Land, or in the Palestine land; during the period when the Master walked in the earth, and there were those takings over of the land previous to that period of the reign by the Romans and those who came into authority.

The entity though very young in years during that period when this portion of the activity began, became very decided *against* the oppressions by taxations; and during those periods when those activities of the Master made for a hope in the development of elderly man, the entity—as Leveudus—hoped for material changes and the material reliefs of the burdens of the peoples during that experience. Hence there came many disappointments and discouragements.

Yet much of the tenderness as experienced by those who may know the entity in the present arises from those lessons the entity gained during that sojourn, in the latter portion of the entity's experience.

The entity then was one who would be called a banker, if his activities were put into present day parlance; though the associations had much to do also with the temple service. For the entity was of those peoples who were in the lineal descent of the priesthood, though never assumed those positions by the entity during that experience, though counseled oft.

Also the entity made and sold musical instruments of that day and period.

In the influences as arise latent and manifested in the experience of the entity in the present will be found the abilities to drive a good bargain, the abilities to choose companions, the abilities to choose associates, the abilities to make for judgments upon individuals or groups as to whether it is their moral life, their material life, their duties, that will prompt them as to their paying their bills or not!

These are definite forces as will be manifested in the experience of the entity during this particular sojourn from that activity in the Holy Land.

The entity also will find that there are certain portions of especially the Sermon on the Mount, the activities of the disciples and the Master just after the crucifixion, that are of the most particular interest to the entity—as they may be read or heard discoursed upon . . .

Q-6. How was I associated with my present wife [578] in Palestine?

A-6. She was then the entity's daughter. Doesn't she try to boss him now?

5252-1   M.29   6/14/44   Louan

. . . the entity was in the Roman land and the Holy Land. The entity was among those who were sent from the Roman land as an overseer, supervisor; not in the soldiery but in the supervising of the collection of the custom or the tax; and thus the individual entity was interested in people's abilities to pay, as well as in their contributing, rather of their free will, which did not work so well in the beginning; but as is the law of the Lord, "Ye will find the seed produceth its own kind." The gentleness with which the entity, as Louan, was active with the peoples in Silicia, Sudan and those portions about the Holy Land, brought results, and there was peace and harmony between those peoples from Antioch. The entity, through its own counsel, even brought the political advisor to the knowledge of the tenets of Jesus. Thus the zealousness with which the entity holds to principles and ideals. But find them first. Not by that which ye hold in your mind, put them in black and white. Put them in writing. They may mean much to others also.

674-3   M.16   9/9/39   Ezekhel

. . . the entity was in the land now known as the Promised Land, during those experiences when there were the activities of the Romans in the land, just after the periods known as the crucifixion, when there were many questionings of those peoples in their various subjects of activity.

For the entity was of those peoples who were of the Promised Land, yet forced into service and activity in the Roman experience; thus not a collector of customs but rather among those who supervised the collectors and the divisions.

Hence the entity became somewhat of a politician, as would be termed in the parlance of the present day . . .

In the experiences there the entity gained, for there were held those periods in which while there were self-preservations these were not at the expense of others, no matter what were the circumstances brought into the experience.

Then the name was Ezekhel.

2030-1   M.21   10/28/39

. . . the entity was in the Roman experience, during those activities in that period when there were dissensions as to "What meaneth the teachings of the man of Galilee?"

There we find the entity was a Roman, and a Roman soldier; but of those activities at *first* in Greece and Cilicia, and later in portions of that land of Palestine and especially that of Herod Archelaus [16] in the northern portion.

There we find the entity came in contact with many of those who had accepted, as well as many of those who persecuted those who followed the Nazarene.

Thus we find a confusion in the experiences of the entity during that sojourn; yet there were the abilities of the entity not merely as a soldier but to interpret for others, and to prevent them from becoming too much in an activity in which turmoils would arise.

Hence we will find, as has been the experience even thus far, the entity is one inclined to be the peacemaker when disputations arise in its associations here and there. For the entity holds not grudges, and yet has *definite, very* definite ideas as to what it thinks; not so much as yet as to what it believes, but what it thinks.

Hence that as has been indicated—the argumentation about minor things or minor details, yet in the deeper things the abilities to bring peace in the experiences of those who are disturbed in some directions.

From the experience we will find the abilities of the entity to meet others, to determine the abilities of others, and thus adding to the characteristics necessary for a *good* salesman.

1650-1   M.37   7/29/38   Pitmumus

. . . the entity was in the Roman land, during those periods when the Romans held a protectorship over the Palestine land; during the days when the Master walked in the earth.

The entity was among the soldiery, and stationed in the garrisons of the Roman soldiery about Bethany and Jerusalem   or to the southernmost gate through which the Master passed! [17]

These the entity saw, though the entity comprehended little, during those periods of the persecutions; though the entity followed the dictates of those that were in authority.

Know, as the experiences then taught the entity, that in whatever place or position an individual may be—whether in a place of authority, a place of confidence, a place of security or of whatever nature the activity may be—no individual is in such a position but that he has merited same for the opportunities of manifesting *in such position* the glory of the Father through his activities with his fellow men!

As ye used throughout that experience those opportunities for learning and gaining a comprehension as to the meaning of life, and the truths as were manifested by those who were the professed and true followers of the teachings of the Master, so may ye apply in thy present experiences, in thy present dealings with thy fellow man those tenets, those laws that were His — and the whole gospel to love the Lord with all thy mind and heart and body, and thy neighbor as thyself; this is the whole law!

The entity gained *throughout* the experience, as Pitmumus; for ye gained much. And ye rose to positions of power, ye rose to places wherein little or no censure could be drawn from thy judgments about thy fellow men, whether they were Roman, Greek, Parthenian or the hated Jew in a portion of thy activity.

Thus may thyself find that He, thy Lord, is not a respecter of persons but to do good unto all men is the whole duty of man.

1467-3   M.33   6/12/38   Philomus

. . . the entity was in the land now known as or called the Promised Land.

The entity, though, was not of the Promised Land; being rather among the Romans who were encamped or engarrisoned in and about Jerusalem during the periods of the persecution of the Master.

The entity knew of, and the entity was acquainted with, much that went on during those experiences. And only later did the entity become the closer associated, or hear of, or understand the teachings in that experience; when there were the persecutions of those followers of the Nazarene by the Jews, as well as the calling upon the soldiery to carry out the orders of many of those rulers.

Hence again we find in the present, as related to those experiences, the desire to hear all sides; the inclination to be too oft the hail fellow well met, in meeting in groups or associations, without considering too well the influences that such may bear upon the associations or *through* the associations into the experiences of self.

THE ROMANS

The entity gained, the entity lost, the entity gained.

In the present, with the deeper study of the happenings during those experiences, there may be much brought back to the entity of the activities as related to the applications of individuals in the teachings through that experience.

The name then was Philomus ("os" called also, but "us" was the name), born in the isle of Cyprus, yet among the Roman soldiery in Jerusalem and in those lands that became the better acquainted with the disciples after the crucifixion.

370-3   M.52   3/25/36   Pontuos

The entity then was among the Roman soldiery; *not* of those that were of the crowds that made for the crucifying, but those that came to *fill* the places of those that rebelled and drew away because of the experiences in the activities of those at that time —then in the name Pontuos.

In the experience the entity fought most within self, for the activities that were *about* the entity convinced his mental mind of those experiences; yet the needs or desires of the flesh made for those things that produced the subduing of the better influences towards those *convincing* experiences of the body.

In the latter portion of the sojourn, when the entity became associated with those to whom the entity had been sent, to persecute, down at Joppa [18] (for *there* the entity was among the Roman guards who were to subdue those that were among those gatherings of the church and of the nobler women), the entity succumbed to not only the deeds of mercy, the deeds of charity, the deeds of kindness shown to those roundabout, but to the beauty of body, the sincerity of purpose, the fearlessness even in those galling ways in which the soldiery acted in the presence and *to* those that were of the faith.

Hence the entity became an outcast; for renouncing its Roman allegiance, it became then one undecided; yet strong sufficient to meet even those in the arena later in its experience, as not a fighter of beasts but of men.

In the present those experiences become as a background or portion of that sought. Hence the tendency in the entity's associations to question those that are teachers or ministers of various groups of individuals, to bring up arguments, and—

most of all—to seek as to what the relationships of the fair sex are to those of the various groups—and these are sought in the entity's experience. These may be well, but they may also become stumbling blocks if they are used for self's own indulgences.

1227-1   F.12   7/21/36   Roslan

. . . the entity was in that land now known as the Roman, during those periods when there were those teachings being spread by the soldiery, by those that returned from that land where those persecutions had begun of those for a faith, for an interpretation, for an understanding.

The entity then was among those of the court, and in the name then Roslan.

In the experience the entity gained through those associations with those that had been in close contact through the teachings by those closely associated with John's sister; and came to know the true teachings of Him that is called lowly, Him that is called the Son of man.

In those understandings and those interpretations came a peace and a harmony; though it brought separations, though it brought persecutions, though it brought misinterpretations by those of the own group or sect as would be called. Yet the entity gained throughout the experience. For the entity ministered not only of its own worldly goods but of itself.

And we will find that those inclinations in the present for the nursing, for those things that will have to do with the care for the unfortunate, for those things that will have to do with such associations, will become a desire. But the greater desire is for the innate love that may find expression without showing emotions in such an activity.

2667-5   M.47   1/20/26   Nebat

. . . in the days when the persecution of the peoples in the country when the Roman rule overran Palestine. The entity then the soldier that led many peoples in the attempt to prevent this yoke or bondage being placed upon the peoples. Then in the name Nebat. The entity then both gained and lost, for the persecution brought self-condemnation to the entity. In this, we find the urges for the love of that country, and its peoples, and the love of freedom, and the love of race.

2496-1   M.54   7/31/26   Remis
. . . the entity among those who were persecuted in the period when the first of the martyrs in the Roman period, for the entity then among the soldiers of that day. Then in the name Remis, and the entity lost and lost, and lost, during that sojourn, for with the position, and with the opportunity to *gain* from those whom the entity contacted, there was little stability in purpose, save as to the self-satisfaction of own self's interest in the earthly fashion . . .

843-9   M.55   10/19/38   Apoloir
. . . the entity was in the land when the Master walked in the earth; being among the Roman peoples that were garrisoned in the Palestine land during and previous to and after the activities of the Master and the disciples and the apostles.

The entity knew much of those activities, and yet kept self in such a manner as to never be in the position of applying direct punishments—as came under the direction of those that were in authority during that experience.

Then the name was Apoloir; and the entity gained and lost, gained and lost. For convictions arose, but owing to circumstance (by which the entity justified self) there was not the true activity in that as the entity believed.

33-1   M.24   8/31/26   Nero: Background
[In July, 1926, Mr. Cayce had this letter from a young man, an ex-coal miner, in West Virginia:

"I was hurt in a car wreck 4 years ago . . . I am paralyzed from my neck down. I have been operated on 3 times but all the doctors don't seem to find what's the matter with me."

The following month Mr. Cayce gave him a physical reading, which said in part:]

Now the experience of this entity through this present physical plane, as a developing entity through earth's experiences, would be more interesting than the physical conditions . . .

For many of these conditions are merited through those actions of the mental and the spiritual forces of the body . . .

[At the end of the reading, in an undertone so that we could hardly hear it, Mr. Cayce said:]

See, this is Nero.

[Report: A form letter sent from our office in 1940 came back marked *"deceased."*

For 18 years he was completely helpless and thus entirely dependent upon charitable Christians for every detail of his care.]

220-1   F.5   11/9/29   Aschell

. . . in the period when there were destructions in the palaces in that city in the hills, when there were being destructions to those believers in the new religion. The entity then was among those of the court of that ruler Nero, and in the name Aschell; losing through this period, gaining only in the last portion of experience in the acceptance of those bonds physical, brought on account of beliefs. In this experience, those innate are the rebellion against authority, yet ever mindful of care, attention, adornment of the body, and unless guided in proper direction this may prove detrimental in the present experience.

5366-1   F.53   7/19/44   Emersen

This entity was among those with that one who persecuted the church so thoroughly and fiddled while Rome burned. That's the reason this entity in body has been disfigured by structural conditions . . .

. . . we find the entity . . . was a companion or associate of that one who persecuted those who believed in, those who accepted faith in righteousness, in goodness, in crucifying of body desires, in crucifying the emotions which would gratify only appetites of a body, either through the physical self or through physical appetites of gormandizing, and of material desire for the arousing more of the beast in individual souls.

In the experience, then, the entity is meeting self in that which was a part of the experience as Emersen.

3031-1   M.40   6/6/43   Loga

. . . the entity was in the Roman land, when there were those influences that caused those in authority to rise or declare against all of those—even in authority—who had proclaimed the name of the Nazarene.

Thus there were periods when the persecutions for activities, for beliefs, were a part of the group activity.

The entity was among those forced—by circumstance, as well as by choice—to contribute to the preparing of means and manners and ways in which such adherents would be tested—and was in the name Loga [?], indicating the manner and way in which those entities—or the entity's forces—were as an aid to the king in authority during that period. This was the name applied to the entity through that experience.

While they were periods of stress, the activities of the entity —while a loss to many—were not all bad, not all good. For, they were the means through which testings were made to the many adherents to those teachings of the Nazarene.

774-5   F.77   4/17/36   Emmalen

... the entity lived in the earth during those periods when there were the turmoils of those that followed closely in the activities of the ministry of Him who had said, had given, "Know thyself; know what *is* the motivative influence in thy life that prompts thee to act in this or that manner toward thy fellow man; for as ye do it unto these, the least of thy brethren, so ye do it unto thy God."

Thus the entity, in those experiences during the oppression of those followers in the days of the emperor in the city upon the hills, or in the Roman land, found self giving expressions to what had been builded in the experiences of its soul through those sojourns in the Egyptian, the Persian, the Mongolian lands; that there were *those forces* that make the creating in the body of the love of good for Goodness' sake, rather than for self-glory, self-indulgence or self-aggrandizements.

Then in the name Emmalen, we find the entity from the material standpoint lost; but from the mental and from the spiritual it gained. For while the years in material activity were cut short by the persecutions, there came the assurance within self that the opportunity for self-expression would come to the entity, to the self, in this experience.

It may be said, then: Use that thou hast in hand today—

today. Thou knowest, thou hast experienced, even as of Him, it is not that people should seek the easier way—but that they themselves should present themselves to be a living example of that they hold as their ideal, even as was set in Him and as taught to thee through those activities as there was the ministry of Paul at Ephesus, at Rome.

The entity was in companionship then of Lydia, that made for the fine linens, the brocadings of the dress for the various estates. Hence these have been, these become a portion of the entity's experiences in the present.

845-1   F.36   3/5/35   Posnell

... the entity was in that land now known as the Roman, during those periods when there were the individual and the group presentations of those tenets that had been gained from the associations of the soldiery; later through the activities of the emissaries as missionaries that came into the Roman land with those tenets of the Nazarene.

The entity then was among those of the ruler's household of the land and came under the influences of those teachings by the applications in self's own experience. In the first portion of the sojourn or experience in the land the entity made for an awareness, an awakening to life as it may be applied in being wasted or being used in an experience of an entity. While it brought in the latter portion material suffering, the mental and the material and the physical forces made for gains during the latter portion of that sojourn; though it brought eventually separations to those of its own household; though it brought to the entity dire disorder and distress from the physical and material angle, yet contentment, peace and harmony arose throughout the latter portion of that sojourn. The entity was in the name then of Posnell.

In the present we find from that sojourn in the earth those tenets of those teachings, especially as presented by Paul, mean much more to the entity than many another portion of the records or the letters or the epistles that were given by the teachers of that day. For the entity came under the direction and under the voice of Paul with Lydia and others that in the latter portion of the sojourn dwelt among those of the faithful of that sect in that particular land . . .

Q-8. *What was my relation to Nero in the Roman experience?*

A-8. Very good friend, and—as would be called today—a pal of his at times.

268-3   F.44   2/15/33   Gracia

. . . the entity was in that land now known as the Roman, during that period when there were the persecutions of the peoples for their belief in a new thought, or those thoughts that came with the peoples then called the Nazarites or Nazarenes. The entity then was among those who in *mental* activity warred against these peoples, for the entity was then of the nobility of the land; of the household of Pompeathiolus, and joined in with those who watched often in the persecutions of the peoples. The entity lost through this experience; yet in the latter portion gained much from that which had been brought over, through the application of self to the tenets within the mental abilities of the entity. The name was then Gracia . . .

Q-5. [*Where have I been formerly associated with*] My niece, [405]?

A-5. In the Roman experience, when there were the associations in the household of Pompeathiolus.

275-11   F.17   10/13/30   Partheniasi

. . . in that period when there were the destructive forces made manifest materially in the land when peoples were persecuted for their religious beliefs. The entity was among those of the household of a ruler who participated in this character of influencing the peoples of that period. Hence in the arena the entity watched *many* an individual perish, and especially was there that expression that brings in the present an influence as to rending of limbs. In this the entity lost. In the latter portion of the experience the entity gained in the manner in which the entity suffered. In the name Partheniasi. In the present the influences as seen are those of outdoor sports, those that partake of that which would remind one of such experiences produce an inexpressible feeling of fear, often causing sensations in the body of the entity—especially if blood be drawn. While the influences also make innate that of the *desire to render aid to the suffering*, rather in the field of preventative measures would the *entity* gain the most, and present a better development from same in the present experience.

275-19   F.18   5/16/31   Partheniasi

During the period in Nero's reign in Rome, in the latter portion of same, the entity was then in the household of Parthesias—and one in whose company many became followers of, adherents to, those called Christians in the period, and during those persecutions in the arena when there were physical combats. The entity was as a spectator of such combats, and under the influence of those who made light of them; though the entity felt in self that there was more to that held by such individuals, as exhibited in the arena, but the entity—to carry that that was held as necessary with the companionship of those about same—laughed at the injury received by one of the girls [301] in the arena, and *suffered* in *mental anguish* when she saw later—or became cognizant of—the physical suffering brought to the body *of* that individual during the rest of the sojourn. The suffering that was brought was of a *mental* nature, and when music—especially of the lyre, harp, or of the zither—was played, the entity *suffered* most; for the song and the music that was played during that experience brought—as it were—the experience to the entity. Hence in meeting same in the present [cancer of the femur], there has been builded that which the entity passes through, or "under the rod"—as it were—of that as of being pitied, laughed at, scorned, for the inability of the personal body to partake of those in the material activities as require the need of all of the physical body . . .

275-22   F.18   10/24/31

Q-2. In the incarnation as Partheniasi, give name of girl that I laughed at.

A-2. One who *suffered* torture *under* the *animal* in the arena, one that is near—*and* dear—to thee in this *present* experience. [See 301-5 on following page.]

Q-3. Give names of other people with whom I was closely associated at that time.

A-3. *All* those who were in the period that suffered persecution, or those who—with that *called* the royalty, or those in power—*looked on.* As to names, *many* of those . . .

Q-4. Have I ever been associated with [301] and her daughter [299] in some other incarnation?

A-4. This has been given in this, and among those whom the entity laughed at during this period—see? . . .

301-5   F.23   6/20/31   Phelemaie

. . . in that land now known as the Roman, and during that period when there were persecutions of those for the new belief, for those who followed the Nazarene, for those who were persecuted for heeding those of the lawyer-tentmaker [Paul]. The entity was then among those who came under this influence; though being of the Roman peoples and of the household of some of the guards in that period, the entity entered wholeheartedly into the aiding of others to know of those lessons, those truths as were taught by those peoples, suffering in body, yet fervent in the spirit of truth as gained. The entity suffered under persecutions in the arena, being torn by those of the beasts, and laughed at by those even associated close with the entity. In the present, as may be seen from this experience of gain throughout by the entity, in the name Phelemaie—in this experience the entity finds those truths that are of the nature that are not of that that would be with sounding of brasses, or of sounding of trumpet, but in the little kindnesses, the little deeds as are done, that that *answers* for that experience. In this experience, the fervency of the desire to know *more* of such though fearful oft of animals in closed ranges, not unmindful of the beauty of, nor the ability of individuals to control same through the use of patience, persistence, and presence of mind —even as the entity did in that experience.

276-2   F.13   2/20/31   Phoebia

. . . in that land now known as the Roman, and during that period when there were the ministering and teaching of those peoples that came up from Judea. The entity was among those who accepted those teachings, and coming in contact with those of that period, taught by the lessons of, the experiences of self and others in the contacts of this new peace, yet suffering in body, by privation—yet able in mind to control those beasts, both of the field and of the dens and lairs that the body was placed in; the body bore same, gaining—gaining—oft the liberation for the teachings again through these *strange* abilities in this particular period; being among those who journeyed again to the Grecian land for the teaching of the peoples, as the entity was carried away from same. In body beautiful, in mind pleasant, in abilities surpassing many in that period; gaining throughout the experience, though suffering in *many* ways and manners. In the name Phoebia.

276-3   F.13   11/20/31

Q-11. Give date of incarnation as Phoebia [in Rome] and describe strange abilities of entity in that period, also as to control of those beasts of the field, dens, and liars.

A-11. This, as we find, was during those periods when man was called upon oft to defend self against the beasts of the fields, in dens, in lairs, in arenas; and the entity through its own development—as had been attained or gained during that period—showed forth the ability to walk with the denizen of the forest without being afraid, also to walk among those in the arena without fear; and no *harm came to* the entity through their activity, but from those that made themselves lower than the beasts; for, as has been given, all may be tamed, but the tongue hath no man tamed! In that day, then, during the first century, as is counted in the present.

1215-4   M.17   6/4/37   Claudiusen

[The sojourn that is the more outstanding] . . . was during those periods when there were the persecutions of those who followed in the way of the teachings of the Nazarene.

The entity then was a Roman soldier, and one given rather to that of self-indulgence—and gloried rather in seeing the suffering of those who held to that principle.

And the entity fought in the arena and watched many that had met the entity fight again with the beasts and with those elements that made for the closer association with the elementals in the sojourn.

The entity saw suffering, and the entity made light of same.

Hence the entity sees suffering in self in the present, and must again make light of same—but for a different purpose, for a different desire, for a different cause.

For again the entity meets self in that wished, that desired on the part of those against whom the entity held grudges.

Hence the entity may find in the present that, in the application of those influences that arose in that period when the entity—known as Claudiusen—brought disturbances in the minds of those with a purpose, that purposefulness must arise within self in the present for meeting those very forces.

And only in Him who *is* life, light and immortality, against whom the entity then sought reactions in the material, may same be met; and it must be as has been given: "Make the paths straight, for straight is the way and narrow is the gate by which the understanding and the wisdom of the use of power, force, mercy or truth may be applied in the experiences of a soul in the material plane."

2444-1   F.16   2/4/41   Tekla

. . . the entity was in the Holy Land, or Palestine; during that experience when the Master walked in the earth.

The entity was among those who heard those tenets, and saw in the activities of His disciples that variation as practiced by Him in the interpreting of the letter of the law *and* the spirit of the law.

Thus the entity gained, though suffering martyrdom through those experiences—being carried to the Roman arena for those activities which *first* were practiced as to individuals of the groups that had embraced or listened to those tenets in the land; this following those periods when many of the Romans had embraced those beliefs.

The entity renounced those tenets when martyrdom was presented; yet suffered death in those periods of exposure and confinement in those groups brought there.

Hence again we may say that the entity gained; for there were the determinations to study, to know those tenets of various groups that had varied religious experiences as related to the political as well as national, as well as *group* truths and tenets.

Then in the name Tekla, the entity gained through the greater portion of the activity. We find that the entity *became* a mother in that experience, during those activities of the nature that may be a part of the present experience—especially its studies in the present for its preparations for its activities. For, while there will be those opportunities for wedded life, the entity *should*—if it will gain the more—have a career before such becomes a part of the experience; as an educator, as a teacher, *especially* of psychological subjects as prepared for the young in its relationships to *activities* of the teen-age children, especially. If the greater development would be made, this should be a part of the entity's experience; not only from the activities as Sister Theresa [American incarnation] but as Tekla also—because of the *determinations* to know and to warn those as to how they, as individuals, may prepare themselves, that there may be a perfect, a better generation in *man's* activity in the earth!

1928-1   F.31   10/18/32   Nalthlai

. . . in that environ when there were those peoples being persecuted for the tenets and beliefs in the new sect; and in the Roman land did the body suffer physically and mentally for those tenets held by self. When there came the period for the bodily injury, else denying the faith, the entity gave way at first, for self-protection, for saving the physical body, bringing to self a mental and material anguish that enabled it (the entity and body) to later stand in defiance of all; in the name Nalthlai. In the arena, then, the body lost its life; gaining through the experience, after there had arisen within self those abilities to control the emotions of the body, mentally and physically, for the glorifying of that held as a high tenet in the inner being; hence in the present those tenets tending towards conditions that deal with the spiritual life, or that called the religious experiences of the entity in the present, have been varied; some that have been held dear at times have been denounced, yet when self has adjusted itself, and when self knows within self what is to be the activity of the body physically and mentally respecting rote, mental reaction, service in body, in mind, in self, *glorious* may be those abilities to find in such that which will answer for every desire of the body, the mind, the soul. The *beauties* of service to the entity are the most wonderful. To attain such for self has so often been felt in the present to be impossible, because of oppression from without and circumstances and variations; yet these will aid in bringing satisfaction, contentment; for—as held innate and manifested from the experience as Nalthlai in the Roman activity—there is no other name, there is no other that has that same saving power, grace or knowledge, save in Him. To whom, to what, then, may one go? . . .

803-1   F.51   1/29/35   Myrtina

. . . the entity was in that land now known as the Roman, during those periods when there were the greater persecutions of those peoples who had held to the tenets that were spread through the activities of the soldiery that returned, when there was the beginning of the ministry of those who had been teachers under the Teacher in Galilee.

The entity then was among those of the household in the ruler's activity, and the entity harkened to much of the beauties and activities indicated in the peace and harmony brought to the lives of those who became adherents to the activities of those people. Yet with the persecutions there came turmoils and strife, and oft the necessity for the entity in its activities to become identified with those gradually brought turmoils and strife. Yet in those activities, in the name Myrtina, being among those who aided those peoples in their meeting and as to the various activities, the entity heard the teachings of both Paul and Peter, also Titus, in the cities about Rome and about those groves and places of meeting that have just begun to be opened in that particular land.

Being of the Grecian people that had entered, or married into the Roman land, made for greater persecution to the entity as an individual; yet much did the entity gain in the mental and the spiritual aspects during that sojourn. Although being among those in the arena when there were the fightings with the animals, the conditions that made for distress to many, the entity—because of its beauty, its gentleness, its activity—did not become a victim to either the beasts or the breaking on the wheel, or the consorts that made for the bringing of material distresses to those people during the sojourn. Rather, with the entity's activity, it was banished to its own land again; where the entity—in the latter portion of the experience—brought much help and aid to many of those that journeyed there for the teachings and activities of the entity.

1175-1   F.61   5/18/36   Marleon

. . . the entity was in the reconstruction activity, as it were, when there were those teachings of the soldiery that had been in the Holy or the Promised Land and in the Roman experience that made for teaching and ministering in those periods. The entity then among the nobles, or of the household of one Phylos [?] [Philoas?].

Then in the name Marleon, the entity made for a social life, as it would be termed in the present; yet activities in same that made for a commanding influence among those in authority.

Yet when the teachings of the lowly Nazarene and His followers who in bondage and in bonds, or even in those periods when there was the use of the entertainments in the fighting with the beasts, or the games that were inaugurated by those peoples for entertainment of the nobles, the ladies and the lords, the entity was rather given to first pity, then to adherence, and then to acceptance of those lowly tenets that "As ye do it unto thy fellow man, so ye do it unto thy Maker."

These brought from the material angle confusions, yet made for a development in the activities of the entity during those experiences.

1718-1   F.37   7/4/30   Lydias

. . . in that land known as the Roman land, when there were the teachings as of Him of Nazareth. The entity then, those that were *offered* in the arena—and the entity fought, or gave life again in the defense of a principle; leading many, being the guide, the counselor, the one that gave hope and courage to many to bear even that of death in defense of a principle. In the name Lydias. In that period the entity gained through the whole of the experience, and the lessons as were gained through the experience are as the lamp to the feet and the light in the pathway the entity would lead. The counsel of those that were martyrs, even as the entity—the sages of that period being the friends of the entity, are *still* as the guides in the daily experiences of the entity.

2123-2   F.34   8/31/31   Arriel

. . . in that land now known as the Roman land, and during those periods when there were oppressions in the land to those peoples who held to an ideal, a new relationship between man and his Maker. The entity then among the peoples of the household of Palatius [?], and sat oft in those boxes that viewed the struggles of man with man, man with beast, as they fought; and in the present comes much of the struggle in the *physical* as was laughed to scorn by the entity in the weakness of those that fought in and for a cause. In the name then Arriel. In this experience the entity lost and gained, and lost. Lost in that the selfishness of self gave *little* of the vision as was given *to* the entity in the earlier portion of its experience. Coming later under the influence of the teachings of those so hated, the entity came to know *much* of that as was given by those teachers, and innately oft does the entity hear the voices of those that rose in *their* beseeching the peoples more than the wailings of those that suffered. Hence easily an understanding comes to the entity in the present experience of the teachings of Paul, of Peter, of Apollus, of those whom the entity was *among* and amid. *Losing* in the latter experience when persecutions came, the entity faltered, yet in the present there comes that stability that may be built by the entity in the present experience; for in *Him* is life, light and immortality; for though the body be burned and ye have not love it is nothing; though ye give all thy goods and have not love it is nothing! This has the entity heard oft in the various experiences in the past, in the present, and will this be made that of the key to that as may be given to others, in song, or in the various relationships with individuals, may again Arriel bring a joyful, an *acceptable* song unto the Throne.

Footnotes

HISTORICAL BACKGROUND
[1] (Covenants to Founding Fathers)
Genesis 3; 6:18; 9:8; 15:7, 18; 17:2, 19; 26:3; 28:13
Exodus 2:24; 6:4
I Chronicles 16:16
II Samuel 7:12; 23:5
Psalms 25:14; 89:3, 28, 34
Isaiah 54:10; 59:21
Malachi 3:1
[2] Isaiah 9:6, 7
Malachi 3; 4
Joel 2; 3
[3] Luke 1:26-38
[4] Matthew 1:18-25
Luke 2:1-7
[5] Luke 2:22-38
[6] Matthew 2:13-18
[7] Matthew 2:19-23
[8] Luke 2:41-50
[9] Luke 2:52
[10] I Kings 18:18-20
II Kings 4:25
[11] Matthew 22:23-33
Mark 12:18-27
Luke 20:27-40
[12] Luke 1:26-38
[13] Luke 1:20
[14] Luke 1:35
[15] Luke 2:1-5
[16] Luke 2:7
[17] Psalm 89
[18] Luke 2:8-20
[19] Luke 2:22-38

PREPARATION FOR HIS COMING
The Essenes
[1] Matthew 3:1-6
Mark 1:2-6
Luke 3:3
[2] Matthew 14:10
Mark 6:16, 27
Luke 9:9
[3] Numbers 35:10-34
Joshua 20
[4] Matthew 26; 57, 59-68

Mark 14:53, 56-65
Luke 22:54, 66-71
John 18:24
[5] Matthew 27
Mark 15
Luke 23
John 19
[6] Matthew 27:55, 59
Mark 15:41, 46
Luke 23:49, 53
John 19:38-40
[7] Matthew 28:10
[8] Matthew 28:1-10
Mark 16:1-11
Luke 24:1-10
John 20:1-18
[9] John 20:24-31
[10] Acts 7:54-60
[11] Acts 8:1-3; 9:1-6
[12] Deuteronomy 11, 12 and following
[13] Leviticus 10:1, 2
[14] Genesis 3; 6:18; 9:8; 15:7, 18; 17:2, 19; 26:3; 28:13
Exodus 2:24; 6:4
I Chronicles 16:16
II Samuel 7:12; 23:5
Psalms 25:14; 89:3, 28, 34
Isaiah 54:10; 59:21
Malachi 3:1
[15] Matthew 16:18; 28:19
Mark 16:15
John 20:21
[16] Acts 24:5
[17] I Kings 18:19
II Kings 4:25
[18] I Samuel 1
[19] Matthew 2:1-12
[20] Matthew 2:1, 2, 7
[21] Matthew 2:6; 27:27-30; 37
Mark 15:16-19, 26
Luke 23:37-38
John 18:33-38
[22] Matthew 2:16
[23] Jeremiah 31:15
Matthew 2:18
[24] Revelation 1:9

[25] I Kings 19:1-4
Romans 11:2, 3
[26] Isaiah 6
[27] Jeremiah 9:1; 10:19-25
[28] Deuteronomy 11
[29] John 2:1-11
[30] Matthew 11:5
[31] John 7:14
[32] John 6:1, 2
[33] Matthew 5
Luke 6:20-49
[34] I Samuel 1:10, 11
[35] I Samuel 8:3-5
[36] Luke 2:19, 51
[37] Matthew 13:55
Mark 6:3; 15:40
[38] John 6
[39] Matthew 2:1
[40] Luke 1:57-59
[41] Matthew 2:16
[42] II Kings 17:23, 24
[43] Deuteronomy 30:3-5
[44] Isaiah 19:20
[45] Matthew 2:16
[46] Acts 12:23
[47] Matthew 23:35
[48] Luke 4:28-30
[49] Luke 3:19-20
[50] Matthew 19:13-15
Mark 10:13-16
Luke 18:15-17
[51] Mark 3:13-19
Luke 6:12-16
[52] Acts 2
[53] Acts 2:4-13
[54] Matthew 28:16-20
[55] Acts 10
[56] Matthew 2:1-12

John the Baptist, Elizabeth and Zachariah
[1] Matthew 11:11
Luke 1:5
[2] Luke 1:13
[3] Matthew 23:35
[4] Luke 3:4; 7:27
[5] Luke 1:13
[6] Luke 1:39, 40
[7] Luke 1:26
[8] Luke 1:8, 9
[9] Matthew 3:5, 6

Mark 1:4, 5
Luke 3:3
John 3:26
[10] Matthew 4:12
Mark 1:14
Luke 3:20
[11] Matthew 14:1-14
Mark 6:14
[12] Matthew 11:2
Luke 7:19
[13] Acts 2
[14] Acts 12:2
[15] Matthew 11:2
Luke 7:19
[16] Luke 1:8, 9
[17] Luke 2:21-38
[18] Matthew 23:35
Luke 1
[19] Matthew 23:35
Luke 1
[20] Matthew 2:13
[21] Luke 1
[22] Matthew 11:4, 5
Luke 7:22
[23] Matthew 3:4; 11:8
Mark 1:6
Luke 7:25
[24] Matthew 14:6
[25] Matthew 23:35
Luke 1:57, 67-80
[26] Luke 7:28
[27] Malachi 4:5
Matthew 11:14; 17:12
Luke 1:17

THE CHOOSING OF MARY
[1] Genesis 14:18
Psalm 110:4
Hebrews 5:6-10; 6:20; 7:1-10
[2] Exodus 1:1-5
Deuteronomy 33
[3] Numbers 6:3
Judges 13:4, 7, 14
[4] Luke 1:26-38
[5] Luke 1:39-45
[6] Matthew 1:20
[7] Matthew 2:13
[8] Matthew 23:35
Luke 1:67-80
[9] Matthew 2:18
[10] Matthew 4:21
Mark 1:19
Luke 5:10
[11] Acts 10:1
[12] Luke 24:13

[13] Matthew 28:1
John 20:1
[14] Matthew 27:55
[15] Luke 2:34
[16] John 19:40
[17] Luke 2
[18] Genesis 3:15
[19] Matthew 2:16
[20] Luke 3:4
[21] John 1:29, 36
[22] Matthew 21:9, 15
Mark 11:9
John 12:13
[23] Acts 1:11
[24] Isaiah 9:6
[25] Luke 2:19

THE BIRTH
Background
[1] Luke 2:4-7
[2] Matthew 1
Luke 3:23-31
[3] Ruth 4
[4] Matthew 1:18
[5] Matthew 1:18
Luke 1:34, 35
Isaiah 7:14

The Inn
[1] Luke 2:7
[2] John 11; 12:1
[3] Matthew 26:39
Mark 14:36
[4] Matthew 2:2
[5] Luke 2:14
[6] Luke 2:41
[7] Matthew 21:9, 15
Mark 11:9
John 12:13

The Shepherds
[1] Luke 2:8
[2] Mark 10:46

Consecration in the Temple
[1] I Samuel 1
Luke 2:36
[2] Luke 1:5, 8

The Wise Men
[1] Genesis 1:28
[2] Matthew 2
[3] Matthew 2:11
[4] Matthew 2:11
[5] Luke 2:36
[6] Matthew 2:1-12

The Flight into Egypt
[1] Matthew 2:16-18
[2] Hosea 11:1
Matthew 2:15

[3] Luke 2:19, 51
[4] Hosea 11:1
[5] Luke 1:26-38
[6] Matthew 2:22, 23
[7] Luke 2:41-52
[8] Luke 23:55, 56
[9] Acts 12:2
[10] Luke 2:19

HEROD'S COURT
[1] Matthew 2:1-12
[2] Matthew 14:6
Mark 6:22
[3] Matthew 14:1-14
[4] Matthew 2:1-12
[5] Isaiah 55:6
[6] John 11
[7] Mark 6:22
[8] Matthew 2:16
[9] Joshua 24:15
[10] Matthew 26:3, 65
Mark 14:63
Luke 22:71
[11] Acts 12:23

THE YEARS PRECEDING HIS MINISTRY
[1] Micah 5:2
[2] Hosea 11:1
[3] Luke 2:41-52
[4] Matthew 12:40
[5] Matthew 28
Mark 16
Luke 24
John 20
[6] Genesis 3
Matthew 3:13
Mark 1:9
Luke 3:21

HIS INCARNATIONS
[1] Genesis 2:7
[2] Genesis 3:17-19
[3] Genesis 3:19
[4] Genesis 5:24
[5] Genesis 14:18
Hebrews 7:3
[6] Genesis 3:6
Luke 1:28
[7] I Corinthians 6:11
John 17:5, 6
[8] Hebrews 4:15
[9] Matthew 3:17
[10] I Corinthians 15:22
[11] Genesis 2:19; 14:18; 15:7; 30:24
I Chronicles 6:39
II Chronicles 5:12

Ezra 2:2
Matthew 1:21
[12] Acts 1:11
[13] I Corinthians 1:12
[14] John 14:15
[15] Joshua 14:6
[16] Isaiah 53
Romans 3:23-25
Matthew 26:28
[17] Joshua 2:1
[18] Genesis 3:15
[19] Joshua 24:15

HIS SISTER AND BROTHERS
[1] Matthew 13:55
Mark 6:3
[2] Luke 24:13
[3] John 11:25
[4] Matthew 3
[5] Luke 4:16
[6] John 11:45
[7] Acts 12:17; 15:13; 21:18
Galatians 1:19; 2:9
[8] Matthew 8:14
Mark 1:30
[9] John 14:11
[10] John 14:16
[11] John 13:23; 19:26; 21:7
[12] John 14
[13] Jude

EVENTS IN THE MINISTRY OF THE MASTER

Random Followers
[1] Matthew 5; 10:1
[2] Matthew 8:28
[3] Mark 2:23
[4] Joshua 24:15
[5] Matthew 8:5
[6] Luke 17:11-19
[7] Matthew 17:14-21
[8] Matthew 17

The Seventy
[1] Luke 10
[2] II Corinthians 1:19
[3] John 6:53
[4] Acts 5:34-39
[5] Acts 22:3
[6] Acts 5:38-39
[7] Acts 5:34-39

The First Recorded Miracle
[1] John 2
[2] Matthew 4:21
Mark 1:20
[3] Luke 1:26, 30

[4] Matthew 4
[5] Matthew 11:18, 19
[6] Matthew 28:1
[7] Mark 6:18
[8] John 14:1-4
[9] II John:1
[10] Matthew 2:16-18
[11] Matthew 2:17

The Samaritan Woman at the Well
[1] John 4:5-7
[2] Acts 1:12-14
[3] Matthew 21:1-11
Mark 11:1-11
Luke 19:29-38
John 12:12-15
[4] Matthew 21:17; 26:6

Peter's Mother-in-Law Is Healed
[1] Luke 4:38
[2] Galatians 2:9-19
[3] Matthew 27:35
Mark 15:24
Psalm 22:18
[4] Luke 7:11-15
[5] John 3:1; 7:50; 19:39
[6] Luke 10:38
John 11
[7] Mark 16:9
Luke 8:2
[8] Acts 1:12-14
[9] Exodus 28:30
[10] John 19:25
[11] Acts 2

The Leper Is Healed
[1] Matthew 8:3
[2] Matthew 9:2

A Widow's Son at Nain Is Healed
[1] Luke 7:11-15

The Parable of the Tares
[1] Matthew 13:24-30
[2] Hebrews 5:8

The Tempest Is Stilled
[1] Matthew 8:23-27

Gadarene Demoniac Is Cast Out
[1] Matthew 8:28-34

Jairus' Daughter Is Healed
[1] Matthew 9:18
Mark 5:22
Luke 8:41

The Woman Who Touched His Gar-
ment
[1] Matthew 9:20-21

The Feeding of the Multitudes
[1] Matthew 14:15-21
Mark 6:32-44
Luke 9:12-17
John 6:1-14
[2] Mark 8
[3] Acts 12:2
[4] Mark 10:15
[5] Matthew 14:22
[6] Matthew 8:32; 14:22
Mark 5:13
Luke 8:33
[7] Matthew 5-7
Luke 6:20

The Teachings at Bethsaida
[1] Mark 6:45; 8:22
John 1:44; 12:21
[2] Matthew 25:40, 45
[3] Psalms 2, 8, 16, 22, 23, 24, 40, 41, 45, 68, 69, 72, 89, 102, 110, 118
[4] Matthew 28
Mark 16:1-14
Luke 24:1-49
John 20:1-23
[5] Matthew 22:32
[6] John 5:39
[7] Matthew 19:13
Mark 10:13
Luke 18:15
[8] Luke 24:18
[9] Isaiah 11:6
Matthew 18:2
Mark 10:15
Luke 18:17
[10] Luke 4:30
[11] Matthew 18:7

Daughter of Syrophoenician Is Healed
[1] Mark 7:26
[2] Mark 7:27-29
Matthew 8:10
[3] John 6:37

An Example for the Disciples
[1] Mark 10:15
Luke 18:17
[2] Matthew 7:5
Luke 6:42
[3] Romans 14
[4] Matthew 18:1, 4
[5] Proverbs 17:5

Luke 6:37
⁶ Mark 16:15-18
⁷ Matthew 22:37, 38
　Mark 12:30, 33
　Luke 10:27
The Adulteress
¹ Luke 10:42
² Matthew 26:13
³ John 8
⁴ Matthew 28:1
⁵ John 20:15
⁶ Acts 8:3
⁷ Luke 8:2
⁸ John 8:7
⁹ John 8
Lazarus Is Raised
¹ John 11:1
² John 8
³ Acts 7
⁴ Acts 2
⁵ I Corinthians 2:2
⁶ Matthew 8:4
⁷ Matthew 9:18
　Mark 5:21-43
　Luke 8:41-55
⁸ John 12:1, 2
⁹ Luke 24:18
¹⁰ Luke 5:27
¹¹ Matthew 14:15-21
　Mark 6:32-44
　Luke 9:12-17
　John 6:1-14
¹² Luke 24:13
¹³ John 12:1-11
¹⁴ Matthew 28
　Mark 16
　Luke 24
　John 20
¹⁵ John 19:26-27
¹⁶ Matthew 16:21
　Mark 8:31
　Luke 9:22
¹⁷ Acts 12:2
¹⁸ John 11:44
The Rich Young Ruler
¹ Matthew 19:16-27
　Mark 10:17-27
　Luke 18:18-27
² Luke 10:25
Blind Bartimaeus Is Healed
¹ Mark 10:46-52
² John 14:3
Zaccheus Entertains the Master
¹ Luke 19:1-10

The Triumphal Entry
¹ Matthew 21:1
　Mark 11:1
　Luke 19:28
　John 12:12
² John 20:22
³ Matthew 27:55, 56
⁴ Matthew 26:32
⁵ Mark 16:15-20
　Luke 24:44-53
　Acts 1:9-11
⁶ Matthew 15:21
⁷ Luke 19:37-40
⁸ Acts 7:54-60
THE LAST HOURS
The Betrayal
¹ Matthew 26
　Mark 14
　Luke 22
　John 18
² John 12:4-6; 13:29
The Last Supper
¹ Matthew 26:17
　Mark 14:12
　Luke 22:7
　John 13:2
² John 13:5-20
³ John 4:34; 17:4; 19:30
⁴ John 13:21
⁵ John 13:16
The Trial
¹ Matthew 26:57
² Matthew 27
　Mark 15
　Luke 23
　John 18:19
³ Matthew 28:9, 10
The Crucifixion
¹ Matthew 27:33
　Mark 15:22
　Luke 23:33
　John 19:17
² Psalm 22
　Matthew 27:46
³ Matthew 27:51
　Mark 15:38
　Luke 23:45
⁴ Acts 23; 24; 25; 26
⁵ Acts 2
⁶ Matthew 27:59, 60
　Mark 15:46
⁷ Matthew 7:22, 23
⁸ Matthew 26:36-39
　Mark 14:32-37
　Luke 22:39-44
⁹ Luke 24:49

¹⁰ John 20:17
¹¹ John 20:27
¹² Luke 24:41-43
¹³ John 21:7
¹⁴ Acts 7
¹⁵ Matthew 27:26-32
The Preparation of His Body
¹ Luke 21
　John 19:39, 40
² Matthew 21:9, 15
　Mark 11:9
　John 12:13
³ John 13:34
⁴ John 19:39
⁵ Matthew 27:57
　Mark 15:43
　Luke 23:50
　John 19:38
The Resurrection
¹ John 11:25
² Matthew 28
　Mark 16
　Luke 24
　John 20:21
³ John 2:19
⁴ Mark 15:34
⁵ Mark 16:9
　John 20:11
⁶ II Kings 13:21
⁷ John 20:25
⁸ Luke 23:34
　John 17:5
⁹ John 14:15, 16, 23
¹⁰ Matthew 25:21
THE PENTECOST
¹ Acts 2
² Acts 1:4
³ Acts 4
⁴ Acts 2:47
⁵ Acts 2:4
⁶ Acts 2:6
THE FOLLOWERS AND THE CHURCHES
¹ Matthew 27:57
　John 3:1; 19:38, 39
² Matthew 26:57-68
　Mark 14:53-65
　John 18:13, 19-24
　Luke 22:66-71
³ Matthew 27:57, 58
⁴ Genesis 29:32
　I Chronicles 5:1
⁵ I Samuel 30:22
　II Corinthians 6:15

FOOTNOTES

6 John 11
7 Exodus 25:10; 37:1
8 Matthew 4:18
  Mark 1:29; 13:3
  John 1:40; 6:8; 12:22
  Acts 1:13
9 John 1:27; 3:30
10 Matthew 4
11 John 6
12 Matthew 26:36
13 Acts 10-12
14 Matthew 14
  Mark 6
  John 6
15 Mark 6:45
16 Luke 10
17 Acts 5; 8:18-23
18 Acts 1:13
19 John 21:18, 19
20 Acts 12:5-19
21 Acts 12:13
22 Matthew 19:14
23 Matthew 13:55, 56; 27:56
  Mark 15:40
24 Acts 12:2
25 Acts 12:12
26 Acts 12:25; 13:5
27 Galatians 2:11
28 Acts 8:20
29 Acts 5:14-16; 16:16
30 Acts 8:9
31 Acts 8:9-24; 16:16-24
32 Acts 10
33 Acts 10:3
34 I Corinthians 13
35 Acts 11:26; 13:1
  Galatians 2:11
36 Acts 2:14
37 Colossians 4:17
38 Acts 13:50
39 Matthew 21:1
40 Luke 24:13
41 Mark 16
  Luke 24
42 John 14:3, 4
43 Matthew 26:60, 61,65
44 Luke 24:13-35
45 Luke 24:18-31
46 Matthew 13:55, 56
  Mark 6:3
47 Matthew 4:21
  Mark 1:20
48 Revelation 1:9
49 Acts 5:39; 22:3
50 Matthew 26:26

Mark 14:22
Luke 22:19, 20
51 Revelation 1
52 I John 2; 3; 4
53 II John
54 Acts 7:58, 59; 12:2
55 Matthew 4:21
56 Matthew 4:21
  Mark 1:19, 20
57 Luke 10:1-24
58 John 6:1-14
59 Mark 1:19
60 Acts 12:23
61 Acts 7
62 John 14:2, 3
63 Acts 7:51, 59
64 John 1:43
  Acts 6:5; 8
65 Matthew 16:19
66 Luke 2:25
67 John 14:11
68 Acts 2
69 Galatians 1:13
  I Timothy 1:13
70 Acts 19:15
71 Acts 19:15
72 II Timothy 4:7
73 Acts 18
74 Acts 27
75 Acts 16:35
76 Acts 12; 16; 20
77 Acts 28:16
78 Acts 14:6
79 II Timothy 1:5
80 Hebrews 11:1
81 Hebrews 5:6
82 Matthew 11:28
83 Acts 15; 16:19
84 Acts 12:5
85 Matthew 16:16
  Mark 8:29
  Luke 9:20
86 Matthew 9:9
87 Titus
88 I Corinthians 2:2
89 Galatians 2:3
  II Corinthians 2:13; 7:6; 13
90 Philemon
91 Luke 19:40
92 Matthew 28:20
93 John 14:2, 3
94 Matthew 23:11
  Mark 10:44
  Luke 9:48
95 Matthew 24:3

96 Matthew 10:3
97 Luke 10
98 Acts 2:4
99 Acts 7:59; 12:2
100 Acts 9
101 I Corinthians 7
  I Timothy 5:14
102 Acts 15:36
103 Revelation 3:15, 16
104 Acts 2:4
105 Matthew 21:1
106 Matthew 21:9
107 Luke 19:40
108 John 11
109 Matthew 21:17
110 Acts 2
111 I Corinthians 7
112 Matthew 27
  Mark 15
  Luke 23
  John 19
113 Luke 10:41, 42
114 Matthew 21:17; 26:6
115 Matthew 19:13
  Mark 10:13
116 Acts 2
117 Matthew 27:56
  John 19:25
118 Acts 12:2
119 John 11; 12:1
120 Acts 12:17; 21:18
121 Revelation 3:16
122 John 5:39

THE ROMANS

1 Luke 3:1
  Acts 11:28
2 Luke 2:1
3 Matthew 27:1-31
  Mark 15:1-19
  Luke 23:1-25
  John 18:28-40; 19:1-15
4 Luke 3:19
5 Matthew 27:19
6 Matthew 27:22
7 John 19:11
8 Luke 2:1
9 John 6:1; 6:23
10 Acts 11:28
11 Acts 23:23, 24; 24:10-25
12 Luke 2:46
13 Luke 24:51
14 Acts 12
15 Acts 27
16 Matthew 2:22
17 Matthew 21
18 Acts 9, 10

Index

Adultery, one taken in 252, 257-260
Alexandrian Library 38, 103, 116, 122, 139, 382, 413, 414, 521
Angels 7, 26, 50-51, 69, 102, 128, 322; Gabriel 50, 186; Michael 51
Annunciation 50-51, 69
Apostles, affluence of 190, 411; seven of the twelve from Galilee 33
Archaeology, research potential 10, 120, 138, 278, 382-383, 438, 442, 522
Art 58, 278, 336, 361; alchemist 97; mosaics 164; raising of Lazarus 278
Ascension 161, 230, 254-255, 291, 513
Astrology 4, 15, 28, 37, 53, 64, 95, 96, 105, 209, 225; Jesus to study 27; Mary's sign 66; Piscean Age 5; signs 5
Atheism 61

Beatitudes 226
Betrayal, the 238, 295-297
Bible, Books of: authors: Job 137; John 461; John, Second Epistle written by John 102, 190, 423; Jude 165, 167; Luke 514; Mark 381-382, 383, 513; Matthew 383, 513; Gospels, contributors to 220, 231, 513-514
Birth—see also Channels, Christmas, Immaculate Conception, Inn
Birth of Jesus 7, 67-108
Brahmanism 21, 133
Buddhism 21, 133-134

Cabala 41
Calendar 67-68, 409, 491, 545
Celibacy 43, 52, 195
Channels, potential, for the birth 49-66, 94, 102, 121, 189, 195
Christian, followers first known as 178
Christianity 514
Christmas 67, 68
Church, the 34, 151, 154, 178, 179, 195, 197, 202, 214, 215, 222, 223, 229, 230, 234, 243, 264-265, 294, 328, 330, 338-344, 350, 353-361, 374, 400, 413, 419-421, 441-443, 445-456, 486, 501, 504, 505, 509, 510, 514-516; Alexandria 382; Antioch 202, 265, 439, 443, 446, 466, 467, 495; Caesarea 169, 365, 387, 443, 527; Caesarea-Philippi 169, 421; Catholic 69, 74, 197, 433, 514; Greece 441; Jerusalem 113, 202, 265, 330, 420, 424, 486, 495, 509, 511; Laodicea 221, 243, 265, 272, 331, 359, 395, 420, 440, 446-457, 467, 468, 487, 494, 501, 510, 511, 512, 513; Patmos 265; Pisidia 445; Pisillia 445; Pygarga 265; Rome 360, 417, 460-461; Thessalonica 336, 442
Comforter, the definition 166
Communion 163, 181, 182, 297, 408, 419
Confucianism 133
Crucifixion 58, 89, 93, 149, 155, 158, 159-160, 190, 203, 288, 289-290, 303-319, 320-321, 325-326, 408-409, 497

David, house of 52, 56, 57, 68

Earth center 124
Egypt, Jesus' early years there 4, 100, 103, 126; Jesus' later years 4, 104, 123, 124, 125; the Flight 5, 46, 81, 99-108
Essenes, defined 17; Elizabeth a member of 48; Jesus a member of 11; Joseph and Mary members of 6; known as Carmelites 262; meetings held in secret 433; met in chambers of Zebedee 11; preparation of potential channels for the birth 49-66; records, preservation of 19-20; school "above Emmaus" 13; their studies 4-5

Faith, defined 160
Faiths of the time discussed 261-262
Feast 87, 269, 274, 277

Glossolalia 34, 57, 328-337, 392, 440, 485, 488, 507
Gnosticism 514
Gospel, see Bible

Hasidees 17
Healings 173, 175, 182, 245, 246, 256, 268, 318; adulteress 201, 252, 257-260; Bartimaeus 283, 285-286; Cephas 434; daughter of Syrophoenician 244-247; Gadarene demoniac cast out 208-210, 224; healed by Peter 385-386; Jairus' daughter 210-214; John Mark 383; Lazarus is raised 263, 264, 266-269, 273, 274, 276-280; leper 204-205; of fever 174; of possession 173, 525; one who did not return to give thanks 175; one whom the disciples could not heal 175; Peter's mother-in-law 196-204, 233; widow of Nain's son 201, 205-207; Pilate's son 528-530; woman who touched His garment 215–216
Helvetians 98

Immaculate conception 5, 6, 24, 50, 72-75, 129, 157, 159; defined 73-74
India, His years there 4, 104, 125-126, 147
Inn, the 6-8, 60, 75-86, 101
Innkeeper, see Names Mentioned: Apsafar
Israel 10, 47, 50, 71, 82, 184, 192; defined 61

Jesus, as musician 298
  attributes as a child 104, 106, 123
  baptism of 124
  birth 8, 67-108
  body, preparation of 281, 292, 315-319
  brothers of, see Names Mentioned: James and Jude
  childhood in Egypt 4, 100
  consecration in the Temple 3, 8, 45, 54, 58, 89-93, 97
  description, physical 169, 215, 297
  education of 4, 22, 27, 42, 104, 106, 122-127, 147
  education of, testing in Egypt 123
  entering materiality, purpose of 21, 68
  entering materiality, through choice 3
  incarnations of 128-141
  influenced all thought that has taught God is One 133-134
  initiate in the pyramid 27, 124, 139
  Jewish authority, was to replace 20
  known as Jeshua 123
  lineal descent 52, 68, 138, 258
  robe of one piece 200, 202
  sister of, see Names Mentioned: Ruth
  "the only begotten son" 139-140, 310-311
  twin soul of Mary 75
Jewry, orthodox, declines 31
Judah 45
Judaism 133, 139

Last Supper 297-300, 436
Law, new 62
Levites 43, 240

Medes 21
Mind is the way 90, 217
Miracles, feeding of the multitudes 216-226, 431; food increased on return from Flight to Egypt 186; Mary cleansed of seven devils 256; the tempest is stilled 207-208; walking on water 224; water turned to wine 185-191, 434; see also Healings
Mohammedanism 133-134
Music of the spheres 7, 65, 81, 84, 86

Names Mentioned:
  Abel-tean 75, 77
  Abighael 174
  Abraham 135, 136, 160
  Achlar 94-95
  Adahr 46
  Adam 129, 130, 131, 135, 136, 137, 139, 319

INDEX

Adynthe 109
Affa 132
Agatha 525-526
Agial 459
Agnosta 278
Agrippa 305, 409, 412
Aiel 465
Alec 17
Alexandria 117
Alphaeus 411
Alphus 181
Amada 360
Amelia 482
Amilius 130-131, 132, 136
Amon-dekar 466
Amorela 302
Ananan 90
Andra 58-59
Andrew, affluence of, 411; associated with 194, 233, 377, 379, 380, 381, 382, 384, 428, 435, 455, 467, 474, 485, 488, 495, 503, 506; at feeding of 5,000 218, 219; characteristics 181-182, 297; employed by James and John 433; incarnated 162, 321, 363; kinsmen of 197, 204, 250, 370, 372; present at resurrection 321; taught in Arabia and the East 379-384
Anilen 246
Ann (Anna, Anne), the mother of Mary 50, 68, 73, 74
Anna, acquainted with 36, 62; daughter of the innkeeper 77; deaconess in the early churches 455; Essene, cousin of Mary 65; Essene prophetess 91; Jesus blessed by 3, 8, 89, 92, 97; maid to Elizabeth and Mary 66; preparation of potential channels for the birth 53, 69; saw Jesus blessed in Temple 54; supervisor in Essene temple 60
Anneuel 515-516
Anniaus 372-373
Antonius 409
Apollo 126
Apollos 445
Apoloir 561

Apsafar 75
Aquila, daughter of 458
Aquilasteben 360
Aran 50
Arcahia 126
Archar 330-331
Archaus 262
Archippus 395
Ardath 169
Ardemetus 349
Ardoen 219
Arestole 5
Armediee 244-245
Armelia 543
Armythar 247
Arriel 573
Artemas 250
Asaph 131, 132
Aschell 562
Ashtueil 94, 95
Astaid 96
Ava 393
Barjon, brother of Peter and Andrew 204
Barnabas, associated with 179, 202, 222, 271, 382, 446, 451, 454, 466-469, 511, 512; at Laodicea 494; collaborated in writing Gospel of Mark 382, 383; disputations 265, 331, 446, 454, 486, 501, 505, 507
Barsaboi 426
Bartellius 242
Bartholomew, associated with 194, 235, 380, 455, 484, 485; characteristics 297; incarnated 162, 166; kinsmen 483
Bartimaeus (Bartaemus) acquaintance of 83, 88, 286; healed by the Master 283, 286; mother of 283, 284-285
Beatrice 318
Belden 447
Bethelda 180
Betrili 37-38
Candace, Queen of 438
Caesars (Augustus, Claudius, Tiberius) 304, 372, 412, 416, 478, 517-525, 538
Caiaphas 117, 118, 300

Caius 546
Caleb 135
Carvett 362
Cassius 531
Cecelia 387
Cecilia, Saint 355
Celeste 243-244
Celicene 389-390
Celopas 471-472
Cephas 197, 434
Cercel 519-520
Cerecea 286
Cerle 424
Chardee 394
Charlene 534-535
Charteuce 535-536
Chloe 235, 240, 381
Cilcia 468
Cineman 165
Cipio 365
Clana 187
Claudius 531
Claudiusen 568-569
Claudiuss 479-480
Clement 376
Clementina 250-251
Cleo 223, 305, 368, 370, 376, 443, 451
Cleoapas 190
Cleodius 11
Cleopas, associated with the seventy 179; blessed by the Master 223; brother-in-law of Peter 368; daughter of Cleopas, who walked on the road to Emmaus 270; elder of the church in which Lucius and Paul ministered 366; mother of Bartaemus 283; of the household of 62, 237, 251; walk to Emmaus, companion in 419
Cleopatia 238
Cleopeo 109-110
Cleopias 316-317
Cleopiasis 341-342
Cleoprates 479
Cleopus 422-423
Constantine Tupela 463
Corine 445
Cornelius, the centurion, acquainted with 34, 36, 55, 392, 397-401; among soldiery of 393-395, 400; companion to 400; daughter of 390-392; incarnated 388
Cyprus 468-469
Cyrenius 372
David 7, 10, 169, 242
Demeutri 339
Duel 205-206
Deunna 293-294
Dienna 293-294
Dora 234-235
Dorcas 335
Dorcohen 452
Duene, Sister 43, 354
Dumuru 110-111
Duors 291-292
Durey 225
Durkon 12
Ederle 394
Edithia 49, 60-62, 64
Elada 214
Elba 298
Elcor 226-227, 230
Eleiza 483-484
Elen 367-368
Elenor 114-115
Eliajah 97
Elias 46, 181-182, 521
Eliazaer 352
Elihu 126
Elijah 4, 17, 19, 22, 48, 49, 54, 105, 201, 262, 351
Elisha 19, 49, 54, 323
Elizabeth, acquainted with 10, 13, 30, 52, 107, 149, 201, 434, 487, 492; Angel Gabriel appears 51; cousin of 240; daughter of 46; education of 126; Essene 48; maid to 66; midwife to 71; mother of John the Baptist 38-41; Romans robbed of mate 32; visited by the cousin 7, 41
Elizeboth Mae 465
Elkanah 19
Elkatma 19, 24
Eloin 286
Eloirn 454
Elois 58, 60, 256, 275, 276, 321
Eloise 12-13, 215, 240, 250, 454

Emersen 562
Emmalen 563
Endoren 553-554
Enoch 129, 131, 135, 136, 140
Enos 5
Erbert 449
Ersa 435
Ersebus 449
Esdrela, Peter's mother-in-law 196-197
Esta 241-242
Ester 307-308
Estes 243
Esthen 285
Esther 221, 231
Eucuo 86-87
Euendi 438
Eunice 30, 34, 36, 465-466
Eve 7, 25, 136
Ex-elor 400
Ezekhel 556
Ezra 135
Felix 305, 544, 548
Fillipe 213-214
Gamaliel 184, 414
Garcia 538
Gardan 219-220
Gassari 361-362
Giovod 380-381
Gracia 565
Guldi 300-301
Haniah 368
Hannah 19, 25, 230
Hannas 142-143
Hedth 377
Helene 421
Herod, associated with 109, 110, 112, 548; beheaded John 10; death of 32, 104, 121; edict of Herod fulfills prophecy 4, 101; entertained at the court of 48, 109, 110, 111, 112, 318; "laid hands upon" James 177; persecutions by 546; provisions of edict 99, 103, 113-114; record to be found 120; rule of 107, 404, 432; slays John the Baptist 64; taken by the edict of 30, 32, 56, 100, 107, 113, 114, 118; wife of 115-121; Wise Men went to 20, 103

Herod Antipas 286, 526
Herod Archelaus 557
Herodias 111
Hunduen 106
Iaundia 246
Idoddxo 379-380
Iola 478
Irman 385-386
Isabodd 457
Isaiah 3, 22
Isalen 424-425
Ishneth 484
Ishmael 210
Istabuel 244
Jabcobin 348
Jacob 135
Jacobeian 354
Jacobing 342-343
Jacobinus 107
Jaelorn 223
Jairus 210-214; wife of 210-211
James, Jesus' brother, son of Joseph and Mary 142, 147; associated with 271, 425; became head of the church 154, 495, 509; elder brother of Ruth 147, 148; known as James the less 376, 377
James, brother of John the Beloved, affluence of 411; associated with 233, 255, 279, 292, 472, 474, 485; at the Last Supper 298; brother of John and of the groom at the wine miracle 186, 187, 189; chief spokesman after Pentecost 329; death of 42, 105, 177, 424, 510; employer of Andrew, Peter, Judas (not Iscariot) 433; first of the martyrs 55; kinsmen of 11, 280, 370, 411, 425; labored in the church of Jerusalem 202, 509; under the care of "the other Mary" 188; wife of 55
Japhter 53
Jarael 36-37
Jason 223-224, 282
Jeanel 237-238
Jeaniel 195
Jeauor 277-278
Jebocel 65
Jenife 77, 79

Jeremiah 22
Jeseuel 231
Jeseuha 420
Jeshua, Jesus known as 123, 131, 132, 135, 136
Jesua 452
Jessica 455-456
Jesus' sister, see Ruth
Jeuel 419
Jhengo 377-378
Jochaim 45, 46
Jochim 496
Joda 276
Jodie 191-192
Joel 3, 87, 180
John the Baptist, Andrew a disciple of 363; associated with 430, 434, 492; became an outcast for a purpose 63; called "The Baptist" after his death 41-42; Essene 24; is slain 64; John Mark healed by 383; kinsmen of 38, 46, 87, 432; least in the kingdom of heaven 48; lineage 52; nurse to 40; was Elijah 48; with Jesus in Egypt 4, 27; Zebedee a follower of 429
John the Beloved, affluence of 255, 411; associated with 195, 220, 233, 247, 279, 292, 340, 377, 422, 423, 439, 472, 484, 485, 502, 511; author of the Epistle of John 102; banishment of 413; brother of James and the groom at the wine miracle 186, 187, 189; characteristics of 297, 367; chief spokesman after Pentecost 327-330; employer of Andrew, Peter and Judas (not Iscariot) 433; incarnated 162, 423; kinsmen of 55, 370, 411, 425, 427-428, 430, 432, 435; labored in church of Jerusalem 202, 510; Mary joins household of 255; Mary Magdalene part of household 255; Master loved the best 166; may incarnate 162; mother of 256; mother of, present at the cross 290; under the care of "the other Mary" 188

John (not identifiable as John the Baptist or John the Beloved), associate of 92, 277; associate of Andrew and Thomas 384
John Louis 369
John Mark (see also Mark), associated with 367, 372, 495; incarnated 381; kinsmen 373; Martha associated with mother of 201; minister 524
Josada, mother of Lazarus 262
Jose 58, 126
Joseph (husband of Mary), age at time of marriage 69; associated with 32, 42, 101, 190, 215, 270, 303, 410; association with Mary prior to wedding 68; death of 4, 102, 147, 159, 161, 410; espoused to Mary; flight to Egypt 100, 101; Gabriel appeared to 51; genealogy 68, 72; informed of his part in birth 69-70; kinsmen 72, 142-167; member of Essenes 6, 68; role in arrival at the inn 6-7, 75; wedding to Mary 69
Joseph 56, 182-183
Joseph of Arimathea 316, 344, 347, 350
Joseph, incarnation of Jesus 131, 133, 135, 136
Josepheush 347
Josephine 452-453
Josephus 318
Joshua 131, 135, 136, 139
Josia 371-372
Josida 446
Josie 33, 58, 88, 101-6, 290-291, 317, 381, 409
Juahn 551
Juana 273-274
Judah 69, 471
Judas, school of prophets 5
Judas, associate of 292; at the Last Supper 297, 436; characteristics 297; incarnated 162, 295; teachings of 271
Judas (not Iscariot) employed by James and John 433
Jude (Jesus' brother), affluence of 411; associated with 194, 271; in-

carnated 162, 165; kinsmen of 411; son of Joseph and Mary 142, 147; younger brother of Ruth 151
Judith 171
Judy 16, 18-21, 23-27, 29, 36, 69, 95, 102, 104, 195, 199, 217, 414, 428, 487, 496, 551
Jueneta 422
Juhel 451
Julia 482-483
Juliah 459-460
Julius 214
Junie 376
Junner 125
Juohean 387
Justin 456
Justine 398
Kshjiar 125
Lacish 367
Lamaas 125
Larue 308
Lascha 242-243
Lazarus, associated with 201, 262, 263, 269, 274, 276-277, 279, 280, 291, 308, 486, 509; brother of Martha and Mary Magdalene 251; incarnated 260, 267; Jesus rests at Bethany 288; kinsmen 251, 267, 268; mother of 262; raising of 76, 149, 255, 256, 263, 268, 273, 274, 280, 510; reconciled with Mary 434
Leah 243
Lectus 473-474
Leoda 392-393
Leonax 15
Lermarn 540-541
Leveudus 554
Levi 255, 473
Lidio 480
Lieoth 437
Lilean Jueanu 461-462
Loda 321
Loga 562-563
Lois 215, 381
Louan 555-556
Louis, see John Louis
Lucei 448
Lucia 506-507
Lucius, among the seventy 485; associated with 44, 105, 179, 195, 202, 203, 231, 272, 336, 391, 448, 449, 452, 454, 455, 499; characteristics of 391-392; church established by 395; disputations 331, 446, 454; faithlessness preached by Paul 264; kinsmen 486, 494, 502-508; Stephen close friend of 264; wife of 494, 501
Lucy 506-507
Luke, associated with 179, 195, 202, 222, 230-231, 251, 272, 382, 391, 435, 469, 495, 502, 504, 519; characteristics of 391-392; disputations 331, 454; genealogy 382, 411; kinsmen 58, 486, 505; known as a physician 340, 503; Stephen close friend of 264; teacher of 145; walk to Emmaus 411
Lydia 226, 331-332, 335-337, 359, 426-427, 564
Lydias 439-440, 441-442, 463-464, 572-573
Lydiaus 464
Lystia 172-173
Lystra 443-444, 462
Macha 51-52
Magan 169-170
Magi, see Wise Men
Mahaieol 204
Maipah 210-211
Malachi 3, 189; book of 17
Mara 529
Marcella 225
Marcellus 305
Marcia 466-467
Marcus 381-382
Marga 516
Margie 236
Margii 70-71, 543-544
Margill 522
Marh 496
Mariaerh, companion to Lucius 453, 488-489, 497, 501, 511
Mariah 220-221
Marian 172
Marie 235, 260
Mark, see also John Mark; associated with 179, 195, 202, 251,

272, 371, 379, 384, 469, 501; characteristics of 391-392; disputations 265, 331, 446, 454; kinsmen 368, 369, 373
Marlan 303
Marleon 572
Martha, of the peoples of Bethsaida 235, 239; cousin of James 280
Martha, sister of Lazarus, associated with 13, 33, 62, 149, 195, 269, 274, 276, 278-279, 280, 291, 307, 308, 486, 496, 509, 510; close relationship with Mary the mother 10; cousin of James 280; incarnated 260, 267, 268, 269; kinsmen 267; reconciled with Mary 434; Saul brought about the death of 255; sister of Mary Magdalene 251, 259-260, 269, 271
Martha, wife of Nicodemus, acquainted with 201, 202; espoused to Nicodemus 200; Essene 201; incarnated 199; made robe for Jesus 200; mother of 200; present at the Crucifixion and Pentecost 203; sister of Peter's mother-in-law 199
Martia 279
Mary, the associate of John Mark 367, 381
Mary, the mother of the Lord, age at time of marriage 69; associated with 11, 42, 106, 149, 188, 190, 195, 201, 215, 264, 270, 303, 410, 487, 509; association with Joseph prior to wedding 68; astrological sign 66; at the inn 6-7; chosen as channel 3, 48-66, 102; education of 126; genealogy 49, 68, 73, 74, 75; handmaid to 101; immaculately conceived 50, 73; kinsmen 65, 73, 88, 142-167, 381; member of Essenes 6, 48, 68; midwife to 70-71; the wedding to Joseph 69; twin soul of Jesus 75, 129; wedding at Cana 186
Mary, the other, acquainted with 33, 201, 277, 279, 307; genealogy 432; incarnated 188-190; kinsmen 185, 431; present at Crucifixion 203
Mary Magdalene, associated with 11, 12-13, 33, 62, 111, 149, 195, 201, 263, 269, 274, 276, 279, 280, 307, 308, 486, 496, 509, 510; characteristics of 253; close associate of John 255, 259; first to see the Master after resurrection 252, 256, 322; incarnated 251-252; incident occurred in early ministry 259; known as Mary of Magdalene 252; mother of 262; prepared spices for Jesus' body 58; present at ascension 254-255; present at the Cross 290; reconciled with Lazarus and Martha 434; sister of Martha and Lazarus 251
Marya 351-352
Maryon 194-195
Matada 187
Mateal 100
Mathias, a companion of the Master 207-208; a witness to the activities of Pilate 301; informed Joseph of his part in the birth 69; Matthew known as 435; of the school of prophets 5; one that was healed 175
Matildah 224
Matildhen 303
Matthew, affluence of 190, 411; associated with 255, 379, 411, 472, 473, 485; disputes with 265; incarnated 471; kinsmen 471; known as Levi 471; known as Mathias 435; prompted to write gospel 247; status as tax collector 249
Mayan 195
Mayrah 208-209
Media 361
Melchizedek 49, 129, 131, 132, 135, 136, 137, 139
Melia 460-461
Mephibosheth 102
Merceden 505-506
Mercia 334-335

Micah 423-424
Midias 523
Mille 374
Morao 232-233
Moses 6, 7, 22, 135, 139, 208, 456, 521
Myra 88, 193
Myrtina 571
Nalthlai 570-571
Naneoi 170-171
Naomi 321, 431-433
Nebat 560
Nehemiah 135
Nero 465, 561-562
Nicholas 281
Nicodemus, acquainted with 344; gift of the robe to the Master 200, 297; husband of Martha 200; kinsmen 275
Niger 442
Nimmuo 507-508, 511, 513
Nylen 442
Og 95
One who returned cloak to the Master 460
Pagosius 445
Palatius 573
Pamphylus 396
Partapathr 374
Partheniasi 565-566
Parthesias 566
Pasquarl 358
Pathaos 265
Patience 377-378
Patricia 343-344
Paul, associated with 179, 202, 222, 272, 336, 360, 382, 445, 446, 454-469, 474-476, 485, 504, 506, 510-511, 528, 530, 547, 564; Laodicea 457, 494; brought misinterpreting and misunderstanding 413; characteristics of 391-392; disputations 197, 264, 265, 331, 424, 446, 454, 486, 495, 501, 506, 507, 511; genealogy 485; had more influence than Paul in bringing correct report of what happened in Jerusalem to Roman conscience 405; translated teachings of Paul into Roman tongue 540; variation in teachings with Peter's 391
Paula 379
Paulos 467-468
Pebelus 380, 472-473
Pebilus 502, 504
Pecbo 399
Pegler 206-207
Pelostos 547-548
Penuel 334
Pergola 397
Perlesus 523
Perseus 299
Peter, affluence of 411; associated with 58, 233, 247, 291, 360, 367, 371, 374-377, 379, 382, 385, 392-394, 428, 435, 439, 445, 455, 474, 485, 495, 506; at the Last Supper 297-298; at the Pentecost 265, 331, 485, 488; characteristics of 182, 297, 367, 391-392; chief spokesman after the Pentecost 329-330; collaborated in writing the Gospel of Mark 382-383; crucified head downward 371; disputations 265, 424, 506; employed by James and John 433; established church in Antioch 446; healed by 385; kinsmen 196, 197, 198, 198-199, 203, 250, 364, 368-372, 376, 469; labored in church of Jerusalem 202; ministry 399; released from prison 373, 374, 375, 382; strengthened church in Caesarea 365; translated teachings of Peter into Roman tongue 540; variation with Paul's teachings 391
Peter's mother-in-law, acquaintance of 203, 204, 233; healed 196-204; incarnation 197, 198; kinsmen 198-199, 203; sister of Jesus present at healing of 159, 161
Petromus 458-459
Petros 207, 384
Phailos 221-222
Pharlos 396-397
Pharsen 393
Phelemaie 567
Pheres 362-363

Philas 328-330, 418
Philcholos 400-401
Philemon 476, 478-479, 528
Philen 442
Philip, a deacon 485; associated with 202, 235, 271, 294, 329, 424, 438-440; characteristics 297; ministered to the needs of visitors 292, 329
Philippi 510-511
Philo 14-15, 523-524
Philoas, husband of Jesus' sister 402-418
Philoas 542
Philolos 531-532
Philomus 558-559
Philon 394-395
Philos 545
Phinehas 19, 24
Phlons 304
Phoebe 193, 294, 321, 554
Phoebia 567-568
Phoenix 321
Phylos 177, 524, 572
Pilate, aided in bringing Pilate before Caesar 524; associated with 318, 528, 533; demands that there be a questioning of Pilate by Caesar 521; guard to 530; kinsmen 340, 520, 530; recall of Pilate to Rome 149, 307, 412, 413-414, 532; son healed 110, 413, 528, 529, 530; wife of 528, 529; witness to the activity of Pilate during trial of Jesus 301
Pilos 179-180
Pinneas 165
Pitmumus 502, 557-558
Pleadila 196
Pleney 419-420
Pluenon 344-345
Polias 370-371
Pollos 395-396
Polymus 353
Polyneius 550
Polyneus 541
Pompeathiolus 565
Pomtplema 546
Pondus 457
Ponticalos 533
Pontifus 535
Pontitutulus 439
Pontius 533
Pontuos 559
Poppipano 552-553
Posnell 513, 564
Priscilla, daughter of 458
Puburus 517-518
Puella 143
Puliduon 546
Puloaus 98-99
Pylemus 520
Quienllo 112-113
Ra 125
Rachel 135
Rachel wept for her children 21, 52, 99, 108, 191
Rata 50
Rebba 401
Rebkah 98
Rehbal 369
Remis 561
Reruhel 430
Rhadahr 111-112
Rhea 331
Rhoda 373-375, 381
Rich Young Ruler 381-383
Roael, Zebedee's son 186, 189
Robolus 481-482
Romacio 410
Romoluen 530
Romual 307
Roselan 249-250
Roslan 560
Ruhel 277
Ruth, sister of Jesus, affluence of 410, 411; associated with 85, 270, 272, 273, 538; birth of 147, 159; education of 273; husband of, see Philoas; incarnated 143-165; Jesus present at wedding of 149, 410; kinsmen 147, 150, 153, 154, 411; present at healing of Peter's mother-in-law 159, 161; present at raising of Lazarus 149; present at the resurrection 161
Ruth 17, 72, 113, 203-204, 241, 332
Ruthen 353
Sachet 332-333
Salamar 203

Salome 88, 111, 126, 357
Salone 371
Salonica 113-114
Samaleuen 349
Samanteherlequen 173
Samantha 241, 526
Samson 25
Samuel 4, 17, 19, 24, 26, 49, 54
San, see Zan
Saparah 530
Sara 79, 436-437
Sarai 209-210
Sarapha 79
Sardenia 303
Sathamantha 91
Saul 19
Saul of Tarsus 12, 255, 265, 485
Schelmezadek 384-385
Selmaa 192-193
Shalmar 54
Sheliah 532-533
Shem 102
Shugard 401
Silas, associated with 179, 222, 284, 371, 467; disputations 486; incarnated 469; kinsmen 202
Silvanus 178
Simean 46
Simeon, associated with 386, 441; in the Essene temple 8, 58, 91; incarnated 435-436
Simon, a teacher 438; associated with 387; rebuking of 365
Simon, a sorcerer 387
Slocombi 87
Smantehn 47-48
Smithene 446-447
Sobol 276-277
Sodaphe 77
Sofa 40-41, 52
Solomon 16
Sopha 306-307
Sophia 175-176, 200, 378-379, 510
Sophie 57-58, 101
Stephen, a deacon 485; a teaching 314; associated with 202, 265, 271, 293, 294, 328, 440; close friend of Lucius 264; ministered to the needs of visitors 292, 329; mother of 11; position in the church 354; stoned for his beliefs 293, 424, 437
Suel 176
Suphor 425
Susana 464-465, 505
Susane 269-271
Susanna 278-279, 356
Sylvanus 202
Sylvesta 353-354
Sylvia 292-293, 438, 476-478
Sylvius 495, 496
Tekla 569-570
Teleman 528
Terteleus 447-448
Teular 194
Thaddeus, a shepherd 86; associated with 255, 474; incarnated 503; son of Lucius 503-504; son of Martha (wife of Nicodemus), also known as Theopolus 202
Thaddues 444
Thardal 274
Thelda 496-497
Theophilus 86
Theopolus 202
Theresa 448-449
Thesea 16, 27, 115-121
Thessi 275-276
Thessile 440
Thomas, affluence of 411; associated with 292, 384, 435, 474, 483, 485; brother of Luke 58; disputations 265; wife of 126
Thurmel 222
Tilda 315
Timothy, a minister 524; acquainted with 439, 506, 530; "not all a Jew" 439
Timous 539
Titus, associated with 474-482, 528, 530; incarnated 474; translated teachings of Titus into Roman tongue 540
Touhpar 211
Tultimustouen 539
Tupela, see Constantine Tupela
Turteltus 234
Tutilius 480
Udraka 125

Uhjltd 95, 135, 138
Ukle 168
Ulai 261-262, 511
Ullen 377-378
Ur 131, 133
Vashti 443
Veldejui 481
Veronicani 9-11
Vesta 498-499, 501, 511
Viola 112
Xaneres 44-45
Xercia 338-341
Xeren 500
Xerxes 423
Zacchaeus 286-287
Zachariah/Zacharias, husband of Elizabeth, associated with 30, 36, 41, 44, 45; death of 5, 32, 40, 45, 46, 48, 51, 492; kinsmen 46; relationship with Essenes 48, 126
Zacheus 38, 430
Zadok 91, 92
Zan 136, 137
Zar 123
Zebedee, affluence of 186, 411, 432; associated with 58, 240, 431, 432; Essenes met in chambers of 11; genealogy 432; in the Essene temple 429; incarnated 427, 428; kinsmen 370, 430, 431, 432, 435; son of the groom at the wine miracle 186, 189; wife of 277
Zebra 532
Zebuden 549-550
Zebulon 31
Zelot 274-275
Zend 95, 131, 136, 137
Zenda Lumi 15-16
Zermada 27-28
Zerubbabel 135
Zioul 365-366
Zoroaster 97, 137
Zu 125
Zxenaw 109
Nazarenes/Nazirites 17, 533
Numerology 4, 53

Original sin 75

Parable of the tares 207
Pentecost 33, 42, 105, 178, 182, 203, 224, 265, 266, 279, 307, 328-337, 440, 451, 485, 488, 493, 507, 509
Persia, His years there 4, 104, 123, 124, 125, 147
Phrenology 4
Platonism 133
Polygamy 340
Prophecy 63, 69; fulfilled 3, 4, 5, 7, 90, 98, 100, 101, 103; records to be uncovered 127, 167
Prophets, school of 4, 17, 18, 19, 54, 262, 433

Race 49
Records, church, preservation of 412, 516
Refuge, city of 10
Resurrection 11, 55, 78, 155, 160, 161, 169, 212, 252, 265, 273, 278, 289, 290, 302, 309, 311-312, 319-327
Roman rule, defined 403-404; extent of 500, 520; Romans refrained from active influence in the religious 228

Saneid 21
Sanhedrin 185, 257, 317
Second Coming 133, 291
Seventy, the 178-185, 430, 485
Shepherds 8, 64-65, 78, 80, 84-88
Shintoism 133
Soul, purpose for entering materiality 71
Syrophoenician people, geography 245

Tax collectors represented by various faiths 98
Temple Beautiful 103
Temples, of Gold 138; of Sacrifice 103
Therapeutae 17
Thummim and Urim on robe of the Master 202
Time 6, 18, 22, 67-68, 125, 139, 338, 379, 409, 545
Transfiguration 175, 177, 521
Trial, the 287, 288, 297, 300-302, 304, 317, 403

Trinity 150
Triumphal entry 64, 83, 159, 195, 287-294, 316, 318, 402, 492
Triune, Holy 217

Upper chamber 11, 193, 202, 264, 288, 290, 298, 311, 370, 436, 497

Vatican, manuscripts, research potential 442, 522

White Brotherhood 17, 103-104, 106
Wisdom, defined 157
Wise Men 18, 20, 28, 32, 37, 45, 60, 64, 77, 78, 80, 85, 87, 93-99, 110, 127, 147, 329, 414
Woman at the well 191-196
Woman's "place" 18, 21, 24-25, 56, 62, 171, 201, 211, 212, 356, 433, 492

Zoroastrianism 137